When Government Helped

When Government Helped

Learning from the Successes and Failures of the New Deal

SHEILA D. COLLINS
and
GERTRUDE SCHAFFNER GOLDBERG

OXFORD
UNIVERSITY PRESS

OXFORD
UNIVERSITY PRESS

Oxford University Press is a department of the University of Oxford.
It furthers the University's objective of excellence in research, scholarship,
and education by publishing worldwide.

Oxford New York
Auckland Cape Town Dar es Salaam Hong Kong Karachi
Kuala Lumpur Madrid Melbourne Mexico City Nairobi
New Delhi Shanghai Taipei Toronto

With offices in
Argentina Austria Brazil Chile Czech Republic France Greece
Guatemala Hungary Italy Japan Poland Portugal Singapore
South Korea Switzerland Thailand Turkey Ukraine Vietnam

Oxford is a registered trademark of Oxford University Press
in the UK and certain other countries.

Published in the United States of America by
Oxford University Press
198 Madison Avenue, New York, NY 10016

Library of Congress Cataloging-in-Publication Data
When government helped : learning from the successes and failures
of the New Deal / [edited by] Sheila D. Collins, Gertrude Schaffner Goldberg.
pages cm
ISBN 978–0–19–999069–6 (pbk. : alk. paper) 1. New Deal, 1933—1939.
2. Depressions—1929—United States. 3. United States—Economic policy—1933–1945.
4. United States—Economic conditions—1918–1945. 5. Recessions—United States.
6. United States—Economic policy—2009- 7. United States—Economic conditions—2009-
I. Collins, Sheila D. II. Goldberg, Gertrude S.
HC106.3.W43 2013
973.917—dc23 2013023621

1 3 5 7 9 8 6 4 2
Printed in the United States of America
on acid-free paper

CONTENTS

Acknowledgments vii
Contributors ix
Introduction xiii

1. Public Attitudes Toward Government: The Social and Political Contexts of the Great Depression and Great Recession 1
SHEILA D. COLLINS

2. A Tale of Two Crises: A Comparative View of the Political Economy of the Great Depression and Great Recession 25
VOLKER JANSSEN

3. The Bottom-Up Recovery: A New Deal in Banking and Public Finance 51
TIMOTHY A. CANOVA

4. A Decade of Dissent: The New Deal and Popular Movements 86
GERTRUDE SCHAFFNER GOLDBERG

5. Labor Militance and the New Deal: Some Lessons for Today 120
RICHARD MCINTYRE

6. The New Deal's Direct Job- Creation Strategy: Providing Employment Assurance for American Workers 146
PHILIP HARVEY

7. The New Deal and the Creation of an American Welfare State 180
GERTRUDE SCHAFFNER GOLDBERG

8. The Democratization of Culture: The Legacy of the New Deal Arts Programs 207
SHEILA D. COLLINS AND NAOMI ROSENBLUM

9. The Rightful Heritage of All: The Environmental Lessons of the Great Depression and the New Deal Response 233
SHEILA D. COLLINS

10. New Deal Agricultural Policy: The Unintended Consequences of Supply Management 266
BILL WINDERS

11. Conclusion: Learning from the Successes and Failures of the New Deal 292
GERTRUDE SCHAFFNER GOLDBERG

Index 325

ACKNOWLEDGMENTS

As editors of this volume, our greatest debt is to our contributors, without whose expertise, enthusiasm for the project, and willingness to engage in multiple rounds of comments and revisions, this book could not have been written. We are indebted to the Warner Fund at the University Seminars at Columbia University for its generous help in publication. Many of the ideas presented here have benefited from discussions in the University Seminar on Full Employment, Social Welfare and Equity. We wish to thank the participants in those seminars for their helpful feedback. Dana Bliss, our editor at Oxford University Press, provided enthusiastic support throughout. We are also grateful to the archivists at the Franklin D. Roosevelt Memorial Library for help in locating photographs and accessing documentary material and to the reference librarians at Adelphi University who assisted in tracking down critical sources. To Richard Wolff, we owe thanks for his initial encouragement in undertaking the project and suggestions for whom we might turn to for certain chapters. Helen Ginsburg provided helpful feedback on the proposal and has been a valuable consultant throughout the preparation of the manuscript. Marguerite Rosenthal and Frank Stricker gave us critical feedback on some of the chapters as well as recommendations of sources. We also thank June Zaccone for her help in leading us to resources. Other colleagues with the National Jobs for All Coalition have been invaluable allies over the years in the struggle to realize the vision of a more just and sustainable world for which the New Deal, at its best, stood.

CONTRIBUTORS

Timothy A. Canova is Professor of Law and Public Finance at the Nova Southeastern University Shepard Broad Law Center in Florida. His work, which crosses the disciplines of law, public finance, and economic history, has been published in numerous articles and book chapters, including academic journals from Harvard, Georgetown, Minnesota, and the University of California. Canova has held high academic and administrative posts at the University of New Mexico and Chapman University. In 2011, he was appointed by U.S. Senator Bernie Sanders to serve on a blue-ribbon advisory panel on reforming the Federal Reserve. Prior to teaching, he served as a legislative assistant to the late U.S. Senator Paul E. Tsongas and practiced law in New York City with Gibson, Dunn & Crutcher, and Mudge Rose Guthrie Alexander & Ferdon.

Sheila D. Collins is Professor Emerita of Political Science and former director of the Graduate Program in Public Policy and International Affairs at William Paterson University. She has written and taught in the areas of American politics, environmental politics and policy, poverty and inequality, globalization, social movements, and religion. Collins is the author or co-author of six books and numerous articles, book chapters, and encyclopedia entries. Among her books are *Washington's New Poor Law* (2001), co-authored with Gertrude Schnaffner Goldberg, and *Let Them Eat Ketchup: The Politics of Poverty and Inequality* (1996). Collins is a member of the Global Ecological Integrity Group, a member of the International Advisory Board of the Toda Institute for Global Peace and Policy Studies, and co-chairs the Columbia Seminar on Full Employment, Social Welfare and Equity and the Seminar on Globalization, Labor and Popular Struggles. She also serves on the board of the National Jobs for All Coalition.

Gertrude Schaffner Goldberg is Professor Emerita of Social Policy and former director of the Ph.D. Program in Social Work at Adelphi University. Her areas of study are full employment, public assistance, the feminization of poverty, and comparative social welfare systems. She has written numerous articles in refereed journals, chapters in edited books, and co-authored or edited six books. With Sheila D. Collins, she co-authored *Washington's New Poor Law: Welfare "Reform" and the Roads Not Taken, 1935 to the Present* (2001). Goldberg was the editor and author of several chapters in *Poor Women in Rich Countries* (2010), the first work to study the feminization of poverty over the life course. Goldberg is co-chair of the Columbia Seminar on Full Employment, Social Welfare and Equity, and co-founder and chair of the National Jobs for All Coalition.

Philip Harvey is Professor of Law and Economics at Rutgers School of Law and Counsel to the Board of the National Jobs for All Coalition. He received his Ph.D. in economics from the New School for Social Research and his J.D. from Yale Law School. A labor lawyer and human rights economist, he practiced law in New York City before joining the Rutgers faculty. He is the author of *Securing the Right to Employment* (1989), co-author of *America's Misunderstood Welfare State* (1990), and has published extensively on the subject of economic and social human rights, with a particular focus on policy options for securing the right to work. Copies of his work can be accessed at www.philipharvey.info.

Volker Janssen is Associate Professor of History at California State University. He specializes in California and United States economic history but has made it a mission to teach economic history to teachers through the National Humanities Center and the Teaching American History grant. He is the editor of *Where Minds and Matters Meet: Technology in California and the West,* and in his own research specializes on the political economy of California's postwar prison system. His monograph on this subject is due to be published with Oxford University Press, and his essay on prison labor camps in postwar California won the Binkley-Stephenson Award of the Organization of American Historians for best article in the *Journal of American History* in 2009.

Richard McIntyre is Professor of Economics at the University of Rhode Island, a faculty member at the Schmidt Labor Research Center, and a fellow of the John Hazen White Center for Ethics and Public Service. In addition to many scholarly articles, he is the author of *Are Worker Rights Human Rights?* (2008) and edits the *New Political Economy* book series for Routledge.

Naomi Rosenblum is an independent scholar who has specialized in the history of photography. Her major work, *A World History of Photography* (1984), is in its fourth edition and has been translated into French, Polish, Japanese, and Chinese. She is also the author of *A History of Women Photographers* (1994). She has arranged exhibits of the work of Walter Rosenblum, Paul Strand, and Lewis Hine for exhibitions in Italy and has written forewords for several books on photography.

Bill Winders is an Associate Professor of Sociology in the School of History, Technology, and Society at Georgia Tech. He studies and writes about national policies, social movements, and the world economy. His book, *The Politics of Food Supply: U.S. Agricultural Policy in the World Economy* (Yale, 2009) won the 2011 Book Award from the Political Economy of the World-System section of the American Sociological Association. In addition, he received the Bernstein & Byres Prize for his 2009 article in the *Journal of Agrarian Change* comparing the U.S. and British food regimes. His current research examines food crises in the world economy, such as the 2007–2008 food crisis that saw food prices and world hunger rise dramatically.

INTRODUCTION

Parallels between the Great Depression of the 1930s and the 2007–2008 global economic meltdown abound. The crisis that hit in 2008 began as severely as that of the Great Depression. In the twelve months following the economic peak in 2008, industrial production fell by as much as it did in the first year of the Depression, while equity prices and global trade fell even more.[1] As in the earlier period, panic swept financial centers across the world, and there was fear that the capitalist system had come undone. Most accounts of the parallels between the two periods, however, deal only with the economic similarities—the asset bubbles that, in the 1930s, resulted in a near complete collapse of the economic system, and the speculative frenzy of the current period that resulted in a near collapse of the global economy. Few, however, have sought to mine that past experience for lessons that might help us resolve the dilemmas of the contemporary crisis.

While the New Deal as a response to the Great Depression has received renewed attention in the current period, that attention has been focused primarily in the realm of fiscal and monetary policy. Yet the New Deal's larger legacy "has been mostly forgotten or expunged except for a few highlights recycled in national memory."[2] Seldom have book-length assessments of the New Deal's response to the Great Depression covered its full range of policy arenas. This book aims to fill that gap. We not only assess the successes and failures of the New Deal's response to economic crisis, but we enlarge the framework for understanding both the Great Depression and our contemporary crisis by including the environmental crises that afflicted both periods. Although these are of different magnitudes, we can nonetheless learn from the New Deal response. In addition, we assess the degree and efficacy of the popular responses to economic crisis in the 1930s with popular responses in the contemporary period.

People are hungry for solutions to the myriad problems we face today, whether these be the corruption and incompetence of government, the high costs of unemployment and mortgage foreclosures, the unfinished business of health care reform, declining wages and incomes, deepening inequality, welfare state cutbacks, costly and unjust wars, the poisoning of our food, air, and water, or the threat of climate catastrophe. Issues such as these are considered in this book with a view to determining the relevance to current crises of New Deal responses to a set of somewhat similar issues.

Politicians and pundits love to analogize from history—take George W. Bush's comparison of Saddam Hussein to Hitler in the run-up to the Iraq war. Yet no period of history is ever an exact replica of the past. That the world is constantly changing is a given, but, for those concerned about making or influencing policy decisions today, it is important to understand the patterns that history imposes. Path dependency theorists have shown us that institutional patterns set in motion in the past often define the limits and possibilities within which choices in the future must be made. American politics and policymaking, for example, is constrained by the framework set by the American Constitution. Yet a crisis of great magnitude can sometimes open up the possibility for path-breaking structural reform. The Great Depression was just such a crisis, setting in motion a period of reform that shaped the limits and possibilities of policymaking for the next fifty years, but which was eroded by the decline of the New Deal order. In this book we ask and attempt to answer why, so far, the crash of 2008 has not opened up another period of progressive reform.

Another pattern imposed by history is the law of unintended consequences. The unintended consequences of a policy meant to correct a social or economic problem in the past may cause new problems at a future time when other circumstances have changed or new knowledge is gained. This is particularly true, as our book shows, in the areas of agricultural and environmental policy. Technological change presents new possibilities, but also new liabilities, raising new questions about both the past and the present in relationship to it. We tend to think that all technological advances are *ipso facto* better than what existed in the past. But a comparison of the two periods of economic crisis raises some questions about this. Despite the long-standing endurance of U.S. political institutions, political realignments do occur—as a result of demographic changes, changes in the configuration and power of dominant economic institutions, changes in international relations, changes in the rules Congress makes for itself, and changes in Supreme Court precedents—and, of course, such realignments have a major bearing on the possibilities for progressive change. Lastly, the changing place of the United States in the international community can also affect domestic policymaking. Domestic policymaking is more constrained when a nation's attention is focused on threats from abroad or when the greater part of its treasury is going into national defense to shore up its position as a superpower. So it is with caution and a great deal of contextualizing that we must approach any attempt to derive lessons for today from the period of the 1930s.

While acknowledging that history never repeats itself in the same way, there are, nevertheless, ways in which the past can help shape our thinking about policy choices in the present and future. Understanding what went wrong in the past can help us avoid making similar mistakes when confronted with similar circumstances;

and it can help alert us to the unintended consequences of our current actions so that, we hope, they can be avoided. But there are also more positive lessons that history can bequeath us. The past, for example, can present us with role models of leadership that can be adapted to different times. It can present us with visionary possibilities for reorganizing our approach to certain contemporary problems now constrained by politics and ideology.

While relying considerably on existing scholarship on the Great Depression and New Deal, this book offers new perspectives on that period and the choices that were taken in light of questions that confront contemporary publics. Through doing so, we hope to demonstrate some possible ways out of our malaise, approaches that were begun but never fulfilled in the 1930s, that were raised as possibilities by popular movements but never allowed onto the political agenda, or approaches that were simply unforeseen in an earlier era. Thus, the book presents a set of guideposts—some beneficial, some cautionary— for the present and future.

Chapters 1 and 2 set the two periods of crisis in context. Chapter 1 teases out the influences of contextual factors on the public's attitude toward government intervention in the economy during the Great Depression and Great Recession, asking why the public became so much more accepting of government intervention in the economy than it is today. It answers this by examining (1) the timing of events and the existence and character of popular social movements in the two periods; (2) the cultural currents at work in society; (3) the changing nature of the communications environment and its effect on politics; (4) the strength and composition of the president's party in Congress; (5) the political skills of the Presidents themselves; (6) the relative political power and cohesiveness of the business class; (7) the international political context; and (8) the environmental context.

Chapter 2 compares the national industrialized consumer economy of the 1920s with today's globalized service and information economy and the economic collapses that occurred in both eras. Dominant economic thought in both eras idealized free markets and rejected government regulations. Changes in consumer culture mark both eras, albeit of different products and mores. Each witnessed increases in productivity and output, consumer credit, and surges in financial speculation. Whereas trickle-down economics in the 1920s spurred domestic industrial employment, it has recently stimulated offshore hiring. One lesson policymakers learned from the Great Depression was to prevent an implosion of the financial system. The quick restoration of market confidence, however, sapped the political will for reforms on behalf of credit consumers and homeowners, and made room for an unproductive preoccupation with the federal deficit.

Chapter 3 examines the fiscal and monetary policies of the New Deal, comparing them with those of the Obama administration. In contrast to the trickle-down approaches of Hoover and Obama, Roosevelt enacted a "public option" or "bottom up" approach to recovery that consisted of steering billions of dollars in Reconstruction Finance Corporation funds into public works, mortgage modifications for millions of homeowners and farmers, and loans to state and local public school districts for school construction and teachers' salaries. This "bottom up" approach was marred by Roosevelt's decision to balance the budget in 1937, but the experience of war time government spending was finally a vindication of this approach, resulting in full employment and economic recovery. In later years amnesia about this lesson set in. In neither the 1930s nor today, however, were structural changes imposed on the management of the banks. But at least during the New Deal, the propped-up institutions of capitalism were supplemented and at times supplanted by more effective and accountable government institutions. A new "New Deal" must go farther than Roosevelt was willing to go—to a truly public option in banking and finance.

Chapters 4 and 5 examine the role of politics from below. Chapter 4 examines the 1930s "decade of dissent" when vibrant social movements contributed to a profound critique of American society and exerted pressure for change in public and corporate spheres. This chapter describes movements of unemployed workers; jobless veterans; employed workers; black workers; the elderly; tenant farmers; and middle- and lower-income persons seeking a more equitable distribution of income and wealth. New Deal responses to popular movements varied from movement to movement and from time to time, depending on the congruity of its goals with movement demands, the strength of the movement and the political threat it posed. The movements, for all their vigor, seldom achieved their goals. In several instances, radical demands served the function of making more moderate New Deal policies acceptable. The New Deal thus pursued a classic strategy of moderate reformers—gaining conservative assent by pointing to the threat of radical alternatives.

Chapter 5 explains the deep decline in U.S. labor which had been a militant force in the 1930s, thanks in no small measure to Communists and their allies in the CIO. Economic gains were made after workers' right to organize and bargain collectively were guaranteed by the National Labor Relations Act. However, labor rights were subsequently curtailed by government policy, particularly red-baiting, that eliminated the movement's most dynamic leaders and organizers. The need for big business assistance during World War II helped to rehabilitate capital, so that industrial stability rather than economic democracy became the priority in labor relations. By positioning labor as an interest group rather than a class, and by eliminating labor's left wing, the "third New Deal" (1937–1945) narrowed the path for radical change and made labor vulnerable to the politics of class fragmentation pursued by the New Right. The "New Deal system" that resulted was more a product of labor's defeat than a truce in the class struggle. The lesson of the New Deal is that a radical labor movement can make real social change even when government is only mildly supportive.

Most progressive economists today seem only to be interested in the macroeconomic effect of the New Deal jobs programs—as if the only thing they have to teach us about combating unemployment is the negative lesson derived from the

Roosevelt Administration's failure to engage in enough deficit spending to end the Great Depression as quickly as it could have. Chapter 6 argues that this misses the most important lessons these programs have to teach us. It misperceives the multiple objectives these programs served in combating the labor-market effects of the Great Depression. It ignores the social-welfare benefits that employment in the programs provided to millions of unemployed workers and their families; it discounts the value of the goods and services they produced for the nation's communities; it overlooks the ability of programs like the WPA to enhance the effectiveness of Keynesian anti-cyclical measures; and it disregards the potential of such programs to achieve the ultimate goal of Keynesian economic policy—sustained full employment. Moreover, direct job creation, as this chapter explains, is a more cost effective model for delivering a macroeconomic stimulus to the economy than the indirect policies and programs progressives have promoted since World War II. The experience of direct job creation during that war taught New Dealers that if it were to become permanent public policy it could be the key to economic prosperity in the future.

Compared to the utter paucity of relief following the 1929 stock market crash, social welfare programs enacted by the New Deal were available and could be readily expanded at the outset of the financial crisis of 2008, thus helping to prevent the ensuing recession from becoming a depression. After discussing the role played by these programs, including their limits, Chapter 7 describes the New Deal's ground-breaking temporary relief measures and Roosevelt's timing and preparation of the public for permanent welfare reform. New Deal social welfare reform, principally the Social Security Act of 1935, is critically analyzed: its relationship to temporary relief; the populations it covered and excluded; security risks included and omitted; the type and level of its benefits; and its potential for expansion. Although Roosevelt and other planners of permanent social welfare reform preferred job creation to direct relief, the Social Security Act included unemployment *insurance* but not employment *assurance*. Although health insurance was considered important by planners of permanent social welfare reform, it was omitted out of fear that the opposition of the medical establishment could topple the entire program. The chapter concludes with a comparison of the Obama and Roosevelt approaches to social welfare reform, especially their timing and skill in preparing and gaining the support of the public.

Chapter 8 examines the unique series of Federal Arts Programs established by the New Deal to provide employment to unemployed cultural workers. It argues that these programs democratized and de-commodified culture, making both the enjoyment of culture and participation in the arts the property of the people, not just the provenance of a few. The chapter examines the difficulties faced by government officials in managing such an enterprise, the extraordinary outpouring of art and culture that resulted, the ways in which it enriched our understanding of the diversity of the country and its history, the tangible and intangible benefits this had for the country, and the lessons we can learn from this experience today as public support for the arts dwindles in the face of budgetary austerity.

Both The Great Depression and Great Recession were characterized by intertwined economic *and* environmental crises. Those drawing parallels between the two periods of economic collapse ignore the significance of the environmental crisis of the 1930s and therefore miss the lessons the New Deal response to that crisis have to teach us. Roosevelt undertook three programs to deal simultaneously with the problems of unemployment and environmental catastrophe: the Civilian Conservation Corps, the Soil Conservation Service and the Tennessee Valley Authority. While acknowledging the shortcomings of these programs, Chapter 9 argues that the lessons we could learn from that experience include the need for presidential leadership with a deep understanding—as FDR had—of ecological science; the importance of going beyond the strictures of the private market; of linking unemployment with environmental conservation and restoration; of the need to invoke the precautionary principle; and most critical of all, national government intervention, long-term planning and financing—not to mention international coordination—to deal with the magnitude of the environmental crisis of the 21st century.

Chapter 10 argues that, although the focus on supply management of New Deal agricultural policy was aimed at alleviating the plight of hard-pressed farmers, the politics surrounding its implementation, particularly the prominent role of Southern Democrats and conflicts that erupted among agricultural stakeholders, resulted in several important unintended consequences with long-term implications. These included reinforcement of regional class structures that benefited the largest and richest farmers, thus strengthening existing patterns of racial and economic inequality; changes in the economic interests of different sectors of agriculture; and the fostering of industrial agriculture with increased reliance on chemical fertilizers, pesticides, and herbicides. Their use has contributed to environmental degradation of rivers and aquifers, harm to wildlife, and global climate change. Overproduction of certain commodities and increased exports, especially of wheat, another unintended consequence, have resulted in the destruction of subsistence farming in parts of the developing world and, as a result, catalyzed political instability. Agricultural policy, the author argues, even during the Depression, was always subject to global trade patterns that limited the effectiveness of national policy. Thus any attempt to deal with it today must take international trade into account.

The final chapter reviews New Deal successes and failures. Achievements in relief, recovery and reform, though considerable, were hampered by Southern control of Congress and antipathy to deficit spending. Today's leaders learned from the past that swift government intervention is necessary to stem economic crisis but didn't apply the New Deal approach to job creation or learn that fiscal austerity stalls recovery or reverses course. It took the exigency of world war for the Roosevelt government to spend sufficient money to create full employment. Convinced that unemployment could be overcome by public policy, Roosevelt, toward the end of the war, proposed a "Second" or "Economic Bill of Rights" in which the "paramount" right was the guarantee of a job at a living wage.

Whereas popular movements contributed to progressive New Deal policies, strong regressive forces and near absence of progressive challenges are today's realities. Unlike FDR, Obama did not use the opportunity to identify culprits and causes of the crisis and to alter perceptions of the political economy. Government intervention stopped the free fall, but the lesson that government *can help* was not drawn, thereby leaving the nation ill-equipped to cope with persisting, high unemployment and an environmental crisis utterly dependent on government for its solution.

Notes

1. "Lessons of the 1930s: There Could Be Trouble Ahead," *The Economist*, December 10, 2011, 1.
2. Richard Walker and Gray Brechin, "The Living New Deal: The Unsung Benefits of the New Deal for the United States and California," Working Paper Series, Institute for Research on Labor and Employment, University of California–Berkeley, accessed July 15, 2013, available at http://escholarship.org/uc/item/6c1115sm.

1

Public Attitudes Toward Government

The Social and Political Contexts of the Great Depression and Great Recession

SHEILA D. COLLINS

At a time when domestic government spending is derided as "socialist" and government attempts to right systemic wrongs, however limited, are seen by many as threats to individual liberties, it seems unfathomable that there was a time when government was seen by a significant sector of the population as beneficent. Yet the Great Depression, after the initiation of the New Deal, was just such a time. How is it that the public attitude toward government was so different in the 1930s? The answer to that question lies in (1) the timing of events and the existence and character of popular social movements; (2) the cultural currents at work in the society; (3) the changing nature of the communications environment and its effect on politics; (4) the strength and composition of the president's party in Congress; (5) the political skills of the president himself; (6) the relative political power and cohesiveness of the business class; (7) the international political context; and (8) the environmental context. This chapter teases out the influences of each of these contextual factors on the public's attitude toward government intervention in the economy during the Great Depression and the Great Recession.

The Timing of Events and the Existence and Character of Popular Social Movements

Presidents Franklin D. Roosevelt and Barack Obama both entered office having inherited from their predecessors two of the worst economic crises in American history. The conditions that brought about the two periods of economic collapse bear striking resemblances. Yet the policy responses of both presidents to the crises and the attitude of the public toward the role of the federal government in both periods are quite different.

When Roosevelt took office in 1933, the Great Depression had been underway for over three years, and for several more before that in rural America. Unemployment engulfed a quarter of the working population, Wall Street had crashed, the American banking system had shut down completely, thousands of businesses had failed, shanties dubbed "Hoovervilles" filled the landscape, bread lines appeared in every major city—in short, the vaunted capitalist economy that just a few years before had been declared by Herbert Hoover to be entering "the greatest era of commercial expansion in history"[1] was in complete collapse. By the time Roosevelt took office, local relief, under the pressure of need and protest movements, had expanded, and most states had begun to provide some relief, but it was not nearly enough. State and local governments were overwhelmed by the extent of need, and the American people had become restive. There were large demonstrations in 1930 in every major city. In 1932 a "Bonus Army," composed of impoverished World War I veterans and their families, had descended on Washington, vowing to camp out at the nation's capital until they got the veterans' pensions immediately that had been promised for 1945, only to be ruthlessly routed and sent packing by President Hoover's army. Unemployed Councils had formed in cities across the land, and rent strikes and resistance to evictions were prevalent. It had taken nearly four years for at least a segment of the population, which had been deeply socialized in the virtues of individualism, to come to the realization that the destitution they were experiencing was not their fault but that of some basic flaw in the system. With state budgets unable to cope, they turned to the federal government for help and to a president who, though not knowing exactly what to do, had said he would do something to ease their pain. Within 100 days of Roosevelt's inauguration, a series of programs was instituted that would begin to permanently enlarge the role of the federal government in the lives of ordinary Americans, bringing hope to millions of the impoverished and unemployed, and stimulating economic recovery.

In contrast, when Barack Obama took office in January 2009, the economic meltdown, though potentially as serious as the Great Depression, was less than a year old; however, as a result of technological changes in the banking system, the panic that gripped investors was much less visible to the average person. Unemployment, though high, was, at 7.8 percent, nowhere near a quarter of the work force. Moreover, reforms that had been put in place by the New Deal such as Social Security, food stamps, unemployment insurance, and federal deposit insurance, as well as Johnson-era programs like Medicare and Medicaid, had helped to cushion the shock of economic decline. Having learned something from the failure of the Hoover administration to halt the economic slide, George W. Bush's Secretary of the Treasury, Henry Paulson, had urged Congress to pass the Emergency Economic Stabilization Act of 2008, a $700 billion bailout of those banks that had brought the global economy to the brink of meltdown.[2] This and subsequent Federal Reserve loans helped stem the erosion of confidence in the credit system and forestalled a complete economic collapse.[3]

With an economy merely stagnating, rather than collapsing entirely, public reaction to the Great Recession was understandably muted in comparison to the Great Depression. After a nearly forty-year corporate and Republican-led campaign to crush labor and discredit the role of the federal government, the only early, popular response came in the form of the right-wing Tea Party movement. Though initially a response to the bank bailout, the Tea Party was quickly co-opted by elements of the financial and corporate elite, becoming an anti-government movement that elected Republicans to office who supported the very policies responsible for the economic breakdown in the first place. It was not until 2011 that a populist movement on the Left arose; but the Occupy Wall Street movement, rather than calling for greater government intervention in the economy or making specific demands of it, took on an anarchist character, in effect, saying a plague on both Wall Street and government.

Cultural Differences Between the Era of the Great Depression and Great Recession

Cultural differences between the era of the Great Depression and today also played a role in the differing responses of the public to government efforts to relieve economic distress. Although there had always been in American political culture a fear of "big government," with the exception of the Civil War and World War I exigencies, the federal government had been largely absent in the lives and consciousness of most Americans. When it was clear that the private economy had collapsed and that the state governments with which the public was most familiar could not cope, there was only one remedy left. Thus, with no real personal residue of resentment against the federal government, most were willing to trust it to respond to their distress.

Trust in the federal government was facilitated by the cultural currents that had shaped many of the New Deal's top players. Foremost among these was the culture of progressivism, a versatile set of ideas that had at its heart a spirit of social reform and optimism in the perfectibility of human society.[4] While historians often tend to think of the Progressive era as having ended around 1919, its cultural influence lived on through the 1920s influencing those who would undertake the reforms that came to be known as the New Deal. Two strains of progressivism, in particular, had had an effect on several of the New Deal architects. One strain was the "social gospel," an intellectual movement that had arisen among some middle-class Christian clergymen toward the end of the nineteenth and early twentieth centuries. As a reaction to the intense socioeconomic turbulence of the Industrial Revolution, its spokespersons preached that Christianity had a mission to transform the structures of society in the direction of equality, freedom, and community.[5] Walter Rauschenbush, one of its major proponents, foresaw a society that embodied the teachings and example of Jesus as a cooperative commonwealth in which producers would be organized on a cooperative basis, distribution would be organized on principles of justice, workers would be treated as valuable ends, not as means to a commercial end, and parasitic wealth and predatory commerce would be abolished.[6] By 1908 the social gospel had succeeded in penetrating the institutional structures of the churches with a "social creed" that was adopted by the mainline denominations. Anticipating by three or four decades many of the reforms enacted in New Deal legislation, the social creed called for the alleviation of Sunday working hours, the abolition of child labor, a living wage, the negotiation and arbitration of labor disputes, social security for workers in old age, disability insurance, poverty reduction, and a fairer distribution of wealth. For about thirty years, the movement called attention to poverty and urban distress, the harsh conditions of working people and immigrants, militarism, and racism.

The still relatively young field of social work with its settlement house work in many of the major cities was another strain that deeply infused the thinking and values of these New Dealers. Settlement houses were established by middle-class reformers appalled by the harsh realities of urban industrial life faced by poor immigrants during the turn of the nineteenth and early twentieth centuries. Imbued with progressivism's spirit of reform, some settlement workers helped assimilate and ease the transition of their impoverished charges into American life by providing them with literacy classes; social services such as health care, daycare, homeless shelters, public kitchens, and baths; recreational activities; and even exposure to and classes in the arts. Settlement houses like Chicago's Hull House and New York's Henry Street Settlement were also a nexus for political activism and research on social conditions, with reformers like Jane Addams (Hull House) and Lillian Wald (Henry Street Settlement) becoming involved in campaigns around public health, against child labor, for civil and human rights (including women's suffrage), fair labor legislation, and world peace.[7] Several of the New Dealers had early experience as social workers in settlement houses like Hull House and the Henry Street Settlement and/or had grown up in households infused with the social gospel.[8] Eleanor Roosevelt considered Addams and Wald her "great mentors and models."[9]

By the time Roosevelt was elected, progressivism was in the process of being transformed from an evangelical belief in the perfectibility of human society to what Leuchtenburg refers to as a "new style liberalism"—which was less interested in moral reform and more in using the power of the federal government to correct certain economic inequities; less rooted in the "old stock middle class of the small towns and cities" and more in the urban masses.[10]

In addition to the kind of social-democratic vision exhibited by progressive New Deal reformers, social movements during the 1930s were setting forth alternative visions of how society and the economy might be reordered.. An activist Communist Party looked to the collective experience of the Soviet Union; the Socialist Party in its "Declaration of Principles" called for resistance to international war and the "bogus democracy of capitalist parliamentarism" in favor of a "genuine workers' democracy"; Townsend Clubs advocated an old age pension financed by a federal sales tax; Huey Long's "Share the Wealth" movement sought a decent standard of living for all Americans by capping personal fortunes through a restructured progressive tax code whose benefits would go into public benefits and public works. Long also called for free higher and vocational education, a guaranteed annual income, a thirty-hour work week, a four-week vacation for every worker, veterans' benefits and health care, a limit on inheritances, and greater regulation of commodities. Upton Sinclair, the muckraking writer, whose exposé of conditions in the meatpacking industry had led to significant social reform, ran as a Democrat for governor of California on a platform of ending poverty by having the State of California take over idle factories and farmland and run them as cooperatives. On the other side of the political spectrum, fascism also claimed some adherents, among them radio priest Father Charles Coughlin. Alive in the culture of the 1930s, this variety of alternative ideas offered a mix of solutions from which New Dealers could draw. In doing so, they could also arrest public support for the more radical of these approaches, at the same time demonstrating that the government was, in some measure, responding to public demands.

By the time Barack Obama was elected president, however, the country had experienced over three-quarters of a century of "big government." The military–industrial complex that had emerged from World War II had given the U.S. government unimaginable global power, and increasing areas of private and economic life were being regulated and surveilled by the federal government. Moreover, there was now a permanent revolving door between big government and big business, which had the effect of corrupting the democratic process and skewing public policy toward the wealthy and powerful. The result was increasing polarization within the polity and in Congress. One side, while still believing that government could help, despaired of a federal government that seemed to side most of the time with big business and acted as an imperialist abroad, while the other side, employing a faux populism, argued that big government was the problem and that, with the exception of defense, it should be cut back as far as possible.

Moreover, the period of optimism in the perfectibility of human society that had characterized many of the architects of the New Deal had given way to a cynicism about large-scale social engineering. Alternatives to the left of the Democratic Party had been thoroughly crushed by anti-communism, by the eclipse of labor militancy as early as the late 1930s, by the globalization of labor (encouraged by government policies) that began in the early 1970s, as well as by continual factional fighting within the left.

A brief resurgence of political optimism accompanying mass movements of the left had erupted in the 1960s, but without an institutional base to codify the message and translate it into political power, it had evolved into a set of postmodern preoccupations centered on race, gender, sexuality, and lifestyle that competed with each other and generated a conservative political backlash that was able to use these as wedge issues to divide what was left of the New Deal coalition and to reassert the values of *laissez-faire* and limited government.[11] The brief optimism during the Johnson administration that society could be massively restructured was quickly crushed by the intransigence of economic racism, by the series of assassinations of political leaders, and by disillusionment over the Vietnam War. The assassination of Dr. Martin Luther King was especially devastating, as he had been moving at the end of his life toward a far more radical critique of American power and capitalism and had been in the process of planning a massive Poor People's Campaign with a campout at the capital similar to the Bonus Army campaign of 1932. Thereafter, the only alternative to the commercial Keynesianism of the postwar period was the return of the idea of *laissez-faire,* which became the rallying cry for a resurgent right that for the next forty years promulgated its benefits through a highly funded campaign consisting of think tanks, research institutes, conservative media outlets, and the religious right, which, for its part, had managed to destroy whatever was left of the vestiges of social gospel thinking in the mainstream denominations.[12] Thus, to insist that government could be a force for good was that much harder in 2009 than it was in 1933.

The Changing Context of the Communications Environment

When the Great Depression broke out, the only media available to the American public to learn about politics were newspapers—which were much more prevalent and varied in every city than they are today—news and opinion magazines, weekly newsreels offered in local theaters, and the radio, which in the 1930s was a relatively new medium. Of all these media, radio was the only one that had the quality of simultaneity.[13] Roosevelt was quick to grasp the potential of the radio to reach a mass audience and used it brilliantly in his "fireside chats"—a series of informal talks in which families gathered in their living rooms around a crackling radio to listen to their president, much as they would gather around a fireplace.[14] Because the radio was such a new phenomenon and seemed almost magical to an audience that had never before heard a live broadcast, these talks—homey, educational, exhortative—"helped make participants—even activists out of his audience."[15] Typical broadcasts would begin with the salutation, "My friends," and then the president would proceed to tell his listeners about what was happening around the country, describe what the New Deal was doing for people in ways that made it personal and brought it home to those listening, tell them what he was planning to do to meet some new problem, exhort them to support these efforts, and ask them to tell him about their troubles and give him their ideas and advice. And the people responded. Hundreds of thousands of letters poured into the White House after each of these chats, some in the grammar of the barely literate, and others in the grammar of the highly educated. "They enclosed editorials, articles, cartoons, and pamphlets they thought the President should see, as well as poems, drawings, photos, stories, jokes, and recipes they wanted to share with him."[16] The fireside chats connected people to their government as well as to other citizens from very different walks and conditions of life in ways that they never had before and probably have not been connected since.

One letter of the many thousands that Roosevelt received sums up the effect he had on ordinary citizens.

> We listened with great interest to your "fireside chat" last evening, and are in accord with your plans and ambitions for the farmer and the less fortunate of our people in this United States. The fact that you go about and observe personally and take the keen interest and have the intelligence to know how to correct the evils which exist, make you the outstanding President of all History. It is such a relief to hear about human beings and natural resources, and not "gold" and "statistics" by the yard. I am one former Republican who voted for you, and been your most devout follower. Your indomitable courage; your never finding any problem insurmountable is a guiding spirit to this nation.[17]

The letter was signed by a woman living in Waltham, Massachusetts. From her language, it is obvious that she was educated and cultured and probably not suffering as much as some others from the Depression. The president had been speaking that day about a trip he took to visit nine states affected by the Dust Bowl.[18] In concretely descriptive language he spoke about the environmental and human devastation he had seen and the farmers who needed government help. The talk created a feeling of empathy between this listener and farmers in another part of the country whose values and lifestyle were probably very different from hers and generated a sense of solidarity and desire to help, turning even a former Republican into a supporter of the Democratic regime.

Roosevelt also made effective use of other sources of communication that were available in his day to inform and educate the public about the programs he was initiating and to tout their benefits. He was the first to initiate the presidential press conference and was more accessible to the press than any president up to that time had been. He also turned the signing of bills into political theater. Public speeches were, of course, staples, and he was a master at political speech. He made ample use of the "special message" accompanying these messages with draft bills.[19] Roosevelt's speeches portray him as having an uncanny ability to give new meaning to traditional values so that they resonated with the American people. Many of his speeches and "fireside chats" were used to educate the public about history, ecology, finance, or any number of other subjects, as well as what his programs were doing to help the economy. Roosevelt's first fireside chat, delivered on the heels of the banking crisis of 1933, is a perfect example. "I want to tell you what has been done in the last few days, and why it was done, and what the next steps are going to be," he began. "I recognize that the many proclamations from state capitols and from Washington, the legislation, the Treasury regulations, and so forth, couched for the most part in banking and legal terms, ought to be explained for the benefit of the average citizen."[20] He then went on to describe in simple terms how the banking system works, why the run on the banks had happened, what effect it had had on the economy, why he had instituted the bank holiday, and how that holiday was to be resolved. He finished, as he usually did, by reassuring the American people and by inviting them to cooperate in resolving the problems.

The New Deal arts programs also provided a variety of ways to promote the role of government—through posters announcing New Deal programs and events, mural paintings placed in public buildings across the country, documentary films, signs and billboards, music, photography, and film. Wherever a New Deal program was in operation, one could usually find a sign or billboard announcing that this was courtesy of the New Deal. And of course, the works programs of the administration directly employing millions of people made their own case for the government.

Although there are many more ways a president today can use the media to reach mass audiences—from television addresses and press conferences to various forms of social media—the effectiveness of that message is drowned out by the multiplicity of competing sources of information and communication that now exist. The wired world of modern-day communications makes the president's voice less salient than it was in Roosevelt's day and, moreover, has fragmented the audience. This fragmentation has had enormous implications for the American presidency. According to Martin P. Wattenberg, the new media landscape has diminished the role of the president and denied him a mass audience for important speeches. As late as the early 1980s, when just three networks dominated the listening public's access to political news, presidents were guaranteed that at least half the public would tune in to important presidential messages and that their message would continue to permeate the public consciousness through news reports for days afterwards.[21] For example, when President Reagan outlined his proposed policies for economic recovery to Congress on prime-time television on February 18, 1981, he received a Nielson rating of 60 percent. In contrast, when President Obama addressed the country on the economic crisis on February 24, 2009—despite the fact that he was covered by more media outlets—his combined rating was only 32.5 percent—a little over half as much. Since the use of the "bully pulpit" has long been considered one of the president's greatest leadership tools, the lack of such public access makes governing all the more difficult.

Changes in the media over the past thirty years have also changed the nature of the audience for political news. When the three major networks (ABC, CBS, and NBC) dominated the airwaves, Americans tuned in to a fairly consistent national narrative. However, with the rise of cable TV, talk radio, the Internet, blogging, and social media, as well as the decline in newspaper reading, Americans are increasingly talking to and hearing from people who think and vote as they do. This echo chamber makes any kind of national consensus about where the country should be going extremely difficult, if not impossible, and even gives rise to disputes about basic "facts." For example, a CBS News/New York Times poll taken as late as April 2011 found that at least 45 percent of Republicans and Tea Party members believed that Obama was not born in the United States, despite his 1961 birth announcement printed in two Hawaii newspapers, verification of his birth by the governor of Hawaii and by Obama himself, who was forced to produce a long copy of his birth certificate.[22]

Despite the difficulties today in attracting attention, the president still commands a bully pulpit, and Obama could have used it to much greater advantage. Given the fact that a third of the stimulus money went for tax breaks rather than jobs (a concession to the incessant Republican mantra against taxes), he could have made more of the fact that an estimated 500,000 to 3.3 million full-time jobs were saved or created by the stimulus.[23] Though Obama touted a figure of 2.5 million jobs in a number of speeches, the fact that those jobs came indirectly through grants to states and were often used to save jobs rather than create new ones made it more difficult for people to see the connection. Still, as economist Alan Blinder has pointed out, Obama was not nearly as effective as Roosevelt in communicating clearly to the American public about what was happening, why it was happening, and what the government was doing about it. The stimulus, Blinder argues, although still insufficient, was much more effective than Obama has been given credit for, and this lack of credit is largely because of the communications failure of his administration.[24] Although some of the infrastructure projects bore signs labeling them a product of the American Recovery and Reinvestment Act, most of the projects consisted of repair of existing infrastructure—road, bridge, and sewer repair, etc.—and thus did not have the same panache as the new dams, hospitals, schools, and post offices to which the Roosevelt administration could point. As Jonathan Alter pointed out, "The bill funded only a fraction of the infrastructure projects listed by the American Society of Civil Engineers as in need of construction or repair. Worse, the project did little to stir the imagination of the public."[25]

The Strength and Composition of the President's Party in Congress

Another difference in the two periods consists of the relative strength and ideological composition of the president's party in Congress. Roosevelt was elected in 1932 by a landslide, with 57.4 percent of the popular vote to Hoover's 39.7 percent and 472 electoral votes to Hoover's fifty nine (an eight to one advantage).

Between 1933 and 1935 Democrats held fifty-nine Senate seats to the Republicans' thirty-six, while in the House the Democrats outnumbered Republicans by more than two and one-half to one. Thus, Roosevelt had a sweeping mandate to change the direction of the country and especially the people's relationship to the federal government. With the economy starting to improve and people being put to work, the midterm elections in 1934 yielded an even greater Democratic majority—more than two thirds—in both houses. Many members of the Seventy-fifth Congress were now clearly to the left of the president, while the election, according to the *New York Times*, had "literally destroyed the right wing of the Republican Party."[26] However, Roosevelt's decision to balance the budget in 1937–1938, which sent the economy once more into depression, resulted in large Republican House gains in the 1938 midterm election.[27] Democrats lost a net of seventy-two House seats, bringing to nearly even the balance of power in the House ((D–48.6 percent to R–47 percent). While losing six seats in the Senate, Democrats continued to hold a commanding lead there (more than two-thirds). The president, however, faced divisions within his own party. Conservative Southern Democrats, by dint of seniority, chaired most of the committees, forcing Roosevelt to bend his programs to mollify their states' rights and racist agenda. Nonetheless, as several chapters in this book attest, while ideological and regional divisions within the Democratic party modified what Roosevelt might have wanted to do, he was able to work with them most of the time, and the New Deal programs, for all their limitations, were the result. By 1938, however, Southern Democrats were becoming more hostile to the president's designs, strengthening a Republican-conservative Democratic coalition that weakened the president's ability to expand New Deal style innovations. In the opinion of most historians, this effectively brought the New Deal to a halt, although, as Leuchtenburg has pointed out, the country still placed more faith in the Democrats, and it wanted none of the reforms undone.[28]

Obama was elected in 2008 with 52.9 percent of the popular vote to McCain's 45.7 percent and 365 electoral votes to McCain's 173 (a two to one advantage). Democrats held a fifty-seven to forty-one majority in the Senate and a 256 to 178 majority in the House. Since the Democratic majority was half that of FDR's, Obama's mandate was not nearly as dramatic as Roosevelt's had been in 1932 or 1936, nor as big as Lyndon Johnson's in 1965–1966 when the bulk of the Great Society programs were enacted.[29] Thus, the opportunity for enacting Obama's agenda was a narrower one. Yet Obama had an advantage that neither FDR nor Lyndon Johnson had in the fact that his Democratic party was more consistently liberal than his predecessors'.[30] As a result, he was able to pass the first major reform of the health care system as well as a massive stimulus bill in his first year in office. These were major accomplishments comparable in significance to some of Roosevelt's reforms, yet not a single Republican voted for the health care bill, and only three Republican senators voted for the stimulus, whereas in 1935 sizable majorities of Republicans in both the House and Senate had voted for the Social Security Act, albeit after offering some resistance in committee.[31] Instead of fueling a resurgence of support for government intervention, as Roosevelt's policies had done, Obama's initiatives were met with hostility from Republicans and tepid support, if not criticism, from many Democrats. With a victory that seemed less than triumphant and unemployment running higher than when Obama took office, the 2010 midterm election turned into a rout for the Democrats, who lost sixty-three House seats, giving Republicans the majority. Although the president's party usually loses seats in midterm elections, this was the largest seat change since the midterm elections of 1938. Thereafter, the intensely partisan—even hostile—nature of the Republicans who had been elected, fueled by Tea Party anger and a rigidly held ideological commitment to reducing government, made getting almost anything done extremely difficult.

The Political Skills of the President

The Democratic rout in the 2010 midterm election resulted, in part, from the surge in radical right-wing candidates elected by the Tea Party and the political gridlock that followed was a function of the redistricting accomplished by Republican legislatures. This gerrymandering enabled Republicans to win congressional seats out of proportion to their numbers.[32] Gridlock was also aided by the increased use by Republicans of the threat of a filibuster. Legislation could be killed by a minority simply by threatening a filibuster. Jacob Hacker and Paul Pierson argue that politics today, where a Republican minority can win victories that are at odds with the moderate center of public opinion—or where they can halt *any* legislative action—defy the logic of the way in which the American political system is supposed to work.[33] Although the right wing rails at the power of the executive branch, in reality, a dysfunctional Congress has become more important and powerful than the president. This makes the role of the legislator in chief, despite being elected by a popular majority, subject to the stranglehold of a minority ideology.

While Obama faces a far more difficult political context than that faced by Roosevelt, at least part of the blame must also rest on the shoulders of the man elected president. To be an effective president requires being a good politician, and this involves a set of the specific political skills and experience that Roosevelt possessed in abundance. Among those skills is the ability to know which advice to listen to, which usually means evaluating not just the person giving the advice but the incentives and political context surrounding that person. During his first term Obama continually misjudged his adversaries. Having come into office with the self-image of someone who could heal the deep polarization that had been building in both the electorate and the Congress for over forty years through the power of reason alone, he failed to understand the emotional undercurrents that govern so much of political life. Fear of an America that was on the decline, fear of a way of life that was changing rapidly and of a population that was becoming less white—a fear personified in the president—was surely fueling much of the animosity among the Republican rank and file. In failing to grasp this fear, Obama could not acknowledge it, could not sympathize with it, could not address it in the way that Roosevelt had been able to do in his 1933 inauguration address and thereafter.

Nor could Obama, whose own economic appointees had failed to place strict limits on Wall Street speculation, challenge the moneyed interests that were exploiting this fear with anything like the candor that Roosevelt did when he excoriated the bankers as "unscrupulous money lenders" and "self-seekers" who had abdicated their responsibility to the American people.[34] Thus, Obama ended up not only alienating members of the opposing party, but disillusioning many of those who had voted for him thinking that he would do something to curb the power of the big banks and restore fairness to the home mortgage industry. The large Democratic loss in the 2010 midterm election was partly due to the fact that a portion of those who had turned out enthusiastically to vote for Obama in 2008—especially the young—failed to go to the polls in 2010.[35]

Even before becoming president, Roosevelt had proven to be a master reconciler, demonstrating his ability to bring together urban working-class machine voters with anti-urban agrarian voters, and after becoming president to reconciling southern conservative Democrats with northern liberal Democrats, at least until 1938.[36] Carefully cultivating the new urban working class ethnic groups (mostly Catholic) that would become the base of his support, he was also careful not to neglect his fellow (mostly middle-class) Protestants, who were thought to be predominantly Republican.[37] Obama, on the other hand, tended to neglect his poor and working-class black and Hispanic base, ignoring the gross inequalities that shaped their lives in his attempt to woo middle class whites and upwardly mobile minorities. Although large majorities of his base continued to vote for him, they had become less enthusiastic by 2010. Despite his attempt to woo white voters, he was able to win no more than 39 percent of the white vote in his 2012 re-election, although it should be noted that it was about the same percentage as won by Clinton in a three-way race in 1992 and exceeded the percentage of the white vote earned by Walter Mondale in 1984, Jimmy Carter in 1980, and George McGovern in 1972.[38]

Political judgment also involves knowing when to stand one's ground, when to compromise, and how to read the public mood. Roosevelt was a canny politician in this regard, although his Supreme Court–packing scheme may seem to be an exception. Paul H. Appleby, who served in the administration, wrote, "Roosevelt would never have expressed himself about a legislative proposal in terms that deprived him of alternative positions and lines of retreat and modification."[39] Rhetorically, at times he could appear very progressive, but when judging that the political context for what he had wanted to accomplish was going to make that impossible, he could draw back to a compromise position, getting some measure of what he had wanted but not giving away the entire store. Obama, on the other hand, made the mistake when he had a Democratic majority of caving in to the opposition too soon, thus giving away whatever leverage he might have had to achieve a compromise that allowed some part of his agenda to be enacted. Having, perhaps, learned that no matter how far he went to appease the Republicans, they would not meet him halfway, he appeared, at the beginning of this second term, to be laying some clearer markers for what he would not accept and asserting that he would go around Congress by issuing executive orders and taking his message to the American people. However, his offer in the 2013 budget standoff with Republicans to reduce Social Security and Medicare, two pillars of the Democratic coalition, in exchange for increased revenue from taxes only angered his base and failed to win over any Republicans. By then it was too late.

It is common knowledge that presidents today live in a self-isolating bubble. Surrounded by layers of security and people who live and work within the radius of Washington, they have few opportunities to mingle for any length of time with ordinary people. Although the technology for gauging the public mood is today vastly superior to that which existed in the 1930s as the science of public opinion polling, focus groups, survey instruments, and sophisticated marketing tools has been perfected, it is doubtful that presidents today have a better way of judging the public mind than they did in Roosevelt's time. Those who have studied public opinion polling have exposed the ways in which polls can often be skewed depending on the way a question is asked or by what are offered and not offered as responses. Polls cannot get at the contradictory opinions most people hold and may only gauge a superficial level of opinion and one that is highly volatile. Since most Americans today do not pay much attention to politics and their knowledge of issues is often confused, they may answer a pollster's questions out of ignorance.

Although limited physically by polio, Roosevelt may have had an advantage in judging the public mood that Obama lacked. Eleanor Roosevelt and the journalists Lorena Hickock and Martha Gellhorn spent time traveling the country listening to the complaints of people suffering from the Depression, gathering data about conditions and feeding back stories and information to Roosevelt and members of the administration. The president himself took several trips around the country during the Depression to survey conditions and to talk to people who were suffering. The feedback he received from the letters sent in response to his fireside chats was another way of gauging the public mood and in Roosevelt's own opinion, constituted the "most perfect index to the state of mind of the people."[40]

The existence of those letters, which can be read at the Roosevelt Library and Museum in Hyde Park, New York, attest also to Roosevelt's ability to connect with and inspire the American people, perhaps the most important quality for a president. Roosevelt had a unique gift for doing this. Frances Perkins wrote in her memoir of Roosevelt,

> His voice and his facial expression as he spoke were those of an intimate friend. After he became President, I often was at the White House when he

> broadcast. . . . As he talked his head would nod and his hands would move in simple, natural, comfortable gestures. His face would smile and light up as though he were actually sitting on the front porch or in the parlor with them. People felt this, and it bound them to him in affection. . . .
>
> . . . It was this quality [*of being one with the people*] that made the people trust him and do gladly what he explained was necessary for them to do.[41]

Some of the skills needed for effectiveness in the presidential office can be learned through experience in jobs with similar requirements. When Roosevelt ascended to the presidency, he had already had significant legislative and executive experience as a member of the New York State Senate, Assistant Secretary of the Navy, and Governor of New York State during the difficult, early Depression years. Such experience not only develops managerial skills and enhances one's understanding of political context, but it also provides a president with a much wider universe of persons whom he can draw on to serve the administration. Many of Roosevelt's choices were distinctly unusual. Roosevelt brought into his "Brain Trust" a large mix of people. Some were bankers and businessmen, but others were farmers and academics and social workers. Moreover, as noted earlier, several of his appointees and advisors—such as Frances Perkins, Harry Hopkins, Adolph Berle, Jr., Henry Wallace, Rexford Tugwell, Harold Ickes, and Henry Morgenthau, Jr.—had had experience in the field of social work and/or had been influenced by the social gospel and Progressivism's reform agenda.[42] This background gave some of them a strong incentive to treat government responses to the Depression, not simply as technical economic fixes, but as remedies that would restore human dignity to those who had been beaten down by the Depression and a sense of pride in the culture, history, and landscape of the country.

In contrast, Obama came into office having served as a member of the Illinois Senate for seven years, but less than one term as a U.S. senator, part of which time he was running for president. As a relative newcomer to national office with no executive experience, he lacked the variety of political experience that Roosevelt had. The result was a naïveté about how to get things done and an over-dependence on Clinton-era appointees, inside-the-Beltway politicians, and Republican defense officials, rather than on people who had come to their offices from varied backgrounds. In contrast to Roosevelt's Treasury Secretary, Henry Morgenthau, Jr., whose Treasury Department funded several of the work programs for artists, and his Federal Reserve Chairman, Marriner Eccles, who, though a banker, was a Keynesian even before Keynes, Obama's economic team, drawn from the Clinton era, consisted of men with deep ties to Wall Street and to the deregulatory anti-government ethos that contributed to the meltdown.[43] Consequently, their approach to economic relief lacked the undergirding in humane values that Roosevelt's advisors had exhibited.

But other presidential skills are not just a matter of previous political experience. They also have to do with personality and character. The most effective presidents have been those who enjoyed the rough and tumble nature of politics. FDR, in particular, was a master politician who reveled in the job. He was said to possess an "irrepressible vitality" whose "vibrant good cheer was contagious."[44] Kenneth S. Davis, while acknowledging that there was a darker side to Roosevelt's personality, wrote that for the most part he exuded an optimistic faith and a *joie de vivre* that "bordered often on the miraculous."

> Every day, in steady stream, people came to him with troubling problems and because of their troubles. Often enough, waiting in the anteroom or their appointed times, they showed themselves unhappy; they were tense, anxious, despairing, angry, their faces drawn with fatigue, their gestures nervous. But almost always, after a quarter hour in his presence, they departed his office smiling and refreshed, their spirits uplifted, their confidence restored, as if they had taken a bath in liquid sunlight and been soaked through by it.[45]

Obama, while praised for his sometimes soaring rhetoric, appeared uncomfortable in the job and often expressed disinterest in playing the "games" that effective politicians must play in order to forge coalitions and win over adversaries. Aloof and reserved, he rarely consulted with members of Congress or met informally with them until his second term and often came across as arrogant, even if that was not his intention. Part of Obama's difficulty, of course, might be traced to the fact that as a black man he had had to earn his way into the elite white male club from which so many presidents are drawn through the strength of his intellect rather than through the circumstances of his birth. And there was no doubt that racism was at the heart of some of the animosity that was generated against him.[46] Roosevelt, on the other hand, was a patrician and perhaps because of his security in this class status could argue that "These unhappy times call for the building of plans that . . . build from the bottom up and not from the top down, that put their faith once more in the forgotten man at the bottom of the economic pyramid,"[47] and he could talk passionately about the inequality that was sapping American freedom and announce to a roaring crowd that he "welcomed the hatred" of the forces of "organized money."[48]

Although both Roosevelt and Obama have been labeled pragmatists, perhaps the most important difference between the two presidents lies in the broader vision for the country that Roosevelt possessed and Obama lacked, a vision that could rally the country to re-elect him four times over. Leuchtenburg has called it his "grasp of the interrelationship of the larger aspects of public policy."[49] This broader vision was most visible in the New Deal arts and culture and environmental programs. But it was also visible in his conception that a new age required a new conception of such old American ideals as "liberty," "security," and "freedom" that could be implemented in new types of public policies. Roosevelt's "Economic Bill of Rights" incorporated in his 1944 State of the Union message spells out that broader vision.

The Relative Power and Cohesiveness of the Business Class

Both the periods leading up to the Great Depression and Great Recession were characterized by increases in mergers and acquisitions resulting in deepening wealth and income inequality. However, the inequality that characterized the two periods was somewhat different. Picketty and Saez,[50] who have done extensive research on income and wealth disparity using tax data, point out that the post–World War I depression and the Great Depression destroyed many businesses and thus significantly reduced top capital incomes. The [income] share of the top decile on the eve of the Great Depression was around 45 percent but dropped during the Great Depression and again during World War II. From the end of that war until the 1970s, it was around 33 percent, when it began to pick up again. Emmanuel Saez, the author of one of the studies, attributes this drop to the regulatory and tax policies enacted by the New Deal as well as to the shock of the war. By the eve of the Great Recession, however, the income share of the top decile had climbed to beyond where it was on the eve of the Great Depression—to 49.7 percent, a level higher than any other year since 1917. While the Great Recession erased some of that income growth for the top decile, it did not do so for long, and the regulatory and tax policies currently on offer by Congress are not likely to undo any of the dramatic increase in top income shares that has taken place since the 1970s.

What is even more interesting about Picketty and Saez's work than what they show about the income share of the top decile over time is what they show about the fluctuations of the income share of the top percentile—the one percent decried by the Occupy Wall Street movement. The top percentile, they point out,

> has gone through enormous fluctuations along the course of the twentieth century, from about 18 percent before WW I, to a peak of almost 24 percent in the late 1920s, to only about 9 percent during the 1960s–1970s, and back to almost 23.5 percent by 2007. Those at the very top of the income distribution therefore play a central role in the evolution of U.S. inequality over the course of the twentieth century.[51]

Top one percent incomes captured more than half of the overall economic growth of real incomes per family over the period from 1993 to 2011, but between 2000 and 2007, the years preceding the meltdown, the top one percent captured even more—two-thirds of income growth.[52]

Even more interesting is the composition of the income of the top one percent. During the Great Depression and World War II periods, most of the income of the top one percent came from capital income (mostly dividend income) and to a smaller extent business income, the wage share being very modest, and thus drops in the stock market seem to account for the large fluctuations during this period.[53] Whereas top wage shares were flat from the 1920s to 1940 and dropped precipitously during the war, top wage shares are now higher than before World War II. Picketty and Saez conclude from this that the working rich have now replaced the coupon-clipping *rentiers*.[54] The high compensation packages that chief executive officers have given themselves and the failure of Congress to limit these packages, even when government money was helping the banks to stay afloat, may be one reason for this.

The precipitous drop in the income of the top one percent in the Great Depression served for a time to weaken and divide the creditor class, making it possible for more progressive government intervention in the economy, including reforms of the financial system that served to reduce income inequality until the 1970s. Today, however, because a greater share of their income comes from wages rather than dividends, the drop in the income of the one percent in 2008 was not as great as in the early 1930s and rather quickly rebounded. In fact, the richest one percent captured 93 percent of income growth during the first year of recovery (2009–2010) while the bottom 99 percent saw income growth of only 0.2 percent.[55] The ability of contemporary CEOs to give themselves enormous salaries and bonuses, even as their businesses face losses, attests to the profound disconnection not only between the managers and shareholders, but between what is good for managers and what is good for the country's economy. This may be one reason why, unlike a significant proportion of the ruling class during the Great Depression, they have vehemently ruled out any measures to redistribute income, in fact, in order to avoid this, calling for more cuts in domestic spending, especially in those areas that benefit the majority and ultimately the economy as a whole. Today, the revolving door between big government and big business—a phenomenon that barely existed in Roosevelt's day—makes government redistribution that much harder. The Supreme Court's decision in *Citizens United v. Federal Election Commission* (2010) that allows corporations and labor unions to spend unlimited amounts of money on advertisements and other political tools calling for the election or defeat of individual candidates is both a reflection of this change in the cohesion of the ruling class and a further enforcer of it. In the absence of tax and regulatory policies that curb the wages of the very rich, as well as changes in campaign financing, the political and economic power and cohesion of the corporate and financial elite will continue to corrupt our democracy and weaken faith that government can be a source for good.

The International Political Context

Roosevelt took office at a time of deep disillusionment over foreign entanglements. World War I—"a dirty, unheroic war"—with its terrible toll of trench warfare and horrendous casualties had been called the "war to end all wars." The American population and much of the Congress vowed never to fight again. As Leuchtenburg put it, "at no time in our history has the hold of pacifism been stronger than in the interlude between the first and second world wars."[56] With the exception of Latin America—in which the United States was engaged in a largely invisible imperialist domination (except, of course, to those who were dominated)—and its Pacific colonies, demobilization had returned the United States to an inward-looking country. Deep protectionist currents in the Congress had resulted in the erection of tariffs on international trade, which, at any rate, the United States was not heavily reliant on, as it had escaped the war with its economy unscathed. With the Crash of 1929, moreover, world trade had come to a grinding halt. Even foreign entanglements meant to keep the peace, such as the League of Nations and the World Court, had been rejected by the Senate. So strong was the isolationist sentiment in Congress that a series of Neutrality Acts was passed that prohibited American ships and citizens from becoming entangled in outside conflicts. While the refusal to use American power to try to mitigate the factors that would eventually lead to World War II seems, in retrospect, mistaken,[57] the absence of foreign entanglement meant that when the Depression hit, the Roosevelt administration could focus on fixing its domestic economy. The end of the war had also turned the United States into a creditor nation, and no military–industrial complex existed to vie for a large chunk of the national treasury. No treaties bound the United States to protect foreign states if they were invaded. No fear of imminent attack led the American people to welcome a national security state.

By the time Obama took office, the United States had become a major superpower with over 700 military bases around the world, a military budget amounting to 58 percent of spending by the top ten military powers in the world[58] and one that ate up by some estimates 58 percent of domestic discretionary spending,[59] the largest nuclear weapons arsenal in the world, and a national security state with vast powers of surveillance and coercion. Moreover, it was engaged in waging two wars at once—in Iraq and Afghanistan—and had committed itself to an unending asymmetrical war against a non-state terrorist enemy that could strike at any time. It existed within an international context of swiftly changing geopolitical dynamics that posed grave and seemingly intractable challenges to world peace and stability and was entangled in a vast web of international trade, investment, and labor flows that dwarfed anything in the 1930s. In addition, unlike the United States in the 1930s that had yet to become an empire, the United States was now an empire in decline, a major debtor facing a rising China and maintaining its self-image of superiority largely in respect to its military might.

The Environmental Context

While the Roosevelt administration faced environmental problems of unprecedented proportions, these problems—deforestation, soil erosion, the need for flood control, the lack of rural electrification—were largely containable within the borders of the United States and, with concentrated attention, could and would be mitigated through wise stewardship and reclamation policies. Though in use, fossil fuels had not yet spawned the massive international cartel that in the twenty-first century would dominate the politics of nations; and the chemical industry had not yet reached its deadly zenith. It was not until the publication of Rachel Carson's *Silent Spring* in 1962 that the country would become aware of what the chemical industry had been pouring into the environment. Nor had nuclear power become an industry that generated a waste stream so deadly that it would have to be sequestered for tens of thousands of years.

The United States now faces an environmental crisis of far greater dimensions and far more complexity than that faced by the Roosevelt administration, and the crisis is now global. Species extinction and climate change, not to mention pollution from the chemicals that are poured into our environment as well as wastes from industrial agriculture, have reached crisis proportions and, in the case of climate change, the timeline for fixing them is very short, if not past. As the world's leading climate scientists had predicted, natural disasters are now occurring more frequently and with greater intensity, causing not only massive human and physical dislocations but straining the ability of even most advanced country governments to deal with them. These problems can no longer be contained within the borders of one country, and thus solutions must be found through international negotiations and treaties. But meeting the environmental challenge in the United States is made all the harder by a powerful campaign funded by the fossil fuel lobby that has convinced the Republican party (a party deeply beholden to this lobby) and a portion of the population that climate change is a "hoax," and that evidence-based science is not a reliable guide for public policy. What is more, we have a Congress that is so ideologically fixated on deficit reduction that it is making it almost impossible to fund the kinds of programs at the level that is necessary to bring about economic recovery and reduce our reliance on fossil fuels. All of these differences in both the international geopolitical climate and the environment make the job of a President of the United States today infinitely harder than it was in the 1930s, notwithstanding the fact that the economy in those years had collapsed entirely, whereas the United States finds itself today in a long, fragile, job-poor recovery.

Despite the fact that the political, cultural, and environmental differences between the Great Depression and Great Recession make it harder today to assert a role for government in mitigating the problems that now beset us—from poverty, unemployment, inequality, lack of affordable housing and healthcare, to environmental degradation and climate change—the contributors to this book still believe that government can and must be part of the solution and that there is much that we can learn from a time when government was indeed viewed as the solution, not the problem.

Notes

1. Herbert Hoover, Speech at San Francisco, July 27, 1928, accessed January 28, 2013, available at http://historymatters.gmu.edu/d/5063.
2. The Emergency Economic Stabilization Act was known as the Troubled Asset Relief Program (TARP), whereby the government was authorized to purchase distressed assets, especially mortgage-backed securities, and supply cash directly to banks.
3. According to an analysis by Bloomberg, altogether the Federal Reserve had, by March 2009, committed $7.77 trillion to rescuing the financial system, more than half the value of everything produced in the U.S. that year. Bob Ivry, Bradley Keoun, and Phil Kuntz, "Secret Fed Loans Gave Banks $13 Billion Undisclosed to Congress," *Bloomberg Markets Magazine*, November 28, 2011,accessed January 17, 2013, available at http://www.bloomberg.com/news/2011-11-28/secret-fed-loans-undisclosed-to-congress-gave-banks-13-billion-in-income.html.
4. Trust-busting; federal income taxation; fair labor standards including the prohibition of child labor; the secret ballot; the direct election of senators; the primary, initiative, referendum, and recall in electoral politics; women's suffrage; and environmental conservation were all a legacy of the Progressive era. So too was the settlement movement that brought together middle-class reformers with impoverished immigrants who were socialized into American society and provided with education, healthcare, and daycare.
5. In addition to New Deal administrators, the social gospel movement contributed leaders to such organizations as the American Civil Liberties Union, the National Association for the Advancement of Colored People (NAACP), and the Fellowship of Reconciliation, among others. Major social gospel clergymen included Walter Rauschenbush, Washington Gladden, Josiah Strong, Richard Ely, Shailer Mathews, George Herron, and Harry Ward. While most of the social gospel spokesmen adhered to a loose set of social-democratic values, Harry Ward was an anti-capitalist revolutionary who called for the complete "overthrow of militarism and of capitalistic industrialism." Gary Dorrien, *Social Ethics in the Making: The Interpretation of an American Tradition* (Malden, MA: Wiley-Blackwell, 2011),113.
6. Ibid., 96.
7. American settlement workers engaged in "the meticulous empirical reconstruction of the ethnic, occupational, industrial and housing patterns within city neighborhoods," contributing to the emerging field of urban sociology. Michael B. Katz, *In the Shadow of the Poorhouse: A Social History of Welfare in America* (New York: Basic Books, 1986), 159. Jane Addams, founder of Chicago's Hull House, was the most prominent reformer of the Progressive era. She fought corruption in Chicago, fostered a more equitable distribution of city services, modernized inspection practices, worked with the Chicago Board of Health, served as the first vice-president of the Playground Association of America, was elected president of the Women's International League for Peace and Freedom in 1915, attended the International Woman's Conference in The Hague, and was chosen to head the commission to find an end to the war. In 1931, Addams was the first American woman to win the Nobel Peace Prize. Lillian Wald, founder of the Henry Street Settlement in New York City, pioneered public health nursing, helping to found the National Organization for Public Health Nursing and Columbia University's School of Nursing. Wald also helped institute the NAACP, the United States Children's Bureau, the National Child Labor Committee, and the National Women's Trade Union League.
8. Secretary of Labor Frances Perkins had once worked at Jane Addams's Hull House settlement in Chicago and later with immigrant girls in Philadelphia. She earned a master's degree in social work and worked for a while with the National Consumers League. Harry Hopkins, FDR's relief administrator and close confidant, had worked in New York City at the Christadora settlement house and then as a case worker for the New York Association for Improving the Condition of the Poor. Subsequent work as executive secretary of the New York City Bureau of Child Welfare, as director of disaster relief for the Red Cross on the Gulf coast, as general director of the New York Tuberculosis Association, as well as his role as drafter of the charter

of the American Association of Social Workers and president of the Association, made him particularly sensitive to the social context in which economic problems arise as well as gave him tremendous experience in the management of large social programs. Adolph Berle, Jr., a member of Roosevelt's Brain Trust and an academic and corporate lawyer, was a critic of corporate concentration and a proponent of government regulation and planning. He had grown up as the son of a Progressive Congregationalist minister who preached the social gospel. He had also worked at the Henry Street settlement in New York City. Henry Wallace, FDR's Secretary of Agriculture, came from a line of committed Progressives. His grandfather had been a Presbyterian minister and farmer who preached the social gospel and viewed his life's mission as helping his fellow farmers, a legacy he passed on to his son and grandson. Rexford Tugwell, an economist and also a member of the Brain Trust, was appointed first as Assistant Secretary and then Undersecretary of the Department of Agriculture. Like Berle, he had also been influenced by the social gospel. Harold Ickes, FDR's Secretary of the Interior and director of the Public Works Administration, was a strong supporter of both civil rights and civil liberties. He had been the president of the Chicago NAACP and supported African American contralto Marian Anderson when the Daughters of the American Revolution prohibited her from performing in the DAR Constitution Hall. Ickes had worked at a settlement house in Chicago and had absorbed the settlement workers' idealism for social justice. Henry Morgenthau, Jr., had worked at the Henry Street settlement in New York and shared Progressivism's concern for social improvement, although he also hewed to the then-dominant belief in balanced budgets and was responsible for pushing Roosevelt to balance the budget in 1937, with disastrous results.

9. Blanche Wiesen Cook, *Eleanor Roosevelt, Vol. 2, 1933–1938* (New York: Viking, 1999), 430–431.
10. William E. Leuchtenburg, *The Perils of Prosperity 1914–1932* (Chicago: University of Chicago Press, 1958), 137–138.
11. Isserman and Kazin contend that although the New Left of the 1960s was thought to have accomplished "nothing," the United States was left both a more politically and socially contentious society but also a more just, open, and egalitarian one as a result of its presence. Maurice Isserman and Michael Kazin, "The Failure and Success of the New Radicalism," in *The Rise and Fall of the New Deal Order*, Steve Fraser and Gary Gerstle, eds. (Princeton: Princeton University Press, 1989), 214. Katznelson, however, argues that the Progressive possibilities of the New Deal had already been delimited by the war and postwar policies of the 1940s. Ira Katznelson, "Was the Great Society a Lost Opportunity?" Fraser and Gerstle, 185–211.
12. For histories of the way in which the right wing engineered a massive sea change in American politics and culture, see: Thomas Byrne Edsall, *The New Politics of Inequality* (New York: W.W. Norton, 1984); Sara Diamond, *Spiritual Warfare: The Politics of the Christian Right* (Boston: South End Press, 1989); Thomas Byrne Edsall with Mary D. Edsall, *Chain Reaction: The Impact of Race, Rights and Taxes on American Politics* (New York: W.W. Norton, 1991); Leon Howell, *Religion, Politics and Power* (Washington, D.C.: The Interfaith Alliance Foundation, undated); Leon Howell, *Funding the War of Ideas, A Report to the United Church Board for Homeland Ministries* (October 1995); Kevin Phillips, *American Theocracy: The Peril and Politics of Radical Religion, Oil, and Borrowed Money in the 21st Century* (New York: Viking, 2006); Jacob S. Hacker and Paul Pierson, *Off Center: The Republican Revolution and the Erosion of American Democracy* (New Haven: Yale University Press, 2005); Thomas B. Edsell, *Building Red America: The New Conservative Coalition and the Drive for Permanent Power* (New York: Basic Books, 2006); Gertrude Schaffner Goldberg and Sheila D. Collins, *Washington's New Poor Law: Welfare "Reform" and the Roads Not Taken, 1935 to the Present* (New York: The Apex Press, 2001), Chapter 5, 103–125.
13. Lawrence W. Levine and Cornelia R. Levine, *The People and the President: America's Conversation with FDR* (Boston: Beacon Press, 2002), 1.
14. Huey Long and Father Coughlin also grasped the power of the radio and used it brilliantly.

15. Levine and Levine, 5.
16. Ibid.
17. Letter from Gertrude Irene Falk, Waltham, Massachusetts, to President Roosevelt, September 7, 1936, in Levine and Levine,153.
18. Franklin D. Roosevelt Fireside Chat, Labor Day 1936, accessed February 19, 2013, available at http://millercenter.org/president/speeches/detail/3306.
19. William E. Leuchtenburg, *The FDR Years: On Roosevelt and His Legacy* (New York: Columbia University Press, 1995), 16.
20. Franklin D. Roosevelt, First Fireside Chat, March 12, 1933, accessed February 19, 2013, available at http://www.americanrhetoric.com/speeches/fdrfirstfiresidechat.html.
21. The average rating for presidential speeches has dropped by at least 40 percent compared to the 1970s and early 1980s. Martin P. Wattenburg, "The Presidential Media Environment in the Age of Obama," in *Obama Year One*, Thomas R. Dye et al., eds. (New York: Longman/Pearson, 2010), 56–58.
22. Another 18 percent of Americans said they did not know where he was born. Stephanie Condon, "One in Four Americans Think Obama Was Not Born in U.S," CBS News/New York Times poll, April 21, 2011, accessed August 30, 2011, available at http://www.cbsnews.com/8301-503544_162-20056061-503544.html.
23. Josh Boak, "CBO: Stimulus Added Up to 3.3M Jobs," *Politico*, November 22, 2011, accessed March 3, 2013, available at http://www.politico.com/news/stories/1111/68965.html. Estimates of the number of jobs saved or created have varied according to the time frame considered as well as the difficulty in estimating such figures.
24. Alan S. Blinder, *After the Music Stopped: The Financial Crisis, the Response, and the Work Ahead* (New York: The Penguin Press, 2013). Journalist Michael Grunwald also argues that Obama's stimulus was much more significant than he has been given credit for. See Michael Grunwald, *The New, New Deal: The Hidden Story of Change in the Obama Era* (New York: Simon & Schuster, 2012).
25. Jonathan Alter, *The Promise: President Obama, Year One* (New York: Simon and Schuster, 2010), 128.
26. Levine and Levine,128.
27. While the continued economic downturn and high unemployment probably played the strongest role in Republican gains, other factors included Roosevelt's much-disliked Court-packing scheme and his effort to defeat certain conservative Southern Democrats in the primaries.
28. William E. Leuchtenburg, *Franklin D. Roosevelt and the New Deal 1932–1940* (New York: Harper and Row, 1963), 274.
29. Brendan Nyhan, "Obama versus FDR and LBJ," March 3, 2010, blog post, accessed February 12, 2013, available at http://www.brendan-nyhan.com/blog/2010/03/obama-versus-fdr-and-lbj.html.
30. Ibid.
31. Ibid. FDR and LBJ, however, had two major advantages relative to Obama—more moderate Republicans and fewer filibusters.
32. For an explanation of the way in which the Republicans have used the gerrymander to increase their congressional power out of proportion to their numbers, see Sam Wang, "The Great Gerrymander of 2012," *New York Times*, February 3, 2013, Sunday Review, 1.
33. Hacker and Pierson.
34. Franklin D. Roosevelt, Inaugural Address, March 4, 1933. National Archives, accessed March 3, 2013, available at http://www.archives.gov/education/lessons/fdr-inaugural.
35. John Nichols, "Young Voter Turnout Fell 60 percent from 2008 to 2010; Dems Won't Win in 2012 if the Trend Continues," *The Nation*, November 16, 2010, accessed December 5, 2013, available at http://www.thenation.com/blog/156470/young-voter-turnout-fell-60-2008-2010-dems-wont-win-2012-if-trend-continues#. The youth vote was down by 10 percent from the last mid-term election of 2006 when Obama wasn't on the ballot.

36. David M. Kennedy, *Freedom from Fear: The American People in Depression and War, 1929–1945* (Oxford/New York: Oxford University Press, 1999), 97.
37. Leuchtenburg, *The FDR Years*,128–129.
38. Chris Cillizza, "The Fix," *The Washington Post*, November 8, 2012, blog post, accessed February 12, 2013, available at http://www.washingtonpost.com/blogs/the-fix/wp/2012/11/08/president-obama-and-the-white-vote-no-problem.
39. Paul H. Abbleby in a letter to William Leuchtenburg, August 30, 1950, in Leuchtenburg, *The FDR Years*, 193.
40. Franklin D. Roosevelt, quoted in Levine and Levine, 5; originally in Louis McHenry Howe, "The President's Mail Bag," *American Magazine*, June 1934, 23.
41. Frances Perkins, *The Roosevelt I Knew* (New York: Harper & Row, 1946/1964), 72.
42. See note 7 for the influence of Progressivism and the social gospel on New Deal leaders.
43. Most of Obama's economic team were protégés of Robert Rubin, who played a role in mentoring people for political office similar to the role Felix Frankfurter at Harvard Law School had played for Roosevelt. Rubin had been Clinton's Treasury Secretary but his résumé also included stints as board member and co-chair of Goldman Sachs and director and senior counselor and chair of Citigroup. Unlike the role played by Frankfurter, however, the U.S. government did not have to bail out Harvard Law School as it did Citigroup. Timothy Geithner, Obama's Treasury Secretary, had been head of the Federal Reserve of New York, which had failed to regulate the banks in the run-up to the 2008 meltdown; Larry Summers, director of Obama's National Economic Council, had helped tear down the wall between commercial and investment banking as Treasury Secretary under Clinton and had been a part-time hedge fund manager. Other Rubin protégés included Jason Furman, Peter Orzag, Michael Froman, Philip Murphy, Gene Sperling, Jacob Lew, Gary Gensler, Diana Farrell, Lewis Alexander, Lael Brainar, and David Lipton. All continued to maintain their ties to Rubin. Alter, *The Promise*, 28–29. The one similarity between Roosevelt's Treasury Secretary, Henry Morgenthau, Jr., and Obama's economic advisors was his belief in balanced budgets.
44. Kennedy, 112.
45. Kenneth S. Davis, *FDR: The New Deal Years 1933–1937* (New York: Random House, 1979), 202.
46. For an analysis of the racialist underpinnings of the ideology of the Republican party, see Sam Tanenhaus, "Original Sin: Why the GOP Is and Will Continue to Be the Party of White People," *The New Republic*, February 10, 2013, accessed February 12, 2013, available at http://www.newrepublic.com/article/112365/why-republicans-are-party-white-people.
47. Roosevelt, radio address, Albany, N.Y., April 7, 1932 in Franklin D. Roosevelt, *The Public Papers and Addresses of Franklin D. Roosevelt, Vol. 1, 1928–1932*, (New York : Random House, 1938), 624.
48. Roosevelt, speech before the 1936 Democratic National Convention, Philadelphia, Pennsylvania, June 27, 1936, accessed February 8, 2013, available at http://www.austincc.edu/lpatrick/his2341/fdr36acceptancespeech.htm
49. Leuchtenburg, *The FDR Years*, 28.
50. Thomas Picketty and Emmanuel Saez, "Income Inequality in the United States, 1913–1998," *Quarterly Journal of Economics*, 118, no. 1, 2003. The authors define income as the sum of all income components reported on tax returns (wages and salaries; pensions received; profits from businesses; capital income such as dividends, interest, or rents; and realized capital gains) before individual income taxes and excluding government transfers such as Social Security retirement benefits or unemployment compensation benefits.
51. Ibid., 12.
52. Emmanuel Saez, "Striking It Richer: The Evolution of the Top Incomes in the United States (Updated with 2011 Estimates)," January 23, 2013, 4, accessed February 13, 2013, available at http://topincomes.g-mond.parisschoolofeconomics.eu/#Country:United%20States.
53. Ibid.

54. Picketty and Saez. In 2011, the top decile share dropped slightly to 48.2 percent but was expected to pick up in 2012, Saez, "Striking it Richer," 3
55. Saez, "Striking it Richer," 4.
56. Leuchtenburg, *The Perils of Prosperity*, 104.
57. See Leuchtenburg's argument on this issue in ibid., 104–119.
58. International Institute for Strategic Studies, "Military Balance," accessed January 30, 2013, chart available at http://www.iiss.org/publications/military-balance/the-military-balance-2012/press-statement/figure-comparative-defence-statistics.
59. See "Cost of War, Security Spending Primer Fact Sheet #2," no author, accessed January 30, 2013, available at http://costofwar.com/media/uploads/security_spending_primer/discretionary_budget_m_vs_nm.pdf.

2

A Tale of Two Crises

A Comparative View of the Political Economy of the Great Depression and Great Recession

VOLKER JANSSEN

Open the newspaper today and it looks as if the entire nation has turned Austrian. No, we are not witnessing mass migration towards the small nation in the European Alps, but a powerful drift towards a body of economic thought widely known as the Austrian school. Similar in principle to the classic economic liberalism of the nineteenth century, the contemporary followers of Ludwig von Mises and Friedrich Hayek hold steadfastly to the notion that economies grow and recover their natural balance of supply and demand on their own, if only prices are allowed to fall freely—especially the price of labor. Any effort of government that impedes the balancing mechanism of price fluctuations—such as the pledge of the business community to Herbert Hoover in 1930 not to lower wages, the Federal Reserve's purchase of mortgage-backed securities since 2008, or the financial support for the struggling American automobile industry by the Obama administration in 2009—is nothing less than an interruption of the "natural" restoration of a market equilibrium.[1] Republican presidential candidate and multimillionaire Mitt Romney took this stand when he recommended in a 2011 interview in Las Vegas, Nevada—ground zero of the imploding housing market—not to "try to stop the foreclosure process" and to "Let it run its course and hit the bottom."[2] Herbert Hoover's Secretary of the Treasury Andrew Mellon summarized this economic view deftly over eighty years ago when he urged his president to "liquidate labor, liquidate stocks, liquidate the farmers, and liquidate real estate." Never too concerned about the fate of ordinary Americans, the multimillionaire treasurer was convinced that this would "purge the rottenness out of the system," by which he meant weak banks and businesses. Such bloodletting, which would come at a high price for most Americans, was part of Mellon's cure. "High costs of living and high living will come down. People will live a more moral life. Values will be re-adjusted, and enterprising people will pick up the wrecks from less competent people."[3] This is economic theory as a morality play—or an exercise in social Darwinism.

The Austrian school notion is that economic recession is a cure rather than an ill. This "wreckage of false expectations" has recently gained a large following among libertarians, Tea Party enthusiasts, and many whose wealth is secure enough to ride through any slump.[4] Historians like Amity Shlaes have given new credence to this return to nineteenth-century economic thinking with her history of the New Deal, *The Forgotten Man*. Shlaes's account blames government intervention for the scope of the Depression and claims that the New Deal did not create new employment, a charge that ignores both the employment numbers for the New Deal years and gross domestic product (GDP) growth rates that averaged 7.7 percent annually between 1933 and 1941.[5] As the nation remains deeply divided over its response to the lingering effects of the Great Recession, and as policymakers determine what lessons are to be learned from the Great Depression, it is hardly surprising that such historical revisionism gains the attention of some pundits and politicians. Shlaes's book is a favorite among Republicans, and Newt Gingrich and the author have a strong mutual affection.[6]

Even Americans who have never heard of Friedrich Hayek, the Austrian school, or Amity Shlaes frequently remember the Great Depression as a "readjustment of values," to paraphrase Andrew Mellon. Local journalists who have turned to survivors for an authentic comparison of the 1930s with the Great Recession have gathered countless anecdotes that contrast past suffering as a lesson in virtue and the fallout of the recent Great Recession as the proper comeuppance for a spoiled generation.

Widespread are the stories of family solidarity and neighborly support, of the stoic endurance of deprivation with humble gratitude and ingenuity. In almost every story, survivors took away the lessons of hard work and frugality. In turn, welfare recipients and the poor tend to get poor marks from Depression survivors who are confused by the different face of poverty today. As stories of perseverance and determination, these accounts of the Great Depression can certainly inspire a younger generation. But as much as Americans lived through the Great Depression as individuals, as families, and as neighbors, they also existed in an economy much larger than their own worlds. It would be too much to ask of Americans to recall, say, the impact of the Federal Deposit Insurance Corporation, which no one notices, since it got rid of the most dramatic memory of an economic downturn, the bank panic of 1933. Nor should we expect the present generation to attribute the standardized thirty-year, self-amortizing home mortgage, and thus the expansion of American homeownership after World War II, to the New Deal's Federal Housing Administration. We should not even begrudge the fact that these memories understate federal relief programs, the lifeline many received through the Civilian Conservation Corps or the Works Progress Administration. And we should not be surprised that they give little mention to lasting institutions such as Social Security or the postwar prosperity that was built on New Deal legacies and was marked less by hard work and frugality than by a new age of consumption. Personal memories are exactly that—personal. They owe the historical context nothing. It is for that reason that any comparison of the Depression era with the early twenty-first century needs to stress the features of the larger political economies. As seductive as the idea of the nation's economy as a morality tale may be, the story is much bigger than that of our grandparents or great-grandparents and different from what Austrian school economists would have us believe.

This chapter compares the political economy of the periods of the Great Depression and Great Recession, highlighting telling similarities and crucial differences in the causes of the two economic downturns. What do we mean when we characterize the economy of the interwar years as a "national industrialized consumer economy," and how does this compare to our globalized service and information economy of today? What infrastructures, technological systems, and scientific standards drove productivity and growth prior to the Great Depression, and what has been behind economic expansion in the last twelve years? What place did the United States assume in the global flow of labor, capital, and goods in the interwar years, and how does this compare to the United States in the world economy today? Finally, how did social, monetary, and fiscal policies shape growth and the distribution of income in the 1920s and today? I begin with a brief summary of the key similarities and differences between the economic collapse of 1929 to 1933 and will conclude with some observations about the different responses of government in the two eras.

The American Way of Life: Then and Now

For young urban Americans in the 1920s, the world looked brand new. There was the jazz that gave the age its name, marathon dancing, body building, and crossword puzzles. They visited speakeasies that illegally sold alcohol in defiance of Prohibition, ate bagels, attended "petting parties," and flirted on "lovers' lanes" in the privacy of their cars. Young women wore low-cut gowns and lipstick, bobbed their hair, and spent their own money. African-Americans discovered a new sense of community and culture in Northern urban neighborhoods such as Harlem, Chicago's Southside, or Los Angeles's Central Avenue. To many rural folks, small town residents, and new urban dwellers, on the other hand, the "Roaring '20s" suggested a corruption of family values, prostitution, racial mixing, bootlegging, and crime. For them, modern life seemed to push traditions and standards off their foundations, and they turned bitterly against what they considered the causes of these undesirable changes—immigrant cultures, labor unions, women's autonomy, science, and the teaching of evolution.[7]

The unbridled enthusiasm for a new age and economy in the 1920s reminds us of the more recent hype about a new online marketplace and community, one in which old traditions and customs no longer count and in which new patterns of consumption and leisure shape a new generation. The conservative reaction—from the surge of religious fundamentalism and anti-immigrant sentiment to the rejection of science—is equally familiar. But to be sure, the changes of the interwar years had been in the making for a generation, just as those of the post-9/11 era did not arise suddenly. The transformation of American life into that of the 1920s consumer society had begun in the late nineteenth century and accelerated remarkably in the 1920s. This transformation extended deep into Americans' culture of work, family life, international relations, and the nation's political culture. At its center, however, stood a surge in mass production, mass consumption, and a new infrastructure geared towards middle class consumerism. Consider the fact that housing began to sprawl into suburbs outside metropolitan centers during that time and that the increasing availability of electricity there as well as in city apartments made possible the use of consumer durables like vacuum cleaners, washing machines, and other household appliances. Only 20 percent of Americans had indoor flush toilets in 1920, but 51 percent enjoyed this amenity ten years later. Central heating was a rarity at the beginning of the decade (one percent of households), but existed in 42 percent in 1930. Radios did not exist in 1920, but four out of ten families owned one by the end of the decade. Most importantly, Americans in the 1920s bought automobiles whenever they could. By 1929, one in every five Americans owned a car, compared to only one in 135 Germans. Large cities like New York, Chicago, and Los Angeles were already familiar with big traffic jams. For the first time in history it seemed that a standard of living once only available to a small elite, if that, was within reach for a large share of the middle-class.[8] A growing number of Americans hoped to ascend to a middle-class lifestyle through education that would qualify them for skilled white-collar work. High school became an American institution, and high school graduation rates rose steadily over the decade.[9]

Part of the change in the national culture of the 1920s was a new embrace of consumer credit, promoted by carmakers and other durable goods producers. A small down payment allowed consumers to "buy now, pay later."[10] The motivation behind this financial innovation was simple: mass consumption did not keep pace with mass production, and only by lowering the thresholds for large household purchases and enticing customers to spend ahead of their earnings could durable goods producers sustain their growth rates. Magazines and the radio broadened Americans' access to information, and advertising campaigns for make-up, ready-made food, and gadgets like personal cameras offered consumption as a lifestyle choice.

Move forward to the early 2000s, and we can observe a very different transformation of consumption and popular culture driving a very similar increase in productivity and output. And both were shaped significantly by new credit-financed consumer experiences. Not cars, radios, telephones, and toasters, but wireless computing and communications, social media, and new online multimedia formats spread rapidly through American households. General Motors and General

Electric shaped consumers' lives and tastes in the 1920s; in the early 2000s, Apple and Google did. The growing demand for consumer durables of the 1920s was part of the political economy of an industrial consumer society in which cars and home appliances furnished the American dream of middle-class family life—much of it dependent on a public infrastructure of transportation, energy, and education. Apple products, Google services, and other agents of the Web revolution have improved the digital access to information, increased worker productivity, and fostered online communities and e-commerce at the expense of traditional communal ties and brick and mortar retail, transcending or bypassing existing public infrastructures rather than reinforcing them.

In the 2000s as in the 1920s, Americans and their economists believed that economic growth derived from increases in worker productivity. The expansion of the Fordist regime of mass production in electrically powered factories certainly increased the output per worker. And there is a good case to be made that the technological change in information and communications in the 1990s reaped significant rewards in the 2000s. Add to that the incorporation of China, India, and the former Soviet bloc into the global post–Cold War economy, and it seems only sensible that economic growth was accelerating. In both cases, however, the evolution of the financial sector altered the scenario considerably, and in both cases consumers relied on credit at an accelerating rate to partake of this growing economy, giving producers and sellers the impression that all was well indeed.[11]

Striking also is the contrast in the way the flagship industries fit into national and global economies. Electricity mobilized industrial power sources in the 1920s and allowed for an increase in continuous flow process methods and the assembly line. The result of such increased industrial productivity was a place like Detroit—the quintessential American city of industry. Since the 1970s, however, revolutions in communications, air travel, and cheap cargo shipment via container vessels have made urban-industrial concentrations like the "motor city" a relic of the past. Global flows of capital, goods, finance, and to some extent even labor have blown a hole in the economic clusters of mid–twentieth century industrial cities. Employment, as a result, takes place everywhere. Apple, the largest U.S. company ever, as measured by its stock market evaluation, has 47,000 employees in the United States, but probably employs up to 700,000 through a network of suppliers that make iPhones, iPads, and other products overseas. By comparison, General Motors employed 77,000 people in the United States in 2011 with market capitalization less than 10 percent of that of Apple.[12]

Between 1921 and 1929, employment in manufacturing industries accounted for much of the 9 million new jobs created. Economic historians have estimated that the average unemployment rate was just 3.3 percent between 1923 and 1929, an average that admittedly obscures the high degree of employment uncertainty and frequent short-term periods of unemployment among factory workers. Workers' productivity grew significantly as a result of technological innovation during this period.[13] Back then, wages and working hours also improved, although the average increase here, too, obscures unequal progress for skilled and unskilled workers. Real earnings between 1900 and 1910 had increased 20 percent, about 12 percent in the following decade, but a full 23 percent between 1920 and 1930.[14] Not all sectors benefited equally, however. Urban industrial workers tended to fare better than their counterparts in rural areas. Women had been part of the American industrial labor force since the early 1800s, but in the 1920s the majority still worked in domestic service or in "pink collar" jobs—the gender-segregated bottom rung of white collar work that comprised secretaries, switchboard operators, and the like.[15] Membership in labor unions declined significantly in the 1920s, from more than 12 percent of the civilian labor force to less than 8 percent on the eve of the Great Depression.[16] Courts were commonly on the side of employers and granted frequent injunctions that temporarily forbade boycotts or picket lines. As a rule, the government did not interfere in these uneven labor relations. Kindled by the Russian revolution, widespread fear of Communism and labor radicalism after World War I undermined public support of unions, while welfare programs at new companies such as Eastman Kodak in Rochester, New York, reduced workers' incentives for organizing their own unions.[17] Finally, the most powerful union, the American Federation of Labor, showed little interest in organizing the unskilled workers of the growing mass-production industries. Employers also exploited religious, ethnic, and racial divisions within the working classes to prevent large-scale unionization.[18]

Similarly, in the first decade of the twenty-first century, the environment for unions was not a friendly one. Large employers like WalMart have worked aggressively to prevent unionization in their stores.[19] A heavy reliance on undocumented immigrant labor in agricultural and some food-processing industries has weakened the ability of unions to fight for workers' rights. At 37.5 percent in 2000, government workers had the highest rate of union membership in the American labor force. In contrast, only 9 percent of workers in the private sector were unionized. Whereas 24 percent of transportation and public utility workers were represented by unions, 18.3 percent of construction workers and 14.8 percent of manufacturing workers were organized. A mere 1.6 percent of employees in finance, insurance, and real estate were union members.[20] That said, basic New Deal labor protections persisted to prevent employers from the openly brutal suppression of labor activism Americans had witnessed in the 1920s and first half of the 1930s.

These differences in labor protections and unionization levels are significant, but there is a more profound difference between the labor force of the Depression era and today: in regard to the type of goods and services produced. In today's globalized economy, manufacturing increasingly takes place abroad, most famously—or notoriously—in China. Cheap-labor competition from developing nations has reduced economic growth in the United States to what Vanek has called "the non-transported goods industries," such as construction, restaurant and hospitality industries, or government goods and services, including the military. These were precisely the sectors that " 'flourished' in recent years or decades."[21]

Not that the economy of the 1920s was without its weak spots. New automotive and electrical industries grew profitably, but other sectors stagnated. The "golden age of agriculture" had passed with the recovery of international commodity markets after World War I and a related drop in crop prices. Stranded with heavy debt and low rates of return, farmers foreclosed at five times the rate in 1929 than in 1923. While the average earnings for all employees in the United States rose, farm income fell from an average of $1,196 to $945 by the end of the decade (comparable to $12,726 in 2013).

Farmers were not the only ones left behind by the new era. In fact, the growth in consumer durables went hand in hand with the stagnation or shrinkage of industries in what Joseph Schumpeter has described as a process of "creative destruction." The telephone replaced the telegraph; the internal combustion engine changed transportation patterns and spelled the ruin of many urban trolley lines.[22] Passenger miles on railroads—the nation's economic engine during industrial development—declined from 47 million in 1922 to 34 million in 1927, and profits remained small. With the exception of oil tankers and some special-purpose vessels transporting fruit from Central America, most ocean shipping depended on government subsidies to remain viable. The expansion of the oil and chemical industries reduced reliance on coal, the fuel on which previous economic fortunes had been built. The coal industry's share of national income shrank from 1.7 percent in 1922 to 0.7 percent in 1929.[23]

The nation's economy of the 1920s did not exist in isolation, of course—although many Americans wished that it did. In the wake of World War I, Americans grew tired of Progressive idealism. Doubtful that foreign diplomacy could "make the world safe for democracy," many subscribed to the notion of isolationism—minimal political involvement with foreign powers. At the same time, America's role in the world and global markets had changed dramatically as a result of the war. The United States had always been a debtor nation, owing some $3.7 billion to foreign investors in 1914. By 1920, the United States had become a creditor nation with $12.6 billion in investments abroad on its balance sheet. Much of this was financial aid the U.S. had provided to its European allies (particularly England and France) during their fight against Germany and the Central Powers. The Allies decided to recover their debt from defeated Germany through reparations, which ultimately led to that nation's monetary collapse in 1923. Under the Dawes Plan, the United States negotiated an international payment system whereby Wall Street and the Federal Reserve provided Germany with loans to be used to pay reparation demands to Allies. This allowed the Allies in turn to meet their obligations to the United States. At the same time, Americans sold more goods abroad than they bought. Congressional tariffs in 1921 and 1922 made it more difficult for Europeans to sell goods to Americans and earn dollars. Without that currency, Europeans had no choice but to pay with the international means of exchange—gold.

The war-related debt and credit triangle between the United States, the Allied Powers, and Germany was one challenge in international finance during that time. Closely tied to this was the burden the gold standard imposed on national economies. Wartime inflation had strengthened a broad desire in much of the world's economies to restore international economic and financial stability through resumption of the gold standard. The volume of a gold standard currency was fixed to its gold reserves and shrank or grew with the amount of gold in the nation's coffers. Some European countries chose exchange rates well below those of the prewar days to give themselves an advantage in trade, while the United Kingdom restored 1913 exchange rates in order to maintain London's position as the center of global finance. This was only accomplished through a major deflationary squeeze, and it pushed Britain's already struggling export industries further into contraction. To add to the struggling British Empire's troubles, international trade was favoring the United States after World War I, increasing the flow of bullion across the Atlantic. In an act of economic nationalism and petty rivalry with the neighbor across the channel, France began to actively buy gold to amass reserves. By 1929, France and the United States had amassed 60 percent of the world's gold reserves. Britain imposed high interest rates to attract foreign investors at the expense of domestic investors in search of credit. And on top of it all, the Bank of England relied on a $500 million commitment by the New York Federal Reserve, whose head, Benjamin Strong, prophetically warned his English counterpart, Montagu Norman, that "domestic considerations would likely outweigh foreign sympathies" in times of "speculative tendencies in the economy."[24]

Under normal conditions, an inflow of payments in gold to the United States would have raised prices, making American goods less competitive, European rivals more successful, and restoring the trade balance. Economists know this as the *price specie-flow mechanism*. It works at the expense of price and market instability in domestic economies—if it is allowed to work. The Federal Reserve wanted gold as well as price stability and stable markets at home and chose instead to manipulate the gold–currency relationship. This prevented inflation in the United States, but it also made banking systems in gold-starved currencies vulnerable.[25]

Isolationism as an ideological position has experienced something of a revival recently, although the resentment against foreign involvement has changed significantly in the late twentieth century and the early twenty-first century. Americans started to home in on the dangers of exporting manufacturing jobs to Mexico and then China during the post–Cold War recession of 1990 to 1992, simultaneously blaming China and American venture capitalists for shipping jobs overseas and depending increasingly on cheaper consumer goods from the growing Chinese manufacturing sector. Progressive critics of globalization were less interested in vilifying Chinese workers or their autocratic government than in speaking out fiercely against the new regime of free trade—represented by such international institutions as the International Monetary Fund (IMF) and the World Trade Organization (WTO). The mission of today's critics of globalization has not been one of economic nationalism, but of restraints on global capital in favor of international collaboration on pressing social and environmental issues. In other words, the critics of globalization wanted to reduce the power of the IMF, to make the WTO less a tool of international capital, and to achieve binding international resolutions to curb greenhouse gas emissions. Beginning with the war on terror under George W. Bush, a new critique of American foreign entanglement focused on the overly ambitious and self-serving efforts of "nation-building" in Iraq and Afghanistan. Since the onset of the Great Recession, however, the inability of European nations to resolve their currency and debt crises and the increasing significance of China, not only as the world's workshop but as a geopolitical force, international creditor to the U.S. bond market, and emerging consumer society, has fostered a popular economic nationalism in fierce denial of U.S. economic interdependence. Although fair-minded economists have also warned about the dependence of the U.S. consumer economy on Chinese capital—the United States has become the world's biggest borrower while China has risen from loser of the Cold War to the world's biggest lender. This fierce neo-isolationism is most pronounced among followers of the Tea Party movement and libertarians. It has even included calls for an end to the Federal Reserve System and a return to the gold standard—something Nobel Prize economist Paul Krugman confessed, in an interview with National Public Radio's Terri Gross, that he would never have thought possible in his wildest dreams.[26]

The gold standard was the monetary regime that governed the U.S. and the international economy of the 1920s. The fiscal regime designed by the élite of the Republican Party was the other. Presidents Warren G. Harding and Calvin Coolidge led most frequently with inaction, but their Secretary of Commerce, Herbert Hoover, put his stamp on Republican economic governance in the 1920s. Hoover effectively invented the role of the modern Secretary of Commerce during his time in the Harding and Coolidge administrations. He revolutionized relations between business and government, playing a central role in the effective regulation of radio broadcasting, aviation, and street traffic. Few would have doubted his capacity to master the nation's most difficult economic crisis, and his solid record as a humanitarian might have led many to expect that Hoover would be the first president to put relief of poverty over the principle that relief was not the province of the federal government.

Tightly connected to their commitment to make the federal government aid the development of American business was the Republican belief that tax cuts at the top could increase federal revenues. While Secretary of the Treasury Andrew Mellon cut taxes for Americans of all income groups in this first installment of trickle-down fiscal policy, his cuts had the biggest impact on those earning $1 million and more, and those who inherited wealth. Tax revenues rose proportionately with GNP, but not more. The share of disposable income for the top 1 percent increased from 14.2 percent to 19.1 percent, which is comparable to the share earners received in 1990 after a decade of President Reagan's policies.[27]

Both the Republican policy makers of the 1920s and advocates of trickle-down Reaganomics since the beginning of Reagan's presidency in 1981 have insisted that less progressive tax rates increased rewards for the owners of capital and thereby stimulated investment and industrial development. They have also claimed that the economic growth that would result from such tax cuts would increase fiscal revenue overall and reduce tax fraud. After World War I, when the United States was the largest manufacturing nation in the world, the latter claim was not unreasonable. Higher earnings on the top could very well have been spent on new manufacturing establishments in the United States—its fastest growing economic sector.[28] How much eventually trickled down to unskilled workers in those new industries is another matter—wage gains for the least skilled workers in industry were minimal during that time. And while the expected revenue increases did not materialize in the 1920s, the spending restraints under Calvin Coolidge meant that the federal government was able to retire some of its debt. Overall, the nation's debt shrank in the 1920s, from $24 billion to $16 billion, or by one-third.

Trickle-down since the Reagan administration has worked in a very different context. At the time, Ronald Reagan's economic advisor, Arthur Laffer, hypothesized that job gains would result from invested income at the top of the economic ladder. But American businesses that were already investing in manufacturing capabilities overseas were simply parking their money offshore. Top earners would have had no reason to let notions of economic nationalism trump their motivation for better gains and business ventures overseas, so whatever "trickled" came "down" many places, and not necessarily in the U.S. labor market. Equally problematic was the claim that tax cuts at the top would stimulate economic recovery and bring in higher levels of fiscal revenue. Even if that had been the case, soaring deficits resulting from increased military spending and war during the Reagan and George W. Bush years created fiscal crises for succeeding administrations.

As was the case with Mellon's original tax cuts, those of the Reagan years were not simply one fiscal policy, but the expression of a set of economic beliefs Peter Temin has termed the "Washington Consensus," a bipartisan economic policy of the post–Cold War years that embraced privatization and deregulation, stable exchange rates, and moderate fiscal policies.[29] This Washington Consensus included the belief that the era of big government was over, that the global economy of the late twentieth century required free-market solutions, and that the firewall between commercial and investment banks in the form of the 1933 Glass-Steagall Act was an obstacle to modern financial markets. Its repeal during the Clinton administration in 1999 marked a turning point in U.S. financial history, the end of an era, and the beginning of new experimentations with structured finance and collateralized debt obligations.

Boom and Crisis: 1929 versus 2008

Stock prices began to move up in 1926 and 1927, and shot upward with increasing speed in 1928 and 1929. A decade earlier, few ordinary Americans would have chosen the stock market over conventional savings accounts, but the marketing of Liberty and Victory bonds during World War I introduced some 22 million Americans to the securities market. The successful bond drives encouraged more corporations to "go public" by offering their shares on Wall Street. A growing number of brokers and investment firms like Goldman Sachs Trading Corporation offered buyers professionally managed investment "portfolios" that contained a diverse range of company shares. *Harper's Magazine* concluded the stock market was no longer an exclusive marketplace for "hard-boiled knights" but a place "for the butcher and the barber and the candlestick maker." The number of shares traded provides a good insight into the increasing activities in the stock market: in 1919, which had been the biggest boom year of the century, a total of 317 million shares were traded. In 1927, the New York Stock Exchange traded 577 million shares; in 1928, a full 920 million. In 1929, Wall Street traders made 1.1 billion share transactions. By the beginning of 1929, new investment trusts emerged at a rate of one a day, doing nothing but selling paper shares in paper portfolios.[30]

American consumers had learned from car dealers and department stores how easy it was to "buy today, and pay later." So, when stockbrokers offered similar deals on their products—paper shares in investment portfolios—it required no giant leap to understand the appeal of buying on margin.

With $100 down and a $900 loan from one's broker, a buyer could purchase 100 shares of a company such as Commercial Solvents at $10 apiece. Assuming that the company's share price rose to $20 in half a year—something that happened frequently in the booming market of 1928–1929—the investor could reap a profit of $1000 on his $100 investment, minus interest payments on the loan and commission fees. Spectacular gains in stock prices made it increasingly difficult for investors to resist margin buying. Buying on margin became so popular that commercial banks began to loan money to brokers, and corporations, too, pumped their own money into brokers' loans. By October 1929, brokers owed $6.6 billion to lenders such as Bethlehem Steel, Standard Oil, and the Chrysler Corporation, as well as $1.8 billion to regular banks.[31]

Many economic indicators at this time suggested that stock prices were increasing for good reasons. Gross national product and per capita income were growing steadily, productivity was increasing, and corporations were reporting profits. But after 1927, the stock market surge was driven by fantasy and speculation rather than by economic facts. Floor traders on Wall Street designed pools—schemes to artificially inflate prices by selling shares back and forth amongst each other, thus creating the allusion of intense market activity around an attractive stock. When buyers outside the pool bought the stock and their demand drove the price higher still, members of the scheme sold quickly and made handsome profits while the manipulated stock fell into a slump. Investors who wanted to make informed decisions had only limited access to information, since Wall Street required very little disclosure from listed companies, and investment bankers produced brochures good for advertising rather than careful assessments of the value of securities. Amidst the general exuberance, voices of caution dissipated. American business, with free rein from the federal government, seemed to have provided the solution to the economic and social problems reformers and unions had struggled with for decades. Typical of the confidence of the time was Democrat John Jacob Raskob, who titled his article in the *Ladies' Home Journal* "Everybody Ought to Be Rich."[32]

Partly because the 1920s witnessed many true stories of economic success, partly because people believed that technological innovations were truly inaugurating a new era, and partly because advertisers sold the illusion of an overall growing prosperity, more Americans were willing to invest with higher levels of risk. During the 1920s, speculation emerged as a major preoccupation of Americans. In 1920, Charles Ponzi of Boston—a former vegetable peddler, forger, and smuggler—convinced thousands of credulous investors that he could deliver a 50 percent return on their investment in his Old Colony Foreign Exchange Company, paying out just enough dividends to allay suspicions of fraud. This "Ponzi scheme" cost its victims everything, and earned its inventor millions—as well as a long prison sentence when the fraud came to light a few months later.[33] This was hardly the last trap for speculators eager for quick riches. The construction boom of the early 1920s produced not only urban sprawl, but also real estate booms in California and in Florida. At the height of Florida's land speculation mania in the summer of 1925, the *Miami Daily News* printed a 504-page issue crammed with real estate advertisements—the largest newspaper issue in history. A hurricane in 1926 brought an end to this euphoria and left many investors stuck with acres of swamp.[34] Speculators then began to look for new opportunities to turn quick profits and moved away from real estate and into the stock market.

The Federal Reserve had been concerned with the irrational exuberance on Wall Street for some time before 1929, believing that speculation drained capital from more productive investments. Fearful of taking more drastic measures such as limiting banks' access to credit, which would have curbed both broker loans and legitimate business loans, "the Fed" tried instead the strategy of "moral suasion"—with little effect. In December 1928, it increased the "discount rate," the interest rate at which banks could borrow from the Federal Reserve, from 4.5 to 5.5 percent. This increase did not make the broker loans unprofitable, but it signaled future restrictions in credit. Other central banks in Europe followed this example. But the stock market's following remained loyal to the bubble. Powerful bankers like Charles A. Mitchell of National City Bank balked at the Federal Reserve policy and promised to pump additional money into the broker's loan market. In the summer of 1929, the Index of Industrial Production headed downward, largely because homebuilding slumped farther for the third year in a row. The Federal Reserve decided to cool the heated stock market by increasing its bond sales in the open market. This meant that money in circulation increasingly went into Treasury savings bonds rather than into stocks.[35]

On September 7, 1929, the Standard and Poor's Composite Stock Index had peaked after the first break in the stock price rally. From September to October, trading volumes increased dramatically, and overall prices declined slowly. On October 24, 1929, panic selling hit the market: thirteen million shares changed hands that day, and the ticker technology was so overwhelmed that buyers and sellers did not know the prices of their afternoon trades until 7:00 PM that night. A group of bankers, including Charles A. Mitchell and J. P. Morgan & Co., tried to stem the tide of selloffs with a $20 million buying pool, and the Rockefellers similarly tried to keep up the price of their Standard Oil stock with a $50 million purchase. It was to no avail. National City Bank's and Standard Oil's stocks dropped precipitously.[36] Trading and the panic resumed on October 28th (Black Monday) and October 29th (Black Tuesday).

The market's decline continued until mid-November, by which time stock prices had fallen to half of their August value. Much of this had to do with the panic selling of stocks that brokers had purchased on margin. News from Wall Street raced around the world and triggered crashes at the London exchange, then in Berlin, in Paris, and finally in Tokyo. President Hoover, economist Irving Fisher, and other market experts assured the public that the American economy stood on solid footing. Such frequent incantations tried to separate the stock market from the American economy like froth on a drink, but they could not prevent the decline. News that industrial production had declined in the third quarter in the United States and that foreign economies were collapsing pushed more investors to cut their losses and bail out of the stock market.

Well into 1930, most stock prices remained above the levels reached in 1926. In the past, observers would have described such market behavior as a "technical adjustment." But in the 1920s, Americans had come to believe that they had entered a "New Era," and the stock market was one of its most illustrious symbols. Thus, falling stock prices hurt the optimistic view of the future and the power of capitalist enterprise. Pessimism spread rapidly. This crippled consumer spending and confidence, without which few were willing to buy goods on credit on the installment plan, the new American custom.[37] And experts at the Federal Reserve still believed that banks failed first and foremost because of poor management, and that the bankruptcies were part of the healthy process of competitive selection in the financial marketplace. Federal Reserve officials thus failed in their most important role, and the collapse of banks continued unabated. Previous market crashes had also produced bankruptcies and unemployment, but their effect had always been most pronounced on the fringes. In 1929 and the ensuing years, the economic plight unseated those who had thought themselves most firmly in the saddle.

In the 1920s, the risks of stock market speculation were significant. In the years after World War II, by contrast, securities fraud became more difficult, thanks largely to the creation of the Securities and Exchange Commission during the New Deal. And yet, it was a stock market crash that ended the twentieth century and inaugurated the new millennium. The burst of the "dot-com bubble" in 2000 shared some significant characteristics with 1929—it depended on an unbridled enthusiasm for new technologies that promised a "new era" seemingly unfettered by the dynamics that brought about economic failures in the past. And it was fed by millions of small middle-class investors rushing into the market hoping to cash in on a trend that seemed to churn out millionaires and hoping to make the financial gains that had eluded them through much of the hollow boom of the 1990s.[38]

Those who had not lost faith in the stock market in 1999 and 2000 might well have lost their nerve in the wake of the Enron, WorldCom, and other accounting scandals that followed soon after. Past the courtrooms and criminal prosecutions, little reckoning followed these corporate corruption cases, and Americans in search of a wiser and safer investment increasingly looked for tangible and seemingly safe assets in real estate. Early in October 2006, the conservative *National Review* celebrated the Bush Boom and compared it favorably to the hollow boom of the Clinton years. This boom "[was] different," explained Jerry Bowyer, since it was "driven by something tangible—profits." "Those who bet on the Bush boom have done well," Bowyer concluded, and "Those who bet against it, lost out."[39]

The occasion for Bowyer's gross mischaracterization of the Bush economy was a record high Dow Jones—an indication that the dot-com bubble had not completely spoiled Americans' appetite for private securities. But even though Bernard Madoff—the Charles Ponzi of the twenty-first century–drew Americans' attention back to the risks of the stock exchange, the biggest boom and bust of the Bush era would happen in the bond market. And American homebuyers were at the heart of it, without their knowledge.

What had made American homebuyers both the agents and the victims of the Great Recession was the proliferation of the sub-prime mortgage industry. Mortgage debt among American consumers had risen since Congress had deregulated the financial industry in 1980, lifted a ban on adjustable mortgage rates in 1982, and made home mortgage interests tax deductible in the Tax Reform Act of 1986.[40] This incentivized a home-loan business model that developed into a predatory lending practice, misleading borrowers about the real cost of their loans with manipulated and hypothetical "teaser rates." Overall, a long-term decline in the regulation of the mortgage industry made possible the explosion of the sub-prime mortgage market. In the 1990s, the biggest year for this segment of the home-financing sector had been a balance of $30 billion. In 2000, it had grown to $130 billion, and by 2005, Americans had borrowed $625 billion in sub-prime mortgage bonds. Seventy-five percent of this loan volume came with floating rates after the first two years. Worse, more than $500 billion of this loan volume had been repackaged and sold on the bond market. The securitization of mortgages had begun in the 1970s to give the government-sponsored enterprise the Federal Home Loan Mortgage Corporation ("Freddie Mac") access to more capital to finance home mortgages. By 1996, almost two-thirds of new home mortgages were traded in the bond market. But the secret to the sub-prime industry's success was an "originate and sell" model that allowed those who signed the loan to sell the debt and the associated risk as a repackaged mortgage bond. It was the packaging into collateralized debt obligations (CDOs) that obscured the true risk of the mortgages and made selling risky assets easy.[41]

Shielded from the risks of default through the securitization of home loans, the financial industries lured both prudent and unqualified buyers towards homeownership, who interpreted the rising housing prices as evidence that the American dream of owning their own home might soon be out of reach and that unconventional loans were both signs of a new age and their lucky break. Those Americans who signed up for "no doc" or "low doc" loans that required no income verification have often been maligned as calculating con artists, but most of them were immigrants and people of color who saw a chance at overcoming their biggest hurdle to ownership—a down-payment—and who could not imagine why anyone would loan them money if they were almost certain to default a few years down the line.[42] As was the case in the 1920s, leading voices in popular culture encouraged Americans to accept a new type of financial risk as the trend of the times. A surge of get-rich-quick literature did the job in 1920s; in the 2000s, reality TV and a rapid cable news cycle multiplied narratives and anecdotes of real estate wealth that were difficult to resist.

Of course, get-quick-rich financial schemes are nothing new and should be expected in a capitalist economy. But what allowed this industry to proliferate was not only the deregulation of the mortgage industry, but of the financial market as well. The Securities and Exchange Commission in particular had loosened the existing regulations for asset-backed securities (ABS) in 1992. In 2003, ABS became exempt from the fraud protections included in the Sarbanes-Oxley Act of 2002, and shortly thereafter ABS was relieved from registration requirements.[43] The purpose was to stimulate the bond market, and that was exactly what happened. Investment banks expanded into asset-backed securities hoping to rebuild their profitability after they had lost significant business in stockbroking to online trading services. Structuring finance meant that asset-backed securities were packed into different tranches of "risk" to be traded as collateralized debt obligations—the now-notorious CDOs. The repeal of the Glass-Steagall Act under the Clinton Administration in 1999 also allowed commercial banks to buy these new papers in large quantities. This meant that loan originators could package their home loans in asset-backed securities and sell them in highly processed form as CDOs to investors at, say, the Bank of America, where there was little understanding of the actual default risks hidden in these assets. Many investors relied heavily on the recommendations of publicly traded ratings agencies whose measure of success was the number of deals they rated for investment banks and the fees associated with it. In order for ratings agencies to keep the business of the mortgage industry, it had to accept the mortgage industries' projections of risk.[44]

In 2005, the Federal Reserve Chairman Alan Greenspan confidently concluded that the sound economic growth was "not altogether unexpected or irrational." To the public, it seemed as if central banks had indeed mastered the art of harnessing the business cycle.[45] But their conviction that the financial system was just a "transmission mechanism" for their monetary policy ignored the ways in which this mechanism had developed a life of its own—one that deregulators had had in mind all along.[46] Consider the fact that between 2000 and 2006, median wages grew by just about 1.7 percent, whereas the sub-prime–driven demand for housing had raised real housing prices by 22 percent.[47] It is difficult to escape the conclusion of Damon Silvers and Heather Slavkin that the deregulation of the mortgage and financial sectors was meant to bolster consumer spending that had stagnated because real income remained flat or was actually falling. With the expansion of credit card debt, mortgages, and home refinancing, American households had leveraged themselves heavily on the bet that growth was now permanent.[48]

Yet the discrepancy between median wages and median housing prices also meant that the bubble of this particular asset was unsustainable. The sub-prime mortgage industry could conceal the poor credit risk of its mortgage holders as long as housing prices maintained a steady growth rate and inventory sold quickly, since that allowed mortgage holders to move on to new property and new adjustable rate mortgages (ARMs). But in 2006, home prices ceased to increase, and in 2007, one of the nation's largest sub-prime mortgage lenders, New Century Financial, had to file for Chapter 11 bankruptcy after the investment banks that had bought their securitized mortgages exercised their right to turn these loans back to this broker firm because borrowers had ceased to make their payments within twelve to eighteen months. New Century's inability to buy back the mortgages ushered it into bankruptcy, but it also left its investors stranded. Bear Stearns was such an investor, and by August 2007, it teetered on the verge of bankruptcy. Around the same time, Countrywide Financial collapsed, and so did a similar outfit in Great Britain: Northern Rock. They were acquired by the Bank of America and Bank of England, respectively. The downturn accelerated in September 2008, when the government-sponsored mortgage insurance enterprises the Federal National Mortgage Association ("Fannie Mae") and Freddie Mac were pulled under by the failure of the secondary mortgage market and became subjects of a federal takeover in September 2008. The two had held the credit risk of more than 50 percent of the U.S. home mortgages, and shareholders lost all their money. One week later, Lehman Brothers went bankrupt, triggering the largest credit crisis in a century, since a large number of firms drew short-term funding for long-term securities from this investment bank. One day later, the Federal Reserve decided not to let the same thing happen to American International Group (AIG) and bought 80 percent of the company's stock at $85 billion.[49]

Fed chairman Ben Bernanke later explained this decision and the commitment to bailouts and the "too big to fail" principle as a lesson learned from the Great Depression. Bernanke credited Milton Friedman with the insight that central bankers bore considerable blame for the Depression, although his own work in economic history had underscored the severe consequences the nation suffered in the 1930s as a result of the disintegration of its financial infrastructure.[50] But this lesson had come to the Federal Reserve chairman only halfway into the crisis. Worse, its own unwillingness to prevent the bubble in the first place by using the powers Congress had provided or by asking Congress for the necessary powers had allowed the economy to boom and bust. To use Joseph Stiglitz's metaphor, the Federal Reserve under Greenspan had grown confident it could easily fix the wreck and never thought about preventing the accident in the first place.[51]

Government Helped—But When?

As banks shut their doors and left their clients out in the cold in the wake of the great crash of 1929, small and large businesses, too, lost their assets and had to declare bankruptcy. An economic historian, Ben Bernanke researched these bank failures and how they affected the credit available to small businesses and how many saw long-term relationships with their lenders end for good. Other banks approached these small businesses far more cautiously and could not evaluate the creditworthiness of new clients easily.[52] Even businesses with access to credit became cautious. Gross investment in the United States declined by over a third between 1929 and 1930, and did so again the following year. By 1932, depreciation of capital goods exceeded investment level.[53]

The Crash of 1929 turned the lives of many Americans upside down, but few Americans probably saw their worldview shaken as much as did the President himself. Hoover's biography reveals that he was convinced that individual self-reliance and voluntarism were the only correct approaches to overcoming the crisis. After the crash in October 1929, Hoover urged his Cabinet members to act as if the panic had not occurred. Well into 1930, he insisted that the downturn was temporary, that the foundations of the economy were solid, and that the source of economic instability had everything to do with the European financial system of reparations payments and nothing with the American economy. He secured pledges from business leaders, governors, and mayors to keep up public spending and investment levels in return for the president's pledge to lower corporate and income taxes to stimulate consumer demand. Fearing declining consumer confidence, businesses reneged on the pledge and began layoffs. Quickly, the remaining parties to the voluntary pact retrenched. The sanguine spending spree based on consumer credit was a thing of the past.

Only in 1931, when it had become clear that the economic crisis was not simply a matter of the financial imbalance between Europe and the United States, did Hoover react more forcefully. The Federal Farm Board, which Congress created under Hoover's guidance, tried to stem falling prices in agriculture by buying up surplus crops, but they did not restrict production. The Board ended up owning several hundred million dollars worth of wheat, and prices continued to decline. In October 1931, Hoover created the National Credit Corporation (NCC), which recruited private bankers to use $500 million for buying up the questionable assets of troubled banks, maintaining their liquidity, and reining in the bank panic. But the bankers at the NCC simply could not bring themselves to buy dubious assets and never made use of the corporation's capital; almost 2,300 banks failed right in front of them. The President's Organization of Unemployment Relief tried to aid existing charities in their efforts, and Hoover tried to lead by example with generous donations. But he balked at direct federal aid to the unemployed, arguing that this would create a class of dependent citizens. He insisted that Americans were sufficiently protected from hunger and cold, but the rising hospital statistics of malnutrition-related deaths said otherwise. In 1932, Hoover's Reconstruction Finance Corporation marked the first significant departure from his voluntary principles. Modeled after government agencies established during World War I, the RFC was authorized to use $2 billion in taxpayer money to loan to banks, the boldest federal anti-depression measure in U.S. history to that point. When most money went to big institutions, however, labor advocates complained that the very economic elite that decried unemployment relief as socialist corruption depended most heavily on government assistance. Hoover still refused emergency funds for food, clothing, and shelter, but he eventually agreed to let the RFC loan money to states for profitable public works projects. Hoover also began to rethink the labor issue and signed into law the Norris-La Guardia Act, which severely restricted the use of injunctions against strikers, something Republican administrations had made ample use of throughout the 1920s.

The impact of federally funded public works on the national economy during the Hoover Administration was negligible. If these projects put additional money into workers' pockets, the administration took it out again with the largest peacetime tax-hike in American history. The 1932 Revenue Act illustrated the conventional political wisdom of fiscal responsibility that the government could not spend more than it received in revenue. Two weeks after passing the Revenue Act, Congress committed another act of fiscal responsibility. It refused to pay out "adjusted compensation certificates"—bonuses—for World War I veterans ahead of their due date in 1945. Congress had granted veterans this bonus in the form of 20-year savings bonds in 1925. Outraged over Washington's thrift at the same time that the government spent public funds on farmers, banks, and railroads, approximately 20,000 veterans from across the country converged on the capitol. President Hoover refused to meet with delegates from this "Bonus Army," at the same time that he received courtesy visits from sports stars and student fraternities. In an effort to disband the mass protest in the heart of the nation's capital, Hoover offered an advance payment of five to twenty dollars per veteran to support their travel home. At the same time, his Secretary of War, Patrick Hurley, announced the clearance of several occupied buildings. When veterans defended themselves against violent police actions, the president ordered the complete removal of the protesters by federal troops under the command of General Douglas MacArthur. Most veterans and their accompanying families fled this show of overwhelming force and the tear-gas attacks. President Hoover defended his general's actions without reservation, convinced that the veterans had threatened the very existence of government. The War Department derided the protesters as a "mob of tramps and hoodlums" and "Communist agitators," and claimed that McArthur had acted with "unparalleled humanity and kindness."[54] Those who saw the photographs of the event did not agree, and veterans' groups—hardly organizations with Communist sympathies—expressed bitter resentment over the Red-baiting. At a time when authoritarian regimes moved with military force against poor and destitute civilians in the waning democracies of Europe, Hoover's harsh reaction to the Bonus Army was unforgivable to most Americans—more so than any blunder in fiscal and economic policy.

Today, we often explain Franklin D. Roosevelt's New Deal as a response to the Great Depression. But the Great Depression only in part explains the New Deal and its popularity. Just as important was Herbert Hoover's administration and its failures. For three successive Republican administrations, Americans had generally appeared to agree with former President Calvin Coolidge's famous dictum that "the business of government is business." By 1932, however, both business and government seemed to have reached their wits' end. The nation had tumbled not only further into economic crisis, but also into a deep political crisis that was the immediate outgrowth of the failed policy responses of the Hoover Administration. Before Roosevelt's New Deal began to turn the tide, the failure of government in the United States and other capitalist nations had shaped the world economy and global instability. The nation's confidence was so shaken by November 1932 that Republican governor Alf Landon of Kansas could speculate aloud that only "the hand of a dictator" could turn the country around. Pennsylvania Senator David A. Reed (R) warned that "if this country ever needed a Mussolini," referring to the Italian fascist dictator, "it needs one now."[55]

The 1932 election was a powerful rejection of Herbert Hoover and an expression of hope in Franklin D. Roosevelt. Not that New York's former governor had an answer to the economic troubles of the time. Like Hoover, he attacked extravagant government spending and actually promised a 25 percent cut in the federal budget. He described the gold standard as a sacred covenant and mocked suggestions by the Farm Board that the answer to agricultural overproduction was plowing under crops in return for government payments. The famous and highly respected columnist Walter Lippmann expressed disappointment with the Democratic challenger.

"Franklin D. Roosevelt is no crusader," he wrote. "He is no tribune of the people. He is no enemy of entrenched privilege. He is a pleasant man who, without any important qualifications for the office, would very much like to be President."[56]

But Roosevelt had learned from his predecessor that he had mustered the political will for experimentation. In a nationwide radio address he advocated "persistent experimentation" in the fight against the Depression and for a "wiser, more equitable distribution of the national income."[57] Historians have noted the many disappointments with Roosevelt's pragmatism, but none can point to a president with a bigger portfolio of accomplishments in real social change.

Roosevelt wasted no time, and the day after his inauguration, he summoned Congress into an emergency session for the coming week to address another round of bank failures. Conservative in nature, the Emergency Banking Act extended government assistance to private bankers to allow them to reopen their banks, authorized the issue of new Federal Reserve bank notes, and penalized the hoarding of cash reserves. Critics on the left were aghast at Roosevelt's adoption of a plan proposed by Herbert Hoover's advisors.[58] But when Roosevelt explained to approximately 60,000,000 Americans in his "Fireside Chat" that it was now safe to return their savings to the banks, they believed him. The next day, cash deposits in banks far exceeded withdrawals in every city. "Capitalism," Raymond Moley later marveled, "was saved in eight days."[59]

Roosevelt's first one hundred days in the presidency had been a whirlwind. Press conferences followed the biweekly cabinet meetings. The president delivered a dozen speeches and guided fifteen major laws through Congress. Roosevelt had promised "action," and he clearly delivered. Regardless of the laws' different impacts, Americans were mostly convinced that the president cared about them and was willing to do whatever it took to bring about economic recovery. Walter Lippmann, the man who had discarded Roosevelt as merely a "pleasant man" a few months prior, now mused: "At the end of February we were a congeries of disorderly panic stricken mobs and factions. In the hundred days from March to June we became again an organized nation confident of our power to provide for our own security and to control our own destiny."[60] Roosevelt's government provided the relief President Hoover had denied. And the New Deal also included legislation intent on reforming the pillars of the American economy: agriculture, industry, banking, and Wall Street.

There is much confusion today about the underlying economic theory that propelled Roosevelt and his Brain Trust. His policies have often mistakenly been associated with Keynesianism—a deliberate federal budget deficit to compensate for the declining private demand with a public demand for goods and services. Many have pointed to the public works projects and relief efforts as evidence of this desire to restore flagging demand with government funds. However, historians have learned from the exchanges between the president and his Cabinet that relief was always the primary objective, and the expansion of demand merely a secondary effect, which

Roosevelt would have sacrificed. And he often did, so that a deliberately countercyclical fiscal policy only became common practice after World War II.

Regardless of the conflict over the importance of demand-management in the Roosevelt administration, the historical data provide strong evidence that the impact of additional government dollars in the economy was, on one hand, unprecedented, and at the same time very weak. This was not only the result of Roosevelt's conservative approach to the federal budget and his conviction that a large deficit was as immoral for government as for individual households. Individual states also shaped the impact of government spending with their own fiscal policies. The additional spending provided by Washington, D.C., was almost entirely canceled out by the shrinking budget of individual states. States had already been frugal in the face of economic crisis before the New Deal, but as the new administration channeled relief funds to state governments, these often decided to cut their own spending even further and let federal monies carry the burden. Economist E. Cary Brown demonstrated in 1956 that in only two years out of seven between 1933 and 1940 did federal expenditures exceed the contracted spending on state and local levels. When it came to fiscal policy, Brown concluded that demand management "seems to have been an unsuccessful recovery device in the thirties—not because it did not work but because it was not tried."[61] In the opinion of Roosevelt advisor Alvin Hansen, the New Deal was best described as "a salvaging program."[62] But this characterization undersells the scale of economic recovery. Between 1933 and 1941, the nation's gross domestic product grew by 7.7 percent per year on average—growth rates this nation's economy has not witnessed since.[63]

As the Great Recession built momentum late in 2007 and early in 2008, the key decision makers in the United States economy were quite familiar with this record. And while none tried very hard to convince Congress of the urgency of the situation to produce a forceful legislative response to the looming asset crisis in the nation's leading investment banks, they all—from Secretary of the Treasury to Ben Bernanke and Timothy Geithner at the Federal Reserve—knew what emergency actions to take. More than anyone else, one of the best students of the financial collapse of the Great Depression, chairman of the Federal Reserve Ben Bernanke, not wanting to repeat the failures of his predecessors in the 1930s, stretched the authority of his institution to the hilt. President Obama followed Henry Paulson's initial stimulus bill with a massive public spending program that directly applied Keynesian economic theory and was far larger as a share of GDP than any spending increase during the New Deal. Although weakened by a compromise with Republicans to turn some of the stimulus into tax cuts—which translated into increased taxpayer savings rather than increased consumer spending—the combined monetary and fiscal response to the financial crisis of 2008 reduced the economic fallout to a recession, rather than a depression. And this recession proved significantly less devastating for Americans who could fall back on unemployment insurance—one of the New Deal legacies and economic stabilizers we take for granted today.[64] In addition, European and Asian economies did not respond to their own entanglement in the financial crisis with hectic reductions in spending but provided generous bailout funds and reduced interest rates.[65] The one lesson that decision-makers around the world learned from the Great Depression was not to allow the implosion of the financial system to happen, and to restore "market confidence."

The reward for the concerted emergency response at the national and international levels was a recession rather than an economic and political calamity. However, the price for averting the breakdown of the economy and political system was a lack of political will for significant interventions on behalf of credit consumers, homeowners, and the poor, and a growing discontent over the slow pace of recovery. It took Republicans fourteen years to recover from the damage their brand had suffered from the Great Depression. It only took Tea Party activists two years after President Obama's victory in November 2008 to overpower the nation's political discourse with a debate about fiscal responsibility and calls for a return to Hoover economics. A similar trend developed overseas, where the seemingly quick aversion of a global economic catastrophe misled policymakers in Germany, England, and other European countries to think that the Continent was experiencing, not an economic slump, but a debt crisis. So, in an ironic twist that only history can deliver, the lessons learned from the Great Depression have helped re-popularize "Depression Economics" in the United States and Europe and revived the very Austrian economics the Great Depression as well as the Great Recession had proven wrong.

Notes

1. Lee Ohanian, "Understanding Economic Crises: The Great Depression and the 2008 Recession," *The Economic Record*, 86 [special issue] (September 2010):2–6; Andrew Leonard, "Herbert Hoover: The Working Man's Hero," *Salon.com,* August 28, 2009, accessed March 12, 2013, available at http://www.salon.com/2009/08/28/pro_labor_herbert_hoover.
2. "Five questions with Mitt Romney," *Las Vegas Review Journal*, Video, October 17, 2011.
3. Herbert Hoover, *Memoirs* (New York: Hollis and Carter, 1952), 30.
4. Lionel Robbins, *The Great Depression.* (New Brunswick and London: Transaction Publishers, 2009 [1934]), 43.
5. Amity Shlaes, *The Forgotten Man: A New History of the Great Depression.* (New York: Harper, 2008). Shlaes accuses FDR of not believing in the capitalist economy, and, of course, his critics on the left think just the opposite.
6. "Lessons of the 1930s: There Could Be Trouble Ahead," *The Economist*, December 10, 2011, accessed March 12, 2013, available at http:www.economist.com/node/21541388/print.
7. Robert S. McElvaine, *The Great Depression: America, 1929–1941* (New York: Times Books, 1984), 18–20.
8. Stanley Lebergott, *The American Economy: Income, Wealth, and Want* (Princeton, NJ: Princeton University Press, 1962), 248–299; Kenneth Jackson, *Crabgrass Frontier: The Suburbanization of the United States* (New York: Oxford University Press, 1985), 163; David M. Kennedy, *Freedom from Fear: The American People in Depression and War, 1929–1945* (Cambridge, MA: Oxford University Press, 1999), 21.

9. Claudia Goldin, "America's Graduation from High School: The Evolution and Spread of Secondary Schooling in the Twentieth Century," *Journal of Economic History*, 58, no. 2 (1998): 345–374.
10. Martha L. Olney, *Buy Now, Pay Later: Advertising, Credit, and Consumer Durables in the 1920s* (Chapel Hill: University of North Carolina Press, 1991).
11. Thomas F. Huertas, *Crisis, Cause, Containment and Cure* (New York: Palgrave MacMillan, 2010), 9.
12. Nick Wingfield, "Apple's Job Creation Data Spurs an Economic Debate," *New York Times*, March 4, 2012, B1; "Apple: We Made 514,000 Jobs," *CNN Money: Economy Blog*, by Charles Riley, March 5, 2012, accessed July 26, 2013, available at: http://economy.money.cnn.com/2012/03/05/apple-we-made-514000-jobs/; *General Motors Company Report to the Securities and Exchange Commission*, Washington, D.C., 2012, 15.
13. Stanley Lebergott, *Manpower and Economic Growth: The American Record since 1800* (New York: McGraw-Hill, 1964) ; R. M. Coen, "Labor Force Unemployment in the 1920s and 1930s: A Re-examination Based on Postwar Experience," *Review of Economics and Statistics*, 55 (1973): 46–55; Alexander J. Field, "Technological Change and U.S. Productivity Growth in the Interwar Years,," *The Journal of Economic History*, 66, no. 1 (March 2006): 203–236.
14. W. Elliot Brownlee, *Dynamics of Ascent: A History of the American Economy* (New York: Knopf, 1979), Chapter 12.
15. Mary P. Ryan, *Womanhood in America: From Colonial Times to the Present*, 3rd. ed. (New York: Franklin Watts, 1983), 229–231, 249.
16. *Historical Statistics, Series D4, D7, D8* (Washington, D.C.: Government Printing Office, 1975).
17. Sanford M. Jacoby, *Modern Manors: Welfare Capitalism Since the New Deal* (Princeton, NJ: Princeton University Press, 1997), 57–58.
18. Lizabeth Cohen, *Making a New Deal: Industrial Workers in Chicago, 1919-1939* (New York: Cambridge University Press, 1990), 94–97.
19. John Dicker, "Union Blues at Wal-Mart," *The Nation*, 275, no. 2 (July 8, 2002): 14–19.
20. Employment by major industry sector, 2000, 2010, and projected 2020, Bureau of Labor Statistics, 2000, accessed July 26, 2013, available at http://www.bls.gov/news.release/ecopro.t02.htm.
21. Jaroslav Vanek, "From Great Depression to Great Recession," *International Review of Economics and Finance*, 20 (2011): 131–134, 133.
22. Roger W. Ferguson Jr. and William L. Wascher, "Distinguished Lecture on Economics in Government: Lessons from Past Productivity," *Journal of Economic Perspectives*, 18, no. 2 (Spring 2004): 3–28, 9; Martin Wachs, "Autos, Transit, and the Sprawl of Los Angeles: The 1920s," *Journal of the American Planning Association*, 50, no. 3 (Summer 1984): 297–310, 302.
23. Barry Supple, "The Political Economy of Demoralization: The State and the Coalmining Industry in America and Britain Between the Wars," *Economic History Review*, 41, no. 4 (1988): 566–591.
24. Liaquat Ahamed, *Lords of Finance: The Bankers Who Broke the World* (New York: Penguin Press, 2009), 228–240; Nicholas Crafts and Peter Fearon, "Lessons from the 1930s Great Depression," *Oxford Review of Economic Policy*, 26, no. 3 (2010): 285–317, 289–290.
25. Milton Friedman and Anna Schwartz, *The Monetary History of the United States,1867 to 1960* (Princeton, NJ: Princeton University Press, 1963), 265–295.
26. Paul Krugman, "The Economic Failure of the Euro," *Fresh Air*, Boston: WHYY-NPR, first aired on January 25, 2011; Peter Temin, "The Great Recession and the Great Depression," *Daedalus* 139, no. 4 (Fall 2010): 115–124, 117.
27. Jeremy Atack and Peter Passell, *An Economic View of American History* (New York: W.W. Norton & Company, 1994), 576–577.
28. Alexander Field, *Great Leap Forward: 1930s Depression and U.S. Economic Growth* (New Haven: Yale University Press, 2011), 69. According to Field, 83 percent of the economic growth of the 1920s came from manufacturing.

29. Temin, 115–124.
30. T. H. Watkins, *The Great Depression: America in the 1930s* (Boston: Back Bay Books, 1993), 38; *Harper's Weekly* quoted by Gordon Thomas and Morgan Witts, *Day the Bubble Burst: A Social History of the Wall Street Crash of 1929* (New York: Doubleday 1979), 191; Steve Fraser, *Every Man a Speculator: A History of Wall Street in American Life* (New York: Harper Perennial 2006), 390; Lawrence E. Mitchell, *The Speculation Economy: How Finance Triumphed over Industry* (San Francisco: Berrett-Koehler Publishers, 2007),269.
31. Michael E. Parrish, *Anxious Decades: America in Prosperity and Depression, 1920–1941* (New York: W.W. Norton & Company, 1992), 229–230.
32. John Kenneth Gailbraith, *The Great Crash of 1929* (Boston: Mariner Books, 1961), 57.
33. Robert Sobel, *The Great Bull Market: Wall Street in the 1920s* (New York: W.W. Norton & Company, 1968).
34. William E. Leuchtenburg, *The Perils of Prosperity, 1914–1932* (Chicago: University of Chicago Press, 1958), 183–184.
35. Parrish, 232.
36. Jeremy Atack and Peter Passell, *A New Economic View of American History from Colonial Times to 1940* (New York: W.W. Norton & Company, 1994), 590.
37. Christina Romer, "The Great Crash and the Onset of the Great Depression," *Quarterly Journal of Economics,* 105 (1990): 597–624.
38. John Cassidy, *Dot.con: How America Lost Its Mind and Money in the Internet Era* (New York: Harper Collins, 2002).
39. Enron Corporation was a Houston-based energy and commodities trading firm that was widely celebrated during the 1990s for its innovation and its generous compensation and benefits packages for its employees. In October 2001, it became apparent that the company had hidden billions of dollars in debt through accounting practices; it also emerged that the company had willfully manipulated energy prices to extreme levels in California the previous year. The bankruptcy eviscerated $11 billion for shareholders, cost 20,000 employees their jobs and Enron-stock dominated 401ks, and led to the dissolution of Arthur Anderson, the accounting firm that had approved Enron's accounting manipulations. A year later, news broke that Worldcom CEO Bernard Ebbers had inflated the value of the company by $3 billion with accounting tricks to uphold the company's stock value. Ebbers was sentenced to 25 years in prison, and Worldcom went through Chapter 11 bankruptcy protection and later emerged as MCI, to be acquired by Verizon. Jerry Bowyer, *The Bush Boom: How a Mis-Underestimated President Fixed a Broken Economy* (New York: Allegiance Press, 2003); Jerry Bowyer, "Perfectly Rational Exuberance," *The National Review Online,* October 4, 2006, accessed July 26, 2013, available at http://www.nationalreview.com/articles/218896/perfectly-rational-exuberance/jerry-bowyer.
40. Alex M. Azar II, "FIRREA: Controlling Savings and Loan Association Credit Risk Through Capital Standards and Asset Restrictions," *Yale Law Journal,* 100 (1990): 149, 153; Patricia A. McCoy and Elizabeth Renuart, "The Legal Infrastructure of Subprime and Nontraditional Home Mortgages," in Nicolas P. Retsinas and Eric S. Belsky, eds., *Borrowing to Live: Consumer and Mortgage Credit Revisited* (Washington D.C.: Brookings Institution Press, 2008), 110; Baher Azmy, "Squaring the Predatory Lending Circle," *Florida Law Review,* 57 (2005): 295, 310–311.
41. For an insightful and engaging exploration of the sub-prime mortgage industry and the people who bet on the implosion of this bond market with credit default swaps, see Michael Lewis, *The Big Short: Inside the Doomsday Machine* (New York: W.W. Norton & Company, 2011), 22–27; Kathleen C. Engel and Patricia A. McCoy, "A Tale of Three Markets: The Law and Economics of Predatory Lending," *Texas Law Review,* 80 (2002): 1255, 1273.
42. Susan E. Hauser, "Predatory Lending, Passive Judicial Activism, and the Duty to Decide," *North Carolina Law Review,* 86 (2008): 1501, 1509–1510; Bob Tedeschi, "Subprime Loans' Wide Reach," *New York Times,* August 3, 2008, RE10.

43. Damon Silver and Heather Slavkin, "The Legacy of Deregulation and the Financial Crisis–Linkages Between Deregulation in Labor Markets, Housing Finance Markets, and the Broader Financial Markets," *Journal of Business & Technology Law,* 4, no. 2 (2009): 304–347, 334.
44. Michael Lewis,. 156–158.
45. Alan Greenspan, "Testimony on the Federal Reserve Board's Semiannual Monetary Policy Report to the Congress," Committee on Banking, Housing, and Urban Affairs, U.S. Senate, February 16th, 2005, accessed July 26, 2013-, available at http://www.federalreserve.gov/boarddocs/hh/2005/february/testimony.htm.
46. Thomas F. Huertas, *Crisis: Cause, Containment and Cure* (New York: Palgrave MacMillan 2010), 7–9.
47. Eric Stein, "Turmoil in the U.S. Credit Markets: The Genesis of the Current Economic Crisis," Testimony of Eric Stein, Center for Responsible Lending, Before the U.S. Senate Committee on Banking, Housing, and Urban Affairs, 110th Congress, Washington, D.C., October 16, 2008, accessed March 11, 2012, available at http://www.responsiblelending.org/mortgage-lending/policy-legislation/congress/senate-testimony-10-16-08-hearing-stein-final.pdf.
48. Damon Silver and Heather Slavkin, "The Legacy of Deregulation and the Financial Crisis—Linkages Between Deregulation in Labor Markets, Housing Finance Markets, and the Broader Financial Markets," *Journal of Business & Technology Law,* 4, no. 2 (2009): 304–347. In 2007, the United States personal (household) savings rate was below 2 percent. Cinzia Alcidi and Daniel Gros, "Great Recession versus Great Depression: Monetary, Fiscal and Banking Policies," *Journal of Economic Studies,* 38, no. 6 (2011): 673–690.
49. Charles P. Kindleberger and Robert Z. Aliber, *Manias, Panics, and Crashes. A History of Financial Crises* (New York: Palgrave McMillan, 2011).
50. "Lessons of the 1930s: There Could Be Trouble Ahead," *The Economist,* December 10, 2011, 1–7; Milton Friedman and Anna Schwartz, *A Monetary History of the United States, 1867–1960.* (Princeton, NJ: Princeton University Press, 1971); Ben S. Bernanke, *Essays on the Great Depression* (Princeton, NJ: Princeton University Press, 2000).
51. Joseph Stieglitz, *Freefall: America, Free Markets, and the Sinking of the World Economy* (New York: W.W. Norton & Company, 2010), 270–271.
52. Ben Bernanke, "Nonmonetary Effects of the Financial Crisis and the Propagation of the Great Depression," *American Economic Review,* 73 (1983): 257–276.
53. McElvaine, 73–74.
54. Roger Daniels, *The Bonus March: An Episode of the Great Depression* (Westport, CT: Greenwood Publishing Co., 1971).
55. Michael Schaller, Robert Schulzinger, John Bezls-Selfa, and Janette Thomas Greenwood, *American Horizons: U.S. History in a Global Context, Volume II: Since 1865* (New York: Oxford University Press, 2012), 882.
56. Walter Lippmann, "The Candidacy of Franklin D. Roosevelt," *New York Herald Tribune,* January 8, 1932, quoted in Sally Denton, *The Plots Against the President: FDR, a Nation in Crisis, and the Rise of the American Right* (New York: Bloomsbury Press 2012), 18.
57. Davis W. Houck, *Rhetoric as Currency: Hoover, Roosevelt and the Great Depression* (College Station, TX: Texas A&M University Press, 2001), 121.
58. William Lemke to the Farmers' Union Convention in Omaha, Nebraska, quoted in "Lorena Hickock to Harry Hopkins, November 23, 1933"; *Hopkins MSS.* See William E. Leuchtenburg, *Franklin D. Roosevelt and the New Deal; 1932–1940* (New York: Harper and Row, Publishers, 1963), 44, note 7.
59. Raymond Moley, *After Seven Years* (New York: Harper & Brothers Publishers, 1939), 155.
60. Parrish, 297.
61. E. Cary Brown, "Fiscal Policy in the 'Thirties': A Reappraisal," *American Economic Review,* 46 (December 1956): 857–879.
62. A. H. Hansen, *Fiscal Policy and Business Cycles* (New York: W.W. Norton & Co., 1941), 84.

63. *Historical Statistics of the United States: Colonial Times to 1970, Part 2* (Washington, D.C.: U.S. Bureau of the Census, 1975), 217–218.
64. Temin, "The Great Recession," 115–124, 122–123; Price Fishback, "US Monetary and Fiscal Policy in the 1930s," *Oxford Review of Economic Policy*, 26, no. 3 (2010): 385–413, 386–387.
65. Felda Chay and Quah Chin Chin, "The Great Depression 2.0? Given the Scale of the Current Financial Turmoil, Will the World See a Repeat of the Depression of the 1930s?" *The Business Times Singapore*, October 27, 2008, 1; Paul Krugman, *The Return of Depression Economics and the Crisis of 2008* (New York: W.W. Norton & Company, 2009); Andrew Leonard, "Paul Krugman's Depression Economics," *Salon.com*, December 8, 2008, accessed July 26, 2013, available at http://www.salon.com/2008/12/08/paul_krugman_2; "Feature: How the World Works; Lessons of the 1930s: There Could Be Trouble Ahead" *The Economist*, December 10, 2011, accessed July 26, 2013, available at http:www.economist.com/node/21541388/print.

3

The Bottom-Up Recovery

A New Deal in Banking and Public Finance

TIMOTHY A. CANOVA

The country needs and unless I mistake its temper, the country demands bold, persistent experimentation. It is common sense to take a method and try it. If it fails, admit it frankly and try another. But above all, try something. The millions who are in want will not stand by silently forever while the things that satisfy their needs are within easy reach.[1]

—Franklin D. Roosevelt, address at Oglethorpe University
Atlanta, Georgia, May 22, 1932

For the first three years of the Great Depression, President Herbert Hoover repeatedly objected to, and occasionally vetoed, public works and work relief programs, calling instead for individual, voluntary, and local aid to the needy.[2] He did, however, direct his newly created Reconstruction Finance Corporation (RFC) to channel more than $1 billion to troubled banks, insurance companies, and railroads on the brink of collapse.[3] Throughout his 1932 presidential campaign, Franklin Roosevelt criticized this approach as "trickle down" while demanding a recovery program "that builds from the bottom up and not from the top down."[4] As president, Roosevelt would eventually steer many billions of dollars in RFC funds into public works, mortgage modifications for millions of homeowners and farmers, and loans to state and local public school districts for school construction and teacher salaries.[5]

This was the public option in banking and finance, made exigent by the collapse in private finance. Like the more recent use of a "public option" in health care policy discussions that contemplate a public insurance program to supplement private insurers, when private banking institutions fail to allocate the nation's credit and capital in a sustainable manner, public institutions could steer resources into relief and recovery.[6] This chapter makes the case that such public options in banking and finance were crucial to the successes of Roosevelt's "bottom-up" approach to recovery. In contrast, President Obama has responded to the most serious economic crisis since the Great Depression with no-strings-attached bank bailouts and indirect stimulus measures that have largely failed to build a sustainable economic recovery.

On the campaign trail, Roosevelt repeated his indictment that the Hoover Administration had encouraged private financial speculation, ignored recovery, delayed relief, and forgotten reform.[7] Roosevelt's New Deal would use a range of policy tools to effectively steer credit and capital away from private speculation and into long-term infrastructure and public works. New federal regulatory agencies would restrict and even prohibit private sector banks from engaging in activities deemed risky, while a parallel system of public banking, flush with resources, would steer credit and capital into the real economy. This changing balance of public and private power was reflected in the shifting priorities of the nation's Treasury Department and its central bank, the Federal Reserve. The orthodox paradigm was being turned on its head, and as a result, a bottom-up recovery soon began. But the successes of the 1930s were incomplete and limited by Roosevelt's premature turn to fiscal austerity. It took the World War II economic boom and its aftermath to provide the clearest vindication of the New Deal approach in banking and finance.

As in the 1930s, today the preconditions exist for a new public option approach in banking and finance. In both periods, market failures—the 1929 stock market crash and ensuing collapse in banking, and the 2008 global financial meltdown—were met with bailout strategies that were not capable of sufficiently restoring private credit and investment. The banking crisis in the early 1930s reached a peak on March 4, 1933, the day of Roosevelt's inauguration, when a nationwide run on the banks led to bank holidays' being declared in every state of the country. The magnitude of the crisis provided Roosevelt with the political opening to push forward on reform, relief, and recovery efforts. In money and banking, as in some other areas of the New Deal, reform was often at odds with relief and recovery. But there were impressive successes on all three fronts before the window of political opportunity started closing in Roosevelt's second term.

In 2008, the financial collapse may have been a bit less visible and dramatic than 1933, but it was no less real, as the global system of financial payments and interbank lending became frozen. Instead of images of thousands of people lining up outside the nation's banks to demand their deposits, the runs on the financial system were now opaque transactions over computer screens, with millions of panic-stricken people and institutions demanding their deposits and redemption of their mutual funds. The Troubled Asset Relief Program (TARP), enacted in the waning days of the Bush Administration, authorized the Treasury secretary to spend up to $700 billion to prop up the financial system.[8] Between TARP and the Federal Reserve's aggressive lending and bond buying programs, the financial system was stabilized—a lesson drawn from the New Deal experience. But with the panic abated, there was less immediate pressure on newly elected President Obama and a Democratic House and Senate to reform the financial system.

The economic contraction was also stopped, both by Obama's $800 billion fiscal stimulus program and counter-cyclical spending—the so-called automatic stabilizers, such as the federal spending on unemployment compensation that traced back to the New Deal. The recession, technically defined as two consecutive quarters of GDP contraction, was ended. Unfortunately, the recession's end did not mean that a depression had been avoided. What had made the 1930s the Depression decade was not recession. For most of the decade, there was actual economic growth. But it was a decade of mass unemployment, long-term joblessness, "underwater" consumers, a deleveraging private sector, and public-sector austerity. Much the same conditions face policymakers today. But in 2009, with financial panic averted, complacency set in, and the political window of opportunity quickly closed in Obama's first term.

The Eight Days That Saved Capitalism

The winter of 1933 is often seen as a defining moment in American political history, with the fate of democracy itself perhaps hanging in the balance.[9] Many histories of the New Deal begin with the dramatic circumstances of Roosevelt's first inauguration. Bank holidays had already been declared in every state to stop the contagion of bank runs. Roosevelt's first act as president was to call Congress into special session and proclaim a four-day national bank holiday that closed down all federally chartered banks.[10] The new president had promised action, and the financial emergency provided justification enough for invoking a little-known provision of the Trading with the Enemy Act of 1917, a provision never intended by Congress to apply to these particular circumstances, now used to close the last remaining banks in the country.[11] After Roosevelt's bank holiday proclamation, there was not a bank open for business in the country. For a week, the country survived on local credit, barter, and IOUs amid uncertainty over whether the panic would resume once the banks reopened. During that week, the window of opportunity was opened wide for a range of possible reforms, from federal guarantees of deposits and the issuing of scrip (government IOUs that are not legal tender) to more far-reaching proposals to nationalize the entire banking system.[12]

As the bank holiday was nearing its end, Congress passed the Emergency Banking Act after barely half an hour of debate, with no committee hearings and few members of Congress having read the bill. (There were very few typewritten copies of the bill.) The House passed the measure with a unanimous shout; the Senate with only seven dissenting votes—the first legislative enactment of the New Deal.[13] The Act expanded the capacity of the Federal Reserve to issue new currency backed not solely by government securities, but by any kind of business obligation, and authorized the Federal Reserve to make loans directly to non-member state banks and business enterprises, which was all considered financial heresy at the time.[14] It also empowered the Reconstruction Finance Corporation (RFC), an independent government agency established in Hoover's last year in office, to subscribe to the preferred stock of banks, an approach that would be followed seventy-five years later when the Congress enacted TARP in 2008 to empower the Treasury to purchase financial stakes in private banks and businesses.

As historian David Kennedy has concluded, the Emergency Banking Act was a "thoroughly conservative measure, which had been largely drafted by Hoover administration officials and private bankers."[15] Hoover was nevertheless unwilling to take these steps in his final months in office. TARP was another conservative measure drafted and passed near the end of the Bush Administration, but largely implemented during the beginning of the Obama Administration.

The top officials of both the Roosevelt and Hoover Treasury Departments worked around the clock to get the banks reopened and, according to monetary economist Lester Chandler, "to do so in such a way as to restore confidence in their solvency and liquidity, to prevent further cash withdrawals, to encourage cash to flow back into the system, and to enable the banks to resume their lending function."[16] Federal banking supervisors surveyed the banks and divided them into three categories: those in good condition would be permitted to reopen quickly; the hopeless cases were closed permanently; and those in the middle were not sound enough to open immediately, but were capable of being saved and given help mostly from the RFC. In addition, a temporary deposit-insurance program was instituted to restore confidence in the safety of deposits, a forerunner of the Federal Deposit Insurance Corporation (FDIC) that would be established three months later.[17]

On the eve of reopening the banks, Roosevelt held the first of his so-called Fireside Chats, a Sunday evening radio address to sixty million people to discuss the banking crisis in terms that could be readily grasped by ordinary citizens. He urged listeners to bring their savings back to the banks where they would be safer than under the mattress. He concluded: "Let us unite in banishing fear. We have provided the machinery to restore our financial system; it is up to you to support and make it work. It is your problem no less than it is mine. Together, we cannot fail."[18]

The country had been stranded for days without cash, and heavy withdrawals were expected when the banks opened for business the next morning. Yet, in every city, deposits exceeded withdrawals.[19] By the end of March, "$1.2 billion in cash had been redeposited with banks; another $700 million flowed back before the end of the summer."[20] The RFC continued to pump large sums into the banks, while the Federal Reserve engaged in large open-market purchases, buying $600 million in government securities from the banks.[21] Soon the banks had reduced their debt to the Federal Reserve from $1.4 billion to only about $100 million late in the year, while amassing about $800 million in excess reserves.[22] According to David

Kennedy, "The prolonged banking crisis, acute since at least 1930, with roots reaching back through the 1920s and even into the days of Andrew Jackson, was at last over."[23]

Raymond Moley, a professor of public law at Columbia University and one of FDR's original "Brain Trust," claimed that "the policies which vanquished the bank crisis were thoroughly conservative policies. The sole departure from convention lay in the swiftness and boldness with which they were carried out."[24] It is true that Roosevelt chose not to nationalize the banking system. Such unorthodoxy, according to Moley, would have "drained the last remaining strength of the capitalistic system" at a time when the new administration was seeking to restore the confidence of the conservative business and banking leaders, and through them, of the public generally.[25]

"Capitalism," Moley later reflected, "was saved in eight days."[26] But it still remained to be seen what kind of capitalism it would be in the future: a reformed system that was more stable, responsible, and accountable; or one that only temporarily limited the freedom of bankers while leaving the institutional foundations of their powers unchanged.[27] The New Deal reforms that would follow were to shift the balance of power between public and private sectors, but it was less certain that the reforms did much to change the self-destructive nature of capitalist institutions, particularly the governance of the big banks and corporations that Washington had to step in and rescue.

Roosevelt apparently saw his reforms in the context of an epic conflict between the state and private finance. In a letter to Colonel E. M. House, who had been President Woodrow Wilson's closest advisor, Roosevelt himself summed up the increasingly chilly relations between his administration and private financiers:

> The real truth of the matter is, as you and I know, that a financial element in the larger centers has owned the Government ever since the days of Andrew Jackson—and I am not wholly excepting the Administration of W.W. [*Woodrow Wilson*]. The country is going through a repetition of Jackson's fight with the Bank of the United States—only on a far bigger and broader basis.[28]

According to Senator Bronson Cutting of New Mexico, Roosevelt's "greatest mistake" was his failure to nationalize the banks when given the opportunity on a silver platter. It could have been accomplished, he said, "without a word of protest."[29] The banks had evaded nationalization, and other far-reaching reform proposals would be stymied during the recovery that followed. To critics on the left, Roosevelt had favored large corporations over smaller firms and guaranteed their survival and ever-increasing power. "Measures to help farmers, workers, and the unemployed were merely palliatives that were sufficient to defuse the threat of disorder but insufficient to disrupt corporate prerogatives."[30]

A far different critique began developing on the right. Once a leading New Dealer, Raymond Moley broke with Roosevelt within a few years, becoming a conservative Republican and a leading critic of the New Deal. For Moley and others on the right, the eight days that saved capitalism were not enough.[31] Jonathan Alter has observed that many wealthy critics of Roosevelt could never admit how close they had come to losing everything. Instead, they would resent and revile the New Deal for taxing and regulating, for disrupting if not reforming the prerogatives of privilege and monopoly.[32]

The Hundred Days

Public opinion responded to Roosevelt's sudden success in stabilizing the banking system. Nearly half a million Americans wrote to Roosevelt in his first week in office. The White House mailroom, which was staffed by a single employee during Hoover's time, now had to hire seventy people to handle a flood of correspondence.[33] Roosevelt took full advantage of his surge in popularity. Within hours, he summoned congressional leaders to the White House and seized the momentum. What followed was the "Hundred Days"—a frenzy of legislative action and reform that is unparalleled in American history.[34]

Any attempt to assess or even summarize the history of the Hundred Days is fraught with challenges. New Deal reforms were at times contradictory, representing diverse responses to the quite different problems of recovery, relief, and reform of the structures of private and public institutions. One strand of reform focused on rationalizing markets by industry self-regulation to stop the deflationary spiral that had undermined the financial foundations of the economy. Since the 1929 stock market crash, prices and wages had been falling steeply, making it more difficult for households and businesses to meet interest and principal payments on debts that were fixed by contract at the previous, higher levels of wages and prices. The National Industrial Recovery Act (NIRA), a centerpiece of the first New Deal, was intended to stop the deflationary spiral. The Act delegated code-making authority to industry trade councils that were dominated by the largest companies. The industry codes that provided a floor on prices in hundreds of industries were soon criticized as a corporatist approach that was cartelizing the American economy by marginalizing and excluding workers, consumers, and small businesses.

The Agricultural Adjustment Act (AAA), also passed during the Hundred Days and intended to stop the relentless fall in farm prices, provided emergency relief to farmers. It attempted to restore farm income and reduce agricultural surpluses by taxing food processing firms and providing subsidies for farmers to restrict their acreage.[35] The AAA was challenged in court as a violation of Congress's interstate commerce powers for extending federal tax, regulatory, and spending authority to local activities; it was struck down by the Supreme Court in 1936, only to be amended two years later and eventually upheld by the Court.[36]

The AAA dealt with far more than farm income. Before the bill was enacted, Congress added an omnibus inflationary amendment by Senator Elbert D. Thomas of Utah, which was passed by the Senate by a three to one margin and then by the House by an even heavier majority[37]—another indication of popular support for attempts to arrest the deflationary spiral in wages and prices. Roosevelt decided to accept the amendment's permissive powers "that otherwise might later be thrust upon him as mandatory."[38] The Thomas amendment provided the president with six discretionary tools for increasing the nation's credit and currency, including giving Treasury the authority to issue $3 billion in United States Notes, the same so-called fiat greenback that Lincoln had used to pay for much of the Civil War. In addition, the Federal Reserve was authorized to make another $3 billion in open-market purchases; if it refused, the president was given authority to adopt bimetallism and issue $200 million in silver certificates in payment of debts to foreign governments.[39]

The emergence of the Thomas amendment reflected a much wider appreciation for the competing methods of currency creation than exists today. The issuance of new currency by either the Treasury (in the form of United States Notes) or the Fed (as Federal Reserve Notes) would provide funds for the administration's recovery and relief programs. In each case, the newly issued currency would be considered "legal tender" for all debts public and private and would be used to purchase federal government bonds.[40] But issuance by the Treasury could reduce overall federal borrowing by retiring government bonds at no cost to the Treasury; in contrast, issuance of currency by the Federal Reserve would merely shift the government's obligations without reducing the deficit itself. Not surprisingly, the forces of wealth and privilege were aghast at the prospect of greenbacks and silver certificates. Lewis Douglas, the Director of the Budget, lamented the Thomas amendment as "the end of Western civilization."[41] According to the conservative orthodoxy then as today, it would be more prudent to vest the power to issue new currency in the hands of private bankers than in elected officials who might debase the currency for short-term political gain.

Other inflation devices were adopted. The Federal Reserve Board was given the authority to increase or decrease the reserve requirements that must be held by private banks; a reduction in the reserve requirement would allow banks to extend more credit. Roosevelt also abrogated the gold clause in public and private contracts, which went back to the time of the first greenback issuance during the Civil War and was intended to protect creditors by requiring repayment of obligations in gold. As a result of Roosevelt's decision, some $100 billion in contractual obligations, including most of the $22 billion of federal debt, could now be discharged upon payment of any currency "which at the time of payment is legal tender for public and private debts."[42] In early 1935, the Supreme Court upheld the administration and struck down the gold clauses for interfering with the constitutional power of Congress to determine the value of its money.[43]

Roosevelt did not ultimately resort to some of the Thomas amendment's more controversial inflationary tools. Instead, deficit financing and dollar depreciation (by raising the price of gold) were his preferred approaches, along with public works projects that provided millions of people with employment and income, thereby inflating wages and reducing debt burdens. It was a bottom-up approach to recovery that reflected the emerging new paradigm in economics that would be associated with the work of the British economist John Maynard Keynes. When the private sector was stalled and deleveraging, according to Keynesian economics, it was the role of the public sector to put resources back to work, which would in turn have positive feedback effects on consumer spending and business investment.

For millions of people, the most important enactments of the Hundred Days were the public works: jobs programs and relief for the unemployed. This was the public option writ large: the public option in job creation and in financing investment. The Civilian Conservation Corps (CCC), the Federal Emergency Relief Act (FERA), the Public Works Administration (PWA), and the Tennessee Valley Authority (TVA) were the first in an alphabet soup of new agencies and programs that provided relief and jobs to the unemployed, directly through federal programs and in loans and grants to states, while accomplishing tangible and lasting results in terms of regional development, energy and public power, and conservation.[44] Within three months of its enactment, the CCC put a quarter million Americans to work in reforestation and flood-control projects in the national parks and forests. Late in the year, Roosevelt diverted funds from the PWA to a new agency, the Civil Works Administration (CWA), which within two months provided jobs to 4.3 million men and women, more than had served in the armed forces during World War I.[45]

By providing jobs and relief to millions of the unemployed, these public works programs contributed to economic recovery. Consumer purchasing power was expanded by a number of work and relief programs, which in turn helped to improve business confidence and investment. Ben Bernanke, in his *Essays on the Great Depression*, considers March 1933 the beginning of economic and financial recovery.[46] For the first time in four years, commercial and industrial failures began to fall,[47] unemployment stopped rising and started to inch downward,[48] and commodity prices and the stock market started to rise.[49]

Roosevelt's approach, to build up a parallel public banking system, had its antecedents in the wartime administration of Woodrow Wilson.[50] But under Roosevelt, the public option in banking and finance was extended with enactment of the Home Owners' Loan Act, the Emergency Railroad Transportation Act, and the Farm Mortgage Act that created the Farm Credit Administration. Meanwhile, Roosevelt expanded the Reconstruction Finance Corporation well beyond support for banks and insurance companies, and the RFC started making larger loans directly to businesses and industry, providing aid to states and cities, helping the real estate mortgage market, and making disaster relief loans.[51] The RFC helped rebuild the building and loan associations, provided funding for federal rural electrification programs, loaned funds to Chicago for teachers' salaries, and supported numerous public works projects, including the construction of the Brooklyn–Battery Tunnel in New York City, the Pennsylvania Turnpike, the Huey P. Long Bridge in New Orleans, and the San Francisco–Oakland Bay Bridge, to name only a few of the many self-liquidating loans made by the RFC.[52]

Jesse Jones, the long-time chairman of the RFC, summed up the success of the legislation that extended the RFC authority to provide self-liquidating loans for public works projects:

> Today the nation is dotted, from coast to coast and from the Rio Grande to the Great Lakes, with useful monuments to the wisdom of that legislation—great bridges, electric power plants and lines, express highways, waterworks, sewer systems, college dormitories, modern low-rent housing, aqueducts, vehicular tunnels, and other facilities.[53]

To many of its supporters and detractors alike, the RFC was a "fourth branch of government."[54]

In 2011, a new eastern span of the San Francisco–Oakland Bay Bridge was manufactured in China and shipped to Oakland for assembly. California officials claimed to have saved hundreds of millions of dollars by outsourcing this infrastructure project to China.[55] State officials apparently were unconcerned about how many jobs were lost or the loss in state revenue from not filling those jobs in California. World Trade Organization (WTO) rules on public procurement tend to make outsourcing of infrastructure that much easier.[56] It is a reminder that there are hidden costs incurred as a result of today's orthodox approaches to public finance and trade—from departing so widely from the New Deal public option approach.

There is no longer a federal RFC to help finance such infrastructure projects and to spur construction and related jobs in the United States. Although Obama has called numerous times for a federal infrastructure bank, it has never been one of his legislative priorities, even though he took office during the worst downturn since the Great Depression, initially had the benefit of control of both houses of Congress, and could have used the example of the RFC to bolster his case for such a bank.[57] TARP also could have served as a type of revolving fund that, like the RFC, could have funded public works and jobs programs by providing funds for state infrastructure banks, help for underwater borrowers to refinance and modify their mortgages, and loans to state and local governments to help pay for teachers' salaries and other essential needs. Unfortunately, the Dodd-Frank Wall Street Reform and Consumer Protection Act of July 2010 (Dodd-Frank) rolled up the TARP program, reduced its spending cap, prevented the Treasury from spending any TARP funds that were received from repayments on earlier TARP loans, and prevented TARP spending for any programs initiated after the enactment of Dodd-Frank.[58] This was an unfortunate concession, completely under the radar and shielded from public debate, that left the Obama Administration without a single major policy tool to provide relief and strengthen recovery in the months leading up to the 2010 midterm elections.

Meanwhile, since late 2008, the Federal Reserve has purchased trillions of dollars in bonds from private-sector banks and hedge funds, but there has been no corresponding effort at the Federal Reserve to fund a bottom-up recovery—for instance, by providing funding for state infrastructure banks. In California, such a mechanism was already in place: the California Infrastructure and Economic Development Bank (the I-Bank). But California governor Jerry Brown never sought to expand its funding sources and instead vetoed several measures that would have strengthened the I-Bank, perhaps at the advice of his "Jobs Czar," a former Bank of America official.[59] This approach to infrastructure investment in the United States is unfortunately reminiscent of the pre–New Deal approach of Herbert Hoover.

While the RFC directed financial resources into important public works and private industries, Roosevelt also took measures to steer the nation's credit and capital away from more speculative activities. During the Hundred Days, FDR signed into law the Truth in Securities Act (the Securities Act of 1933) to protect investors from fraud and misrepresentation, and the Glass-Steagall Act (the Banking Act of 1933) to separate commercial from investment banking.[60] The Glass-Steagall Act resulted in the breakup of several of the nation's largest banks. For instance, J. P. Morgan & Company chose to become a commercial bank, while its underwriting department and partners split off into Morgan Stanley, a newly formed investment bank.[61] Both measures were greatly aided by the Pecora Investigation of the Senate Banking Committee, named after Ferdinand Pecora, the fourth and final chief counsel of the investigation that riveted the nation for weeks with testimony about the widespread frauds on Wall Street and evidence of how the banks had been caught up in the speculative mania.[62] The dearth of official hearings since 2008 is quite a contrast: a tamped-down Senate committee and the Financial Crisis Inquiry Commission (the Angelides Commission), with only a few days of public hearings to question Wall Street executives.[63]

The 1933 Securities Act was the beginning of a most significant federal effort to bring transparency to the securities markets. The Securities Exchange Act of 1934 created the Securities and Exchange Commission (SEC). The Glass-Steagall Act would stand for sixty-six years and would survive numerous attempts by Republicans to repeal it until finally signed away in 1999 by President Bill Clinton, a Democrat. The Banking Act also created the Federal Deposit Insurance Corporation (FDIC) on a temporary basis (later made permanent), thereby establishing federal insurance of bank deposits. Milton Friedman would later call the FDIC the "single most important structural change" in the economy since the Civil War.[64] The FDIC was given authority to regulate and supervise all commercial banks for the first time, including state-chartered banks that were not members of the Federal Reserve System.[65] It prohibited the paying of interest on checking accounts and limited interest on savings accounts, a reform that helped maintain stability in the banking sector for more than half a century.[66]

In June 1934, Roosevelt signed into law an amendment of the Federal Reserve Act, a new clause, Section 13(b), that authorized the Fed to "make credit available for the purpose of supplying working capital to established industrial and commercial businesses."[67] This was breaking much new ground for the Federal Reserve by departing from the orthodox view that the Fed should only lend to banks. But the interests of finance and industry were diverging. As the banks relied more and more on Federal Reserve assistance both before and after the bank holiday, and as the private banking sector failed to meet so many pressing financing needs, the administration embraced the unorthodox. For each of the twelve regional Federal Reserve Banks, Section 13(b) created Industrial Advisory Committees consisting of three to five individuals "actively engaged in some industrial pursuit." The committees were to review loan applications and make recommendations to the regional Reserve banks.[68]

The 1934 Act opened the floodgates by authorizing the Reserve banks to extend credit to business enterprises "for working capital purposes with permissible maturities of up to five years and without any limitations as to the type of security."[69] The Act also authorized the RFC to engage in commercial lending, another departure from the Hoover Administration, which had limited RFC lending to banks and insurance companies and few other businesses. In total, nearly $280 million were available for such lending by the Federal Reserve, or about 0.43 percent of gross national product (in today's terms, about $65 billion).[70] In the first eighteen months, the Fed would make nearly 2,000 loans totaling about $124 million, a sizable boost to the economy. The RFC, with fewer restrictions, would lend much more to Main Street.

While much of Roosevelt's New Deal was ad hoc experimentation, the Hundred Days contained the framework for a new paradigm in public finance and financial regulation—a framework that would be followed throughout Roosevelt's thirteen years in office. The primary objective of this paradigm was to shift the balance between private and public sectors in the allocation of credit and capital. Regulation would limit the freedom of bankers and impose greater transparency on the markets, provide stability to the private financial sector, and thereby reduce the need for government bailouts and subsidies in the future. The RFC, the Federal Reserve, and other parallel public banking institutions would boost investment in infrastructure and public works projects. The resulting job creation and income support would reduce private-sector debt burdens, thereby contributing further to banking sector stability and recovery. Reform, relief, and recovery were mutually reinforcing.

Not uncommon is the argument that Roosevelt's legislative successes were owed to large Democratic majorities in Congress, an argument that is often offered as an explanation of why similar reforms are not possible today. This interpretation, however, overlooks Roosevelt's ability to bring public opinion to bear on members of both parties. Although Democrats in 1933 commanded the House by a wide margin and had 60 of 96 Senate seats, their ranks included a large number of Southern conservative Democrats.[71] Roosevelt's ability to move legislation through Congress and to maintain Democratic party discipline while pulling more liberal Republicans on board lay partly in the progressive populist appeal of his policies. He also understood that the moment for reform could end quickly and that he had to strike while the iron was hot.[72]

Roosevelt's success in 1933 suggests that a newly elected president's power may be at its zenith soon after election, particularly when succeeding a failed presidency in an atmosphere of crisis.[73] Throughout the Hundred Days, Roosevelt rode a wave of public enthusiasm while shaping popular opinion. He called Congress into special session, gave ten major speeches, sent fifteen messages to Capitol Hill demanding immediate action on specific problems, and Congress passed fifteen major laws. As Nathan Miller concluded:

> Most of the measures were controversial; some were of doubtful constitutionality. But Roosevelt had no intention of making a revolution or creating a new institutional structure for the nation. Rather, he was attempting to cure the temporary ailments of a capitalist society and to nurse it back to health. Experimental cures were being tried only because the conventional nostrums no longer worked.[74]

The achievements of the Hundred Days were rewarded by another landslide victory for Roosevelt in the 1934 midterm elections. Democrats gained nine Senate seats, more than enough to break any filibusters, which at the time required a two-thirds vote.[75] Reform, relief, and recovery—including massive public works and jobs programs—were all good politics. This stands in stark contrast to the history of Obama's first term, where he shied away from relief and recovery efforts after the one-shot stimulus, watched the agenda slip from his grasp with each successive adjournment of Congress, and subsequently lost the 2010 midterm elections to a Tea Party wave that rode the crest of populist impatience and anger.

The Second New Deal

Roosevelt followed up on the success of the 1934 congressional elections with the "Second Hundred Days," another burst of legislative activity that included some of the New Deal's most important reforms: the Social Security Act and the National

Labor Relations Act (the Wagner Act). It also included further relief and recovery efforts. The Emergency Relief Appropriations Act authorized Roosevelt to create a new federal relief agency. The Works Progress Administration (WPA) would employ another 3.2 million at its peak, including Ronald Reagan's father, Jack, as a local director, as well as Reagan's older brother, Neil.[76] The WPA built thousands of schools, hospitals, highways, and airfields across the country, while providing work for many thousands of unemployed writers, actors, artists, and musicians. The National Youth Administration (NYA) employed about 1.5 million young men and women, often in part-time jobs that kept them in school.[77] It is easy to appreciate that millions of Americans who found hope and dignity in New Deal jobs programs, and many of their loved ones, would feel strong, even mystical connections to Roosevelt. Ronald Reagan would vote for Roosevelt four times.[78]

The range and scale of the New Deal public works programs were enormous and a telling contrast to President Obama's approach, which has relied almost exclusively on repeated tax holidays and tax credits to try to spur private-sector job creation. From the beginning of his first term, Obama stated that the public sector cannot create jobs, that only the private sector can be the engine of job creation.[79] Austan Goolsbee, the chairman of his Council of Economic Advisers, went unchallenged in his view that the public sector has never created a single job. With such a mindset, it would hardly seem to matter how large a majority the Democrats had in the House and Senate during Obama's first two years.[80] In accepting a trickle-down approach to recovery and appointing economic advisors with this view, the Obama Administration undermined its own popularity and the public approval that would come with successful public-sector job creation. The result was the 2010 midterm election fiasco and a hopelessly divided Congress that would keep the agenda fixed on austerity and deficits into Obama's second term.

Roosevelt and Obama took diametrically opposite approaches to the sequencing of reforms.[81] Relief and jobs programs were the essence of the New Deal: a new social contract between the American people and their government. To many, reform could sometimes look like rearranging deck chairs on the Titanic, while relief and recovery were more real and personal, even if consisting simply of a temporary job and cash enough to pay for the necessities. By providing relief in the form of public works and jobs programs and boosting recovery with public banking facilities like the RFC in his first two years, Roosevelt was rewarded in the 1934 midterm elections with larger majorities in Congress that allowed him to move forward on more far-reaching reforms in 1935, such as Social Security. In contrast, the Obama Administration propped up the banks without providing the relief of public works and jobs programs. Instead, in his first two years, Obama moved forward with his signature health care reform (which gave up a public option in health insurance), a measure that invited the Tea Party backlash, contributed to the 2010 election losses, and thereby made future relief and reform efforts that much more difficult.

Roosevelt's Second New Deal included other important structural changes. The Public Utilities Holding Company Act of 1935 brought the nation's electric utility companies under federal regulation, including provisions to force divestitures and break up the concentration of an industry that was mostly controlled by eight large conglomerates.[82] This reflected the anti-monopoly and anti-trust impulse in the administration's reform efforts—efforts that were often impeded by the administration's recovery priorities and later, the war effort.[83]

The Banking Act of 1935 owed much to Marriner Eccles, Roosevelt's chairman of the Federal Reserve Board. Eccles was a banker and industrialist, a Mormon from Utah, who testified along with dozens of other bankers to the Senate Finance Committee in early 1933, just prior to Roosevelt's inauguration.[84] He was the only witness who departed from calls for austerity and balanced budgets, and he quickly got the attention of the incoming administration. His ideas on public works projects, deficit financing, and demand stimulus anticipated Keynesian economics.[85] After serving briefly as an aide to Treasury Secretary Henry Morgenthau, Jr., Eccles was appointed by Roosevelt to chair the Federal Reserve Board. Like many of Roosevelt's appointments to regulatory agencies and Cabinet posts, Eccles was not a captive of Wall Street or big business interests.[86] Although a Republican who had voted for Hoover, Eccles was guided by the principle that "laissez faire in banking and the attainment of business stability are incompatible" and that the only remedy was "conscious and deliberate control" of banking and finance by federal regulation.[87]

The Banking Act of 1935 reformed the structure of the Federal Reserve System. Eccles and the administration had proposed making the chairman and vice-chairman of the Federal Reserve Board removable at will by the President. Other proposals sought by the administration and key members of Congress included proposals for a unified central bank, a national monetary authority, government ownership of the regional Reserve banks, and a policy declaration granting the Federal Reserve more regulatory control over private banking and finance.[88] None of these was included in the final bill. Instead, the administration's influence was further diminished by the removal of the Secretary of the Treasury and the Comptroller of the Currency as *ex officio* members of the Board.[89] However, the Board's power was enhanced in several ways. The presidents of the regional Federal Reserve Banks, each of whom sat on the Fed's Open Market Committee (FOMC) that conducts monetary policy, now had to be approved by the Board, although only after election by the directors of their regional banks. The FOMC would now consist of the seven Federal Reserve Board governors (appointed by the President for fourteen-year terms), along with the twelve regional Federal Reserve Bank presidents (only five of whom could vote on the FOMC at any one time). In addition, the Board was given authority to double the reserve requirements for member banks.[90]

As long as Eccles was Board chairman, the Roosevelt Administration would have tremendous influence on Federal Reserve policies. The Banking Act made it a stronger Federal Reserve, but, unfortunately, one that could more easily be co-opted by the private banking interests once Eccles was gone. It was an example of structural reform that left in place an undemocratic structure that, with the passage of time and changes in leadership, could become anti-democratic (openly hostile to the fiscal and regulatory policies of the administration and Congress). The failure to reform the most troubling features of institutional structures that had caused financial calamity and depression would threaten stability and prosperity in the future.

Landslide, Missteps, and Shortcomings

Roosevelt ran for reelection in 1936 on the strength of his massive public works projects and jobs programs, financed by the emerging system of public banking institutions. Once again, it proved to be good politics. He won by a record eleven million votes, more than 60 percent of the popular vote, and an Electoral College landslide of 523 to 8. The Democrats picked up another seven Senate seats for a total of 76 of 96 Senate seats, and another twelve House seats for a total of 331.[91] It was the most dominant position of any administration in modern American political history.

With such commanding majorities in both houses of Congress, Roosevelt made two major missteps. The first was his plan to pack the Supreme Court, a proposal that proved highly unpopular. The Judiciary Reorganization Bill, introduced early in 1937, would have allowed Roosevelt to appoint an additional justice to the Supreme Court for every sitting justice over the age of 70, six of the justices at the time. Although the Constitution does not limit the size of the Supreme Court, Roosevelt's plan came under sharp attack in Congress and from Bar associations and the public.[92]

Roosevelt had been frustrated through 1936 by a series of Supreme Court decisions striking down some of the most important New Deal programs, including the National Industrial Recovery Act (NIRA), the Agricultural Adjustment Act, and the Railroad Retirement Act. A unanimous Court rejected the NIRA industry trade councils and industry codes as violations of the commerce clause, as well as the private non-delegation doctrine (preventing delegation of law-making authority to private entities).[93]

There was concern about what would come next, perhaps a constitutional attack on Social Security or some other popular and vital New Deal program. By the time NIRA was struck down in 1935, its strategy of setting a floor under prices and wages by limiting production was well in retreat. Limiting production would not grow the economy and create jobs. Keynesian demand-side strategies were quickly supplanting the NIRA approach. Perhaps the Court did the New Deal a favor by striking NIRA down.

Roosevelt backed away from his Court-packing plan, and the Supreme Court backed away from its obstruction and began upholding major New Deal programs in five to four decisions. Since then, the Court has routinely upheld the authority of administrative agencies through a more expansive interpretation of the Commerce Clause, while largely ignoring the delegation challenges as long as Congress provides some intelligible principle in the delegation.[94] John Hart Ely, in *Democracy and Distrust*, lamented the demise of the non-delegation doctrine as a "death by association" with pre-1937 substantive due-process decisions and narrow readings of the Commerce Clause: "when those doctrines died the non-delegation doctrine died along with them."[95]

Ever since, there has been a nagging, persistent scholarly critique of this lack of judicial scrutiny of democratic processes—a critique that is more easily ignored than refuted. Theodore Lowi derided Congress's habit of making overly broad delegations to administrative agencies.[96] How much worse it is when the delegation is made to private self-interested parties. Alan Brinkley has argued that an anti-populist critique of deliberative democracy is visible in the "extraordinary, and largely unchallenged, authority of presumed experts on the Federal Reserve Board to chart the course of our economy."[97] Unfortunately, the Banking Act of 1935 only further entrenched the Federal Reserve's problematic institutional structure, which looks much like a NIRA trade council.

Roosevelt's failed attempt to cloak private cartels with the protection of public law is strangely tied to the rise of cartels in more recent decades. Some would say that the Federal Reserve is "the poster child of an unconstitutional private delegation."[98] Like the NIRA, the Federal Reserve is dominated by private actors. The presidents of the regional Reserve banks participate on the Fed's Open Market Committee and are appointed by privately selected regional board members.[99] Meanwhile, unlike other public agencies, the Federal Reserve does not rely on Congress for budgetary appropriations, since it is effectively able to print money. In addition, the Federal Reserve is exempt in whole or in part from much of the tapestry of administrative procedural requirements that apply to most other federal agencies.[100]

There have been numerous challenges to the Federal Reserve since Roosevelt's time, most notably in the 1970s and 1980s, on private non-delegation and Appointments Clause grounds claiming that its regional Reserve Bank presidents are federal officers who should be appointed by the President and confirmed by the Senate, rather than selected by private boards of directors dominated by the big banks. All have been dismissed on narrow procedural grounds by the gatekeepers on the U.S. Court of Appeals for the D.C. Circuit, and the Supreme Court has denied *certiorari*.[101]

Those who praise the New Deal for its wise policies in banking regulation and public finance often ignore its shortcomings on reform, arguably including the role of the Banking Act of 1935 in entrenching the fox in the henhouse. Over the past two decades, evidence has mounted that suggests the Federal Reserve is largely in the hands of powerful private financial institutions and their representatives. There are occasional progressive voices in the Fed, either on the Board of Governors or in the regional Reserve banks, but those are too often marginalized or ignored within the Fed itself. This may explain why the Federal Reserve failed to regulate or supervise the declining lending standards of the biggest banks prior to the 2008 crash. It also helps explain why the Fed under Ben Bernanke appeared to be in no rush to exercise its full authority to lend to business enterprises and infrastructure projects as it did under the enlightened leadership of Marriner Eccles in the 1930s and 1940s. Instead, it preferred to confine its largesse to purchasing bonds from its banking and hedge fund clientele.

Roosevelt's second major misstep so soon after his landslide reelection was his decision to cut spending in 1937, a foolhardy attempt to balance the budget, or at least reduce the deficit, by reducing spending on work projects and relief programs. He was siding with his Treasury Secretary, Henry Morgenthau, Jr., against the advice of his Fed chairman, Marriner Eccles, who counseled more spending, not less.[102] In 1937, federal spending was reduced by more than five percent from the previous year.[103] Appropriations for the WPA were cut from $689 million to less than $500 million; there were also huge cuts in spending on agricultural adjustment and defense programs.[104] Unfortunately, these cuts happened to coincide with the first year of payroll tax collections for Social Security and the Federal Reserve's own misstep. In fearing inflation in commodity markets, the Fed raised reserve requirements too quickly.[105] The payroll tax reduced consumer and private-sector spending, while the higher reserve requirements contributed to a squeeze of private credit.

What followed was the Roosevelt recession, an economic contraction beginning in 1937 that exceeded in severity (though not in longevity) the downturn following the 1929 stock market crash.[106] It was Roosevelt's greatest economic failure as president, and for the first time it took the wind out of the sails of reform. Manufacturing output fell by nearly 40 percent; the unemployment rate, which had been reduced from 25 percent when Roosevelt took office to 14 percent in 1937, jumped back up to 19 percent.[107]

Even before Roosevelt's turn to austerity in 1937, the state and local government sector was in decline. For most of the 1930s, fiscal austerity and an anemic private sector undermined the tax base and reduced tax revenues for all levels of government, making it more difficult to provide needed relief. The federal government could borrow, but state governments had to keep raising taxes and cutting spending because they did not have sufficient access to the bond markets and often had constitutional mandates to balance their budgets. According to E. Cary Brown, the macroeconomic effects of the federal New Deal stimulus of public works and jobs programs were largely erased by the aggregation of spending cuts and tax increases at the state and local levels.[108] That is why New Deal spending was so important yet insufficient throughout the 1930s and why it took much larger federal spending in World War II to finally end the Depression.[109]

The resulting economic downturn became a significant political liability. The 1938 midterm election was a huge defeat for the Democrats, who lost seven Senate seats and 70 House seats.[110] They still had large majorities in each house that, however, included conservative Southern Democrats who would impede reform. Obama's turn to fiscal austerity in 2010 is reminiscent of Roosevelt's 1937 blunder. Roosevelt waited four years to make such a mistake: productive years in terms of reform, relief, and recovery. Unfortunately, Obama turned to austerity in his second year as president, slowing the recovery and contributing to a political backlash in the 2010 midterm elections.

The politics of Obama's shift from stimulus to austerity are confusing. In January 2010, the Senate rejected a proposal for a commission on fiscal consolidation and deficit reduction by a vote of 53 to 46, with six Republican co-sponsors voting against it after Obama announced his support for such a commission.[111] Among the Republican co-sponsors who voted against the commission were several of the most conservative senators. But barely two weeks later, Obama created the Commission on Fiscal Responsibility and Reform by executive order, and named as the co-chairs of the Commission Alan Simpson, a leading Republican deficit hawk, and Erskine Bowles, a leading Democratic deficit hawk and member of numerous corporate boards, including top financial firms such as Morgan Stanley.[112]

Obama could easily have created a commission on economic recovery and jobs, but instead he turned to a deficit-reduction agenda. The Commission on Fiscal Responsibility and Reform was a gift to Republicans, one of many self-inflicted wounds by Obama's turn to austerity. However, as Obama's reelection indicates, many of his constituents have suffered far more than Obama's political fortunes. The Commission could have played out much differently if he had appointed two Progressives as co-chairs, perhaps Keynesian economists like Joseph Stiglitz or Paul Krugman (both Nobel laureates), or politicians on the left of the spectrum—people who would recognize the need to reduce the deficit by putting people back to work, starting with the public sector, rather than trying to reduce the deficit by cutting expenditures and laying off the tax base. But Obama's appointments of Simpson and Bowles, as well as many key officials in the Treasury department and the Federal Reserve, reflects a strongly conservative bias and an acceptance of a pre–New Deal and pre-Keynesian orthodoxy, particularly foolish during a time of massive long-term unemployment, ongoing deleveraging, and a stagnant recovery. With the creation of the Commission, the national discourse shifted quickly from stimulus to austerity, which in turn helped close off political possibilities for more active government responses to the economic crisis.

Instead of public works and jobs programs in 2010 (a time when the Democrats still had working majorities in both houses of Congress), Obama presided over premature spending cuts.[113] Federal government employment, as a percentage of the population, fell to its lowest level since before the 1950s.[114] The federal budget did not sufficiently come to the aid of state and local government finances, which took a nosedive as in the 1930s, because of the collapse in state and local tax revenues in 2008 and 2009.[115] More than half a million state and local government workers lost their jobs in Obama's first term.[116] Schoolteachers, police officers, firefighters, and many other public-sector occupations witnessed massive job cuts and hiring freezes.[117] The decline in public-sector jobs did not help the private sector. Direct federal spending cuts meant declining revenue for private-sector government contractors and lower aggregate spending by consumers (through a reverse multiplier effect).[118]

If the 1934 and 1936 elections were proof that public works and jobs programs can be politically popular in a depression, 2010 is evidence that forgoing such public options can be a political loser. Although fiscal and monetary stimulus and bank bailouts had averted a worse crisis, the official unemployment rate was higher in 2010 than when Obama first took office.[119] While voter turnout fell in the midterm election, for Democrats it fell by ten million more than for Republicans. According to ABC News exit polls, more than four out of every ten people who had voted for Obama in 2008 did not bother voting in 2010, a decline of more than 29 million votes.[120] Democrats lost control of the House of Representatives, lost their filibuster-proof majority in the Senate, and lost all hope of a workable recovery and reform agenda.

Roosevelt's failed experiment in austerity was short-lived. In the last nine months of 1938, he once again boosted federal spending, including funding for the WPA. The recovery began in mid-1938, but employment would not regain the 1937 level until the United States entered World War II. The Federal Reserve chairman, Marriner Eccles, was still defending public spending as the means for economic recovery and business prosperity, but the 1938 midterm election results and shifting public opinion were beginning to undermine support for new relief and reform.

It was not too long before the drums of war, sounding across the ocean, were having salutary effects on the U.S. economy. In 1940, Britain was in dire need of American arms and supplies and fast running out of money. The U.S. Neutrality Act required belligerents to pay cash for arms, and loans were prohibited to nations like Britain that had not paid their debts from World War I. Roosevelt solved the problem with a "flash of genius": the United States would lend or lease the supplies and equipment to Britain in return for British overseas military bases that Britain could ill afford to defend.[121] The Lend-Lease program eventually provided more than $50 billion worth of American supplies to Britain and other allied nations. U.S. foreign military assistance provided a dramatic stimulus to American industry and labor, which were increasingly reoriented into military production. The Lend-Lease boom was a portent of even bigger changes to come for the U.S. economy.

War and Nation-Building: Vindication and Amnesia

It has been suggested that each generation rewrites history to suit its own ends.[122] The history of the New Deal, particularly in money and banking, seems to follow such a pattern. In the early post–World War II period, in the heyday of corporate liberalism when organized labor was near the zenith of its power and influence, the dominant view was to see the New Deal as a great epoch of reform that was stalled by its pragmatic compromises with corporate power and its failure to solve the problem of unemployment.[123] In more recent years, as private finance and corporate power extended its reach at home and abroad, the New Deal legacy in banking and finance was turned on its head and largely swept aside. Such a sea change in policy required a kind of historical amnesia, a "creative forgetfulness" and rewriting of New Deal history.[124]

It is common to hear conservative critics of Roosevelt point out that the New Deal did not end the Depression, that it was World War II that finally brought it to an end, as if that somehow discredits the New Deal Keynesian precepts of active fiscal policy, public works and jobs programs, and public options in banking.[125] Of course, the reverse is much more accurate. The war brought a fiscal revolution. In the first six months of the war, the federal government placed over $100 billion in orders for war contracts, thereby demanding more goods than the economy had ever produced in a single year.[126] The portion of the economy devoted to war production more than doubled in 1942—from 15 to 33 percent of the economy. Total wartime spending was more than $320 billion, twice as large as all previous federal spending in the history of the Republic combined.

The dramatic increase in federal spending translated directly into an enormous economic boom.[127] The nation's gross national product (GNP) grew from $99.7 billion in 1940 to $211.9 billion in 1945. The mobilization of resources—human, industrial, technological, and financial—exceeded the efforts of all other belligerents combined. By any measure, World War II was the most impressive economic expansion in American history, with real (inflation-adjusted) economic growth rates exceeding 15 percent a year during the war's three peak years and averaging double digits throughout the war.

War came to the rescue of the American economy. By the end of the war, the jobless rate was 1.2 percent. A hyperactive fiscal policy had ended the Great Depression. It confirmed the Keynesian prescription that higher levels of government spending can bring higher growth rates, just as the 1937 recession confirmed the futility and dangers of cutting government spending in a weak economy.

There were fears that the war's end would bring another depression.[128] Sixteen million American military personnel would be returning to the civilian economy. How would they be employed, and by whom? Would wages fall as a result of an oversupply of labor? Was a debt deflation about to harm borrowers and threaten banks and financial institutions yet again?

As the end of the war approached, Congress passed the Servicemen's Readjustment Act of 1944, the so-called G.I. Bill of Rights, to assist newly returning veterans with jobs, training, education, and health care, and low-cost business loans and home mortgages. In the G.I. Bill, one could see shades of so many New Deal programs, now all wrapped into one.[129] The war's mass conscription now translated in peacetime into the basis of a Keynesian full employment and social policy on a grand scale. Conscription spread the G.I. Bill's benefits to an enormous portion of the population, nearly one-quarter of the civilian workforce. More than sixteen million new veterans benefited from subsidized low-interest mortgage loans and tuition-free university education, along with living stipends.[130] Veterans received more than $13 billion for education and training, a significant part of the federal budget. Higher education boomed, and the domestic economy continued to boom.

Peter Drucker considered the G.I. Bill of Rights to be perhaps the most important single event of the twentieth century, signaling an important shift to a technologically advanced "knowledge society."[131] According to historian Michael Bennett, there would not have been the political support for a Marshall Plan if sixteen million Americans and their families had not successfully readjusted to civilian life thanks to the G.I. Bill.[132] The Marshall Plan and other U.S. foreign aid programs in turn helped rebuild, on democratic foundations, war-torn economies throughout Western Europe and Japan, a powerful inoculation against any turn to either communism or fascism.

The Marshall Plan was the largest peacetime foreign aid program in U.S. history, consisting of more than $13 billion in grants (rather than loans) between 1947 and 1951. This also represented about 13 percent of the total U.S. budget, the equivalent of more than $400 billion today (compared with recent U.S. foreign aid budgets, which are barely $50 billion a year and 1.5 percent of the federal budget).[133] It was a huge spending program, and it had an immediate, positive impact: recipient countries experienced economic growth rates of nearly 40 percent over the next four years; and the U.S. economy, already getting a shot in the arm from the G.I. Bill, now got a double dose from the Marshall Plan's boost in exports, manufacturing, and employment.

Throughout the 1940s, in both wartime and post-war, the Federal Reserve and the RFC continued to channel credit into the real economy (i.e., into actual industries that produced tangible goods, as opposed to the paper economy of Wall Street). The Fed made sure Treasury could borrow and spend at near-zero interest rates. The RFC, following the New Deal public investment model, more directly pumped billions of dollars into investments in defense plants, building 2,300 factories at a cost of more than $9 billion dollars.[134]

The decade of the 1940s provides vindication of the role of big government in a modern mass industrial economy. This active role necessarily extended to money and finance. The 1940s decade turned all the metrics in public finance upside down. Federal spending and borrowing quickly grew to enormous levels, compared to both the 1930s and the present time. In 2012, federal spending was about 25 percent of GDP; in the 1940s it peaked at nearly 45 percent. In 2012, the federal debt held by the public was about 70 percent of GDP; in the 1940s, it peaked at over 114 percent. In the 1940s, the federal deficit peaked at more than 30 percent of GDP; in 2012 the federal deficit was about 8 percent of GDP (in Greece, after 2008, it peaked at little more than 10 percent of GDP). Although the 1940s may be taken as a vindication of military Keynesianism, far more could be accomplished in terms of employment and quality of life if the same level of resources were invested in the civilian economy.[135]

The higher spending and borrowing levels of the 1940s did not coincide with rising inflation or rising interest rates precisely because of the New Deal legacy in financial regulatory reform and the public option in banking. Of crucial importance was the administration's control of the central bank. From 1942 to 1951, the Federal Reserve was directed by the White House and Treasury to peg interest rates at three-eighths of one percent on short-term Treasury debt and 2.5 percent on long-term Treasury debt. During this so-called pegged period, it was the Federal Reserve's duty to purchase government securities in any amount and at any price needed to maintain the interest rate pegs.[136]

Since 2008, the Federal Reserve has purchased trillions of dollars in Treasury securities and mortgage-backed securities, also to keep interest rates low on Treasury debt and the rest of the U.S. economy. Yet the recovery has been slow and tepid. The Fed's monetization of debt has propped up the balance sheets of banks and helped the stock market,[137] but at the same time, federal spending is actually being pinched by the turn to austerity. Without public works and jobs programs, long-term unemployment remains disturbingly high. Meanwhile, the slow growth economy and its lagging tax receipts contribute to ongoing government deficits, resulting in more calls for spending cuts and budget austerity.

In his *Essays on the Great Depression*, Ben Bernanke described how the Federal Reserve's bond-buying programs in the 1930s left the banks with excess reserves without stimulating recovery. He credited this insight to Milton Friedman and Anna Schwartz: that the growing level of liquidity created an illusion of easy money, and that, in reality, lenders were shifting away from making loans, in large part because of the continued weakness of debtors (often upside-down and out of work). The banks instead preferred to hold safe and liquid investments: government securities.[138] Likewise, today the banks have amassed more than $1.5 trillion in excess reserves, thanks also to the Federal Reserve's quantitative-easing programs of purchasing bonds from those banks. And once again, the banks are propped up but not lending sufficiently to finance a vibrant economic recovery, for much the same reasons of mass unemployment and the deleveraging of consumers and businesses.

Bernanke's view of the Depression seemed to be marked by selective amnesia. If one lesson of the Great Depression is that the Federal Reserve must be ready to expand the money supply (Bernanke's main point), another lesson that he did not seem to recognize is that monetary expansion alone will not renew growth for the economy when consumers and businesses are underwater, there is mass unemployment, and people's liquidity preferences are elevated because of weak confidence in the economy.[139] In the 1930s, Marriner Eccles said that, under such conditions, the use of monetary policy is like "pushing on a string." He argued that a far more active fiscal policy was necessary, that tax cuts are also limited in effectiveness in such an environment, and therefore that public works projects are of paramount importance.

Although the Federal Reserve was monetizing a significant amount of Treasury debt in the 1940s, the Treasury was spending such funds on gigantic projects that resulted in full employment: the war, the G.I. Bill, and the Marshall Plan. Instead of the 1930s' liquidity trap, in the 1940s there was booming confidence, and the Federal Reserve's focus had to shift from prodding banks to make loans to restraining them instead from extending credit for speculative purposes. But thanks to New Deal banking law reforms, the Federal Reserve and other federal agencies used their authority to set margin requirements and minimum down-payments on loans for stock purchases, real estate, automobiles, and consumer durable goods.[140] The modern administrative state was able to prevent any hyperinflation of consumer prices or asset markets during the greatest economic boom in the nation's history.

If the economic policies and performance of the 1940s stand as a vindication of the New Deal's Keynesian approach to economic recovery, that analysis must be tempered with the realization that the New Deal left unfinished much of its ambitious reform agenda. Alan Brinkley has written about the assumptions of early New Deal reformers: "that the nation's greatest problems were rooted in the structure of modern industrial capitalism and that it was the mission of government to deal somehow with the flaws in that structure."[141] Large corporate enterprises were seen as particularly problematic and requiring institutional reform at several levels, including reform of corporate governance and more robust anti-trust policy to rein in the cartels that were exploiting consumers, workers, and taxpayers. According to Brinkley, the rapid economic recovery and expansion during World War II reduced the impetus for anti-trust and other reforms, while the war-planning bureaucracy itself helped entrench the self-regulation of big business.[142]

For instance, both Congress and the Securities and Exchange Commission (SEC) considered proposals to reform corporate governance to make management more accountable to the interests of shareholders and other stakeholders. In 1934, congressional concern extended to deficiencies in the federal proxy rules that allowed corporate insiders to control the process of electing corporate directors. It was not until 1942 that the SEC proposed a rule to require corporations to include shareholder-nominated director candidates in their proxy statements, but the SEC proposal was roundly criticized by corporate management as unworkable, confusing, and potentially costly to the war effort, so the SEC abandoned the proposal.[143] While in postwar Europe, corporate governance would be reformed to enhance the voice of various corporate constituencies, such as workers and consumers, in the U.S., large private-sector corporations became more hierarchical and less accountable to non-management and non-shareholder interests. U.S. corporate elites would preside over industries that were increasingly cartelized after the 1970s and therefore increasingly profitable. The corporate pie would be divided more unequally than in the past, with top management and shareholders claiming larger shares at the expense of rank-and-file workers, consumers, and taxpayers.

As the U.S. economy expanded in the war and post-war periods, there was a general amnesia in American politics about the need for structural reforms. The watering down of anti-trust efforts coincided with a retreat from state economic planning. Corporate elites would fill the vacuum. For instance, in the late 1940s, General Motors, Firestone Tire, Greyhound Bus, Mack Truck, and Standard Oil of California colluded in creating front companies that bought up more than a hundred electric trolley, rail, and bus lines around the country. Each of these companies enjoyed a dominant position in increasingly cartelized and oligopolistic industries. Together, they formed a super cartel that would remake cityscapes and transportation patterns across the nation. After taking control of previously public-transit systems, they promptly shut down the electric trolley lines and replaced them with gas-powered buses.[144] The railcars and tracks from the Los Angeles electric rail system (at the time the largest system in the country) were simply dumped in the ocean. Los Angeles and a hundred other cities and locales were increasingly motorized at the expense of air quality and the quality of life; commuters would pay more, and corporations would reap bigger profits. The General Motors–led cartel was also a disturbing portent of the dangers of private planning when the public sector surrenders all voice and all public options.

In time, corporate dominance would shift from such industrial cartels (oil, steel, and autos, for instance) to a cartel in banking and finance with global reach. After the nation-building period of the G.I. Bill and Marshall Plan, the RFC was allowed to lapse, and the Federal Reserve scaled back its lending to non-bank business interests. Public options in banking and finance were in retreat. In 1951, with Eccles no longer serving as chairman of the Federal Reserve, but still serving as a Fed governor, the Federal Reserve rebelled against Treasury and White House control. What followed was the Federal Reserve–Treasury Accord of March 1951, by which the Fed regained its control over monetary policy and the setting of interest rates. It was a far cry from the New Deal proposals to bring the central bank under government ownership and control.

As the Federal Reserve fortified its independence from the political branches of government, it increasingly became the captive of the private financial and banking interests that owned and directed the regional Reserve banks. A couple of dozen big banks, their satellite hedge funds and interrelated credit ratings agencies, located primarily in seven wealthy countries (the G-7 countries), would receive guidance and protection from "independent" central banks.

The amnesia about New Deal reform crossed party lines. In 1999, as noted, Bill Clinton, a Democratic president, signed away the Glass-Steagall Banking Act of 1933 that had kept commercial banks out of the "casino economy" for more than half a century. During that time, banking and finance were generally far less risky industries. From the 1930s through the 1970s, there were only 198 U.S. bank failures, an average of fewer than six bank failures a year, resulting in about $124.3 million in FDIC losses. Deregulation changed everything. By the late 1980s, there were hundreds of bank failures a year, and the savings and loan industry collapsed, at much larger cost to taxpayers. The end of Glass-Steagall and the deregulation of derivative financial markets in late 2000 (in Bill Clinton's final month in office) let the genie out of the bottle.[145]

By the end of the Clinton era, the entire financial system was turning on its head. Without public options in banking, the public sector was increasingly starved of resources. On a per capita basis, federal civilian employment fell to its lowest levels since the 1950s. With regulation of banks and financial markets reduced, the financial system became far riskier. The New Deal model in banking regulation and public finance gave way to industry self-regulation and speculative financial markets. By the twenty-first century, it was common, and for good reason, to refer to the distribution of wealth, income, and power as resembling a New Gilded Age. This set the stage for the 2008 financial collapse, the most significant meltdown in banking and financial markets since 1929 and the early 1930s.

The Need for a New Deal Today

In 1933, as in 2008, private finance had utterly collapsed into the hands of the state, which chose to prop up the banks with public funds in each case. In 1933, it was the RFC that pumped capital into the banks; in 2008 and 2009, it was the TARP bailout fund that bought non-voting stakes in the banks. In both periods, the Federal Reserve provided massive help with few strings attached. In neither period were structural changes imposed on the management of the subsidized banks. But at least during the New Deal, the propped up institutions of capitalism were supplemented and at times supplanted by more effective and accountable government institutions.

Despite the several big responses by the Bush and Obama administrations to the financial and economic collapse of late 2008—the Troubled Asset Relief Program (TARP), the American Recovery and Reinvestment Act (ARRA) of early 2009, and the Dodd-Frank Wall Street Reform and Consumer Protection Act of July 2010—none of these measures showed much learning from the experience of the New Deal in the 1930s and 1940s. In fact, each showed how little was learned from the successes and shortcomings of the New Deal era. TARP funds were used to keep big banks afloat, but without sweeping out the actual bankers who had made such terrible decisions. The few-strings-attached nature of TARP suggested a view that what was good for Wall Street was good for the United States. But there were large costs in propping up the banks with taxpayer funds without bringing them under government control. The banking élites were able to continue with many of the same speculative financial practices, while using their corporate treasuries to lobby Congress and the administration to limit reforms. There was also a significant political cost, as the TARP bailout helped fuel the Tea Party backlash in the 2010 midterm elections.[146]

Although the Obama stimulus provided direct employment for several hundred thousand people, these jobs were mostly already in the pipeline. Obama called them "shovel-ready" jobs for construction projects that had already reached a point of planning where workers could be quickly employed to begin work.[147] In contrast, Roosevelt's public works programs were not shovel-ready in the same sense—instead, they provided jobs (and in the case of the CCC, actual shovels) for unemployed Americans who had no prospects, and they started new projects that had not previously been on the drawing board. Moreover, the size and duration of Obama's stimulus was far too small and short-lived for the magnitude of the crisis facing the American economy, and the design was flawed by not focusing on direct job-creation.[148]

The Dodd-Frank Act delegated authority for new regulations to many of the same federal departments and agencies that were largely captured and staffed with Wall Street operatives. In late 2012, Treasury Secretary Timothy Geithner was able to exempt foreign exchange swaps and forwards from the rules under the Dodd-Frank Act that were intended to reduce risk and increase transparency in derivative markets. The exemption would protect a four-trillion-dollar-a-day global market and one of the largest sources of derivatives-trading revenue for the biggest banks.[149]

In restricting the ability to use TARP for any future industrial lending, the Dodd-Frank Act curtailed the administration's ability to finance any new public works projects or jobs programs. After the House fell under Republican control in late 2010, the Obama Administration turned increasingly to an austerity agenda. With the elected branches unable to agree on budgets and arguing over extension of the debt-ceiling limit, the Federal Reserve played a larger role in trying to nurse a recovery. The Fed's quantitative easing programs pushed trillions of dollars in newly created money into the banks, but too little trickled down to the real economy and to real job creation.

There are several factors that explain Obama's failure to follow up on the successes of financial stabilization with a more vibrant agenda of reform. Prior to his election, and since, Obama's top advisors on economic and finance issues were people with Wall Street ties. Obama all too readily accepted their perspective that the public sector cannot create jobs, thereby ruling out public works as well as the public option in banking.[150] Likewise, Obama accepted the "free trade" and *laissez-faire* assumptions that globalization, trade, and capital flows could not be slowed, regulated, or taxed.[151] With the exception of his initial "stimulus" in early 2009, Obama's approach to the problems in private and public finance often resembled Hoover's trickle-down approach, and like Hoover's, was an insufficient impulse for action.

One of Obama's momentous decisions was to reappoint Ben Bernanke to chair the Federal Reserve. Bernanke had been a Republican appointee (first as chair of President George W. Bush's Council of Economic Advisers, and then as Fed chairman), and he was averse to having the Federal Reserve intervene beyond helping Wall Street. Since the 1930s, the central bank had the authority under Section 13(3) of the Federal Reserve Act to open its discount window to non-bank enterprises "in unusual and exigent circumstances." The Dodd-Frank Act retained the Fed's Section 13(3) authority to lend directly to individuals, partnerships, and corporations in unusual and exigent circumstances, but only if it were part of a program or facility with "broad-based eligibility."[152] For the Federal Reserve to establish a broad-based facility or program, it would first have to obtain permission from the Treasury Secretary, and at least five members of the Board of Governors would have to agree with the credit advance.[153] It was easy to imagine a number of programs or facilities with broad-based eligibility that could help pull the economy out of its slow-growth trajectory while providing relief and jobs to millions of unemployed, including: loans to federal agencies for public works and infrastructure projects; loans to state infrastructure banks for capital investments; loans to or purchases of mortgages from Fannie Mae and Freddie Mac and other lenders for the objective of modifying mortgages; or loans to or purchases from holders of student loans, also to modify loan repayments. Unfortunately, it was far more difficult to imagine a Federal Reserve willing to assert its Section 13(3) authority to finance such a recovery program.

In the fall of 2008, as credit and capital markets froze across the world and as large banks and financial institutions teetered on the brink, there was hope for change. But throughout Obama's first term, very little changed in terms of the dominant models and approaches to banking regulation and public finance. New regulations were either piecemeal or delegated to the captured agencies for drafting and implementation. Most significantly, doors were closed on public options in banking, in turn closing the door on possibilities for significant infrastructure investment, public works, and jobs programs. Trickle-down was the dominant strategy across the board, an unfortunate contrast with the approach of Franklin Roosevelt, who recognized that any sustainable recovery must be a bottom-up recovery that provides jobs and better wages and incomes to ordinary folks. Roosevelt understood that such a recovery depended on an active public sector to lead the way, through institutions like the Reconstruction Finance Corporation, to underwrite a large and comprehensive program of infrastructure investment and public works. Roosevelt's New Deal approach in financial regulation and public finance provides a lodestar for today's troubled economy.

Notes

1. Franklin D. Roosevelt, Address at Oglethorpe University, Atlanta, Georgia, May 22, 1932; quoted by Kirsten Carter in "Bold, Persistent Experimentation," in *Roosevelt History*, Oct. 22, 2010, FDR Presidential Library and Museum blog, accessed July 20, 2013, available at http://fdrlibrary.wordpress.com/tag/digital/.

2. Broadus Mitchell, *Depression Decade: From New Era Through New Deal, 1929–1941* (New York: Holt, Reinhart and Winston, 1947), 87.
3. David M. Kennedy, *Freedom from Fear: The American People in Depression and War, 1929-1945* (New York: Oxford University Press, 1999), 84.
4. Nathan Miller, *FDR: An Intimate History* (New York: Signet, 1983), 262.
5. Mitchell, Appendix IX, 442; Jesse H. Jones, *Fifty Billion Dollars: My Thirteen Years with the RFC* (New York: MacMillan, 1951).
6. Timothy A. Canova, "The Public Option: The Case for Parallel Public Banking Institutions," New America Foundation, June 2011, available at http://www.newamerica.net/publications/policy/the_public_option.
7. Miller, 285.
8. Andrew Ross Sorkin, *Too Big to Fail* (New York: Penguin Books, 2009), 507.
9. Jonathan Alter, *The Defining Moment: FDR's Hundred Days and the Triumph of Hope* (New York: Simon & Schuster, 2006), xiii.
10. FDR's bank holiday proclamation suspended all banking transactions, embargoed all gold and silver shipments, prohibited hoarding, and made violations punishable by a fine of $10,000 or ten years' imprisonment. Franklin D. Roosevelt, "Proclamation 2039—Declaring Bank Holiday," March 6, 1933. Gerhard Peters and John T. Woolley, *The American Presidency Project*, accessed July 20, 2013, available at http://www.presidency.ucsb.edu/ws/?pid=14661. FDR took office on Saturday, March 4th, and the proclamation was made effective just after midnight on Monday, March 6th, so as to keep from profaning the Sabbath; Miller, 309.
11. A year later, the U.S. Supreme Court would uphold a state's emergency legislation that imposed a moratorium on foreclosures in the face of a constitutional challenge. "Emergency does not create power," wrote Chief Justice Hughes. "Emergency does not increase granted power [or] diminish the restrictions imposed upon power [granted]. While emergency does not create power, emergency may furnish the occasion for the exercise of power." *Home Building & Loan Association v. Blaisdell*, 290 U.S. 398, 54 S.Ct. 231, 78 L.Ed. 413 (1934).
12. Miller, 309.
13. Kennedy, 135–136.
14. Mitchell, 134.
15. Kennedy, 136.
16. Lester V. Chandler, *The Economics of Money and Banking*, 5th ed. (New York: Harper & Row, 1969), 464.
17. Ibid.
18. Miller, 311; Kennedy, 136.
19. Miller, 311.
20. Chandler, 464.
21. Ben S. Bernanke, *Essays on the Great Depression* (Princeton, NJ: Princeton University Press, 2000), 62.
22. Chandler, 464.
23. Kennedy, 137.
24. Raymond Moley, *After Seven Years* (New York: Harper & Brothers Publishers, 1939), 155. According to one congressman at the time: "The President drove the money-changers out of the Capitol on March 4th—and they were all back on the 9th." Alter, 251.
25. Moley, 155; Miller, 311; Alter, 251.
26. Moley, 155; Miller, 311.
27. Broadus Mitchell feared "that an economic system which had come so near to self-destruction was scarcely worth the passionate loyalty" expressed by Moley. Mitchell, 136.
28. Franklin D. Roosevelt, *F.D.R.: His Personal Letters*, ed. Elliott Roosevelt (New York: Duell, 1947–1950), 373; Miller, 249, 334.
29. Alter, 230.
30. Anthony J. Badger and William Hughes, *FDR: The First Hundred Days* (New York: Farrar Straus & Giroux, 2009), 163.

31. An eight-day week may have been enough for Roosevelt to save capitalism, but it was apparently not enough to show he cared about the capitalists.
32. Alter, 231.
33. Kennedy, 137. "Thereafter mail routinely poured in at a rate of four to seven thousand letters per day."
34. Miller, 313.
35. Ibid., 314.
36. The Court struck down the Agricultural Adjustment Act of 1933 on a restrictive commerce clause analysis in *United States v. Butler*, 297 U.S. 1, 56 S. Ct. 312, 80 L. Ed. 477 (1936). Six years later, the Court upheld the 1938 Agricultural Adjustment Act with a more expansive commerce clause reading, in *Wickard v. Filburn*, 317 U.S. 111, 63 S. Ct. 82, 87 L. Ed. 122 (1942).
37. Mitchell, 137.
38. Ibid.
39. Ibid.
40. Ibid.
41. Ibid.
42. Ibid., 138.
43. *Norman v. Baltimore & Ohio Railroad Co.*, 294 U.S. 240 (1935); Mitchell, 138.
44. Miller, 315–316; Kennedy, 144.
45. Miller, 339.
46. Bernanke, 62.
47. Mitchell, Appendix, 439.
48. Charles P. Kindleberger, *The World in Depression, 1929–1939* (Berkeley, CA: University of California Press, 1973), 233.
49. Ibid., 221.
50. The New Deal approach to public finance had its antecedents in Wilson's War Finance Corporation, a new federal credit institution that helped finance railroads, banks, and utilities. Jordan A. Schwartz, *The New Dealers: Power Politics in the Age of Roosevelt* (New York: Vintage, 1993), 18. According to Schwartz, the Wilsonians also "abhorred socialism or unwarranted intervention in the marketplace, but when capital was timid or crisis threatened, bold and visionary men in Washington recalled that government itself was enterprise.... Thus began the emergence of American state capitalism" (p. 14).
51. Jones, 146–152, 173–205.
52. Ibid., 163–172, 203–205, 211–213.
53. Ibid., 163.
54. "Brother, Can You Spare a Billion? The Story of Jesse H. Jones," PBS, accessed July 20, 2013, available at http://www.pbs.org/jessejones/jesse_bio3.htm. According to the *Saturday-Evening Post*, "Next to the President no man in the Government and probably in the United States wields greater power," accessed July 20, 2013, available at http://www.pbs.org/jessejones/index.htm. Roosevelt reportedly came to calling Jones "Jesus H. Jones." Merle Miller, *Plain Speaking: An Oral Biography of Harry S. Truman* (New York: Berkley Books, 1974), 196.
55. David Barboza, "Bridge Comes to San Francisco with a Made-in-China Label," *New York Times*, June 26, 2011, A1.
56. Lori Wallach, "U.S. Foreign Economic Policy in the Global Crisis," Statement by the Director of Public Citizen's Global Trade Watch to the Subcommittee on Terrorism, Nonproliferation and Trade, Committee on Foreign Affairs, U.S. House of Representatives, March 12, 2009, accessed July 20, 2013, available at www.citizen.org/documents/WallachTestimony031209.pdf. The Agreement on Government Procurement that is currently in force was part of the Clinton administration's trade liberalization agenda. It was signed in Marrakesh on April 15, 1994 at the same time as the Agreement Establishing the World Trade Organization and was entered into force on January 1, 1996. "Overview of the Agreement on Government Procurement," Trade Topics: Government Procurement, World Trade Organization (Washington, D.C.

2013), accessed July 20, 2013, available at http://www.wto.org/english/tratop_e/gproc_e/gpa_overview_e.htm.

57. Michael Likosky, *Obama's Bank: Financing a Durable New Deal* (New York: Cambridge University Press, 2010), 7–18.
58. Dodd-Frank Wall Street Reform and Consumer Protection Act, 124 Stat. 1376, P.L. 111–203 (July 21, 2010), Section 1302 (amending Section 115(a) of the Emergency Stabilization Act of 2008), accessed July 20, 2013, available at www.gpo.gov/fdsys/pkg/PLAW-111publ203/.../PLAW-111publ203.pdf.
59. In 2011, Governor Jerry Brown vetoed AB 750, a bill to create a commission on chartering a state-owned bank; he would also veto bills to enhance the authority of the I-Bank. Adam Weintraub, "Calif. Gov Names Retired BofA Exec as Jobs Adviser," *Associated Press*, August 18, 2011, accessed July 20, 2013, available at http://news.yahoo.com/calif-gov-names-retired-bofa-exec-jobs-adviser-143916977.html.
60. Miller, 315–317.
61. Matthew Josephson, *The Money Lords: The Great Finance Capitalists 1925–1950* (New York: Webright and Talley, 1972), 173.
62. Michael Perino, *The Hellhound of Wall Street* (New York: Penguin Press, 2010), 4–7; Mitchell, 154–157.
63. *The Financial Crisis Inquiry Report, Final Report of the National Commission on the Causes of the Financial and Economic Crisis in the United States* (Washington, DC: U.S. Government Printing Office, 2011), accessed July 20, 2013, available at http://www.gpo.gov/fdsys/pkg/GPO-FCIC.
64. Alter, 305 (quoting Friedman).
65. Milton Friedman and Anna Jacobson Schwartz, *A Monetary History of the United States, 1867–1960* (Princeton, NJ: Princeton University Press, for National Bureau of Economic Research, 1963), 434–440.
66. Timothy A. Canova, "The Transformation of U.S. Banking and Finance: From Regulated Competition to Free-Market Receivership," *Brooklyn Law Review,* 60 (1995): 1295, 1298–1303.
67. David Fettig, "Lender of More Than Last Resort," Federal Reserve Bank of Minneapolis, December 2002, 15, accessed July 20, 2013, available at http://www.minneapolisfed.org/publications_papers/pub_display.cfm?id=3392.
68. In 1932, Hoover had reluctantly agreed to an amendment in a highway construction bill (ten days after vetoing similar legislation) that granted the Federal Reserve the authority to lend directly to "individuals, partnerships, and corporations" (therefore, not solely to banks), but only in "unusual and exigent circumstances." With the Fed's rather orthodox leadership at the time, the power was used sparingly: "Just 123 loans were made over four years" by all twelve regional Reserve banks, totaling about $1.5 million; the largest single loan was for $300,000. The Emergency Banking Act of 1933 authorized similar loans to non-banking corporations by the regional Reserve Banks, but such loans had to be secured by direct obligations of the United States, and the loans were limited to 90-day advances. Fettig, 18–19.
69. Ibid., 19 (quoting Howard Hackley's useful but out of print *Lending Functions of the Federal Reserve* [Washington, DC: Board of Governors of the Federal Reserve System, 1973]); Hackley was the Board's General Counsel.
70. Ibid., 45.
71. David Woolner, "How Obama Can Fight Back: FDR, the 'Populist Backlash' and the 1934 Election," Roosevelt Institute, accessed July 20, 2013, available at http://www.rooseveltinstitute.org/new-roosevelt/how-obama-can-fight-back-fdr-populist-backlash-and-1934-election; *The American Heritage Book of the Presidents*, Vol. 10 (New York: Dell Publishing, 1967), 898.
72. As Senator Burton Wheeler put it, in early March 1933, Congress would "jump through a hoop" if Roosevelt asked: Miller, 313. But only for a time, and FDR knew to take advantage of the moment.

73. Nathan Miller pointed out that "honeymoon" circumstances assisted Roosevelt: "Hoover was an easy act to follow. The country was at rock bottom, with no place to go but up." Because of the financial crisis, the honeymoon was more intense than usual. Miller, 314 (quoting Robert E. Sherwood).
74. Miller, 318–319.
75. In 1975, the Senate reduced the number of votes required for cloture from two-thirds to three-fifths, or sixty of the current 100 senators.
76. "Ronald Wilson Reagan, Life before the Presidency," American President: A Reference Resource, Miller Center, University of Virginia, accessed July 20, 2013, available at http://millercenter.org/president/reagan/essays/biography/2. According to some accounts, "the family would have starved" had Reagan's father Jack and older brother Neil not obtained employment with the Federal Emergency Relief Administration. William Kleinknecht, *The Man Who Stole the World: Ronald Reagan and the Betrayal of Main Street America* (Philadelphia: Perseus Books, 2010), 37.
77. Miller, 367–369.
78. "Reagan, Life," *supra* note 76; Kleinknecht, 37.
79. "The Myth of Job Creation," *New York Times,* October 22, 2012, A22.
80. "Scarecrow's Nightmare: Austan Goolsbee Defends President Romney's Economic Plan," *Firedoglake.com (FDL),* June 5, 2011, accessed March 25, 2013, available at http://my.firedoglake. com/scarecrow/2011/06/05/austan-goolsbee-defends-presidents-romneys-economic-plan/; "Colbert or Goolsbee: Who's the Clown?" Institute for Public Accuracy, June 6, 2011, accessed March 25, 2013, available at http://www.accuracy.org/release/colbert-or-goolsbee-whos-the-clown/
81. Empirical evidence suggests that the success of a policy may often depend on the correct sequencing of reform, perhaps putting wider social interests ahead of the interests of capital markets in the policy queue. Eswar Prasad, Kenneth Rogoff, Shang-Jin Wei, and M. Ayhan Kose, "Effects of Financial Globalization on Developing Countries: Some Empirical Evidence," International Monetary Fund, March 17, 2003, 5, accessed July 20, 2013, available at http://www.imf.org/external/np/res/docs/2003/031703.pdf. The authors conclude that financial integration should be approached cautiously, with the pace and sequencing of integration dependent on country-specific circumstances and institutional features. (Rogoff was the IMF Chief Economist and Director of Research at the time of the report.)
82. Leonard S. Hyman, *America's Electric Utilities: Past, Present and Future* (Vienna, VA: Public Utilities Reports, 1988), 74; Mitchell, 173.
83. Alan Brinkley, *The End of Reform: New Deal Liberalism in Recession and War* (New York: Vintage Books, 1995).
84. Investigation of Economic Problems, Hearings Before the Committee on Finance, United States Senate, 72nd Congress, 2nd Sess., Pursuant to S. Res. 315, Feb. 13–28, 1933, 703–733 (Washington, DC: U.S. Government Printing Office, 1933), available at Federal Reserve Bank of St. Louis, accessed July 20, 2013, available at http://fraser.stlouisfed.org/docs/meltzer/ecctes33.pdf.
85. Marriner S. Eccles, *Beckoning Frontiers: Public and Personal Recollections,* ed. Sidney Hyman (New York: Alfred A. Knopf, 1951); Sidney Hyman, *Marriner S. Eccles: Private Entrepreneur and Public Servant* (Stanford, CA: Graduate School of Business, Stanford University, 1976).
86. Conrad Black, *Franklin Delano Roosevelt: Champion of Freedom* (New York: Public Affairs, 2003), 260. Black concluded that Roosevelt was "very leery of big industrialists, financiers, and corporate lawyers" in making his Cabinet appointments.
87. Mitchell, 168.
88. Ibid., 171.
89. Ibid., 168–169.
90. Ibid., 169.
91. *The American Heritage Book,* 898–899.

92. "Franklin Delano Roosevelt's 'Court Packing' Plan," United States Senate Committee on the Judiciary, Recess Reading, accessed July 20, 2013, available at http://www.judiciary.senate.gov/about/history/CourtPacking.cfm.
93. *A. L. A. Schechter Poultry Corp. v. United States,* 295 U.S. 495, 550 (1935). Justice Cardozo, in his concurring opinion, characterized the delegation to the private industry trade council as a "delegation running riot." Ibid., 553.
94. John Hart Ely, *Democracy and Distrust: A Theory of Judicial Review* (Cambridge, MA: Harvard University Press, 1980), 132.
95. Ibid., 132–133.
96. Theodore J. Lowi, *The End of Liberalism: The Second Republic of the United States,* 2nd ed. (New York: W.W. Norton, 1979), 96–97.
97. Alan Brinkley, "The Challenge to Deliberative Democracy," in *The New Federalist Papers: Essays in Defense of the Constitution,* Alan Brinkley, Nelson W. Polsby, and Kathlen M. Sullivan, eds. (New York: W.W. Norton & Co., 1997), 23, 25.
98. Timothy A. Canova, "Black Swans and Black Elephants in Plain Sight: An Empirical Review of Central Bank Independence," *Chapman Law Review,* 14 (2011): 237, 301. John Hart Ely is credited for the colorful description.
99. *The Federal Reserve System: Its Purposes and Functions,* 2nd ed. (Washington, DC: Board of Governors of the Federal Reserve System, 1947), 53–54, 62–64.
100. See Freedom of Information Act, 5 U.S.C. Section 552(b)(5), providing exemptions for certain Federal Reserve directives and information that are part of its deliberative process; Federal Advisory Committee Act, 5 U.S.C. App. Section 4(b) (2007), exempting any advisory committee of two entities, the Federal Reserve System and the Central Intelligence Agency.
101. *Melcher v. Federal Open Market Committee,* 836 F.2d 561 (DC Cir. 1987), dismissed on grounds of equitable discretion; *Committee for Monetary Reform v. Board of Governors of the Federal Reserve System,* 766 F.2d 538 (DC Cir. 1985), dismissed for lack of standing; *Riegle v. Federal Open Market Committee,* 656 F.2d 873 (DC Cir. 1981), dismissed on grounds of equitable discretion; *Reuss v. Balles,* 584 F.2d 461 (DC Cir. 1978), cert. denied, 439 U.S. 997 (1978), dismissed for lack of standing. When the plaintiff has been a U.S. Senator, the court has created the doctrine of "equitable discretion" to avoid ruling on the substantive merits. If standing and justiciability are somehow found in a future challenge (perhaps for a private financial institution or state government plaintiffs), the next roadblock could be redressibility.
102. Brinkley, *The End of Reform,* 15, 23–28.
103. Mitchell, 43. Federal spending was reduced from $8.47 billion in 1936 to $8 billion in 1937.
104. Ibid., 44.
105. Ibid., 21–22, 43–44.
106. Brinkley, *The End of Reform,* 23.
107. Kennedy, 350.
108. E. Cary Brown, "Fiscal Policy in the 'Thirties': A Reappraisal," *American Economic Review,* 46 (December 1956): 857–79; Christina D. Romer, "What Ended the Great Depression?" *Journal of Economic History,* 52 (December 1992): 757–784.
109. For most of the 1930s, fiscal policy was a wash; about the only real federal stimulus was monetary, in the form of dollar devaluation and gold inflows. Romer, 757–784.
110. *The American Heritage Book,* 899.
111. "McConnell reverses position on Conrad-Gregg budget commission," *Tampa Bay Times,* February 1, 2010, accessed July 20, 2013, available at http://www.politifact.com/truth-o-meter/statements/2010/feb/01/mitch-mcconnell/mcconnell-reverses-position-conrad-gregg-budget-co/.
112. Executive Order 13531—National Commission on Fiscal Responsibility and Reform (Washington, D.C.: White House, February 18, 2010), accessed July 20, 2013, available at http://www.whitehouse.gov/the-press-office/executive-order-national-commission-fiscal-responsibility-and-reform.

113. The foolishness of austerity should have been as apparent in 2010 as it was in 2008, and the history of 1937–1938 should have been clear. Canova, "Massive Stimulus." May Be Needed to Stem Crisis," *Wall St. Journal, Real Time Economics*, October 22, 2008, accessed March 25, 2013, available at http://blogs.wsj.com/economics/2008/10/22/massive-stimulus-may-be-needed-to-stem-crisis
114. Ezra Klein, "John Boehner's Funny Numbers," *Washington Post Wonkbook*, February16, 2011, accessed March 25, 2013, available at http://voices.washingtonpost.com/ezra-klein/2011/02/john_boehners_funny_numbers.html. "In 1953, there was one Federal worker for every seventy-eight residents. In 1989, there was one Federal employee for every 110 residents. By 2009, the ratio had dropped to one Federal employee for every 147 residents. The picture that emerges is one of a Federal workforce that has significantly shrunk compared to the overall U.S. population, as well as compared to the size of Federal expenditures and the work that the Federal Government is called upon to perform." *Analytical Perspectives: Budget of the U.S. Government, Fiscal Year 2012* (Washington, DC: Office of Management and Budget), 103, accessed July 20, 2013, available at http://www.whitehouse.gov/sites/default/files/omb/budget/fy2012/assets/spec.pdf.
115. State revenue fell by 11.8 percent from 2008 to 2010, and states faced budget shortfalls in the range of $291 billion for fiscal years 2009 and 2010, and more than $100 billion in fiscal year 2011. *Analytical Perspectives: Budget of the U.S.*, 279.
116. Travis Waldron, "Last Three Years Were Worst on Record for Public Sector Job Losses," *Think Progress*, April 9, 2012, accessed March 25, 2013, available at http://thinkprogress.org/economy/2012/04/09/460380/worst-ever-public-sector-job-loss.
117. Unfortunately, neither Bar associations nor government agencies seem to keep statistics on public-sector job losses for lawyers. It seems clear to observers of the legal job markets that hiring freezes and layoffs have resulted in thousands of fewer jobs across the country in the wide range of public-sector offices that employ lawyers (including district attorneys, public defenders, environmental enforcement, and many regulatory agencies at all levels of government).
118. The authors of a January 2013 International Monetary Fund Working Paper, Olivier Blanchard (the IMF's chief economist) and David Leigh, "deduced that IMF forecasters have been using a uniform multiplier of 0.5, when in fact the circumstances of the European economy made the multiplier as much as 1.5, meaning that a $1 government spending cut would cost $1.50 in lost output." Howard Schneider, "An Amazing Mea Culpa from the IMF's Chief Economist on Austerity," *Washington Post WonkBlog*, January 3, 2013, accessed March 25, 2013, available at http://www.washingtonpost.com/blogs/wonkblog/wp/2013/01/03/an-amazing-mea-culpa-from-the-imfs-chief-economist-on-austerity. In this IMF Working Paper, the authors also accepted findings by Alan Auerback and Yuriy Gorodnichenko that U.S. "fiscal multipliers associated with government spending can fluctuate from being near zero in formal times to about 2.5 during recessions." Olivier Blanchard and Daniel Leigh, "Growth Forecast Errors and Fiscal Multipliers," IMF Working Paper WP/13/1 (Washington, DC: International Monetary Fund, January 2013), 4.
119. "Labor Force Statistics from the Current Population Survey," Databases, Tables & Calculators by Subject (Washington, DC: Bureau of Labor Statistics), accessed July 20, 2013, available at http://data.bls.gov/timeseries/LNS14000000. The official U.S. unemployment rate rose from 7.8 percent in January 2009 when Obama took office, to 9.8 percent in November 2010, the month of the midterm elections (it peaked at 10.0 percent in October 2009).
120. "Obama's No-Shows: 29 Million," *ABC News*, November 3, 2010, accessed March 25, 2013, accessed July 20, 2013, available at http://abcnews.go.com/blogs/politics/2010/11/obamas-no-shows-29-million.
121. Miller, 460.
122. Eric Foner, "Preface," in *Who Owns History? Rethinking the Past in a Changing World* (New York: Hill and Wang, 2002), xi.

123. Alonzo L. Hamby, "Introduction," in *The New Deal: Analysis and Interpretation* (New York: Webright and Talley, 1969), 1, 4–8.
124. Foner,, xii–xiii, quoting Friedrich Nietzsche.
125. Amity Shlaes, *The Forgotten Man: A New History of the Great Depression* (New York: Harper Perennial, 2007).
126. Timothy A. Canova, "Democracy's Disappearing Duties: The Washington Consensus," Chapter 11, in Yoav Peled, Noah Lewin-Epstein, Guy Mundlak, and Jean L. Cohen, eds., *Democratic Citizenship and War* (London: Routledge, 2011), 202.
127. Lynn Turgeon, *The Advanced Capitalism System: A Revisionist View* (Armonk, NY: M.E. Sharpe, 1980), 47.
128. Lynn Turgeon, *Bastard Keynesianism: The Evolution of Economic Thinking and Policymaking Since World War II* (Westport, CT: Greenwood Press, 1996), xv, 8.
129. Glenn C. Altschuler and Stuart M. Blumin, *The G.I. Bill: A New Deal for Veterans* (New York: Oxford University Press, 2009), 6–9.
130. In passing the G.I. Bill of Rights, Congress had learned from the mistakes of the past, when World War I veterans were forgotten and ignored. When the veterans' "Bonus Army" encamped in the Capitol demanding their pensions, President Hoover sent in the Army with guns and bayonets to burn down their makeshift village. Paul Dickson and Thomas B. Allen, *The Bonus Army: An American Epic* (New York: Walker & Co., 2005).
131. Peter F. Drucker, *Post-Capitalist Society* (New York: Harper Business, 1993), 3.
132. Michael J. Bennett, *When Dreams Came True: The GI Bill and the Making of Modern America* (Herndon, VA: Potomac Books, 1999). See also Robert Sobel, *The Great Boom 1950–2000* (New York: St. Martin's Press, 2002); Suzanne Mettler, *Soldiers to Citizens: The G.I. Bill and the Making of the Greatest Generation* (New York: Oxford University Press, 2005).
133. "Foreign Assistance and the U.S. Budget," Center for Global Development, Washington, DC, accessed July 20, 2013, available at http://www.cgdev.org/page/foreign-assistance-and-us-budget.
134. Jones, 315.
135. Robert Pollin and Heidi Garrett Peltier, "The U.S. Employment Effects of Military and Domestic Spending Priorities," Working Paper 51 (Amherst, MA: Political Economy Research Institute, University of Massachusetts, October 2007), accessed July 20, 2013, available at http://scholarworks.umass.edu/cgi/viewcontent.cgi?article=1122&context=peri_workingpapers.
136. Chandler, 482. In addition, federal income tax rates were at an all-time high during the 1940s, with the statutory top marginal tax rate over 90 percent. Yet the economy performed brilliantly. Thomas L. Hungerford, "Taxes and the Economy: An Economic Analysis of the Top Tax Rates since 1945," *CRS Report for Congress* (Washington, DC: Congressional Research Service, Sept. 14, 2012).
137. The Fed's bond-buying program has had other tangible benefits for the bankers. By propping up the balance sheets of big banks, it allowed top management to quickly repay their TARP funds, thereby allowing them to evade the TARP-imposed limits on executive compensation that had reached historic levels. It also allowed these banking CEOs to remain in office where they would continue to use corporate resources to lobby Congress and the administration against reform.
138. Friedman and Schwartz, 449–462.
139. Canova, "Massive Stimulus."
140. Timothy A. Canova, "Financial Market Failure as a Crisis in the Rule of Law: From Market Fundamentalism to a New Keynesian Regulatory Model," *Harvard Law & Policy Review,* 3 (2009): 369.
141. Brinkley, *The End of Reform,* 5.
142. Ibid., 118, 189–190.
143. Jill E. Fisch, "From Legitimacy to Logic: Reconstructing Proxy Regulation," *Vanderbilt Law Review,*. 46 (1993): 1129, 1162–1164.

144. Russell Mokhiber, *Corporate Crime and Violence: Big Business Power and the Abuse of the Public Trust* (New York: Random House, 1988), 221–228.
145. Timothy A. Canova, "Legacy of the Clinton Bubble," *Dissent* (Summer 2008): 42, 45–47, 50.
146. The Tea Partiers objected to the bailout on ideological grounds. As proponents of *laissez-faire*, many of them thought the market should have allowed the troubled banks to fail.
147. Manuel Roig-Franzia, "Obama Brings 'Shovel-Ready' Talk into Mainstream," *Washington Post*, January 8, 2009, accessed March 25, 2013, available at http://articles.washingtonpost.com/2009-01-08/news/36771075_1_shovel-ready-obama-plugs-obama-era.
148. At its peak, the American Recovery and Reinvestment Act may have directly employed more than 700,000 Americans on construction projects, research grants, and other contracts. "That number doesn't include the jobs saved or created through its unemployment benefits, food stamps, and other aid to struggling families likely to spend it; its fiscal relief for cash-strapped state governments; or its tax cuts for more than 95 percent of workers. Top economic forecasters estimate that the stimulus produced about 2.5 million jobs and added between 2.1 percent and 3.8 percent to our gross domestic product." Michael Grunwald, "Five Myths about Obama's Stimulus," *Washington Post*, August 10, 2012, accessed July 20, 2013, available at http://articles.washingtonpost.com/2012-08-10/opinions/35492297_1_stimulus-recovery-act-tax-cuts. If true, that the stimulus directly and indirectly created 2.5 million jobs, that would be barely a quarter of U.S. jobs lost in the wake of the 2007–2008 Great Recession.
149. "A Step Back for Derivatives Regulation," *New York Times* editorial, November 20, 2012, A26.
150. "The Myth of Job Creation," *New York Times* editorial, October 21, 2012, A22; Institute for Public Accuracy, "Colbert or Goolsbee: Who's the Clown?"
151. Barack Obama, *The Audacity of Hope* (New York: Three Rivers Press, 2006), 174–175. Obama seems to equate any tariff (presumably, even a multilateral tax on financial transactions) with doomed protectionist efforts to slow globalization. The speed of globalization is a flawed analogy. If the problem is that globalization is off course, then it is the direction, not the speed, that must be corrected by regulatory strategies of control.
152. Sections 1104 and 1105 of Dodd-Frank, discussed in Weil, Gotschal & Manges LLP, "Financial Regulatory Reform: An Overview of The Dodd-Frank Wall Street Reform and Consumer Protection Act," 7, Financial Regulatory Reform Center, accessed March 25, 2013, available at http://financial-reform.weil.com/recent-posts/financial-regulatory-reform-overview/#axzz2HSt7SVYe.
153. In addition, the Reserve bank extending the credit must show that such credit was not available elsewhere: Fettig, 47. The FDIC Improvement Act of 1991 amended Section 13(3) of the Federal Reserve Act to allow the Federal Reserve to lend directly to securities firms during times of emergency. The Federal Reserve would flirt with these powers throughout the 1970s and even into the 1990s.

4

A Decade of Dissent

The New Deal and Popular Movements

GERTRUDE SCHAFFNER GOLDBERG

During the Great Depression many vibrant social movements arose, contributing to a profound critique of American society and exerting pressure for change in government and corporate spheres. Indeed, the 1930s was not only a decade of Great Depression but also of *great dissent*. The interest here is not only in the character and range of these popular movements, but in how the New Deal both responded and influenced them, and in the closely related issue of their impact on the New Deal and public policy.

This is a difficult task for several reasons, an obvious one being that policies are multi-determined. Among the influences on federal government policies, in addition to popular movements, were: the views of the "slightly left of center" New Deal president himself;[1] FDR's advisors such as the Brain Trust and members of his administration; elected representatives from the South intent on preserving white supremacy and the region's low-wage economy; members of Congress who proposed Progressive policies during and prior to the New Deal; liberal business leaders; conservative business leaders; local and state government officials; public opinion; and combinations of these. Some of these actors, of course, were influenced by popular movements. In addition to social protest, the prolonged and largely unrelieved deprivation wrought by the Depression gave rise to disorderly group behavior such as the widespread looting of food and a consequent need to restore political, economic, and social order.[2]

Direct evidence of policymakers' response to particular organizations or protests is sought. However, because political élites may not admit they are responding to pressure, particularly from disorderly or radical lower-income groups, making these connections risks committing a *post hoc* fallacy. Another problem is the frequent failure of general historians of the New Deal to downplay or even denigrate radical-led organizations; on the other hand, writers on the left may tend to exaggerate the size and impact of such movements.

This chapter attempts to identify the effect on New Deal policies of movements by and on behalf of unemployed workers; jobless workers who sought relief *qua* veterans; employed workers; black workers; the elderly; tenant farmers; and middle- and lower-income persons seeking a more equitable distribution of income and wealth, sometimes referred to as "levelers."

The Unemployed Workers' Movement

The Movement: 1929–1933

Poor people typically lack resources for organized protest—other than their numbers and the urgency of their need. This weakness can be overcome by using the resources of radical organizations.[3] Following the stock market crash of 1929, some unemployed men and women initiated action on their own behalf, but many who sought relief, perhaps most, were aided by radical organizations that offered leaders, money, and strategies. "Throughout America in the early 1930s unemployed workers, sometimes under the leadership of radical activists,... sometimes on their own initiative, formed a variety of local jobless associations aimed at meeting the staggering individual and societal problems of Depression unemployment."[4] Communists were the first to aid the unemployed and the most active in the early years following the stock market crash of 1929.[5] In time, other radical groups provided these resources: the Workers' Committees organized by members of the Socialist Party and other groups of socialists and the Unemployed Leagues led by the left-wing labor minister, labor educator, and activist A. J. Muste.[6] However, most members of unemployed organizations were not politically affiliated, much less radical.[7] According to Frances Fox Piven and Richard A. Cloward, this was "the largest organization of the unemployed this country has ever known."[8]

Only a few months after the stock market crash, demonstrations by the unemployed took place in almost every important American industrial and commercial center, some involving serious and violent clashes with the authorities.[9] Although the Communist press probably exaggerated when it claimed that "millions" demonstrated on March 6, 1930, large numbers did take part, many of them at the instigation of the local Unemployed Councils (UC).[10] According to Irving Bernstein, "Bleeding heads converted unemployment from a little-noticed to a page-one problem in every important city in the United States. No one could any longer afford to ignore it."[11] Although violence raised people's consciousness of the problem, it could also be a deterrent to participation. Among the "formidable barriers" faced by the movement were "persistent and often violent repression by government...."[12] On the other hand, sociologist Steve Valocchi maintains, repression was not "the dominant response," and the successes of the movement are due not only to its attributes but to a government that could have repressed it but did not.[13] Yet, there is ample evidence of violence at the local level, particularly if protesters were identified with

Communists, and, in some cases, there was a combination of both brutality and concession by local officials.[14]

The goals of the radical organizers went way beyond relief and even reform, for they viewed the organizations as "transmission belts" to Communist Party membership and commitment to revolutionary goals.[15] Yet, in order to build a movement, it was necessary to address the immediate, urgent needs of the unemployed for relief and protection against evictions and foreclosures. The array of strategies included direct resistance to eviction, sit-ins at relief centers, resolution of grievances, and local, state, and national hunger marches.[16] Communists in Chicago led, organized, or participated in 2,080 mass demonstrations in the first five years of the Depression.[17] In New York, in less than six months in 1931, a Workers Committee formed by Socialists and independent organizers "sprouted into a citywide movement of over 10,000 unemployed; within a year it flowered into sixty locals and 25,000 members."[18]

Direct relief of suffering was the chief activity of the organizations that arose throughout the country, but from the start, federal unemployment insurance and federal appropriations for relief were goals for which movement organizations lobbied at city and state levels.[19] The unemployed movement contributed to a revival of interest in unemployment insurance.[20] Significant, particularly in view of virulent racism in the 1930s, was the priority that Communist-led groups gave to interracial councils. Indeed, in some Southern cities, the Unemployed Councils were the first interracial organizations in the area.[21]

Roy Rosenzweig, who has studied the organizations led by Communists, Socialists, and Musteites, writes that "Easily two million jobless workers engaged in some form of activism at some time in the thirties, and their participation affected not only their own outlook, but also how society looked at and treated them."[22] Still, Rosenzweig holds that, despite the heroism and imagination of radical leaders, it was "neither a revolutionary force nor even a truly mass movement." He estimates that the active membership never included even one percent of the unemployed at the height of the Depression.[23] Writing specifically of Chicago, Lizabeth Cohen recognizes that actual rank-and-file members of the Communist and Socialist unemployed movements were relatively few, but that when an action such as a hunger march took place, many more joined in. "Even those who stood on the sidelines, because they were employed or wary of joining a 'radical' cause, were influenced by the strategies and demands of the more militant."[24] In considering membership in unemployed organizations, one should bear in mind the inherent barriers to organizing the unemployed: their tendency toward blaming themselves rather than the economy for their condition, loss of self-confidence, the deterrent effect of militant strategies or of being labeled "Red" or subversive, and the potential for violence already mentioned.[25] In any case, social protest of this sort is probably never a majority phenomenon, and it is hard to say how large the numbers of activists, how frequent the actions, and how skilled the strategists need to be in order to have a "truly mass movement" and one with a significant influence on public policy.

Before the New Deal, the major gains of the unemployed movement were raising public consciousness of the extent and devastation of unemployment, stopping evictions, increasing relief levels, and adding rent allowances to relief benefits. In the cities he visited, wrote one author of a magazine article, the amount of relief was proportionate to the strength of the Unemployed Councils.[26] The movement had some success in reversing cutbacks. For example, a hunger march of 50,000 in Chicago in October 1932 forced the rescinding of an announced 50 percent reduction in relief.[27] According to the editors of *Fortune*: "...the sharp rise in relief expenditures...is due more than you might think to Communist agitation. By mass demonstrations, stubborn, insistent and vociferous protests, the Unemployed Councils...have indeed improved the lot of the jobless." [28]

Since municipalities lacked sufficient resources to meet the mounting needs that the unemployed movements were forcing them to address, city governments exerted pressure on higher levels of governments for funds. In fact, the National Conference of Mayors was established in 1932 with the express purpose of lobbying for federal relief, and immediately after its founding, a delegation of big-city mayors was dispatched to Washington to lobby federal officials.[29] Thus the mayors became "lobbyists for the poor."[30]

Beginning in 1931 with New York under then-governor Franklin Roosevelt, the states responded to the need and the inability of local governments to meet it by opening up their own limited coffers. It is not clear how much FDR was influenced by the unemployed movement to initiate the state's Temporary Emergency Relief Administration (TERA), although New York City was a hotbed of unemployed protest, and Roosevelt later claimed that as governor he had resisted pressure to call out the National Guard.[31] Directed by future federal relief administrator Harry Hopkins, TERA was a state-level version of the subsequent New Deal Federal Emergency Relief Administration (FERA).[32] By 1933, the majority of states had followed New York's lead,[33] but their resources, too, were limited.

Judging by the revolutionary aims of its radical organizers, New Deal historian Irving Bernstein considers the unemployed movement a failure: "Its principal achievement was to raise relief standards in some communities and to hasten the coming of federal relief."[34] That, however, seems like quite an accomplishment from the perspective of the unemployed and public policy.[35] One historian of labor in the twentieth century holds that when Franklin D. Roosevelt took office in 1933, his decision to provide direct relief was influenced by the insurgency of the organized unemployed.[36] Other writers have noted that experience with the organizations of the unemployed prepared some participants for other movement activity, particularly in the labor struggles of the New Deal era.[37] "Many organizers in the CIO," according to Cohen, "would come directly out of the unemployed movement."[38]

The New Deal and the Unemployed Movement.

To Labor Secretary Frances Perkins, one of FDR's closest advisors, the case for federal relief was compelling, and the reasons included indirect consequences of the unemployment movement:

> It is hard today to reconstruct the atmosphere of 1933 and to evoke the terror caused by unrelieved poverty and prolonged unemployment. The funds of many states and localities were exhausted. The legal debt limit of many states had been reached, and they could borrow no more, even for so urgent a matter as relief. The situation was grim in city, county, and state. Public welfare officers had reached the end of their rope.... The Federal Government and its taxing power were all one could think of.[39]

Further, Perkins recalled: "Hunger marchers were on parade. Food riots were becoming more common. Crime, born of the need for food, clothing, and other necessities of life, was on the upsurge."[40] Thus the magnitude of need, depleted local and state resources, partly the result of relief expansion achieved by agitation of the unemployment movement, and disorder played a part in the unprecedented assumption of relief by the federal government.

Most writers emphasize a decline in movement activity in response to New Deal relief, but Albert Prago presents a different picture of the early years: the inadequacy of early New Deal reforms prompted "mounting protests involving large numbers of people and with the organizations of the unemployed mushrooming." During the period from 1933 to 1935, there were militant daily struggles at relief bureaus that were met with police brutality.[41] According to the American Civil Liberties Union (ACLU), "time and again strikes and demonstrations on F.E.R.A. [Federal Emergency Relief Administration] projects have resulted in the adjustment of unfair wage-scales and stopping discrimination."[42] When the brief but large Civil Works Administration was terminated after four months, there was a considerable outcry from numerous sources, a march led by Socialist leader Norman Thomas, 60,000 protest letters, strikes and demonstrations by CWA workers, but to no avail. Roosevelt, under pressure from Southern Democrats and Budget Director Lewis Douglas, and worried about the cost of the CWA, did not bow to pro-CWA forces.[43]

Despite continuing to agitate, the Communists, according to Prago, "simply did not have the resources in manpower and finance, to provide the necessary leadership for the many millions scattered in so vast an area."[44] Moreover, the movement lost some of its ablest members who were among the first to get work when unemployment abated, while others became labor organizers with the resurgence of the labor movement.[45] Yet, by early 1935, the UCs claimed to have chartered 859 units in forty-two states, with 300,000 carrying membership cards, plus scores of affiliated organizations that issued their own cards.[46] Both an indication of continued protest and New Deal respect, if not encouragement, is what the WPA's labor relations director had to say early in 1936: "They are irreconcilable...because they never stop asking....They crowd through the doors of every relief station and of every WPA office. They surround social workers in the street. They exhibit the American spirit of determination...."[47]

The fight for unemployment insurance, one of the early demands of the unemployed movement, was an important focus of the left in this early period. In a personal communication to Piven and Cloward, who saw lobbying as a departure from the movement's earlier militancy, Herbert Benjamin, leader of the UCs, maintained that theirs was not the usual approach to lobbying, that they engaged in "mass lobbying...angry delegations besieging reactionary members of Congress in their offices. We marched and picketed and were arrested."[48]

Early in 1934, Representative Ernest Lundeen (Farm Labor–Wisconsin) introduced the first version of what was known popularly as the Workers' Unemployment Insurance Bill—a federal bill, financed by general revenues, available to all the unemployed regardless of need, and administered under a democratic plan with local representation by recipients. The Interprofessional Association for Social Insurance, founded at the time that Lundeen introduced his bill in 1934, had twenty-one chapters within a year, one in every major city in the Northeast but also in the Midwest and far West. In January 1935, a national conference in Washington convened to support Lundeen's Workers' Unemployment Insurance Bill; it was composed of 2,506 elected delegates from trade unions, including 742 AFL locals, scores of unemployment organizations, African-American organizations and social work groups.[49] Inserted in the record of House of Representatives hearings on the Lundeen bill was a list of original sponsors that included 3,000 local unions, over sixty city councils, county and municipal bodies, and hundreds of clubs and fraternal organizations.[50] In testimony before the House Committee on Labor, Herbert Benjamin of the Unemployed Councils said his office had published over a million copies of the bill and sold them at two dollars a thousand to organizations that distributed them free to individuals, and over 650,000 postcards in favor of the bill were sold for $1.50 per thousand for mass distribution.[51] The bill was supported by the House Committee on Labor, but through maneuvers of the administration, never went to the House floor.[52] According to Seymour, it had not the remotest chance of passing. Dona and Charles Hamilton write that conservative Republicans helped to get it out of the Labor Committee and added amendments, hoping this would render social security legislation unacceptable to the majority of Congress.[53]

University of Chicago economist Paul Douglas, later a Democratic Senator from Illinois, wrote that the Communists were initially the "main driving force" behind the Lundeen bill but that many non-Communists came to support it because it was "the most thorough-going and adequate proposal...for taking care of the unemployed." Douglas further observed that although the AFL officially opposed it, support came from many city federations and a much larger number of local unions and "by a surprisingly large number of social workers."[54]

Unemployment insurance, as adopted by the Social Security Act, however, fell far short of the demands of the left. It was Douglas's position that the radical proposal of the left had "enabled the administration forces to say to the indifferent and conservatives that unless they accepted the moderate program put forth by the administration, they might later be forced to accept the radical and far-reaching provisions of the Lundeen bill." In short, Douglas pointed out, it was the traditional strategy of the center using the left "as a club against the right."[55]

In the early New Deal years, unemployed workers, in a remarkable show of solidarity with their employed brothers and sisters, lent support in some of the decade's critical strikes. For example, the Musteite Unemployed Leagues played a central role in the Electric Auto-Lite strike in Toledo, where they organized workers, not to get relief and jobs for themselves, but to engage in mass picketing to help striking workers.[56] Largely under Socialist control, the Milwaukee Workers' Committee on Unemployment sent 13,000 unemployed workers into the picket lines just as the 1934 Milwaukee Streetcar Strike was on the verge of collapse.[57] In the Minneapolis General Drivers' strike of 1934, there was "extraordinary activity in the unemployed field involving jobless union members, direct relief clients and WPA workers."[58]

What leading historians have to say of the movement after the advent of the New Deal is more characteristic of the Workers Alliance of America (WAA) that united the formerly rivalrous unemployed workers organizations in 1936. According to Rosenzweig, "The New Deal did not wipe out the problems of the unemployed, but the small gains and the more optimistic tone of Roosevelt's administration... probably helped to pacify some jobless and made them less likely recruits for the Leagues [the Unemployed Leagues led by A. J. Muste]."[59] Piven and Cloward hold that "more liberal relief machinery... diverted local groups from disruptive tactics and absorbed local leaders into bureaucratic roles."[60] Each year, according to one study that reported fewer sit-ins, strikes, and picket lines, there was "a gradual evolution from the position of a purely conflict group to an organized and responsible relationship with the authorities."[61] There is another explanation as well. Recognizing Roosevelt's popularity and that jobless workers put their trust in FDR more than in the radical left, WAA leaders, according to Rosenzweig, felt the need to develop a sympathetic relationship with FDR and the New Deal and to gently prod it toward incremental improvements. The Popular Front mentality no doubt contributed to Communists' *rapprochement* with other radical groups as well as with the New Deal. The result was a "symbiotic relationship" between the WAA and the New Deal, including not only WPA administrators but Roosevelt himself.[62] According to WAA's chairman David Lasser and its executive secretary Herbert Benjamin, Roosevelt liked having an organization pushing from the left for support of his programs to counter the inevitable pressure from the right.[63] Indicative of the friendly relationship between the WAA and WPA administrators, Harry Hopkins and Aubrey Williams, was the recognition of the WAA as the bargaining representative of WPA workers. The right to strike, however, was contested.[64]

Local protest, if diminished, nonetheless continued after the merger that created the WAA. For example, five thousand hunger marchers entered the New Jersey legislature in protest over cutbacks in August 1936, and a similar action took place in the Pennsylvania state capitol. Later that year, short "folded arms strikes" for a "living wage" were conducted by the WAA in WPA projects throughout the country.[65] Despite the "symbiotic relationship" with New Dealers, the WAA greeted the announced cutbacks and firing of 475,000 WPA workers late in 1936 with a wave of protest actions, sit-downs, sit-ins, stoppages, picketing, demonstrations, mass meetings, delegations to city officials, resolutions, and telegrams to Congress, the president, and Harry Hopkins. To oppose the cutbacks, the U.S. Conference of Mayors called a special meeting in Washington and sent telegrams to the president. The mass layoffs were called off. Once again, the support of local officials was important to the unemployed movement.[66] Although Karsh and Garman write that the WAA moved increasingly away from organizing the unemployed and "job actions" and toward lobbying for legislation to protect the unemployed, they note that as late as 1939 it mounted a nationwide strike of WPA workers protesting cutbacks and layoffs on relief projects.[67]

In 1938, the WAA was attacked by the Dies Committee (House Committee for Investigation of Un-American Activities) for being under Communist domination. FDR thought that if there were a chance to save the WAA, "liberals should make the fight and not simply withdraw," and wrote as much to Aubrey Williams, deputy WPA director. On the letter was a handwritten comment by Eleanor Roosevelt: "FDR wld [*sic*] like to see Dave Lasser change name & purge communists who put Russia first."[68] This would seem to indicate that Roosevelt did find the WAA a useful WPA ally. Williams, it should be noted, had spoken admiringly of Lasser and the WAA, and for this and other examples of outspokenness he paid dearly—in Roosevelt's unwillingness, despite exemplary service, to appoint him to succeed Hopkins as WPA director.[69]

Jobless Veterans

The thousands of veterans who descended on Washington, D.C., in the late spring of 1932 demanded a different form of relief from the organizations that represented all unemployed workers, but they were in similar states of joblessness and destitution. They sought a special form of relief for veterans, an advance on bonuses (Adjusted Compensation Certificates) that were not due until 1945; their future bonus was the only asset most of them had.[70] Compared to ongoing relief for millions of unemployed workers, including veterans, theirs was a small order. Two-thirds were entitled to about $1,000, according to an estimate of the Veterans Administration.[71] The veterans did not call for relief for all the unemployed and were, in fact, criticized for the narrowness of their focus.[72] Yet this "Bonus Army" (Bonus Expeditionary Force or B.E.F) and its violent rout by the U.S. Army did much to dramatize the plight of the jobless, and contributed to the election of Franklin Roosevelt or the size of his triumph and perhaps to the New Deal's federal relief policies. Whereas most other protests by poor people depended on outside resources, the B.E.F. was largely a spontaneous phenomenon. Communists, trying to take credit for originating what was a "ready-made revolutionary engine," staged a march to the Capitol.[73] They were, however, reviled by most of their fellow veterans. [74]

The march to Washington was sparked by a bill introduced by Representative Wright Patman (D-Texas) providing for immediate payment at full maturity value of bonuses otherwise not due until 1945. The first contingent set out from Oregon:

> Early in May 1932, some World War veterans in Portland, Oregon, contemplated the fact that the one nest egg they had left was the government's promise of payments on... the bonus for their wartime services.... If the money was really theirs, why should they not have it when they needed it? Tired of watching their children grow pale on a diet of stale doughnuts and black coffee, tired of community neglect, tired of official gabble, tired, above all of waiting, the men in Portland decided to bring their plight home to the country by marching on Washington. They chose as leader an unemployed cannery superintendent and former World War sergeant named Walter Waters... who had not worked for eighteen months. Under his command, the group set out, riding the rods and living on handouts along the way. Its principles were "no panhandling, no drinking, no radicalism."... [75]

A confrontation with the Illinois National Guard over their trying to board a Baltimore and Ohio freight train in Illinois—"the Battle of the B & O"—became a front-page story,[76] evidently encouraging other veterans to follow the Oregon vanguard to the nation's capital.

Bernstein refers to the gathering of an estimated 22,000 veterans and family members in Washington to lobby and demonstrate on behalf of the Patman bill as "a remarkable display of jobless transiency."[77] It was to be "the most explosive demonstration that Washington had ever experienced."[78] On May 19, the first contingent of 300 from Oregon arrived; "a flood tide of servicemen followed."[79] Theirs was no one-day march. According to Waters: "We are going to stay until the veterans' bill is passed."[80] Theirs was a "new kind of lobbying" combining public demonstrations with an energetic and persistent presence in the halls and galleries of the Capitol.[81] The House of Representatives passed the Patman bill by a large margin, but it was defeated overwhelmingly in the Senate. Herbert Hoover was against special treatment for veterans, as were FDR, then running against him for the presidency, and liberals like Republican Fiorello LaGuardia of New York, who held that ex-servicemen had been treated generously by Congress and that it should consider the plight of millions of other equally needy unemployed men and women.[82]

There remain questions regarding Hoover's assent to police action resulting in the killing of two veterans and the subsequent violent eviction by tear gas and bayonets of unemployed veterans by the United States Army under General Douglas MacArthur. MacArthur and Secretary of War Patrick Hurley justified the brutal attack on the nation's impoverished veterans as putting down a Communist conspiracy. President Hoover, for his part, expressed relief that the "Red plot" had been checked.[83]

Although agreeing with Hoover regarding early payment of the bonus, FDR disagreed sharply with his handling of the protest (but refrained from commenting publicly about his opponent's behavior). At the time, FDR told Brain Truster Rexford Tugwell his views concerning the use of force that were already noted. "Suppression," he held, was "not good enough."[84] Instead, he said he would have given them jobs developing the Shenandoah National Park and would have hoped to stimulate states and municipalities to offer similar types of jobs in public works.[85] Roosevelt believed that his election had been made much more likely by the eviction of the veterans.[86] "It is probable," writes Irving Bernstein, that "no act of Hoover's proved so unpopular as his decision to drive out the BEF."[87]

Early in the New Deal, a second bonus march, largely in response to cuts in veterans' disability payments resulting from FDR's Economy Act of 1933, descended on Washington. Roosevelt clearly controlled their protest, but he did follow his dictum that suppression was not good enough. He issued a regulation barring loitering in public parks or grounds and located the veterans in a camp at some distance from the city. He drove out to the camp, waving his hat at them, and asked Mrs. Roosevelt and his close aide Louis Howe to visit the camp and be sure to bring coffee. In one of her early acts as First Lady, Eleanor Roosevelt, apologizing that she could bring them no news about their bonuses, waded through the mud to speak with the veterans and brought sandwiches in addition to coffee as well as uplifting talk about her gratitude for those who had served their country.[88] Thereafter the veterans met regularly with presidential assistant Howe.[89] FDR rid Washington of the veterans by offering them free transportation home or jobs in the Emergency Conservation Works, a forerunner of the Civilian Conservation Corps. Encouraged by FDR, most of the marchers took the jobs, and others were transported home.[90] The veterans did get their bonuses but did not have the New Deal President to thank for them. A New Deal Congress voted for it in 1936, overriding FDR's veto. It has been suggested that the fear of another army of unemployed veterans was one of the motives for the Servicemen's Readjustment Act of 1944 (G.I. Bill) that provided cash allowances, tuition for higher educations and other benefits that removed World War II veterans from the ranks of the jobless.[91]

Employed Workers

The Depression decade began with union membership at a low ebb. In 1930, union density was 12 percent, membership having fallen by about 1.7 million since the end of World War I.[92] (This is about the proportion of the work force that belonged to unions in 2007 when the Great Recession began.)

Government did much to wake up the nation's labor movement. The Norris-La Guardia Act of May 1932, the initiative of two progressive Republicans, outlawed "yellow-dog" contracts or pledges that employees would not join a union and restricted the use of federal court injunctions against strikes, picketing, and boycotts.[93] The next important step was a New Deal measure, Section 7(a) of the National Recovery Act of 1933. The Act gave something to both business and labor in order to encourage cooperation that would facilitate recovery. Section 7a gave labor collective bargaining rights. William Green, President of the American Federation of Labor, called Section 7(a) "a Magna Charta for labor."[94] John L. Lewis, President of the United Mine Workers (UMW), Sidney Hillman of the Amalgamated Clothing Workers of America (ACWA), and David Dubinsky of the International Ladies Garment Workers' Union (ILGWU) recognized the significance of Section 7(a) and responded by launching vigorous organizing drives and other militant actions. "The resurgence of union activity…was mobilized by the industrial unions with the strongest fighting traditions, the miners and the garment workers."[95] Lewis compared Section 7(a) to the Emancipation Proclamation and committed the UMW's entire treasury to the drive.[96] According to Bernstein, this New Deal measure was "the spark that rekindled the spirit of unionism within American labor."[97] A UMW official described the fantastic response of the miners: They "moved into the union *en masse*…. They organized themselves for all practical purposes."[98]

Resistance to Section 7(a) by capital was enormous. Where employers responded to 7(a) by establishing company unions, the law was actually a setback for resurgent unionism.[99] Senator Robert Wagner (D-New York) who headed the National Labor Board established by Roosevelt to oversee the implementation of 7(a) became discouraged with the Board's insufficient authority. Convinced that enforceable rules were necessary for the guarantee of collective bargaining rights, he proposed the National Labor Relations Act, which would not only grant the right to collective bargaining, but establish administrative machinery with quasi-judicial powers to implement it. The Board would be a permanent independent agency to conduct elections that would determine appropriate bargaining units and outlaw "unfair labor practices" such as company unions, discharging workers for union activities, or refusing to bargain with workers.[100] FDR and Labor Secretary Perkins were initially cool to the NLRA, and Perkins wrote that it was not part of FDR's program, that "all the credit goes to Senator Wagner."[101] As Bernstein points out, "Roosevelt had more confidence in the power of the state to promote the welfare of wage earners than he had in their capacity to do so themselves by means of trade unions," and this point of view was either shared with Perkins or reflects her influence.[102] It should be noted that despite the fact that over the decade labor became a part of the New Deal coalition, the right of workers to organize and bargain collectively was not included in FDR's 1944 proposal for an Economic Bill of Rights.[103]

Why did Roosevelt suddenly throw the weight of his influence behind the NLRA? Leuchtenburg writes that the reasons were "not wholly clear."[104] The background of resistance to unionization on the part of capital and the bitter, intensive, numerous, and violent labor strikes during 1934 and 1935 may have influenced his decision to support the NLRA, whose proponents argued it would reduce such conflicts and facilitate recovery.[105] The bill had already passed the Senate by a huge majority of 63–12 and had been reported out of the House Committee. Roosevelt did make the decision before the Supreme Court ruled the NRA unconstitutional, thus ending Section 7(a), although he may have anticipated the decision from the Court's ruling against the Railroad Retirement Act a little earlier.[106]

Along with other Progressive labor leaders, Lewis urged the AFL to expand the labor movement by organizing on an industrial union rather than on a crafts basis. The AFL, evidently preferring to have control of a small organization rather than to lose it in one double or triple the size, refused.[107] Another reason was longstanding disdain for the less skilled workers by the craft unionists and related snobbery and nativism.[108] Lewis and other Progressive labor leaders like Sidney Hillman and Philip Murray left the AFL and formed the Congress of Industrial Organizations (CIO), which sought to organize the unorganized in the mass production industries.[109] This was enormously important for the nation's semi-skilled and unskilled industrial workers and, because the CIO organized interracial unions, for black workers as well. It was the CIO, pushed ahead by militant rank and file members, that led the drives that won collective bargaining rights in the nation's leading mass-production industries. In the Minneapolis Teamster strike, local unionists had proceeded in opposition to their national union, and in the general strike in San Francisco, conservative national leaders were overruled by the militant members of the longshoremen's union.[110]

Employers resisted the Wagner Act on the grounds that they expected it to be declared unconstitutional, and militant labor groups for their part took the law into their own hands with a spate of sit-down strikes shortly after FDR's second-term victory. When courageous rank and file workers at the General Motors plant in Flint, Michigan, sat down without Lewis's authorization, he nonetheless supported them to the hilt.[111] In the critical showdown at Flint, Roosevelt and Perkins refused to condemn the sit-down. Instead, they supported the efforts of Michigan's governor, Frank Murphy, to achieve a peaceful settlement and to delay the enforcement of a court order to end the strike.[112] The result was a momentous victory for the labor movement: recognition of the United Auto Workers as the company's bargaining unit by General Motors (GM), then the largest corporation in the world. It was "the most important single strike confrontation of the century...."[113] Following on its heels was another great accomplishment, union recognition by the United States Steel Corporation. Roosevelt subsequently explained why he acted as he did: "Little do people realize how I had to take abuse and criticism for inaction at the time of the Flint strike. I believed and I was right, that the country, including labor would learn the lesson of their own volition without having it forced upon them by marching troops."[114]

In a press conference with newspaper publishers soon after the constitutionality of the National Labor Relations Act was upheld by the Supreme Court, Roosevelt was asked why he had not spoken out against what one of the publishers described as "an epidemic of sit-downs." The President acknowledged that the sit-downs were illegal but held that both sides had made mistakes. He predicted that "we are going to get a workable system but we won't get it by antagonism and threats and demands." The labor people, he observed, were beginning to realize that sit-downs were wrong, that they were "damn unpopular" and that "labor cannot get very far if it makes itself unpopular with the bulk of the population of the country." It would take time to realize this, "perhaps two years, but that is short time in the life of a nation...."[115]

Roosevelt's restraint in aid of the labor movement could be seen as reciprocating labor's substantial support for his candidacy in 1936. However, soon after, FDR failed even to condemn the violence in the Memorial Day massacre at Republic Steel that resulted in the fatal shooting of ten marchers and the wounding of twenty-eight more.[116] Roosevelt took a neutral stance in relation to the drive to organize the Republic plant, making the oft-quoted remark at a press conference that "The majority of the people are saying just one thing, a plague on both your houses." That was usually reported as if this were his own opinion.[117] He had rejected Perkins's advice to intervene.[118] According to Lewis's biographers, Dubofsky and Van Tine, Roosevelt, having been warned by advisors that he had little to gain, "acted as he did for good political reasons."[119] This one could infer from his remark concerning public attitudes toward the strike. It was, however, interpreted by Lewis as a betrayal of the heavy UMW support for his presidential campaign: "It ill behooves one who has supped at labor's table...to curse with equal fervor and fine impartiality both labor and its adversaries when they become locked in deadly embrace."[120] The CIO failed to unionize "Little Steel" (a term that refers to steel companies other than the United States Steel Corporation), thanks partly to FDR's hands-off policy. The "Roosevelt Recession," moreover, contributed to labor's loss of steam that began with the failure at Republic. In the ensuing years, the Democratic Party would fail to reciprocate labor's consistent support.

The relationship of the New Deal to the labor movement in the late 1930s is a complicated one. It involves the rivalry between the AFL and the CIO, a business counterattack, and a Red-baiting campaign to discredit the labor movement and the National Labor Relations Board (NLRB). The AFL attacked the NLRB for being both pro-CIO and Communist-led, and it Red-baited the CIO as well. These charges were readily received and promulgated by the House Committee on Un-American Activities (Dies Committee). The AFL joined the National Association of Manufacturers (NAM) in this attack against the rival union and the NLRB. FDR acted by enlarging the NLRB governing board, thereby diluting both the alleged "Red" influence and CIO bias, replacing one of the board members most linked to Communism, appointing a chairman with an unvarnished record for both judiciousness and competence, and at the same time intervening to prevent passage of legislation directed against the NLRB and the Wagner Act.[121]

Concurrently, the courts weighed in on the side of employers. The Supreme Court upheld the constitutionality of the Wagner Act in 1937, but the courts otherwise limited labor rights, notably making the sit-down illegal. James Green concludes, "the courts allowed unions to engage in collective bargaining over a limited range of issues, but prohibited them from using the kind of militant, direct action that had built the CIO."[122]

The state thus gave and then took away. The limiting of labor's power continued with the Administration's exacting a no-strike pledge during World War II and then, when the war emergency was no longer a justification for reining in the unions, Congress went even further with the Taft-Hartley Act by enacting it and then sustaining it over President Harry Truman's veto. Regardless of the pull-back, the New Deal had given more support to organized labor than any previous administration. Labor, it should be noted, tripled its membership between 1933 and 1941.[123]

Black Workers

Neither long-established civil rights organizations nor the radical interracial groups that arose during the 1930s were able to muster significant pressure to advance civil rights for African Americans. The Unemployed Councils had not only crossed the color line in their protest but had supported such measures as non-discrimination in rehiring and legislation like the Lundeen bill, which, in contrast to the insurance programs of the Social Security Act, would have included all workers. Testifying in favor of the Lundeen bill, the National Urban League's (NUL) acting executive secretary pointed out that it would cover farmers, domestic and personal service workers—occupations employing two-thirds of Negro workers.[124] Because Negroes' experiences with state-administered programs had been unsatisfactory, the NUL favored another attribute of Lundeen: federal administration of benefits for the unemployed. Hamilton and Hamilton suggest that the NUL's advocacy of legislation associated with the Communist Party is an indication of how much the League valued the Lundeen Bill.[125] The NAACP and the NUL tried to add anti-discrimination measures to the Social Security Act, the National Labor Relations Act of 1935, and the Fair Labor Standards Act of 1938, but were unsuccessful.[126]

Progress in civil rights would have to await militant action by blacks as well as proper timing. Wartime production provided that opening. Many of the unemployed were being absorbed in defense industries, but discrimination robbed blacks of the benefits of this upswing. "As Negroes saw wages skyrocket in plants holding large defense contracts and as they saw no change in the rigid anti-Negro policy in industry, they developed a program of drastic action."[127] Previous to the decision to employ militant tactics, black leaders had met with Roosevelt to protest discrimination in defense employment and in the military, and they had felt he was with them, only to be disillusioned when a short time later he supported segregation in the military: "the policy of the War Department is not to intermingle colored and white enlisted personnel in the same regimental organizations."[128] Putting an end to discrimination in the military had been a principal goal of their delegation.

A.Philip Randolph, president of the Brotherhood of Sleeping Car Porters, had been part of the delegation to the Oval Office. He decided that such delegations were not going to get them anywhere, and that it was time to take to the streets.[129] Consequently, Randolph formed the National March on Washington Committee and threatened to march on the capitol to protest this discrimination. The idea caught fire, and Randolph was able to predict 100,000 marchers. Despite appeals to desist from allies like Eleanor Roosevelt and Mayor LaGuardia, Randolph did not back down.[130] A march of this magnitude in the capital would have been disruptive of the defense build-up and national unity in a time of impending war, so Roosevelt made concessions. The result of bargaining between FDR and black leaders was Executive Order 8802, the Fair Employment Practices Commission (FEPC), which held that there should be no discrimination based on race, creed, color, or national origins in the employment of workers in defense industries. The March on Washington bargainers had asked for much more: including ending discrimination in the civilian sector of the federal government, rooting out discrimination and segregation in the armed forces, and denying discriminatory unions the benefits of the Wagner Act. "A much reduced compromise" is how Bernstein describes Executive Order 8802.[131] It should be noted that an executive order does not require the assent of Congress. Clearly, the FEPC did not abolish discrimination in defense-related employment, but blacks made gains in defense industries as a result, particularly in factories organized by CIO affiliates.[132] This, of course, was not the end of the story. The FEPC had little support from the Roosevelt Administration, but it was still the general consensus of the civil rights organizations that "the experiences of black workers during the war would have been quite different without it."[133]

The successful use of black power in 1941 reverberated in a number of ways, such as black pressure in CIO unions for a change in racist hiring practices, and it served to encourage subsequent protest.[134] Randolph went on to play a leading role in the civil rights movement of the 1960s. Indeed, he initiated and planned another march on Washington that did take place: the 1963 March on Washington for Jobs and Freedom.

Southern Tenant Farmers

Tenant farmers, severely disadvantaged to begin with, were made more so by New Deal agricultural policies. (Tenant farmers is a general term for landless Southern farmers, the most numerous and worst off of whom were sharecroppers.)[135] In order to curtail production, the federal government paid farmers for crop reduction. Since payments were based on equity in crop production, landlords got a disproportionate share of the money. Furthermore, landlords often pocketed sharecroppers' payments, and when they complained, landlords changed their status to wage-hands in order to disqualify them.[136] Robert Leighninger points out that landlords took the money, evicted tenants, and in some cases used it to buy farm machinery, further reducing the need for tenants.[137] "The New Deal was not to blame for the social system it inherited, but New Deal policies made matters worse."[138]

With the encouragement and support of outside resources, particularly Socialist Party leader Norman Thomas and a small group of Arkansas socialists, the beleaguered white and black tenant farmers banded together in 1934 to form the Southern Tenant Farmers Union. (STFU).[139] Here, as with the organization of the unemployed, outside resources were necessary for a poor people's movement.[140] Immediately the STFU encountered fierce opposition from planters and their allies, including violence and jailing of protesters and prohibiting members to speak. Planters used their political and economic power against the STFU, padlocking church doors and packing schoolhouses with bales of hay to deter union rallies, and flogging sympathetic croppers.[141] In a national radio broadcast, Thomas, who, on one occasion, was prevented from speaking and escorted to the Arkansas border, described the situation as a "reign of terror" directed against the Southern Tenant Farmers Union in Arkansas.[142] The heart of the protest was in Arkansas, the home state of Senate Majority Leader Joseph Robinson who, like local landlords, smeared the union as Communist, socialist, the work of outside agitators. Roosevelt, speaking in Arkansas, did not mention the union or condemn violence directed against one of the STFU strikes.[143]

Thomas waged a relentless campaign to inform the public of these "Forgotten Men of the New Deal," taking his message to the highest government officials, including the president, and gaining support from religious groups and civil rights organizations as well as the AFL, which unanimously adopted a resolution condemning "the inhuman levels to which the workers employed in the cotton plantations had been reduced" and calling for a federal investigation of the condition of the workers.[144] Groups that could not be accused of radicalism corroborated the reports of Thomas and others, and a number of articles about the hardships of the sharecroppers appeared in national magazines and Northern newspapers.[145] The STFU's most effective weapons were said to be agitation and publicity, not strikes or collective bargaining, although it did mount some successful strikes.[146]

Early in 1935, when liberals within the Agricultural Adjustment Administration (AAA) attempted to provide legal protection to the tenants, the AAA administrator demanded their dismissal from the agency. Roosevelt was said to be sorry and to have the highest regard for the liberals who were purged, but he made no attempt to save them.[147] The President was moved by the plight of the sharecroppers but nonetheless did not move on their behalf; as the organ of the STFU put it, "Too often he has talked like a cropper and acted like a planter."[148] Protection of the tenant farmers ran up against the formidable opposition of Southern congressional leaders. When Senator Wagner was urged to include agricultural workers in the NLRA, he replied that they were excluded only because he thought it would be better to pass the bill for the benefit of industrial workers than not to pass it at all.[149]

As the 1936 election drew closer, government officials made some concessions, probably in response to the condemnation of the treatment of the tenant farmers by mainstream groups. At the Democratic Convention, the STFU leader, H. L. Mitchell, won Majority Leader Robinson's consent to include platform planks protecting the sharecroppers' civil liberties and their right to organize.[150] During the campaign of 1936, Roosevelt responded by urging Senator Bankhead (D-Alabama) and Representative Marvin Jones (D-Texas) to formulate plans for a federal program to reduce farm tenancy. Soon after his re-election, Roosevelt appointed the President's Committee on Farm Tenancy; its efforts laid the groundwork for the Bankhead-Jones Farm Tenancy Act of 1937 and for establishment of the Farm Security Administration (FSA). The STFU considered it a recognition of its power that Roosevelt appointed one of its members to the Committee.[151]

The report recommended the establishment of a Farm Security Administration in the Department of Agriculture to carry out a program of "land for tenants," that is, federal loans for the purchase of land. The STFU member of the Committee, W. L. Blackstone, dissented from the majority proposal.[152] What the administration recommended to Congress was "cautious and conservative," according to an historian of the movement; even so, Roosevelt's proposals were further scaled down by Congress. [153] There were approximately 2.9 million tenant farmers in the United States in 1935, and by the end of 1941, the Farm Security Administration had given loans to only 20,748 tenants for the purchase of farms—less than one percent. According to the FSA, it received about twenty applications for every loan it made.[154] Like so many other problems, some relief of the dreadful suffering of tenant farmers and their families had to await the stimulus of World War II. A popular movement of very poor people, aided by a determined and eloquent advocate and the mainstream support he aroused, had achieved only token concessions from the New Deal.

The Elderly Become a Political Force

The elderly formed one of the most significant social movements of the decade of dissent. It was widespread, mainstream, and American, and hence not vulnerable to attacks as radical or "Red." According to a plan of California doctor Francis E. Townsend, persons sixty years and older would be eligible for a pension of $200 a month, providing they were unemployed and spent it all during the month they received it. The plan would aid a group hit very hard by the Depression, and, through its spending requisite, expand consumption and aid recovery. It did not matter to the millions of elderly persons who joined Townsend that the numbers did not work out. Nine percent of the U.S. population at the time, the elderly would be getting benefits equal to 60 percent of national income.[155] The plan would transfer to the aged money otherwise spent by the general population, and the two percent "transfer tax" that was intended to finance the benefits would only raise a sum sufficient for benefits of $60 rather than $200 a month.[156] Nonetheless, the plan was attractive to its beneficiaries, and the means of selling it, devised by Townsend's partner, real estate promoter Robert Clements, were entrepreneurial and innovative for a social movement. The establishment of "Townsend clubs," especially in the West, provided companionship and recreation to elderly members who joined, paid dues, and participated in advocacy, principally, in the early days, a massive petition campaign. Dr. Townsend probably exaggerated the size of the movement and the number of petitions in support of the plan, but his critics conceded there were at least ten million signatures.[157] Interestingly, the Townsend movement eclipsed the more conventional organizations that had studied and advocated benefits for the elderly for a number of years.[158]

The Struggle for Old Age Security: Act One, 1934–1935

"Before his inauguration," recalled Frances Perkins, "Roosevelt had agreed that we should explore at once methods for setting up unemployment and old age insurance in the United States."[159] As New York governor, FDR had publicly endorsed and promulgated unemployment insurance but stated a distinct preference for old-age insurance over non-contributory pensions for the elderly in a system of contributions beginning at an early age.[160]

Prior to the Administration's plan for social security, the Dill-Connery bill to establish a federal-state program of old age benefits passed the House and would have passed the Senate were it not that FDR withheld his support. The bill called for federal matching grants of one-third of states' expenditures for relief to the elderly. Thomas Eliot, who drafted the Social Security Act, explained the administration's delay: that recovery measures had priority at the time, not long-term reform.[161] Paul Douglas believes that the failure to act "helped...to create the Townsend movement which arose in the summer of 1934."[162] What about this suggestion—that the Townsend movement might not have arisen had the Dill-Connery bill been enacted? On one hand, Townsend and his adherents were by no means pleased or satisfied with the Social Security Act and might have reacted similarly to the Dill-Connery Act, which promised no more than the Old Age Assistance program in the Social Security Act. Nonetheless, Townsend and his lieutenants might have had a hard time mobilizing millions of elderly people if Congress had already taken action on their behalf.

According to Frances Perkins, who headed the Administration's Committee on Economic Security (CES) that was planning the security legislation, the pressure of the Townsendites and other radicals was tremendous:

> One hardly realizes nowadays how strong was the sentiment in favor of the Townsend Plan and other exotic schemes for giving the aged a weekly income. In some districts the Townsend Plan was the chief political issue, and men supporting it were elected to Congress. The pressure from its advocates was intense. The President began telling people he was in favor of adding old-age insurance clauses to the bill and putting it through as one program.[163]

Roosevelt also told CES members, "Congress can't stand the pressure of the Townsend Plan unless we have a real old-age insurance system, nor can I face the country without having devised... a solid plan which will give some assurance to old people of systematic assistance upon retirement."[164] According to a historian of the movement, FDR "over-assessed Townsend claims of popular support," but, in any case, he "countered the political threat inherent in the mushrooming pension movement by utilizing this public clamor for old-age pensions to justify the enactment of a moderate social security program of his own." [165] In the opinion of CES director Witte, FDR's strategy of keeping the entire social security program together was critical because of the various programs, only old-age assistance would have gone through.[166]

It is important to point out the differences between what Townsendites advocated and the provisions for the elderly in the Social Security Act. Townsendites wanted an equal or flat benefit payable to *all* the elderly without a means test—a universal demogrant. Even the combination of benefits for the elderly in the Social Security Act, Old Age Insurance and Old Age Assistance, was much less comprehensive and generous.

The Lundeen and Townsendite movements, the one advocating more progressive unemployment insurance than the New Dealers, and the other more expansive benefits to the elderly, did not attempt to combine forces in 1935. Together they might have been formidable, but they were far apart politically, and while the Lundeen plan was carefully thought out, the first Townsend plan was considered "crackpot." Later Dr. Townsend did join forces with other dissidents, though not with leftists, in a failed third-party attempt in 1936.

What did the Townsendites get on the first round? Perhaps left to its own devices the administration would have omitted pensions for the elderly, including only Old Age Insurance, which Roosevelt preferred to pensions.[167] The insurance program would have afforded no current benefits to the elderly. That the SSA version of benefits, Old Age Assistance, was somewhat more generous than Dill-Connery could be credited to Townsend pressure. Instead of matching one-third of state benefits, the federal government would match up to 50 percent of the first thirty dollars.[168] It should be noted that many states were not willing to grant enough funds to take advantage of the full benefit.[169]

The Struggle for Old Age Security Act Two, 1935–1939

The second act in advocacy for the elderly did not result in a universal demogrant for older people or a generous pension, but it did achieve considerable improvement of Old Age Insurance and a small change in Old Age Assistance. The Townsendites continued to fight for better, more adequate benefits for the elderly. After some setbacks to Dr. Townsend and the organization, the movement emerged stronger and was joined by other pension-promoting groups. As one historian of the movement put it, prior to the elections to the Seventy-sixth Congress in 1938, pension advocates were aided by a number of conditions: deficiencies in coverage and benefits of the Social Security Act, dissatisfaction with the SSA's payroll taxes on the part of businessmen, and the recession of 1937–1938, which left more people in need and the states less able to pay their shares of Old Age Assistance (OAA).[170] One of the movement's strategies was to endorse congressional candidates who agreed to support their plans for the elderly. Ninety Republicans with some commitment to the demands of the elderly were elected in 1938. Harry Hopkins laid Republican victories in that election to the pension issue: "Democratic Congressmen were pitched out and... Republican Congressmen went in because they promised bigger and better old-age pensions." The pension movement could be credited with the prominence of the pension issue and the electoral advantage of candidates who supported "bigger and better pensions."[171]

How did the Roosevelt Administration respond to this successful move by a popular movement? As Holtzman put it, "To conciliate the national demand for increased old-age security, to head off the demands by radical pension lobbyists, and to cut the ground from under the Republicans, the Democratic leadership undertook to liberalize its Social Security Act."[172] Their proposals were based on a Senate Advisory Committee considerably and adroitly influenced by the Social Security Commissioner, Arthur Altmeyer, with Roosevelt's encouragement.[173] These efforts were in motion by the fall of 1937, well before the Republican gains in the election of 1938. In putting forth the administration's proposals for liberalization, Roosevelt urged Congress to reject "untried and demonstrably unsound panaceas,"[174] a not very subtle jibe at the Townsendites. Not all the administration's proposals held sway, but Old Age Insurance was changed from a narrowly conceived annuity for retired workers to a family program: benefits for workers' dependent spouses and the workers' widows and dependent children. Moreover, payments to lower-wage workers were increased, and the date at which payments began was moved up so that newly retired claimants were receiving what amounted to a "pension-like" benefit to which they had contributed very little. The amendments fell short of the administration's proposals, primarily the refusal of Congress to extend coverage to farm and domestic workers. The pension advocates did not get what they wanted, but older people and their families got more. The New Deal once again used the radical demands of a popular movement to gain approval of its preferred, moderate reforms.

Levelers

While the unemployed and labor movements advocated for particular population groups, other social movements, sometimes referred to as levelers, campaigned for a more egalitarian distribution of income or wealth.[175] The leaders of the two most prominent of these latter movements, Senator Huey Long (D-Louisiana) and Father Charles E. Coughlin, were initially for Roosevelt and the New Deal. "Roosevelt or Ruin" and "The New Deal Is Christ's Deal" were Coughlin's slogans. Long favored Roosevelt's nomination in 1932 and helped keep the Mississippi delegation to the Democratic convention in his camp.[176]

By 1934, however, both Long and Coughlin were disappointed in the New Deal: Coughlin because it was too close to the banks and did not do enough to spur inflation, Long because its policies did not go to what he considered the heart of the matter, the grossly unequal distribution of wealth. Both men, like Roosevelt, were excellent orators and used the radio to attract followers. Coughlin had the largest regular radio audience in the world.[177] A Catholic priest, born outside the United States (Ontario), he was not a potential rival for the presidency, but Long was. Among the dissenters, "Long was the shrewdest operator and the most thoroughly professional politician. He had brains, money, ambition, extravagant oratorical skill, a gift for political theater.... He was the radical most likely to succeed."[178] In the Senate, Long was not alone in his dissent. Despite his outrageous behavior, he was "liked and even admired" by senators who were increasingly alienated from both major parties. A Southerner, Long voted often with such Midwestern or Western Progressives as William Borah, Lynn Frazier, Robert La Follette, Jr., George Norris, Gerald Nye, and Burton Wheeler.[179]

Early in the second year of the New Deal, Long invited his radio audience to join his Share Our Wealth Society (SOW), a nationwide system of local clubs. Share Our Wealth was a plan whereby the rich would be taxed highly in order to provide an income guarantee for everyone. The guarantee of two to three thousand dollars annually was enticing, particularly in view of the fact that half the nation's families earned less than $1,250, the amount considered necessary for a minimal standard of living.[180] The numbers, however, did not add up. The taxes on the rich would not yield enough for the guarantee, and Long acknowledged it, saying "when they figure that out, I'll have something new for them."[181] Nonetheless, as historian Alan Brinkley points out, Long, in focusing on the distribution of wealth, was addressing "an issue of genuine importance" and a major cause of the Depression.[182]

Both Long and Coughlin founded organizations. Early in 1935, Reverend Gerald L. K. Smith, the skilled, tireless organizer of the Share Our Wealth clubs, claimed he was enlisting 20,000 recruits a day and that the organization had passed the five-million mark in membership. "No one could either verify or dispute his claim, but few could disagree with his statement that 'The popular appeal of our movement can't be discounted. . . .' "[183] Coughlin also established an organization, the National Union for Social Justice, which stood for monetary reform, nationalization of key industries and protection of the rights of labor.[184] "Social justice" was to substitute for capitalism in a political order "strikingly similar to that of Italian corporatism."[185]

Brinkley writes that in the spring of 1935, when Congress was debating the Social Security Act, the Share Our Wealth clubs and Coughlin's National Union for Social Justice appeared to be "vibrant growing movements with almost limitless political potential." Yet Brinkley concludes that "they were far from the kind of coherent, centralized organizations that could easily be transformed into an effective third party."[186] Nor were their predominantly middle and lower-middle class constituents—people with something to lose—the stuff of revolutions. In fact, both movements included people unwilling to desert the New Deal, and the more Coughlin, for example, criticized Roosevelt, the more support he lost.[187] Whether they could be designated "movements" is also questionable, for "there was nothing for members of either organization to do, if they obeyed their leaders, besides write letters to the President and listen to the radio."[188] Interestingly, Brinkley identifies a problematic effect of the movements' organizing strategies. While the radio gave Long and Coughlin immediate access to millions of people, earlier populists who lacked such mass media were obliged to engage in vigorous grass-roots organizing. This, in turn, gave their followers "a strong sense of connection with dissident politics" and a more active engagement with the organizations than the relatively passive act of listening to the radio.[189] (The heavy dependence on the Internet as the medium for organizing protest today would seem to pose an even greater challenge to the creation of a vital social movement.)

Even if a third party or powerful social movement was not likely to emerge from the actions of these dissidents, Long was a serious political threat. He boasted of a "Share the Wealth" ticket in 1936. His strategy was to be a spoiler in 1936 by throwing the election to a Republican, and by 1940, the nation's plight would be so desperate that voters would be ready for him.[190] Wary of Long, even when he had helped him to secure the nomination, Roosevelt told Brain Truster Rexford Tugwell that

Huey Long was "the second most dangerous man in this country."[191] In response to Long's strident criticism, Roosevelt blocked federal patronage to the Long machine in Louisiana and ordered an Internal Revenue Service investigation of Long and his political associates.[192] Roosevelt vacillated more with Coughlin, who was initially less strident than Long, but he nonetheless cut off relations with the radio priest by mid-1934, and was also responsible for investigating his finances and checking his citizenship, as well as trying to get the Roman Catholic Church to silence him.[193] Both Long and Coughlin were flawed as leaders, the former by his dictatorial rule in Lousiana and the latter by pro-fascism and anti-Semitism later in his career.

A "scientific" poll taken by Democratic Party leaders in the spring of 1935 found that Long, particularly if he enjoyed the support of Coughlin and other dissenters, could hold the balance of power in the 1936 presidential election, perhaps throwing victory to the Republicans.[194] In response to this threat, Roosevelt tried co-optation—in addition to the deprivation and opposition already invoked against Long. In the summer of 1935, partly to "steal Huey's thunder," FDR proposed a tax on undistributed profits, stepped-up inheritance taxes, and increased levies on the very wealthy.[195] It is not clear how much Roosevelt wanted this Wealth Tax Act to be enacted in that particular session of Congress.[196] In any case, Congress eliminated the inheritance tax and reduced the graduated corporation income tax to "no more than symbolic importance." Actually, it would not have changed the distribution of wealth significantly nor done much to raise revenues.[197] Long initially said "Amen," but several days later inserted into the *Congressional Record* a letter challenging Roosevelt to support his whole Share Our Wealth Plan.[198] To what extent this did steal Long's thunder is an unanswerable question because of Long's assassination a few months later, but in the time between the proposal of the Wealth Tax Act and his death, Long's personal and organizational strength was growing.[199] It is not clear how much further Roosevelt would have gone to steal Long's thunder, but had Long lived, he might have forced Roosevelt to move further to the left and do more to redistribute income than the gestural Wealth Tax Act. The encounter with Long shows that where a challenger posed a threat, not only to his policies, but to his presidency, it would take more than simply ignoring the dissent, depriving him of privileges that were at the disposal of the president, or attacking him.

Without Long, the opposition to the New Deal was greatly weakened. Roosevelt had predicted that "when it comes to show-down these fellows [*the various dissident groups*] cannot all lie in the same bed."[200] The Union Party, which mounted a third-party challenge to Roosevelt in 1936, was a complete misnomer for very incompatible, rivalrous bedfellows: principally Father Coughlin, Dr. Francis Townsend, and Long's successor, the Rev. Howard L. K. Smith. "Since all three men were prima donnas, a compromise candidate was needed."[201] With that standard bearer—Representative William Lemke of North Dakota—the Union Party went down to resounding defeat, taking less than two percent of the popular vote away from Roosevelt and the New Deal.[202]

Conclusion: The New Deal and Popular Movements

New Deal responses to popular movements varied from movement to movement and from time to time. Take the relationship between the New Deal and organized labor, a movement with which it was thought to be allied. The New Deal encouraged unionization through its National Recovery Administration. When Section 7(a) of the NRA proved unenforceable in the face of capital's resistance, labor rights were strengthened very considerably by the National Labor Relations Act, the work of Senator Robert Wagner that Roosevelt supported tardily (and perhaps reluctantly as well). Capital continued to defy the law, and rank and file labor resorted to sit-downs that clearly infringed on property rights. Nonetheless, Roosevelt refused to condemn the Flint sit-down strikes, consistently opposed the use of force to suppress popular protest, and supported Governor Frank Murphy in his successful avoidance of violence. The New Deal stance at Flint was pro-labor as well as reciprocation for Progressive labor leaders' vigorous support and participation in Roosevelt's 1936 campaign for reelection. However, only a few months later, during labor's drive to unionize Little Steel, FDR condemned labor and capital equally, evidently thinking that that was the view of the public. The New Deal needed working-class votes, but organized labor still represented a minority of the working-class, many of whom may well have condemned militant union tactics. State support, a critical contributor to the gains labor made, was abating by the end of the decade, particularly in the Supreme Court and Congress, and the Executive branch was either unwilling or unable to do much to protect labor's gains.

New Deal enactments were more moderate than popular movement demands for unemployment insurance and benefits for the elderly. Title III of the Social Security Act established a federal-state program for unemployment compensation that was consistent in its general framework with the preferences of such New Dealers as Roosevelt and Perkins: although Perkins was deeply disappointed in the restrictions on coverage imposed by Treasury Secretary Morgenthau and Congress. Given his druthers and without the Townsend pressure, Roosevelt would have avoided pensions for the elderly, but Title I, Grants to States for Old-Age Assistance, fell far short of Townsend demands. Old Age Insurance, initially a very limited program for retired workers, underwent structural change as a result of the 1939 amendments. The amendments were close to administration proposals and made possible by congressional representatives of both parties whose pledges to support the pension movement could be fulfilled by voting for the more moderate administration proposals. The overall pattern with respect to social welfare is that the social movements served the purpose of moderate New Deal reform.

Did the movements ever succeed in moving the New Deal farther than it wanted to go? Its support of the National Labor Relations Act was partly a response to labor militancy but at the same time was initially opposed by the Communist Party. Whereas the NLRA did guarantee an important right to labor, albeit one that was weakened even before the end of the 1930s, this was not the case with Roosevelt's response to a political rival, one who could have threatened the very existence of the New Deal. Redistribution of wealth was not a New Deal policy. Roosevelt's proposed Wealth Tax Act was co-optative, an attempt to "steal Huey's thunder." FDR did not seem to care whether Congress passed the Wealth Tax Act, nor did he rail against it for weakening his proposals. Nonetheless, the opinion of an unidentified Democratic senator suggests that Huey Long in particular, and movements in general, had pushed the New Deal further left: "We are obliged to propose and accept many things in the New Deal that otherwise we would not because we must prevent a union of discontent around him; the President is the only hope of liberals and conservatives: if his program is restricted, the answer may be Huey Long."[203] On the other hand, historian Robert McElvaine points out that in most of the 1934 elections in which plausible candidates to the left of Roosevelt appeared, they won. From these results he infers:

> This was a firm indication of the direction in which many Americans, particularly those on whom Roosevelt's political future depended, wanted to move. The votes for these candidates were not anti-Roosevelt votes—at least not yet. But the possibilities that such voters would turn against the President if he did not produce more constructive change was a real one.[204]

Despite the blatant oppression of Southern tenant farmers, the Roosevelt administration initially turned a deaf ear to reports of their suffering and of the "reign of terror" that greeted the movement that arose to fight for sharecroppers' rights. Roosevelt was apparently sympathetic but trapped by the Southerners on whom the New Deal depended for enactment of its programs. Some support for the tenant farmers was expressed during the 1936 election campaign. However, the results were limited, bordering on token support for this very oppressed group.

The New Deal did occasionally bow to the pressure of the Workers Alliance of America, a more moderate successor to the unemployed movement and friendlier to the Roosevelt administration than its predecessor. Whereas the Roosevelt Administration withstood protest against the decision to shut down the CWA in 1934, it did accede to WAA protest over announced, severe cutbacks of the WPA in 1937. This was perhaps because it valued the program and needed WAA support to balance anti-WPA forces. The New Deal also gave into threatened black protest over discrimination in the defense industry that would perhaps have been disruptive of preparations for war and that could be achieved through an order without the assent of Southern legislators.

Crisis can be a fertile ground for social movements, and the economic collapse of 1929 and its aftermath, coupled with a paucity of public policies to cope with it, contributed to widespread protest by a number of deeply distressed populations. A welfare state that has often been considered "reluctant" or a laggard by international standards may nonetheless be one reason for the relative lack of popular protest in the early stages of the Great Recession. The outside resources, particularly parties of the left, that were important ingredients in protest movements of the poor during the 1930s were conspicuous in their absence during the nation's second great economic crisis and another reason for limited social protest.

The popular movements of the 1930s were relatively large and characterized by great commitment, courage, and skill. They were diverse in class, race, political persuasion, and demands, and they peaked at different times during the decade. Given this diversity, they were seldom allied in their protest, and this may be one reason why their contributions to permanent reform were relatively modest. Perhaps, it is an axiom of social protest that a great deal of effort often yields only a modicum of social change. Still, one might have expected more far-reaching change from economic crisis and the burst of social action to which it gave rise. Part of the answer lies in the New Deal itself and in the political skill and persuasion of Franklin Roosevelt, as well as his administration's dependence on a Congress led by Southern legislators. The moderate policies with which the "slightly-left-of-center" Roosevelt was most comfortable were aided by the movements, and, along with co-optation and some token benefits, were sufficient to restore social order and bring the New Deal victories at the polls.

Notes

1. This is how Roosevelt described himself to *New York Times* columnist Anne O'Hare McCormack. Marion Turner Sheehan, ed., "A Little Left of Center," November 25, 1934, in *The World at Home: Selections from the Writings of Anne O'Hare McCormick* (New York: Alfred Knopf, 1956), 248–258.
2. Irving Bernstein refers to organized looting of food as a "national phenomenon." The "most remarkable illustration of illegal self-help" was anthracite bootlegging, described by Bernstein: "an entire industry in northeastern Pennsylvania that nonetheless had the approval of authorities and public opinion." Bernstein, *The Lean Years: A History of the American Worker 1920–1933* (Boston: Houghton Mifflin, 1972), 422–423.
3. See, e.g. Steve Valocchi, "The Unemployed Workers Movement of the 1930s: A Reexamination of the Piven and Cloward Thesis," *Social Problems*, 37, no. 2 (May 1990): 191–205; and Steve Valocchi, "External Resources and the Unemployed Councils of the 1930s: Six Propositions from Social Movement Theory," *Sociological Forum*, 8, no. 3 (1993): 451–470.
4. Roy Rosenzweig, "'Socialism in Our Time': The Socialist Party and the Unemployed, 1929–1936," *Labor History*, 20, no. 4 (Fall 1979): 486. In addition to these dominant organizations, "innumerable local associations sprang up, built ordinarily around an individual, and either independent of or breaking away from existing organizations." Helen Seymour, *When Clients Organize* (Chicago: American Public Welfare Association, 1937), 6.
5. Roy Rosenzweig, "Organizing the Unemployed: The Early Years of the Great Depression, 1929–1933," *Radical America*, 10, no. 4 (1974): 40. According to Albert Prago, "Of all the radical groups, the Communists were the most active, reacted earliest to the problems of the jobless, and had the greatest influence." "The Organization of the Unemployed and the Role of Radicals, 1929–1935" (Ph.D. diss., Union Graduate School, Yellow Springs, OH, 1976), 11.
6. For the Socialists' Unemployed Leagues, see Rosenzweig, "'Socialism in Our Time,'" 485–509; for the Musteites, see Rosenzweig, "Radicals and the Jobless: The Musteites and the Unemployed Leagues, 1932–1936," *Labor History*, 16 (1975): 52–77. There was inter-organizational

competition among the movement groups in the early stages that, in Valocchi's view, contributed to the numbers and types of insurgency because each group tried to outdo the other. Valocchi, "Unemployed Workers Movement," 193, draws on the work of Prago, 189–211.

7. Seymour, 3.
8. Frances Fox Piven and Richard A. Cloward, *Poor People's Movements: Why They Succeed, How They Fail* (New York: Pantheon, 1977), 41.
9. Daniel J. Leab, "'United We Eat': The Creation and Organization of the Unemployed Councils," *Labor History*, 8 (1967): 306.
10. Ibid. According to an account of movements of the unemployed by one who took part in the struggles of the 1930s, there were 100,000 or more in New York and Detroit, 50,000 in Boston and Chicago, 30,000 in Philadelphia, 25,000 in Cleveland, and 20,000 in Youngstown and Pittsburgh; and "at least 125,000 demonstrated in a total of two dozen other cities across the country." That would add up to around half a million. Frank Folsom, *Impatient Armies of the Poor: The Story of Collective Action of the Unemployed 1808–1942* (Niwat, CO: University Press of Colorado, 1991), 55.
11. Bernstein, 427. These demonstrations may have raised consciousness of the problem but the Hoover administration continued to underplay and resist relief throughout its tenure. Similarly, Leab (p. 318) writes that the demonstrations "had broken through the generally optimistic tone of a press which had talked of little but quick recovery and happy days."
12. Rosenzweig, "Organizing the Unemployed," 56.
13. Valocchi, "Unemployed Workers Movement," 196. Valocchi points out that the unemployed movement used the political resources of local élites who found it in their interest to support the movement's demand for national relief. This is discussed below.
14. See, e.g., American Civil Liberties Union, *What Rights for the Unemployed? A Summary of the Attacks on the Rights of the Unemployed to Organize, Demonstrate, and Petition* (New York: Author, February 1935), 6, accessed July 18, 2013, available at http://debs.indstate.edu/a505w5_1935.pdf. The ACLU reports this example of violent response and concession: In a demonstration of the Unemployed Councils at New York's City Hall, the leaders were arrested and treated with brutality, but the next day the New York City Board of Estimate appropriated one million dollars for relief (p. 6).
15. Leab, 361. Similarly, "the day-to-day economic action of the Councils was looked upon in the party as meaty bait to attract the workers and as an effective demonstration that they could hope to get nothing from "a capitalistic government which was in the throes of decay." Bernard Karsh and Phillips L. Garman, "The Impact of the Political Left," in *Labor and the New Deal*, Milton Derber and Edwin Young, eds. (Madison: University of Wisconsin Press, 1961), 90.
16. Rosenzweig, "Organizing the Unemployed"; see also Leab.
17. Rosenzweig, "Organizing the Unemployed," 40.
18. Rosenzweig, "'Socialism in Our Time,'" 491.
19. Also part of a platform adopted in March 1930 by the Unemployed Councils were: no discrimination in rehiring because of race, religion, or sex; exemption from taxes and mortgage payments for the jobless; and a fair distribution of all available employment. Leab, 309, citing the Communist *Daily Worker*, March 7, 1930. Valocchi, "Unemployed Workers Movement" (p. 196) calls attention to lobbying, not simply direct action.
20. Rosenzweig, "Organizing the Unemployed," 52; see also Prago, Chapter VI.
21. Rosenzweig, "Organizing the Unemployed," 41–43; see also Prago, 110–111.
22. Rosenzweig, "'Socialism in our Time,'" 486.
23. Rosenzweig, "Organizing the Unemployed," 38.
24. Lizabeth Cohen, *Workers Make a New Deal: Industrial Workers in Chicago, 1919–1939* (Cambridge, UK: Cambridge University Press, 1990), 263.
25. See Rosenzweig, "Radicals and the Jobless," 64, for inherent barriers. Seymour (p. 3), writes that "By 1932, repeated disorder, violence, police arrests, and unfriendly publicity contributed to bring the Councils into disrepute." Other reasons such as fear of being branded a "reliefer," "conservatism and inertia" of the rank and file, and distrust of Communists are given

by E. Wright Bakke, *Citizens Without Work: A Study of the Effects of Unemployment upon the Workers' Social Relations and Practices* (New Haven, CT: Yale University Press, 1940), 71–84. Communists, particularly, were adept at helping unemployed workers to overcome the tendency toward self-blame or to achieve a "transformation from personal troubles to public grievances" (Valocchi, "External Resources," 456-457).

26. C. R. Walker in *The Forum*, September, 1932, cited by Prago, 145–146.
27. American Civil Liberties Union, 6.
28. *Fortune*, September 1934, 69, 159, cited by Prago, 188. *Fortune*, a business magazine founded in 1929 by Henry Luce, was known for having a social conscience during the Depression. It's interesting, given the Party's eyes on larger goals, that responsiveness to immediate needs is noted.
29. Melvin G. Holli, *American Mayor: The Best & the Worst Big City Leaders* (University Park: Pennsylvania State University Press, 1999).
30. Piven and Cloward, 91. See also, Valocchi "The Unemployed Workers Movement" (p. 196) who mentions as well governors, social workers, and labor leaders. See also Josephine Chapin Brown, *Public Relief, 1929–1939* (New York: Henry Holt, 1940), 106–141 who emphasizes the compelling testimony of social workers and labor leaders at Congressional hearings on relief measures.
31. See below for Roosevelt's approach to protest expressed at the time when the Hoover Administration used armed force against the encampment of unemployed veterans in Washington.
32. For a description of TERA, see Emma Octavia Lundberg, "The New York State Temporary Emergency Relief Administration," *Social Service Review*, 6, no. 4 (1932): 545–566.
33. Brown, 96.
34. Bernstein, 434.
35. While acknowledging the Communists' role in stopping evictions, improving conditions in relief centers, and promoting unemployment insurance, Schlesinger also comments that "they won credit for much that could more soberly be ascribed to conditions than to agitation." Arthur M. Schlesinger, Jr., *The Crisis of the Old Order 1919–1933* (Boston: Houghton Mifflin, 1957), 295, 219. However, need alone is seldom a sufficient reason for governments to meet it.
36. James R. Green, *The World of the Worker: Labor in Twentieth-Century America* (New York: Hill and Wang, 1980), 138.
37. Karsh and Garman, 197; see also Leab. Folsom studied the unemployed movement during the entire decade. Referring to the Workers Alliance that succeeded the earlier movements, he writes: "the alliance and its predecessors had created a body of thousands of workers who had learned a great deal about how to organize and get results"(p. 431).
38. Cohen, 265.
39. Frances Perkins, The Roosevelt I Knew (New York: Harper and Row, 1946/1964), 182.
40. Ibid., 183.
41. Prago, 180.
42. American Civil Liberties Union, 6.
43. Arthur M. Schlesinger, Jr. *The Coming of the New Deal* (Boston: Houghton Mifflin, 1957), 277; William E. Leuchtenburg, *Franklin D. Roosevelt and the New Deal* (New York: Harper, 1963), 122.
44. Prago, 188.
45. See, e.g., Seymour, 9.
46. Prago, 188. The source of the claim was Herbert Benjamin, the leader of the UCs who could be quite critical of the movement. See his "The Unemployment Movement in the U.S.A. from March 6, 1950, through the Second 'New Deal' Year," *The Communist*, 14 (June 1935): 528–547.
47. Nels Anderson, "Pressure Groups," *Survey Graphic* (March 1936): 168–170, 189.
48. Herbert Benjamin, in Piven and Cloward, 87.
49. Prago, 242–245.
50. Ibid., 248–249.
51. Ibid., 249–250.

52. Paul H. Douglas, *Social Security in the United States: An Analysis and Appraisal of the Federal Social Security Act* (New York: McGraw-Hill, 1939), 81–82.
53. Seymour, 9; Dona Cooper Hamilton and Charles V. Hamilton, *The Dual Agenda: Race and Social Welfare Policies of Civil Rights Organizations* (New York: Columbia University Press, 1997), 31.
54. Douglas, 76–77.
55. Ibid., 82.
56. Rosenzweig, "The Radicals and the Jobless," 68; Irving Bernstein, *The Turbulent Years: A History of the American Worker* (Boston: Houghton Mifflin, 1970), 217–227.
57. Rosenzweig, " 'Socialism in Our Time,' " 499. The unemployed union in Camden, New Jersey, assisted in organizing workers at Campbell's Soup and RCA.
58. Seymour, 6.
59. Rosenzweig, "The Radicals and the Jobless," 63.
60. Piven and Cloward, 76. See their full discussion, 76–91. Similarly, Cohen (p. 265) writes that, by the mid-1930s, the unemployed movement "became more centralized and bureaucratized under the aegis of a national coalition." For a different position regarding the decline of insurgency that includes the effect of federal relief but not bureaucratization, see Valocchi, esp. 197.
61. Irene Oppenheimer, "The Organizations of the Unemployed, 1930–1940," (unpublished MA thesis, Columbia University, 1940), 36, cited by Rosenzweig, "'Socialism in Our Time,' " 502.
62. Rosenzweig, " 'Socialism in Our Time,' " 505.
63. Ibid., 507–508. Evidently Mrs. Roosevelt, who became a friend of Lasser, was an honorary member of the WAA. For the relationship of WAA leaders to New Dealers, including FDR, see also Prago, 257.
64. "While federal rulings did not touch upon the legality of WPA strikes, relief organizers interpreted the right to organize as implying the right to strike. State and local administrators frequently ruled differently." Seymour, 8.
65. Karsh and Garman, 94. For actions in New Jersey, Pennsylvania, and New York, see Folsom, 419–421.
66. Folsom, 423, based on information in a WAA pamphlet, "How to Win Work at a Living Wage or a Decent Standard of Relief with the Workers Alliance of America," 1937.
67. Karsh and Garman, 94.
68. Joseph P. Lash, *Eleanor and Franklin: The Story of Their Relationship Based on Eleanor Roosevelt's Private Papers* (New York: W.W. Norton, 1971), 602. Lash cites Eleanor Roosevelt's marginal note on Aubrey Williams' letter to her, November 11, 1939.
69. John A. Salmond, *A Southern Rebel: The Life and Times of Aubrey Willis Williams, 1890–1965* (Chapel Hill: University of North Carolina Press, 1983), 102–103, 168–169. Roosevelt told him he was "a political liability."
70. Bernstein, *Lean Years,* 437.
71. Lucy G. Barber, *Marching on Washington: The Forging of an American Political Tradition* (Berkeley: University of California Press, 2002), 75.
72. The Socialist Party and its leader, Norman Thomas, supported the Bonus Army but criticized the veterans for not broadening their demands to include general relief for all of the unemployed and the needy. According to Donald J. Lisio, theirs was a "non-radical, essentially middle class outlook." Donald J. Lisio, *The President and Protest: Hoover, Conspiracy, and the Bonus Riot* (Columbia: University of Missouri Press, 1974), 84. At one point Commander Waters did try to say that the B.E.F. was "the vanguard of a general rising of the unemployed." Schlesinger, *Crisis of the Old. Order,* 259, but there was no evidence of a program beyond the bonus.
73. Bernstein, *Lean Years,* 446.
74. Schlesinger points out that "B.E.F. leaders were tireless in denouncing Communist activity, destroying their leaflets and throwing their leaders out of the camps. *Crisis of the Old Order,* 260. See also Lisio, Chapter 5, 87–108; see also, Barber, 90.
75. Schlesinger, *Crisis of the Old Order,* 257.

76. Ibid.
77. Bernstein, *Lean Years*, 437. A crude census of cantonments in July put the size of the army at 23,000. The Washington Superintendent of Police put the size at peak at 22,000. Bernstein, *Lean Years*, 441, citing papers of the police superintendent, Pelham D. Glassford, and other sources. See, e.g., Bernstein, *Lean Years*, 441–443; Lisio, 51–53 and *passim*.
78. Lisio, 50.
79. Bernstein, *Lean Years*, 441.
80. Ibid.
81. Barber, 88.
82. Lisio, 109. Roosevelt tried to persuade the New York contingent to return home from Washington, offering them free transportation and jobs, but they refused, saying they would stay in Washington until they got their bonuses. Lisio, 84.
83. Lisio, 219 and *passim*.
84. Rexford Tugwell, *Brains Trust* (New York: Viking, 1968), 358.
85. Lisio, 283.
86. Tugwell, 358. Lisio (p. 285) refers to a conversation between Roosevelt and his advisor Professor Felix Frankfurter, who was visiting him in Hyde Park at the time of the rout in which Roosevelt said that this incident and Hoover's behavior would elect him.
87. Bernstein, *Lean Years*, 454. A lengthy account of the aftermath of the rout shows that initially public opinion favored the President for ridding the nation of subversives, but in time, owing to the Attorney General's report that many of the veterans were criminals and a refutation by Superintendent of Police Glassford, the tide turned against Hoover a bare two months before the presidential election. See Lisio, 226–257.
88. Blanche Wiesen Cook, *Eleanor Roosevelt, Vol. 2, 1933–1938* (New York: Viking, 1999), 46.
89. While Eleanor Roosevelt's visit was largely symbolic, FDR's Veterans Administration director, Frank T. Hines, is said to have done much to ensure that the demonstration remained peaceful by housing the marchers away from the capital and attending to their needs. Lisio, 292.
90. Lisio, 293.
91. Paul Dickson and Thomas B. Allen, *The Bonus Army: An American Epic* (New York: Walker and Company, 2005), 266–277.
92. Green, 133. Milton Derber reports that union membership was 3.4 million in 1929, having declined 1.7 million from its post–World War I peak or by about one-third. "Growth and Expansion," in Derber and Young, 3.
93. "Thanks to the Norris-LaGuardia Act of 1932... capital could no longer look to the federal courts for help." David M. Kennedy, *Freedom from Fear: The American People in Depression and War, 1929–1945* (New York: Oxford University Press, 1999), 289.
94. Bernstein, *Turbulent Years*, 34.
95. Green, 140.
96. Bernstein, *Turbulent Years*, 34, 41.
97. Ibid., 37.
98. Ibid., 41.
99. Green, 141.
100. Leuchtenburg, 151.
101. Perkins, 239.
102. Bernstein, *Turbulent Years*, 3; Murray Edelman makes a similar point about FDR and the influence of Perkins in "New Deal Sensitivity to Labor Interests," in Derber and Young, 180. See also Schlesinger, *Coming of the New Deal*, 402, regarding FDR's somewhat paternalistic attitude of having government do things for working people rather than gaining them through union power.
103. Franklin D. Roosevelt, Annual Message to Congress, January 11, 1944, accessed April 22, 2013, available at http://www.fdrlibrary.marist.edu/archives/address_text.html. See Chapter 11 in this book for a discussion of the Economic Bill of Rights.
104. Leuchtenburg, 151.

105. See, e.g., J. Joseph Huthmacher, *Senator Robert F. Wagner and the Rise of Urban Liberalism* (New York: Athenaeum, 1968), 192. See McIntyre, Chapter 5 in this book, on the bill as both pro-worker and anti-Communist. In 1934, nearly 1.5 million workers took part in some 1,800 strikes. See Robert S. McElvaine, *The Great Depression: America, 1929–1941,* 2nd ed. (New York: Times Books, 1993), 225.
106. On May 6, 1935, the Railroad Retirement Act was declared unconstitutional by the Supreme Court in *Railroad Retirement Board v. Alton Railroad Co.*, 295 U.S. 330.
107. Melvyn Dubofsky and Warren Van Tine, *John L. Lewis: A Biography* (New York: Quadrangle/New York Times Book Co., 1977), 232, citing C. P. Howard to Sidney Hillman, February 3, 1936, Sidney Hillman Papers, CIO Folder, 1935–1936.
108. Dan Tobin of the Teamsters, one of the AFL officials most opposed to industrial unionism, referred to the heavy industry workers as "the rubbish," and another remarked, "My wife can always tell from the smell of my clothes what breed of foreigners I've been hanging out with." Schlesinger, *Coming of the New Deal*, 411, citing Edward Levinson, *Labor on the March* (New York: Harper, 1938), chapters 3, 4.
109. For fuller discussion of the rupture, see Bernstein, *Turbulent Years*, 352–431.
110. McElvaine, 226.
111. Bernstein, *Turbulent Years*, 257.
112. Sidney Fine, *Sit-down: The General Motors Strike of 1936–1937* (Ann Arbor: University of Michigan Press, 1969). See also, Bernstein, *Turbulent Years,* esp. 523–551.
113. Green, 155.
114. Bernstein, *Turbulent Years,* 550. This was in a letter to his advisor and speech writer Samuel Rosenman following his reelection in 1940.
115. Press Conference, April 15, 1937. See *Complete Presidential Press Conferences of Franklin D. Roosevelt,* Introduction by Jonathan Daniels (New York: Da Capo Press, 1972), vol. 9, 304–307.
116. Bernstein, *Turbulent Years,* 485–490.
117. Dubofsky and Van Tine, 314.
118. Bernstein, *Turbulent Years,* 494.
119. Dubofsky and Van Tine, 315.
120. Leuchtenburg,. 243.
121. Bernstein, *Turbulent Years,* 663–671.
122. Green, 166.
123. Green, 173. The increase was from 2.8 million to 8.4 million.
124. Hamilton and Hamilton, 31, citing the statement of T. Arnold Hill, February 8, 1935, House Committee on Labor, *Unemployment, Old Age, and Social Insurance, 74th Congress, 1st sess., 326.328.* Hamilton and Hamilton point out that the NUL testimony put the proportion of Negro workers excluded at two-thirds, whereas the NAACP estimate was one-half.
125. Ibid.
126. Ibid., 27.
127. John Hope Franklin, *From Slavery to Freedom: A History of Negro Americans,* 5th ed. (New York: Alfred A. Knopf, 1980), 426.
128. Kennedy, 765–766, cites Jervis Anderson, *A. Philip Randolph: A Biographical Portrait* (New York: Harcourt, Brace, Jovanovich, 1973), 241–241, for examples of discrimination; and Ulysses Lee, *United States Army in World War II Special Studies: The Employment of Negro Troops* (Washington: Department of the Army, 1963), 76, for the War Department policy.
129. Kennedy, 766, citing Anderson, 247–253.
130. Franklin, 426–427.
131. Irving Bernstein, *A Caring Society: The New Deal, the Worker, and the Great Depression* (Boston: Houghton Mifflin, 1985), 296.
132. Bernstein, ibid., 294–296; August Meier and Elliott Rudwick, *From Plantation to Ghetto*, 3rd ed. (New York: Hill and Wang), 268.

133. Hamilton and Hamilton, 54; Green, 180.
134. Green, 130.
135. In the system that emerged after Reconstruction, landowners assigned landless farmers small tracts of land and provided them with food, shelter, clothing, necessary seeds, and farm equipment. When the crop was harvested, part of the proceeds went to tenants after deduction of the cost of items furnished by the landlord. Sharecroppers got a smaller part of the proceeds than share tenants whose portion depended on what they could pay for themselves, and cash tenants paid a fixed rent and kept all the proceeds of the harvest.
136. Jerold S. Auerbach, "Southern Tenant Farmers: Socialist Critics of the New Deal," *Labor History,* 7, no. 1 (Winter 1966): 4–5.
137. Robert D. Leighninger, Jr., *Long-Range Public Investment: The Forgotten Legacy of the New Deal* (Columbia: University of South Carolina Press, 2007), 151.
138. Leuchtenburg, 137.
139. Auerbach (p. 17) writes that although the STFU claimed to be interracial and both races were welcome, the overwhelming number of unions were either black or white or with one white or one black member only. Surveys of STFU membership are the basis of his conclusion.
140. According to the chief STFU organizer, Harry L. Mitchell, whose salary was paid by the Socialist Party, they could not have continued without outside support. Auerbach, 9–10.
141. Ibid., 9–12.
142. M. S. Venkaratamani, "Norman Thomas, Arkansas Sharecroppers, and the Roosevelt Agricultural Policies, *Mississippi Valley Historical Review,* 137, no. 2 (September 1960): 236.
143. Auerbach, 15.
144. Venkaratamani, 238.
145. Ibid., 239.
146. Auerbach, 17.
147. Venkaratamani, 229, 231. The account regarding Roosevelt is taken from Schlesinger's review of a number of sources, including the AAA papers and interviews. See *Coming of the New Deal,* 597.
148. Schlesinger, ibid., 379, quotes *The Sharecropper's Voice.*
149. Venkaratamani, 237, citing a letter from Wagner to Norman Thomas, April 2, 1935.
150. Auerbach, 16.
151. Ibid.
152. Venkaratamani, 244. Blackstone expressed disagreement with the philosophy of small homesteads for tenants.
153. Ibid.
154. Ibid., 245.
155. Leuchtenburg, 104, citing several critics of the plan.
156. Abraham Holtzman, *The Townsend Movement: A Political Study* (New York: Bookman, 1963), 108–109.
157. Leuchtenburg, 106. Amenta writes that the doctor claimed there were 2,000 clubs promoting the plan in December 1934, and a little later, 300,000 members. Examination of the Townsend Plan's financial records show that the figures for both are about half what Townsend claimed. Edwin Amenta, *When Movements Matter: The Townsend Plan and the Rise of Social Security* (Princeton, NJ: Princeton University Press, 2006), 58–59.
158. See Roy Lubove, *The Struggle for Social Security, 1900–1935* (Cambridge, MA: Harvard University Press, 1968). A similar overshadowing of more conventional organizations occurred in the 1950s and 1960s when the Southern Christian Leadership Conference and the Student Non-Violent Coordinating Committee temporarily displaced long-established civil rights organizations like the NAACP and the Urban League. This is not to compare the reasonable demands of the civil rights leaders of the 1960s with the unrealistic ones of the Townsendites.
159. Perkins, 278.

160. Roosevelt, The Annual Message to the Legislature, January 7, 1931. In *The Public Papers and Addresses of Franklin D. Roosevelt, 1928–1932* (New York: Random House, 1938), 103.
161. Thomas H. Eliot, "The Legal Background of Social Security, delivered at a general staff meeting at Social Security Administration Headquarters, Baltimore, Maryland, February 3, 1961, accessed May 6, 2013, available at http://www.ssa.gov/history/eliot2.html.
162. Douglas, 12.
163. Perkins, 278–279.
164. Ibid., 294.
165. In January 1935, the Townsend national publicity director wrote to movement co-founder Robert Clements that newspapers were sold on the movement's strength. "Our big job is to get that strength before our strength is actually measured." Letter from Frank Peterson to Robert E. Clements, January 20, 1935, cited by Holtzman, p. 89, who gave this as evidence of Roosevelt's over-assessment.
166. Witte, 78–79. Witte added that it was smart of Thomas Eliot, who drafted the bill, to make Old Age Assistance "Title I."
167. Amenta, 87–88. See also Holtzman, 94–100.
168. Amenta, 91–92.
169. The average OAA benefit was under $20 throughout the 1930s. Eveline M. Burns, *The American Social Security System* (Boston: Houghton Mifflin, 1951), 313.
170. Holtzman, 115.
171. Holtzman, 104, cites Hopkins's address at Grinnell College quoted by Robert Sherwood, *Roosevelt and Hopkins: An Intimate History* (New York: Harper, 1948), 20.
172. Holtzman, ibid.
173. Arthur J. Altmeyer, *The Formative Years of Social Security* (Madison: The University of Wisconsin Press), 89–90 and *passim*; Amenta, 169–171.
174. House Ways and Means Committee, *Hearings Relative to the Social Security Act Amendments of 1939*, Vol. 1, 1–2, cited by Amenta, 171.
175. The emphasis here is on national movements. A fuller treatment of popular movements would include End Poverty in California (EPIC). Based on Upton Sinclair's plan to give the unemployed the opportunity to produce for their own use on lands purchased or leased by the state, EPIC won its author the Democratic nomination for governor in 1934. Also worthy of discussion is the Midwestern Farmers' Holiday Association, organized by Milo Reno in 1932 to deal with the problem of over-production in agriculture.
176. Leuchtenburg, 7.
177. Ibid., 100. It was estimated at thirty to forty-five million by the end of 1932.
178. Kennedy, 234.
179. Alan Brinkley, *Voices of Protest: Huey Long, Father Coughlin, and the Great Depression* (New York: Alfred Knopf, 1982), 77–78.
180. William Ivy Hair, *The Kingfisher and His Realm: The Life and Times of Huey P. Long* (Baton Rouge: Louisiana State University Press, 1991), 270.
181. Ibid., 272. Hair cites an interview with one of Long's associates, H.C. ("Happy") Sevier in the Interview Collection in T. Harry Williams' Papers, Hill Memorial Library, Lousiana State University, Baton Rouge,
182. Brinkley, 74. Hair (p. 272) makes a similar point: that "hunger and rags in the midst of plenty was real enough" and "inadequate distribution of income a prime cause of the Depression." James MacGregor Burns also points out that Long was describing "a fundamental dilemma of American democracy." MacGregor Burns, *The Crosswinds of Freedom* (New York: Knopf, 1989), 60.
183. Brinkley, 173.
184. Kennedy, 233.
185. Leuchtenburg, 102. The reference is to the fascistic corporatism of Italian dictator Benito Mussolini.

186. Brinkley, 179.
187. Brinkley, 201–203, 246, 248; Kennedy, 243.
188. Brinkley, 193. See also McElvaine, 240.
189. Brinkley, 193.
190. Ibid., 174–175.
191. Tugwell, 433. In answer to Tugwell's question, FDR said the most dangerous was General Douglas MacArthur.
192. Kennedy, 237.
193. Brinkley, 126–128. See also, Leuchtenburg, 100–102.
194. Ibid., 207–209. See also Kennedy, 240–241.
195. Roosevelt admitted to Brain Truster Raymond Moley that he was indeed trying to steal Long's thunder. Moley, *After Seven Years* (New York: Harper, 1939), 312, cited by Kennedy, 276.
196. Leuchtenburg, 153–155.
197. Ibid.,154; Brinkley, 207–209.
198. Hair, 307.
199. Brinkley, 80.
200. Kennedy, 243, citing Elliott Roosevelt, *FDR: His Personal Letters* (New York: Duell, Sloan and Pearce, 1970), 452–453.
201. MacGregor Burns, 84.
202. Lemke, a Progressive Republican, was, like Coughlin and Long, originally pro-New Deal but became embittered by the Roosevelt Administration's intervention to defeat the Frazier-Lemke Act, which called for government refinancing of all farm mortgages and major inflation of the money supply. See Brinkley, 154.
203. Arthur Krock, "In Washington Ways Are Sought to Counteract Huey Long's Program," *New York Times*, January 10, 1935, 18.
204. McElvaine, 236–237.

5

Labor Militance and the New Deal

Some Lessons for Today

RICHARD MCINTYRE

Only seven percent of private-sector workers in the United States currently belong to unions. While the public-sector rate is over one third, public-sector unionization is under attack in a number of traditionally union friendly states such as Wisconsin, Michigan, and Ohio. For fifty years, even when the Democrats have controlled the presidency and both houses of Congress, organized labor has been unable to win any federal legislation that would spur union growth or increase what little political and economic leverage it still has.

Unionization rates have also declined in most of the rich countries, but the United States is an exceptional case. Decline started earlier in the United States, beginning in the late 1950s, and has been more severe. Perhaps the most relevant comparison is Canada, which had a similar unionization rate in the 1950s and 1960s and then saw unionization *increase* in the 1970s and 1980s, declining slightly thereafter. Canada's overall rate is now 30 percent compared to 11 percent in the United States.[1] Unionization in most European countries is significantly higher, and it is no accident that organized labor there has been much more successful in countering the agenda of organized capital.

Unions now have little impact on wages or working conditions for most Americans. This has not always been the case. Indeed, in the 1930s and 1940s, labor was a militant force for social change, and this militancy helped create key social protections such as the forty-hour working week, the minimum wage, unemployment insurance, old age insurance, and the right to unionize itself.

How did such a powerful force three-quarters of a century ago become the weak and divided entity that U.S. organized labor is today? There is no single explanation for labor's decline; in fact, there are nearly as many explanations as there are scholars who have studied the question: bad leaders, excessive bureaucracy, exogenous economic forces, shifts in the composition of the labor force, cultural shifts, excessive wage premiums, employer resistance, presidential and congressional opposition, and the nature of the American legal system are just a few of the explanations given for the exceptional decline of the American labor movement.[2]

Answering this question has become more urgent since the financial crisis of 2008 and the resulting "Great Recession." Many Progressives see this as a crisis of the free market capitalist or "neoliberal" model that displaced the "New Deal" model around 1980, and they now hope for a return to a more regulated capitalism. But this nostalgia for the New Deal model is generally not for the working-class solidarity and power that produced it but for the economic gains made under the New Deal by the (especially white, male) working class.

These gains are often imagined to be the product of a "limited post-war capital-labor accord" in which capital accepted organized labor's right to exist and labor accepted capital's right to rule the work place.[3] Yet a careful accounting of historical scholarship since the 1980s shows the idea of a truce between labor and capital to be inaccurate and misleading: inaccurate because it creates an image of a golden age that never was, and misleading in that it suggests a politics of social cooperation that has no material basis.[4] Capitalists as a class never accepted anything resembling such an accord, nor is there any indication that support for progressive reform would be forthcoming today in the absence of a serious mass movement for radical social change.

Rather than an accord, the labor relations system in the United States in the New Deal era (ending roughly in 1980) is better understood as the product of the radical labor upsurge in the 1930s that was then shaped and limited by wartime government and capitalist counterinsurgency. The "New Deal system" that resulted was more a product of labor's defeat than of any truce in the class struggle. This system was institutionalized in workers' right to organize and bargain collectively by both craft and industry as guaranteed by the National Labor Relations Act (1935), known as the Wagner Act; limits on workers' ability to challenge incumbent union representation based on National Labor Relations Board cases (1940s), so that the law came to protect unions more than workers; and elimination of the radical cadre of union organizers through both Red-baiting, which began in the late 1930s, and continued with the loyalty clause of the Taft-Hartley Act (1947).

In other words, by the early 1950s when labor reached its peak coverage of about a third of the workforce, unions had achieved government protection against employer attacks *and* against the most radical elements of the working class. This did allow unions to achieve economic gains for their members through collective bargaining and strike activity, but it also made them vulnerable to a change in government policy and cut them off from their most dynamic organizers and leaders. When that change occurred in the late 1970s and early 1980s, what had been a long slow decline turned into a rout.

Three Labor Relations Systems

There are three distinct periods in the story of American labor relations since the Civil War: the formative pre–Great Depression era (1870s–1920s), the New Deal era (1930s to about 1980), and the era of conservative hegemony since the late 1970s. In the late nineteenth century, the United States had the world's largest market and largest capitalist establishments (i.e., very big employers with tens of thousands of employees), with no parallel at the time in Western Europe and Japan. In this period, the American state played less of a role in industrialization than did those in continental Western Europe and Japan. Comparatively speaking, capital had an extreme anti-statist ideology. Social Darwinism and a fierce defense of managerial prerogative became deeply ingrained, and employers became used to a unilateral way of operating, free of government influence (though with government assistance for infrastructure). Although labor struggles during this period were fought with an intensity that frequently erupted into open warfare, labor was mostly ineffective in challenging management prerogative. Ultimately, unionism was largely confined to residual groups of highly skilled trades, and radical attempts at mass unionization of industry, such as the "Wobblies" (International Workers of the World), were repeatedly crushed. Large and small employers alike could count on courts stocked by right wing judges to fiercely defend any and all prerogatives.

Finally, unlike European economies, U.S. manufacturers did not develop effective employer associations or cartels, and with unionization fragmented along regional and occupational lines, wages were not taken "out of competition," creating a strong incentive for employers to crush unions that would make them uncompetitive. In the early twentieth century, European capitalist classes generally faced more prominent left parties than in the United States and sometimes found collective bargaining a useful route to working-class co-optation and thus a reasonable class strategy. They were also more likely to curtail radical or socialist tendencies through various social welfare measures. Prior to the 1930s, the American left and labor movements did not gain the kind of traction that would have made a strategic acceptance of collective bargaining possible, much less likely.[5]

American employer hostility was both a cause and effect of early defeats of the U.S. labor movement. These defeats—uniquely violent and large in scale—helped produce a very careful and largely non-radical labor movement.[6]

The labor movement's weakness in the wake of these violent defeats had a self-reinforcing quality. For instance, because wages were never effectively taken out of competition on the national level, individual employers had a greater incentive to vigorously and violently repress organizing initiatives that would raise labor costs for them but not for their competitors. Without a traditional aristocracy that put a premium on social stability, the U.S. labor movement and its allies had few opportunities to make alliances over the heads of the bourgeoisie, as was possible in some

European countries. For example, the limitation of the working day in England would not have been possible without the support of the landed aristocracy. Such alliances were less possible in the United States where no such aristocracy existed.[7] By the 1920s well-organized, large, and independent U.S. corporations faced a weak labor movement. Economic policy and company and industry-level industrial relations were, at that time, distinctly employer-dominated.

Accompanied by vast and militant social movements, the economic and political crisis of the Great Depression dislodged capital from its unilateral power position, partly because of the perception that capital was responsible for the Depression. At first the Roosevelt Administration sought to stabilize economic conditions through the promotion of economic planning and the funding of conventional public works—both authorized by the National Industrial Recovery Act (NIRA)—and by engaging in a halting effort to reform the delivery of public relief to the unemployed through both direct relief and government job creation, a process that culminated in the establishment of the Works Progress Administration (WPA) in 1935. This "First New Deal" of 1933–1934 dealt with economic survival in a variety of industries, including banking, agriculture, railroads, and manufacturing. The first New Deal created a legal basis for union organizing under Section 7(a) of the National Industrial Recovery Act. Though the legality of that Act was immediately and successfully challenged, new unions based on industry (coal, steel, autos) rather than craft (pipefitters, carpenters, etc.) began to organize unskilled and semi-skilled workers. These workers and their militant leaders were critical to the electoral landslide for the Democrats in 1934 at a time when American capital was discredited and politically weak.

That landslide, and continuing agitation by labor radicals, produced an unprecedented three-year window (1935–1937) when the "second New Deal" could be launched. This second New Deal dealt with general economic security through the National Labor Relations (Wagner) Act, the Social Security Act, the Farm Security Administration, the Housing (Wagner-Steagall) Act of 1937, and the Fair Labor Standards Act, which regulated working hours and minimum wages.

Social Security, the right to organize and bargain collectively with employers, and the rise of the Congress of Industrial Organizations (CIO)—the industrial alternative to the craft-based American Federation of Labor—all occurred in a period of unusual weakness for employer interests. These developments will be analyzed in detail in the next section. The key issue here is that the second New Deal *did not* become the basis for the "New Deal system." Rather, the "second ND" was modified dramatically by changes in government policy and capitalist organizing.[8]

Recent scholarship has identified a third New Deal, from 1938–1945.[9] The economic downturn of 1937–1938, rising conflict between the AFL and the CIO, and Republican electoral victories in 1938, which left Democrats in control of Congress but ended the progressive majority, led to this third phase. A coalition of

Republicans and Southern Democrats was able to curtail direct relief programs. The need for big business assistance in the war effort helped to rehabilitate big capitalists, so that industrial stability, rather than economic democracy, came to be the priority in labor relations.

By the New Deal "system," I mean this last set of conditions. It was modified in important ways by National Labor Relations Board decisions in the 1940s and the Taft-Hartley Act of 1947, but its basic outlines were clear by the beginning of World War II. Collective bargaining was embedded as a right administered by the state for the promotion of industrial and social stability. Union officials in pursuit of the same goal were generally protected from being challenged by their own members. Taft-Hartley, which was passed in the wake of the postwar strikes and rising anti-Communist hysteria, officially eliminated the influence of the labor left, but this influence had already been tightly contained as labor purged the most class-conscious of its own members.

The Influence of Radical Labor Action on New Deal Legislation

In discussing the role of the radical labor movement during the New Deal, two issues are of importance: the influence of radical labor action on New Deal legislation, and the impact of radical labor leadership on class struggle in the workplace. With regard to the first issue, I will focus on the National Labor Relations (Wagner) Act, which gave most private-sector workers the right to organize and bargain collectively and to strike. By "radical" labor I mean trade unions controlled by or generally supportive of the positions of the U.S. Communist Party, by far the most important group on the left at that time.

There have been three general explanations of the major laws passed during the second New Deal, especially the Wagner and Social Security Acts. One, associated with William Domhoff, emphasizes corporate élite involvement in writing those laws. This position is difficult to reconcile with the historical record on the National Labor Relations Act, as virtually all organized capitalist groups opposed the Act. The "state autonomy" theory of Theda Skocpol explains that state actors, strengthened by their experience with the National Industrial Recovery Act and the election results of 1934, were responsible for passing Wagner, but Skocpol and her co-authors provide little documentary or statistical evidence. The "social movement" theories of Michael Goldfield and Frances Fox Piven and Richard Cloward emphasize popular unrest due to general strikes and other actions led by radicals in the labor movement, but they do not establish a direct link between radical labor actions and legislation.[10]

An interesting study by Peter Philips resolves some of these problems.[11] Using oral history, legislative hearings, and analysis of interlocking membership in élite social clubs, Phillips makes a direct link between the remarkable social unrest of 1934 and the formation of the Liberty League, "the pivotal point for the splitting of the U.S. upper class."[12] Liberty League members were drawn from boards of directors of some of the largest corporations in the United States and saw the New Deal as nothing but socialism under another guise. These business conservatives took direct action to fight New Deal legislation, but they were largely ineffectual in the short run. However, the ties built between various business groups in the fight against the New Deal were to bear fruit in a coordinated ideological mobilization to promote a free-market vision of the economy and a union-free workplace after World War II.

Although labor unions had little role in writing the Wagner Act, radical trade union activity inside and outside the workplace created the context in which the Act became possible. A crucial aspect of the social unrest of this period is the link between the new industrial unions and broader social movements, especially the Communist Party (CP) but also movements of the unemployed, black workers, and single-issue groups and political parties, such as the Farmer-Labor party in Minnesota, the Progressive Party in Wisconsin, New York's American Labor party, and groups like California's EPIC, Huey Long's Share the Wealth, and the Townsend movement.[13] General strikes in Toledo (May 1934), Minneapolis (May–August 1934), and San Francisco (July 1934), as well as a huge strike in the textile industry in the same year, created an atmosphere of panic among business élites in 1934–1935, and confusion over how to deal with this. The conservative wing, represented by the newly formed Liberty League, advocated violent repression. They had been fine with much of the National Industrial Recovery Act, which allowed business coordination of industry, but they wanted minimal regulation and balanced budgets, and they resisted Section 7(a) Giving workers the right to organize and bargain collectively was anathema to big business in general; but in this unique period of capitalist class confusion and disorganization, civil unrest led to a critical division within the ruling class. The increasing radicalization of the labor movement in the context of a general social uprising gave corporate liberals and Southern Democrats in Congress a sense that something needed to be done. The Wagner Act, which drew on a series of national and state level precedents and which was opposed by the Communist Party, was near at hand. The Act was meant to provide most private-sector employees rights to freedom of association and collective bargaining and to create a National Labor Relations Board to organize elections and to adjudicate disputes.

In 1934, Wagner had introduced a labor law bill similar to the 1935 Act, but the bill failed. Although communism and radical action had been mentioned in the 1934 hearings on that bill, it had not frightened legislators sufficiently. Roosevelt did not support it, nor did he support the 1935 bill until the very end of the legislative process. By 1935, however, there was "a qualitatively stronger concern [among members of the political class] about communism and radical insurgencies."[14] During the hearings, for example, Lloyd Garrison, dean of the University of Wisconsin Law School, said, "I regard organized labor as our chief bulwark against communism and other revolutionary movements."[15] That the Communist Party opposed the Act made it easier for its proponents to sell it as both pro-worker and anti-Communist. The 1935 version passed without a roll call in the House and by 68–12 in the Senate. Most Republicans and most Southern Democrats supported it. Phillips argues that voting for the Wagner Act allowed Representatives and Senators to appeal to working people while at the same time taking on the mantle of anti-communism, as the bill was seen as creating the conditions for restoring labor peace. Democrats, who increasingly counted on the labor vote, hoped to gain a return to economic normalcy by constraining strikes through collective bargaining.[16] Democratic politicians were looking to secure labor support without grossly exceeding the bounds of what was acceptable to capital.[17]

The congressional election of 1934, which added a veto-proof Democratic majority in the Senate to existing Democratic dominance in the House of Representatives, "was in good part the result of the activities of broad social movements among the urban unemployed, farmers, Afro-Americans, and others, and of the 1934 labor upsurge."[18] The Communist Party opposed Wagner because it limited minority unionism by granting exclusive bargaining rights and involved employers in dues collection. Furthermore, the Communists feared government-controlled unions would result in loss of the right to strike. However, the CP had moved to a Popular Front strategy and was strongly supportive of the National Labor Relations Board by the time the act was declared constitutional by the Supreme Court (1937). One could say this was typical of the Party's unstable line, although one could also say that the CP was right on both counts: as argued below, after 1940 the NLRA did narrow union activities in a kind of repressive tolerance, even before the Taft-Hartley amendments. At the same time it protected the right to strike more or less effectively until the 1980s. Moreover, the first Board under the Wagner Act (up to 1940) was generally supportive of industrial unions, where the Communists had their strongest presence.[19]

Southern planters' support was critical to passing the Wagner Act and to the New Deal coalition. Through their control of key committee chairs they were able to directly influence the shape of New Deal legislation. Their initial support of Wagner and eventual defection from the pro-labor coalition is an important and little-told part of this story. Unlike conservative capitalists, Southern planters supported the regulation of production and state income supports as long as these did not interfere with their control of black workers and the low-wage Southern labor market. Sixty-eight percent of Southern senators supported the Wagner Act. That this number was lower than Southern support for the Agricultural Adjustment Act (AAA) or Social Security shows that labor policy was tricky for Southern Democrats, even in 1935. Still this is equal to overall support for Wagner from the Northeast where labor was strongest. [20]

All of these laws were tailored to the needs of the planters. The Wagner Act excluded farm workers, just as AAA payments went directly to landowners, with no requirement they be shared with tenants or sharecroppers. Old age and unemployment insurance similarly excluded agricultural and domestic workers, and other Social Security (SSA) programs were locally controlled. Southerners removed language from the original bill requiring state benefits for the elderly to provide "reasonable subsistence compatible with decency and benefits." Southern legislators expressed concern that younger people might stay home from the fields, living off their grandparents' benefits.[21]

Still, it is not entirely clear why the planters did not simply block the SSA and Wagner. Winders speculates that increased income in urban areas might raise demand for agricultural goods and negate the impact of food price increases due to agricultural price supports, encouraging urban Democrats to support AAA in return for Southern support of Wagner, but he provides no evidence that this was true.[22] It is also the case that the SSA meant a permanent infusion of federal money for broke Southern states, but this cannot explain Southern support for Wagner.

Winders argues that, while Southern planters' support of the SSA and AAA was based on shared economic interests with capitalists and farmers outside the South, their support for Wagner was a calculated political move designed to secure the New Deal coalition and thus became subject to change when the political winds shifted. And that is exactly what happened, as I discuss below.

In sum, radical labor action in the context of general social upheaval and perceived crisis led to a law that placed the federal government in the position of, according to the Wagner Act's preface, "encouraging the practice and procedure of collective bargaining...protecting the exercise by workers of full freedom of association, self-organization, and designation of representatives of their own choosing, for the purpose of negotiating the terms and conditions of their employment or other mutual aid or protection."[23] While capitalists largely opposed the Act, they were divided, and the Great Depression had weakened their influence. Wagner was supported by Southern planters who were able to exclude domestic and agricultural workers from the Act, shoring up the Democratic coalition while preserving the semi-feudal relations of production in the South.[24]

The Impact of Radical Labor Leadership on Class Struggle in the Workplace

The second aspect of radical labor action during the early New Deal period was the effectiveness of radical unions in the workplace. Today it is generally forgotten that Communists and their allies in the CIO created a vibrant and powerful radical left movement in the 1930s and 1940s. Communists were influential at both the local and national level in most of the CIO unions, with roughly 30 percent of CIO members either Communists or non-Party members generally supportive of Party positions.[25]

Communist and Communist-allied unions were more likely to challenge capitalist hegemony in the workplace and society in the 1930s and 1940s without sacrificing the immediate bread and butter interests of their membership. Precisely why they were successful, whether due to their approach to shop-floor organizing as a mission or calling, their discipline, an ideology that gave them hope, or their long-term focus, is beyond our scope here. But understanding their role is critical to achieving clarity on what the New Deal can teach us in the twenty-first century.

Communist influence on labor radicalism was not a function of their numbers. Twenty-five percent of New York City Teachers Union members were in the Communist Party, but this was unusual. Communists were about only two percent of union membership in the "Red" unions, though the percentages at the leadership level were much higher. Even in a "mainstream" or "non-radical" union like the Steelworkers, roughly 30 percent of full-time staff were Party members in the late 1930s. Moreover, many independent leftists were dedicated union activists, and while they did not caucus with Party members, their positions on key issues were similar.[26]

There are many critical comments to be made about radical unionism in the 1930s and 1940s; the point here is that despite these failures the Red and "semi-Red" unions effectively challenged capitalist hegemony in the workplace, including on issues such as wages and benefits, hours, and work rules.[27] Most Party members and independent leftist union members were effective trade unionists with a penchant for pursuing anti-capitalist goals in written contracts, not simply ideologues.[28]

While pluralist and some Marxist theories of industrial relations traditions argue that unions tend to incorporate the working class and thus stabilize capitalism, the history of these unions shows that with leadership committed to anti-capitalist struggle, unions can and have succeeded in encroaching on capital's dictatorship in the workplace and in society.[29]

Whereas industrial relations scholars and labor historians have claimed that Communist leadership made no difference to the results their unions achieved, quantitative research by Stepan and Zeitlin and qualitative work on individual unions by Rosswurm tell a different story. Looking at a sample of 236 collective bargaining agreements between 1937 and 1955, Stepan and Zeitlin found that contracts negotiated by locals of Communist-led unions were significantly more likely to limit management "rights," reject strike prohibitions and long-term contracts, and incorporate grievance procedures favorable to unions. They found this to be true regardless of industry structure, and also found that the political orientation of union leadership had no impact on bread and butter issues such as wages.

Communist-led unions opposed speedup and other methods of raising productivity on the ground that this increased the rate of exploitation. Based on ethnographic data, Stepan and Zeitlin conclude that contract provisions were mirrored by actual shop-floor practices.[30]

In the context of the social crisis of the 1930s, the growing weight of labor radicals in general and Communist Party members in particular was critical to the early functioning of the National Labor Relations Board. According to labor historian Melvin Dubofsky, "By the time the NLRB was up and running, the policies of the CIO, the CPUSA, and the New Deal as well were in harmony."[31] Things began to change after 1938 with the split between the AFL and CIO, internal conflicts in the CIO over the issue of Communist influence, and Roosevelt's reshaping of the National Labor Relations Board in response to congressional attack and red-baiting.

The older craft unions of the AFL were always leery of Wagner, as they saw collective bargaining as a private matter between employers and unions. They saw unions themselves, rather than the law, as determining who had the right to belong to a union. Now rights to organize and bargain collectively had become individual civil rights created and enforced by the state, with unions existing only as representatives of administratively determined groups of workers. That the NLRB seemed to favor the CIO unions in disputes between the two federations only increased the AFL's conflict with the Board. Searching for allies, the AFL embraced reactionary forces in and out of government. "The AFL leadership could sustain its position only through a more explicit alliance with the elements outside the labor movement—the Congressional conservatives and the employer groups—who were attacking the Wagner Act itself."[32]

In its early years (up to 1939), the National Labor Relations Board had been chiefly concerned with workers' self-organization and its own authority. By 1939, with war looming, there was growing concern in the Roosevelt Administration about autonomous rank and file activity (i.e., wildcat strikes). Roosevelt reconstituted the Board to placate his conservative critics, with the result that stable collective bargaining became the *only* goal of federal labor relations policy. By the early 1940s, workers' right to associate in unions of their own choosing was made subordinate to stability and order in business.[33]

After Germany attacked the Soviet Union, the Communist Party strongly supported the war effort, and, in particular, the no-strike pledge. However, contracts negotiated during the war were still more likely to be pro-labor in Communist than in non-Communist locals: "wartime contracts won by the Communist-led unions were far *less* likely than those of their rivals on the Right to cede management prerogatives, to sign away the right to strike, or to have cumbersome grievance procedures."[34] Whatever the national Party line, Communists and their allies in the trade unions sought to balance national unity with worker power at the point of production.

Capital's Ideological Offensive Against the New Deal

The creation of new workers' rights, vast expansion of union density, and the rapid growth of the state sparked an immediate response from many sectors of capital, beginning in the late 1930s. Employer hegemony was threatened in three ways—a loss of unilateral managerial prerogative in all aspects of the employment relationship, economic security provided by the state and not employers, and loss of the national narrative about American capitalism. These threats initiated an "ideological jihad."[35] Both individual and collective capitalist activism aimed to reverse all three losses.

First, employers fought to regain a measure of shop-floor control, weaken and undermine collective bargaining, and resist efforts to expand unionization beyond its early post–World War II high mark. There was a broad movement to create a non-union industrial relations alternative that took root and rapidly expanded from the 1950s through the 1970s. These developments have long been known to careful readers of postwar industrial relations' history.[36] I have already noted the shift in National Labor Relations Board policy from 1940, with industrial stability taking precedence over workers' self-activity. There is also strong evidence from the late 1930s on for an ideological and political campaign waged to reestablish capitalist hegemony. The two-fold goal of this movement was to label labor and the state in general as Communist and a threat to American democracy and to promote these ideas through a variety of channels.

Conservative ideologues and journalists and a growing number of American businessmen worked to create a dense network of right wing institutes, a new political language and to harness these new ideas in political campaigns. Spanning the late 1940s to the mid-1960s, these ideological campaigns were organized around candidates, national anti-labor legislation, and state right-to-work laws. Capitalist funding for employer-associated institutes such as the Foundation for Economic Education and the American Enterprise Association (precursor to the American Enterprise Institute) and right wing journals like the *National Review* were part of this process, which had the dual mission of restoring *laissez-faire* and rolling back Soviet-style Communism.[37]

The central signifier of this political and ideological effort was free enterprise. For the past four decades, hundreds of thousands of business students have passed through the ranks of "Students in Free Enterprise" (SIFE). This Wal-Mart-funded project first flourished in small southern Christian business schools and has become a massive international organization seeding extreme pro-business ideology in countless universities and colleges.[38]

Elizabeth Fones-Wolf's *Selling Free Enterprise* (1995) details the 1940s' origins of this movement. In propaganda campaigns, waged in the employer-controlled workplace, in communities, in the halls of state capitals, and in Congress, individual employers and their associations (especially the National Association of Manufacturers and the Chamber of Commerce) aimed squarely at changing societal understandings about labor and the state. Union legitimacy was especially targeted. Says Fones-Wolf:

> ... unions, business leaders complained, had drenched the minds of workers in a "reckless propaganda of distortion, deceit, and phoney [*sic*] economics." ... [B]usiness not only sought victory at the bargaining table and in the halls of Congress but also sought to win the hearts and minds of American workers. To accomplish this task ... employers [*sought*] to send a message that business had solved the fundamental ethical and political problems of industrial society, the basic, "harmony between the self-interest of our economic institutions and the social interests of society."[39]

These efforts dovetailed with the top-down creation of a conservative intellectual movement to carry forward the fight against liberal (in the U.S. political sense) hegemony. Right wing thinkers such as Friedrich Hayek and his circle in the Mont Pelerin Society attracted strong business support, providing a language and analysis for this fight.[40] Small-business owners had reacted strongly to Roosevelt's effort to pack the Supreme Court, and this reaction promoted an alliance between large and small business. The older anti-monopoly stance of organizations representing small business faded as it increasingly identified itself with the interests of capital in general. This occurred as conservative economists were abandoning their critique of monopoly power.[41]

Hayek's uncompromising indictment of welfare as "The Road to Serfdom" was an instant hit in this new business alliance. In 1945, *Reader's Digest* published an abridged reprint of his attack on burgeoning social democracy, which quickly reached a million households in the United States. Right wing activists forged thick connections between the Mont Pelerin Society and a broad network of conservative American intellectuals and businessmen in the 1950s.[42] Early leaders in this movement, like Lemuel Boulware, the infamous labor relations director of General Electric and a chief propagandist and organizer for the capitalist reaction, made the extraordinary claim at the height of anti-Communist paranoia that unions and the welfare state were far greater threats to American employers than the Soviet Union itself.[43]

As employers joined this ideological movement, they also operated directly to thwart the spread of unionism. The defeat of the CIO's postwar Operation Dixie campaign (1946–1953) preserved the South as a political and economic bulwark against the New Deal and labor. At the level of the firm, many large Northern/Midwestern capitalists moved immediately after the Wagner Act to confront the emerging "New Deal industrial system" of unionized collective bargaining by creating what Jacoby calls "vanguard welfare capitalism."[44] Corporations such as

Thomson Products, Sears, Kodak, and IBM led the way in creating an alternative to unionism based on "humane" management methods, company unions or works councils, and modest benefits for long-term workers. While only a minority of American corporations adopted the full package of welfare capitalism, the existence of an alternative model provided a base from which to critique the New Deal system as unnecessary. The discrediting of the New Deal industrial relations system was well underway by the 1940s.

Even where organized capital appeared to be accepting of social democracy, this acceptance was tied to the restoration of employer hegemony in the workplace. Jennifer Klein's *For All the Rights* (2003) explains how American capital prevented the expansion of the welfare state, particularly thwarting national health care. Insurance companies were key early advocates and specialists in developing welfare capitalism in the 1910s and 1920s. Insurance companies first persuaded, and then collaborated with, large corporations, using private "welfare" policies to compete with unions and the state for employees' loyalty. The first step was an embrace of Social Security by insurance companies and some other capitalists in 1936 and 1937. Key employer associations opposed efforts to repeal Social Security, preferring instead to make peace with it while hemming it in. The approach was to keep it as a basic "safety net" to be supplemented by additional "security" provided by employer pensions. The next step in the early 1940s was to compete with emerging community health models supported by unions. To do so, insurance companies successfully promoted the idea of providing group health insurance benefits to employees. This costly investment paid several dividends for employers in their struggle to regain hegemony over employees. It bound employee's loyalty to their "good employers," and it also forestalled a move towards national health insurance, which would have reduced employers' control of their employees, not to mention the blow to health insurance companies.

The Exclusion of the Radicals

The legal taming of labor radicalism began in the early 1940s. Both the National Labor Relations Board and the courts narrowed allowable collective action. Though Roosevelt Administration labor policy during the war had favored membership growth, it restricted what labor could do, limiting the ability to strike and imposing a mandatory cooling-off period before strikes could begin. Union leaders were increasingly concerned that subordination of union power to the war effort was spreading apathy and resentment among their members.[45] While the Wagner Act had legalized collective bargaining, its interpretation had also reduced workers' potential for economic disruption.

Business leaders and their conservative allies, however, opposed even this narrow scope of union power; that is, the government-labor-management tripartism that was key to the war effort but that also legitimated organized labor, and the consequences of consolidated union power at the ballot box. Anti-union campaigns from the 1940s to the present day have had the dual goal of restoring capitalist hegemony in the workplace and at the polls.

With the Taft-Hartley Act in 1947, federal labor policy actively halted union growth. This revision of the Wagner Act prohibited political solidarity and wildcat strikes, required union officers to sign non-Communist affidavits, and allowed states to pass laws prohibiting union shops. By then capital had repaired its rifts, and the coalition supporting Wagner had frazzled. Senators from farm states both in and outside the South abandoned their support of Wagner. The AFL-CIO split, and the growing salience of anti-Communism meant that it was impossible to produce a united labor front. Labor's leverage was also reduced because it had become so firmly wedded to the Democratic Party, a party that did not return its love. While President Truman vetoed Taft-Hartley, "only seventy-one House Democrats voted to sustain the President's veto while 106 voted to override it. In the Senate twenty Democrats voted to override the veto, and twenty-two voted to sustain it."[46]

Once agricultural workers were excluded, a majority of Southern senators supported the Wagner Act. But they became increasingly wary of *any* labor legislation after the Southern Tenant Farmers Union (STFU) began to organize tenants and sharecroppers in the South in the mid-1930s. These tensions increased with the dramatic growth in union strength during and immediately after the war. Between 1939 and 1953, union membership rose faster in the South than in the rest of the country. War-time growth was followed by postwar organizing drives by both the AFL and CIO, and while these largely failed, they were seen as a direct attack on the Southern labor system, causing planters to join Northern capitalists in opposing Wagner. Eighty-five percent of Southern senators supported Taft-Hartley, and by 1953, every Southern state except Louisiana had passed a right-to-work law. Groups representing farmers outside the South, such as the Farm Bureau, also supported Taft-Hartley because they saw strikes and secondary boycotts as limiting their ability to get crops to market. The split between labor and various kinds of farmers allowed capitalists to heal their divisions, and the alliance of Southern Democrats and Northern Republicans was sealed by the results of the 1946 congressional election. This conservative shift was itself partly due to the strike wave of 1944–1946 and capitalists' ability to organize against labor's agenda for the postwar recovery.[47]

From the depths of the Depression to the late 1940s, a progressive option had been on the table in the United States involving national economic planning and shared corporate governance. It was only at the end of the 1940s that progressive forces in the labor movement were forced to accept "the pursuit of economic security through a private, depoliticized system of collective bargaining" with a state that largely limited itself to pursuing high consumption through monetary and fiscal policy only.[48] Those who were fully included—unionized workers and the expanding group of white collar workers—found a definition of the good life in which leisure was superior to work, individual expression was valued over social solidarity, and private family life over public civic life. The older language of workers' control and payment for the "full fruits of our labor" gave way in the 1940s and 1950s to a rhetoric of personal satisfaction for the semi-skilled operatives whose lot was improved by the New Deal.

The system that emerged included decentralized and highly detailed collective bargaining at the individual firm or plant level, minimal social welfare spending, and labor market segmentation. The end game for a more radical labor strategy was between 1946 and 1948, when business and conservative interests blocked labor's attempt to create a social democracy based on planning and social solidarity. "This forced retreat narrowed the political appeal of labor-liberalism and contributed both to the demobilization and division of those social forces which had long sustained it."[49] Of course, much of the labor movement had never embraced a class vision of unionism. After 1948, labor as a whole developed an interest-group politics based on growth and productivity gain sharing, and it was even this narrow view of the good society that was lost, post-1980.

Labor's ambitious postwar social agenda had included support for Roosevelt's "Four Freedoms" and his "Economic Bill of Rights," a continuation of tripartite planning mechanisms established during the war, full employment and national health insurance. This had been prefigured by the CIO's wartime tripartite governance plan, "an admixture of Catholic social reformism and New Deal era faith in business-labor-government cooperation."[50] Labor progressives in the 1940s assaulted traditional management power in the name of economic efficiency and the public interest, usually through "tripartism," the notion that cooperation among unions, management, and government at the national level was key to prosperity and social stability. In Europe, many right wing capitalists were legitimately seen as having been collaborators or appeasers and thus were open to tripartism as a way to rehabilitate themselves, but conservative American business leaders had *improved* their social standing during the war and saw little need for the forms of labor–management cooperation or worker voice that were developing in Germany, France, Italy, and the Nordic states. Moreover, as the economy rebounded from the short but sharp 1945 recession, Keynesian economists began to think that the economy could be stabilized through fiscal and monetary policy without a structural shift in the distribution of power.

One of labor's key demands after the war was a reconversion wage increase to make up for wartime inflation and to sustain aggregate demand. This had few supporters outside union ranks. Still, the strike wave of 1945–1946 showed that labor radicalism was still alive. General strikes in Oakland, Pittsburgh, and Rochester led to union victories, and smaller ones in Lancaster, Stamford, and Akron constituted a national movement. The United Auto Workers (UAW) demanded that General Motors raise wages by 30 percent without increasing car prices or "open their books" to union inspection to show why this was not possible. GM's successful resistance to these demands indicated that progressive labor's hope of reshaping class relations in American society as a whole faced long odds. Instead, by the early 1950s, the UAW worked for privatized welfare that succeeded in providing security for employed autoworkers while giving up on national programs based on citizenship alone.

This wave of strikes, resulting in pay increases, and capitalists' ability to raise prices subsequently led directly to Republican victories in the congressional elections of 1946 and the campaign for Taft-Hartley. That law, in addition to curbing inter-union solidarity, eliminated the radical cadre and contained the labor movement demographically and geographically. It "encouraged contractual parochialism and penalized any serious attempts to project a class-wide political-economic strategy."[51] The elimination of the radicals removed both an important source of activism promoting class solidarity and any class analysis of the situation facing labor. Women, white-collar workers, and people of color were over-represented in the expelled unions. Indeed, labor segmentation and consequent narrowing of the basis for labor politics in the postwar era is at least partly traceable to the expulsion of the radical unions.

The best estimate is that between 17 and 20 percent of CIO members were expelled from the organization, or between 750,000 and 900,000 people.[52] Most of these were people working outside manufacturing, and they reflected the diversity of the working class more fully than those unions that remained in the CIO. For instance, the United Office and Professional Workers (UOPWA) had organized thousands of insurance agents and clerical workers and had begun successful organization of New York banks and Wall Street. Management certainly thought UOPWA was a threat, one indication being a flurry of articles on declining worker morale and the dangers of unions which appeared in the trade press in the mid-to-late 1940s.[53] When these groups were expelled from the CIO, any hope for a labor-based civil rights movement, a socialist labor federation, or a working-class political party went with them.

Subsequent to the general strikes of 1945–1946, labor suffered a series of defeats whose longer-term consequences were devastating. Operation Dixie, the attempt to organize the South, was a total failure. A series of organizing drives had already been defeated in textile factories in 1946. In the broader Dixie campaign, CIO leaders excluded Communists (even before Taft-Hartley) and "fellow travelers" such as members of the Highlander Center.[54] Two of the most dynamic unions in the South, the Union of Mine, Mill and Smelter Workers and the Food, Tobacco, Agricultural and Allied Workers, were heavily black and hospitable to Communists. They were largely avoided by non-radical unions before Taft-Hartley and systematically raided after. The New Deal's agricultural policy would eventually proletarianize millions of blacks and transform the Democratic Party, but in the short run it mainly created a labor surplus. The early postwar labor policy did nothing to organize that surplus labor, although conditions were ripe, given the organizing efforts of radical multiracial unions during the Depression and the World War.[55]

In the North in the 1940s, mass unionization was central to the struggle for civil rights. Although racist discrimination in hiring was still rampant, the rise of the industrial unions and the existence of the National Labor Relations Board generated a class-based rights consciousness. In fact, according to Korstand and Lichtenstein, "By the mid-1940s, civil rights issues had reached a level of national political salience that they would not regain for another fifteen years."[56] But the employer offensive of the late 1940s isolated left wing black leaders and destroyed the Popular Front.

This management offensive was especially destructive of newly organized locals that had especially large numbers of black members. The narrowing of the collective bargaining agenda meant it was more difficult to develop a labor politics specific to black workers. Remaining unions, race-based organizations, and liberal advocacy groups began to take a legal/bureaucratic rather than an organizing approach to civil rights. In other words, rather than seeking power in the workplace, they sought redress through law and the courts. "The rise of anti-communism shattered the Popular Front coalition on civil rights, while the retreat and containment of the union movement deprived black activists of the political and social space necessary to carry on an independent struggle."[57] The working-class-based civil rights movement of the 1940s had little impact on or participation in the movement that would arise a generation later. That the later movement was based in the churches and student groups rather than the unions may partly explain why it failed so completely to solve the difficult economic problems faced by the great numbers of lower-income blacks. Martin Luther King's increased emphasis on economic and not just civil rights at the end of his life was an attempt to address this, an attempt that failed in the wake of his death.

The closing scene in this tragedy might be Henry Wallace's insurgent presidential campaign in 1948. His program included friendlier relations with the Soviet Union and an end to the emerging Cold War, ending segregation, with full voting rights for blacks, and universal government-sponsored health insurance. The campaign foundered for a number of reasons beyond our focus here, but also because it ran up against the two pillars of the emerging Cold War consensus: barring Communists from labor organizations domestically and the anti-Communist rhetoric of the Marshall Plan internationally. As Nelson Lichtenstein has written, the failure to build an independent labor party may have been "over-determined" by the peculiarities of American politics, Cold War ideology, the highly uneven geographical development of union representation, ethnic and racial divisions of the working class, and other factors, but the costs of that failure were very high.[58] The South was preserved as a union-free underdeveloped colony within the United States. Even in the North, unions rarely played any role greater than junior partner in the Democratic coalition. They had no way to exert systematic pressure on the party at either state or national level and no way to create a union culture within the party. Along with the prosperity of the postwar era, this explains the gradual demobilization and depoliticization of the working class, as its consciousness came to be shaped by the vague populism of the Democrats or the narrow interests of their individual unions.

The defeat of the Communists and their CIO allies eliminated the major barrier to the management-friendly contracts that came to characterize the post–World War II period. Writing in the early 1990s, Stepan and Zeitlin observed, "This defeat, not capitalism's cunning, accounts for the unions' capitulation to management and for the unchallenged hegemony of capital in the regnant political regime of production in the United States today."[59] If capital was hegemonic in the early 1990s, how much more so today, with private-sector unionization below 10 percent and worker rights jeopardized in supposed labor strongholds like Wisconsin and Michigan?

The Communists were defeated, not because they were poor unionists, but because of the overwhelming power of business conservatives and their allies, the willingness of non-Communist trade unionists to sacrifice them for the survival of bread and butter unionism, and their own tactical errors. After the expulsion of leftists, the CIO merged with the AFL, attempts to organize the unorganized were abandoned for the most part, and the merged federations failed to challenge the politics of capitalist hegemony on the shop floor or in the state. We will never know how far a third, radical labor federation could have pushed an anti-capitalist agenda in production, by limiting management "rights," rejecting strike prohibitions and long-term contracts, and pushing grievance procedures favorable to unions. The evidence from the radical remnants—the United Electrical Workers and the International Longshore and Warehouse Union—indicates there was a possibility for a vital, left-led organized working class had the CIO not fragmented.

Despite the best efforts of United Auto Workers president Walter Reuther and others, the expansion of the state in the sphere of domestic policy was also stopped in this period. Most labor leaders initially rejected cost-of-living adjustments (COLAs) in collective bargaining agreements as they sought a large increase in real living standards through a general reconversion wage increase, and they wanted to avoid the down escalator when a period of deflation developed, as it had in the 1930s. The UAW saw its immediate postwar contract agreements as a holding action. Nonetheless, the 1950 "Treaty of Detroit," which connected wage increases to the rate of inflation and increases in productivity and established pension and health insurance plans for GM workers became the archetypal union contract. Labor agreements patterned on the GM contract accepted the existing income distribution, corporate hegemony in the workplace, and privatized pensions and benefits. According to *Fortune* magazine: "It is the first major union contract that explicitly accepts objective economic facts—cost of living and productivity—as determining wages, thus throwing overboard all theories of wages as determined by political power and of profits as 'surplus value.'"[60] Cost-of-living adjustments, private pensions and private health care, the security enjoyed by the unionized working class, were part of the retreat from the earlier, progressive postwar agenda.

The same forces of organized capital that had gutted the Full Employment Act of 1946 and promoted Taft-Hartley destroyed the attempt to raise the social wage. "Nothing more clearly distinguishes the post-war political climate of the USA from that in Great Britain than the almost unqualified refusal of its legislature to respond to proposals for social reform."[61] "Pattern bargaining," by which wage and benefit conditions in union strongholds were imagined to spread to other sectors, had "a remarkably anemic life. As a result, wage disparities increased dramatically within the postwar working class."[62]

One legacy of the immediate postwar period then was the erosion of working-class solidarity. Workers felt doubly taxed: by union dues for their own pensions and health care and by government for the minimal welfare provided to the poor.[63] This perceived double taxation lay at the root of working-class racism. Thus support for the New Deal welfare state eroded even within the organized working class. Once universal health and full employment programs were defeated, labor took care of the interests of its members through collective bargaining and largely withdrew from the struggle over the structure of the political economy. This had debilitating consequences, opening up the working class to conservative cultural appeals and eliminating what might have been a dissonant voice in the celebration of the "American way of life."

The late Truman and Eisenhower years solidified the "commercial Keynesian" consensus—capitalism worked just fine if government used fiscal and monetary policy to create reasonable levels of employment and collective bargaining, and union threat effects made sure that workers got "their share." This settlement was contested by an increasingly organized and influential right wing reaction but not by an active and organized left.

A new wave of social turmoil arose in the 1960s, but the possibility of its developing into a drive for social democracy had largely been closed off by the nature of the defeat in the 1940s. The United States did not turn to the left at the end of the sixties, not because of some timeless American antipathy to socialism, but because of the closing off of the social democratic initiative in the 1940s; that is, the shutdown of the New Deal's left wing and the victory of the corporate crusade for the hearts and minds of workers through the campaign for free enterprise, a campaign that accelerated in the 1960s and 1970s. In both the Kennedy and Johnson years, economists committed to commercial Keynesianism became increasingly influential and had no use for state involvement in capital and labor markets. Presidents John F. Kennedy and Lyndon B. Johnson both went out of their way to pander to business interests.[64]

The failure to transform the South through organizing meant that the Democrats' commitment to civil rights and economic abundance for all—dragged out of the Kennedy brothers by Martin Luther King, Jr., and pushed successfully by Johnson—required extraordinary judicial action in the absence of the popular support that might have been forthcoming from a unionized South. Of course, those extraordinary judicial actions were met by violence. Great Society policymakers "imprisoned by the 1940s ideological framework they inherited, lacked the necessary intellectual autonomy and clarity."[65]

Lessons for Today

The incorporation of labor within a set of governing institutions in the "Third New Deal" limited what it could accomplish and sowed the seeds of its decline. By positioning labor as an interest group rather than a class and by eliminating labor's left wing, the New Deal system narrowed the path for radical change and made labor vulnerable to the politics of class fragmentation pursued by the New Right.

The heightened ideological class struggle waged by capitalists and their allies in the 1970s and 1980s led to the erosion of what union power remained and a gross increase in inequality and exploitation. It is not surprising that progressives would be nostalgic for the days when unions had a positive impact on wages and working conditions, but as we have seen, the limited gains made in living standards and social solidarity associated with the New Deal were powerfully driven by socialist and Communist forces in the labor movement. No one starts a revolutionary organization to achieve reform; nonetheless, this was one effect of labor-movement radicalism. Without a significant revolutionary presence in today's working class, contemporary calls for a "New, New Deal" are pure fantasy or wishful thinking. Even if such a "New, New Deal" could be achieved, there is no reason to believe it could be sustained without a program challenging capitalists' control of the economic surplus and the ideological apparatuses.

Is a militant labor movement even possible today? Globalization of production means that in some industries (such as electronics, apparel, and footwear), taking wages out of competition necessarily involves organizing across national boundaries and vast national differences in wages. Yet the communications revolution associated with globalization also means that we are aware of these differences as never before, and response to remote suffering now occurs on an almost real-time basis. The exploitive policies of the most-admired companies, such as Apple, are widely publicized.[66] This seems to be affecting the speed with which reform occurs. Compare, for instance, the nearly half century it took between the initial establishment of factory regulation in England and the effective enforcement of that regulation with the current speed of change in factory conditions in China.[67]

The shift from manufacturing to services is also seen as a barrier to militant labor in that services have traditionally been difficult to organize. Yet some of the most militant unions in the United States today are in health care and hospitality services. The National Nurses United made common cause with Occupy Wall Street to demand a "Robin Hood tax" to heal America. Hotel workers, many of them first-generation immigrants, have organized corporate campaigns that pressure large hotel chains by stimulating and utilizing grassroots energy. Many of these immigrants come from cultural backgrounds in which solidarity and even socialism are more powerful concepts than individual gain. These campaigns are based on collaboration between grassroots, working-class leadership and progressive, college-trained activists with roots in the student anti-sweatshop and immigrant-rights movements.[68]

There is no question that creating a new, militant movement of working people faces daunting challenges. In addition to globalization and deindustrialization, there is the very real possibility of a secular decline in labor demand due to technological change. Yet there are reasons to be hopeful. Perhaps because of its weakness, segments of the American labor movement are as innovative and dynamic as any in the developed world. Because women and racial minorities form a disproportionate share of public-sector workers, increasing union membership there has changed the American labor movement's racial and gender composition. For instance, women comprised only 19 percent of American union members in the mid-1950s, but today nearly half of union members are women.[69]

The best survey data indicate that workers want unions more than ever and that union members continue to enjoy superior compensation and more say over working conditions.[70] Employer resistance is the most important reason why unions find it hard to grow. Where employers do not resist, unions have success. In the public sector and in the case of some private employers where workers have free choice to join a union, they are as likely as they ever were to join. If workers knew they had a government committed to workplace democracy, another union revival might be possible.

Union growth tends to come in spurts, when workers are willing to overthrow the rational calculation of short-term self-interest for the joy of participating in a common project. These brief periods of social upheaval usually involve major demonstrations and strikes when large numbers see their fellow workers publicly demonstrating a shared commitment to the collective project. In a survey of thirteen countries between 1880 and 1985, Gerald Friedman found that 67 percent of union growth came in only five of those 105 years, and 90 percent in only ten of those years.[71]

Such a shared collective project is unlikely to be inspired by calls for a "New, New Deal," for better labor–management cooperation, or for any other slogan associated with reformist liberalism. It is more apt to come out of the immigrant communities, especially the second generation for whom just being in America will not be enough, and to take shape fully when native-born Americans can make common cause with immigrants around workplace and social justice. The lesson of the New Deal is that a radical movement can make real social change when government is even only mildly supportive.

The success of the anti–New Deal coalition in first limiting and then undermining the New Deal also provides an important lesson. Sticking to first principles and developing one's arguments over a long period of time, while building alliances with like-minded and somewhat like-minded groups, can pay off when the world changes in such a way that what was once considered crazy becomes common sense. The "free market" cause seemed hopeless to some in the 1930s and 1940s, but intellectuals like Hayek and management theorists like Boulware kept the faith. Those hoping for a more just and equal society might learn something from the opponents of the New Deal as well.

Notes

1. Kris Warner, "Protecting Fundamental Labor Rights: Lessons from Canada for the United States," Center for Economic and Policy Research, Washington, D.C., August 2012, accessed January 15, 2013, available at http://www.cepr.net/documents/publications/canada-2012-08.pdf.
2. For detailed discussion see John Godard, "The Exceptional Decline of the American Labor Movement," *Industrial & Labor Relations Review*, 63, no. 1 (2009):82-108, accessed January 10, 2013, available http://digitalcommons.ilr.cornell.edu/ilrreview/vol63/iss1/5/; Jon Schmitt and Alexandra Mitukuewicz, "Politics Matter: Changes in Unionization Rates in Rich Countries, 1960–2010," Center for Economic and Policy Research, Washington DC, November 2011, accessed January 15, 2013, available at http://www.cepr.net/documents/publications/unions-oecd-2011-11.pdf.
3. Most progressive economists and sociologists in the United States accept such an accord uncritically. The classic statement is David Gordon, Richard Edwards, and Michael Reich, *Segmented Work, Divided Workers: The Historical Transformation of Labor in the United States* (Cambridge, MA: Cambridge University Press, 1982).
4. Richard McIntyre and Michael Hillard, "Capitalist Class Agency and the New Deal Order: Against the Notion of a Limited Capital-Labor Accord," *Review of Radical Political Economics*, 45, no. 2 (June 2013): 129–148.
5. Sanford Jacoby, "American Exceptionalism Revisited: The Importance of Management," in *Masters to Managers: Historical and Comparative Perspectives on American Employers*, Sanford Jacoby, ed. (New York: Columbia University Press), 173–200; Wolfgang Streeck and Kozo Yamamura, eds., *The Origins of Nonliberal Capitalism: Germany and Japan in Comparison* (Ithaca, NY: Cornell University Press, 2001); David Montgomery, *The Fall of the House of Labor: The Workplace, the State, and American Labor Activism, 1865–1925* (New York: Cambridge University Press, 1989); Nelson Lichtenstein, *State of the Union: A Century of American Labor* (Princeton, NJ: Princeton University Press, 2002).
6. For a more detailed discussion, see Michael Hillard and Richard McIntyre, "Historically Contingent, Institutionally Specific: Class Struggles and American Employer Exceptionalism in the Age of Neoliberal Globalization," in *Heterodox Macroeconomics: Keynes, Marx, and Globalization*, Jonathan P. Goldstein and Michael G. Hillard, eds. (New York: Routledge, 2009), 189–199.
7. The classic treatment is Karl Marx, *Capital: A Critique of Political Economy*, Vol. 1, Chap. 10, parts 6 and 7, accessed September 2, 2013, available at http://www.marxists.org/archive/marx/works/1867-c1/ch10.htm. The role of the factory inspectors and middle-class reformers is emphasized in Richard P. McIntyre, *Are Worker Rights Human Rights?* (Ann Arbor: University of Michigan Press, 2008), Chap. 7. The alliance among workers, middle-class lawyers, and Southern planters in passing the Wagner Act is a possible, largely unexplored exception.
8. Lichtenstein, 53; Theda Skocpol and Kenneth Finegold, "Explaining New Deal Labor Policy," *American Political Science Review*, 84, no. 4 (December 1990): 1297–1315.

9. John W. Jeffries, "A Third New Deal? Liberal Policy and the American State, 1937–1945," *Journal of Policy History*, 8, no. 4 (October 1996): 387–409.
10. G. William Domhoff, "The Wagner Act and Theories of the State: A New Analysis Based on Class-Segment Theory," *Political Power and Social Theory*, 6 (1987): 159–185; Theda Skocpol, "Political Response to Capitalist Crisis: Neo-Marxist Theories of the State and the Case of the New Deal," *Politics & Society*, 10 (March 1980): 155–201; Michael Goldfield, "Worker Insurgency, Radical Organization, and New Deal Labor Legislation," *American Political Science Review*, 8, no. 4 (1989): 1257–1282; "Explaining New Deal Labor Policy," *American Political Science Review*, 8, no. 4 (December 1990): 1298–1314; Frances Fox Piven and Richard A. Cloward, *Poor People's Movements: How They Succeed, Why They Fail* (New York: Vintage Books/Random House, 1979); *Regulating the Poor: The Functions of Public Welfare* (New York: Vintage Books/Random House, 1972).
11. Peter Phillips, "The 1934–35 Red Threat and the Passage of the National Labor Relations Act," *Critical Sociology*, 20, no. 2 (July 1994): 27–50.
12. Ibid., 43.
13. Goldfield, 1269.
14. Philips, 46
15. Ibid., 47.
16. Bill Winders, "Maintaining the Coalition: Class Coalitions and Policy Trajectories," *Politics and Society*, 3, no. 3 (September 2005): 393. In the mid-1930s industrial and craft workers voted together for the Democratic Party, a switch in that industrial workers had previously supported Republicans. The fight between the AFL and CIO would split the labor movement within a few years, but there was unity at the time of Wagner.
17. Whether Wagner received anything beyond passive support from capital is still a matter of controversy. The few capitalists that did express open support were executives of already unionized firms hoping that the unionization of their competitors would level the playing field. Thomas Ferguson claims that some corporate liberals from export-oriented, capital-intensive industries traded off support for Wagner for Roosevelt's commitment to pursue bilateral free trade agreements, but he provides little evidence. Thomas P. Ferguson, "From Normalcy to New Deal: Industrial Structure, Party Competition, and American Public Policy in the Great Depression," *International Organization*, 3, no.1 (Winter 1984): 41–94. Peter Swenson has argued that some employers gave "signals" to New Deal policymakers that indicated that while they could not publically support Wagner, they could live with it, but once again the evidence is spotty. Peter Swenson, "Varieties of Capitalist Interests: Power, Institutions, and the Regulatory Welfare State in the United States and Sweden," *Studies in American Political Development*, 18, no. 1 (April 2004): 1–29.
18. Goldfield, "Explaining New Deal Labor Policy,"1305.
19. See, generally, James A. Gross, *The Making of the National Labor Relations Board: A Study in Economics, Politics, and the Law, 1933–1937* (Albany: State University of New York Press, 1974).
20. Winders, 416.
21. See Chapter 7 in this book where the hearings that demonstrate this are discussed.
22. Winders, 387–423.
23. Pub. L. 74-198, 49 Stat. 449, codified as amended at 29 U.S.C. § 151–169.
24. On the postbellum South as a form of feudalism, see Serap Kayetkin, "Sharecropping and Feudal Class Processes in the Postbellum Mississippi Delta," in *Re/Presenting Class: Essays in Postmodern Marxism*, J.K. Gibson-Graham, Stephen Resnick, and Richard D. Wolff, eds. (Durham, NC: Duke University Press, 2001).
25. Judith Stepan-Norris and Maurice Zeitlin, "'Red' Unions and 'Bourgeois' Contracts?" *American Journal of Sociology*, 9, no. 5 (March 1991): 1151–1200.
26. Steve Rosswurm, ed., *The CIO's Left-Led Unions* (New Brunswick, NJ: Rutgers University Press, 1992).

27. The most important way in which the independent radicals differed from the Communists was over the Party's unquestioning loyalty to the Soviet Union. Thus when Germany invaded the Soviet Union, Party members became vociferous in their support of the war effort, including the alliance with "progressive capital." In fact, they became so supportive of Roosevelt that they "failed to politically educate millions of 'new' workers to the realities of capitalism." Rosswurm, 10. The Party's militant secularism inflamed the hostility of Catholic working people. "The most fundamental criticism to be made of the CP and its trade-union cadre is that it failed utterly in its professed mission to build a socialist movement" (ibid., 11). Its penchant for secrecy also undermined movement building in a fundamental way.
28. Ibid., 12.
29. Marxists have long debated the limits that organized labor might be able to impose on capital within the sphere of production. This is a question both of the ability of unions to affect the relations of production on the shop floor and whether the political orientation of union leadership makes a difference. Because the capital–labor relationship is an incomplete contract, the political regulation of the workplace is not fully defined by capitalist relations of production. Regulation is partly accomplished through law, but laws themselves are responses to the class struggle in the workplace and society. The political regime of production is always contingent on a host of other factors. This perspective is most closely associated with Antonio Gramsci, who argued that trade unions take on a determinate historical form only as its members propose the policies and programs that define it. See Frank Annunziato, "Gramsci's Theory of Trade Unionism," *Rethinking Marxism*, 1, no. 2 (1988): 142–164. The evidence presented by Stepan and Zeitlin can be seen as a criticism of Lenin's pessimistic approach to trade unions.
30. Judith Stepan-Norris and Maurice Zeitlin, *Left Out: Reds and America's Industrial Unions* (Cambridge: Cambridge University Press, 2003).
31. H-NET online discussion, 1995, accessed January 12, 2012, available at http://h-net.msu.edu/cgibin/logbrowse.pl?trx=vx&list=hlabor&month=9504&week=c&msg=vXMp9oRI4vbGtahoNsUt%2BA&user=&pw=.
32. Christopher Tomlins, *The State and the Unions: Labor Relations, Law and the Organized Labor Movement in America, 1880–1960* (Cambridge, MA: Cambridge University Press, 1985). See also James Gross, *The Reshaping of the National Labor Relations Board: National Labor Policy in Transition* (Albany: State University of New York Press, 1981), 200–225.
33. On the campaign against the board, see Gross, ibid.,151–225; and on the result, see Tomlins, 148–251. See also Karl Klare, "Judicial Deradicalization of the Wagner Act and the Origins of Modern Legal Consciousness, 1937–1941," *Minnesota Law Review*, 6, no. 3 (March 1978): 265–340.
34. Stepan and Zeitlin, "Red Unions," 1184.
35. Sanford Jacoby, *Modern Manors: Welfare Capitalism since the New Deal* (Princeton: Princeton University Press, 1998), 242.
36. See especially Jacoby.
37. Right wing intellectuals and journalists actively solicited employer support for this new propaganda campaign—figures like Leonard Read, William Baroody, and William Buckley, a story told especially well by Kim Philips-Fein, *Invisible Hands: The Businessmen's Crusade Against the New Deal* (New York: W.W. Norton, 2010), 26–86.
38. Bethany Moreton, *To Serve God and Wal-Mart: The Making of Christian Free Enterprise* (Cambridge, MA: Harvard University Press, 2009).
39. Elizabeth Fones-Wolf, *Selling Free Enterprise: The Business Assault on Labor and Liberalism, 1945–60* (Champaign: University of Illinois Press, 1994), 67. The two quotes she cites here are from John W. Hill, "Industry's Iron Curtain," *Public Relations Journal*, 2 (November 1946): 3; and "Basic Elements of a Free, Dynamic Society," *Harvard Business Review*, 29 (1951): 57.
40. Robert van Horn and Phillip Mirowski, "The Rise of the Chicago School of Economics," in *The Road from Mont Pelerin: The Making of the Neoliberal Thought Collective*, Philip Mirowski and Dieter Plehwe, eds. (Cambridge, MA: Harvard University Press, 2009), 139–180; Philips-Fein.

41. Nelson Lichtenstein; Bethany Moreton; Robert Van Horn, "Jacob Viner's Critique of Chicago Neo-liberalism," in *Building Chicago Economics: New Perspectives on the History of America's Most Powerful Economics Program*, Robert Van Horn, Philip Mirowski, and Thomas A. Stapleford, eds. (Cambridge: Cambridge University Press, 2011), 279–300.
42. Philips-Fein, 41–51.
43. Ibid., 263.
44. Jacoby, 32.
45. Nelson Lichtenstein, *Labor's War at Home: The CIO in World War II* (Philadelphia: Temple University Press, 1981), 67–81.
46. Alexander Cockburn, "How Many Democrats Voted for Taft-Hartley?" *Counterpunch*, September 6, 2004, accessed September 2, 2013, available at http://www.counterpunch.org/2004/09/06/how-many-democrats-voted-for-taft-hartley/.
47. Winders, 403.
48. Steve Fraser and Gary Gerstle, eds., *The Rise and Fall of the New Deal Order, 1930–1980* (Princeton: Princeton University Press, 1990), xv.
49. Nelson Lichtenstein, "From Corporatism to Collective Bargaining: Organized Labor and the Eclipse of Social Democracy in the Postwar Era," in Fraser and Gerstle, 123.
50. Ibid.,125.
51. Ibid.134
52. Rosswurm.
53. Sharon Strom, "'We're No Kitty Foyles': Organizing Office Workers for the Congress of Industrial Organizations, 1937-1950," in *Women, Work and Protest: A Century of Women's Labor History*, Ruth Milkman, ed. (London: Routledge, 2012), 206–234.
54. The Highlander Folk School (now called the Highlander Research and Education Center) was founded in 1932 by activist Myles Horton, educator Don West, and Methodist minister James A. Dombrowski in Grundy County, Tennessee, as a safe place for workers throughout the South to meet to discuss grievances and to obtain education and training in labor organizing. The Center also saw itself as conserving the indigenous culture of the region. During the 1950s and 1960s, it served as the training ground for many of the leaders of the civil rights movement. It was often the victim of anti-Communist witch hunts.
55. Robert Korstad and Nelson Lichtenstein, "Opportunities Found and Lost: Labor, Radicals, and the Early Civil Rights Movement," *The Journal of American History*, 7, no. 3 (1988):786–811.
56. Ibid., 787, 799. See also Gross, *The Reshaping*, 5–41; Michael Honey, *Southern Labor and Black Civil Rights: Organizing Memphis Workers* (Urbana: University of Illinois Press, 1993).
57. Korstad and Lichtenstein, 811.
58. Lichenstein, "From Corporatism to Collective Bargaining," 139.
59. Stepan and Zeitlin, "Bourgeois Unions," 1191.
60. Cited in Lichtenstein, "From Corporatism to Collective Bargaining," 142.
61. Ibid., 142, quoting English political scientist Vivian Vale.
62. Ibid., 144.
63. Of course the expansion of social spending in the 1960s largely benefited middle-income households, especially through Medicare, but this was not always the perception.
64. Philips-Fein, 140–142.
65. Fraser and Gerstle, xxiii.
66. These problems include unpaid overtime, unsafe working conditions, violation of child labor laws, etc. See Charles Duhigg and David Barbosa, "In China, Human Costs Are Built into an iPad," *New York Times*, January 25, 2012, accessed April 1, 2012, available at http://www.nytimes.com/2012/01/26/business/ieconomy-apples-ipad-and-the-human-costs-for-workers-in-china.html?pagewanted=all&_r=0.
67. Keith Bradsher and Charles Duhigg, "Signs of Changes Taking Hold in Electronics Factories in China," *New York Times*, December 26, 2012, accessed April 1, 2012, available at http://www.nytimes.com/2012/12/27/business/signs-of-changes-taking-hold-in-electronics-factories-in-china.html?pagewanted=all.

68. Julius G. Getman, *Restoring the Power of Unions: It Takes a Movement* (New Haven, CT: Yale University Press, 2010).
69. U.S. Bureau of Labor Statistics, "Union Membership, 2011," USDL-12-0094, accessed January 15, 2013, available at http://www.bls.gov/opub/ted/2012/ted_20120130.htm; and Gerald Friedman, "Labor Unions in the United States," February 1, 2010, accessed January 15, 2013, available at http://eh.net/encyclopedia/article/friedman.unions.us.
70. Richard B. Freeman, "Do Workers Still Want Unions? More Than Ever." EPI Briefing Paper #182, February 22, 2007, Washington, D.C.: Economic Policy Institute, accessed January 10, 2013, available at http://www.sharedprosperity.org/bp182/bp182.pdf.
71. Friedman.

6

The New Deal's Direct Job-Creation Strategy

Providing Employment Assurance for American Workers

PHILIP HARVEY

> *Our greatest primary task is to put people to work. This is no unsolvable problem if we face it wisely and courageously. It can be accomplished in part by direct recruiting by the Government itself, treating the task as we would treat the emergency of a war, but at the same time, through this employment, accomplishing greatly needed projects to stimulate and reorganize the use of our natural resources.*
>
> —Franklin D. Roosevelt, First Inaugural Address, March 4, 1933

Of all the programs and legislative reforms comprising the Roosevelt Administration's response to the Great Depression, none is more emblematic of the New Deal than the era's direct job-creation programs—most famously the Works Progress Administration (WPA) and Civilian Conservation Corps (CCC). It might be supposed, therefore, that when Progressive economists consider whether the New Deal has anything to teach us about responding to the problem of unemployment, these are the initiatives that would attract their attention. But the only attribute of these programs that appears to interest Progressive economists today is their macroeconomic effect—as if the only thing they have to teach us about combating unemployment is the negative lesson derived from the Roosevelt Administration's failure to engage in enough deficit spending to end the Great Depression as quickly as it could have. The jobs provided to WPA and CCC workers simply do not register in their assessment, either because they assume those jobs are already accounted for in the multiplier effect of the deficit spending that created them, or because their Keynesian bias has blinded them to the possibility of addressing aggregate shortfalls in employment by means other than accelerating economic growth.

This chapter argues that this view of the New Deal's direct job-creation programs misses the most important lessons they have to teach us. It misperceives the multiple objectives they served in combating the labor-market effects of the Great Depression. It ignores the social welfare benefits that employment in the programs provided to millions of unemployed workers and their families; it discounts the value of the goods and services they produced for the nation's communities; it overlooks the ability of programs like the WPA to enhance the effectiveness of Keynesian anti-cyclical measures; and it disregards the ability of such programs to achieve the ultimate goal of Keynesian economic policy—sustained full employment.

To fill these gaps in our appreciation of the Roosevelt Administration's response to the problem of unemployment the chapter (1) reviews the history of the New Deal's direct job-creation initiatives; (2) describes the policy vision that motivated their establishment; (3) discusses the advantages of this strategy for achieving genuine full employment;[1] and (4) explains why the New Deal strategy would have would have constituted a better response to the "Great Recession" than the Keynesian strategy advocated by most progressive economists.

The Origins of New Deal Employment Policy

When the Roosevelt Administration assumed office in early 1933, a consensus existed across the relevant political spectrum that some form of government intervention in the economy was necessary to meet the relief needs of the population, reduce unemployment, and facilitate a return to prosperity. The continuing debate concerned the form this intervention should take. The Roosevelt administration was eclectic and pragmatic in the strategies it pursued, guided by varied and often conflicting visions of how the economy should be structured. It also had to contend with other centers of power and interest, both inside and outside government.

The policies that emerged in this context reflected compromises, not the pure application of a particular ideological agenda. The strategies pursued had various goals—to "prime the pump" of business activity, increase consumption, stabilize the financial system, increase the money supply, ease the availability of credit, promote "business confidence," reduce industrial strife, or introduce a measure of economic planning into the management of the economy. Ironically, in light of his reputation as a spendthrift, the one firm belief Roosevelt held regarding federal economic policy was that balancing the federal budget—if it were possible—would hasten the economy's recovery. Roosevelt was not alone in holding this view, and he made sure it was well represented in his administration—principally in his choice of Secretaries of the Treasury. When his advisors finally agreed the time was right to rein in spending, the result was the disastrous recession of 1937–1938 that delayed the economy's full recovery by several years.

Despite their differences, however, the New Dealers shared a common view of the general nature of the nation's joblessness problem. This view directly contradicted the presumption embedded in the nation's existing Poor Law system (and supported by the teaching of classical and neo-classical economists) that joblessness was a voluntary condition.[2] The New Dealers believed that joblessness was caused by a lack of jobs, not by a failure on the part of jobless individuals to seek or accept work. They believed that cutting wages would increase joblessness, rather than reduce it, because of its depressing effect on consumer purchases. The goal of government initiatives to combat joblessness should be to close the economy's job gap, not to correct the supposed moral failings of jobless individuals or to put pressure on them to seek and accept presumably available work. Concerns about the negative effects public assistance might have on jobless individuals persisted, but they were overwhelmed by concerns about the negative effects of joblessness itself. The New Dealers believed that society had an obligation to offer aid to persons denied the opportunity to be self-supporting, and that the stigma associated with the receipt of such assistance under the nation's existing Poor Law system was inappropriate.

Consistent with the eclecticism of the Roosevelt administration, a variety of reforms were initiated to address the joblessness problem. Some of these reforms focused directly on the problem of unemployment, such as the administration's direct job-creation initiatives. Others focused on problems that had an indirect effect on unemployment, such as the widespread use of child labor or the lack of old age pensions. All of the reforms they implemented pursued a common strategy consistent with the New Dealers' shared view of the nature of the unemployment problem. Their goal was to narrow the economy's job gap either by increasing the number of jobs available or by reducing the number of job seekers.

The most obvious strategy devised to achieve this goal was to use public funds to create jobs. They did this in two ways. The first was to increase federal funding for contracted public works. The second was to establish public employment programs for needy workers in which the government itself acted as the employer. In addition to the direct job-creation effect of these initiatives, it was believed they would stimulate job creation in the private sector by increasing both consumer purchasing power and capital goods orders.[3]

Contracted Work: The Public Works Administration

The New Deal's contracted public works initiative was implemented mainly through the Public Works Administration (PWA), established in the summer of 1933 with an initial \$3.3 billion authorization.[4] This was a sizable fiscal commitment for a government whose expenditures in 1933 totaled only \$3.4 billion[5] in an economy whose GDP equaled only \$56.4 billion.[6] Congress intended for these funds to be fully committed, if not fully spent within two years, so the net fiscal stimulus contemplated was on the order of 2–3 percent of GDP a year. All PWA project hiring was done by private contractors.

The program took much longer to spend its authorization than was contemplated, and other job-creation programs were adopted in the interim, but the PWA remained the primary source of funding for large-scale public works in the United States between 1933 and the end of the decade. Reauthorized and granted additional funding several times during this period, the PWA made grants totaling about $2.3 billion to state and local governments and another $1.8 billion to other federal government agencies for the support of public works construction projects. State and local governments contributed another $1.9 billion to this effort, though a significant portion of their contribution was initially financed with loans furnished by the PWA.[7] Thus, a total of approximately six billion dollars was spent on PWA projects between mid-1933 and the end of the decade, an average of about 1.3 percent of GDP annually.[8]

Between their establishment in mid-1933 and March 1939, PWA projects furnished approximately 1.7 billion hours of direct employment and paid wages averaging seventy cents per hour ($10.59 in 2012).[9] The maximum work week for individuals employed on these projects was originally set at thirty hours, though this was later raised to the industry standard of forty hours.[10] Based on this work week, the program provided an average of 183,204 jobs at any point in time, a figure that amounted to only three-tenths of 1 percent of the nation's labor force.

For each dollar spent on direct labor costs, however, PWA projects spent an average of $1.79 on materials, and the U.S. Bureau of Labor Statistics estimated that approximately 2.5 jobs were created in producing those materials for every job created within the PWA itself.[11] Adding these jobs to the average of 183,204 jobs provided directly on PWA projects results in an estimated employment effect of 485,000, or about 0.9 percent of the nation's labor force at the time.

This estimate of the program's employment effects is still incomplete, however, because it does not include the full multiplier effect of program expenditures. If the tail-end of the multiplier effect of PWA expenditures equaled fifty percent of the 485,000 jobs attributed to the program's direct purchases of labor and materials,[12] the overall employment effect of the program equaled about 750,000 jobs, or about 1.5 percent of the nation's labor force—in exchange for an annual investment that we have noted averaged about 1.3 percent of GDP between 1933 and 1939. The program was phased out during World War II, with its functions transferred to the Federal Works Agency in 1943.[13]

Direct Government Job Creation

Although the difference is often overlooked, it is important to distinguish the PWA's conventional public works model (which relied on private contractors funded by the government to hire workers and carry out projects) from the New Deal's direct job-creation initiatives (in which the federal government itself hired workers and carried out projects). The New Deal's direct job-creation effort was embodied in four major programs: the Civilian Conservation Corps (CCC) established in the spring of 1933 ; the Civil Works Administration (CWA), established as an emergency initiative using PWA funds in the winter of 1933–1934; the WPA, established in 1935; and the National Youth Administration (NYA) also established in 1935 (originally as the youth division of the WPA but later reorganized as a freestanding program).[14] The CWA lasted only four months, but the CCC, WPA, and NYA all continued to operate until the early 1940s, when they were phased out as spending on World War II and a dramatic expansion of the armed forces pushed the unemployment rate down to the genuine full employment level (1.9 percent in 1943).

Why, if Roosevelt believed in balancing the budget, was he willing to engage in deficit spending to fund programs like these? The principal reason was that there was one thing Roosevelt considered even more important than balancing the budget. That was the duty of government to fulfill its obligation to secure what he viewed as the right of every member of society to economic security. Simply stated, although he may have thought that balancing the federal budget was the road to recovery, Roosevelt believed the fulfillment of the government's social welfare obligations to the American people took priority over that goal.

Roosevelt's views on this point were always clear. In his principal campaign address on the federal budget in 1932, candidate Roosevelt excoriated President Hoover for his administration's failure to balance the federal budget, but he also made it clear that he was willing to operate in the red to meet human needs. After summarizing his strategy for cutting government expenses, he offered the following caveat.

> At the same time, let me repeat from now to election day so that every man, woman and child in the United States will know what I mean: If starvation and dire need on the part of any of our citizens make necessary the appropriation of additional funds which would keep the budget out of balance, I shall not hesitate to tell the American people the full truth and ask them to authorize the expenditure of that additional amount.[15]

This attitude created an opportunity for the president's social welfare advisors to play a particularly prominent role in shaping his administration's response to the problem of unemployment. Joblessness was not just an economic problem to be solved by promoting the economy's recovery. It was also a social problem that required the immediate intervention of government to provide for the needs of unemployed workers and their families. The most important and creative aspects of the New Deal's response to the problem of unemployment were viewed by the New Dealers themselves in this light—as social welfare rather than economic policy measures—and the social welfare strategy embodied in those measures was conceived and developed by the President's social welfare advisors rather than his economic advisors.

Harry Hopkins was Roosevelt's public relief administrator. A social worker with strong administrative experience, he was appointed by the president to head the Federal Emergency Relief Administration (FERA) established in the spring of 1933 to distribute $500 million in federal funds appropriated by Congress to shore up the nation's state-based and locally administered public relief system.[16] Hopkins's principal aide was another social worker, a white Southerner named Aubrey Williams, who grew up in poverty and was a lifelong champion of civil rights.[17]

Frustrated by the narrow range of reforms the FERA was empowered to make in the nation's existing social welfare system, Hopkins and Williams developed an alternative model for the delivery of public aid to the unemployed. In a conceptual memo outlining their plan, Williams wrote that "relief as such should be abolished."[18] Instead, the unemployed should be offered real jobs paying good daily wages, doing useful work suited to their individual skills. In other words, instead of offering the unemployed public relief, they should be offered quality employment of the sort normally associated with contracted public works. However, to minimize both the cost of the undertaking and the amount of time needed to launch it, the government should serve as its own contractor, and the projects undertaken should be both less elaborate and more labor-intensive than conventional public works.

In late October 1933, Hopkins pitched a job-creation proposal to President Roosevelt based on the model he and Williams had devised. Disappointed by the slow pace in getting the PWA up and running, and concerned about growing political unrest among the unemployed, Roosevelt was quick to embrace Hopkins's proposal. A week later, the Civil Works Administration (CWA) was formally established by executive order, with Hopkins at its head and an initial budget allocation of $400 million diverted from the PWA.[19]

The program was funded only through the winter of 1933–1934, but it still stands as the largest public employment program ever established in the United States. With a peak employment of 4.3 million in a labor force of fifty-one million, the CWA provided employment to about 8.4 percent of the nation's work force during its short existence.[20] The administrative task of establishing the CWA—which moved from nothing more than an idea to a fully operational program with four million employees in about ten weeks' time—was gargantuan. It employed seven and one-half times as many people as the rest of the federal government (civilian and military) combined.[21] A program of similar relative dimensions in the United States today would have to create almost thirteen million jobs.

Also, though it fell short of realizing the policy goals Hopkins and Williams had formulated for the reform of public aid for the unemployed—the creation of a program that offered unemployed workers jobs that were indistinguishable from regular employment and devoid of associations with public relief—it embodied enough features of that model to mark a sharp and definitive break with the nation's existing public relief system.

The most important constraint Hopkins and his associates faced in implementing their reforms was that they had only enough funding to create 4 million jobs at a time when 1) there were over 12 million unemployed workers[22] and 2) they had a continuing responsibility under the FERA to provide support for existing recipients of public assistance, about 40 percent of whom were families headed by unemployed workers enrolled in locally administered, poor-quality work relief programs of the sort Hopkins was intent on replacing.[23] If the CWA had been funded and authorized to provide jobs for all unemployed workers, the existing population of unemployed relief recipients could have been directed to apply for work in the program on the same basis as other unemployed workers. However, with only enough funding to create about 4 million jobs, the decision was made to reserve approximately half of the positions in the CWA for public assistance recipients (so that all FERA work relief participants could be transferred to the CWA) while using normal skill- and experience-based hiring criteria (subject to a statutorily mandated preference for war veterans) to fill the other half.[24]

Another constraint limiting Hopkins' options was that the CWA's initial $400 billion in funding was subject to the same statutory restrictions as the PWA. These included a requirement that the funds be used only for the planning and execution of construction projects. To allow for the employment of persons for whom such work would not be suitable, Hopkins used his limited pot of FERA funds to establish a parallel Civil Works Service (CWS) program for white-collar and professional workers (both male and female),[25] and a Women's Division (transferred to the CWA from the FERA) to provide non-construction projects for working-class women and to encourage the hiring of women in the CWS and in non-construction positions in CWA construction projects.[26]

Although it accounted for less than 5 percent of total program employment,[27] the CWS was quite successful and included some of the CWA's most innovative projects.[28] The Women's Division was far less successful. The U.S. work force was approximately 25 percent female at the time, and while confirmatory data are hard to find, there is no reason to believe they suffered less unemployment than men during the 1930s.[29] Nevertheless, only 12.4 percent of all CWA applicants were women, and only 7.5 percent of all program jobs went to women.[30] Hopkins' goal was to provide jobs for about 400,000 women—approximately 10 percent of total expected program employment—but the Women's Division struggled in its efforts to recruit women and to develop appropriate projects to employ them. The Division's staff consisted mainly of FERA personnel with backgrounds in voluntary charity work, and they tended to hold more traditional views of the functions of work relief than the engineers Hopkins hired to run the program's construction projects. This contrast was especially marked at the state and local level, and the Women's Division's very capable director, Ellen Woodward, had trouble getting her field staff to develop projects other than the sewing rooms associated with traditional public assistance. It is hardly surprising, therefore, that working-class women had trouble figuring out whether the CWA was offering them work or just a continuation of conventional public assistance.[31]

The Women's Division had more success developing appropriate work projects in collaboration with the CWS. These collaborative projects employed women in a wide range of endeavors, including nursing, education, social work, public health, child care, library work, and the collection of statistical data.[32] But given that the CWS created a total of only 211,000 jobs, it could hardly make up for the more limited employment opportunities provided women in the rest of the CWA.

African Americans and other people of color were also shortchanged. Discrimination on the basis of race or color was prohibited in the application of eligibility and wage standards, but the eligibility rule was a hard one to enforce at the local level where the actual hiring occurred. Moreover, segregated work assignments and, in some instances, wholly segregated work projects were tolerated. It was also common for skilled minority workers to be discriminatorily categorized as unskilled. The CWA staff in Washington did not direct or approve of this discrimination, but they did not object to it, either.[33]

On the other hand, non-white workers were paid the same as white workers with the same job classification, and this was enough to precipitate significant political opposition to the CWA in the South, where whites resented the idea of blacks' being paid the same wages they received, and employers relied extensively on cheap black labor. The experience of African Americans with the CWA was accordingly mixed, particularly in the South, where discriminatory practices were most common—and since almost 80 percent of the African American population of the United States still lived in the South at the time, it was the way the program functioned there that defined the experience most African Americans had with it.

Despite these shortcomings, 9 million people applied for the approximately 2 million CWA jobs that were not reserved for public relief recipients. This is a stunning figure, since national unemployment stood at less than 11 million at the time outside of FERA work relief programs.[34] To emphasize the non-relief character of this hiring, it was performed by the newly organized United States Employment Service (USES) rather than local relief offices. At the same time, however, it is worth noting that local relief offices were swamped with new applicants for public aid, since job seekers quickly realized that qualifying for relief was a surer means of getting a CWA job than applying for one through the USES.[35]

Special hiring procedures were also adopted for skilled craftsmen. Instead of requiring applicants for these positions to apply through the USES, unions were allowed to refer their members in accordance with customary procedures for the trades in question. More importantly, the CWA agreed not to fill these positions from among USES applicants unless a local union failed to refer enough qualified workers. In other words, the CWA formally adopted a union-shop policy for the skilled trades; however, local CWA administrators often ignored this policy unless local unions insisted on its observance.[36] It should be noted, however, that while this policy was supportive of unions, it reduced the access of African Americans to skilled work in the CWA because the craft unions that benefited from the policy were among the most racially discriminatory in the American labor movement at the time.[37]

The CWA's wage policies broke even more decisively with traditional relief practices than its eligibility standards. Customary practice in work relief programs had been to limit an individual's earnings to the family's "budget deficiency"—the difference between the family's available resources and their "need" as determined by local relief officials. Consequently, the number of hours an individual was required to work in a traditional work relief program depended on the size of the individual's budget deficiency, and this was true of FERA-funded work relief projects as well.[38] Thus, despite a minimum wage (30 cents per hour) that would have generated a twelve-dollar weekly income for a forty-hour work week, actual earnings on FERA-funded work relief projects averaged less than five dollars per week in the period immediately preceding the establishment of the CWA.[39]

No individual working-hour limitation existed under the CWA. Hourly wage minimums were generally higher than those paid in FERA work relief programs, but the more important difference was that everyone worked the same number of hours. The result was that average weekly earnings among CWA workers (about $15, until program funds began to run short in mid-January) were three times as great as the benefits received by individuals enrolled in FERA-funded work-relief projects.[40] In fact, average CWA earnings during this period were the highest of any New Deal direct job-creation program.[41]

The CWA's hourly wage scale was the same as the PWA's.[42] It was also national policy (though frequently ignored by program administrators at the state and local level) to recognize locally negotiated union contracts in the construction trades as determinative of prevailing wage rates.[43]

The hourly rates paid by the CWA were controversial because they were often higher than what employers in particular regions (especially the South) or industries (especially agriculture) were accustomed to paying. What this debate tended to ignore, however, was that the program's 30-hour work week limited the earnings of program employees below what their hourly wage rates suggested. Moreover, as program funds began to run short in mid-January, the program's work week was shortened to 24 hours in order to spread the remaining work as widely as possible. As a result, average program earnings declined from about fifteen dollars per week to about $11.30 per week, compared to average weekly earnings by privately employed workers of about $20 in 1933.[44]

Although Hopkins's goal was to give unemployed worker jobs that utilized their existing skills, statutory and practical limitations made this impossible in most cases. First, as previously noted, statutory restrictions limited the CWA to construction projects. Second, a pre-existing FERA policy required that projects be performed only on public property. Third, no project was supposed to be undertaken that would duplicate work normally performed by state and local government employees. Fourth, no projects were supposed to be approved that could qualify for funding by the PWA.[45]

Project selection was further constrained by timing issues and the desire to maximize the program's employment effect. This meant projects had to be labor-intensive and capable of completion in a short period of time. It also meant they could not require significant advance planning or be hard to shut down on short notice. Finally, project selection was subject to weather and political constraints.

Although the CWA hired its own work force and administered its own projects, the program relied on other government agencies (at the federal, state, or local level) to sponsor the projects it undertook. The involvement of state and local government sponsors was limited to providing plans for the projects and contributing the cost of the materials and supplies used to complete them. At the federal level the CWA assumed all program costs but still relied on the sponsoring agency to propose and plan the projects it undertook.

The quality of the sponsored projects varied widely. First, by taking over all FERA-funded work projects from the local relief officials who had been administering them, the CWA burdened itself with an initial portfolio of poor-quality activities. While the CWA gained direct administrative control over these projects, it took time to implement significant improvements in their quality.

A second large group of projects originated with suggestions for new undertakings by local government officials. Approval authority for these projects was exercised by state CWA administrators whose review of the projects was often cursory. The quality of these projects varied greatly. Where sponsors had already developed plans for suitable construction projects, the activities tended to be quite successful and provided good value. Where advance planning had not been completed, the results were less satisfactory, though the CWA's newly recruited and very competent Engineering Division was, over the life of the program, able to achieve steady improvement in the quality of the program's construction work.

A third large group of projects originated at the federal level. These projects were sponsored by a variety of federal government agencies, including the Treasury Department, the Departments of the Interior and Agriculture, the Commerce Department, and the War Department. Most were developed in collaboration with CWA staff and also required the approval of a special office established within the Engineering Division that vetted them for quality control purposes. By all accounts, the CWA's highest quality projects were found in this group.

As for the type of work performed, the single largest category of CWA projects consisted of road work, which accounted for 35 percent of all project expenditures and employed close to half the program's entire work force. The road work consisted mainly of minor repairs and improvements rather than new construction, and in many rural areas this was the only type of CWA work available.[46]

The CWA administration was not happy with the predominance of road work in the program's activities since it was associated both historically and in the public's mind with the kind of work relief the CWA was supposed to replace. Indeed, a significant proportion of these projects were taken over from FERA-funded programs. The difference between these earlier programs and their CWA counterparts was not immediately apparent to the public walking or driving by a CWA work crew. The fact that these projects were more visible than other, higher quality projects also made it more difficult for the CWA leadership to explain the innovative character of the CWA to the public.[47]

Nevertheless, it would be wrong to underestimate the social utility of this work at a time when state and local governments lacked the funds needed to maintain, let alone improve, the roads and highways upon which local commerce depended. The CWA built or improved over 250,000 miles of roads. In rural areas, improving farm-to-market roads was a priority. In urban areas, significant repairs and improvements were undertaken—such as a Chicago project that employed 11,500 CWA workers to lay brick pavement in a major street-improvement project.[48]

The next-largest category of CWA projects consisted of construction and repair work on public buildings. Accounting for about 15 percent of project expenditures, approximately 60,000 public buildings were repaired or constructed, two-thirds of which were schools. Public health and sanitation activities constituted another major activity. Almost 2,300 miles of sewer lines were laid or repaired, swamp-drainage projects to fight malaria employed 30,000 CWA workers, and 17,000 unemployed coal miners were employed sealing abandoned coal mines to protect ground-water supplies. CWA workers also were employed in emergency disaster relief—either fighting floods or assisting in post-flood cleanup and repair work.[49]

Other CWA project categories included improvements to public recreational facilities and to public transportation and utility systems. The program constructed 4,000 athletic fields, 2,000 playgrounds, 350 swimming pools, and 150,000 privies. Surprisingly, the CWA built 469 airports and improved another 529, but this was the dawning of the aviation age, and the facilities in question mainly consisted of unpaved landing fields.[50]

Because the CWS was not limited to construction projects and employed professionals, the projects it undertook were more varied. And since most of these projects were sponsored by federal government agencies, they also benefited from the attention of the CWA's Washington staff. Professional associations also assisted in the design and management of many of these projects.

Education projects provided jobs in local schools for 50,000 laid-off teachers. Another 13,000 kept small rural schools open through the winter, while 33,000 were employed in adult education and nursery school programs. Adult education classes staffed by CWS teachers were attended by 800,000 people during the winter of 1933–1934, and 60,700 preschool children attended CWS nursery schools. The latter were generously staffed and provided warm clothes, hot meals, medical care, and parent-education services in addition to childcare.[51]

Twenty-three thousand CWS nurses staffed a nationwide child health study, and 10,000 more were employed in a variety of other programs. The U.S. Coast and Geodetic Survey sponsored a triangulation and mapping project that employed 15,000 CWS workers. An aerial mapping project charted hundreds of U.S. cities and employed another 10,000 CWS workers. The National Park Service and the Library of Congress undertook a survey of the nation's historic buildings that provided work for 1,200 draftsmen. Over 70,000 people were employed in CWS pest-eradication campaigns, and a group of ninety-four Alaskan Indians was employed restocking the Kodiak Islands with snowshoe rabbits.[52] Descriptions of CWS cultural projects are described in Chapter 8.

The single largest category of CWS employment, though, consisted of work performed on statistical surveys. The Department of Commerce employed 11,000 CWS workers to conduct a census of real property in sixty cities. An Urban Tax-Delinquency Survey documented the fiscal condition of 309 cities. The CWA's own Statistical Division employed 35,000 CWS workers to collect and record data and documentation concerning program operations, labor market conditions, and the nation's public relief problem.[53]

The establishment of a program as large, as complicated, and as innovative as the CWA within a span of weeks was a major administrative achievement. A War Department engineer assigned to study the program compared it favorably to the country's mobilization effort in World War I.[54] A New Deal historian has called the CWA "one of the greatest peacetime administrative feats ever completed" in the United States.[55] It was a remarkable experiment, more ambitious in its goals than any other New Deal employment program. It contemplated nothing less than the replacement of means-tested work relief with a promise of public employment paying good wages and doing work of genuine social utility.

The quick demise of the program shows how controversial that idea was. Criticism of the program by conservatives was fierce, and support for it within the Roosevelt Administration was by no means unanimous. The president's own support for the program was ambiguous. He was not yet ready to commit the federal government to the operation of a massive, year-round public employment program for unemployed workers. Still, Hopkins and his associates continued to work toward their broad reform goals, hoping that by stepwise movement they could win the political support needed to establish a more sustainable, if less ambitious, version of the CWA. We shall see that this is exactly what they achieved with the establishment of the WPA in 1935.

New-Deal Work Relief in the 1934–1935 Period

Following the termination of the CWA, the FERA once again assumed responsibility for funding the nation's relief effort. Hopkins and his associates continued to direct that effort, and even though the CWA was politically unsustainable, they made a concerted effort to preserve as much as they could of the CWA model in FERA work relief programs. But, once again, the FERA had to rely on local relief officials to administer the work relief projects it funded, with employment on those projects limited to persons on relief. The common work week established under the CWA was also lost, as hours of work were once again determined by applying the "budget deficiency" principle. Work relief participants worked as many hours as were necessary to "earn" their family's public assistance grant. At first, the thirty-cents-an-hour minimum wage rate that had previously applied to FERA-funded work relief programs was reinstated. However, under political pressure from low-wage employers, particularly in the South, the thirty-cents- per-hour minimum was abandoned in November 1934. Henceforth, wage rates depended exclusively on locally prevailing wages, with no minimum wage floor.[56]

Under Hopkins's leadership, the FERA established a number of special programs that experimented with new forms of work relief. One was a part-time employment program for needy college students who might otherwise have been forced to drop out of college—the prototype for today's College Work Study program. Another was a Transient Program that provided both residential camps and work for a population that today would be referred to as "homeless."[57] Perhaps the most interesting of the FERA's innovations during this period, however, were "production for use" projects undertaken in cooperation with the Federal Surplus Relief Corporation (FSRC). The FSRC purchased surplus agricultural commodities in an effort to maintain farm prices and hence the livelihoods of farmers. These commodities were processed by FERA workers (including the canning of fresh fruits and vegetables and the production of clothing and bedding from surplus cotton) and then distributed to relief recipients outside market channels. This distribution was accomplished on an "over-and-above" basis, to prevent local relief agencies from counting the commodities received from the FSRC in determining the budget deficiencies of relief recipients.[58]

Business interests strongly opposed the FERA's "production for use" initiatives. One frequently voiced complaint was that the projects competed with private producers and hence reduced unsubsidized employment—despite the fact that the commodities at issue were distributed at no cost to people who otherwise would not have been able to afford them. The real source of business opposition was more accurately reflected in complaints that the projects challenged the private enterprise system and constituted a dangerous step down the road to government control of all industry. This opposition was strong enough that Hopkins was forced to abandon the production-for-use model by the time the WPA replaced the FERA in the spring and summer of 1935.[59]

Employment Assurance and the WPA

In June of 1934, shortly after the termination of the CWA, President Roosevelt appointed a Cabinet-level Committee on Economic Security (CES) to develop a comprehensive social welfare strategy that would be responsive to the American people's desire for "some safeguard against misfortunes which cannot be wholly eliminated in this manmade world of ours."[60] Chaired by Secretary of Labor Frances Perkins, the other members of the committee were Secretary of the Treasury Henry Morgenthau, Attorney General Homer Cummings, Secretary of Agriculture (later Vice-President) Henry Wallace, and Harry Hopkins.

The committee's report, officially delivered to the president in January 1935, proposed a two-legged social welfare strategy—one leg to address the economic security needs of those members of society who could support themselves if adequately paid work were available for them, and the other to address the economic security needs of people who were either unable or not expected to be self-supporting.[61]

The first leg of this strategy adopted the plan Hopkins and Williams had developed and tested with the CWA. Specifically, the report proposed that the federal government provide unemployed workers with "employment assurance" in both good times and bad.

> Since most people must live by work, the first objective in a program of economic security must be maximum employment. As the major contribution of the Federal Government in providing a safeguard against unemployment we suggest employment assurance—the stimulation of private employment and the provision of public employment for those able-bodied workers whom industry cannot employ at a given time. Public-work programs are most necessary in periods of severe depression, but may be needed in normal times, as well, to help meet the problems of stranded communities and overmanned or declining industries.[62]

The second leg of the CES strategy relied on the establishment of a series of income-transfer programs designed to insure that everyone who was either unable or not expected to be self-supporting would be assured a reasonable subsistence. The best-known of the programs proposed by the CES to perform this function was the contributory old-age pension system that subsequently came to be known as Social Security; but the CES report included proposals addressing a range of other income security needs as well.[63]

Given Hopkins's role in developing the CES's employment assurance proposal, it is hardly surprising that it reflects the reform vision he and Aubrey Williams had previously developed. At the same time, that vision is enhanced in the CES report by its linkage to reforms proposed to meet the economic security needs of persons who cannot rely on work for their support. If fully implemented, the two legs of the social welfare system proposed by the CES would have effectively secured what subsequently came to be called the "right to work" and the "right to income security" in international human rights law.[64]

Given the expansiveness of the CES's employment assurance proposal, it is striking how far short of that goal the Roosevelt Administration aimed its implementation efforts—especially when compared to the virtually complete incorporation of the CES's income security proposals in the Social Security Act.[65] Established by executive order and a budgetary enactment a few months before the Social Security Act passed,[66] the WPA did not even attempt to provide work for all unemployed workers. Instead, it aimed only to provide work for unemployed workers who qualified for public relief. Moreover, in contrast to the reasonably good wages paid by the CWA (an average of $15.00 per week at first for 30 hours of work), the WPA paid a below-market "security wage" designed to provide an incentive for program workers to accept regular employment when it became available.[67]

It is true that Hopkins did his best, with partial success, both to minimize the onerousness of the program's means test and to raise program wages over time. Still, the program's eligibility requirements and low wages constituted a step backward (compared to the CWA) in Hopkins's efforts to sever the job creation he promoted from its continuing associations with public relief. The program also failed to eliminate the gender and race discrimination that tarnished the CWA.[68]

On the other hand, the program's administrative structure and the very substantial contributions it made to the country's physical and social wealth demonstrated Hopkins's sharp break with the past. As was true of the CWA, the vast majority of WPA projects were sponsored by state and local governments. These sponsors were responsible for providing all drawings for construction projects, and paid an average of about 20 percent of total program costs—usually in the form of purchases of supplies and materials. It was the WPA, though, that hired and supervised the program work force.[69] The WPA also adopted the CWA model of having federal agencies sponsor some of the program's more innovative projects—like the program's famous Art, Theatre, Music, and Writers' Projects.[70]

The WPA staff worked proactively with local governments and non-governmental organizations to develop new ideas for projects, especially in the non-construction fields. Since the WPA possessed a wealth of information concerning widely diverse projects operated under a variety of circumstances, WPA staff served as a viaduct for the dissemination of new ideas and best practices throughout the country. Program evaluators from the National Resources Planning Board who studied the WPA's operational model described it as achieving the advantages of both decentralized and centralized government control. The projects selected responded to local needs, while national standards of performance in carrying out the projects were maintained.[71]

This administrative structure permitted the WPA to operate its work projects on an "enterprise" rather than a "relief" model—notwithstanding the program's low wage scale and need-based eligibility standards. Once they qualified for the program, applicants were hired to fill specific job classifications on the basis of their experience and qualifications relative to other qualified applicants. When hired, they became federal employees who received a monthly paycheck in exchange for work performed—not a local welfare grant based on their "budget deficiency." If the income they received from their WPA earnings left them poor enough to qualify for relief (a fairly common occurrence for WPA workers with large families), they could still apply for public assistance from their local relief agency—on the same basis as privately employed workers and without involving the WPA in any way. Though low, WPA wage rates did vary with skill level and by region; a common work week was observed; and normal workplace discipline was maintained. WPA workers were covered by workers' compensation and were permitted to organize unions.

What accounted for the WPA's hybrid character—with one leg still stuck in the public relief tradition, while the program's organizational structure reflected the CES's reform goals? Moreover, why did Roosevelt allow the CES to advocate an employment assurance plan he was not prepared to fully implement (and which he might not have been able to get through Congress if he had tried)? It's a puzzling question. The CES also developed a national health insurance proposal, but when it became clear that the American Medical Association had both the intention and power to scuttle it, the president told the CES to drop the proposal from its published report.[72] Why didn't he tell the CES to scale back its job-creation proposal to match what he was prepared to implement?

One possibility is that Roosevelt was hesitant to commit to the employment assurance goal because he did not know how much it would cost to achieve it. No one knew in 1935 how many unemployed workers there were in the country because the government had not yet begun to collect unemployment data. The size of the fiscal commitment required to provide "employment assurance" to the nation's work force was therefore unknown, and given how many people had applied for work on the CWA—9 million in a matter of weeks—the president may have wondered whether the federal government really could take on the task. Any concerns he had on that score would have been encouraged by fiscal conservatives within his administration who applied constant pressure on him to restrict federal spending.

It is also possible that he remained unpersuaded that the federal government should assume responsibility for the task even if it could afford to do so. He knew the business community would be unalterably opposed to the idea—based on its concerted opposition to the CWA. He also knew, though, that the CWA model lacked strong institutional support among liberals. The social work profession, which one would have thought Hopkins and Williams represented, had considerable misgivings about the CWA experience because it dispensed with the individual casework that social workers viewed as the *sine qua non* of their professional role in assisting the poor.[73] The engineers and managers who had administered the CWA's work projects were strongly invested in completing the projects, but they did not view their mission as providing work for the unemployed.[74] Union members were happy for the jobs the program provided, but the role of unions in the CWA model was both unclear and unsettling for union leaders accustomed to representing private sector employees.[75] Civil rights organizations supported job-creation efforts but were disappointed by the Roosevelt Administration's failure to rid them of racist practices.[76] The list could go on. There simply was no organized liberal constituency that placed job creation for unemployed workers at the top of its agenda, and the president surely knew that.

In any case, Roosevelt made it clear in his 1935 State of the Union message, delivered as he was preparing to forward the CES report to Congress with his recommendations, that the "program for putting people to work" he would advocate was limited to creating security-wage jobs for those unemployed workers who qualified for public relief.[77] He made no mention whatsoever of the CES's employment assurance goal—which was thereby abandoned before it was even published.

But why, then, let the report be published with that recommendation intact—a recommendation that served as the foundation for the CES's entire economic security program? It may simply be that the report had already gone to press by the time Roosevelt made his decision to ignore the committee's employment assurance proposal. Another possibility may be the importance Roosevelt attached to the principle of societal obligation on which the employment assurance proposal was based—even if he was not prepared to press for its adoption. Roosevelt believed very strongly that society had an obligation to its members to insure their ability to support themselves. In a widely reported campaign address delivered to the Commonwealth Club of California in the fall of 1932, then–presidential candidate Roosevelt explained his views on this matter in the following terms.

> Every man has a right to life; and this means that he has also a right to make a comfortable living. He may by sloth or crime decline to exercise that right; but it may not be denied him. We have no actual famine or death; our industrial and agricultural mechanism can produce enough and to spare. Our government formal and informal, political and economic, owes to every one an avenue to possess himself of a portion of that plenty sufficient for his needs, through his own work.[78]

Roosevelt made it clear in the same speech that he assigned primary responsibility for securing this right to those he referred to as the "princes of property," who "claim and hold control of the great industrial and financial combinations which dominate so large a part of our industrial life." Only if they failed to fulfill their responsibility, he continued, would it fall upon government to "assume the function of economic regulation . . . as a last resort." He also made it clear that he had not yet given up hope, in the fall of 1932, that the "princes of property" would fulfill their duty in this regard. "As yet there has been no final failure, because there has been no attempt, and I decline to assume that this nation is unable to meet the situation."[79]

Four years later, in 1936, Roosevelt made it clear in his acceptance speech at the Democratic National Convention that the "princes of property"—whom he now referred to as "the royalists of the economic order"—had failed the test he set for them four years earlier; and in doing so he once again referred to the right to work as the touchstone by which the legitimacy of their power should be judged.

> The royalists of the economic order have conceded that political freedom was the business of the government, but they have maintained that economic slavery was nobody's business. They granted that the government could protect the citizen in his right to vote, but they denied that the government could do anything to protect the citizen in his right to work and his right to live.[80]

In short, the assertion of the CES that government should assume the duty of providing jobs for workers whom the private sector could not employ was an article of faith for Roosevelt, even if, as "Politician in Chief," he knew better than to ask Congress to authorize him to do it, and as "Fiscal Officer in Chief" he thought it was not something he could justify funding with additional deficit spending. Still, we might speculate that the broader commitment the CES advocated was close enough to his heart that he was willing to let it remain in the CES report.

It is also important to note that, even with the limited mandate given the WPA, it made a far greater dent in the nation's unemployment problem than is generally recognized. This accomplishment is obscured by the unemployment statistics commonly reported for the New Deal period, which count workers employed in these programs as unemployed rather than employed. If workers employed in direct job-creation programs are counted as employed (as they are in unemployment statistics today), we see that the nation's unemployment rate dropped from 22.9 percent to 10.0 percent during President Roosevelt's first term in office, rather than the commonly reported drop from 23.0 percent to 17.0 percent. The difference between the two sets of figures is attributable entirely to the effect of hiring by the FERA, CWA, and WPA. The WPA alone reduced unemployment by 4.4 percentage points during its first year of operations—8.9 percentage points, if we count as unemployed the workers who received public relief on a "budget deficiency" basis in locally administered work relief programs replaced by the WPA.[81]

Learning from the New Deal: The Social and Economic Benefits of Direct Job -Creation

As the CWA's accomplishments during its brief, four-month existence illustrate, the New Deal's direct job -creation programs also enriched the country with a profusion of new public goods and services at a time when normal budgetary considerations would have ruled out virtually all such undertakings. The forced idleness of the nation's work force was turned into a wealth-producing asset in service of the public good. As Leighninger points out, the incalculable legacy of this public investment in infrastructure, health, education, recreation, environmental conservation, and culture has been little recognized, even by historians.[82] Indeed, had the government not undertaken such a vast public-investment program, the United States almost surely would not have been as prepared as it was to enter World War II. Nor would we have emerged from the war with as much economic momentum as we did. Conventional public works spending by the PWA accounted for only about 30 percent of the New Deal's total investment in the country's physical and social infrastructure during the 1930s. It was the era's direct job-creation programs that accounted for most of it—approximately 70 percent of the total.

Moreover, by tapping this idle productive capacity, the federal government gave back to millions of unemployed workers and their families precisely what the Depression had taken from them—the opportunity to support themselves in dignity. The jobs provided by the New Deal made it possible for them to put their broken lives back together again while they waited for the private economy to recover. The value ordinary people attached to this is indicated by the 9 million applicants for the CWA's 2 million non–means-tested jobs.

Nevertheless, among progressive economists, the prevailing view of the New Deal's direct job-creation strategy is that it was nothing more than a delivery device for a Keynesian fiscal stimulus. Noting that it was World War II spending that finally brought the Depression to an end, these economists see no reason to emulate the Roosevelt Administration's direct job-creation strategy because there are far easier ways to boost aggregate demand. Of course they should advocate for the allocation of stimulus spending to socially useful purposes, but except for differences in the multiplier effect of different categories of stimulus spending, they can cite no economic reason to prefer one type of deficit spending over another. As Keynes himself famously noted, if there are political difficulties that prevent a sensible allocation of stimulus spending, engaging in otherwise wasteful spending would be preferable to doing nothing at all. A government could even bury bank notes in bottles at the bottom of abandoned mines, fill the mines with trash, and then invite capitalists to dig them up.[83] From this perspective, there is no reason for progressives to pursue the administratively challenging and politically fraught direct job-creation strategy when responding to a recession. It's not that progressive economists argue against using the strategy. They simply ignore it when fashioning their policy proposals.

Ironically, this tacit dismissal of the direct job-creation strategy overlooks the role played by military enlistments in achieving full employment during World War II. Between 1943 and 1945—a three-year period during which the nation's civilian unemployment rate fell below 2 percent—an average of 10.9 million able-bodied workers were employed in the U.S. military.[84] That was three-and-a-half times the average number employed in the New Deal's direct job-creation programs between 1936 and 1940. In short, even though it was not the reason for the military buildup, the achievement of full employment during World War II actually did rely on direct job creation—with the military replacing the New Deal's direct job-creation programs as the vehicle for providing the jobs.

Still, the Keynesian critique of the New Deal response to the Great Depression is clearly correct in its condemnation of the Roosevelt Administration's fiscal conservatism. Figure 6.1 shows the U.S. unemployment rate from 1933 through 1947. The top line shows the rate as it is normally reported—that is, with persons employed in the New Deal's direct job-creation programs counted as unemployed. The lower line shows the unemployment rate as it would be reported today, with persons employed in these programs counted as employed.

The first thing Figure 6. 1 illustrates is the disastrous effect of President Roosevelt's ill-conceived attempt to balance the federal budget in 1937. It took the economy three years to recover from the economic reversal precipitated by that action, confirming Keynes's argument concerning the beneficial effect of deficit spending.

The second thing the figure shows, however, is the dramatic impact the New Deal's direct job-creation programs had on the level of unemployment over and above the beneficial multiplier effect of program spending on the private sector. The employment effect of a direct job-creation program has two components. The first is the program's direct employment effect—the jobs that are created in the program itself. The second is its indirect (i.e., multiplier-induced) employment effect on private-sector hiring. It is this dual employment effect that makes the direct job-creation strategy such a potent means of responding to economic downturns.[85]

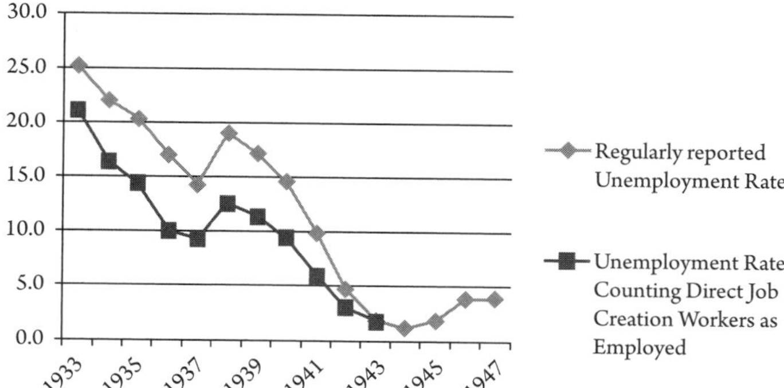

Figure 6.1 U.S. Unemployment Rate from 1933–1947.

If, instead of funding programs like the CWA and WPA, the Roosevelt Administration had used the same amount of stimulus money to pay for other types of government benefits (such as unemployment insurance), the private sector probably would have recovered at the same pace shown by the top line in Figure 6.1; but it would have sacrificed the additional, direct job-creation effect shown by the difference between the top and the bottom lines in the figure.

The third thing Figure 6. 1 shows is that Keynesian critics of the New Deal are correct in noting that the Roosevelt Administration could have achieved a full recovery from the Great Depression far more quickly if it had engaged in more deficit spending during the 1930s. What the figure also shows, however, is that the best way to have spent that money would have been to implement the employment assurance proposal contained in the CES report.

If, in 1936, the WPA had been expanded to provide 4.7 million jobs instead of the 3.3 million actually provided, the economy's unemployment rate could have been reduced to the full employment level of 2 percent in 1937, rather than waiting for wartime spending (and the draft) to do it in 1943. If they had also spent enough to increase the WPA work week to a standard 40 hours for full-time workers, and increased program wages to market levels, those jobs would have been fully comparable to their private-sector counterparts. The additional spending required to achieve that goal probably would have doubled the New Deal's direct job-creation budget—from $2.6 billion (2.2 percent of GDP) to $5.2 billion (4.4 percent of GDP, or the equivalent of about $690 billion in 2012). The fiscal stimulus provided by that additional spending would have caused private sector unemployment to decline more rapidly as well; and if the mistaken 1937 attempt to balance the federal budget had been avoided, the private sector probably would have fully recovered by 1939 instead of 1943—and possibly with lower overall levels of spending on direct job-creation than were actually incurred during that period.

Why would this strategy have been superior to the standard Keynesian strategy—i.e., spending stimulus dollars on budget items other than the WPA? Both strategies would have achieved full recovery from the Great Depression at about the same rate. The difference is that the standard Keynesian strategy would have forced unemployed workers and their families to wait for that recovery in order to get their lives back on track, while the direct job-creation strategy would have given them the benefits of full employment immediately rather than years later.

Learning from the New Deal: Securing the Right to Work

As noted earlier, President Roosevelt was naturally inclined to view the "right to live" and the "right to work" as entitlements that society has a duty to secure for its members. In light of that predisposition, it required no great conceptual leap on his part to describe the New Deal's social welfare goals (which were most fully expressed in the CES's 1935 report) in similar terms. The rhetorical turning point came in Roosevelt's 1941 State of the Union Address to Congress—his famous "four freedoms" speech. In it, he identified "equality of opportunity" and "jobs for those who can work" as the first two things the American people expect of their government; and he famously included "freedom from want" as one of the "four freedoms" World War II was being fought to secure, not just in the United States and Europe, but "everywhere in the world." This was "no vision of a distant millennium," he declared, but a "definite basis for a kind of world attainable in our own time and generation."[86]

At the time the president delivered his Four Freedoms speech, the National Resources Planning Board (NRPB)—a research and advisory body housed in the Executive Office of the President—was engaged in a detailed assessment of the social welfare initiatives undertaken by the Roosevelt Administration since 1933 as a guide for planning the social welfare institutions it believed the country would need at the end of World War II. In other words, it was tasked with carrying on the work of the CES.

Recognizing the link between "freedom from want" and the goals of its own planning initiative, the NRPB undertook the task of developing a nine-point "Declaration of Rights" that would "translate" the "freedom from want" into a list of specific economic and social entitlements. Drafted in close consultation with President Roosevelt, this declaration was first published in a pamphlet bearing the title "Our Freedoms and Our Rights." The first two rights listed in the declaration were the "right to work" and the "right to fair pay."[87]

President Roosevelt's framing of the war effort as a human-rights struggle also inspired the American Law Institute (ALI) to undertake the drafting of a "Statement of Essential Human Rights." A highly influential and quintessentially mainstream organization of judges, lawyers, and academics dedicated to the improvement of the law, the ALI convened an international drafting committee to enumerate the human rights on which a lasting peace could be based following the end of World War II. The effort took three years of study and discussion, and the final "Statement," like the NRPB Declaration, recognized a range of economic and social entitlements as human rights—including the right to work and the right to reasonable wages, hours, and other conditions of work.[88]

In 1944, with the end of the war in sight and a presidential election scheduled for the following fall, Roosevelt chose to use his State of the Union Message to restate his belief that the employment and social welfare entitlements his administration had sought to secure during the preceding eleven years were in fact human rights that the federal government had a duty to secure. Invoking both the country's Declaration of Independence and its Constitution, Roosevelt opined that the United States "had its beginning, and grew to its present strength, under the protection of certain inalienable political rights" secured by the country's Constitution. However, as the nation grew and its economy industrialized, these rights (which he described as "our rights to life and liberty") proved inadequate to "assure us equality in the pursuit of happiness." Claiming that "these economic truths have become accepted as self-evident," he asserted that "we have accepted, so to speak, a second Bill of Rights under which a new basis of security and prosperity can be established for all—regardless of station, race, or creed." He then listed the economic and social entitlements included in this second bill of rights—a refinement of the NRPB's earlier nine-item list, and, like it, beginning with the "right to a useful and remunerative job" and the "right to earn enough to provide adequate food and clothing and recreation."[89]

Framing these entitlements as "rights" rather than "economic policy objectives" may not guarantee that the government will actually fulfill its obligations, but there was nothing wide-eyed about the New Dealers' willingness to make the commitment. They believed that policies were available that actually could secure the rights in question—beginning with the right to decent work. As President Roosevelt stated in his Four Freedoms speech, it was not a "vision of a distant millennium." It was an agenda for reaching an immediate and achievable goal.

Beginning with the key insight that jobs could be provided for unemployed workers in the same way that other social-welfare benefits could, the New Dealers had fashioned a strategy for providing employment assurance that was eminently doable. When wartime spending appeared to confirm Keynes's premise that a market economy could spend its way to full employment without going to the trouble of operating programs like the WPA, it merely reinforced the confidence of progressives in their ability to secure the right to work while giving them a less contentious way of describing their objective—the achievement of full employment.

The tragedy is that they forgot they had two strategies for achieving full employment and also forgot the association of that goal with securing the right to work. Fully embracing the Keynesian full-employment strategy, they abandoned both the New Deal direct job-creation strategy and the rights-based claims the New Dealers asserted to describe their employment and social welfare policy goals. Generations of progressive economists came to believe that their job in the battle against unemployment was to induce the economy to grow fast enough to achieve full employment—without ever asking how successful they were in securing the right to work.

The CES had a more balanced view. The Committee's report recognized that the "stimulation of private employment" was an important part of the strategy for providing workers with employment assurance, but they saw no reason to rely exclusively on the success of that effort. The Committee's employment assurance strategy was shaped by social workers who knew from long experience that the scourge of unemployment had never been limited to economic downturns, nor to slackers angling for a handout. Harry Hopkins expressed their view in the following terms:

> [*People*] suggest that we make relief as degrading and shameful as possible so that people will want to get "off." Well—I've been dealing with

> unemployed people for years in one way and another and they do want to get off—but they can't, apparently, get "off" into private industry. Well—if they can't get off into private industry, where can they turn if they can't turn to their government? What's a government for? And these people can be useful to America; they can do jobs no one else can afford to do—these slums, for instance. No private concern can afford to make houses for poor people to live in, because any private concern has got to show a profit. Why, we've got enough work to do right here in America, work that needs to be done and that no private concern can afford to touch, to lay out a program for twenty years and to employ every unemployed person in this country to carry it out.[90]

Therefore, while acknowledging the government's obligation to do what it could to stimulate private-sector employment, the CES report recognized the need for the federal government to back up that effort with a commitment to provide "public employment for those able-bodied workers whom industry cannot employ at a given time," and to do so, not only in "periods of severe depression," but in "normal times" as well.[91]

Given the nature and scope of this commitment—and particularly its focus on filling whatever employment gap the private sector failed to close—it may be fair to say that the principal goal of the New Deal's direct job-creation strategy was not to end the Great Depression but to help people survive it. It was a social-welfare strategy whose synergy with Keynesian economic policy was not perceived at the time—for the simple reason that the strategy was conceived and implemented before Keynes's *General Theory* had even been published.

The progressive economists who embraced Keynes's work a few years later lack this excuse for failing to recognize the advantages of using a direct job-creation strategy to deliver a Keynesian fiscal stimulus to a depressed economy. Moreover, their blindness to the social-welfare contribution of the New Deal strategy also prevented them from truly comprehending the value of the New Deal strategy apart from its fiscal impact.

The true irony, though, is that the full implementation of the CES's employment assurance strategy would have automatically incorporated the benefits of Keynesian countercyclical policy without anyone knowing it was doing so. The reason for this is simple. Spending on a direct job-creation program designed to secure the right to work would be naturally countercyclical in its effect—just like spending on unemployment insurance, another social welfare program conceived without the benefit of Keynesian economic theory. In other words, even if the countercyclical virtues of Keynesian fiscal policy had never been discovered, the New Deal's direct job-creation strategy could have functioned perfectly well to both secure the right to work and dampen the business cycle.[92] Unfortunately, the same is not true of Keynesian measures implemented in ignorance of the virtues of direct job creation.

The Great Recession

In February of 2009, President Obama proposed, and Congress enacted, the American Recovery and Reinvestment Act (ARRA), a two-year $787 billion Keynesian fiscal stimulus. It was estimated at the time that the ARRA would "save or create" 3 to 4 million jobs, and subsequent analyses have confirmed that the programs did indeed perform as predicted, even though its job-creation effect was disguised by the fact that the recession's negative effect on employment levels was greater than the ARRA's positive effect.[93]

I have argued elsewhere that if the New Deal's direct job-creation strategy had been pursued with the same resources, it could have reduced the national unemployment rate either to its pre-recession level of 4.5 percent or to the genuine full-employment level of 2 percent in less than a year, while providing a substantially larger fiscal stimulus than the ARRA furnished to the private sector.[94]

The job-creation program I modeled would have provided not only officially unemployed workers, but also involuntary part-time workers and discouraged workers with their preference of either part-time or full-time employment producing relatively labor-intensive public goods and services.[95] I assumed the jobs would have paid the same wages as similar jobs in the private or regular public sectors of the economy, and program participants would have been provided the same health insurance benefits as federal government employees. To the extent possible, persons employed in the program would have been offered positions comparable in skill level and responsibility to those they previously occupied. Employment in the program would also have been treated as regular employment for tax purposes, for establishing eligibility for government benefits, and for asserting legal rights—including the right to unionize.

Based on these assumptions, I estimated the program's average job cost at $46,800 annually.[96] However, because such a program would generate additional government revenues (e.g., income and payroll taxes) and savings (e.g., reduced unemployment insurance and Medicaid expenditures), the additional funding required to cover its true "net cost" would have averaged only $24,189 per job. Based on these figures, the *budgeted* cost of creating the 12.2 million jobs that I estimated would have been needed to reduce the nation's unemployment rate to its pre-recession low of 4.5 percent would have been approximately $571 billion the first year, but the program's *net cost* would have been only $295 billion. Reducing the nation's unemployment rate another 2.5 points to the genuine full employment level of approximately 2.0 percent would have increased the program's first-year net cost by another $130 billion, bringing the program's' total net cost to $425 billion.

How much the program would have cost the second year would have depended on the size of the program's multiplier effect and how quickly private sector investment recovered from its recessionary levels. My model projects that the multiplier effect of program spending would have induced private sector employers to create 4.9 million jobs over and above those created in the program, with most of that job creation occurring during the program's second year. That means the program would have needed approximately that many fewer jobs during its second year of operations, for a net program savings of about $170 billion, compared to the program's first-year cost. The program's total two-year net cost accordingly would have been about $679 billion—about a $100 billion less than Congress voted to spend on the far-less-effective ARRA.

Why is the New Deal strategy so much more effective at creating jobs than the standard Keynesian strategy exemplified by the ARRA? There are several reasons, but the two most important ones are what I call the direct job-creation strategy's "twofer" effect (as in "two for the price of one") and the government's ability to create jobs at a lower average cost in such a program than the cost of stimulating the private sector to create the jobs.

The "twofer" effect of a direct job-creation program refers to its ability to create jobs both directly and indirectly.[97] When you use stimulus dollars to pay for SNAP benefits (food stamps), the government in effect pays for two benefits. The first is the benefit that food stamps provide to their recipients. The second is the private-sector job-creation induced by the government's expenditures on the program (assuming additional deficit spending is used to fund the benefits). When you use stimulus dollars to provide jobs in a direct job-creation program, both of the effects you purchase consist of jobs. First, you get the jobs provided by the program itself, but you also get the private-sector job-creation induced by the government's spending on the program.[98] This is the program's "twofer" effect. Add to it the value to the community of the additional public goods and services produced by the direct job-creation program, and you have a third benefit for taxpayers.

The same effect occurs, of course, when the government uses stimulus dollars to purchase goods or services from private businesses and the businesses hire unemployed workers to produce them; but that brings us to the second major reason why the direct job-creation strategy is more effective in creating jobs than the Keynesian strategy. It turns out, for a variety of reasons, that a job can be created in a direct job-creation program for about half of what it costs the government, on average, to induce the private sector to create one. The reasons for this advantage include the following:

1. The tendency for private businesses to increase the hours of work of already employed workers rather than add new workers to their payrolls—especially during a recession;
2. The tendency for direct job-creation programs to employ more labor-intensive methods of production than the private sector uses, and to deliberately choose labor-intensive over capital-intensive projects;

3. The fact that the money used to create jobs in a direct job-creation program is not diminished by the earnings paid to owners of private businesses or the depreciation allowance the owners of those businesses retain as compensation for the use of pre-existing capital goods that are not replaced (or whose replacement is delayed until after the recession is over);
4. The fact that unemployment tends to be concentrated among lower-wage workers rather than higher-wage workers, so that the average wages paid by a program that provides jobs only to unemployed workers tends to be lower than the average wages paid to a cross-section of the national labor force—the typical profile of employment generated by a stimulus-induced increase in the economy's overall rate of economic growth.

Taken together, the "twofer" effect and the lower cost per job of the direct job-creation strategy mean that a billion dollars spent on direct job-creation is likely to produce two to four times as many jobs as the same expenditure on unemployment insurance and SNAP benefits (which are representative of the types of stimulus spending that generate the biggest multiplier effect on private-sector employment). Compared to types of stimulus spending with a small multiplier effect (e.g., the retention of the so-called Bush-era tax cuts) the direct job-creation strategy is ten to twenty times as cost effective.[99]

As if this were not enough, the New Deal direct job-creation strategy has four other economic advantages over the standard Keynesian strategy for combating unemployment. First, its job-creation effect is achieved much faster. It is "front-loaded" in the sense that most of the jobs attributable to the strategy are provided immediately—or as soon as the program can be up and running—whereas the peak employment effect of a standard Keynesian stimulus takes about eighteen months to achieve.

Second, the New Deal strategy has a natural tendency to target its job-creation effect on the individuals, population groups, and communities that most need jobs. The burdens of joblessness are unequally distributed, with disadvantaged population groups bearing substantially more than their fair share of the pain. Unfortunately, the job-creation effect of conventional Keynesian stimulus strategies does little or nothing to correct this imbalance. The same economic forces that cause private-sector job losses to be concentrated among disadvantaged workers tend to direct private-sector job gains away from them. A direct job-creation program that provided work for all job seekers would disproportionately benefit the members of disadvantaged population groups, and it would do so automatically. A direct job-creation program that provided work for only some of the unemployed could achieve the same goal with eligibility requirements that take the length of time a person has been unemployed and his or her need for work into consideration in allocating employment opportunities.

The third advantage of the New Deal strategy is that it delivers its private-sector fiscal stimulus in a way that is likely to maximize its anti-cyclical effect. The revenue losses that businesses suffer during a recession flow primarily from rising unemployment rather than whatever economic problems triggered the recession in the first place. Businesses that are otherwise healthy and well-managed lose their customers because their customers lose their jobs. The fiscal stimulus provided by a direct job-creation program would reverse this process. The resumption of ordinary consumer spending by re-employed workers would fill the very same gap in the balance sheets of local businesses that rising unemployment created in the first place. Why does this matter? Under conventional stimulus approaches, the government increases spending in places and in ways (e.g., new infrastructure projects) that bear little immediate connection to the losses most businesses have suffered. Eventually, the multiplier effect of the stimulus spending spreads through the economy, but it takes time, and this delay can mean the difference between life and death for stressed businesses. Because it would deliver its fiscal benefits to the very same segments of the economy that suffered income losses as unemployment grew, the direct job-creation strategy would help insulate otherwise healthy firms from the harmful effects of the recession, and in doing so, it would provide a more stable foundation for the resumption of self-sustaining economic growth.

Finally, the New Deal strategy is much better designed than the Keynesian strategy to stop recessions from feeding on themselves. The rapid deployment of a large, direct job-creation program at the beginning of a recession could reduce the depth of the recession more than the deployment of a large Keynesian stimulus package like the ARRA. This is because, as just noted, most of the job losses and attendant economic harm that occur during a recession are the consequence of earlier job losses rather than being linked to the tendencies or events that triggered the economic contraction in the first place. It is this downward spiral of job losses leading to further job losses that turns a business correction into a recession. If the initial job losses associated with a recession could be stopped from triggering further job losses, periodic slowdowns in economic activity would still occur. There might even be recessions, but they would not be as deep. By offering immediate re-employment to laid-off workers, a direct job-creation program would prevent their job losses from triggering further job losses. That alone might be enough to stop a recession in its tracks, but even if it did not, it would lessen its severity.

Sadly, the employment-assurance leg of the CES's overall strategy for securing everyone's right to an adequate income has languished, with progressives failing even to understand what their predecessors abandoned as a result of their pursuit of the seemingly easier path to full employment promised (but only rarely delivered) by the Keynesian strategy. The advantages of the direct job-creation strategy over the Keynesian strategy are so clear and so great that the attachment progressives continue to show to the latter seems almost perverse. It is long past time for progressives to shed their Keynesian bias and start learning from the New Deal.

Notes

1. The definition of *full employment* (or "genuine" full employment) used in this chapter is grounded on William Beveridge's widely cited 1944 description—provided we ignore his gendered language. "It means having always more vacant jobs than unemployed men, not slightly fewer jobs. It means that the jobs are at fair wages, of such a kind, and so located that the unemployed men can reasonably be expected to take them; it means, by consequence, that the normal lag between losing one job and finding another will be very short." William Beveridge, *Full Employment in a Free Society*, London: G. Allen & Unwin Ltd. (1944), 18. While my usage of the term is consistent with Beveridge's, I define it more precisely as equivalent to securing the "right to work" recognized in the Universal Declaration of Human Rights. See Philip Harvey, "Why Is the Right to Work So Hard to Secure," in *The State of Economic and Social Human Rights: A Global Overview*, Alanson Minkler, ed. (New York: Cambridge University Press, 2013), 135–172. As a practical matter, I believe this requires the achievement of an unemployment rate in the neighborhood of 2 percent. See Philip Harvey, *Securing the Right to Employment: Social Welfare Policy and the Unemployed in the United States* (Princeton, NJ: Princeton University Press, 1989), 13.
2. For a more detailed account of these views and a discussion of their historical origins, see Philip Harvey, "Joblessness and the Law before the New Deal," *Georgetown Journal on Poverty Law and Policy*, 6 (1999): 1–41.
3. National Resources Planning Board, *Security, Work and Relief Policies* (Washington, D.C.: U.S. Government Printing Office, 1942), 234, note 42.
4. National Industrial Recovery Act, sec. 201 *et seq.*, *Statutes at Large* 48 (1933), 195 *et seq.*
5. U.S. Bureau of Economic Analysis, National Income and Product Account Tables, Table 3.2 (Federal Government Current Receipts and Expenditures), accessed May 6, 2013, available at http://www.bea.gov/iTable/iTable.cfm?ReqID=9&step=1#reqid=9&step=3&isuri=1&910=X&911=0&903=87&904=1933&905=1933&906=A.
6. U.S. Bureau of Economic Analysis, National Income and Product Account Tables, Table 1.1.5 (Gross Domestic Product), accessed May 6, 2013, available at http://www.bea.gov/iTable/iTable.cfm?ReqID=9&step=1#reqid=9&step=3&isuri=1&910=X&911=0&903=5&904=1933&905=1933&906=A.
7. Because of the limited fiscal capacity of state and local governments at the time, many were not in a position to finance their required 55–70 percent share of the cost of PWA-funded projects. To address this problem, the PWA not only established a bonding unit that purchased state and local government securities to finance their share of the cost of PWA projects, it helped state governments rewrite their laws to allow for the necessary borrowing and actively assisted both state and local governments in creating agencies to undertake PWA-funded financing and construction activities.
8. Arthur E. Burns and Edward A. Williams, *Federal Work, Security, and Relief Programs*, Works Progress Administration, Division of Social Research, Research Monograph XXIV (Washington, D.C.: U.S. Government Printing Office, 1941), 70–71.
9. Public Works Administration, *America Builds: The Record of PWA* (Washington, D.C.: U.S. Government Printing Office, 1939), 19.
10. Ibid., 86.
11. Ibid., 18–30.
12. This is roughly equivalent to assuming a multiplier of 1.5 for program expenditures.
13. Franklin D. Roosevelt, "Executive Order 9357—Transferring the Functions of the Public Works Administration to the Federal Works Agency," July 2, 1943, available at http://www.presidency.ucsb.edu/ws/?pid=16423.

14. For more detailed descriptions of these four programs than this chapter provides (and of the PWA), see Burns and Williams; and National Resources Planning Board, *Security, Work and Relief Policies* (Washington, D.C.: U.S. Government Printing Office, 1942).
15. Franklin D. Roosevelt, "Campaign Address on the Federal Budget" in Samuel I. Rosenman, comp., *The Public Papers and Addresses of Franklin D. Roosevelt, Vols. 1–5 (1928–1936)* (New York: Random House, 1938), Vol. 1, 810.
16. Federal Emergency Relief Act, *Statutes at Large* 48 (1933), 55.
17. Williams was particularly hated by Southern Democrats in Congress, who succeeded in blocking his elevation to head the WPA when Hopkins resigned from the post to become Secretary of Commerce in 1938, and again when Roosevelt nominated him to head the Rural Electrification Administration in 1945. He lived long enough, though, to attend the March on Washington in 1963 and died in 1965 railing against the Vietnam war to a former protégé from his New Deal days—Lyndon Baines Johnson. See John Salmond, *A Southern Rebel: The Life and Times of Aubrey Willis Williams, 1890–1965* (Chapel Hill, NC: University of North Carolina Press, 1983).
18. Bonnie Fox Schwartz, *The Civil Works Administration, 1933–1934: The Business of Emergency Employment in the New Deal* (Princeton NJ: Princeton University Press, 1984), 36.
19. Franklin D. Roosevelt, "Executive Order 6420-B—Establishing the Federal Civil Works Administration," Nov. 9, 1933, in Franklin Delano Roosevelt, *The Public Papers and Addresses*, Vol. 2, 456.
20. Burns and Williams, 31, Table 2.
21. Susan Carter et al., eds., *Historical Statistics of the United States: Millennial Edition* (Cambridge, UK: Cambridge University Press, 2006): series Ea932 and Ea933, accessed April 24, 2013, available at http://hsus.cambridge.org/.
22. Ibid., series Ba474 and Ba477.
23. Burns and Williams, 133, Supplementary Table 2.
24. Schwartz, 43–44.
25. Burns and Williams, 32; Schwartz, 133.
26. Schwartz, 156–180.
27. National Resources Planning Board, Appendix 5.
28. For descriptions of some of these projects, see Schwartz, 133–139.
29. The only authoritative comparison of male and female unemployment rates that I am aware of from the era is from the 1940 census, which found an identical rate of 9.6 percent for both male and female labor force participants. Carter et al., *Historical Statistics*, series Ba353 and Ba354.
30. Schwartz, 179.
31. Ibid., 158–164.
32. For descriptions of CWS projects developed for women workers, see ibid., 172–178.
33. John Charnow, *Work Relief Experience in the United States* (Washington DC: Committee on Social Security, Social Science Research Council, 1943), 40–41.
34. Carter et al., series Ba475.
35. Charnow, 11; Schwartz, 43.
36. Schwartz, 105–109.
37. Richard L. Worsnop, "Racial Discrimination in Craft Unions," *Editorial Research Reports 1969*, Vol. II (Washington, D.C.: CQ Press, 1969), accessed April 29, 2013, available at http://library.cqpress.com/cqresearcher/cqresrre1969112600.
38. Burns and Williams, 26.
39. Charnow, 51.
40. Burns and Williams, 34.
41. When the WPA was established in 1935 it provided average monthly earnings of about $50 (Charnow, 52). Over the seven-year life of the program, average WPA earnings increased. In 1940, the average was about $55 per month (Burns and Williams, 62). In 1942 the average

was over $60 per month generally and over $65 per month on certified defense projects (Charnow, 52). The CCC paid all enrollees $30 per month plus subsistence valued at another $30 per month (ibid., 122–123). Earnings in FERA-funded work relief projects increased following the demise of the CWA, averaging about $28 per month (ibid., 51).

42. Schwartz, 117–118. The minimum hourly rates for unskilled workers under this scale were $.40, $.45 and $.50, depending on the area of the country in which the program operated, with the exception of highway construction work, for which the usual rates paid by state highway departments were used, subject to a national minimum of $.30 per hour. The minimum rates for skilled workers were $1.00, $1.10, and $1.20 per hour, depending on the region. Charnow, 58, note 23.
43. Schwartz, 118–125.
44. Charnow, 51; Burns and Williams, 33–34.
45. Charnow, 103–106, 108–109; Burns and Williams, 32–33.
46. Schwartz, 182.
47. Ibid., 53–54.
48. Burns and Williams, 34; Harry Lloyd Hopkins, *Spending to Save: The Complete Story of Relief* (New York: WW Norton, 1936), 120–121; Schwartz, 182.
49. Schwartz, 183–184; Hopkins, 121–122.
50. Schwartz, 59, 183, 185; Hopkins, 122; Charnow, 82; Searle F. Charles, *Minister of Relief: Harry Hopkins and the Depression* (New York: Praeger, 1974), 65.
51. Schwartz, 136, 176–178, 186; Hopkins, 113.
52. Schwartz, 135, 174–176, 183, 186.
53. Ibid., 69, 138, 178; Burns and Williams, 35.
54. Arthur M. Schlesinger, Jr., *The Coming of the New Deal* (Boston: Houghton Mifflin Co., 1958.), 271.
55. Charles, 65.
56. In some regions, wage rates were reduced to as little as $.10 or $.15 an hour by local relief officials. Earning on FERA work relief projects averaged between only $5.50 and $7.25 a week from the spring of 1934 (when the FERA program was reinstated following the demise of the CWA) through the end of 1935 (by which time it had been replaced by the WPA). Burns and Williams, 11; National Resources Planning Board, 44.
57. Burns and Williams, 43, 45; National Resources Planning Board, 44.
58. Nancy Rose, *Put to Work: Relief Programs in the Great Depression* (New York: Monthly Review Press, 1994), 65–70.
59. Ibid., 76–80, 85–87.
60. Committee on Economic Security, *Report of the Committee on Economic Security*, reprinted in *The Report of the Committee on Economic Security of 1935 and Other Basic Documents Relating to the Development of the Social Security Act* (Washington, D.C.: National Conference on Social Welfare, 1985), 70.
61. See Philip Harvey, *Securing the Right to Work: Social Welfare Policy and the Unemployed in the United States* (Princeton, NJ: Princeton University Press, 1989), 16–20.
62. Committee on Economic Security, 74–75.
63. These included a non-contributory old-age pension system, an unemployment insurance system, an income support program for needy children who lacked a father's support, a state-administered system of residual relief for persons of working age who were unable to be self-supporting, and a range of public health initiatives, including a national health insurance system (though this latter proposal was withheld from the final report when it became clear that it lacked the political support necessary to be enacted). See ibid.
64. United Nations, Universal Declaration of Human Rights, G.A. Res. 217A (III), 1948, arts. 22 and 25. It is important to distinguish the right to work proclaimed in the UN's Universal Declaration of Human Rights and generally recognized in international human rights law from

the willful misappropriation of the term by anti-union groups in the United States to describe laws outlawing union security agreements.

65. The only noteworthy deviation from the CES's income security proposals was the exclusion of agricultural and domestic workers from the Unemployment Insurance and contributory old age pension systems established by the act. The CES report opposed any such exclusions, though it supported some others (e.g., public employees). It is often asserted that Congress excluded agricultural and domestic workers from these programs to appease Southern Democrats who wanted to deny the benefits in question to African Americans, but this view has been challenged on the grounds that it was Secretary of the Treasury Henry Morgentheau who promoted the exclusion out of concern for the difficulties involved in collecting payroll taxes from the employers of these categories of workers. The exclusion had in fact been originally proposed by the CES staff on the grounds later cited by Morgenthau, but the CES itself overruled that recommendation because Hopkins and Frances Perkins felt strongly that the programs in question should be universal. Morgenthau, himself a member of the CES, undercut the official CES recommendation in his Congressional testimony, citing concerns by the Internal Revenue Service. See Larry DeWitt, "The Decision to Exclude Agricultural and Domestic Workers from the 1935 Social Security Act," *Social Security Bulletin*, 70, no. 4 (2010): 49–68.
66. Emergency Relief Appropriations Act of 1935, Pub. Res. 74-11, 49 Stat. 115 (1935); Franklin D. Roosevelt, "Executive Order 7034—Creating Machinery for the Works Progress Administration," May 6, 1935, accessed July 23, 2013, available at http://www.presidency.ucsb.edu/ws/?pid=15053.
67. Burns and Williams, 61–64.
68. See Rose, 100–104.
69. Burns and Williams, 39, Table 7.
70. For a slide-show introduction to the WPA in general and to its various art projects in particular, see Franklin D. Roosevelt Presidential Library and Museum, "FDR, the WPA and the New Deal Arts Programs," accessed July 23, 2013, available at http://www.fdrlibrary.marist.edu/pdfs/ppDIRwpa.pdf.
71. National Resources Planning Board, 393–394.
72. See Social Security, the Official Website of the U.S. Social Security Administration, Social Security History, "CES—Unpublished Study on Health Insurance," accessed May 1, 2013, available at http://www.ssa.gov/history/reports/cesmedical.html.
73. Schwartz, 221–225.
74. Ibid., 234–237.
75. Ibid., 102–128.
76. Dona Cooper Hamilton and Charles V. Hamilton, *The Dual Agenda: The African American Struggle for Civil and Economic Equality* (New York: Columbia University Press, 1997), 9–27.
77. Franklin D. Roosevelt, "Annual Message to the Congress, January 4, 1935" in *The Public Papers and Addresses*, Vol. 4, 18–22; National Resources Planning Board, 237.
78. Franklin D. Roosevelt, "Campaign Address to the Commonwealth Club of California, September 23, 1932," in *The Public Papers and Addresses*, Vol. 1, 754.
79. Ibid., 754–755.
80. Roosevelt, "Acceptance of the Renomination for the Presidency, Philadelphia, PA, June 27, 1936," in *The Public Papers and Addresses*, Vol. 5,233–234.
81. Author's calculations using data from National Resources Planning Board, Appendix 1; and Carter et al., eds., series Ba470, Ba474, Ba477.
82. Robert D. Leighninger, *Long Range Public Investment: The Forgotten Legacy of the New Deal* (Columbia: University of South Carolina Press, 2007), xv. That legacy included schools and university buildings, courthouses and prisons, bridges, viaducts, tunnels and dams, hospitals and clinics, waterworks and incinerators, ports and zoos, golf courses and tennis courts, stadiums and auditoriums, botanical gardens and museums, fairgrounds and farmers' markets, city

halls and fire stations, parks and trails, shelters and lodges. For a quantitative accounting of some of these public works, see National Resources Planning Board, 342, notes 4, 5.

83. John Maynard Keynes, *The General Theory of Employment, Interest, and Money* (New York: Harcourt Brace, 1936), 129.
84. Robert Goralski, *World War II Almanac: 1939–1945* (New York: Putnam's Sons, 1981).
85. For a more extended discussion of this point, see Philip L. Harvey, *"Back to Work: A Public Jobs Proposal for Economic Recovery"* (New York: Demos Policy Brief, 2011), 20–23, accessed May 3, 2013, available at http://www.demos.org/sites/default/files/publications/Back_To_Work_Demos.pdf.
86. Franklin D. Roosevelt, "The Annual Message to Congress, January 6, 1941," in Samuel I. Rosenman, comp., *The Public Papers and Addresses of Franklin D. Roosevelt, Vols. 6–9 (1937–1940)* (New York: Macmillan, 1941), Vol. 9, 670–72.
87. The balance of the list consisted of: (1) the right to adequate food, clothing, shelter, and medical care; (2) the right to security, with freedom from fear of old age, want, dependency, sickness, unemployment, and accident; (3) the right to live in a system of free enterprise, free from compulsory labor, irresponsible private power, arbitrary public authority, and unregulated monopolies; (4) the right to come and go, to speak or to be silent, free from the spying of secret political police; (5) the right to equality before the law, with equal access to justice in fact; (6) the right to education, for work, for citizenship, and for personal growth and happiness; and (7) the right to rest, recreation, and adventure; the opportunity to enjoy life and take part in an advancing civilization. National Resources Planning Board, "Our Freedoms and Rights," quoted in Marion Clauson, *New Deal Planning: The National Resources Planning Board* (Baltimore, MD: Johns Hopkins University Press for Resources for the Future, 1981), 183–184.
88. The other economic and social rights recognized in the ALI *Statement* were the right to education, the right to adequate food and housing, and the right to social security (including access to medical care and compensation for loss of livelihood). American Law Institute, *Statement of Essential Human Rights* (New York: Americans United for World Organization, 1945), 281–286.
89. Franklin D. Roosevelt, "Message to the Congress on the State of the Union, January 11, 1944," *The Public Papers and Addresses*, Vol. 13, 40–41.
90. Quoted in William E. Leuchtenburg, *The FDR Years: On Roosevelt and His Legacy* (New York: Columbia University Press, 1995), 74–75.
91. Committee on Economic Security, 70.
92. For a description of how the direct job-creation strategy could be funded by a polity that operated under a balanced-budget constraint, see Philip L. Harvey, *"Securing the Right to Work at the State or Local Level"* (Berkeley, CA: Institute for Research on Labor and Employment Big Ideas for Jobs Report, 2011), accessed May 3, 2013, available at http://www.philipharvey.info/securing.pdf.
93. Alan Blinder and Mark Zandi, "How the Great Recession Was Brought to an End" July 27, 2010, accessed August 11, 2010, available at http://www.economy.com/mark-zandi/documents/End-of-Great-Recession.pdf; Congressional Budget Office, "Estimated Impact of the American Recovery and Reinvestment Act from January 2010 through March 2010," May 2010, accessed May 3, 2013, available at http://www.cbo.gov/sites/default/files/cbofiles/ftpdocs/115xx/doc11525/05-25-arra.pdf.
94. See Harvey, "Back To Work"; Harvey, "Securing the Right to Work at the State or Local Level."
95. My assumed program budget includes one dollar of funding for non-labor costs for every three dollars spent on employee compensation.
96. This average assumed that approximately 85 percent of all program jobs would be full-time (averaging forty hours per week) and the balance, part-time (averaging twenty hours per week). The average budgeted cost per full-time-equivalent (FTE) job would have been $53,300.

97. It should be noted that the same is true of spending devoted to hiring regular public-sector workers, so using stimulus dollars for that purpose would be as effective as the operation of a direct job-creation program.
98. This indirect job-creation effect is attributable to government purchases of materials and supplies for the program and to purchases of privately produced goods and services by program workers with their program wages.
99. Harvey, "Back to Work," 6, Table 2.

7

The New Deal and the Creation of an American Welfare State

GERTRUDE SCHAFFNER GOLDBERG

We can never insure one hundred percent of the population against one hundred percent of the hazards and vicissitudes of life, but we have tried to frame a law which will give some measure of protection to the average citizen and to his family against the loss of a job and against poverty-ridden old age.... This law, too, represents a cornerstone in a structure which is being built but is by no means complete. It is a structure intended to lessen the force of possible future depressions.

—Statement of President Franklin D. Roosevelt in Signing the Social Security Act, August 14, 1935

Social Welfare: Then and Now

When Franklin Roosevelt took the oath of office in March 1933, there was no American welfare state to cope with the ravages of a Great Depression. Since 1930, the nation had weathered a severe collapse and mounting unemployment—nearly 25 percent by 1933. Roosevelt's predecessor, President Herbert Hoover, opposed direct federal relief to millions of hungry and homeless people, even though aid from lower levels of government and private sources was disastrously deficient. "For three severe winters, 1930, 1931, and 1932," wrote Harry Hopkins, the administrator of federal relief in the Roosevelt administration, "the unemployed of the United States had suffered untold misery."[1]

Historian Arthur Schlesinger, Jr., described the utter paucity of resources to cope with the severest depression in the nation's history:

> And so, through the winter of 1931–32, the third winter of the depression, relief resources, public and private, dwindled toward the vanishing point. In few cities was there any longer pretense of meeting minimum budgetary standards. Little money was available for shoes or clothing, for medical or

> dental care, for gas or electricity. In New York City, entire families were getting an average of $2.39 a week for relief. In Toledo, the municipal commissary could allow only 2.14 cents per meal per person per day. In vast rural areas, there was no relief coverage at all.[2]

Three-quarters of a century later, when the Great Recession struck, the U.S. welfare state was able to cushion some of the effects of mass unemployment. Elected, like Franklin Roosevelt, in a time of crisis, President Barack Obama inherited social welfare programs initiated by Roosevelt's New Deal. The Roosevelt administration first mounted temporary relief programs to reduce the "untold misery." Not long after, Roosevelt and his fellow New Dealers began a campaign for permanent economic or social security programs in a nation long schooled in self-reliance. What were the temporary relief measures of the New Deal? What role did the New Deal play in the achievement of permanent social welfare programs? What other forces were at play? How significant were the permanent programs? How did the programs born in the Great Depression mitigate suffering in the Great Recession? Finally, what can the New Deal teach us about meeting current challenges to economic and social security?

The New Deal Legacy and the Great Recession

When the Great Recession struck, social welfare programs were on hand to reduce mass suffering and privation. Instead of the deep downward spiral of diminishing consumption, rising unemployment and collapsing production of the early years of the Great Depression, its twenty-first-century counterpart remained a recession—a *Great* Recession, but nonetheless much lower on the Richter scale of economic cataclysm.

Feeding the hungry in the Great Recession did not require a three-year struggle for new federal relief. Food stamps (SNAP), a program born in the Depression, could feed increasing numbers of hungry people. In the first two years of the Great Recession, food stamp beneficiaries increased by 14.3 million.[3] According to the president of a national anti-hunger organization, "The program's almost a model countercyclical program, in the sense that as more people are unemployed, as more people's wages fall, food stamps can step in quickly and effectively to pick up some of the slack and ameliorate some of the pain."[4] The cost of its expansion was paid for, in part, by funds from the American Recovery and Reinvestment Act (ARRA, or the "Obama stimulus"). Another New Deal program, unemployment insurance (UI), was available to aid millions of jobless workers. UI expenditures increased nearly fivefold (4.84) between 2007 and 2010, keeping 3.3 million Americans out of poverty in 2009.[5] The length of time that a worker can collect benefits during normal times, usually 26 weeks, was increased by an extended benefits program enacted by Congress in 1970 and by the Emergency Unemployment Compensation

Program (EUC) of 2008. Workers who exhaust regular UI and EUC benefits are eligible for additional coverage, depending on the level of unemployment and the laws in their states. In July 2012, after reduced coverage in six states, benefit length for newly unemployed workers ranged from forty-six to ninety-nine weeks, with the modal number being seventy-three, and 58 percent of the states covering seventy or more weeks.[6] Unemployment insurance is a New Deal program available since the mid-1930s, and there has been a precedent since 1970 for extending its benefits with federal financial support during periods of recession.[7]

The availability of social welfare programs and the relative ease with which they were expanded early in the recession may be one reason why, for three years after the crash, there was little protest from the unemployed, underpaid, or foreclosed—until public service workers, threatened with loss of collective bargaining rights, struck back in Wisconsin, and Occupy Wall Street, protesting a wide range of inequities. Contrast this with the three years following the stock market crash of 1929, when the neglect of catapulting need aroused substantial organized protest by and on behalf of the unemployed (see Chapter 4 for discussion of popular movements during the Great Depression).

Social welfare, though meeting some need in the Great Recession, has its limits. Food stamps, even with fewer holes than other safety net programs, has very low benefits and was serving just 75 percent of potentially eligible individuals or families in 2010.[8] Moreover, to paraphrase a placard of Occupy Wall Street: "We didn't get an education to be on food stamps." Even though suffering was less widespread than in the early 1930s, it was still severe. Although the proportion of jobless workers collecting benefits rose during the height of the recession, a report early in 2013 put the rate at less than half; extended benefits, moreover, do not last forever.[9] On average, not even 50 percent of a worker's earnings are replaced by UI.[10]

Has the rest of the social welfare system stood the test of a Great Recession? The old age and disability insurance system, known popularly as Social Security—the foremost legacy of New Deal social reform—continues to pour billions of dollars into the hands of the elderly, the disabled, and the widows and children of retired, deceased, and disabled workers, thereby maintaining their purchasing power. Moreover, the reduction of the Social Security payroll tax became a source of relief to workers and a stimulus to consumption when Congress lowered it in 2011 and 2012.

One program that did not respond to the economic crisis was public assistance for needy families with children. Aid to Families with Dependent Children (AFDC), one of the public assistance programs established by the Social Security Act (initially "Aid to Dependent Children"), was repealed in 1996 and replaced by Temporary Assistance for Needy Families (TANF). The new program has lifetime limits on benefits and strict work requirements that were hard for many recipients to meet before the crisis and impossible for many more in its wake. According to Chairman of the Senate Finance Committee Max Baucus, "A welfare system focused on jobs can work when there are plenty of jobs, . . . But that kind of system poses harsh realities when a recession sets in."[11] What the senator overlooks is the chronic shortage of jobs and the very low wages of those that do exist, particularly for women with the labor market handicaps of many single mothers.[12] Public housing, also enacted during the New Deal, has never been an entitlement in the sense of providing shelter to all who are eligible. In Dallas, when the housing authority began accepting applications for the first time in five years, 21,000 people applied for 5,000 places.[13] Yet Congress reduced the 2012 budget of the Department of Housing and Urban Development (HUD) by nearly $4 billion.[14]

New Deal Emergency Relief

There was no question that the federal government would provide relief when Franklin Roosevelt became president. That had been a promise of the Democratic Party platform and its standard-bearer. While Roosevelt held that the expenditures of cities, states, and the federal government must be reduced, he was "utterly unwilling that economy should be practiced at the expense of starving people." It was the obligation of government to prevent the starvation of those who try but are unable to maintain themselves—"not as a matter of charity, but as a matter of social duty." If lower levels of government are unable to fulfill this obligation, "it then becomes the positive duty of the Federal Government to step in to help." Quoting the Democratic national platform, he said that the federal government has a " 'continuous responsibility for human welfare, especially for the protection of children. That duty and responsibility the Federal Government should carry out promptly, fearlessly and generously.' "[15] Roosevelt's rhetoric, however stirring, often exceeded the New Deal's deeds. With the Federal Emergency Relief Administration (FERA) of 1933, however, the New Deal broke historical precedents by financing direct relief to millions of needy Americans. According to the most knowledgeable officials, the combined budget for relief and public works was just over a fourth of what was needed.[16] Nonetheless, social-welfare historian Walter Trattner regards FERA as "a tradition-shattering statute that opened up an era of federal aid that had momentous consequences for social welfare."[17] Appointed administrator of FERA, Harry Hopkins had directed New York State's Temporary Emergency Relief Administration, established by then-Governor Franklin Roosevelt.

Hopkins, it should be noted, had spent his life working for the poor. Indeed, the Roosevelt Administration included a number of other persons with lifelong commitments to social reform or civil rights, like Labor Secretary Frances Perkins, Interior Secretary Harold Ickes, Jr., and, though she had no official position, First Lady Eleanor Roosevelt, the preeminent New Deal humanitarian. One searched for advisors and appointees with such qualifications in the first Obama Administration. An exception was Labor Secretary Hilda Solis. A former congresswoman, Solis had a strong background in worker and immigration rights but, as a member of the Cabinet, she was barely visible to the public, much less a vocal advocate for an extension of labor rights. As this discussion will show, Hopkins particularly, and Perkins as well, stand out as proponents within the FDR administration of more progressive social welfare measures, available to all workers and, in Hopkins's case, without invidious distinctions among various needy populations. In referring to the close relationship between Roosevelt and Hopkins, Perkins wrote "Roosevelt was greatly enriched by Hopkins's knowledge, ability, and humane attitude toward all facets of life."[18] The presence of outstanding reformers in the Obama Administration might have made such differences, but the choice of advisors is, of course, that of the president.

FERA either shared the cost of relief with the states or, if states lacked the wherewithal, picked up most of the tag. The federal share of FERA relief was approximately 70 percent, but in some states, notably in the South, where revenues were especially depleted, Washington paid 95 percent or more of relief expenditures.[19] Innovation in temporary relief programs went beyond financing. Some aid was in the form of work relief—currently called "workfare"—in which recipients worked for their relief checks. Hopkins preferred work programs like those in the Works Progress Administration (WPA), established later in the New Deal. The unemployed who got jobs in the WPA, Hopkins wrote, were inclined to think of themselves as "working for the government" instead of being on relief.[20]

Another FERA innovation was more adequate benefits. Average relief grants for the country as a whole about doubled in less than two years, between May 1933, when FERA was initiated, and January 1935.[21] According to a representative of the American Association of Social Workers, "perhaps the greatest thing that has been done to the worker by the Federal Emergency Relief Administration is that it has for the first time given assistance... that was way over and above anything that we have known in our state poor laws."[22] Nonetheless, as Hopkins himself regretted, "We have never given adequate relief."[23]

The New Deal and Social Welfare Reform

The Social Security Act of 1935 and the 1939 amendments that significantly expanded it are the principal social welfare reforms of the New Deal. The complicated history of this legislation is well beyond the scope of this chapter. In a time when confidence in government's ability to solve problems remains low, it is important to understand how New Dealers took advantage of an economic crisis to make a case for a larger government role in economic security. The timing of reform was important to New Dealers, and is also of contemporary interest, given President Obama's advocacy of health care reform rather early in the course of a Great Recession. The provision of federal relief to the unemployed was a clear break with tradition, but it was temporary. How did the unemployed fare with the permanent measures? Finally, how much economic security would be met by the permanent social welfare reform, and how conducive was its framework to further expansion of social provision?

Framing the Message

Soon after becoming president, Roosevelt told a *New York Times* reporter, "We'll be social-minded enough in another year to make a beginning in a great social reform which must be carefully adapted to our special conditions and needs." The "great social reform" was social insurance. Despite what the Depression should have taught the American people, Roosevelt held that "a nation has to be educated to the point where reforms can be assimilated without dangerous spasms of indigestion."[24] Popular movements, of course, help with digestion and often include not only those who advocate for themselves but "conscience constituents" who favor benefits or justice for others.[25] Evidently, FDR was not being too cautious about the need to educate the public. Frances Perkins who headed the Cabinet-level Committee on Economic Security (CES) that planned the Social Security Act, reminded her colleagues that "this was the United States in the years 1934–35." Thus, their recommendations needed to take into account "the needs of our country, the prejudices of our people, and our legislative habits."[26]

According to political scientist George Edwards III, even presidents renowned for their communication skills do not change the minds of those they govern. Instead, they focus the public's attention on a particular issue, framing or setting the terms of the debate.[27] Rather than changing values, they point out the applicability of widely held values to a policy they favor.[28] Once is not enough: "It is likely that reaching the public will require frequent repetition of the president's views."[29]

The New Deal security message was frequently intoned, usually associating it with enduring values and with prevention of depressions or aid to its casualties. Historian Elmer Cornwell, Jr. observed:

> F.D.R.'s tactic was much more than mere repetition, though this was useful, no doubt, in lending familiarity to the ideas involved. He attempted also to clothe the apparently unorthodox in the garb of the familiar. Over and over he insisted that what he was going to propose was not alien to American values, but a mere fulfillment or rediscovery of elements already present.[30]

In his message to Congress in June 1934, Roosevelt declared his intention to undertake "the great task of furthering the security of the citizen and his family through social insurance."[31] He set forth the themes that were to be repeated by him and his associates in their effort to make the nation more "social-minded" and more receptive to the idea of government-assured security. "Security" was concerned with common desires for decent homes, productive work and "some safeguards against misfortunes which cannot be wholly eliminated in this man-made world of ours." The objectives themselves were traditional, but they could no longer be achieved "through the interdependence of members of families upon each other and of the families within a small community upon each other." In modern society, there were unavoidable "misfortunes" or what Roosevelt also referred to as "the hazards and vicissitudes of life." It was not just a matter of individual responsibility or self-reliance. This being the case, "we are compelled to employ the *active interest of the Nation as a whole through government* in order to encourage a greater security for each individual who composes it [*emphasis added*]." To allay fears of a radical departure, he pointed out: "This is not an untried experiment. Lessons of experience are available from States, from industries and from many nations of the civilized world."

An important theme was the relationship of economic security to freedom. In Harrodsburg, Kentucky, Roosevelt looked forward to giving to all the people of the nation "the fulfillment of security, of freedom, of opportunity, and happiness which every American asks and which every man [*sic*] is entitled to receive."[32] This was one of many attempts to integrate security with the old social philosophy that put political liberty on a pedestal. In a Fireside Chat in November 1934, this weaving of old and new was apparent: "I prefer and am sure you prefer that broader definition of liberty under which we are moving forward to greater freedom, to greater security for the average man [*sic*] than he has ever known before in the history of America."[33] Thus Roosevelt was creating a new social paradigm consonant with reform and at the same time integrating it with traditional American values.

Repetition was important. Roosevelt referred to the bill no less than twenty-five times in press conferences from February 1934 to August 1935.[34] Other New Dealers joined in popularizing the security concept. Urged by Roosevelt to discuss the issue as much as possible, Frances Perkins made more than 100 speeches, "always stressing social insurance as one of the methods for assisting the unemployed in times of depression and in preventing depressions."[35]

Timing: Recovery and Reform.

Less than a year and a half into his first term, when he started to promote permanent social welfare reform, Roosevelt could point to the administration's accomplishments: "On the side of relief we have extended material aid to millions of our fellow citizens. On the side of recovery we have helped to lift agriculture and industry from a condition of utter prostration."[36] The country was somewhat better off than when he took office, but the road to recovery was still long and uncertain. In 1934, unemployment was almost 20 percent but nonetheless down 14 percent from the previous year; progress in industrial production was better, up almost 30 percent since its 1932 nadir.[37] Things were better, but "the surge of recovery subsided," and between the spring of 1934 and the spring of 1935, "the country rode at anchor."[38] Nonetheless, Roosevelt was determined to move ahead, for he thought 1936 might bring a change of administration.[39] Furthermore, he felt the opportunity for reform was a narrow window that could be shut by recovery. The historian David Kennedy alludes to Roosevelt's "sensitivity to the relationship between economic crisis and political opportunity," citing a reference in his second inaugural address to improvements in the economy as "portents of disaster!"[40]

Other New Dealers also wanted to seize the day. Perkins told a conference of social workers that "this is an opportune time to launch a far-sighted security program.... Recovery has not proceeded to the point that we have forgotten the social ills produced by the depression."[41] *Carpe diem* was also urged by Senator Robert Wagner (D-New York) in introducing the Economic Security Bill: "While the horror of depression is still fresh upon our memory we are taking decisive steps to shake off its lingering aftermath, to prevent its recurrence, and to set up safeguards for those who may suffer in the future from economic forces beyond the control of the individual"[42] Note Wagner's reference to the insufficiency of self-reliance.

The midterm elections of 1934, some months after Roosevelt began to push for social insurance, were a resounding victory for his party and encouraging to reform. By contrast, Barack Obama made healthcare reform the priority of his first two years in office, even though unemployment was higher than when he took office, and he lost control of Congress in a midterm election in which the achievement of reform was, if anything, a liability. In the 1934 midterm election, Democrats gained a three-to-one lead in the House and Senate, the greatest majority ever held by either party and the only time in modern history that the party holding the White House has increased its standing in midterm elections.[43] Yet the 1930s Democratic Party was a mix, with some to the left of Roosevelt and Southern legislators protecting their region's low-wage economy and white supremacy. Nonetheless, to Hopkins, the election results were a golden opportunity: "Boys—this is our hour. We've got to get everything we want—a works program, social security, wages and hours, everything—now or never."[44] In the following year, both a works program and Social Security were enacted. Wages and hours came later, in the 1938 Fair Labor Standards Act.

Reform and Relief

Only a few weeks before proposing the Economic Security Bill (later Social Security Act) to Congress, Roosevelt declared, "The federal government must and shall quit this business of relief." He then proceeded to say what would be done for the 5 million people then on federal relief rolls. About 1.5 million were, through no fault of their own, unable to maintain themselves independently. In the past they were dependent on the states, counties, towns, cities, churches, and private welfare agencies. FDR stated that "Local responsibility can and will be resumed," and the security legislation he would soon propose would assist state and local governments to provide relief for the group he designated as "unemployable."

The remaining larger group on the federal relief rolls numbered 3.5 million. These were "victims of a nation-wide depression caused by conditions which were not local but national." The federal government, Roosevelt held, "is the only governmental agency with sufficient power and credit to meet this situation." For this group he proposed a new program of emergency public employment. He outlined its principles: that all work undertaken should be useful, " in the sense that it affords permanent improvements in living conditions or that it creates future new wealth for the Nation." Another principle was that compensation on emergency public work projects would be in the form of security payments, larger than a "relief dole" but not large enough to be a disincentive to private employment. The public works program would be an emergency measure: the Works Progress Administration was enacted as the Emergency Relief Appropriation Act of 1935 in April of that year and renewed annually until its demise in 1943.[45] According to Josephine Brown, an administrator in the federal relief program and author of a definitive history of public relief in the 1930s, "These changes were entirely consistent with the original intention of the Federal Administration to attack the unemployment problem by providing work. The FERA was looked upon as a temporary expedient, a stop-gap, to be liquidated as soon as possible."[46]

How well did the WPA and other federal work programs like the Civilian Conservation Corps meet the needs of the unemployed? In early 1936, the number on work projects was about 3.85 million, the vast majority on WPA. On average during the period from 1935 to 1940, the total number served by federal work programs averaged from 2.3 to 4.6 million. At its peak, the number employed represented less than half of the estimated unemployed, and throughout the period the average number served was between one-quarter and one-third of the unemployed.[47]

The Permanent Programs

The Social Security Act of 1935 was primarily interested in the future security of the American people and in prevention or easing of the effects of future depressions. It enacted the nation's first national social insurance programs, available on the basis of the contributions of employers and employees and hence without the stigma of relief. Unemployment insurance was an acknowledgement after centuries of blaming those without work for their condition that unemployment could be involuntary and through no fault of their own. There would also be a permanent federal presence and financial contribution to public assistance. In that sense, the federal government did not entirely "quit this business of relief" but did reduce its financial commitment to the 1.5 million. Whereas it had been footing 70 percent or more of the relief bill, it would be sharing with the states a smaller proportion of the assistance programs, but, it should be noted, all of the costs of the work programs. The assistance programs were presumably for unemployable people, but as the numbers showed, there were many employable people not served by the work programs, and further, the term "unemployable" was inaccurate because many men and women who might seem unemployable had been made temporarily so by prolonged unemployment and poverty. Many of those people became employable when employment opportunity was abundantly available during World War II.

As the description of each of the Social Security programs will show, they were limited in the risks they covered and the level of benefits. In signing the Social Security Act, Roosevelt hailed it as an historic achievement but acknowledged that it "represents a cornerstone in a structure which is . . . by no means complete."[48] Indeed, the cornerstone could give rise to a larger and more secure structure over time that would cover more risks and more vulnerable population groups. Nonetheless, the division of the Act into insurance and assistance programs has created an enduring divide between the beneficiaries of the insurance programs, who see themselves as having earned their benefits through the contributions of employment and payroll taxes by themselves or their breadwinners, in contrast to the recipients of means-tested benefits that are perceived as unearned. Harry Hopkins, for his part, had advocated for a more progressive approach: that relief and social insurance be lumped together, that relief payments be called "unemployment" or "old age insurance," and that payment be made as a matter of right and not of need. Roosevelt, however, saw this as the very thing he had been against for many years—"the dole."[49]

Social Insurance

The two major risks to income security covered in the Social Security Act were only for a portion of the workforce. The CES proposed that unemployment insurance cover employees in all firms employing four or more persons, but the House Ways and Means Committee exempted agricultural labor, domestic service in a private house, and employment in the nonprofit sector. Similarly, the CES recommended that the old age insurance system be for all employed persons.[50] However, persuaded by members of his department that it would be difficult to collect taxes from these types of workers, CES member and Treasury Secretary Henry Morgenthau, later recommended that the House Ways and Means Committee exclude farm laborers, domestic servants, and employees in establishments employing fewer than ten people.[51] However, it seems certain that the Southern-dominated Congress would have excluded them anyway. According to Witte, Perkins was strongly opposed to this amendment.[52] She later wrote, "This was "a blow."[53] It was a blow to African Americans, 50 to 70 percent of whom were employed as farm laborers and domestic servants.[54]

The change in Old Age Insurance between 1935 and 1939 offers one of the most important lessons for current advocates of social reform. The Townsend Movement, which had advocated a benefit of two hundred dollars a month for every person over sixty years of age, did not stop when the Social Security Act fell far short of its goals. It continued to agitate and was joined by other groups, some focusing at the state level, in what became a pension movement.[55] In 1939, even with a loss of New Deal strength in Congress, the movement played a part in gains for the elderly at a time when Congress neglected other needs, although it once again did not come near to achieving the movement's goals.[56]

The 1939 amendments made several important changes in Old Age Insurance (OAI). Most importantly, OAI coverage was extended to dependents and survivors, thus transforming a program for retired workers that closely resembled private insurance into a family program, or social insurance. With this change, a worker with dependents could collect more in benefits than a worker without dependents who had comparable lifetime wages.[57] Furthermore, OAI benefits were to begin two years earlier than scheduled, thus providing income to persons who could not have contributed much to them. It also instituted a weighted-benefit formula that provides a higher proportion of benefits to contributions to lower- than to higher-wage workers. Expansion of the program continued. In 1948, the excluded domestic service workers were covered, and in 1950, agricultural laborers. Risk coverage extended to disability insurance in 1956; inflation with automatic-cost-of-living increases in 1972; and partial cost of health care for the elderly (Medicare) in 1965 and for the disabled, after two years of receipt of disability insurance, in 1972. Clearly, the structure of Old Age Insurance was expandable.

Unemployment insurance has been less expandable. However, coverage was provided to excluded groups in the 1970s. Also in 1970, as noted in discussion of benefits during the Great Recession and its aftermath, the length of time unemployed workers can collect benefits is extended in periods of high unemployment and with partial or full federal support.

Adequacy

Security is not only a matter of risk and population coverage but of adequate benefits. There were no requirements regarding benefit levels in either of the insurance programs. The wages on which benefits were based could be very low. In unemployment insurance, the duration of benefits is related to adequacy. Typically, benefits have been for 26 weeks or less, leaving longer-term jobless workers without benefits. As noted, even with some added federal benefits, current allowances remain low.

OASI benefits were very low in the early years of the program. A survey of seven cities by the Social Security Board found that in 1940 and 1941 the income from all sources of between three-fourths and four-fifths of aged beneficiaries fell below the Maintenance Budget of the federal Works Progress Administration, one considerably below a Bureau of Labor Statistics City Workers' Budget.[58] Reluctance to burden the workers and employers during a severe depression was a factor in the size of benefits. However, different funding sources, such as federal general revenues, could have boosted them.[59] Benefits in recent times have risen somewhat but are still low. In 2010, the average retired worker had an annual benefit about 8 percent higher than the near poverty level (125 percent of the very meager poverty standard).

Taxation

Who pays for a social welfare program can, of course, be as important as who benefits. In the case of Old Age Insurance, payroll taxes levied on workers came under fire for several reasons: as a burden to workers, as a deduction from their wages, as a regressive tax, and for reducing consumption, and hence recovery, during a depression. Because of the limit on taxable wages, workers above the cutoff pay a lower proportion of earnings than those below. Roosevelt, for his part, was clear about the value of payroll taxes in both of the insurances. In conferring with public administration specialist Luther Gulick, who had questioned their value, Roosevelt responded:

> I guess you're right on the economics. They are politics all the way. We put those pay roll contributions there so as to give the contributors the legal, moral, and political right to collect their pensions and their unemployment benefits. With those taxes in there, no damn politician can ever scrap my social security program. Those taxes aren't a matter of economics. They're straight politics.[60]

It has been suggested that this was merely a rationale of the preferences of other actors and that employees did not contribute to unemployment insurance. [61] However, according to Gulick, Roosevelt referred to the effect of contributions in destroying the "relief attitude."[62]

Federally Aided Public Assistance Programs

Categorical Assistance

The Committee on Economic Security and the Social Security Act went against the recommendations of the Advisory Committee on Public Employment and Relief consisting of representative social workers and leaders in the field of public welfare and appointed by CES chairperson Frances Perkins. The Committee had recommended Federal grants to the states for general relief for *all* persons in need who could not be provided for on the work programs. Instead, Congress followed the recommendation of the CES that the federal government only share in the cost of assistance to certain categories of the needy. The CES proposed that only the needy elderly and dependent children be covered in the federally aided programs, and Congress added the blind.

Categorical aid was a characteristic of the Poor Laws with their emphasis on aiding only the "worthy poor." The U.S. Children's Bureau, a division of the Department of Labor, had long championed and maintained some oversight over state Mothers' Aid programs. These had been a progressive departure in the early decades of the twentieth century from the previous prohibition of any aid to the poor in their own homes. In any case, the Children's Bureau had prepared a report to the CES arguing that attempts to provide security for the unemployed would not benefit families whose breadwinners were absent. For these families, "special provision must be made."[63] However, they could have been provided for by making federally aided relief non-categorical. The Bureau, like others in the social services, had favored careful supervision of single-mother families, and this may be the main reason for its report's having advocated "special provision." Whereas the state mothers' aid programs had usually been restricted to white, native-born widows, the Children's Bureau proposals did not specify the marital status of the single parent or caretaker of the dependent child.[64] This opened the door to unmarried and divorced parents as well as to African American and immigrant women, although relief authorities, especially in the South, found ways of discriminating against them.[65]

Aid to Dependent Children was itself restrictive, for it did not cover all needy dependent children. Although it was named "Aid to Dependent Children," the Social Security Act limited coverage to children in single-parent families or those in which a second parent was disabled.[66] Thus, most needy children in two-parent families were denied aid throughout the history of the program. Confining AFDC to one-parent families, overwhelmingly single-mother families, meant that if fathers were either marginally employed or jobless, their families could be better off financially without them. Thus AFDC was viewed as an incentive to single parenthood. How frequently the program provided such an incentive is not known, but the perception contributed to its unpopularity and ultimate repeal in 1996.

If African Americans were not excluded from ADC on specifically racial grounds, discrimination against them in the South was rampant until the 1960s, when both the civil rights and welfare rights movement brought millions of African Americans onto the rolls. An important source of discrimination was the "suitable homes" policy made possible by the congressional stipulation that "a state may…impose such other eligibility requirements—as to means, moral character, etc.—as it sees fit."[67] "Suitable homes" was really a euphemism for "legitimate children."[68] Since out-of-wedlock births were much more common among African Americans, the "suitable homes" policy was used to deny aid to thousands of black children, until it was terminated at the end of the Eisenhower Administration.[69]

In time, the denial of aid to two-parent families would stigmatize AFDC by race as well as single motherhood. When the rolls expanded in response to the civil rights and welfare rights movements, the number of black recipients increased, although they were never the majority.[70] The combination of racism and restriction based on family composition contributed to the unpopularity and repeal of AFDC.

Figure 1 The Unemployed Union of Camden, New Jersey marching south on Broadway. The 1930s was a decade of dissent. Courtesy: FDR Library

Figure 2 Unemployment Insurance in operation. Unemployed workers receive their checks. Courtesy: FDR Library

Figure 3 CCC workers at an experimental farm in Maryland. Records showed that the men gained weight, muscle and height, and their disease and mortality rates were lower than the national average for men of their age group. Courtesy: FDR Library

Figure 4 CCC workers planting trees. The CCC planted over three billion trees, essentially reforesting a country that had decimated its forests. Courtesy: FDR Library

Figure 5 CCC boys from camp F-167, Salmon River National Forest, Idaho ready to transplant beaver from a ranch to a forest watershed where they will help conserve the water supply. Courtesy: FDR Library

Figure 6 CCC enrollees being trained in auto mechanics. Vocational education, as well as academics and on-the-job training were offered to enrollees. Courtesy: FDR Library

Figure 7 Soil Conservation Service. CCC workers putting sod along a gulch to prevent soil erosion. Courtesy: FDR Library

Figure 8 Eleanor Roosevelt talking with a project superintendent in Des Moines, Iowa, June 8, 1936. This project, sponsored by the WPA, planned to convert a city dump into a waterfront park. Courtesy: FDR Library

Figure 9 Norris Dam, one of over two dozen dams built by the TVA in the Tennessee Valley to bring electrification to an area that had been the U.S.'s "Third World." Courtesy: FDR Library

Figure 10 Children working on art projects at the Walker Art Center, Minneapolis, MN, one of some 100 community art centers established around the country by the WPA Art Project. Both experienced artists and amateurs could take free classes in drawing, painting, sculpture and many other forms of artistic expression. Courtesy: FDR Library

Figure 11 Kathleen Wilson of the Federal Art Project/WPA in Arizona directing children in a radio program. Courtesy: FDR Library

Figure 12 Violin teacher and students, Federal Music Project/WPA. Music classes for all ages and ability levels were offered in parts of the country and to populations that had never had access to such instruction before. Courtesy: FDR Library

Figure 13 John Steuart Curry Painting Mural for the Federal Art Project/WPA. Murals like this can be seen in countless schools, hospitals, post offices, and courthouses around the country, built or embellished by the WPA. Courtesy: FDR Library

Figure 14 Crowds outside the Lafayette Theatre in NY's Harlem, April 14, 1936, trying to see the Federal Theatre's production of *Macbeth*, set in Haiti, performed by an all-black cast, and staged by twenty-one year old Orson Welles,. The *NY Times* reported that the theatre "rocked with excitement" and that police had to hold back the crowds outside. Courtesy: FDR Library

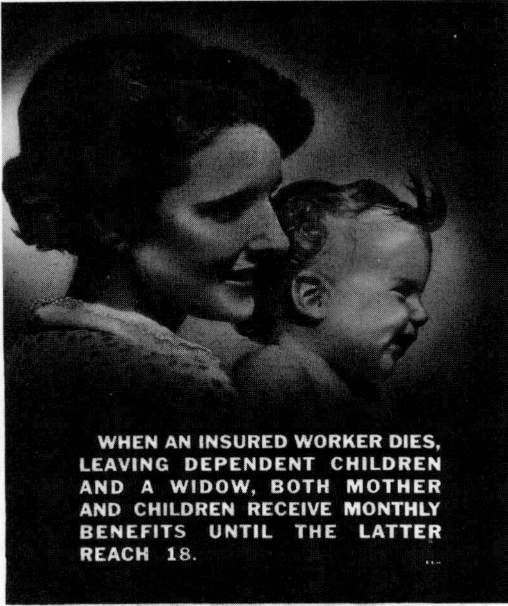

Figure 15 Poster advertising the Social Security program. As a result of the 1939 amendments to Old Age Insurance, it was now a family program providing security to widows and their dependent children. Courtesy: FDR Library

Figure 16 A public health nurse visiting a rural family made possible by the Social Security Administration's Maternal and Child Health program. Courtesy: FDR Library

There were other important omissions to the federal categories of assistance. The disabled, except for the blind, were excluded, and employable persons not accommodated by the work programs—including two-parent families with children in which neither spouse was disabled—would be ineligible. Then and now, individuals and families who do not fall into the federally aided categories are relegated to general relief which, in most states, is less adequate and sometimes only available on an emergency, short-term basis.

Beyond the Poor Laws

Although the assistance programs bore marks of the traditional Poor Laws, there were some differences, in addition to partial payment by the federal government. A very important step forward was the stipulation in the law that assistance benefits meant "money payments," thus providing the choice that comes with cash rather than in-kind benefits. The 1939 amendments specifically excluded payments to persons in public institutions, thus ruling out federally assisted relief to inmates of poorhouses. Individuals whose claims to benefits were denied had a right to a fair hearing before a state agency. Residence requirements that restricted the mobility of the poor and lessened the financial obligations of local authorities were retained but limited in length.[71] Later, the Supreme Court ruled all residence rights unconstitutional.[72]

The 1939 amendments outlawed the practice of publicly identifying relief recipients by requiring states to "provide safeguards which restrict the use or disclosure of information concerning applicants and recipients" of both Old Age Assistance (OAA) and Aid to Dependent Children (ADC), and they required that personnel standards for state administering agencies be on a merit basis. These amendments specifically stated that in determining eligibility states were to take into consideration the income and resources of an individual claiming old-age assistance, but it is likely, given their limited resources and the tradition of the Poor Laws, that states were applying the means and asset tests from the inception of the program.[73]

The inadequacy of assistance benefits was another poor law vestige. The CES recommended that states must furnish assistance to provide "when added to the income of the aged recipient, a reasonable subsistence compatible with decency and health."[74] Senator Harry Byrd (D-Virginia) led the successful opposition to this requirement, arguing that it would place a financial burden on states like his own and would also be a form of "dictatorial power" over the states by the federal administrator.[75] Fifty years later, Wilbur Cohen, on the staff of the CES and later Secretary of Health, Education and Welfare (now Health and Human Services), wrote that Byrd was responsible for the bill's "most significant long-range loss . . . the fatal blow that still prevents any effective nationwide quantitative standards in federal-state welfare. . . . "[76] In the House, representative Howard W. Smith's (D-Virginia) opposition clearly showed that an adequate benefit would threaten low-wage labor. Smith pointed out that if the average farm laborer who earned between $20 and $30 a month were put on a pension of $30 a month at age sixty-five, it was "not only going to take care of him, but a great many of his dependents . . . who could much better be employed working on a farm."[77] In short, they would not be available to pick cotton. While it has been argued that excising the "reasonable subsistence" requirement was primarily a means of keeping both white and black labor cheap, Witte held that "at least some Southern Senators feared that it could serve as an entering wedge for federal interference with the handling of the Negro question in the South."[78] In some Southern states, benefits for blacks were even more inadequate than for whites because federal matching funds were not contingent on paying all classes of people at the same rate.[79]

Employment Assurance

The report of the Committee on Economic Security to FDR stated that "the first objective of economic security must be maximum employment," and consequently it proposed "employment assurance" through public works and stimulation of private employment not only in periods of deep depression but in normal times as well."[80] Recognizing that unemployment would continue to be a problem well after the Depression, Roosevelt and Hopkins considered creating a permanent government employment program for those still jobless after receiving short-term unemployment benefits, typically sixteen weeks in the early years of the program.[81] Hopkins had convinced Roosevelt that the social security bill should be combined with his job creation program. Witte writes that the acting budget director objected, and the president agreed to present the bills separately, but the reasons against a permanent, expensive work program probably go deeper, including likely conservative opposition to such a permanent program or an admission that unemployment was there to stay.[82] As noted, WPA was enacted as a temporary program that had to be renewed annually, lasting until wartime employment temporarily solved the unemployment problem.[83] As Perkins wrote in the mid-1940s, "Unemployment insurance stands alone as the only protection for people out of work."[84]

As unemployment rose after World War II, the United States concentrated primarily on short-term cash benefits for the unemployed, except for a few years during high unemployment in the 1970s when government job creation and training or "active" labor market policies were enacted.[85] As a result of the failure to assure employment opportunity, millions of workers and their families—in good times and bad—have suffered economic privation and been vulnerable to the myriad of social problems associated with unemployment. As Amartya Sen has written, unemployment has many far-reaching effects other than loss of income: "psychological harm, loss of work motivation, skill and self-confidence, increase in ailments and morbidity, and even mortality rates, disruptions of family relations and social life, hardening of social exclusion, and accentuation of racial tensions and gender asymmetries."[86]

Today, as well, the United States has only a passive labor market policy or cash benefits for short-term unemployment but still lacks an active labor market policy of job creation or public employment for workers who suffer longer periods of unemployment. The New Deal planners had their eye on the insecurity of normal times. They recognized the tendency of capitalist economies to generate unemployment unless government employs or creates jobs for those whom the private sector fails to accommodate. In a typical month in the year 2000, when unemployment was at a thirty-year low of 4.0 percent, 5.7 million people were officially unemployed and another 7.4 million "hidden unemployed" were either working part-time because they could not find full-time work, or wanted jobs but were not looking, so were not counted in official statistics—a total of 13 million.[87] The CES planners and FDR recognized that unemployment was a serious, permanent problem, but they and the Congress addressed it with only a temporary, partial solution, albeit an innovative and relatively large one.

Housing

In the famous phrase of his second inaugural address, Roosevelt referred to "one-third of a nation ill-housed...."[88] The housing problem was not addressed in the Social Security Act, but measures to deal with it had been enacted during Roosevelt's famous First Hundred Days. Two years after passage of the Social Security Act, Senator Wagner's name would be on another piece of liberal legislation, the United States Housing Act of 1937 (Wagner-Steagall Act).

When Roosevelt took office, 1,000 home loans were foreclosed each day.[89] In response, the New Deal created the Home Owners' Loan Corporation (HOLC), which bought mortgages from failed banks and modified the terms so families could make affordable payments and keep their homes, providing HOLC judged they had sufficient income to make loan payments. In fact, it would not loan to unemployed people and foreclosed on 100,000 homes during the economic downturn in 1938.[90] HOLC often counseled delinquent borrowers and readjusted payment schedules in order to delay or prevent foreclosures when borrowers fell behind on their payments. On average, loans were delinquent two years before foreclosure.[91] In another example of how New Deal programs discriminated against African Americans, HOLC instituted the policy of "redlining" or refusing loans to homeowners in black or racially or ethnically mixed areas.[92] HOLC refinanced about 10 percent of non-farm, owner-occupied dwellings and about 20 percent of those carrying a mortgage.[93]

With mounting foreclosures in 2008, then-Senator Hillary Rodham Clinton (D-New York) proposed a new version of HOLC to help homeowners refinance their mortgages. Clinton argued that "if we are going to take on the mortgage debt of storied

Wall Street giants, we ought to extend the same help to struggling, middle-class families."[94] Unfortunately, federal policy has been inequitable in the way Clinton feared; the Troubled Asset Relief Program was supposed to aid 3 to 4 million troubled homeowners, but by the end of 2010, only about 750,000 had been helped.[95]

The Federal Housing Administration (FHA), created in 1934, also attempted to stimulate the housing industry and to facilitate homeownership by offering insurance for loans for upgrading existing housing or construction of new. However, the FHA followed HOLC's racially discriminatory evaluation practices, thus disadvantaging those probably in greatest need of help.[96] Today, the FHA lends disproportionately to African Americans and Hispanics.[97] It has contributed to the growth of homeownership from 40 percent of U.S. households in the 1930s to almost 70 percent currently.[98]

Resettlement of displaced farm or factory workers was a New Deal housing venture that joined the goals of relief, employment, and conservation. Both the Public Works Administration (PWA) and FERA had homestead divisions. Their resettlement communities combined subsistence farming and part-time employment, offered a chance for home ownership, and fostered a spirit of cooperation. Together, FERA and PWA developed nearly sixty such projects. These were taken over by the Resettlement Administration of 1935, which added over thirty more communities, developed camps providing temporary, decent housing for migrant Okies, and created the famous "greenbelt" towns.[99] Four model communities were anticipated: "garden suburbs, protected by encircling belts of farm and woodland, easily accessible to cities, but with the space and tranquillity of the countryside"; however, only three were built.[100] The greenbelt towns were very forward-looking ventures prefiguring the contemporary "smart growth" movement, which also recognizes the value of linking housing to jobs and recreational space and a sense of community and place.

Housing reformers and organized labor lobbied vigorously for public housing legislation—labor standing to gain from jobs in construction as well as housing for workers.[101] The result was the National Public Housing Act of 1937, which established publicly owned and operated housing, a reform in which the United States was preceded by a number of European nations. The act, as housing experts Peter Marcuse and Dennis Keating maintain, "was liberal in that it relied on direct public construction by local housing authorities, which built, owned and managed the housing under federal government oversight." On the other hand, it was made more acceptable to conservatives by limiting eligibility for public housing to persons with such low incomes that they were not in the private housing market. As Marcuse and Keating point out, its meager funding also limited any competition with the private sector.[102]

A recent review of the legislative process that ended with passage of Wagner-Steagall credits it with a victory for the reformers.[103] If it was, the victory was short-lived. In the first three years of the program, the dollar value of new public housing construction was $300 million, compared to $6.8 billion for private construction.[104] Pointing to its appropriations and the number of projects that had been built by 1940, New Deal historian William Leuchtenburg concluded that "the federal housing venture was notable more because it created new precedents for government action than for the dimensions of its achievements. Measured by the needs or by the potentialities, Roosevelt's public housing program could make only modest claims."[105] Yet, millions of Americans, though not nearly enough, escaped homelessness, budget-breaking housing costs, or substandard housing.

Health Care

A major omission in the Social Security Act of 1935 was health insurance. Harry Hopkins was said to be "more interested in it than in any other phase of social insurance," but even he realized it would "have to be handled very gingerly."[106] As Perkins recounts, "Powerful elements of the medical profession were up in arms over the idea of any kind of government-endorsed system."[107] Even an announcement of a CES study of health insurance, along with a long list of other studies, evoked an outpouring of protests to President Roosevelt and an editorial in the *Journal of the American Medical Association* stating that the administration was trying to railroad health insurance through Congress without consulting the profession.[108] The AMA and its insurance and Christian Science allies had crushed state health insurance initiatives in what historian Roy Lubove describes as "a complete disaster." The medical profession, Lubove wrote, "emerged from the struggle with an awareness of its political power and a determination to use it to protect its corporate self-interest."[109]

The only health protection in the Social Security Act was grants to the states for maternal and child health services and services for crippled children (Title V). Witte pointed out that these may have compensated some for the omission of health insurance, or were advocated by opponents of health insurance as a means of "killing the proposal for health insurance."[110]

President Harry Truman proposed a national health insurance plan that was turned down by Congress in 1950, a move that led to an expansion of workplace coverage and a consequent, prodigious growth in the power of private insurance companies. Medicare was enacted in 1965, as was Medicaid, which provides health-care to some groups of the poor. In 2009, when Barack Obama became president, there were 49 million persons in the United States without either private or public health care coverage.[111]

Learning from the New Deal

In response to the mass unemployment and widespread poverty of the Great Depression, Franklin Roosevelt's New Deal mounted large-scale federal relief programs. After coping with the emergency, FDR launched a campaign for permanent programs, in the case of the insurances, resembling those initiated by some other industrial countries a half century earlier. The enactment of major social welfare reform, the Social Security Act of 1935, was the result of a combination of political factors, including executive leadership and powerful social movements. The focus of one of those movements, the Townsend Movement on behalf of the elderly, had a lasting effect on the nation's social programs: a tilt toward one group in the population and a tendency to neglect some other populations and risks equally worthy of attention. On the other hand, the continued advocacy of the pension movement, though it did not achieve the universal, generous program for the elderly that it sought, was a factor in the transformation of a program of limited benefits for retired workers into a family program covering workers' dependents and survivors.

New Deal social reform left much need unmet—risks ignored, populations, particularly minorities, covered poorly or not at all, and meager benefits. The insurances were, on one hand, contributory but financed by regressive taxes. One historian called the United States a "semi-welfare state."[112] Yet a federal government that had previously eschewed responsibility for the economic security of its people had now stepped permanently into the arena of social welfare. For a nation steeped in individualism and *laissez-faire*, it was a considerable achievement.

The achievement of modest reform, we learn from the 1930s, can be a cornerstone rather than a stone wall. The social movement on behalf of the elderly was not strong enough to achieve its goals in 1935, but it did not fold its tents. In the next four years, it grew in strength, added new organizations on behalf of the elderly, and exerted pressure that influenced the previously noted improvements in old age insurance.

The Patient Protection and Affordable Care Act of 2010 (hereafter, Affordable Care Act or ACA) has been compared to the limited Social Security Act of 1935 that nonetheless proved expandable.[113] That would imply that health advocates should follow the example of 1930s advocates for the elderly by continuing to mobilize and fight for improvements. However, Dr. Steffie Woolhandler, a professor of public health and co-founder of Physicians for a National Health Program, which advocates a single-payer program without private insurance intermediaries, does not consider the Affordable Care Act comparable to the Social Security Act: "this is a little like saying that we are going to start Social Security by handing it over to the private pension fund."[114]

A private option in Social Security was, in fact, a distinct possibility that Roosevelt thwarted. An amendment to the Social Security Act, introduced by Senator Bennett Clark (D-Missouri), proposed exempting from the tax for Old Age Insurance employers with industrial pension plans paying benefits at least as liberal as the federal program's. Roosevelt threatened to veto the bill if it contained this amendment. The result was a decision to deal with the issue in the next session of Congress.[115] In all likelihood, Roosevelt not only realized that a private option would undermine the system but took on the private pension movement because it was weak. According to economic historian Steven Sass, "The Great Depression of the 1930s sent a massive shock wave through the nation's fragile private pension system."[116] By the time Congress would have taken up the issue, insurance industry representatives no longer feared a loss of business because the SSA had awakened interest and investment in private insurance as a supplement to low Social Security payments.[117] Arthur Altmeyer, chairman of the technical board of the CES and chairman of the Social Security Board in its formative years, gives a different reason: that employers and insurance companies recognized the difficulties in developing a private option, and that, in any case, strict governmental controls would have to be imposed.[118] Whereas the private pension system was weak in 1935, private health insurance was formidable in 2010. Still, introducing a public option into health care for the non-elderly or disabled and the poor was a compromise between expensive, private intermediaries and a wholly public single-payer system--one that seems to have been yielded too easily.

Even if one takes Dr. Woolhandler's position, it is still important for health advocates to build a stronger movement for universal, affordable care. According to Richard Kirsch, who was the national campaign manager of Health Care for America Now (HCAN), the beyond-the-Beltway grassroots campaign that contributed significantly to passage of the Affordable Care Act, "the fight goes on."[119] In less than two years after its passage, the Supreme Court upheld the constitutionality of the ACA. Nonetheless, healthcare advocates face a harder battle than did their 1930s counterparts for social insurance reform: not only fighting for expansion and improvement but opposing conservative efforts to repeal it. After Old Age Insurance was declared constitutional in 1937, reformers had only the task of improving it.

Pressure exerted on Congress and the Roosevelt Administration by the Townsend Movement contributed to the passage of the Social Security Act. Indeed, many Republicans said "aye" to Social Security, fearing reprisal at the polls if they voted against a bill that contained benefits for the elderly. In the words of the title to Edwin Amenta's book on the Townsend Movement, this was a time "when movements mattered."

Executive leadership also mattered—in strategic use of pressure from advocates of more Progressive reform, in timing and in focusing and shaping public opinion. The forces to the left served moderate reform in several important ways. First, the more radical proposals like those of the Townsendites and advocates of more progressive financing and taxation made the administration's proposals seem a moderate, acceptable alternative. Roosevelt's insistence on an omnibus bill was also important, for there is some reason to doubt that public assistance for children, old age insurance, perhaps even unemployment insurance, would have been enacted had the administration not insisted on an omnibus bill that used the coattails of the elderly to gain passage of less popular measures that were nonetheless important to economic security. It should be noted that neither title for the elderly met the demands of the pension movement for a flat, universal or non-means-tested benefit for the elderly or a universal demogrant. Instead, the Social Security Act initiated a small relief program for the needy elderly, partially funded by the federal government, and work- and wage-determined insurance for retired workers and, beginning in 1939, their dependents and survivors.

Timing was an important element of executive leadership. Roosevelt began the campaign for security legislation relatively early in his administration but not too early to point to some accomplishments—in relief, modest recovery, and reconstruction. Conditions had improved, and, although recovery had stalled, Roosevelt had the public's confidence, as demonstrated a few months later by the unprecedented victory for his party in the midterm elections. It was a time when Republican and other opponents to the right were still relatively weak, although conservative Southern Democrats in the president's party watered down the legislation before voting for it.

New Dealers' push for reform began after moderate recovery, but they did not want improvements to have progressed to the point where the memory of the terrible insecurity of the Depression had faded. Roosevelt, aided by other New Dealers, focused public attention on security. They not only drove home the need for measures that would prevent insecurity, but Roosevelt, in particular, showed how an industrial order required government to supplement the traditional sources of economic security, namely, the individual, the family, and the community. Furthermore, Roosevelt was a master at making reform more acceptable by emphasizing its compatibility with traditional American values.

At a time like the present, when anti-government ideology forms a wall of resistance to reform, New Dealers' rationale for expanded government is a lesson for those whose goals depend on weakening that wall. As the former HCAN director Richard Kirsch observed, "the push to repeal the Affordable Care Act is part and parcel of a broader attack on the role of government overall and in particular in health care."[120]

Those who mount a counterattack on the ideology that undermines reform could draw a lesson from history. They could make the public more aware of how the absence of government programs led to enormous suffering and near economic collapse following the stock market crash of 1929. They could contrast the conditions that led to "untold misery" with the very different aftermath of a severe crash eighty years later—when the legacy of New Deal government programs mitigated mass suffering and helped to prevent a second Great Depression.

Notes

1. Harry L. Hopkins, *Spending to Save: The Complete Story of Relief* (Seattle: University of Washington Press, 1936), 95.
2. Arthur M. Schlesinger, Jr., *The Crisis of the Old Order, 1919–1933* (Boston: Houghton Mifflin, 1957), 174.

3. Center on Budget and Policy Priorities, *Policy Basics: Introduction to the Food Stamps Program* (Washington, DC: Author, 2010), accessed November 20, 2010, available at http://www.cbpp.org/cms/index.cfm?fa=view&id=2226. In the two decades following the Great Depression, Food Stamps was discontinued in favor of distribution of surplus commodities, but it was revived by President John F. Kennedy early in the 1960s and expanded in the 1970s under the Nixon and Carter presidencies in response to revelations of widespread hunger and an anti-hunger movement. The program was officially renamed the Supplemental Nutrition Assistance Program or "SNAP."
4. James Weill, president of the Washington-based Food Research and Action Center (FRAC), cited in Lizzy Rattner, "Food Stamps vs. Poverty," *The Nation*, January 2, 2012, 14.
5. Regarding expansion: *Unemployment Insurance Benefits and Family Income of the Unemployed* (Washington, DC: Congressional Budget Office, 2010), accessed November 26, 2010, available at http://cbo.gov/ftpdocs/119xx/doc11960/11-17-UnemploymentInsurance.pdf; regarding poverty, Robert Greenstein, *Statement on Census' 2009 Poverty and Health Insurance Data* (Washington, DC: Center on Budget and Policy Priorities, 2010), accessed November 20, 2010, available at http://www.cbpp.org/cms/index.cfm?fa=view&id=3292.
6. "Policy Basics: How Many Weeks of Unemployment Compensation Are Available?" (Washington, DC: Center on Budget and Policy Priorities), July 2, 2012, accessed July 8, 2012, available at http://www.cbpp.org/cms/index.cfm?fa=view&id=3164.
7. For information about Unemployment Insurance, including the Extended Benefits (EB) program and Emergency Unemployment (EU) compensation, see Chad Stone and William Chen, "Introduction to Unemployment Insurance" (Washington, DC: Center on Budget and Policy Priorities, February 6, 2013), accessed April 14, 2013, available at http://www.cbpp.org/cms/index.cfm?fa=view&id=1466.
8. The percentage of eligible individuals choosing to participate in SNAP was 75 percent in fiscal year 2010, with states ranging from 55 percent to 100 percent. *Reaching Those in Need: State Supplement SNAP Participation Rates in 2010, Summary* (Washington, DC: U.S. Department of Agriculture Food and Nutrition Service, December 2012), accessed April 14, 2013, available at http://www.fns.usda.gov/ora/MENU/Published/snap/FILES/Participation/Reaching2010_Summary.pdf.
9. Stone and Chen. The EU was scheduled to expire at the end of 2013.
10. Stone and Chen. In 2011, the latest year available at this writing, the average unemployed worker collecting UI had benefits equal to 46 percent of previous earnings.
11. "Baucus Hearing Statement on Welfare Reform: A New Conversation on Women and Poverty" (Washington, DC: United States Senate Committee on Finance, September 21, 2010), accessed March 10, 2012, available at http://finance.senate.gov/newsroom/chairman/release/?id=62f7c15c-ce76-48b1-92cc-2f0ae81d671c.
12. Prior to the recession, 1 million poor mothers were without either work or welfare every month. Sharon Parrott and Arloc Sherman, *TANF at 10: Program Results Are More Mixed Than Often Understood* (Washington, DC: Center on Budget and Policy Priorities, 2006), accessed June 16, 2012, available at http://www.cbpp.org/files/8-17-06tanf.pdf. For labor market conditions for poor single mothers, see Gertrude Schaffner Goldberg, "Feminization of Poverty in the United States," in *Poor Women in Rich Countries*, Gertrude Schaffner Goldberg, ed. (New York: Oxford University Press, 2010), 230–265.
13. Patrick Markee, "The Deep Freeze in Housing Aid," *The Nation*, January 2, 2012, 25.
14. *HUD Program Funding for 2012* (Washington, DC: Center on Budget and Policy Priorities, November 8, 2011), accessed March 13, 2012, available at http://www.cbpp.org/files/9-27-11-IPmemoHUDapprops.pdf. While the voucher program is likely to be sustained at present rates that nonetheless continue to fall very short of meeting need, other areas, including capital repairs for public housing, suffered sharp cuts.
15. Franklin D. Roosevelt, radio address on unemployment and social welfare, Albany, N.Y., October 13, 1932, in Franklin D. Roosevelt, *The Public Papers and Addresses of Franklin*

D. Roosevelt, Vol. 1, *The Genesis of the New Deal, 1928–1932* (New York: Random House, 1938), 788–789. In part of his address he was quoting from a speech he had made to the New York State Legislature in 1931.

16. Rexford. G. Tugwell, "Protagonists: Roosevelt and Hoover," *Antioch Review,* 13, no. 4 (1953): 430. The officials were Senators Robert Wagner (D-NY) and Robert LaFollette, Jr. (R/Progressive-WI).
17. Walter I. Trattner, *From Poor Law to Welfare State: A History of Social Welfare in America,* 6th ed. (New York: Free Press, 1989), 284.
18. Frances Perkins, *The Roosevelt I Knew* (New York: Harper & Row, 1946), 191.
19. Arthur E. Burns and Edward A. Williams, *Federal Work, Security and Relief Programs,* Research Monograph XXIV, Federal Works Agency and Works Projects Administration (Washington, DC: U.S. Government Printing Office, 1941), 37. For high federal shares in some states, see Edith Abbott, *Public Assistance,* 3 vols. (Chicago: University of Chicago Press, 1940), 3, 763.
20. Hopkins, 114. For a full description of the work programs, see Chapter 6 in this book.
21. Burns and Williams, 26–27.
22. U.S. Senate Committee on Finance, Statement of Dorothy Kahn, *Hearings Before the Committee on Finance, United States Senate, Seventy-fourth Congress, First Session on S.1130, A Bill to Alleviate the Hazards of Old Age, Unemployment, Illness, and Dependency, to Establish a Social Insurance Board in the Department of Labor, to Raise Revenue, and for Other Purposes* (Washington, DC: U.S. Government Printing Office, 1935), 652.
23. Hopkins, 99.
24. Anne O'Hare McCormick, as cited by Elmer E. Cornwell, Jr., *Presidential Leadership of Public Opinion* (Bloomington: University of Indiana Press, 1965), 118.
25. Bob Edwards and John D. McCarthy, "Resources and Social Movement Mobilization," in David A. Snow, Sarah A. Soule, and Hanspeter Kriesl, eds., *The Blackwell Companion to Social Movements* (Malden, MA: Blackwell, 2004), 116–162.
26. Perkins, 286.
27. George C Edwards, III, *Strategic President: Persuasion and Opportunity in Presidential Leadership* (Princeton, NJ: Princeton University Press, 2009), Chapter 3.
28. Ibid., 64.
29. Ibid., 105.
30. Cornwell, 129.
31. Franklin D. Roosevelt, Message to the Congress reviewing the broad objectives and accomplishments of the Administration, June 8, 1934, *The Public Papers and Addresses of Franklin D. Roosevelt,* Vol. 3, 1934 (New York: Random House, 1938), 287–292. Hereafter *PPA.*
32. Roosevelt, Address at George Rogers Clark Celebration, Harrodsburg, Kentucky, November 16, 1934, *PPA,* 3, 458.
33. Roosevelt, "Second 'Fireside Chat' of 1934," November 30, 1934, *PPA,* 3, 422.
34. Cornwell, 122.
35. Perkins, 278.
36. Roosevelt, *PPA,* 3, 287.
37. The figures, based on official sources, are from Broadus Mitchell, *The Depression Decade: From New Era Through New Deal, 1929–1941* (Armonk, NY: M.E. Sharpe, 1947), 446, 451.
38. William E., Leuchtenburg, *Franklin D. Roosevelt and the New Deal* (New York: Harper & Row, 1963), 94.
39. Perkins, 281.
40. David M. Kennedy, "What the New Deal Did," *Political Science Quarterly,* 124, no. 2 (2009): 261.
41. "Asserts Law Lags Behind Social Need: Miss Perkins Tells Social Work Session in Montreal," *New York Times,* June 11, 1935, 19.
42. Robert F. Wagner, "Wagner Statement on Bill's Objectives," *New York Times,* January 18, 1935, 16.

43. Leuchtenburg, 116, regarding the margins; Robert S. McElvaine, *The Great Depression: America, 1929–1941*, 2nd ed. (New York: Times Books, 1993), 229, regarding the unprecedented increase in mid-term outcome.
44. Robert Sherwood, *Roosevelt and Hopkins: An Intimate History* (New York: Harper, 1948), 65.
45. Franklin D. Roosevelt, Annual Message to the Congress, January 4, 1935, The American Presidency Project, accessed April 14, 2013, available at http://www.presidency.ucsb.edu/ws/?pid=14890.
46. Josephine Chapin Brown, *Public Relief 1929–1939* (New York: Henry Holt, 1940), 301.
47. Burns and Williams, 74.
48. "Social Security Bill Is Signed; Gives Pensions to Aged, Jobless," *New York Times*, August 15, 1935, 1.
49. Perkins, 284.
50. Edwin Witte, *The Development of the Social Security Act* (Madison: University of Wisconsin Press, 1962), 152–153. The CES overruled staff who had also recommended exclusion of these workers. Universality was largely at the insistence of Hopkins but also favored by Secretary Perkins.
51. Witte, ibid.; Perkins, 298. Kennedy, 268–269, offers another reason for Morgenthau's exclusion of these workers: on one hand, that Roosevelt was opposed to meeting future obligations out of general revenues, and on the other, the fear of the deflationary effects of levying sufficient taxes to cover such a large number of workers.
52. Witte, 153.
53. Perkins, 197–198.
54. Bernstein, 295, estimates 70 percent. The National Urban League estimated two-thirds, and the NAACP, half. Dona Cooper Hamilton and Charles V. Hamilton, *The Dual Agenda: Race and Social Welfare Policies of Civil Rights Organizations* (New York: Columbia University Press, 1997), 31.
55. Edwin Amenta, *When Movements Matter: The Townsend Plan and the Rise of Social Security* (Princeton, NJ: Princeton University Press, 2006), chapters 5–7.
56. Amenta, Chapter 8; see also Abraham Holtzman, *The Townsend Movement: A Political Study* (New York: Bookman Associates, 1963), 101–120.
57. For example, the average benefit for an individual in 1940 was $23 for a retired male worker, $37 for a worker and eligible wife, and $51 for a widow and three or more children. Eveline M. Burns, *The American Social Security System* (New York: Houghton Mifflin, 1951), 97.
58. Ibid., 100.
59. This was not done, partly because the government was operating at a deficit and because of what Perkins referred to as "the President's prejudice about the 'dole.'" See Perkins, 296.
60. Luther Gulick, Memorandum on conference with FDR concerning Social Security taxation, Summer 1941, accessed April 20, 2021, available at http://www.ssa.gov/history/Gulick.html.
61. G. William Domhoff and Michael J. Webber, *Class and Power in the New Deal: Corporate Moderates, Southern Democrats, and the Liberal-Labor Coalition* (Stanford, CA: Stanford University Press, 2011), 176. Domhoff and Webber maintain that Roosevelt gave in to "the liberal-labor coalition" that did not want employee contributions for unemployment insurance. Perkins, 290, felt that unemployment was a "natural risk" of industry, part of the cost of doing business and that only employers should contribute.
62. As noted, this was an important goal to FDR. As governor of New York, he stated his preference for old age insurance over state pensions: "the next step to be taken should be based on the theory of insurance by a system of contributions commencing at an early age." Roosevelt, *PPA*, 1, 103.
63. U.S. Committee on Economic Security, *Social Security in America; The Factual Background of the Social Security Act as Summarized from the Staff Reports to the Committee on Economic Security*, Social Security Board Pub. No. 20 (Washington, DC, 1937), 229–230. For a discussion of the role of the Children's Bureau in the design of the ADC program, see Gertrude

Schaffner Goldberg and Sheila D. Collins, *Washington's New Poor Law: Welfare "Reform" and the Roads Not Taken, 1935 to the Present* (New York: Apex Press, 2001), 28–56.

64. The Chief of the Children's Bureau, Katharine Lenroot, who had co-authored the ADC program, had been supporting the extension of mothers' aid to unwed mothers for more than a decade, although she and her colleagues favored careful supervision of single-mother families. Katharine Lenroot and Emma O. Lundberg, *Illegitimacy as a Child Welfare Problem,* Children's Bureau Pub. No 75 (Washington, DC: U.S. Government Printing Office, 1921), 67, cited by Marguerite G. Rosenthal, "Social Policy for Delinquent Children: Delinquency Activities of the U. S. Children's Bureau, 1912–1940" (Ph.D. diss., State University of New Jersey, 1982), 142–144.
65. Reportedly, Perkins thought in terms of widows or married women with disabled or deserting husbands, but not unwed mothers. She thus felt misled by the Children's Bureau for its having written the program to include the unwed mothers. Gerald Reilly, "Madame Secretary," in *The Making of the New Deal: The Insiders Speak,* ed. Katie Louchheim (Cambridge, MA: Harvard University Press, 1983), 175. Reilly was on the legal staff of the Department of Labor, 1934–1941.
66. "The term dependent child means a child under the age of sixteen who has been deprived of parental support or care by reason of the death, continued absence from the home, or physical or mental incapacity of a parent, and who is living with his father, mother, grandfather, grandmother, brother, sister, stepfather, stepmother, stepbrother, stepsister, uncle, or aunt, in a place of residence maintained by one or more of such relatives as his or their own home." Social Security Act of 1935, Title IV, Grants to States for Dependent Children, Sec. 406, accessed May 13, 2013, available at http://www.ssa.gov/history/35activ.html.
67. U. S. House of Representatives, Report No. 615, 75th Cong., 1st sess., 24 (1935).
68. James T. Patterson, *America's Struggle Against Poverty, 1900–1950* (Cambridge, MA: Harvard University Press, 1981), 69.
69. For a history of the effect of the "suitable homes" policy, see Winifred Bell, *Aid to Dependent Children* (New York: Columbia University Press, 1964).
70. In 1994, just prior to the repeal of Aid to Families with Dependent Children, just over one-third of the caseload was black (36 percent) and another 20 percent was Hispanic. U. S. House of Representatives, Committee on Ways and Means, *1996 Green Book: Background Material and Data on Programs within the Jurisdiction of the Committee on Ways and Means* (Washington, DC: U.S. Government Printing Office, 1997), 474.
71. Social Security Act of 1935, Title I, Grants to the States for Old Age Assistance, accessed April 15, 2013, available at http://www.ssa.gov/history/35act.html#TITLE I.
72. In *Shapiro v. Thompson,* 394 U.S. 618, 1969, the Supreme Court ruled that the residency requirement violates the constitutional right to travel between states.
73. Social Security Act Amendments of 1939, Title I—Amendments to Title I of the Social Security Act, accessed April 15, 2013, available at http://www.ssa.gov/history/pdf/1939Act.pdf.
74. Witte, 144.
75. U.S. Senate Committee on Finance, *Hearings Before the Committee on Finance, Seventy-fourth Congress, First Session on S. 1130* (Washington, DC: U.S. Government Printing Office, 1935), 579.
76. Wilbur J. Cohen, "The Social Security Act of 1935: Reflections Fifty Years Later," in Committee on Economic Security, *The Report of the Committee on Economic Security of 1935, 50th Anniversary Edition* (Washington, DC: National Conference on Social Welfare, 1985), 8.
77. U.S. House of Representatives, Committee on Ways and Means, Hearings on H.R 4120, 74th Cong., 1st sess. (Washington, DC: U.S. Government Printing Office, 1935), 974. The "reasonable subsistence" language was also troubling because it was feared that a state would be forced by the federal statute to spend more than it wanted or could afford, 974–978.
78. Witte, 143–144.

79. Mary Poole, *The Segregated Origins of Social Security: African Americans and the Welfare State* (Chapel Hill: University of North Carolina Press, 2006), 51–52, citing Confidential Hearings before the Committee on Finance, United States Senate, May 1935, 17, and other archival material.
80. Report of the Committee on Economic Security, Summary of Major Recommendations, Employment Assurance, accessed April 15 2013, available at http://www.ssa.gov/history/reports/ces5.html.
81. Perkins, 188–189. See also Hopkins, 182–184.
82. Witte, 77. For some other reasons, see June Hopkins, *Harry Hopkins: Sudden Hero, Brash Reformer* (New York: Palgrave Macmillan, 2009), 195–196; Searle F. Charles, *Minister of Relief: Harry Hopkins and the Depression* (Syracuse, NY: Syracuse University Press, 1963), 95–101.
83. According to Irving Bernstein, p. 149, "throughout its history, both the President and the Congress considered the WPA a 'temporary' if not 'emergency' agency slated for oblivion as soon as severe unemployment disappeared."
84. Perkins, 189.
85. The Comprehensive Employment and Training Administration (CETA) ran from 1973 until 1982. It provided classroom and on-the-job training, work experience, basic and remedial education, counseling, job-search assistance, supportive services, and public service employment to jobless individuals. See, e.g., Helen Ginsburg, *Full Employment and Public Policy: The United States and Sweden* (Lexington, MA: Lexington Books, 1983), 51–54.
86. Amartya Sen, *Development as Freedom* (New York: Knopf, 1998), 94.
87. U.S. Bureau of Labor Statistics, "The Employment Situation for June 2000," tables A-1, A-4, accessed May 30, 2013, available at http://www.bls.gov/news.release/history/empsit_07072000.txt. For monthly figures on real and hidden unemployment, visit the website of the National Jobs for All Coalition, http://www.njfac.org.
88. Franklin D. Roosevelt, The Second Inaugural Address, January 20, 1937, *PPA*, 6, 5.
89. David C. Wheelcock, "The Federal Response to Home Mortgage Distress: Lessons from the Great Depression," *Federal Reserve Bank of St. Louis Review*, May–June 1, 2000, 138, citing *Fifth Annual Report of the Federal Home Loan Bank Board*, 1937, 4, accessed April 15 2013, available at http://research.stlouisfed.org/publications/review/08/05/Wheelock.pdf.
90. Leuchtenburg, 165.
91. Wheelcock, 142, citing C. Lowell Harris, *History and Policies of the Home Owners' Loan Corporation* (New York: National Bureau of Economic Research, 1951).
92. Douglas S. Massey and Nancy A. Denton, *American Apartheid: Segregation and the Making of the Underclass* (Cambridge, MA: Harvard University Press, 1993), 51–52.
93. Wheelock, 142.
94. Hillary Rodham Clinton, "Let's Keep People in Their Homes," *Wall Street Journal*, September 25, 2008, accessed June 15, 2012, available at http://online.wsj.com/article/SB122230767702474045.html#articleTabs%3Darticle.
95. *New York Times: Times Topics*, "The Obama Housing Plan," updated February 1, 2012, accessed May 20, 2012, available at http://topics.nytimes.com/top/reference/timestopics/subjects/c/credit_crisis/housing_plan/index.html.
96. Massey and Denton, 53–54.
97. Albert Monroe, "How the Federal Housing Administration Affects Home Ownership," Harvard University Department of Economics, November 2011, 3, accessed May 12, 2012, available at http://www.jchs.harvard.edu/sites/jchs.harvard.edu/files/monroe_w02-4.pdf.
98. U.S. Department of Housing and Urban Development, "Federal Housing Administration," undated, accessed May 25, 2012, available at http://www.reference.com/browse/Federal_Housing_Administration.
99. Robert D. Leighninger, Jr., *Long-Range Public Investment: The Forgotten Legacy of the New Deal* (Columbia: University of South Carolina Press 2007), Chapter 9. The Resettlement

was transferred to the Department of Agriculture in 1937 and renamed the Farm Security Administration.

100. Arthur M. Schlesinger, Jr. *The Coming of the New Deal* (Boston: Houghton Mifflin 1958), 371. Leighninger, 157–163, regarding fewer communities.
101. Peter Marcuse and W. Dennis Keating, "The Permanent Housing Crisis," in *A Right to Housing: Foundation for a New Social Agenda,* eds. Rachel G. Bratt, Michael E. Stone, and Chester Hartman (Philadelphia: Temple University Press, 2006), 139–162.
102. Ibid., 142.
103. D. Bradford Hunt, "Was the 1937 U. S. Housing Act a Pyrrhic Victory?" *Journal of Planning History,* 43 (August 2008): 195–221.
104. Marcuse and Keating, 143, citing U.S. Department of Commerce, 1975. Currently, Marcuse and Keating report, public housing is about 1 percent of U.S. housing stock.
105. Leuchtenburg, 136.
106. Witte, 174. Perkins "likewise believed in health insurance, although originally she was doubtful whether it was immediately feasible," Witte, 187. According to Perkins, 289, Roosevelt told a conference held by the CES that it was "highly desirable."
107. Perkins, 289.
108. Witte, 174.
109. Roy Lubove, *The Struggle for Social Security 1900–1935* (Cambridge, MA: Harvard University Press, 1968), 89. For discussion of the pre–New Deal health insurance campaigns, see 66–70.
110. Witte, 172–173.
111. Carmen DeNavas-Walt, Bernadette D. Proctor, and Jessica C. Smith, *Income, Poverty, and Health Insurance in the United States: 2010, U.S. Census Bureau, Current Population Reports,* P60–P239 (Washington, DC: U.S. Government Printing Office, 2011), Table 8, 26, accessed May 1, 2012, available at http://www.census.gov/prod/2011pubs/p60-239.pdf.
112. Michael B. Katz, *In the Shadow of the Poorhouse: A Social History of Welfare in America,* rev. ed. (New York: Basic Books, 1996), esp. 254–255.
113. Katherine S. Newman and Steven Attewell, "Learning to Live with the Healthcare Bill," *The Nation,* May 17, 2011, 22–24.
114. Steffie Woolhandler in "Healthcare Debate: As Supreme Court Hears Landmark Case, Does Law Do Enough to Fix Health Crisis?" *Democracy Now,* March 27, 2012, accessed April 16, 2012, available at http://www.democracynow.org/2012/3/27/healthcare_debate_as_supreme_court_hears.
115. Witte, 159–162.
116. Steven A. Sass, *The Promise of Private Pensions: The First Hundred Years* (Cambridge: Harvard University Press, 1997), 88, as cited by Domhoff and Webber, 155.
117. Nancy J. Altman, *The Battle for Social Security: From FDR's Vision to Bush's Gamble* (New York: John Wiley, 2005), 95–96.
118. Arthur J. Altmeyer, *The Formative Years of Social Security* (Madison: University of Wisconsin Press, 1966), 42. Controls would have to be imposed "to assure actuarial soundness, proper investment and control of funds, and protection of beneficiaries' rights."
119. Richard Kirsch, *Fighting for Our Health: The Epic Battle to Make Health Care a Right in the United States* (Albany, NY: Rockefeller Institute Press, 2011), 357–372.
120. Ibid., 367.

8

The Democratization of Culture

The Legacy of the New Deal Arts Programs

SHEILA D. COLLINS AND NAOMI ROSENBLUM

Striking industrial workers and protests by unemployed councils were not the only form of social agitation in the Great Depression. Lack of employment affected those in cultural and clerical fields as well. Intellectuals had their own picket lines and were among the most politically leftist members of the working class.[1] As Robert Whitcomb, secretary of the Unemployed Writers' Union, wrote in 1934 to the Civil Works Administration:

> The unemployed writers of New York City do not intend to continue under the semi-starvation conditions meted out to them.... If the government does not intend to formulate some policy regarding the class of intellectual known as the writer, who is trained for nothing else in this economic emergency, then the writer must organize and conduct a fight to better his condition.[2]

The federal work programs that were intended to take the place of the demeaning dispersals of money and goods known as "relief" were at first centered on building and repairing the nation's infrastructure and taking care of the land. Eventually, however, New Deal administrators recognized that lack of employment affected those in cultural fields as well as industrial workers and youth. The result was what has been called "a governmental adventure in cultural collectivism, the like of which no nation has experienced before or since."[3]

Prior to the establishment of the federal arts programs, most cultural workers had to depend on a network of wealthy patrons to support their work and to get it presented to a wider audience. Not only did the Depression dampen private support for the arts, but technological changes—the invention of the radio, phonograph, and movies—were fast displacing live performance artists. Some 30,000 musicians had been displaced by these new technologies, and the government estimated that well over 30,000 theater workers were made expendable by the mid-1930s.[4] Aside from the immediate effect of reducing the relief roles, these projects had an unprecedented effect on the practice and appreciation of the arts in the United States—an effect that has left an indelible, if often unrecognized, mark some eighty years later. This chapter looks at the origins of the various federal arts programs, the difficulties faced by government officials in managing such a unique series of enterprises, the extraordinary outpouring of art and culture that resulted, the tangible and intangible benefits this had for the country, and the lessons we can learn from this experience for today.

Origins of the Federal Arts Programs

The nation's legacy from this period of cultural expansion has been little praised and sometimes mocked, and in general was little known until recently, other than by specialists. For many years, the social content and recognizable styles of many of the public works of art produced during the New Deal years were deemed old-fashioned, if not faintly ridiculous. With reference to the visual arts especially, we were and remain much more aware of the influences emanating from Europe in the early years of the twentieth century—that is, before the rise of fascism and the Depression. Then, cubism, abstraction, and surrealism, as practiced in Europe, were the experimental modes that attracted a small coterie of American artists who were, for the most part, from a prosperous, urbanized middle class and élitist collectors.[5] However, during the 1920s, there were few sales of modern American art, and artists were unable to make a living from their art, despite the existence of several galleries devoted to marketing their work; the few who were in a position to collect works of art were oriented toward the European product.

The federal programs initiated in the 1930s had both economic and cultural goals. They were intended to alleviate the economic hardships experienced by those occupied in cultural areas of work—and perhaps as important, to popularize art among a much wider segment of the population than just a small coterie of enthusiasts living in urban centers, notably New York City. Though he had no particular knowledge of or judgment about the arts, Roosevelt had many friends who were artists, and when the Civil Works program was getting underway, it was his decision to include artists. These programs made possible literary, musical, theatrical, and visual expression under a variety of alphabetical entities—the Public Works of Art Project (PWAP), the Treasury Relief Art Program (TRAP), the Federal Art Project/Works Project Administration (FAP/WPA), and the Farm Security Administration (FSA). Various movers and shakers, among them George Biddle, Harry Hopkins, Hallie Flanagan, Harold Ickes, Edward Bruce, Holger Cahill, Henry Alsberg, Nikolai Sokoloff, and Roy Stryker, were charged with seeing that these projects were initiated and completed; they also ran interference with congressional critics who found expenditures on culture to be politically radical or unnecessary.

The Treasury Art Programs

In 1933, the idea that art might enhance public life had been suggested to President Roosevelt by painter George Biddle. Biddle had been impressed by government-funded Mexican murals (in particular those painted by Diego Rivera and José Clemente Orozco) that made use of themes from that country's history. (Both Mexican artists later received privately sponsored mural commissions in the United States.) As a consequence of the interest of Roosevelt and Biddle in public art, the federal government established several public art projects. Though established for different periods and under different names, all had in common that their products—mostly murals, sculptures, and paintings—were to enhance and decorate public buildings. They were, of course, economic programs designed to put money in people's pockets, but they also had a less tangible purpose—to boost public morale during a time of deep stress and pessimism. It is well known to psychologists that exposure to the arts and participation in creative activity can have a beneficial effect on people's sense of well-being.[6]

The Public Works of Art Project

The first such experiment in employing cultural workers was the Public Works of Art Project (PWAP), which, in its short life (December 1933—June 1934) and with funds transferred from the Civil Works Administration, put 3,700 unemployed graphic artists (about a third of the nation's estimated unemployed artists) to work in beautifying public buildings and parks and producing over 15,000 works of art. Its guidelines stressed that "artists were to improve the craftsmanship of furnishings" of public buildings; embellish federal, state, and municipal buildings and parks; and make pictorial records of such national projects as the CCC dams.[7] Taking a phrase from a speech given by Franklin Roosevelt on December 6, 1933, Edward ("Ned") Bruce, an attorney and the program's director, called the PWAP an example of the president's desire to give Americans "a more abundant life" with "the first completely democratic art movement in history." [8] Bruce set the PWAP in motion quickly to preempt political blowback because many people thought that government funding of art was frivolous and a waste of taxpayers' money. Within days, all sixteen regional directors, selected by Bruce, had accepted their jobs and were forming volunteer committees to identify artists across the nation. Within eight days, the first artists had their checks, and within three weeks they all did—an amazing administrative accomplishment.[9] The legacy of the PWAP was: 99 carvings; 1,076 etchings; 42 frescoes; over 1,000 mural designs and projects; 3,821 oil paintings; 1,518 prints; 43 pieces of Pueblo pottery; 2,938 watercolors, plus an array of bas reliefs, drawings, light fixtures, mosaics, Navajo blankets, portraits, poster prints, stage sets, and tapestries.[10] In 1934, the Corcoran Gallery in Washington held an exhibit of the works, to an overwhelming response. The *New York Times* gave a glowing review, and members of Congress, as well as Cabinet secretaries lined up to request paintings for their offices.[11]

Treasury Section of Painting and Sculpture

As the PWAP was running out of money another program was begun to employ artists and sculptors. Called by various names (Treasury Section of Painting and Sculpture, or simply, the Section), and also headed by Edward Bruce, it operated from October 1934 through July 1943. Unlike the PWAP, however, this program was not a relief program. Instead, it sought to employ artists through a selective competition regardless of whether or not they were penurious. Once chosen, an artist essentially became an independent operator, signing a contract to complete a specific project, rather than assuming a regular salaried position, thus making it a precursor of the much-later National Endowment for the Arts. One of the benefits of the program was that it allowed lesser-known artists, including a large number of women, to compete with more established painters and sculptors.[12] The Section had five main goals: 1) to secure the best-quality art to embellish public buildings; 2) to stimulate the development of American art; 3) to employ local talent wherever possible; 4) to secure cooperation of the art world in selecting artists for this work; and 5) to encourage project proposal competitions where practical. Seeking to make art a part of everyday life, the Section commissioned outstanding pieces to be located in places such as post offices, court houses, schools, and hospitals that citizens would visit frequently and at no cost.[13] The Section was administered with central oversight to ensure that themes that appeared in the art were neither radical nor embarrassing to the New Deal. Ultimately some artists saw this as censorship and protested that their creativity was being stifled. By December 1942, when the program was terminated, over 1,100 towns and cities could boast federal buildings with New Deal murals and sculpture embellishing both exteriors and interiors.[14] These works remain a legacy to this day, though many people who see them may have no knowledge of the history that produced them.[15]

The Treasury Relief Art Project

The Treasury public art programs culminated in the Treasury Relief Art Project (TRAP) under Olin Dows and Cecil Jones. TRAP ran from July 1935 to June 1939. It expanded its focus to include all kinds of art, not just murals and sculptures. At least 75 percent of participants had to qualify for relief in addition to being competent artists. One percent of construction costs for new buildings was set aside for the purchase or commissioning of artwork. For the TRAP endeavor, painted and frescoed scenes of historical events and everyday life that might also embrace themes promoting New Deal reformist ideas were chosen by competition among the artists. Their works, selected on the sole basis of quality, adorned the walls of post offices, state and federal offices, schools, libraries, and airports. It is safe to say that few ordinary Americans at the time were knowledgeable about many of the painters involved or aware of the varied aspects of life that their works revealed. For example, the decoration of the Interior Department building in Washington, D.C., included scenes of indigenous life painted by a little-known Native American artist. TRAP was finally closed by the Treasury Department as the result of a dispute between the Artists Union and the program director over the issue of quality versus quantity. It was meant to be a small program, yet there were more people clamoring for jobs than the funding could sustain. During its active period, 356 artists completed 85 murals, 30 sculptures, and 10,215 easel paintings.

The Federal Arts Projects/WPA

With unemployment still raging and the arts and cultural community becoming more restive, a more elaborate arts program was eventually established under the WPA. The WPA Art Project, known as Federal One, which was to include theater people, visual artists, writers, dancers, musicians, conservators, and clerical workers, became the best known of the New Deal arts and culture programs. Its contributions to American culture are incalculable. Under the national directorship of Holger Cahill, Federal One was begun in August 1935 and was to last until 1943. Federal One programs differed from the other New Deal arts programs in that they were decentralized and largely run at the state or municipal level (albeit with federal oversight and often federal guidelines). Regional directors worked with state federal art programs and community committees to carry out tasks of public improvements and service. The WPA provided wages while state or local entities and sponsors were responsible for providing materials and equipment. This decentralized structure, however, could often make for friction between state-level WPA officials and national leadership, and it led to a somewhat chaotic and conflictual experience. Nevertheless, the output of Federal One through all of its various programs was vast and varied.

The Federal Art Project

By far, the best known of all the New Deal visual arts programs was the Federal Art Project (FAP/WPA) initiated in 1935 as part of Federal One and lasting until March 1942. Employing at the height of its tenure more than 5,000 artists, the majority of whom would otherwise have been applicants for relief, it maintained an easel painting division, a graphic arts section, and its own relatively small mural effort. Among the now well-known artists supported by this effort were painters Thomas

Hart Benton, Stuart Davis, Arshile Gorky, Philip Guston, Willem de Kooning, Lee Krasner, Jacob Lawrence, Jackson Pollock, Mark Rothko, Raphael and Moses Soyer, Lucienne Bloch, and sculptor Louise Nevelson.

The FAP underwrote projects to supply posters and illustrations for books and theater and eventually the war effort.[16] The fully furnished print workshops set up under the WPA prepared the ground for the flowering of the graphic arts in the United States, which until that time had been limited in both media and expression. Moreover, since prints were portable and cheap and were allocated to schools, libraries, museums, hospitals, government offices, and army bases, they became a vehicle for broadening the public's understanding and appreciation of the creative arts.[17] Under the FAP/WPA aegis, artists also made a pictorial record of all manner of vernacular objects. This compendium of 22,000 plates provided the nation with its first *Index of American Design*. The program expanded the appeal of this commonplace material—much of it folk art—from a fancy held by a coterie of well-to-do "connoisseurs," to one that a wider public might experience—a forerunner perhaps of PBS's *Antiques Roadshow*. Small works of art, both easel paintings and prints, produced in workshops throughout the nation were given to government offices, while murals completed under the aegis of FAP were seen mainly on the walls of schools, libraries, post offices, and hospitals. Over the course of its eight years, the WPA commissioned over five hundred murals for New York City's public hospitals alone. The breadth of the imagination to which the public was exposed can be seen in the finely preserved collection of the Norwalk, Connecticut Transit District. Murals commissioned for public buildings in that city depicted not only scenes from American history and contemporary life and work, but also stylized scenes from Chinese, Egyptian, and Venetian cultures, as well as illustrations depicting famous literary works.[18]

One of the unique features of this program was the community art centers—some one hundred of them established in twenty-two states—but particularly in areas where opportunities to experience and make art were scarce. These centers included galleries, classrooms, and community workshops, and served an estimated 8 million people.[19] Here, both experienced artists and amateurs, including children, could take classes in drawing, painting, sculpture, and other forms of artistic expression. This effort afforded individuals who may never have seen a large painted scene or a piece of sculpture an exceptional opportunity not only to experience a finished work of art but also to participate in the actual process of creation. According to Smithsonian author David A. Taylor, "the effect was electric. It jump-started people beginning careers in art amid the devastation."[20]

The Federal Writers' Project

The Federal Writers' Project, under Henry Alsberg, provided employment and experience for some 6,686 writers, editors, art critics, researchers, and historians, many of whom later flowered in the genres of the novel and poetry. In finding a way to employ writers, many of whom had leftwing sympathies, Alsberg and his team came up with the idea of putting them to work writing well-researched state and regional guidebooks that were to portray the social, economic, industrial, and historical background of the country. In this way, their political sympathies were not likely to intrude into their writing and thus upset conservative critics who were critical of the entire arts enterprise.

The implementation of the program was fraught with conflict from the beginning. Determined to have writers' projects creating guidebooks in all forty-eight states, the Project's directors often found it difficult to find qualified writers or experienced project managers in regions far from urbanized cultural centers. According to Jerre Mangione, who served as coordinating editor of the Project, in addition to attacks from Congress and the press, which characterized the project as a blatant boondoggle, conflicts between national Project directors and state-level WPA directors—frequently men with engineering backgrounds who had no understanding of the literary requirements—often erupted. Field offices often fell short of meeting deadlines, and professional writers occasionally rebelled against having to write according to national guidelines or to meet the demands of self-appointed censors, who, "in the name of patriotism or civic pride, objected to New Deal attitudes expressed in some Project publications."[21]

By 1942, despite these difficulties and the constant threat by Congress to cut off the Project's funding, the Writers' Project had produced an estimated one thousand books and pamphlets, although, according to Mangione, no one knows exactly how many published items it produced, as many have since been lost or destroyed.[22] Among the works were guidebooks to each of the 48 states, to cities, small towns, major regions, and interstate roadways—a vast treasury of Americana from the ground up that included facts and folklore, history and legend, histories of the famous, the infamous and the excluded, embracing, as one observer noted, a pluralism "that countered racism at home and fascism abroad."[23] There were, as well, the *Slave Narratives*—seventeen-volume oral histories of the last people who could give first-person accounts of what it was like to have lived under slavery. These volumes, now held in the Library of Congress, have been an invaluable resource to historians. An additional set of folklore and oral histories of 10,000 people from all regions, occupations, and ethnic groups are now part of the Library of Congress's *American Memory* collection. Despite the almost incessantly negative press received during the Project's buildup, by the time it was finished, the critics were generally favorable. Robert Cantwell wrote in the *New Republic* in 1939 that the guidebooks to cities, towns, and regions represented the first effort to write American history in terms of its communities. In the past, he wrote, American history had been written in terms of its "leading actors and its dominant economic movements but never in terms of the ups and downs of the towns from which the actors emerged and in which the economic movements had their play."[24] Bernard De Voto saw the books as an "educational force, and even a patriotic force, an honorable addition to our awareness of ourselves and our country."[25] Alfred Kazin summed up the serendipitous nature of the entire collection:

> So the WPA state guides, seemingly only a makeshift, a stratagem of administrative relief policy...resulted in an extraordinary contemporary epic. Out of the need to find something to say about every community and the country around it, out of the vast storehouse of facts behind the guides—geological, geographical, meteorological, ethnological, historical, political, sociological, economic—there emerged an America unexampled in density and regional diversity.[26]

The Writers' Project thus produced an unparalleled store of American history and folkways that continued to provide help to writers and editors in the development of characters and locales long after the program's demise.[27]

Although many writers were ashamed at the time to be "on the dole" and even afterwards tried to ignore their role in these programs, the experience of working in the New Deal programs gave many who would go on to become this nation's most famous literary figures a means to survive at a time when joining the Project was a matter of life and death, and set them on the road to their future careers. One of the fringe benefits of the Project for young writers was that of associating with published authors. The poet, Margaret Walker, for example, received valuable advice from Nelson Algren when she showed him her unfinished poem, "For My People," which later won the Yale Award for young poets.[28] It also gave them material and techniques that appeared later in novels and plays.[29] Richard Wright, who had been a Post Office employee before joining the project, found new material through his work for the Writers' Project that would later appear in his books. Studs Terkel used the oral history techniques learned through his work with the Writer's Project to write his famous collection of oral history books. Ralph Ellison might never have written *The Invisible Man* had it not been for the Writer's Project. Ellison is quoted in a Library of Congress document as saying that the Writers' Project helped him better understand the powerful connection between serious literature and folkways.[30] With their publications, the Writers' Project authors contributed not only to their own development, but in absorbing, in the course of their work, genetic information about their country and its people, they could "destroy false myths, dethrone phony heroes, eliminate racial barriers, and promote assistance for disadvantaged Americans."[31] Among the other now-famous writers to benefit from the Project were Conrad Aiken, Nelson Algren, Saul Bellow, Arna Bontemps, Malcolm Cowley, Edward Dahlberg, Ralph Ellison, Zora Neale Hurston, Claude McKay, Kenneth Patchen, Philip Rahv, Kenneth Rexroth, Harold Rosenberg, Studs Terkel, and Frank Yerby.

The Federal Theatre Project

Long before the Great Depression, changes in the theater industry had limited quality theater productions to a select metropolitan clientèle, leaving the Middle West, the Far West, and large parts of the South deprived of first-rate theatrical entertainment. By the late 1920s, technology was replacing even those who did find work in the theater business. Large numbers of actors, stagehands, technicians, musicians, and vaudeville performers were displaced by the movie industry. "Sound films had replaced the orchestra; recorded music replaced live performance; the training of actors became less important than publicizing the Hollywood star. The popularity of radio and a change in public taste added to the plight of those who were often thought of as a 'dispensable luxury' anyway."[32] With the onset of the Depression, theater doors, even in New York City, the theater capital of the country, were closed, leaving thousands of people without jobs or means of support, except for sporadic help from theatrical unions.

Under the leadership of Hallie Flanagan, who had been recruited from her post as director of the Vassar Experimental Theatre by WPA Administrator Harry Hopkins, all this was to change. Hopkins believed that society had an obligation to conserve the talents of men and women in the arts as well as of those in the factories. This belief also coincided with the desires of Eleanor and Franklin Roosevelt for a national theatrical project or projects that would provide musical and dramatic entertainment for small and remote communities.

The Federal Theatre Project was the first and only attempt to create a national theater in the United States. In writing a brief for the program, Flanagan pointed out that ancient Athens and the modern countries of "France, Germany, Norway, Denmark, Sweden, Russia, Italy and practically all other civilized countries appropriate money for the Theatre."[33] But beyond the fact that most other countries supported the theater, there was the fact that thousands of unemployed actors, dancers, directors, playwrights, designers, stage technicians, ushers, box office personnel, and clerical staff "could get just as hungry as unemployed accountants and engineers, but—and this was much more revolutionary—that their skills were as worthy of conservation." Harry Hopkins, she pointed out, "believed that the talents of these theatrical workers, together with the skills of painters, musicians, and writers, made up a part of the national wealth which America could not afford to lose."[34] Flanagan was also convinced that theater could be an agent of change. In a report on the first summer Federal Theatre, she expressed her belief in the socially transformative function of theater.

> By a stroke of fortune unprecedented in dramatic history, we have been given a chance to help change America at a time when twenty million unemployed Americans proved it needed changing. And the theatre, when

> it is any good, can change things. The theatre can quicken, start things, make things happen. Don't be afraid when people tell you this is a play of protest. Of course it's protest, protest against dirt, disease, human misery. If, in giving great plays of the past as greatly as we can give them, and if, in making people laugh, which we certainly want to do, we can't also protest—as Harry Hopkins is protesting and as President Roosevelt is protesting—against some of the evils of this country of ours, then we do not deserve the chance put into our hands[35]

It was Flanagan's conviction that the project must not just repeat theatrical forms of the past but be responsive to the technological, economic, and cultural changes the country was undergoing. In addition to performances of classical plays by well-known playwrights, circuses, dance performances, musical comedies, puppet shows, light opera, children's theater, pageants and spectacles, vaudeville, and religious drama were all given space, not only "in city Theatres, but in parks and hospitals, in Catholic convents and Baptist churches, in public schools and armories, in circus tents and universities, in prisons and reformatories and in distant camps. . . ."[36] Touring companies brought plays to parts of the country where drama had been nonexistent and provided training and experience for new actors who would later became prominent.

One important, but overlooked, aspect was the program's emphasis on preserving and promoting minority cultural forms. At a time of strict racial segregation, with arts funding non-existent in African American communities, black theater companies were established in Birmingham, Boston, Chicago, Hartford, Los Angeles, New York, Newark, Philadelphia, Raleigh, San Francisco, and Seattle. Foreign language companies for which funding had become impossible also performed works in French, German, Italian, Spanish, and Yiddish to eager audiences. In addition, the Federal Theatre Project employed photographers in every major city who recorded performances, rehearsals, and images of performers and also captured behind-the-scenes work, stage sets, costumes, audiences, and theaters.[37]

The Federal Theatre project, however, was not an easy program to pull off. As one historian of the theater has written:

> The organizational problems were, of course, always aggravated by the financial limitations and by the hostility and obstructionism of certain elements both inside and outside the government. Congressional disapproval, WPA regulations, and anti-Roosevelt newspaper columns vilified the efforts of the Theatre project from the beginning. Even professional theatre people opposed Federal theatre performances at nominal prices, charging they took business from the commercial theatre.[38]

The Federal Theatre Project was especially effective in bringing controversial social and economic issues to the foreground, making it one of the most embattled of all the New Deal programs. Plays about labor disputes, economic inequality, racism, and other such issues infuriated a growing chorus of political critics who sought to shut the program down and at other times threatened and then succeeded with funding cuts. One innovation, the Living Newspaper unit, which dramatized stories from the newspapers, was especially offensive. Even though plays about controversial issues were wildly popular with audiences, Flanagan recognized that the Federal Theatre Project had to walk a careful line between producing "safe" plays and more controversial ones if it were to survive.[39] In contrast to the amount of criticism of the program, fewer than 10 percent of the plays dealt with issues that were likely to draw fire. Nevertheless, the program had become "a microcosm of all the New Deal represented to the enemies of the administration, notably in its spending policy and its liberal attitude toward labor, aliens, and minorities."[40]

Flanagan had hoped that this experiment in national theater might lead "toward an art in which each region and eventually each state would have its unique, indigenous dramatic expression, its company housed in a building reflecting its own landscape and regional materials, producing plays of its past and present, in its own rhythm of speech and its native design, in an essentially American pattern."[41] Sadly, this vision was not to come to fruition, although the development of local community theater in many places in the country may be seen as one legacy of this experiment. Falling victim to the House Committee to Investigate Un-American Activities under Chairman Martin Dies, and the House Committee on Appropriations, the Federal Theatre Project was finally shut down by an act of Congress in 1939. Nevertheless, the program, however, brief, had left a lasting legacy. Seventy-seven new plays had found audiences in more than one city. Thousands of aspiring actors, directors, stagehands, and playwrights were either supported or got their start in the Federal Theatre Project,[42] among them many now-famous theatrical figures such as Orson Welles, Joseph Losey, John Houseman, Helen Hayes, and Eugene O'Neill. The creative formats that characterized many productions greatly enlarged the contours of dramatic presentation. Thus, it would be difficult to conceive of present-day theater and even film culture without reference to the aesthetic developments in the 1930s WPA theater productions.

The Federal Music Project

The Depression arrived in an era of flourishing popular music—both jazz and folk. Nevertheless, thousands of professional musicians were unemployed. To provide these musicians with opportunities to perform, former director of the Cleveland Symphony Nickolai Sokoloff promoted live concerts of such music at low cost or for free under the aegis of the Federal Music Project. The Project provided financial assistance for existing symphony and concert orchestras and created new ones in states and cities that had never had an orchestra. The musical menu was not limited to this fare, however; band concerts and opera were among the offerings, and work by popular American musicians—ethnic ensembles, musical comedies, and jazz—were also highlighted. A lesser effort, though not insignificant, resulted in the gathering and recording of the folk music heritage of the nation. John and Alan Lomax's collection, now housed at the American Folklife Center in the Library of Congress, stands as an incomparable product of this effort.[43]

One important aspect of the program was education. Music classes for all ages and ability levels were offered in parts of the country and to populations that had never had access to such instruction, and lectures on music theory and appreciation were also offered. In 1939, an estimated 132,000 children and adults in 27 states received instruction every week.[44] There was even a "Composers' Forum Laboratory" where composers could play their compositions before an audience and get feedback from it. According to one music scholar, the Federal Music Project increased the technical ability of many musicians who were employed by it.[45] The music project eventually became the largest and most expensive of the arts projects, employing more than 15,000 instrumentalists, composers, vocalists, and teachers.

The Farm Security Administration Photography Program

The Farm Security Administration (FSA) photography program, under Roy Stryker, oversaw the production of more than 80,000 photographs, produced as part of the effort to make the nation aware of the plight of displaced rural populations. These images—produced by a changing group of photographers—among them such luminaries as Jack Delano, Walker Evans, Dorothea Lange, Russell Lee, Gordon Parks, Arthur Rothstein, Ben Shahn, John Vachon, and Marion Post Wolcott—were used in news and magazine articles and at country fairs and exhibitions, helping to humanize the verbal and statistical reports of the terrible poverty and turmoil in the agricultural sector of the economy. Categorized at the time as "documentary" photography, this approach to image-making remained a viable form of expression into the postwar period, with the result that this body of work continued to receive considerable attention, unlike much of the graphic art and painting of the 1930s. The photographs provide a vivid picture of the many faces of the Depression that remain iconic to this day. Photographs were also produced under the auspices of the WPA; its most complete project, *Changing New York,* was the work of photographer Berenice Abbott and historian Elizabeth McCausland.

The Democratization of the Arts

During the nineteenth and early twentieth centuries, visual art expression in the United States had been considered a somewhat suspect activity—indeed, it was thought by some to be a pursuit for dilettantes. The notion that there should be government support for the arts was unheard of. Other than portraitists and those few who provided commemorative painting and statuary for public purposes, only individuals with unusual interests involved themselves in making art, while to acquire art objects required knowledge and means. The New Deal Arts programs had changed all that. Art making and appreciation had gone from being an activity valued and practiced by a relatively small group of the "enlightened" to an experience that gained participants from a wider range of the American public, including population groups and artistic subjects and styles that would normally have been ignored. Hundreds of Hispanic Americans, Native Americans, and African Americans were now contributing their talents and their worldviews to the country's heritage. Art historian Milton W. Brown commented that the lack of a color line in the arts had "a telling effect on racial relations in the United States."[46] As one historian of the period has estimated, projects that produced graphic art reached an audience of millions. In that many more people came in contact with "art"—whether they recognized it as such or not—their ideas about artists and their products evolved. One has only to note the current large museum attendance to acknowledge the lasting effects of WPA efforts to make art experience available to the people. Art had been democratized and, for a time, de-commodified. The legacy of experiencing visual art in all its many forms, which the art projects made possible, remained a potent force long after the initial programs had ended.

Not only did more people get to experience art during this period, but they also were able to participate in making it. Classes for young and old in the various visual and plastic arts and in both the appreciation and performance of music were held in settlement houses, community centers, and schools, where they acquainted a generation with the idea that art was not merely a frill but something they might themselves aspire to, or at least want to experience in an intelligent way. In the New York City area alone, an estimated 50,000 children and adults participated in classes under the Federal Art Project auspices each week. (As a 10-year-old child, one of the authors was a thankful recipient of these programs, studying painting and sculpture in settlement house classes in the mid- to late 1930s.) Community art centers in impoverished rural areas were visited by some 3 million people who had no previous experience with art production of any kind.

Additionally, the arts programs were thought to have turned American artists away from their attraction to European styles and reintegrated them with their homeland experiences. Support for artists by government agencies during the Depression years was accompanied by resurgent interest in American history and in ordinary people and events. During the early years of the twentieth century, this direction had already been demonstrated in literary works such as Edgar Lee Master's *Spoon River Anthology* and in visual works produced by the so-called Ash Can painters whose subjects were frequently drawn from urban street life. The subject matter of the somewhat later "American scene" painters of the Twenties expanded that vision. Edward Hopper and Charles Burchfield, for instance, were drawn to rural life in places like Gloucester, Massachusetts, and Taos, New Mexico, as well as to that in cities. A later group known as Regionalists concentrated almost entirely on rural themes. But interest in the American landscape and experience expanded during the New Deal. Artists like Thomas Hart Benton, John Steuart Curry, and Grant Wood sought to express what they considered a uniquely American experience, highlighting the significance of the agricultural sector and presenting it in a positive light. In contrast, other Thirties artists known as Social Realists were concerned with city life and its disparities and travails; often, but not invariably, their political orientation was to the left of the overall spectrum. Whatever their subject matter and political orientation, these painters for the most part rejected the modernist styles emanating from Europe in favor of portraying aspects of reality in an accessible manner. One consequence of both more accessible formal language and the wider existence of art works during this time was that many more people were able to see and understand examples of visual expression. Still, there was also government support for artists who adhered to more abstract styles in their work, notably Stuart Davis and Burgoyne Diller. The fact that there were differing ways of handling reality was also a factor in opening up public understanding of visual art. These developments helped prepare the way for a continuing national interest in the visual arts—even after the programs were terminated.

In past eras, American artists had gathered together in societies mainly to acquire exhibition space and promote their work, but the tenor of the times now led them to join together to affect economic and political developments on the national and local levels. The Artists' Congress, organized in 1936, embraced those with differing styles and attitudes about artistic production as well as those with various political views. To deal specifically with the economic problems and issues of censorship that arose with the development of publicly supported artwork, the Artists' Union was formed. Its publication, *Art Front,* featured writers—among them Harold Rosenberg and Meyer Schapiro—who later became esteemed critics of the new art of the postwar period. In the mid-Thirties, photographers of the urban scene came together in the Photo League to promote the kind of imagery that portrayed working-class people in their neighborhoods, both to celebrate an unheralded aspect of society and call attention to deplorable slum housing.[47]

While the Federal Art programs were greeted with high expectations by many artists—and not only because they made it possible for them to live while producing art—ideas about their efficacy and quality varied. Acknowledging that art enriched ordinary life, some supporters held that the American government had long needed to catch up with European countries in underwriting the arts. It was, to some, a social necessity for democracy and the welfare of the people, and should be given a permanent bureau in the government—a sort of Fine Arts Ministry. Others felt that art programs were a necessary part of a democratic ethos but should be run by state agencies rather than by a centralized federal bureaucracy that promulgated rules often deemed nonsensical. Still other artists felt that government interference in artistic matters did not accord with the general *laissez-faire* principles on which society was predicated, or with the right to choose style and subject matter according to one's individual interests. Business interests sometimes complained that federal projects (such as an effort to revitalize glass-blowing in New Jersey) competed with private enterprises, even though the objects produced were not sold but donated to public institutions so as to avoid this kind of conflict. Still other voices at the time referred to government support of the arts as "boondoggling," that is, a waste of the taxpayers' money. And a virulent and noisy few suggested that the programs were prone to exploitation by left wing interests. This latter argument against government support of the arts gained strength toward the end of the Thirties, with denunciations that claimed that various aspects of the programs were infiltrated by radical political ideas, in particular, Communism.

Arts in the Postwar Period: Neglect and Re-commodification

With the onset of United States entry into World War II, federal support for the arts was discontinued, with the exception of some programs that contributed to the war effort. The WPA arts program, however, ended in 1943, and for nearly sixty years the U.S. government paid little or no attention to the disposition of hundreds of thousands of works of art that it had commissioned. Consequently, the art

> languished in warehouses, was offered to public agencies, given to museums, was thrown out, taken home by employees, sold as scrap, and otherwise disseminated throughout the country. Few records were kept, hardly anyone knew what was going where and, as a result, many of the pieces that were not destroyed or kept within public agencies ended up in private hands.[48]

It is only in recent years—in the 1990s—that the General Services Administration has initiated efforts to locate, identify, and catalogue WPA art, realizing its unique importance for the country. The products of the WPA Writers' Project suffered a similar fate. Because the American Guidebooks were not published by any one publishing house, they had not been brought together as an entire series, so many ended up in dustbins or, as in the case of the original *Idaho Guidebook*, were destroyed in a warehouse fire.[49] Much of the original source material that could have been valuable to scholars and manuscripts that never made it into print but might have been published had sponsors and publishers been found in time were subsequently lost to history when the program was closed.[50] Jerre Mangione was later to lament, "the general indifference to the [*Writers'*] Projects unpublished materials constituted a shocking waste of a precious national resource."[51]

As previously suggested, however, in some important respects the effects of the WPA arts programs were long-lasting. Prior to the Thirties, the United States government had not acknowledged either art or artists as an occupation or group worthy of support, but this attitude was no longer tenable in the postwar years. While the WPA was no longer the paymaster for artists as teachers, some found employment in colleges, universities, and trade schools as a result of other federal legislation. As these institutions expanded their art offerings to accommodate those taking advantage of the educational opportunities funded by the federally mandated GI Bill, artists were able to fill this niche.

In the immediate post–World War II period, the economic scene was more optimistic than it had been in a long while, and money had become available for spending on culture as well as on consumer goods. The taste for books, concerts, and artworks, which had been nurtured by the federal programs, now carried over, as individuals who formerly were unaccustomed to acquiring cultural goods began to do so and, due to the economic recovery, could now afford to do so. However, without the federal programs that as a matter of policy employed artists, performers, and writers, the funding dynamics were profoundly altered. On the federal level, the National Endowment for the Arts (NEA) was established by Congress in 1965, modeled on a similar organization initiated as the New York State Council of the Arts.[52] Philanthropic foundations, such as the Guggenheim Foundation, took over one aspect of support for the arts by awarding fellowships on a competitive basis. Indeed, competition became the significant factor in deciding which individuals and projects might receive awards. Ostensibly decided by one's peers in the field under consideration, this process also invited favoritism, depending to some extent on one's friendships in the particular area under consideration. This format was quite different from one that in theory supported individuals on the basis of need, no matter the opinions or styles of one's colleagues.

It also returned the artist to a state of individualism in that he or she became free to produce an art object that might be difficult to comprehend or that was purely decorative, and to work in any style that appealed to its maker or to the art market. While the postwar period did not reestablish Paris as a mecca to which artists must travel, it did renew their interest in earlier European experiments with form, such as abstraction and non-objectivity.

The purchase of art objects became a greatly expanded commerce, with hundreds of art galleries centered at first mainly in New York City, and then on the West Coast, handling the work of individual artists. Decisions about quality were predicated on what was saleable and left up to gallery owners and art critics. These figures directed the attention of the art-buying public to what they believed aesthetically important, often promoting work that was difficult to understand or purely decorative.

Despite this expansion of the art market, it is doubtful whether most visual artists today are able to make a living from their art. In other words, a business model for the arts became the norm. Concerts and theatrical events flourished, but they, too, became commercial enterprises, although often still requiring philanthropic and government support. Visual art remained accessible to the public at museums, where attendance grew enormously throughout the postwar period, even after these formerly free-access institutions initiated fees. With some notable exceptions, the distribution of public works of art such as murals and large sculptural pieces now became the province of architects in charge of erecting commercial or public edifices. Influenced by the commercial art market, such endeavors often favored abstract or decorative works rather than those with public messages.

Lessons of the New Deal Support for the Arts

In the archives and memoirs of those who participated in the Federal Art Project there can be found numerous anecdotes "illustrating the insensitivity of bureaucrats, the clumsiness of politicians' interventions, the attacks of censors and the perils of centralized control."[53] Despite Harry Hopkins's vow that the WPA would never institute censorship, censorship did happen, although there was never an official federal policy. State and local officials prodded by conservative critics of the New Deal were the most likely to be censorious, particularly because of the leftist political nature of some of the art.

In retrospect, however, the arts programs' extraordinary accomplishments far outweigh the criticisms that have been leveled at them, both then and more recently. In terms of sheer output, the program's effects are staggering. Between 1933 and 1942, 10,000 artists produced some 100,000 easel paintings, 18,000 sculptures, over 13,000 prints, 4,000 murals, over 1.6 million posters, and thousands of photographs. As noted above, the Writers' Project produced more than a thousand books and pamphlets, and the Federal Theatre Project produced thousands of plays in its relatively short life. WPA projects were highly popular with audiences and critics, and reviews were generally favorable. In summing up the legacy of the Federal Theatre Project, for example, Hallie Flanagan explained,

> Quite aside from their primary and most important function, that of enabling people to live decently and happily by the practice of their profession, these public theatres indicated certain things which no one knew when Federal Theatre started: that the government could operate theatres, sign leases, pay royalties, raise curtains, and take in admissions; and that millions of Americans want to go to the theatre if it can be brought geographically and financially within their range.... This audience proved that the need for theatre is not an emergency. Either the arts are not useful to the development of the great numbers of American citizens who cannot afford them—in which case the government has no reason to concern

> itself with them; or else the arts are useful in making people better citizens, better workmen, in short better-equipped individuals—which is, after all, the aim of a democracy—in which case the government may well concern itself increasingly with them. Neither should the theatre in our country be regarded as a luxury. It is a necessity because in order to make democracy work the people must increasingly participate; they can't participate unless they understand; and the theatre is one of the great mediums of understanding.[54]

One example of the way in which the Federal Theatre Project moved audiences that had never been exposed to theater before was in the overwhelming enthusiasm met by the production of *Macbeth,* set in Haiti, performed by an all-black cast, and staged by the then-unknown 21-year-old Orson Welles in New York's Harlem on April 14, 1936. Reporting the day after the opening, the *New York Times* observed that the Lafayette Theatre, packed to overflowing, "rocked with excitement," and that police had to hold back the crowds outside.[55] Another little-noticed legacy of the Federal Theatre Project was the new uses for theater talents that it developed in an exploratory way in the fields of education, therapeutics, diagnosis, and social and community work.[56] The contemporary use of psychodrama, role play, dance, and music therapy, and many other forms of theatrics to heal and educate may be seen as a legacy of this period.

Another little-recognized lesson of the New Deal arts programs was the way in which they served to promote the New Deal itself. Posters and photographs made by WPA artists, for example, were used to advertise and recruit for the CCC, to advertise to the public the New Deal's musical and theatrical events and the availability of music and art lessons, to tout the accomplishments of the Resettlement Administration, the TVA, and the Soil Conservation Service. The New Deal posters were also used to inculcate in the public values such as environmental conservation, the importance of visiting the great outdoors, of reading, of the dignity of manual labor and to promote such efforts as noise abatement, good nutrition, better housing, fire prevention, and other beneficial causes.[57] Musicians and filmmakers were also employed in this way. Woody Guthrie, "the People's Troubadour," was hired in 1941 by the Bonneville Power Administration, a federal agency created to market and distribute electricity from the Columbia River hydroelectric projects, to write a set of songs about the federal projects to gain support for federal regulation of hydroelectricity. Songs such as *Roll On, Columbia, Grand Coulee Dam,* and *Pastures of Plenty,* which came out of this period, are among the iconic folksongs of the twentieth century. Documentary films, like *The Plow That Broke the Plains* (1936), with music by Virgil Thompson, and *The River* (1937) were also commissioned to educate the public about the agricultural practices that had led to the Dust Bowl and the great Mississippi and Tennessee River floods. The focus of WPA photographers on everyday life in the cities and in rural America served to awaken those who were not so dramatically affected by the Depression to the suffering of those less fortunate. In this way, the New Deal arts programs served as a kind of indirect propaganda machine for the importance and role of the federal government in the lives of ordinary people and, more importantly, for the values that are essential to a viable democracy. This democratizing function of the New Deal arts programs is all the more remarkable when we realize that it was occurring at the same time as art in Germany was being used to inculcate the values of racial superiority and militarism.

In the more than half a century since its existence, many factors have influenced the ways that art is made and received, but there can be little question that before the advent of the federal art projects, neither art nor artists had much of a presence in the American consciousness. The recognition of the change that the arts projects had rendered in the country was recognized as early as 1934 by George Biddle, who observed that the New Deal had made "America art conscious as never before" and the artist "conscious of the fact that he is of service to the community."[58] But it is perhaps best summed up by Roosevelt in a speech in 1941 dedicating the National Gallery of Art.

> A few generations ago, the people of this country were often taught by their writers and by their critics and by their teachers to believe that art was something foreign to America and to themselves—something imported from another continent, something from an age which was not theirs—something they had no part in, save to go to see it in some guarded room on holidays or Sundays. But... within the last few years—yes, in our lifetime—they have discovered that they have a part. They have seen in their own towns, in their own villages, in schoolhouses, in post offices, in the back rooms of shops and stores, pictures painted by their sons, their neighbors—people they have known and lived beside and talked to. They have seen... rooms full of painting and sculpture by Americans, walls covered with painting by Americans—some of it good, some of it not so good, but all of it native, human, eager, and alive—all of it painted by their own kind in their own country, and painted about things that they know and look at often and have touched and loved. The people of this country know now... that art is not something just to be owned but something to be made: that it is the act of making and not the act of owning that is art. And knowing this they know also that art is not a treasure in the past or an importation from another land, but part of the present life of all the living and creating peoples—all who make and build; and, most of all, the young and vigorous peoples who have made and built our present wide country.[59]

The arts projects not only gave many who later became icons of American culture both the support they needed at a critical time in their lives, but also new subjects, new aesthetics, and new audiences. For example, since the program did not discriminate between representationalism and abstract expressionism, it gave artists like Jackson Pollack and Lee Krasner a start before Abstract Expressionism developed a commercial audience. Moreover, poor, minority, and working class people who would never have had access to the so-called higher arts were invited to participate both in the making and enjoyment of those arts. Sometimes politically embarrassing subjects like slavery and class exploitation were also portrayed for American audiences, thus giving Americans a truer picture of their own history. Writers, filmmakers, historians, actors, artists, photographers, and musicians not only found a way to sustain themselves through hard times, but also got training for careers that would produce some of the country's best-known works of art and culture.

The epitaph for the federal arts programs is best given by Roger G. Kennedy and David Larkin in their stunning book on the period, *When Art Worked*: "Throughout the long chronicle of redemption of the American dream, artists have often been summoned 'to coax the soul of America back to life.' In the New Deal period, that was their most important work."[60] The WPA arts programs not only brought hope and beauty and a new sense of accomplishment into the lives of ordinary people at a time of immense economic distress, but they made significant contributions to the country's lasting cultural heritage, a realization that has only recently begun to be acknowledged by museums, historians, and even the federal government. According to John Cole, who has worked on cataloguing the material from the Federal Writer's Project for the Library of Congress, "it's an amazing collection. The Federal Writers' Project helped us rediscover our heritage in a more detailed and colorful way than it had ever been described."[61] Such a legacy can also provide inspiration for future artists as illustrated by the gifted young composer Gabriel Kahane, who produced to critical acclaim in 2013 a new musical work, "Gabriel's Guide to the Forty-eight States," based upon excerpts from the *American Guide* series. Interviewed by the *New York Times*, Kahane said that he was "immediately spellbound by the aesthetic values of those books, and by their craftsmanship."[62] We may finally be coming to the acknowledgement of Roosevelt's prophetic remark to his friend and Secretary of the Treasury, Henry Morgenthau, Jr., that "one hundred years from now my administration will be known for its art, not for its relief."[63] The question for us today is: Are we now neglecting our contemporary national heritage? One writer has suggested that a modern FWP, employing laid-off journalists, might document the ground-level impact of the Great Recession, chronicle the transition to a green economy, or capture the experiences of the thousands of immigrants who are changing the American complexion.[64]

Although the recession that began in 2008 is not as deep as the Great Depression, its effects—joblessness, anemic growth—seem likely to continue well into the future. Under the threat of tight budgets, arts programs in the public schools are being slashed, and government funding at all levels for the arts has fallen precipitously since 1990. Between 1990 and 2011, government per capita arts funding (adjusted for inflation) dropped by 48 percent. While private funding for the arts is much higher, it, too, has dropped by about 18 percent since the start of the Great Recession.[65] This means that regional theaters are closing for lack of patrons; public libraries around the country are closing or on shorter hours; and the National Endowment for the Arts, the National Endowment for the Humanities, and the Institute of Museum and Library Services have all faced significant cuts, threatening their ability to support cultural activities throughout the country. What is more, public funding for the Corporation for Public Broadcasting, some of which goes to PBS, one of the few sources of fine arts programming in a sea of crass, commercial culture, has been cut and is under constant threat from conservative politicians who would like to eliminate it entirely. With a significant segment of Congress that views such programs as a waste of taxpayer dollars and would like to do away with nearly all federal funding except for the military, the future of the arts as both a heritage of democracy and as a contributor to it does not look very hopeful.

Numerous people today lament the fact that our nation is not producing enough scientists and mathematicians in order to compete in the global world. While more emphasis in our educational systems should certainly be directed toward math and science, equally important is support for arts education. Cognitive scientists recognize that there are many ways of learning and many forms of intelligence that are distributed differently within a population. The arts provide a path to knowledge and understanding that offer benefits that other kinds of learning may not provide and that may even transfer to other kinds of learning. Music, for example, has been connected to spatio-temporal reasoning as well as math and reading.[66] New research offers empirical evidence that reading literature can help us become more empathetic toward others.[67] Empathy, including feeling for those less fortunate, is something that our society could use more of. It could help to soften the harshness of our current social philosophies. The arts can also contribute to our sense of happiness and well-being. Preliminary results from a large research project on happiness have found that of the top six most happiness-inducing activities after intimacy/making love and exercise, the other four are all arts-related. They include: theater, dance, concerts, singing or performing, attending exhibitions at a museum, and hobbies or arts and crafts.[68] Making art may also operate like yoga and other mindfulness exercises to mediate depression and anxiety and create a feeling of well-being and connectedness to the whole.[69] The noted settlement house founder Jane Addams, with whom some of the New Dealers had worked in the early part of the twentieth century, had early understood this function of the arts as providing solace, comfort, beauty, and joy to those suffering from the stress of social deprivation, and thus the arts were an integral part of her program for impoverished immigrants.[70]

A large body of studies present compelling evidence connecting student learning in the arts to a wide spectrum of academic benefits—including greater proficiency in reading, language development, mathematics, and critical thinking—and social benefits, such as self-confidence, self-discipline, self-control, conflict resolution, collaboration, empathy, and social tolerance.[71] Critical thinking and social tolerance are other characteristics that are badly needed in our society. One national study using a federal database of over 25,000 middle and high school students found that students with high arts involvement performed better on standardized achievement tests than students with low arts involvement. Moreover, the high arts-involved students also watched fewer hours of television, participated in more community service, and reported less boredom in school.[72] Other researchers contend that support for arts education should not have to rely on its supposed benefits for doing well on standardized tests, but should be supported for its own intrinsic benefits. Students who study the arts seriously, they find, "are taught to see better, to envision, to persist, to be playful and learn from mistakes, to make critical judgments and justify such judgments."[73] Parents' groups across the country have objected to the de-funding of arts education in the schools, reflecting what a Harris poll, conducted in 2005, showed—that 93 percent of the public agree that the arts are vital to providing a well-rounded education for children, and 79 percent agree that incorporating the arts into education is the first step in adding back what is missing in public education today. [74]

If art, literature, music, dance, and drama are critical to the development and education of the young, they are even more critical to the spiritual health—the soul—of a people, and the creative talents and expression they give voice to are essential to the development of a collective imagination that is needed if we are to resolve the enormous challenges that confront us in the twenty-first century. It may be useful to speculate that had a Federal Writers' Project been able to continue to nurture a true picture of the diversity of the American people, or had Hallie Flanagan's vision for the Federal Theatre been extended—a theater that could "interpret region to region, emphasize the united aspect of the states and illuminate the United States for the other Americas"[75]—perhaps the country might have been able to escape the polarizing tendencies that so cripple our democracy and dull our imaginations about how to move toward a future of justice, peace, and ecological sustainability. The lessons of the New Deal arts programs are, if anything, more important than ever.

Notes

1. Jerre Mangione, who served as coordinating editor of the Federal Writers' Project, reported that intellectuals in the 1930s were particularly attracted to the radical ideology of the Communist Party, and many of them were members of the left wing John Reed clubs, and later, the CP's popular front organization, the League of American Writers. Jerre Mangione, *The Dream and the Deal: The Federal Writers' Project, 1935–1943* (New York: Avon Books, 1972), 29–50.
2. Whitcomb, quoted in Mangione, 36.
3. Mangione, 42.
4. Don Adams and Arlene Goldbard, *New Deal Cultural Programs: Experiments in Cultural Democracy*, 1986, 1995, accessed May 2, 2012, available at http://www.wwcd.org/policy/US/newdeal.htm.

5. William E. Leuchtenburg, *The Perils of Prosperity, 1914–1932* (Chicago: University of Chicago Press, 1958), 141.
6. Seymour B. Sarason, *The Challenge of Art to Psychology* (New Haven: Yale University Press, 1990).
7. National New Deal Preservation Association, "Art Projects," accessed May 16, 2012, available at http://www.newdeallegacy.org/art_projects.html.
8. David A. Taylor, "What's the Deal About New Deal Art?" *The Smithsonian*, May 19, 2000, accessed May 16, 2013, available at http://www.smithsonianmag.com/arts-culture/Whats-the-Deal-about-New-Deal-Art-.html.
9. Ibid.
10. Kathryn A. Flynn, *The New Deal: A 75th Anniversary Celebration* (Salt Lake City: Gibbs Smith Publisher, 2008), 28.
11. Taylor, 2.
12. Eleanor Mahoney, "Post Office Murals and Art for Federal Buildings: The Treasury Section of Painting and Sculpture in Washington State, 1934–1943, The Great Depression in Washington State," Pacific and Northwest Labor and Civil Rights Projects, University of Washington, accessed May 16, 2013, available at http://depts.washington.edu/depress/Section.shtml#_edn7.
13. Ibid.
14. This was probably a reaction to the public furor that had erupted over the image of Vladimir Lenin that Diego Rivera had painted in a mural commissioned by the Rockefeller family for New York's Rockefeller Center. Flynn, 30. The mural was eventually chiseled off the wall at Nelson Rockefeller's request.
15. Surprisingly, there is no national archive of what the New Deal bequeathed to every state in the nation. Several groups around the country, spurred by the current recession, are seeking to remedy this ignorance. See, for example, the website of the Living New Deal, accessed February 17, 2013, available at http://livingnewdeal.berkeley.edu/;
16. For a collection of these posters, see Posters for the People, accessed May 16, 2013, available at http://postersforthepeople.com.
17. Milton Meltzer, *Violins and Shovels: The WPA Arts Projects* (New York: Delacorte Press, 1976), 76–77.
18. These murals can be found at Norwalk Transit District, available at http://www.norwalktransit.com/ntd_murals.htm.
19. Adams and Goldbard.
20. Taylor, 1.
21. Jerre Mangione, *The Dream and the Deal: The Federal Writers' Project, 1935–1943* (New York: Avon Books, 1972), 193.
22. Ibid., 352.
23. William Robin, "Traveling 48 States by Orchestra," *New York Times*, April 21, 2013, AR 12.
24. Robert Cantwell, quoted in Mangione, 353.
25. Bernard De Voto, quoted in Mangione, p. 360.
26. Alfred Kazin in *On Native Grounds: An Interpretation Of Modern American Prose Literature* (1942), quoted in Mangione, 365.
27. Mangione, 366.
28. Ibid., 123.
29. Adams and Goldbard.
30. Ibid.
31. Mangione, 373.
32. As early as 1910, increased costs of railroad travel made touring companies less profitable and by 1929–1930, the movies had supplanted most touring companies. Lorraine Brown, "Federal Theatre: Melodrama, Social Protest and Genius," accessed August 1, 2012, available at http://memory.loc.gov/ammem/fedtp/ftbrwn00.html.

33. Hallie Flanagan, "Brief Delivered Before the Committee on Patents, House of Representatives, February 9, 1938," Library of Congress, accessed February 14, 2013, available at http://memory.loc.gov/cgi-bin/ampage?collId=ftscript&fileName=farbf/00040002/ftscript.db&recNum=0,1.
34. Ibid.
35. Hallie Flanagan, "Theatre as Social Action," in "First Summer Federal Theatre: A Report," in *Federal Theatre*, ed. Piere de Roban (June–July 1937): 36. A project newsletter is available in the Federal Theatre Project collection, Library of Congress, accessed June 15, 2013, available at http://historymatters.gmu.edu/d/5103/.
36. Ibid.
37. "Coast to Coast: The Federal Theatre Project, 1935–1939," Library of Congress, February 17–July 16, 2011, accessed March 16, 2013, available at http://myloc.gov/Exhibitions/federaltheatre/Pages/default.aspx#__utma=37760702.2104218719.1315239933.1344196243.1344360594.5&__utmb=37760702.21.9.1344360854700&__utmc=37760702&__utmx=-&__utmz=37760702.1344360594.5.3.utmcsr=google|utmccn=(organic)|utmcmd=organic|utmctr=(not%20provided)&__utmv=-&__utmk=40777568.
38. Brown, "Federal Theatre."
39. Ibid.
40. Ibid.
41. Hallie Flanagan, *Arena: The History of the Federal Theatre* (New York: Benjamin Blom, 1965 [original copyright 1940]), 371.
42. At its peak, the Project supported 12,700 people. Flanagan, Brief Delivered Before the Committee on Patents.
43. The Lomax Collection houses approximately 650 linear feet of manuscripts, 6,400 sound recordings, 5,500 graphic images, and 6,000 moving images of ethnographic material created and collected by Alan Lomax and others in their work documenting song, music, dance, and body movement from many cultures. The collection includes field recordings and photographs Lomax made in the Bahamas, the Caribbean, England, France, Georgia, Haiti, Ireland, Italy, Morocco, Romania, Russia, Scotland, Spain, the United States, and Wales, 1930s–2004. A guide to the collection can be found at http://www.loc.gov/folklife/lomax/.
44. Adams and Goldbard.
45. You Young Kang, "The WPA Federal Music Project and Its Enduring Legacies," lecture given at Scripps College, March 21, 2011, accessed July 7, 2012, available at http://www.youtube.com/watch?v=hWv1XKAla0Q.
46. Milton Brown, quoted in Meltzer, 87.
47. For a visually stunning and inspiring history of the Photo League, see the film *Ordinary Miracles: The Photo League's New York*, by Daniel V. Allentuck, Nina Rosenblum and Mary Engel, available at http://www.thephotoleaguefilm.com/about-ordinary-miracles/about-the-film/.
48. "The Government Wants Its WPA Art Back," accessed May 16, 2012, available at http://www.artbusiness.com/wpa.html. For a film documenting the GSA's effort to retrieve New Deal art works, see "Returning America's Art to America" available at: http://www.gsa.gov/graphics/admin/recovering_americas_art.swf.
49. The *American Guide* series, available at http://www.senate.gov/reference/resources/pdf/WPAStateGuides.pdf. In recent years, however, the *American Guide* series has begun to be recognized as a valuable resource. Some state governments have reissued works, and books in the series have now become valuable collectors' items.
50. Mangione, 370.
51. Ibid., 371.
52. The NEA is the largest annual funder of the arts in the United States. It solicits proposals and makes grants for performances, exhibitions, festivals, artist residencies, and other arts projects throughout the country in a number of different disciplines/fields, including artist communities, arts education, dance, design, folk and traditional arts, literature, local arts agencies, media

arts, museums, music, musical theater, opera, theater, and visual arts. "NEA at a Glance," available at http://www.nea.gov/about/Facts/AtAGlance.html.

53. Adams and Goldbard, "Federal One in Retrospect".
54. Flanagan, *Arena*, 372.
55. "Crowds Jam Street as *Macbeth* Opens," *New York Times*, April 15, 1936, accessed April 14, 2013, available at http://query.nytimes.com/mem/archive/pdf?res=F50A17FB3D5E167B93C7A8178FD85F428385F9.
56. Flanagan, *Arena*, 372.
57. Meltzer, 79.
58. George Biddle, "The Artist Serves His Community," *Magazine of Art*, 27, no. 9 (September 1934, Supplement): 31–32. Quoted in Roger G. Kennedy and David Larkin, *When Art Worked: The New Deal, Art and Democracy* (New York: Random House, 2009), 26.
59. Franklin D. Roosevelt, Address at the dedication of the National Gallery of Art, March 17, 1941. The American Presidency Project, accessed May 23, 2013, available at http://www.presidency.ucsb.edu/ws/?pid=16091.
60. Kennedy and Larkin, 323, quoting from a letter written to Aubrey Williams from the sculptor Gutzon Borglum in Robert E. Sherwood, *Roosevelt and Hopkins: An Intimate History* (New York: Harper, 1950), 59.
61. Douglas Brinkley, "Unmasking Writers of the WPA," *New York Times*, August 2, 2003, accessed March 1, 2012, available at http://www.nytimes.com/2003/08/02/books/unmasking-writers-of-the-wpa.html?pagewanted=all.
62. Robin, AR 13.
63. Henry Morgenthau, Jr., in an interview with Erica and Lewis Rubenstein for the Archives of American Art, November 9, 1964, the Smithsonian Institution. Quoted in Kennedy and Larkin, 25.
64. Mark I. Pinsky, "Write Now: Why Barack Obama Should Resurrect the Federal Writers Project and Bail Out Laid-off Journalists," *The New Republic*, December 8, 2008, accessed February 26, 2013, available at http://www.tnr.com/article/politics/write-now?id=428819dc-f4bf-4db3-a6e8-1b601c8fe273.
65. Samantha Cook, "Government Support for Arts Down Dramatically over Time," Remapping Debate, March 27, 2013, accessed May 23, 2013, available at http://www.remappingdebate.org/map-data-tool/government-support-arts-down-dramatically-over-time. Information was gathered from data on appropriations to the National Endowment for the Arts, as well as from state and local arts agencies and from private corporations, foundations, bequests, and individuals. Sources included: National Endowment for the Arts, National Assembly of States Arts Agencies, Americans for the Arts, and "Giving USA: The Annual Report on Philanthropy 2012," published by Giving USA Foundation. The author cautions, however, that private giving includes support for non–arts-related institutions, like science and technology museums, so the data may actually underestimate the percentage by which it has fallen for the arts.
66. Larry Scripp, "An Overview of Research on Music and Learning," in *Critical Links: Learning in the Arts and Student Achievement and Social Development*, J. Richard Deasy, ed., (Washington, D.C.: Arts Education Partnership, 2002), 143.
67. Raymond A. Mar, Keith Oatley, Maja Djikic, and Justin Mullin, "Emotion and Narrative Fiction: Interactive Influences Before, During, and After Reading," *Cognition & Emotion*, 25, (2011): 818–833,
68. Clayton Lord, "Art and Happiness: New Research Indicates 4 out of 6 Happiest Activities are Arts-related(!)," *ArtsJournal.com*, December 2, 2011, accessed May 26, 2013, available at http://www.artsjournal.com/newbeans/2011/12/art-and-happiness-new-research-indicates-4-out-of-6-happiest-activities-are-arts-related.html. Lord is reporting on email correspondence he had with London School of Economics researcher George MacKerron, who is conducting a large-scale study of the environments that are conducive to happiness.

69. Cathy Malchiodi, "The Healing Arts: The Restoring Power of the Imagination," *Psychology Today*, September 27, 2011, accessed May 26, 2013, available at http://www.psychologytoday.com/blog/the-healing-arts/201109/art-and-happiness-is-there-connection.
70. The very first building erected for Hull-House contained an art gallery, to be followed by studios for practicing art, music classes, concerts and recitals, and drama. Jane Addams, *Twenty Years at Hull-House*, Chapter 16 (New York: The MacMillan Company, 1910), 371–399.
71. Sandra S. Rupert, *Critical Evidence: How the Arts Benefit Student Achievement*, National Assembly of State Arts Agencies, 2006, 11–14, accessed May 26, 2013, available at http://www.nasaa-arts.org/Research/Key-Topics/Arts-Education/critical-evidence.pdf. See also the articles in Deasy, ed., *Critical Links*.
72. James S. Catterall, *Involvement in the Arts and Success in Secondary School*, Americans for the Arts Monographs 1, no. 9, 1–10, accessed July 17, 2013, available at http://www.americansforthearts.org/NAPD/files/9393/Involvement%20in%20the%20Arts%20and%20Success%20in%20Secondary%20School%20('98).pdf.
73. Robin Pogrebin, "Book Tackles Old Debate: Arts Education in the Schools," *New York Times*, August 4, 2007, accessed May 20, 2013, available at http://www.nytimes.com/2007/08/04/arts/design/04stud.html?_r=0.
74. Harris poll cited in Rupert, 5.
75. Flanagan, *Arena*, 373.

9

The Rightful Heritage of All

The Environmental Lessons of the Great Depression and the New Deal Response

SHEILA D. COLLINS

I see an America whose rivers and valleys and lakes—hills and streams and plains—the mountains over our land and nature's wealth deep under the earth—are protected as the rightful heritage of all the people.
—Franklin D. Roosevelt, Cleveland, Ohio, November 2, 1940

Those who have sought to mine the history of the Great Depression for its economic lessons have tended to forget that the Great Depression was not only an economic disaster, but an environmental one as well. Most environmental historians have been equally ignorant of the meaning of the Great Depression, either treating the environmental conditions of the time as a "blank space" in the country's environmental narrative, or interpreting the New Deal's administrative state as antithetical to environmental protection.[1] Even scholars of the New Deal have neglected its environmental aspects. Nor have they seen how central conservation was to the New Deal agenda and to Roosevelt himself;[2] and fewer still have understood that financial crises and environmental crises are interlinked. In fact, they represent twin peaks of a systemic civilizational crisis of unprecedented but entirely foreseeable and preventable proportions. Clearly, the climate crisis we currently face is unprecedented, yet there are parallels between the two periods that extend beyond the purely economic. Understanding both periods as times of unprecedented, intertwined economic *and* environmental crises may help us see lessons for current citizens and policymakers. This chapter will survey the environmental crisis of the Great Depression era, examine both the philosophy and practice of the New Deal's approach to environmental conservation, including both its accomplishments and limitations, and look at the lessons for environmental policy making today that can be drawn from the specific programs enacted by the New Deal.

The Environmental Crisis of the 1930s

The financial collapse of the 1930s, as Joseph Stiglitz has argued, was a consequence of deeper problems in the real (i.e., productive) economy that had been building for decades before the official Depression started. Stiglitz attributes the problem to declining prices and increasing productivity in agriculture that resulted in unemployment and a credit crunch in a sector that employed a fifth of the nation's workers.[3] Stiglitz's explanation, however, confuses the symptoms with the causes. A deeper explanation requires that we look at the relationship between the land and its human ecosystem, something Roosevelt and his Brain Trust understood far better than most of today's economists. As Miller and Rees recently observed, "Rather late in the play, we are beginning to recognize that a necessary prerequisite for both economic security and social justice is ecological stability."[4]

By the 1920s, something had gone terribly wrong with our relationship with the ecosystem, and that most fundamental of activities—the growing of food—was the first to exhibit the symptoms of the disease. In the 1920s, rural poverty was rampant. Farmers in the Deep South, the Appalachian region, the Tennessee Valley, the Midwest, and the Great Plains were facing bankruptcy, and would soon experience what would turn out to be the greatest environmental disaster in American history. By the start of the Great Depression, commodity prices had fallen by 50 percent below their prewar levels, and per capita farm income was one-third the national average. Only 16 percent of farm households earned incomes above the national median. Ninety percent of farms relied on gas engines, horses, mules, and hand labor for power and kerosene lamps for light. Seventy-five percent had no indoor plumbing. Illiteracy was twice as common in rural areas as in cities. The causes of rural poverty differed slightly for each region, but both economic and environmental devastation were linked by a common thread: capitalism's rampant disregard for the integrity of the ecosystem, the ruthless, competitive greed that it engendered, and the social divisions that it exploited in the human ecosystem.

The rural southeastern part of the United States was the poorest. Nearly one million children between the ages of seven and thirteen had no schooling. Health care was largely nonexistent. More than 1,300 rural counties containing 17 million people had no general hospital and lacked even a public health nurse. Unattended childbirths were frequent; malnutrition, pellagra, malaria, hookworm, and other parasites were rampant. Lorena Hickock, an Associated Press reporter who traveled through the region in 1933, reported to Harry Hopkins, a key member of the Roosevelt Administration:

> I just can't describe to you some of the things I've seen and heard down here.... I shall never forget them—never as long as I live. Southern farm workers, half starved whites and blacks struggle in competition for less

> than my dog gets at home, for the privilege of living in huts that are infinitely less comfortable than his kennel.[5]

The causes of Southern poverty were twofold: the legacy of the slave system and the sharecropping system that succeeded it. Both systems treated human beings, not as ecological entities themselves, whose well-being was intimately tied to the functional integrity of the non-human ecosystem, but as tools for extracting products from the land that would then be appropriated by others. To get the most bang for the buck, they relied on a monocropping system that had robbed the soil of its nutrients, destroyed natural biodiversity, and deprived the exploited human "capital" of the knowledge needed for its own survival. An economic system based on extreme social exploitation was exacerbated by the overproduction (made possible by new technology) required by World War I, so that when postwar demand slackened, crop prices fell by as much as one-third to two-thirds. Rising prices for farm machinery and fertilizer, coupled with ignorance about soil conservation methods, were also at fault.

The Appalachian region, stretching from the southern tier of New York State through the northern regions of Alabama, Mississippi, and Georgia, amounted to America's own Third World. Like many sub-Saharan African countries today, it had been repeatedly robbed of its natural resources—lumber, coal, oil, gas—by exploitative corporations, leaving behind a devastated land that, well before the stock market crash of 1929, failed to sustain even subsistence mountain agriculture. Here, in the heart of the coal industry, electricity was nonexistent. Families lit their shacks with kerosene, cooked on wood-burning stoves, dumped their garbage into the mountain "hollers," and eked out a bare subsistence. In some counties, unemployment was as high as 80 percent. In the Tennessee Valley (covering Tennessee, parts of Alabama, Mississippi, Kentucky, Georgia, North Carolina, and Virginia) an estimated one-third of the population suffered from malaria. Overproduction had also driven Midwestern family farmers into bankruptcy. By the early 1930s, produce was selling at 50 percent or less of the cost of its production. In response to slashed prices, farmers dumped millions of gallons of milk, plowed under their surplus, and slaughtered their hogs and cattle in a futile effort to boost prices, even at a time when people across the country were facing malnutrition and starvation. But farm foreclosures multiplied, and many farmers organized to try to prevent eviction. So radicalized were farmers becoming that Edward O'Neal, president of the Farm Bureau Federation, warned Congress that "unless something is done for the American farmer we will have revolution in the country within less than twelve months."[6] Altogether, 750,000 family farms would be lost during the Great Depression.

Deforestation also added to the inability of the land to sustain its human occupants. Despite warnings as early as the 1870s that deforestation would result in streams overflowing their banks, causing floods, by the 1930s fully seven-eighths of the nation's original forests had been destroyed.[7] Farmers who had tried to earn money by lumbering had stripped the forests throughout the South, resulting in deep, rain-washed gullies that left land unsuitable for growing other crops like grains and vegetables. In other parts of the country, timber barons had stripped the land clean and lobbied to prevent Congress from legislating sound forest-management practices. Moreover, by 1933, every major white pine region in the country had been severely affected by blister rust, an alien tree disease that threatened to eradicate white pine completely from the nation's forests.

One result of deforestation was the Great Mississippi Flood of 1927, the most destructive river flood in the history of the United States up to that time. Rains of biblical proportions began in the winter of 1926, and by the spring of 1927, the Mississippi River broke its levee system in 145 places, flooding 27,000 square miles in ten states. One levee breech in Mississippi unleashed a violent cascade of water with the force of Niagara Falls, containing more water than the falls itself and the river behind it. An area up to eighty miles wide was inundated to a depth of thirty feet. The flood caused over $400 million in damages (about $5.3 billion in 2013), killed 246 people in seven states, and displaced over a million people.[8] In the words of historian Stephen Ambrose, the Great Mississippi Flood created "more water, more damage, more fear, more panic, more misery, more death by drowning than any American had seen before, or would again."[9] Ironically, these words were written in 2001, just four years before Hurricane Katrina, which killed 2,000 people and destroyed over 100,000 homes.[10] Then, as now, the Army Corps of Engineers had assured the affected populations that the levees would hold, that technology would outwit nature.

On the Great Plains, a region that stretches from Canada to Texas and from the Rocky Mountains east, crossing seven states, farmers in the late 1920s were beginning to face what has been called the greatest sustained environmental disaster of the twentieth century.[11] The full meaning of what came to be known as the Dust Bowl, its causes and the remedies that were eventually devised in an effort to recover from it, have been forgotten by an American public that is likely to face a similar environmental disaster within the next decades.

The Dust Bowl was a man-made disaster. During the latter half of the nineteenth century, the great American heartland that had supported Native American populations for thousands of years but from which they had been ruthlessly dispossessed was opened up to exploitation through the Homestead Acts, despite a warning by Major John Wesley Powell to the Interior Department in 1878 that the prevailing methods of land distribution and agriculture would not work in the arid West.[12] The Homestead Acts relieved overcrowded Eastern cities by offering "public" land to any adult for little more than an $18 filing fee, provided the claimant moved onto the land and developed it for personal use. After five years, applicants could file for a deed to the land after demonstrating that improvements had been made. From 1862 to 1938, some 287.5 million acres, or 20 percent of the so-called public domain, was granted or sold to homesteaders.[13] The Homestead Acts unleashed a frenzy of greed and speculation, fueled by unscrupulous developers who promised those who had lost out in earlier land grabs overnight riches in wheat production and cattle ranching. "Railroads, banks, politicians, and newspaper editors all played a variation of the theme."[14] Soon, millions of acres of prairie grass were being plowed up or overgrazed. With rainfall more abundant in the first few decades, the hyperbole of the developers seemed to bear fruit. In less than ten years, homesteaders went from virtual poverty to being masters of wheat estates, directing harvests with wondrous new machines, at profit margins that in some cases were ten times the cost of production.[15] World War I more than doubled the price of wheat, and production increased by fifty percent with government-guaranteed prices. But in the postwar decade, even though the need for wheat was now reduced, the expansion continued, as did the ripping up of the product of thousands of years of evolution.

Much of the Great Plains should never have been settled. A region unique in its flatness and lack of forest cover, it constituted 21 percent of the entire land area of the United States and Canada, making it the largest single ecosystem on the continent outside the boreal forest. The Great Plains amounted to a gigantic inland sea of perennial grasses that had evolved over 20,000 years or more. A dense root system had allowed these grasses to hold moisture a foot or more below ground level, a perfect fit for the sandy loam of the region and the fierce winds and periodic droughts that swept through it.[16] Before whites had driven the indigenous people off the land, the region had been home to millions of buffalo, nearly all of which would subsequently be slaughtered, in addition to other creatures that had evolved to fit the land.

Given the nature of this ecosystem, the bonanza promised by the developers could not last. Starting in the late 1920s, the region suffered the onset of a long drought that was to last for much of the decade and in some places into the 1940s. Temperatures rose above 100 degrees Fahrenheit for weeks on end. Lakes, ponds, and reservoirs shrank. Fish, frogs, toads, and salamanders died by the millions.[17] With no grass to hold the calcified soil and no water to irrigate crops, nothing would grow. On the Plains, the fierce winds whipped across the fields raising billowing clouds of dust into the sky as high as 10,000 feet or more, rolling like moving mountains.[18] The Dust Bowl was also a health crisis. Physicians across the Midwest reported thousands of cases of what came to be known as "dust pneumonia," which sometimes resulted in death.[19] On the northern Plains, the heat and drought hatched a plague of grasshoppers that darkened the sky and ate everything from corn on the stalk to garments hung on clotheslines.[20] To those who lived through it, the Dust Bowl had the character of a biblical apocalypse. Periodically, the "dusters," as the storms were called, would darken skies from Canada south to Texas and east to Washington, D.C., and New York. One particularly bad storm blanketed ships in dust as far as 300 miles off the Eastern Seaboard and dropped 12 million tons on Chicago.[21] The worst duster of all, which occurred on April 14, 1935, carried in one day twice as much dirt as was dug out of the earth to create the Panama Canal, which had taken seven years to build.[22] By 1934, an estimated one-sixth of the nation's topsoil had blown away or was going.[23]

The Dust Bowl created the first great migration of environmental refugees in the modern age. An estimated 2.5 million people between 1932 and 1940 left their homes on the Great Plains and headed West to seek work. But a country suffering from a depression was ill equipped to deal with this great dislocation. Some found poorly paid work in the fruit and vegetable fields as migrant laborers, but many were turned away at state borders, and many often endured squalor in roadside ditch encampments or as hoboes who rode the rails. In the context of the times, the environmental disasters of the 1920s and 1930s were monumental ecological and human disasters, comparable in relation to this country to the predicted world-wide devastation wrought by global warming .

The Environmental Knowledge of the Great Depression Era

While the concept of conservation had been implanted as an American value during the Progressive era and enshrined in legislation, it was still a limited and somewhat utilitarian view that prevailed in public policy.[24] A portion of the public domain was to be set aside in perpetuity as wilderness, and public forests were to be managed wisely so that they would continue to be economically productive. Teddy Roosevelt and his chief forester, Gifford Pinchot, along with the naturalist John Muir, are justly credited with the establishment of the National Parks system and with conceiving of conservation as a democratic virtue. It was in this period that the National Forest Service was established, along with the nation's system of wildlife refuges and the first commission to investigate the condition of the country's navigable waterways. Also a product of the Progressive Era was protection of human health as a legitimate goal of conservation, resulting in the Meat Inspection Act and the Pure Food and Drug Act. The concept of sustainability of the nation's natural resources for future generations was also a result of Progressive-era thinking. But in 1933, the year Franklin Roosevelt took office, Aldo Leopold's *Sand County Almanac,* with its more holistic understanding of ecosystems, was still sixteen years into the future, and Rachel Carson's *Silent Spring,* which demonstrated that the destruction of nature and human health were part of the same misuse of technology in the service of so-called "progress," was eighteen years away.

Roosevelt would build on the legacy left by his predecessors but give the environment a new meaning and significance. His approach to the environment was more complex, more a product of scientific interrogation of natural systems and thus closer to that of Leopold and Carson than to that of his cousin Theodore, and it would take into account the need to develop some kind of balance between human well-being and environmental conservation. Franklin Roosevelt was a more modern environmentalist than his predecessors and is still ahead of any of his presidential successors.

The New Deal's Economic and Environmental Vision

Though Franklin D. Roosevelt was no radical, the American people were fortunate to have elected as their president in 1932 a man who was suited to the exigencies of the times. From his experience with polio, Roosevelt knew about human suffering. He had, as the focus of his policies, the "forgotten man [*sic*]"—the common worker, the unemployed, the homeless and the destitute.[25] But beyond that, he had an uncommon understanding of ecological principles and a visceral empathy for the natural world. As Schlesinger wrote, "he felt the scars and exhaustion of the earth almost as personal injuries."[26] Another historian wrote:

> By innate character and formative experience he was a country gentleman, invincibly, personally rural in his outlook upon a gigantically mechanized and urbanized America. Stronger in him than in most men was a profound instinctive feeling for living nature. Something deep in his spirit vibrated in rare sympathy with the rhythms of seasonal change and weather change, of river flow and sea tide, and the growth of green-growing things, trees, and grass, food plants and flowers.... thrusting their way out of the living soil into sunlight and air, ripening there in open air, then dying back into the soil whence they came.[27]

Roosevelt's love of nature was formed during his boyhood on the family estate at Hyde Park, New York, where he developed an interest in the site from both an historical and ecological perspective. Here he collected species of all the birds on the estate, noted the effects of soil erosion and deforestation, and became committed to the need for reforestation and land conservation. Roosevelt's approach to environmental protection was based on an organic feeling for and knowledge of the land's specific ecology. His *Farm Journal* on the land at Hyde Park, which he kept from 1911 to 1917, reveals "a level of attention rivaling the chronicle of an agronomist's forest science log."[28] His interest in the land was less romantic than that of a Henry Thoreau or a John Muir; and in contrast to TR, for whom "wild" nature was something against which to test one's masculinity, FDR's nature was more domesticated, the nature of field and farm and productive forest. The land was a set of relationships—between humans and between humans and the natural world—that had evolved over time. The result of that relationship had often been destructive. Thus, the land had to be carefully husbanded if it was to be able to regenerate itself and therefore to support its human inhabitants. Sustainable land management was, for Roosevelt, the foundation of a democratic society.[29]

From the time he first entered public life, Roosevelt had sought to make conservation a key focus of public policy. His sensitivity to the integrity of the natural world had been publicly defined as early as 1912 when, as chair of the Agriculture Committee of the New York State Senate, he spelled out in a speech the rudiments of what we now call ecological ethics, among whose principles could be discerned the ideas of generational and intergenerational equity. The speech could just as well have been written about the United States today as of the country in 1912. In it he laments both the loss of forests to clear cutting and the reckless use of land resulting from private ownership, connecting the health of the land to the health of the human community. In so doing he created a definition of "liberty" that pertained not only to the individual, but to the community, thus imbuing time-honored values with new meaning.

> There are many persons left to-day that can see no reason why if a man owns land he should not be permitted to do as he likes with it.... They care not what happens after they are gone and I will go even further and say that they care not what happens even to their neighbors, to the community as a whole, during their own lifetime. The opponents of Conservation who, after all, are merely opponents of the liberty of the community, will argue that even though they do exhaust all the natural resources, the inventiveness of man and the progress of civilization will supply a substitute when the crisis comes.... I have taken the conservation of our natural resources as the first lesson that points to the necessity for seeking community freedom, because I believe it to be the most important of all our lessons.[30]

For Roosevelt, the health of the human community required not only that the piece of land on which a particular community lived be handled sustainably, but that Americans had a national—long distance—responsibility to each other to care for the land, whether that be in Hyde Park or North Dakota. In a speech to the rather prosperous members of the Home Club of Hyde Park, he said:

> if a farm family is on the verge of starvation in North Dakota, we people in the town of Hyde Park are helping to pay to keep that family from actual starvation; if we have made mistakes in the settling of the country in the past, we in the town of Hyde Park have got to pay to correct those mistakes. In other words, that we have a definite stake, not merely the spiritual side of it, or the social side of it, or the patriotic side, but the actual financial side of it.[31]

As chairman of the New York State Senate's Forest, Fish and Game Committee, Roosevelt publicized threats to the state's natural resources and introduced eight bills aimed at conserving them; and as the governor of New York State, he designed a rural program that enlisted the support of the state's farmers and foresters as well as national forestry leaders to expand the state's forests, defying upstate power companies that sought to acquire leases on forest preserves in order to create reservoirs for generating hydroelectric power. He also successfully sponsored an amendment to the state constitution which gave the state government authority to purchase and reforest abandoned and sub-marginal land. It was the nation's largest reforestation program to date.

When he assumed the presidency of the United States in the midst of the greatest economic and environmental catastrophes the country had ever seen, Roosevelt immediately set to work on three programs that uniquely spoke to the combined concerns of unemployment, underdevelopment, and environmental crisis: the Civilian Conservation Core, the Soil Conservation Service, and the Tennessee Valley Authority. All three programs were FDR's brainchildren,[32] all were introduced and initiated within the first 100 days of his presidency, and all benefitted from his eagerness to push them through in the face of opposition and ridicule from some special-interest groups.

In the conception and carrying out of these programs, we can see a progression in Roosevelt's ecological understanding—an understanding that immeasurably benefited the people and without which the United States might not have emerged as the economic power it did after the Second World War. Central to the New Deal environmental programs was the idea of careful land management and planning based on scientific research that attempted to reconcile ecological and human patterns of evolution. For New Deal planners, the landscape was a middle ground between the needs of civilization and the needs of wild nature. Thus, prevention, recovery, and restoration of destroyed landscapes, as well as conservation, were placed on the public agenda. This represented a significant—indeed a watershed—shift from a public ethos in which decentralization, atomistic thinking, and short-term decision making had led to tremendous waste, inefficiency, and environmental destruction. It also differed from the Progressive-era ethos in which "wild" nature was to be preserved as much as possible in its pristine state so that human beings, leaving the realm of "civilization" behind, could partake of its wonders. Education of the public about these changing ideas of nature and humanity's role were also part of the New Deal approach to the environment.[33] The third characteristic of the New Deal approach, which demonstrates its very modern character, was the idea of holistic planning. Problems such as soil erosion, flooding, deforestation, disappearing wildlife, unemployment, and poor health were not seen as isolated issues but as interrelated, thus requiring that they be treated together.

The Civilian Conservation Corps

The most popular of the New Deal work programs was the Civilian Conservation Corps (CCC), a semi-militarized voluntary work program for impoverished young people. From its inception in 1933 as the Emergency Conservation Work program (its name was changed in 1937) to its termination in 1942, the CCC employed an estimated 3 million youths, 85,000 Native Americans, and 225,000 World War I veterans, making it the largest peacetime manpower mobilization in history.[34] The program was conceived as fulfilling a double mission—serving as a work program for unemployed youth and as a way of halting the erosion of the nation's neglected natural resource base—thus bringing together two wasted resources in an attempt to save both. But in its implementation, it also served four other functions: it provided extra financial assistance for urban families on relief; it infused local communities with much needed financial and technical aid; it improved the health of its impoverished and malnourished recruits; and it provided education and training for them. In urging passage of the program, Roosevelt said:

> This enterprise is an established part of our national policy. It will conserve our precious natural resources. It will pay dividends to the present and future generations. It will make improvements in national and state domains which have been largely forgotten in the past few years of industrial development.... We can take a vast army of these unemployed out into healthful surroundings. We can eliminate, to some extent at least, the threat that enforced idleness brings to spiritual and moral stability. It is not a panacea for all the unemployment but it is an essential step in this emergency.[35]

At the same time the program was also a politically clever move, as it served as a hedge against widespread social turbulence that was then imminent.[36]

Membership in the CCC was for young people whose parents were on relief, with the exception of the separate programs for veterans and Native Americans. In 1937, Congress dropped the relief requirement. CCC workers were to be put to work to carry out a broad natural resource conservation program on national, state, and municipal lands. Passage of the legislation setting up the CCC met with expected criticism from Republicans and business interests that the wages were not to compete with the private sector, and from labor leaders that the low wages proposed—$1 per day—would drive wages down for all workers. Some objected to what at first appeared to be an overly militaristic program reminiscent of the Nazi and Soviet youth programs, as the Army was to be put in charge of logistics. To this Roosevelt replied that the corps was a *civilian* corps, explaining that since most of the young men lived in the East and most of the work projects were to be in the West, the Army was the only agency capable of handling the logistics of such an ambitious program in such short order.

There had never before been an organization like the CCC. Prior to the New Deal, the federal government hardly touched the lives of ordinary Americans. With the exception of Civil War veterans' pensions, most Americans' experience of government had been with their local and state governments. Yet this was an experiment in top-level management designed to prevent red tape and political wrangling from strangling the newborn effort. In order to get the legislation passed, details that would be likely to generate political backlash if embedded in the legislation were largely left to the president.

The program required the cooperation of four different federal departments. The Labor Department was charged with hiring; the War Department with physical training, transportation to specially constructed work camps, clothing, housing, and day-to-day running of the camps; and the departments of Agriculture and Interior with finding the work projects, in conjunction with state and local governments. In order to appease labor, the entire operation was directed by Robert Fechner, a vice-president of the Machinists' Union and of the AFL. Unemployed local woodsmen were hired to supervise the work, and within a few months a voluntary education program was developed providing academic subjects, vocational classes, and job training. Ninety percent of enrollees participated in some aspect of the educational program, which was run by the military camp commanders with the help of civilian educational personnel.

As noted earlier, Roosevelt was personally and viscerally concerned about forest conservation. In response to a rather ignorant question from a reporter as to what the CCC men would do in the forests, Roosevelt replied with a lecture on forestry that displayed his knowledge of the forest as a living ecosystem and his concern for the proper management of the country's forests. The passage below is typical of the kind of "teaching" that Roosevelt conducted during his presidency.

> We have to have another class here on it. The easiest way to explain it is this: Taking it all through the East where, of course, the unemployment is relatively the worst with far more people, nearly all of the so-called forest land owned by the Government is second, third or fourth growth land—what we call scrub growth which has grown up on it. What does that consist of? Probably an average of four or five thousand trees to the acre little bits of trees, saplings, and so forth. Proper forestation is not possible; in other words, you will never get a marketable timber growth on that kind of land—plenty of cordwood and that is about all. But the timber supply, the lumber supply of the country, at the present rate of cutting we are using lumber somewhere around three to four times the rate of the annual growth. In other words, we are rapidly coming to an end of the natural lumber resources and the end is within sight and, unless something is done about it, we will become a very large lumber importing nation, the figures showing that it will be from 20 to 40 years when that will come about. Now, take this second, third, fourth growth land.... Say there are five thousand of these saplings to the acre.... They go in there and take out the crooked trees, the dead trees, the bushes and stuff like that that has no

> value as lumber, and leave approximately one thousand trees to the acre. That means that they are sufficiently spaced to get plenty of light and air and there is not too much of a strain on the soil. Those trees then eventually will become a very valuable lumber crop. That is the simplest way of explaining the operations so far as the trees themselves go.[37]

The practicality and wisdom of Roosevelt's plan to have the CCC reforest the country had been questioned by some foresters, but praised by another as "the most unique and outstanding of its kind in the history of American forestry."[38] The latter appraisal turned out to have been the correct one. Thanks to Roosevelt's vision, by the end of the program in 1942, nearly three billion trees had been planted, white pine blister rust had been brought under control, and the eradication of tree-killing insects resulted in the preservation of forests. In addition to these measures, the CCC, in cooperation with a remarkable cadre of architects, engineers, landscape designers, and park planners, had created an estimated 800 new state and county parks and an infrastructure for their ongoing maintenance, as well as trails, overnight cabins and shelters, campgrounds, dams, and ski runs to facilitate their recreational use.[39]

Thousands of acres of grazing lands in the West were re-grassed by the CCC, fences and bridges built, and rodent-control schemes enacted. One feature of the effort to recover the Great Plains was Roosevelt's own idea, pushed over the objections of most professional foresters. This was a "shelterbelt" of drought-resistant trees that were planted in 100-mile wide rows crosswise to the prevailing winds in order to break the winds, anchor soil, and retain moisture. By the end of the decade, shelterbelts of over 22 million trees had become a prominent feature of the Plains landscape and had achieved all the success predicted by their proponents.[40] Moreover, by 1942, the CCC's firefighting efforts had succeeded in reducing the acreage lost by fire to its lowest point ever, even though a record number of fires were reported. The CCC also successfully fought seventeen subterranean coal fires that had been burning for years in Wyoming. [41]

By the start of the Depression, the United States had experienced nearly 300 years of unchecked wildlife destruction, which was revealed by the President's Committee on Wildlife Restoration, appointed in 1934. At the Committee's insistence on action, a wildlife restoration program was devised, and the CCC was used in its implementation.[42] CCC enrollees developed sub-marginal land as wildlife refuges; built fish-rearing ponds and animal shelters; developed springs; planted food for animals and birds; constructed nesting areas and reintroduced wildlife to depleted areas; stocked streams, dams, and rivers with fish; and collected, treated, and released sick or injured creatures on federal refuges. Some camps were involved in wildlife research, and many more were tasked with the monitoring of wildlife. By 1938, the most serious aspects of wildlife wastage had been ameliorated, and funding for wildlife administration had increased by 450 percent. Other activities included the preservation of historical sites and monuments and irrigation and flood control projects, including the construction of major dams.

Despite Roosevelt's desire to make the CCC permanent and its director's plea for a permanent CCC before the Senate Unemployment and Relief Committee in 1938, the return to nearly full employment during World War II meant that the program could no longer justify its existence to its critics. There were certainly functions that a reorganized permanent youth service corps could usefully perform. Preservation and restoration of the environment, after all, would be an ongoing necessity; but the exigencies of its origins, the opposition of conservatives to any permanent work program, and the attention now focused on preparing for the United States's involvement in World War II meant that it was doomed to temporary status.

The Soil Conservation Service

As we have seen, soil conservation had also been central to Roosevelt's early development as an environmentalist. Although some farmers practiced soil conservation, soil erosion continued to be a problem in the late nineteenth and early twentieth centuries, and none of the agricultural agencies created during the latter half of the nineteenth century saw soil conservation as a priority.[43] By 1933, however, dirt from the Dust Bowl had settled over the halls of Congress and the Department of Agriculture, where soil conservation scientists were still trying to figure out what had gone wrong. In 1929, a dynamic soil scientist, Hugh Hammond Bennett, who had made a reputation as both an alarmist and an evangelist for soil conservation, had been hired to head up what was called the Soil Erosion Service in the Interior Department. Seeking a firmer legislative foundation for soil conservation, Bennett successfully promoted passage of the Soil Conservation Act of 1935, which created a Soil Conservation Service in the United States Department of Agriculture (USDA). Bennett served as its first chief until his retirement in 1951. Travelling by train across the United States in 1934, Roosevelt had seen for himself the devastation that improper farming methods had wrought on the northern Plains. As he rode toward Green Bay, Wisconsin, he had a vision of America that one of his biographers described as an "organismic watershed concept":

> There was in Roosevelt's mind a vivid, though vaguely defined, sense of water, flowing water, as means and organizing principle of Union. The watershed became metaphor. It bespoke the unity of nature and the bitter wages of man's sinning against this unity. By the same token, it bespoke the natural necessity and the basis in nature for defining individual freedom as a cooperative enterprise in any truly civilized human society, especially one of advanced technology. The America it stood for would be possessed

> of that "which a young Franklin Roosevelt... struggled so hard to describe two decades ago...."[44]

Following Roosevelt's vision, the Soil Conservation Service was to set up a series of Soil Conservation Districts to be selected, wherever possible, on a watershed basis. The program represented the first major federal commitment to the preservation of privately held natural resources.[45] Roosevelt saw that if members of Congress could see the positive effects on the reduction of flood heights and the deposition of silt from rolling uplands, they would be more likely to fund the program. Within a few weeks, Bennett had selected a staff "notable, even among New Deal agencies, for zealous, youthful dedication to its work."[46] Within a few months, forty erosion control projects encompassing 4 million acres were operating in thirty-one states, and scores of CCC camps were working with local farmers.

The Coon Valley Project in southwestern Wisconsin established the model for the rest of the soil conservation projects. Here everything was interconnected by running water. Water not only compelled cooperation among farmers, but created interdependencies and cooperation among a variety of technical experts—agronomists, soil chemists, foresters, wildlife specialists, agricultural engineers, agricultural economists. All these came into Coon Valley to make a concerted attack on soil erosion in cooperation with CCC'ers and local farmers. In less than a year there was marked improvement in both Coon Valley's physical appearance and, interestingly, in the growth of community among its inhabitants—an outcome Roosevelt had foreseen in his early conviction that ecological health was necessary for community health. Within four years of the Soil Conservation Service's inception, over half the farms were operating in accordance with complete farm conservation plans.[47] By 1938, the CCC had developed more than 500 soil project areas in forty-four states, employing about 60,000 youths annually. Their work consisted of demonstrating practical methods of soil conservation to farmers, actual work on private land in cooperation with landowners, and the development and improvement of erosion control techniques through research. The agency's work and staff spread nationwide, eventually cooperating with nearly 3,000 locally organized conservation districts. The conservation districts proved to be very popular in the field.

The Tennessee Valley Authority

The Tennessee River and its tributaries had always been volatile; relatively placid in some seasons and wild and uncontrollable in others. The Mississippi flood of 1927 had established flood control as a continuing responsibility of the federal government, and one of the initial purposes of the Tennessee Valley Authority (TVA) was to control hillside erosion through proper soil conservation and to create a series of reservoirs and dams to mitigate flooding and harness the river's potential to provide power and navigation to the region. Roosevelt's vision of the project was a multidimensional one and perhaps the boldest challenge to the established order, as it had the potential to demonstrate that planning and community cooperation could work and that a government-owned business could compete successfully with private enterprise.[48] It would link water power, flood control, forestry, conservation, reclamation, agriculture, and industry in one vast experiment that, if successful, could be replicated in other major watersheds around the country. It was to be the basis of a new kind of economy. "Could the valley be so transformed by regional planning," he asked, "as to support not only those now living in it, and at a decent standard of living, but also others who moved in, myriads of others who now, jobless and hopeless, walked the city streets?" His vision was of a kind of back-to-the-land movement where people could be spiritually and physically restored through useful work in small industries "where the people can produce what they use, and where they can use what they produce, and where, without dislocating the industry of America, we can absorb a lot of this unemployment, and give the population a sound footing on which it can live."[49]

In the structure of its governmental relations, the TVA was without organizational precedent, occupying a place midway between the national government and the states. Directed by a three-person board appointed by the president, it was nevertheless accountable not only to the federal government, but to state, county, and local governments. This required a complex network of agreements with states, cities, counties, the U.S. Forest Service, the Fish and Wildlife Service, the Agriculture Department, the U.S. Public Health Service, and many private organizations such as farmers' cooperatives. In the complex federal structure of the United States, with its myriad levels of government each having different jurisdictional authority, often in competition with each other, and with the endemic fear of "Big Government" that had been built into the political culture from the founding, this was no easy task. As one of its staff members recalled, the TVA became an illuminator of a number of dichotomies that had plagued—and still plague—American political life: centralization vs. decentralization; uniformity vs. diversity; regionalism vs. sectionalism; public vs. private realms. Amazingly, the TVA was able to hold both sides of these dichotomies in creative tension, at least for a period of five years. It was a centralized agency working in a decentralized manner that actually empowered states and local governments, giving them responsibilities not formerly within their province. Employing the vision of a unified region defined by its particular ecosystem required diversity in organizational structure, procedures, and methods. The TVA sought to build a strong regional economy that could contribute to a stronger national economy. While recognizing the importance of the work of specialists, it insisted on an integrated approach to development.[50] Each issue TVA faced—whether it was power production, navigation, flood control, malaria prevention, reforestation, or erosion control—was studied in its broadest context and weighed in relation to the others.

The TVA built locks and cleared channels for river transportation, exorcised the curse of periodic floods, developed fertilizers, taught farmers how to improve crop yields, improved agricultural tools, replanted forests, controlled forest fires, and improved habitats for wildlife and fish. With passage of the Flood Control Act of 1936, policies to control floods were put in place that endure to this day. The remarkable engineering projects carried out by the Corps of Engineers have saved billions of dollars in property damage and protected hundreds of thousands of people from anxiety, injury, and death.

Prior to the establishment of the TVA little attention had been given to water quality, and little knowledge was available. The TVA undertook a survey of the extent of stream pollution. The facts collected provided a basis for the development of the first stream pollution legislation in various states and laid the groundwork for implementation of the 1948 Federal Water Pollution Control Act.

Within sixteen years of the TVA's operation, malaria had been completely eradicated through a scheme of water fluctuation measures for its reservoirs, creating an environment in which the larvae of mosquitoes were unable to thrive. Unlike the modern tendency to treat insect infestation with chemicals, in this case an ecologically consonant remedy was found. By collaborating with health institutions in the search for knowledge and control, the TVA helped stimulate greater interest in malaria control in areas far beyond the zone of direct influence.[51] Fertilizer production was revolutionized not only in this country but abroad, so that fertilizer is now made with the aid of TVA technology.[52] But the most dramatic change came from the electricity generated by TVA dams. Within a decade, the TVA had built 21 dams, and by the early 1940s, one out of every five farms had been electrified. Electric lights and modern appliances made life easier and farms more productive. Electricity also drew industries into the region, providing desperately needed jobs.

Limitations of the New Deal Programs

While providing very important and lasting legacies for generations to come, neither the CCC, the TVA, nor any of the other stimulus programs devised by the Roosevelt Administration was able to bring the country out of the Great Depression. The business community refused to allow government stimulus spending anywhere near what was needed, and Roosevelt himself did not veer from his commitment to a balanced budget until he was persuaded to reverse his disastrous 1937 budget balancing decision and to increase WPA spending substantially, though not enough to end the Depression. Thus, the works programs of the New Deal that brought hope to so many and did so much to conserve the environment and culture, improve health, and build the infrastructure that is still in use today were doomed to be temporary, all of them ending with the onset of World War II.

This is not to say that there were no problems in the execution of these programs. In an era of deep racial segregation, with congressional committees headed by Southern Democrats and a federal system dictating that most programs had to be implemented by the states, blacks in work programs faced discrimination both in hiring and pay scales. The CCC was an exception. Roosevelt stipulated that the CCC employ African Americans, which it did in about the same proportion as their representation in the population, yet they had to serve in segregated units. So too, when the TVA built model communities, they were racially segregated. Like so many of the New Deal work programs, the CCC was conceived as a males-only program, depriving women of the opportunity to gain new skills and to contribute to the nation's conservation; and the New Deal's emphasis on development often clashed with Native Americans' cultural rootedness in the land. Moreover, the CCC's educational program, tacked on after it had begun, was never well supported at either the local or highest administrative levels, preventing it from achieving even more significant educational gains.[53]

Although the idea of combining relief with environmental conservation was a "brilliant idea" and contributed to the program's popularity, this combination was also its undoing. As sociologist Robert Leighninger has noted, "the balance of conservation and relief was more delicate than Roosevelt understood. Underneath the compelling synthesis were several issues that posed threats of cleavage: education, class, and military control."[54] As time went on, Roosevelt himself lost sight of the program's double mission, with the result that critics from both the right and left were able to weaken Congress's commitment to the program's being made permanent. For example, conservative critics were able to redefine the program as a relief program and thus to characterize the work as "make-work." Isolationists, on the other hand, criticized the program's military orientation, and Roosevelt, himself, finally had to resort to defending the program on the basis of its contribution to war readiness. The fact that protection of the environment amounted to a national security issue as much as war preparedness and that a permanent civilian conservation corps could contribute to two ongoing national needs—countercyclical employment and environmental protection, conservation, and restoration—were lost in the fights over the program's extension.[55]

Not all of the New Deal's environmental programs were environmentally beneficial, due in part to the conflict inherent in attempting to balance the needs of the natural environment against those of a growing population, in part due to the still-incomplete scientific understanding of ecology existing at the time. Opening up the national parks to human traffic made possible by the CCC was a point of contention between the wilderness preservation and conservationist wings of the environmental movement of the time, and is a point of tension with many environmentalists today.[56] The CCC's planting of the kudzu vine, a non-native species, to prevent soil erosion in the Southeast, proved to be an ecological disaster as it spread quickly and widely, smothering native growth. It was finally declared a weed by the USDA in 1953 and outlawed for use in soil erosion.

Despite many New Dealers' assertions that humans had to adapt to the harsh environment of the Great Plains, and some, like Harold Ickes, who recommended not doing anything to help people remain on the Great Plains so that the land could return to nature, Roosevelt's commitment to saving both people and land resulted in a kind of compromise between the two, even though the scientist in him counseled that "at least one hundred million acres of land now under the plough ought not to be cultivated again for a whole hundred years."[57] The report of the government's Great Plains Committee had called for a "new economy based on conservation and effective use of all the water available. Intelligent adjustment to the ways of Nature," the *Report* said, "must take the place of attempts to 'conquer' her."[58] Consequently, techniques such as fallowing, greater crop diversity, contouring, and stubble retention allowed farming and grazing to continue, but it had to be supported with federal subsidies.[59] The CCC's aggressive fire prevention and suppression activities were later criticized by scientists who came to understand the role played by fire in forest progression.[60]

The TVA was always more controversial than the CCC, since it required the cooperation of so many different interests; challenged those of private energy companies which complained that the government had an unfair advantage in that it could borrow unlimited funds at low interest rates and deprive private energy investors of their equity; and required people at the local level to change their land-use habits.[61] The dams built by the TVA and the other large dams constructed by the New Deal, while bringing electricity, industry, and development to underdeveloped areas, also displaced thousands of families from their homes and made land that could have been used for agriculture unavailable. Another example of the law of unintended consequences due to insufficient understanding of environmental systems is the fact that large dams, once thought to be "clean" sources of energy, have been found to interfere with fish runs and have recently been discovered to be producers of methane gas, a more potent contributor to global warming even than carbon dioxide.[62] Moreover, in providing electricity at cheaper rates than private companies, the TVA inadvertently invoked "Jevons Law."[63] The increased demand for electricity that resulted was not, in hindsight, an ecologically sound basis for energy conservation, because it led to increased use of coal that resulted in strip mining and eventually nuclear power, unleashing powerful entrenched interests in those industries that are now resisting the need to move toward a clean energy economy.[64]

In addition, within five years, the comprehensive vision for the region that had enlivened Roosevelt became narrower as TVA officials found themselves capitulating to local political interests. A bill that had envisioned the development of seven regional authorities modeled on the TVA fell afoul of state's rights interests, lobbying by power companies and political infighting over turf within the Roosevelt Administration.[65] The TVA's laudable focus on grassroots involvement also meant that Southern conservatives could influence the implementation of the program, steering its benefits to already existing political institutions, such as the white land-grant colleges and to white grassroots communities, depriving African Americans of access to the benefits of this national program.[66] The TVA eventually devolved from a grand experiment in national planning into a government wholesale power supplier.

Learning from the New Deal Environmental Experience

Perhaps one of the most important lessons to be derived from the limitations of the New Deal's environmental programs is that protecting and preserving the environment both for current and future generations requires an ongoing commitment of national and international political will, resources, and energy. Population growth, technological change, and consumption habits driven by capitalist growth imperatives continuously threaten to destroy the natural basis of all economic activity. We can learn much from the conservation and reclamation efforts of the New Deal administration about the resiliency of eroded natural systems, given the right mix of policy responses. However, without an ongoing international, national, and, of course, regional and local commitment to continuous environmental preservation, conservation, and reclamation, the earth's carrying capacity—its ability to sustain human life itself and all economic activity—will eventually die. Ecologists tell us that as a species we are now in a condition of "overshoot." We are currently using up, in less than a year, more biocapacity than the entire earth produces in one year. As of 2008, humans were demanding 1.52 planets to maintain their lifestyles, 2.5 times more renewable resources than were required in 1961. Moderate United Nations scenarios suggest that if current population and consumption trends continue, by the 2030s, we will need the equivalent of two Earths to support us.[67]

A long-term commitment to the environment requires national planning. Roosevelt had been very clear in his views on this. As early as 1933, he established the National Planning Board (later the National Resources Planning Board- NRPB) which was tasked with taking an inventory of both the human and natural resources of the country with a view to planning for the long-term sustainability of both. In his State of the Union message in 1935, FDR, reiterating his commitment to "the security of the men, women, and children of the Nation" as his defining mission, spoke of environmental sustainability as requisite to the security of the American people. Indeed, he placed it first, and hinted that long-term planning involved far more than the concrete environmental programs he had already initiated.

> A study of our national resources, more comprehensive than any previously made, shows the vast amount of necessary and practicable work which needs to be done for the development and preservation of our natural wealth for the enjoyment and advantage of our people in generations

> to come. The sound use of land and water is far more comprehensive than the mere planting of trees, building of dams, distributing of electricity or retirement of sub-marginal land. It recognizes that stranded populations, either in the country or the city, cannot have security under the conditions that now surround them.[68]

As he had when he had described his vision in 1933 for the Tennessee Valley as one of planning, not only for an entire region, but for "generations to come,"[69] so in response to a reporter's question about whether the Ohio River flood of 1937 was going to result in more flood control work, Roosevelt responded with even more specificity about planning:

> . . . we have in the last three or four years been developing a synchronized program to tie in the entire field of flood prevention and soil erosion. That is one reason why I hope, in the Reorganization Bill, we can have a Central Planning Authority, which will be responsible for, let us say in the case of all of the waters of the Mississippi, responsible for a plan which will cover all of the watersheds that go into the Mississippi. And then all the work that is being carried on will have some relationship to the work that is being carried on at some other point.[70]

Since the TVA experiment, however, there has been no governmental emphasis on long-term planning. In 1977, President Jimmy Carter tried to raise the need for a national energy policy to deal with growing demand and diminishing resources, but he was drowned out by the then still largely invisible propaganda campaign of the fossil fuel industry and Republican right, and his energy proposal went nowhere. In 1980, instead of the "pessimistic" realist who had urged the nation to face the facts, the country elected Ronald Reagan, the sunny optimist, who immediately took the solar panels off the White House, killed funding for mass transit and alternative energy programs, and steered the country toward dominance by large, wealthy corporations—especially the fossil fuel industry.[71] More recently, President Obama suggested that we need to plan for the future by creating a modern energy grid, developing every source of American-made energy and investing more heavily in renewable energy, but he has not pushed these ideas very hard, afraid that in a volatile climate any suggestion of planning may be labeled as "socialism" or "government control" by his political adversaries. And unlike Carter, he has not dared to suggest that perhaps Americans should try to reduce their energy consumption. The result, which the White House even brags about on its webpage, is that energy consumption has steadily increased during the Obama Administration.

The tendency of capitalist economies to treat the environmental effects of productive activity as "externalities" makes applying the lesson about long-range planning extremely difficult, especially in the United States where free-market fundamentalism seems to permeate the national culture more than in any other country. The denial of the centrality of the environment to human development is also exacerbated by the short-term nature of the decision-making process that is built into the American political system. Long-term planning and long-term commitment are made extremely difficult by election cycles that, for all practical purposes, have gotten shorter and shorter. As the TVA experience shows, national planning is also hampered by the long-standing ideology of states' rights which is a product of the American federal system, by the multitude of powerful private interests that would be threatened by such planning, and by the entrenched fiefdoms that exist in a federal bureaucracy that came into being at differing times.

The complexity of the natural environment dictates that we cannot know ahead of time what consequences our actions will have on it. Thus, another lesson to be drawn from the negative experiences of the New Deal's attempt to conserve the environment is the need to apply the precautionary principle to every new policy, program, and technology that has environmental consequences, using the best science that is available at the time. Had Roosevelt's foresters made use of the precautionary principle, they might not have been so ready to use kudzu to prevent soil erosion or have allowed energy demand to grow without placing some limitations on its use and the sources from which is derived. Fortunately, we have today so much more knowledge of how natural systems work than we had in the 1930s as well as analytical tools developed by complexity theorists to anticipate many of the effects that our actions will have on the environment. We should therefore be able to apply the precautionary principle with a great deal more precision. What is lacking is the political will.

Despite the numerous limitations of the New Deal environmental programs and the lessons we could derive from them, there are also many positive lessons that can be drawn from these experiences of massive social and physical engineering. Foremost among them were a president and administration that were willing to think big and to go far beyond the strictures of the private market. Especially important was tackling the root causes of the environmental crises, rather than treating them as temporary aberrations. As Woolner has noted, it is thanks to the New Deal's Soil Conservation Service and the Great Plains Shelter Belt that we have not experienced another Dust Bowl—even in the face of such severe conditions as the droughts of 1956 and 2012.[72] Second was the enlightened vision and political skills of President Roosevelt himself. As Tarlock has noted, more than any other president, FDR "had an acute awareness of the potential limits that the environment places on humans and the need to understand those limits."[73] The application of science-based ecological principles to solve long-standing environmental problems was a critical aspect of this leadership, as illustrated by the eradication of malaria in the Tennessee Valley, not through the use of pesticides, but by using the life cycle of the mosquito against itself. Other aspects of Roosevelt's leadership were his understanding of the interrelationships of human and non-human ecologies, his ability to bring creative, visionary leadership into his administration, his capacity to promote the institutional changes needed to carry out the vision, and his recognition that the public needed to be educated about conservation if they were going to support it.

Contrast this with contemporary administrations. While the findings of science itself were disdained by the George W. Bush Administration, the Obama Administration, which claimed to restore science to its rightful place in policymaking, often capitulated to the interests of the fossil fuel industry and to the consumer-driven quest for greater energy consumption. Unlike Roosevelt, Obama did not use the bully pulpit to educate the American public about how the environment works. His tepid support of climate legislation saw the legislation go down to defeat. Nor did he seek aggressively enough to rally the country to reduce greenhouse gas emissions or to prepare for the adjustments that will have to be made in our lifestyles as climate change deepens. His public pronouncements fell short of the deep understanding of ecology that Roosevelt demonstrated seventy-five years ago.

While Obama faced far greater political obstacles to effective environmental policy making than Roosevelt—a Republican Party that has been wholly captured by the now powerful fossil fuel industry and a Democratic Party that is deeply divided over energy issues—he could still have used the mandate he was elected with in his first term far more effectively than he did. In the areas where he had complete control, he failed tragically to exhibit the kind of leadership required of a president facing looming environmental problems. He gave tepid support to his first environmental regulator, Lisa Jackson, in her effort to strengthen clean air regulations. To the consternation of many environmentalists, he pushed so-called "clean coal" and nuclear energy, supported hydraulic gas fracturing, and after placing a moratorium on offshore oil drilling following the disastrous Gulf Oil spill, eventually capitulated by promising to allow exploration of oil off the Atlantic waters within five years. He opened up a large chunk of Wyoming public land to coal mining, and, after being pushed by a massive environmental civil disobedience campaign to place a moratorium on the Keystone XL pipeline, he again capitulated by agreeing to the building of a southern section, which environmentalists argue is just a wedge into completion of the pipeline in the future. While giving lip service to environmental protection and enacting some positive measures through executive orders, such as increased auto fuel efficiency standards and funding some energy efficiency and renewable energy projects with the stimulus bill, the best that can be said about Obama's first term is that he helped fend off an all-out assault on environmental policies and regulations by the Republicans and their Tea Party and fossil fuel supporters.[74]

After the massive destruction of Hurricane Sandy on the East Coast in the fall of 2012, Obama came out more forcefully, at least in rhetoric, at the start of his second term about the need to tackle climate change, vowing to use his executive powers if Congress did not act. In contrast to his first term's commitment of public lands to oil and gas leasing, near the start of his second term he designated five new national monuments which will preserve thousands of acres of wilderness.[75] Yet he failed to commit himself to any of the most important steps to halt climate change, such as calling for a carbon tax, and he remained wedded to an "all of the above" energy policy, refusing a request from the governors of eight states to waive the federal requirement that corn-based ethanol be blended with gasoline,[76] continuing to expedite oil, natural gas, and nuclear power leases while also funding renewable energy and calling for a market-based approach to greenhouse gas reduction. Despite his new rhetoric, he appeared to be oblivious to the contradictions embedded in his approach to energy policy and continued to support economic growth without acknowledging that the kind of growth we have been pursuing is destroying the planet. Moreover, hidden in his 2014 budget is a proposal to privatize the highly popular Tennessee Valley Authority that has provided the region with low-cost energy, navigation, land management, and flood control for over eight decades.[77]

Another lesson of the New Deal experience is that hiring young unemployed people to work in conserving the environment is far more cost-effective than using that same money in other ways, such as tax reduction, and meets two needs at once. Throughout the tenure of the New Deal, critics on the right complained that the work-relief programs were costing too much. Nevertheless, the long-lasting achievements of the CCC are incalculable and far outweigh the yearly per capita cost of $1,004, which in 2012 inflation-adjusted dollars comes to about $17,731. Compare this figure with the cost of Obama's stimulus program, which, as of the first quarter of 2011 had cost $666 billion and produced or saved between 2.4 and 3.6 million jobs at a cost per job of $278,000 as estimated by the conservative *Weekly Standard*, or somewhere below $100,000 per job as estimated by the liberal Economic Policy Institute.[78] Or compare it to the estimated $1.4 million the Pentagon spent in 2012 to deploy each soldier in the Middle East.[79] For a mere fraction of the cost of either the stimulus or our bloated military budget, the CCC essentially reforested a country whose original forest cover had been decimated, adding 20 million acres in the East and Midwest to the nation's forests. A 1960s study noted that half the trees ever planted in the United States up to that time were planted by the CCC. The program added more park acreage than Teddy Roosevelt's administration, turning the National Park System into a truly *national* system exhibiting much more diversity and including culture as well as nature preservation. It more than doubled the number of national wildlife refuges; and, in conjunction with the Soil Conservation Service, restored much of the nation's topsoil to health. The CCC's hiring of so many landscape architects generated a new interest in the field, leading to rising pursuit of interest in professional degrees in landscape-related fields, as well as new programs to provide such training.[80] And both the CCC and TVA contributed greatly to the future environmental movement, creating a base of knowledge about what works and does not work to preserve and restore the landscape.

Moreover, the role of the CCC as a conserver of the human resource base can in no way be measured economically. Despite the limitations of the CCC educational program, by June 1941, over 100,000 illiterate persons had learned to read and write, over 25,000 had received eighth-grade diplomas, over 5,000 had graduated from high school, and 270 were awarded college degrees.[81] The on-the-job technical vocational education was, of course, a component as well, providing many graduates of the program with skills that they could turn into paid work upon completion.[82] A Library of Congress study concluded that the CCC "is now one of the important educational organizations in the country."[83] As one historian remarked, the young men of the CCC did more "than reclaim and develop natural resources. They reclaimed and developed themselves."[84] When the program started, the majority of enrollees were malnourished. Records showed that the men gained weight, muscle, and height, and their disease and mortality rates were lower than the national average for men of their age group. They had not only gained education and health but new vistas for future employment, an appreciation for the natural environment, hope for the future, and a new faith in the country and its possibilities. In addition, their pay, which was required to be sent home, helped sustain their desperate families during the worst years of the Depression.

During crises of such magnitude as those experienced in the Great Depression, when local communities can see the benefits of federal help flowing to their entire community, Americans' traditional fear of big government and top-down planning greatly diminishes. The CCC was the most popular of all the New Deal programs, and few in the TVA region would wish that the federal government had never been involved in rural electrification or ridding the region of periodic floods and malaria. Moreover, the program's focus on environmental conservation engendered a national dialogue about the meaning of conservation that forced members of the Roosevelt Administration to accept a more holistic and increasingly ecological approach to federal planning.[85] Through aggressive educational campaigns that used print, film, and photography as well as presidential addresses, the idea of conservation had been broadened in the public mind into what we would now call an ecological understanding of the deep relationship between human development and sound earth-management principles. Human health, human development, human community, human rights, and even human spiritual well-being were all tied to the health of the land. The evolution in Roosevelt's own thought and in the thought of his Brain Trust is exemplified in his desire to make the National Resources Planning Board permanent. In 1942 the NRPB issued a report that was an effort to craft the blueprint for continuing to expand the government's social welfare and employment programs in the years after the New Deal. While a permanent work program to conserve the environment was not foreseen by the NRPB's report, the need for an ongoing federal commitment to full employment was; and since ongoing work to restore and sustain the environment had been in Roosevelt's original vision for the Board,[86] it is not inconceivable that, had such a national planning agency been established, it might have added environmental programs as new environmental challenges in the years ahead made their appearance.[87]

The CCC had laid the groundwork for the national environmental movement that emerged in the late 1960s. Thousands of former enrollees in the CCC went on to take jobs in the field of conservation and to join or form environmental organizations, while the next generation who learned to love the outdoors through family camping experiences became the environmental activists of the 1970s. It was only through the efforts of those environmental activists of the 1970s and some sympathetic members of Congress that the United States has any environmental regulations today. Perhaps Roosevelt's own assessment, made in a speech in 1937, best sums up the lessons of these years:

> If, for example, we Americans had known as much and acted as effectively twenty or thirty or forty years ago as we do today in the development of the use of land in that great semiarid strip in the center of the country that runs from the Canadian border all the way down to Texas, we could have prevented in great part the abandonment of thousands and thousands of farms in portions of ten states and thus prevented the migration of thousands of destitute families from those areas.... We would have done this by avoiding the plowing up of great areas that should have been kept in grazing range and by stricter regulations to prevent over-grazing. And at the same time we would have checked soil erosion, stopped the denudation of our forests and controlled disastrous fires.[88]

To bring the lessons of this aspect of the New Deal programs up to date, it is worth speculating that, had the CCC, the Soil Conservation Service, and the TVA not existed, the nation might have experienced the tipping point for climate change and species destruction much earlier in our history. Indeed, had the work of the CCC and the Soil Conservation Service not happened, the 2012 drought experienced in the Southwest and Midwest would have immediately turned into a dust bowl.

Tragically, however, the more impressive accomplishments of the New Deal programs lost much of their momentum and support by the end of World War II. But even as early as 1937, the New Deal had been losing ground as a result of the fight over expansion of the Supreme Court and a weakening economy, which Roosevelt's turn to deficit reduction only exacerbated, with the result that the country suffered a "depression within the Depression." The New Deal as an attempt to restructure the American economy virtually ground to a halt in 1938.[89] The war itself ended the CCC, but with the untimely death of Roosevelt in 1945, the forces of reaction were able to mobilize more effectively. The TVA was to be the first and only experiment in comprehensive regional development; and the National Resources Planning Board, which had drawn up plans for the demobilization of the war machinery, a postwar full-employment economy, and an expanded welfare state was disbanded even before the war's end, the victim of fierce attacks by conservatives in Congress.[90]

Today, the family farms that once dotted the Great Plains are gone, leaving in their wake a string of ghost towns except in the areas where newly discovered oil and natural gas have created overnight boom towns. The Southern Plains and the Southwestern part of the United States are facing a water shortage as great as that faced by those who experienced the Dust Bowl.[91] In the last three or four years, parts of the United States have been hit with an increasing series of environmental disasters—hurricanes, tornadoes, floods, wildfires, droughts—yet not enough is being done to mitigate the greenhouse gases that scientists say may be largely responsible for the increasing frequency and severity of these disasters.

Moreover, a recent study revealed that in 737 U.S. counties out of more than 3,000 (most in the region that New Deal policies were meant to improve), life expectancies for women declined between 1997 and 2007, reversing nearly a century of progress in public health, a trend not seen since the great influenza epidemic of 1918.[92] The natural and physical infrastructure of the nation has been badly eroded, yet budget cuts have closed state and local public parks, threatened food safety inspection, and other vital public services. The immanence of possibly catastrophic climate change means that we must move very quickly to make our economy environmentally sustainable. This makes national government intervention, planning, and financing—not to mention international coordination—all the more urgent; yet even here we see the failure of the Obama Administration to respond to the severity of the problem. At both the 1999 Copenhagen and 2012 Rio Earth summits, the United States played a conspicuous role in dampening efforts to achieve a coordinated international attack on greenhouse gases, pushing instead for vaguely worded national voluntary efforts.

The situation today, differs, of course, in several important respects from that faced by the Roosevelt Administration, making the solving of these problems infinitely more complex. Unlike in the 1930s, the United States is now a debtor nation. To move at the speed and with the resolve displayed by the Roosevelt administration would require taking on more public debt—at least in the short run—a course that appears at the moment politically unsolvable unless, of course, we decide to create different ways of financing these programs. In contrast to the United States in the 1930s, we are now saddled with an enormously powerful military industrial complex that eats up over half the discretionary federal budget. With its tentacles in every congressional district in the country, providing jobs, revenue to state and local budgets, and campaign contributions, it has become almost impossible to dislodge.[93] Reducing the military budget to that which is needed to defend the country from attack would be one important revenue stream, but that is not even on the political radar screen. The National Guard could provide the quick logistical support needed to get a national Youth Service Corps something like the CCC off the ground. Such a corps, while engaged in ongoing needed work, could also be trained and mobilized quickly to provide emergency relief and recovery in cases of national disasters, like hurricanes Katrina and Sandy. Here again, the New Deal provides a precedent. WPA workers were mobilized in just this way during the great Ohio River flood of 1937. According to a local journalist,

> Trained military forces could hardly have done a better job of flood rehabilitation than did Fifth District WPA workers.... They were everywhere, from start to finish, doing all kinds of jobs—constructing sanitary toilets over sewer manholes to protect the city's health; carrying relief supplies over precarious catwalks, cooking, and serving meals for refugees, soldiers, and coast guardsmen, disposing of garbage and refuse, rescuing livestock and persons, cheering, and entertaining refugees.[94]

Not only has the idea of national or regional planning been abandoned, but any attempt, howsoever mild, to suggest that the federal government should do more to regulate business and stimulate the economy, let alone plan for the future, is stifled by the pejorative labels "socialism" and "big government." Our scientific knowledge of the environment has progressed way beyond the conservation underpinnings of the New Deal programs; yet a significant sector of our political establishment and the public (including some scientists)—misinformed by a well-funded global warming denial campaign waged by the fossil fuel industry, by an unwillingness to go against views held by their primary reference group, or by a reluctance to change comfortable lifestyles—is in denial about the preponderance of scientific evidence pointing to human-induced climate change.[95] Presidential leadership thus far seems woefully lacking in the kind of organic understanding of the relationship between human development and the environment that was present among New Deal leadership. And, finally, we face today an entire country that must be radically reconstructed on a sustainable basis. So the lessons of the New Deal are still applicable. The need to relearn them is urgent, and to the extent that they apply, they may well serve as lessons in many other parts of the world.

Notes

1. A. Dan Tarlock, "Rediscovering the New Deal's Environmental Legacy," in *FDR and the Environment*, Henry L. Henderson and David B. Woolner, eds. (New York: Palgrave Macmillan, 2005), 157.
2. Paul Sutter, "New Deal Conservation: A View from the Wilderness," in Henderson and Woolner, 88.
3. Joseph Stiglitz, "The Book of Jobs," *Vanity Fair*, January 2012, accessed February 12, 2012, available from http://www.vanityfair.com/politics/2012/01/stiglitz-depression-201201.
4. Peter Miller and William E. Rees, "Introduction," in *Ecological Integrity: Integrating Environment, Conservation and Health*, David Pimental, Laura Westra, and Reed F. Noss, eds. (Washington, DC: Island Press, 2000), 6.
5. Lorena Hickock, quoted in David M. Kennedy, *Freedom from Fear: The American People in Depression and War, 1929–1945* (New York/Oxford: Oxford University Press, 1999), 192–193.

6. Adam Cohen, *Nothing to Fear: FDR's Inner Circle and the Hundred Days That Created Modern America* (New York: Penguin Books, 2009), note 3.
7. In the early 1870s, Arnold Hague of the U.S. Geological Survey warned that deforestation would produce floods. In 1874, Dr. Franklin B. Hough, in a report to President Ulysses Grant's Secretary of Agriculture, noted that the nation's forests were being illegally harvested and were rapidly disappearing; in the late 1870s, Rutherford B. Hayes's Secretary of the Interior, Carl Schurz, had tried unsuccessfully to institute professional forest management but was shot down by Congress. Philip Shabecoff, *A Fierce Green Fire: The American Environmental Movement* (New York: Hill and Wang, 1993), 61.
8. President Calvin Coolidge did nothing. Despite pleas from governors, mayors, and other officials in the flooded states, he refused to visit the area. Stephen Ambrose, "Great Flood," *National Geographic*, May 1, 2001, accessed April 14, 2012, available at http://news.nationalgeographic.com/news/2001/05/0501_river4.html.
9. Ibid.
10. Hurricane Facts, accessed February 19, 2012, available at http://www.hurricane-facts.com/Hurricane-Katrina-Facts.php.
11. American meteorologists rated the Dust Bowl the number-one weather event of the twentieth century. Historians say it was the nation's worst prolonged environmental disaster. "In no other instance was there greater or more sustained damage to the American land," wrote Timothy Egan in *The Worst Hard Time* (Boston/New York: Houghton Mifflin, 2006), 10. It was recently listed as one of the ten worst environmental disasters in history. See Maura O'Connor, "The Ten Worst Man-Made Environmental Disasters," May 3, 2010, accessed February 17, 2012, available at http://www.globalpost.com/dispatch/global-green/100502/oil-spill-environmental-disasters.
12. Major John Wesley Powell was a Civil War veteran, explorer, and geologist with the U.S. Geographical and Geological Survey. He had intensively studied the soil, rainfall, water resources and flora and fauna of the West. His report, delivered to the Interior Department in 1878, was entitled, *Report on the Lands of the Arid Region of the United States*, available at http://digital.library.unt.edu/ark:/67531/metadc125/m1/1/.
13. The Enlarged Homestead Act (1909) targeted land suitable for dryland farming (mostly not very productive land), increasing the number of acres to 320. The Stock-Raising Homestead Act (1916) targeted settlers seeking 640 acres of public land for ranching purposes.
14. Egan, 33.
15. Ibid., 42–43.
16. Ibid., 19.
17. T. H. Watkins, *The Hungry Years: A Narrative History of the Great Depression in America* (New York: Henry Holt and Company, 1999), 422.
18. Egan, 5.
19. David Woolner, "Is the Drought a New Dust Bowl? No, Thanks to the New Deal," Roosevelt Institute, July 26, 2012, accessed May 13, 2012, available at http://www.nextnewdeal.net/drought-new-dust-bowl-no-thanks-new-deal?utm_source=Next+New+Deal+Newsletter&utm_campaign=7240140a61-NND_Weekly_7_26_127_25_2012&utm_medium=email.
20. Watkins, 422.
21. Ibid.
22. Ibid., 8.
23. John A. Salmond, *The Civilian Conservation Corps, 1932–1942* (Durham, NC: Duke University Press, 1967), 4. The *Yearbook of Agriculture* for that year announced that approximately 35 million acres of formerly cultivated land had been destroyed for crop production, 100 million acres then in crops had lost all or most of the topsoil, and an additional 125 million acres were rapidly losing topsoil.
24. An opposing view—that of naturalists like John Muir—saw nature as a transcendental realm that should not be interfered with by man. This more romantic view helped in

the promotion of the idea of the national park system, but it was Teddy Roosevelt's chief forester, Gifford Pinchot's, more utilitarian view of nature that ultimately prevailed in public policy.

25. Though he had grown up as a patrician, Roosevelt was sensitized to the economic suffering of the time through the influence of his wife, Eleanor, who would take trips across the country meeting with poor and unemployed people and listening to their stories. She would then badger Roosevelt to take action on what she had found. Earlier, she had introduced him to the suffering documented by settlement workers and to women trade unionists.
26. Arthur M. Schlesinger, Jr., *The Coming of the New Deal, The Age of Roosevelt,* Vol. II (New York: Houghton Mifflin, 1958), 224–225.
27. Kenneth S. Davis, *FDR: The New Deal Years 1933–1937* (New York: Random House, 1979), 386.
28. Brian Black, "The Complex Environmentalist: Franklin D. Roosevelt and the Ethos of New Deal Conservation," in Henderson and Woolner, 25–26.
29. For more detailed accounts of the evolution of Roosevelt's environmental ethic, see Henderson and Woolner, 7–83.
30. 16 Franklin D. Roosevelt, "Speech before the Troy, New York People's Forum," March 3, 1912. *Franklin D. Roosevelt and Conservation* Vol. 1, 1911–1937, Edgar B. Nixon, comp. and ed. (Washington, DC: U.S. General Services Administration), available at http://www.nps.gov/history/history/online_books/cany/fdr/part1.htm.
31. Franklin D. Roosevelt, Remarks at Welcome Home Party, Hyde Park, New York, August 30, 1934, accessed May 2, 2012, available at http://docs.fdrlibrary.marist.edu/php83034.html.
32. The idea of a civilian conservation corps was not uniquely Roosevelt's. It is likely that he had known about similar programs that had been instituted by 1932 in Bulgaria, the Netherlands, Norway, Sweden, Denmark, Austria, and Germany. Roosevelt himself had created a prototype as governor of New York. Salmond, 5.
33. Black, 37–40.
34. "Manpower mobilization" refers to the program's military character. In the first three months of World War I, 181,000 were enrolled, compared with 275,000 during the first three months of the CCC. Many more, of course, were employed by all of the New Deal's work programs. Robert D. Leighninger, Jr. *Long Range Public Investment: The Forgotten Legacy of the New Deal* (Columbia: University of South Carolina Press, 2007), 13.
35. Franklin D. Roosevelt, "Three Essentials for Unemployment Relief," speech to Congress, March 21, 1933, available at http://newdeal.feri.org/speeches/1933c.htm.
36. In May of 1933, the first contingent of a new Bonus Army—3,000 desperately poor, embittered World War I Army veterans descended on Washington demanding a bonus that had been promised them for service in the war. An earlier Bonus Army had been routed by General MacArthur under orders from President Hoover with nothing to show for their efforts; but this time, President Roosevelt sent emissaries to listen to their grievances, and defused their anger with the promise of jobs in the FERA.
37. Franklin D. Roosevelt, press conference, March 15, 1933, in Nixon, Vol. 1.
38. 113 *[Enclosure 2]* James Lathrop Pack, "Reforestation as a Means of Emergency Employment: Is it Really Practical or Altogether Wise?" July 11, 1932; and 114 *[Enclosure 3]* James O. Hazard to Charles L. Pack, July 19, 1932, in Nixon, Vol. 1.
39. Ren Davis and Helen Davis, *Our Mark on This Land: A Guide to the Legacy of the Civilian Conservation Corps in America's Parks* (Granville, OH: The McDonald and Woodward Publishing Co., 2011), 48–50.
40. Davis, 386.
41. Salmond, Chapter 7. The CCC spent nearly 6.5 million days fighting fires, a period equivalent to the constant efforts of more than 16,000 men working for a whole year on the basis of an eight-hour day. Forty-seven enrollees lost their lives.
42. Ibid.

43. Douglas Helms, "Soil Conservation Is an Old Time Religion," in *Readings in the History of the Soil Conservation Service*, U.S. Department of Agriculture Soil Conservation Service Historical Notes No. 1, 20–22, available at http://www.nrcs.usda.gov/Internet/FSE_DOCUMENTS/stelprdb1043484.pdf.
44. Davis, 392.
45. Woolner, "Is the Drought a New Dustbowl?"
46. Ibid., 389.
47. Ibid., 393.
48. Robert S. McElvaine, *The Great Depression: America, 1929–1941* (New York: Random House, 1993), 168–169.
49. Roosevelt, quoted in Arthur M. Schlesinger, Jr., *The Politics of Upheaval, the Age of Roosevelt*, Vol. III *1935–1936* (New York: Houghton Mifflin, 1960), 323.
50. Gordon R. Clapp, "The Meaning of TVA," in Roscoe C. Martin, ed., *TVA: The First Twenty Years, A Staff Report* (Knoxville, TN: University of Alabama Press and University of Tennessee Press, 1956), 11–13.
51. O. M. Derryberry, M.D., "Health," in Martin, 195–200.
52. Leighninger, 116.
53. Salmond, 168.
54. Leighninger, 12.
55. Ibid, 21–26.
56. Aldo Leopold, for example, lamented in the September 1935 issue of *The Living Wilderness* that the "hammer of development" now threatened "the remaining remnant of wilderness" though it was wilderness that "gave value and significance to its [*the New Deal conservation program's*] labors." Aldo Leopold, "Why the Wilderness Society?" *The Living Wilderness*, 1, no. 1 (September 1935): 6. Quoted in Sutter, 89.
57. 583 Roosevelt to Hendrik Willem Van Loon, South Norwalk, Connecticut, February 2, 1937, in Nixon, Vol. III, (Washington, DC: U.S. General Services Administration), available at http://www.nps.gov/history/history/online_books/cany/fdr/part3.htm.
58. 577 [*Enclosure*]Summary of the Final Report of the Great Plains Committee on the Future of the Great Plains, January 22, 1937, in Nixon, ibid.
59. Tarlock, 165.
60. Davis and Davis, 53–54.
61. Wendell Willkie, president of the Commonwealth and Southern Company, the largest power company in the South and a presidential candidate in 1940, led the fight against the TVA, calling it not only a threat to private industry, but unconstitutional.
62. "Environmental Impacts of Dams," *International Rivers*, accessed March 14, 2013 available at http://www.internationalrivers.org/environmental-impacts-of-dams; Philip Fearnside, "Greenhouse Gas Emissions from Hydroelectric Dams: Controversies Provide a Springboard for Rethinking a Supposedly 'Clean' Energy Source," *Climatic Change* 66, nos. 1–2 (2004): 1–8.
63. Jevons Law or Jevons Paradox, as it is sometimes called, refers to the observation made by the English economist, William Stanley Jevons in 1865, that technological progress that increases the efficiency with which a resource is used tends to increase the rate of its consumption. He made this observation in relation to the increased efficiency of coal use. In this case, the reduced cost of electricity made possible by publicly- owned utilities facilitated an exponential growth in the use of energy.
64. Until this time, the philosophy of private power had been to keep rates high and consumption low. Schlesinger, *Politics of Upheaval*, 374.
65. William E. Leuchtenburg, *The FDR Years: On Roosevelt and His Legacy* (New York: Columbia University Press, 1995), 159–195. After reviewing the evidence, Leuchtenburg concludes that, while state and private pressure groups played their part, the proposal for seven TVAs was scrapped primarily because of territorial infighting among administration officials—particularly between Henry Wallace, who headed the Agricultural Department, and Harold Ickes of the Interior. Part of this conflict was personal. Ickes was not an affable person, and many in the

administration felt that he was trying to create his own fiefdom in the Interior Department. But it was also a function of the conflict between functional and geographical structure. Agricultural policy was a functional issue, whereas the TVA crossed geographic lines, subsuming all functions within it. Wallace, who should have been for such regional development across the country, felt that the TVA's monopolization of agricultural policy would make it subordinate to the Department of the Interior, headed by Ickes.

66. For example, the black agricultural colleges had no place in the fertilizer program, and the number of blacks on the extension service in the field had not been utilized. Moreover, the leadership of the agricultural department had been turned over to men with explicit racial biases. Philip Selznick, *TVA and the Grassroots: A Study in the Sociology of Formal Organization* (New York: Harper & Row, 1966), 112.
67. *Biocapacity* refers to the amount of renewable resources needed to sustain a given population plus handle all its wastes. "World Footprint," Global Footprint Network, accessed February 12, 2013, available at http://www.footprintnetwork.org/en/index.php/GFN/page/world_footprint.
68. Franklin D. Roosevelt, Annual Message to Congress, January 4, 1935, The American Presidency Project, available at http://www.presidency.ucsb.edu/ws/?pid=14890.
69. 126 Speech by Roosevelt, Montgomery, Alabama, January 21, 1933, in Nixon, Vol. 1.
70. Franklin D. Roosevelt Press Conference, January 26, 1937, in Nixon, Vol. II.
71. Carter had warned the nation that the failure to plan for future energy needs "is a problem we will not solve in the next few years, and it is likely to get progressively worse through the rest of this century.... Our decision about energy will test the character of the American people and the ability of the President and the Congress to govern. This difficult effort will be the 'moral equivalent of war'—except that we will be uniting our efforts to build and not destroy." Jimmy Carter, "Proposed Energy Policy," speech delivered on April 18, 1977, available at http://www.pbs.org/wgbh/americanexperience/features/primary-resources/carter-energy/.
72. Woolner, "Is the Drought a New Dust Bowl?"
73. Tarlock, 158.
74. For summaries of Obama's environmental record, see: Michael Arria, "Obama's an Environmental Failure: An Interview with Journalist Joshua Frank," *Motherboard*, May 9, 2012, accessed May 26, 2012, available at http://motherboard.vice.com/2012/5/9/obama-s-an-environmental-failure-an-interview-with-journalist-joshua-frank--2; and "Forum: Assessing Obama's Record on the Environment," multiple authors, *Forum 360*, July 25, 2011, accessed May 26, 2012, available at http://e360.yale.edu/feature/forum_assessing_obamas_record_on_the_environment/2427/.
75. The national monuments include the First State National Monument in Delaware and Pennsylvania, the Rio Grande del Norte National Monument in New Mexico, the San Juan Islands National Monument in Washington State, the Charles Young Buffalo Soldiers National Monument in Ohio, and a monument commemorating Harriet Tubman and the Underground Railroad in Maryland.
76. Environmentalists and food experts claim that growing corn for ethanol uses up too much land that could be used for growing food, contributes to higher food and gas prices, lowers vehicle fuel efficiency, and may be contributing to air pollution. See Diana Furchtgott-Roth, " With Ethanol, Obama Ignores Common Sense," *Real Clear Markets*, November 20, 2012, accessed July 21, 2013, available at http://www.realclearmarkets.com/articles/2012/11/20/with_ethanol_obama_skirts_common_sense_99997.html; Mario Parker & Alan Bjerga, "Obama Said to Reject Request to Ease Corn-based Ethanol Law," Bloomberg News, November 16, 2012, accessed July 21, 2013, available at http://www.bloomberg.com/news/2012-11-16/obama-said-to-reject-request-to-ease-corn-based-ethanol-law.html.
77. Ironically, it is the region's free-market Republican congressional representatives who are objecting most vocally to this proposal. Gar Alperovitz and Thomas Hanna, "Shocker: Republicans Fight Obama Plan to Privatize the Hugely Popular, Cheap Energy Source of the TVA," *Alternet*,

May 19, 2013, accessed May 20, 2013, available at http://www.alternet.org/economy/shocker-republicans-fight-obama-plan-privatize-hugely-popular-cheap-energy-source-tva.

78. *The Economic Impact of the American Recovery and Reinvestment Act of 2009*, Seventh Quarterly Report, Executive Office of the President, President's Council of Economic Advisors, July 1, 2011, accessed 29 March 2012, available at http://www.whitehouse.gov/sites/default/files/cea_7th_arra_report.pdf. The conservative *Weekly Standard* accused the President of spending $278,000 per job, but the White House correctly pointed out that not only had the magazine used the lower jobs estimate, but not all of the stimulus money went to salaries, but to long-term investments in infrastructure, education, and the like. The liberal Economic Policy Institute estimated the actual cost per job was somewhere under $100,000. Jake Tapper, "$278K per Stimulus Job? White House Says No," *ABC News*, July 5, 2011, accessed March 29, 2012, available at http://abcnews.go.com/blogs/politics/2011/07/278k-per-stimulus-job-white-house-says-no/. See also Stephen Clark, "White House Disputes Study Saying Stimulus Cost Taxpayers $278,000 Per Job," *Fox News*, July 5, 2011, accessed March 29, 2012, available at http://www.foxnews.com/politics/2011/07/05/white-house-disputes-study-saying-stimulus-cost-taxpayers-278000-per-job/.
79. Todd Harrison, *Analysis of the FY 2012 Defense Budget, Center for Strategic and Budgetary Assessments*, accessed March 22, 2012, available at http://www.csbaonline.org/wp-content/uploads/2011/07/2011.07.16-FY-2012-Defense-Budget.pdf.
80. Tara Mitchell Mielnik, *New Deal, New Landscape: The Civilian Conservation Corps and South Carolina's State Parks* (Columbia: University of South Carolina Press, 2011), 25–26.
81. Irving Bernstein, *A Caring Society: The New Deal, the Worker, and the Great Depression* (Boston: Houghton Mifflin Company, 1985), 159.
82. Vocational education was generally related to CCC work. Classes were given in truck driving, mechanics, equipment maintenance and repair, landscaping, surveying, carpentry, forestry, and wildlife conservation, as well as in skills related to management of the program such as typing, accounting, journalism, newspaper production, cooking, and baking.
83. Bernstein, 159.
84. Schlesinger, *The Coming of the New Deal*, 339.
85. Neil Maher, *Nature's New Deal: The Civilian Conservation Corps and the Roots of the American Environmental Movement* (New York: Oxford University Press, 2007).
86. See 310 Roosevelt to Congress, January 25, 1935 in Nixon, Vol. 1, Part 2.
87. The Department of the Interior created what it called the National Planning Board (NPB). In 1939, it was transferred to the Executive Office of the President, and renamed the National Resources Planning Board (NRPB). A new "Bill of Rights," going beyond the rights enunciated in the U.S. Constitution, had been at the heart of the philosophy of the National Resources Planning Board. But while beginning as an enormously ambitious project, the NRPB's report languished as Pearl Harbor interfered. The NRPB was terminated in 1943 due to political opposition. Charles E. Merriam, "The National Resources Planning Board: A Chapter in American Planning Experience," *American Political Science Review*, 37, no. 6 (December 1944): 1079–1080. See also *Security, Work, and Relief Policies: A Report by the National Resources Planning Board*, 1942, available at http://www.ssa.gov/history/reports/NRPB/NRPBreport.html.
88. Roosevelt, speech at the dedication of the Bonneville Dam, Oregon, September 28, 1937, in Richard D. Polenberg, ed., *The Era of Franklin D. Roosevelt 1933–1945: A Brief History with Documents* (Boston/New York: Bedford/St. Martin's Press, 2000), 67.
89. Kennedy, 356–363.
90. For discussions of the National Resources Planning Board, see Alan Brinkley, *The End of Reform: New Deal Liberalism in Recession and War* (New York: Vintage Books/Random House, 1995), 227–264; Merriam, 1075–1088.
91. For a detailed analysis of the coming water shortage, see Frank Ackerman and Elizabeth A. Stanton, *The Last Drop: Climate Change and the Southwest Water Crisis* (Somerville, MA: Stockholm Environment Institute–US, February 2011), accessed April 3, 2013, available

at http://sei-us.org/Publications_PDF/SEI-WesternWater-0211.pdf; William deBuys, *A Great Aridness: Climate Change and the Future of the American Southwest* (New York: Oxford University Press, 2011).

92. Noam N. Levey, "Life Expectancy for Women Slips in Some Regions," *Los Angeles Times*, June 15, 2011, accessed June 29, 2011, available at http://www.latimes.com/news/science/la-na-womens-health-20110615,0,1751262,full.story. Researchers attributed the decline in life expectancy to smoking and obesity, with some relationship to income inequality. While this study did not measure the effects of environmental pollutants on health, it is possible that the health effects were also exacerbated by toxic pollutants. Over half of the top 20 most polluted states are in the South. See Pete Altman, "The 'Toxic Twenty': States with the Highest Levels of Air Pollution from Power Plants," July 20, 2011, Natural Resources Defense Council, accessed June 22, 2013, available at http://switchboard.nrdc.org/blogs/paltman/the_toxic_20_states_with_the_h.html.

93. As of this writing, there is growing evidence of public dissatisfaction with the cost of the nation's commitment to the military, even among normally hawkish members of Congress. Thus, we may begin to see some change in this area.

94. John A. Ellert, quoted in "Ohio River Flood of 1937," The Lilly Libraries, Indiana University, Bloomington, available at http://www.indiana.edu/~liblilly/wpa/flood.html. Original source: *Work Relief under John K. Jennings, 1931–1939,* Chapter 3, "The Ohio River Flood." The flood left 1 million homeless, 385 dead, and property losses reaching $500 million ($8 billion in 2012 dollars). "Flood of '97, Infamous Floods," *The Cincinnati Enquirer*, accessed March 3, 2013, available at http://www.enquirer.com/flood_of_97/history5.html.

95. Andrew C. Revkin, "Skeptics Dispute Climate Worries and Each Other," *New York Times*, March 8, 2009, accessed June 6, 2012, available at http://www.nytimes.com/2009/03/09/science/earth/09climate.html?pagewanted=all; Justin Gillis and Leslie Kaufman, "Leak Offers Glimpse of Campaign Against Climate Science," *New York Times*, February 15, 2012, accessed June 6, 2012, available at http://www.nytimes.com/2012/02/16/science/earth/in-heartland- institute-leak-a-plan-to-discredit-climate-teaching.html?_r=1&pagewanted=all. For more on the climate change denial campaign, see *Koch Brothers Exposed: Fueling Climate Denial and Privatizing Democracy,* a film by Robert Greenwald available from Brave New Foundation, at http://www.BraveNewFoundation.org. For the psychological mechanisms involved in climate change denial, see Dan M. Kahan, Ellen Peters, Maggie Wittlin, Paul Slovic, Lisa Larrimore Ouellette, Donald Braman, and Gregory Mandel, "The Polarizing Impact of Science Literacy and Numeracy on Perceived Climate Change Risks," *Nature Climate Change*, May 27, 2012, accessed June 6, 2012, available at http://www.nature.com/nclimate/journal/vaop/ncurrent/full/nclimate1547.html; S. Stoll-Kleemann, Tim O'Riordan, and Carlo C. Jaeger, "The Psychology of Denial Concerning Climate Mitigation Measures: Evidence from Swiss Focus Groups," *Global Environmental Change,* 11, no. 2 (2001): 107–117.

10

New Deal Agricultural Policy

The Unintended Consequences of Supply Management

BILL WINDERS

...the real and lasting progress of the people of farm and city alike will come, not from the old familiar cycle of glut and scarcity, not from the succession of boom and collapse, but from the steady and sustained increases in production and fair exchange of things that human beings need.

—Franklin D. Roosevelt, Statement on Signing the Agricultural Adjustment Act of 1938, February 16, 1938

New Deal agricultural policy was undoubtedly a response to the Great Depression as it affected agriculture and, to a lesser extent, the environment. Yet, this response was neither inevitable nor automatic. Just as with the recent financial crisis and recession, the Great Depression was preceded by a world economic crisis in agriculture that rested on several factors: unstable prices, expanding production (beyond demand), environmental degradation, and a faltering system of international trade in agriculture.[1] Overproduction and price instability, in particular, plagued farmers in the United States and around the world as early as the mid-1920s. The eventual New Deal response was bold and among the most extensive economic interventions created as it regulated prices and production of agricultural commodities through the Agricultural Adjustment Act of 1933 (hereafter, AAA) and its policy of supply management. These elements aimed to coordinate and regulate agricultural production and markets in ways that would alleviate overproduction and market collapses. Other elements of New Deal agricultural policy aimed to redistribute land and expand opportunities in rural areas or to ease the environmental degradation brought by expanding and industrializing agriculture at the time. Thus, agricultural policy in the New Deal not only intended to regulate agriculture and smooth out markets, but it also aimed at increasing farm income, reducing rural poverty, and promoting conservation in farming.

Despite this boldness, New Deal agricultural policy eventually came to reinforce existing patterns of inequality and industrialization in agriculture. For example, the number of farms decreased, and average farm size increased as agriculture became more concentrated. And by reinforcing the inequalities in agriculture, some of the core elements of New Deal agricultural policy promoted some farming practices and technologies that contributed to environmental decline: much greater use of chemical fertilizers, pesticides, and herbicides, as well as intensive irrigation in some regions such as the Great Plains—which had been struck by the Dust Bowl in the 1930s.

To understand fully this long-term development, however, we need to start with the origins in the agricultural depression beginning in the 1920s. The next section, then, explores various agricultural aspects of the nascent depression in the 1920s as well as the initial political responses. Then the chapter will explore New Deal agricultural policy and how it was won. What political forces and context brought forth the policy of supply management? Next, the heart of the chapter examines the development and consequences of supply management policy in the mid–twentieth century, as this New Deal policy ultimately resulted in several important yet unintended consequences: changes in regional class structures, production patterns, and farmers' economic interests. This section also examines how the long-term trajectory of New Deal agricultural policy is apparent today. The chapter ends with a reflection on the lessons of New Deal agricultural policy for the current era of economic troubles and political debates about government economic policy. It all starts, however, in the early twentieth century.

The Depression in Agriculture and Early Political Responses

During and immediately after World War I, agriculture prospered as prices for cotton, wheat, corn, and other agricultural commodities increased significantly as a result of increased exports to Europe. Between 1914 and 1919, cotton prices rose from about 7 cents per pound to about 35 cents per pound; wheat went from 97 cents a bushel to $2.16 a bushel; and corn rose from 67 cents a bushel to $1.44 a bushel. At the same time, gross farm income more than doubled, from $7.6 billion to $17.7 billion.[2] After the brief postwar recovery of European agriculture, this prosperity was interrupted by a short but intense depression from 1920 to 1921 as market prices fell by more than 50 percent: cotton fell to 17 cents a pound, wheat to $1.03 a bushel, and corn to 46 cents a bushel. Likewise, gross farm income fell to $10.5 billion in 1921—a drop of more than 40 percent in two years (see Figure 10.1).

Market prices rebounded somewhat in 1924 and 1925, but this rebound ended as prices resumed their downward slide between 1926 and 1930: cotton prices

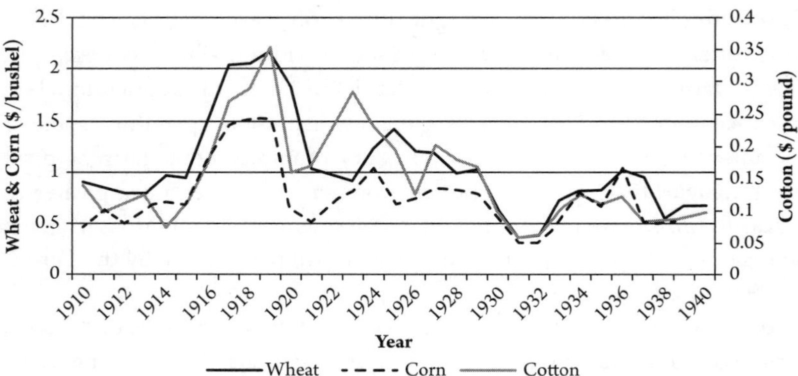

Figure 10.1 Wheat, Corn, and Cotton Prices, 1910–1940.

averaged about 16.8 cents a pound, wheat about $1.10 a bushel, and corn about 80 cents a bushel. This represented a decline of at least 20 percent from the cotton and corn prices in 1924, and from the wheat price in 1925. Furthermore, agricultural prices began a continuous decline in 1927 that would not end for about six years. A few years before the U.S. stock market crash in October of 1929, then, agriculture had begun to slip into depression.[3]

After 1929, agriculture markets collapsed as the entire economy was enveloped by the Depression. In 1932, agriculture hit bottom along with the rest of the economy. Wheat was a mere 37.5 cents per bushel by 1932—a decline of more than 70 percent from 1925. Cotton prices fared just as poorly. After rising to about 23 cents a pound in 1924, cotton prices fell to 5.7 cents a pound in 1931—a drop of about 75 percent in only seven years. Finally, corn prices experienced a similar decline: after reaching $1.06 in 1924, corn fell to 32 cents a bushel in 1932—a 70 percent decline.

The collapse in agricultural prices, of course, led to a sharp decline in overall farm income, as this economic crisis affected everything from wheat, to hogs, to tobacco.[4] Average income per farm fell from $2,051 in 1926 to $953 in 1932—a drop of about 54 percent in seven years.[5] Per-farm income for cotton farmers fell even faster, by 68 percent between 1929 and 1932, from $1,245 to $397.[6] With farm prices and income in a free-fall, farmers throughout the country increasingly faced bankruptcy and bank foreclosure on their mortgages. The rate of farm foreclosures and bankruptcies in the United States more than doubled, from 18.7 per 1,000 farms in 1931 to 38.8 per 1,000 farms in 1933.[7] Thus, the depression of the late 1920s and early 1930s devastated U.S. agriculture.

What factors lay behind this depression? How did farmers come to be faced with prices that collapsed to a mere fraction of their previous levels? Part of the answer rests in U.S. agricultural production levels, and part of it is found at the level of the world economy. The fundamental problem was that American cotton, wheat, and corn farmers began to face a serious economic crisis due to overproduction and declining exports during the mid-1920s. Between 1920 and 1925, for example, annual U.S. cotton production averaged about 12 million bales. In 1926, however, cotton farmers produced a record 18 million bales of cotton. Over the next several years, cotton production declined slightly but still remained high, averaging more than 15 million bales between 1926 and 1931. At the same time, the average yearly surplus of cotton more than doubled, from 2.5 million bales between 1921 and 1925 to 5.6 million bales between 1927 and 1932.[8] Increased production in the world economy also posed a problem for cotton: annual world cotton production increased from an average of 20 million bales in 1921–1925, to almost 27 million bales per year between 1926 and 1931, with an increase of 55 percent during the entire period between 1922 and 1931. The situation was similar for other commodities: U.S. and world production increased in the 1920s, leading to a glut on world markets and decreased exports. Farmers in the United States and elsewhere faced the daunting problems of overproduction and surplus.

Regarding exports, two factors created a context in which U.S. exports would be expected to decline. First, agriculture in Europe recovered from the devastation of World War I, and consequently Europe's market for American agricultural products declined. Furthermore, many European nations began to rely on agricultural exports to help pay down debts accumulated during the war. As a result, European farmers began competing with American farmers for export markets. Second, the United States came out of World War I as a creditor nation rather than the debtor nation it had previously been. This status increased the value of the dollar relative to other currencies, thereby increasing the cost of U.S. goods, including cotton and wheat. Thus, the nation's creditor status made American exports less competitive.

Several factors contributed to the increased cotton and wheat production, including "better seeds, improved control of diseases, more efficient specialization, and the adoption of mechanized equipment."[9] Perhaps most importantly, however, cotton and wheat acreage in the United States expanded. Cotton production expanded westward out of the Southeast into Arkansas, Oklahoma, and Texas. In these states, cotton acreage increased from 15 million acres in 1921 to almost 27 million acres in 1926. In Texas alone, cotton acreage increased from 10.7 million acres to 18.3 million acres. Wheat acreage also increased by more than 20 percent between 1924 and 1929, from 52 million acres to 63 million acres. This expansion in cotton and wheat acreage led to increased production and contributed to surpluses that drove down the prices of these commodities. This expansion of farming in the middle of the United States also laid the foundation for one of the most alarming environmental crises in agriculture: the prolonged Dust Bowl that ravaged the Great Plains in the 1930s. But the crisis of the 1920s was one of economics—overproduction, unstable prices, and the collapse of global markets.

Despite the roots of this crisis in agriculture, the proposed political solutions during the Republican administrations of Calvin Coolidge (1923–1928) and Herbert Hoover (1928–1932) did not automatically focus on production, prices, and exports.[10] Each of these administrations saw the problem in agriculture as deriving from a lack of economic coordination and therefore opposed policy solutions that required significant involvement in the economy, such as directly influencing prices or production. Rather than such direct intervention in the economy, Coolidge and Hoover each supported legislation that aided and strengthened farmer cooperatives as a means of improving market coordination.

In contrast, many members of Congress from farm regions increasingly did favor more extensive action by the federal government. In an effort to win such policies, senators and representatives from the South, the Wheat Belt, and the Corn Belt formed the Farm Bloc in 1921.[11] In 1924, Senator Charles McNary (R-Oregon) and Representative Gilbert Haugen (R-Iowa) introduced bills in the Senate and House, respectively. The McNary-Haugen bills, as these proposals came to be known, called for the federal government to raise agricultural prices by purchasing surpluses and selling them abroad at world market prices. Domestic prices would be protected by a tariff, further helping to raise agricultural prices relative to those in industry that had long been protected by tariffs. The difference between the higher domestic price and the lower world price would be covered by an "equalization fee" charged to farmers based on their production. The equalization fee would not only help pay for the program, but, proponents hoped, it would reduce the risk of overproduction as well. The key is that the McNary-Haugen bills would regulate prices in a way that was favorable to farmers as well as alleviate overproduction by removing the surplus from the market.

These bills, none of which passed, were effectively a precursor to the New Deal agricultural policy of supply management. Presidents Coolidge and Hoover each stood in the way of their passage: Coolidge vetoed two versions of the McNary-Haugen bills, in 1927 and 1928; soon after taking office, Hoover signed the Agricultural Marketing Act, which provided financial and managerial support for agricultural cooperatives.[12] Although the Farm Bloc stretched across party lines to include both Democrats and Republicans, it did not have enough influence in the Republican Party to enact supply management policy.

In the South, cotton prices and farm income declined so much that public officials and farm leaders grappled desperately with the cotton crisis. The dire economic situation in world cotton markets led many Southern cotton producers and politicians to advocate mandatory reductions in production in order to raise prices and farm income. In 1931, Mississippi Governor Theodore Bilbo proposed that cotton states pick only two-thirds of the crop, and the Hoover Administration then proposed that cotton farmers plow under every third row.[13] Huey P. Long, governor of Louisiana, proposed a year's "Cotton Holiday" during which the South would produce no cotton in 1932. Long recommended that Southern states create laws mandating that farmers abstain from growing cotton and levy fines on any farmers who violated the holiday. A cotton holiday conference held in New Orleans in August 1931 was attended by state officials, planters, merchants, newspaper reporters and editors, and congressional representatives and senators from Southern states. The conference endorsed Long's proposal for a cotton holiday.[14] In the end, five Southern states—Arkansas, Louisiana, Mississippi, South Carolina, and Texas—enacted mandatory cotton-reduction legislation in 1931.[15] Thus, prior to the New Deal, there was significant support in the South for an agricultural policy that would directly regulate production.

Support for production controls by individual states, however, was by no means unanimous. Alabama's governor, for example, refused to support legislation to mandate a reduction in production. With several cotton states likewise failing to pass reduction legislation, the cotton-reduction movement in the South died.[16] Nonetheless, even before the creation of the AAA, parts of the South already demonstrated that they favored the cornerstones of the AAA: production controls and price supports. Still, the goal of supply management was elusive, even with Southerners firmly supporting the policy. The political power necessary to win supply management policy came with the election of Franklin Delano Roosevelt in 1932.

A New Deal for Agriculture: The Creation and Expansion of Supply Management Policy

Franklin Roosevelt defeated the incumbent, Hoover, in the 1932 presidential election by a landslide, winning 89 percent of the electoral vote and 57 percent of the popular vote. In addition, Democrats won substantial majorities in the U.S. House (313–117) and Senate (59–36). Roosevelt's New Deal brought national policies that significantly departed from those of the Republican administrations of the 1920s: a more activist government, by which he meant a government that intervened more in the economy. This was territory into which neither Coolidge nor Hoover was willing to venture.

The Agricultural Adjustment Act

One of the first of President Roosevelt's "alphabet programs" aimed at alleviating the Great Depression was the Agricultural Adjustment Act (AAA), which he signed on May 12, 1933. The AAA set up two central programs—price supports and production controls—with the objective of raising farm prices by controlling the supply of agricultural commodities. This policy built on the various production controls of the McNary-Haugen bills and the cotton-reduction legislation passed by Southern states. To administer supply-management policy, the AAA created a few new bureaucracies and made use of some existing ones.

The Commodity Credit Corporation (CCC) was created in 1933 to administer price supports through "nonrecourse" loans. If the market price rose above the loan rate, then farmers could sell their crop and pay back the CCC loan, earning a profit on the difference between the higher market price and the loan rate. If prices remained below the loan rate, however, then the "nonrecourse" element of the loan operated: farmers had no recourse other than to forfeit their crop to the CCC, and the CCC could take no action against farmers who forfeited their crop. Consequently, farmers would receive an "adequate" price for their crop, and the CCC would effectively reduce the supply of commodities on the market with the expectation of stabilizing or even raising market prices. In essence, when market prices fell below price support levels, the CCC purchased basic commodities from farmers at the price support level as a means of pulling the commodities off the market, controlling supply and raising farm income.

Price supports aimed to raise agricultural prices—and hence, farm income—relative to other consumer and industrial prices. To accomplish this, price supports were based on "parity," which gave agricultural commodities "the same purchasing power in terms of goods and services farmers buy that the commodities had" in the period from 1909 to 1914, when agricultural prices reached historic heights relative to other prices.[17] Price supports, then, gave agricultural prices parity with industrial prices, based on the ratio of prices between 1909 and 1914.

Production controls were administered by the Agricultural Adjustment Administration and were a means of limiting the supply of agricultural commodities. The AAA required farmers to adhere to acreage allotments that were determined by growers' historical production of basic commodities. For example, farmers who had historically grown cotton on large numbers of acres were given large cotton allotments. Farmers who did not adhere to production controls would not receive price supports. Because historical production levels determined acreage allotments, the AAA was biased in favor of larger farms. The AAA also created set-aside programs that paid farmers to leave land idle.[18]

In addition to restrictions on acreage, the AAA also created marketing agreements between farmers and processors. The Secretary of Agriculture could mediate the terms of the agreements to limit the supply of commodities that farmers could market, and impose a fine on farmers who exceeded their marketing allotment. In this way, if farmers ignored controls on acreage, the United States Department of Agriculture (USDA) could still head off any potential surplus by limiting how much made it to the market.[19] Whether through restrictions on acreage or marketing, production controls under the AAA sought to eliminate surpluses and their downward pressure on agricultural prices and farm income.

Under the AAA of 1933, government subsidies to farmers from price supports and production controls were funded by a tax on processors of agricultural commodities. Because the basic commodities—wheat, corn, cotton, tobacco, hogs, and rice—all needed to be processed in some fashion before they could be consumed, the processing tax was easy to administer. (The required processing also made it relatively easy to monitor production levels.) The Secretary of Agriculture set the level of the processing tax based on the difference between farm prices and parity prices. The "tax was placed on the 'first domestic processing' of agricultural commodities"—except for cotton ginning, which was exempt from the tax.[20] The aim of the processing tax was to prevent the cost of payments to farmers from straining the federal budget.

What factors influenced the shape of the AAA and Roosevelt's decision to pursue a policy of supply management based on price supports (through CCC loans) and production controls (acreage allotments and marketing agreements)? The bipartisan McNary-Haugen bills of the 1920s and the production control measures proposed in the South in 1931 certainly had an influence, as did the composition of Roosevelt's USDA and his selection of Henry A. Wallace for Secretary of Agriculture. Wallace had favored price supports and production controls before joining Roosevelt's cabinet. Importantly, each of these components of the foundation of the AAA rested on the Farm Bloc, a political coalition of corn, wheat, and cotton interests.[21]

Of particular significance, New Deal legislation had to be acceptable to—and was influenced by—the Southern Democrats in the House and Senate. In Congress, Southern Democrats held powerful positions, including Senate Majority Leader Joseph Robinson of Arkansas, House Majority Leader Joseph Byrns of Tennessee, the chair of the Senate Committee on Finance, Pat Harrison of Mississippi, and the chair of the House Ways and Means Committee, Robert Doughton of North Carolina.[22] The dominance of Southern Democrats over such key legislative positions gave them much influence over the shape and substance of New Deal policies.[23] For example, the social insurance programs of the Social Security Act of 1935 and the National Labor Relations Act of 1937 both explicitly excluded agricultural workers. As a result, most Southern blacks were effectively excluded from these federal policies. In each instance, Southern Democrats were protecting the racial political economy of the South.

This was especially true with the AAA. First, Southern Democrats played key roles in the passage of the AAA: Marvin Jones of Texas was the chair of the House Agricultural Committee, John Bankhead of Alabama headed the Senate's Agriculture Committee and as Majority Leader Joseph Robinson guided the AAA through the Senate. More than 80 percent of Southern senators voted for the AAA in 1933.[24] Second, Southern support for and influence over the AAA was likewise evident in the implementation of supply management policy. For example, Oscar Johnston—president of the largest cotton plantation in Mississippi—was the finance director of the Agricultural Adjustment Administration.[25] Furthermore, Southern planters dominated local agencies administering AAA programs.[26] The influence of planters pervaded the AAA, from the federal government to the local administration. Thus, understanding supply management policy is impossible without acknowledging the role of Southern Democrats and Southern planters in making and shaping the policy. Supply management policy bore the imprint of the Southern class structure.

How successful was this policy at controlling production and raising prices and farm income? Southern cotton production fell from 13 million bales in 1933 to 9.6 million bales in 1934 and increased very slightly to 10.6 million in 1935. And after averaging 39.5 million acres between 1929 and 1932, total American cotton production averaged 28 million acres between 1934 and 1936. The AAA cotton reduction program facilitated changes in the rural class structure of the South by pushing tens of thousands of tenant farmers and sharecroppers off the farm since the land was often left fallow, for pasture, or for other uses that required less labor than did cotton.

In the Midwest, corn and wheat farmers cut back their acreage and overall production. U.S. corn acreage fell from 110 million in 1932 to 93 million in 1936, and wheat acreage fell from 57 million to 49 million—a decline of about 15 percent for each commodity. Production levels fell even more dramatically: corn production fell from about 82 million metric tons (MMT) in 1932 to 40 MMT in 1936, and wheat production fell from 25.6 MMT to 17.1 MMT during the same period. The decreased production was also due, in part, to a severe drought that hit parts of the Corn and Wheat Belts in 1934. Nonetheless, production controls seemed somewhat effective: between 1932 and 1935, the production of cotton fell by almost 20 percent, corn fell by 10 percent, and wheat by 25 percent.

This policy of supply management achieved its goal of boosting farm income by making the State deeply involved in the market economy. Between 1932 and 1936 cotton prices almost doubled, and wheat and corn prices almost tripled. Increased prices then led to higher farm income: after falling from $1,746 per farm in 1930 to $953 in 1932, it rose to $1,583 in 1936—an increase of more than 65 percent in four years.[27] On each count, therefore, the AAA was successful to some degree: farmland in use and overall production declined, and commodity prices and farm income increased.

The AAA and Conflict Within Agriculture

Despite the initial success of price supports and production controls, the AAA faced serious political challenges and created significant conflict within agriculture. First, some farmers opposed AAA's price-fixing and production dictates. Such opposition from farmers tended to come from the Corn Belt.[28] Second, conflict emerged over the extent to which the AAA should attempt to reform agriculture. Within the Agricultural Adjustment Administration, some officials believed that New Deal agricultural programs should aim to alleviate rural poverty and inequality—especially in the South—through social reforms. Third, and perhaps most important, many corporations that processed agricultural commodities—such as grain processors, cotton mills, and meat packers—opposed being forced to finance supply management. The processing tax created by the AAA rested squarely upon these corporations.

Farm organizations that opposed the AAA tended to do so for one of two reasons: either because the AAA failed to provide enough support to farmers, or because the policy went too far in imposing "regimentation" and government control on farmers.[29] The National Farmers' Union (NFU), which was strongest in the Wheat Belt, was the largest farm organization to oppose the AAA for providing too little support to farmers. The NFU instead favored support based on the cost of production (including the cost of seed, fertilizer, land, and so on).[30] John Simpson, president of the NFU, criticized the administration's focus on parity, which Simpson argued would give farmers less than half of the cost of production.[31] The Roosevelt Administration, however, opposed cost-of-production because the USDA was unable to calculate the cost of production for agricultural commodities.

By contrast, a few small-farm organizations—rarely surpassing several hundred members—opposed the AAA for imposing unnecessary and "un-American" controls on farmers. Most notable among these organizations was the Farmers Independence Council (FIC). Led by Dan Casement, who owned a large cattle farm in Kansas, the FIC expressed significant concerns that the federal government would take control of agriculture. Supported by meat processors, the FIC was particularly opposed to the processing tax that funded relief payments. In doing so, Casement and the FIC claimed to be protecting the liberty and independence of farmers from the control of the government. Other organizations, such as the National Farmers Process Tax Recovery Association (FPTRA), emerged in opposition to the processing tax of the AAA, arguing that processers simply paid lower prices to farmers to make up for the processing tax.[32] In addition, the Corn Belt Liberty League organized farmers in opposition to production controls. Thus, these and other organizations opposed the AAA because they saw supply management policy as an unacceptable expansion of the federal government's reach. Nonetheless, such organizations had little to no influence on New Deal agricultural policy.[33]

The AAA also created conflict among segments of agriculture over another aspect of the policy: rural reform. The most notable conflict emerged in the South between tenants and sharecroppers on one hand, and planters on the other. Disagreement existed over what portion of AAA payments—if any—tenants and sharecroppers should receive. Under the AAA, landowners signed contracts to restrict their acreage and limit production, and AAA payments were sent directly to landowners with the instructions that "a sharecropper was to receive one-half of the payments, a share-tenant two-thirds, and a cash-tenant all."[34] But many planters refused to share the AAA payments with their tenants or sharecroppers. Consequently, a political battle over the distribution of AAA payments emerged both within the federal government's agricultural bureaucracy and in the cotton fields of the South.

A division emerged within the Agricultural Adjustment Administration over the distribution of AAA payments and the use of agricultural policy as a means of rural reform. Opposed to such efforts was a group of "conservative agrarians" that included Chester Davis, Chief of the Production Division; Oscar Johnston, Head of the Finance Division; and, Cully Cobb, who headed the Cotton Section. George Peek, the head of the Agricultural Adjustment Administration, tended to agree with this group that supply management policy took precedence over rural reform. The primary focus of these conservative agrarians was raising farm prices through production controls. Rural reform was largely absent from their agenda. A core group of "urban liberals" who were mostly lawyers from the Northeast argued that landowners ought to be required to share AAA payments with tenants and sharecroppers. They also proposed confiscating some of the planters' land and redistributing it to allow tenants and sharecroppers to become small, independent farmers.[35] This group was led by Rexford Tugwell, Undersecretary of Agriculture, and Jerome Frank, General Counsel of the AAA. Several members of this group, including Gardner "Pat" Jackson, were in the Consumer Division of the AAA.

Outside the Department of Agriculture, the Southern Tenant Farmers Union (STFU) advocated for the rights of tenants and sharecroppers, particularly to share in the benefits distributed by the AAA. Founded and led by H. L. Mitchell and Clay East in Arkansas in July 1934, the STFU organized strikes and lobbied for assistance to tenants and sharecroppers, but their efforts were met with violence and intimidation. Nonetheless, the STFU found little support from the Roosevelt Administration, in part because Arkansas was the home state of Joseph Robinson, the Senate Majority Leader, who was central to the passage of Roosevelt's New Deal legislation. The president avoided offending Southern Democrats like Robinson who were important to the success of other administration policies. Likewise, the STFU found little support in the USDA or the AAA. Davis, Cobb, Johnston, and others opposed upsetting the organization of the rural South, and their contacts in the South told them that Mitchell and Clay were "Communists" trying to start "uprisings" among black tenants and sharecroppers.[36]

Yet the urban liberals did advocate for the STFU and the interests of tenants, croppers, and poorer farmers. In February 1935, Jerome Frank "issued a telegram to all state AAA offices in the South" to enforce cotton program contracts in a manner that favored tenants,[37] with the result that Chester Davis demanded that Secretary Wallace "authorize him to request the resignations of [Jerome] Frank, ... ['Pat'] Jackson" and several other urban liberals.[38] Wallace agreed, largely because taking a stance behind Frank's interpretation of the cotton contracts would have cost Wallace his Cabinet post and endangered other New Deal programs. Southern Democrats and planters were politically powerful enough to exact such a high price for undermining their interests. As a result, the STFU's strongest advocates were removed from government in what became known as the "liberal purge."

Despite the liberal purge, new regulations created in 1938 required landowners to share AAA payments with tenants and sharecroppers. Following this legislation, however, planters frequently expelled tenants from their land and hired sharecroppers and tenants as wage laborers who had no legal claim to federal farm subsidies. In this way, the planters won the battle over the distribution of AAA payments.

Ironically, as I explain later, this policy ultimately undermined the very system that planters and conservative agrarians fought to protect: the Southern plantation system.

The final political battle surrounding the AAA was the tax on agricultural processors that provided funds for price support and production control payments. Various processors sued the government, claiming that this tax was an undue burden and was therefore unconstitutional. Indeed, more than 1,700 lawsuits had been filed against the AAA by the end of 1935. In December 1935, the Supreme Court heard the case of *United States v. Butler,* which challenged the constitutionality of the processing tax used to fund AAA benefits. The primary claimant was the Hoosac Mills Corporation, a bankrupt cotton milling corporation in Massachusetts.[39] The administration defended the AAA based on the government's right to tax and regulate interstate commerce. The Court's majority, however, rejected this reasoning. On January 6, 1936, the Supreme Court declared in a 6 to 3 decision that two core elements of the AAA were unconstitutional: the tax on processors used to fund subsidies to farmers and the regulation of production by using acreage allotments tied to benefit payments.[40]

Congress responded to the Supreme Court's ruling on the AAA by quickly passing the Soil Conservation and Domestic Allotment (SCDA) Act in February 1936. This legislation—influenced by droughts in 1934, 1935, and 1936—paid farmers to reduce their production of "soil-depleting" crops, which tended to be defined so as to overlap with the commodities that were overproduced. Payments under the SCDA Act were funded by general Treasury funds rather than processing taxes. In these ways, the SCDA Act avoided the two primary points of contention that the Supreme Court had with the AAA: federal regulation of agricultural production that the Court majority saw as a state power; and processing taxes upon which the Court looked unfavorably. The constitutionality of the SCDA Act was strengthened by the claim that the reduction of soil-depleting commodities was in the interest of the general welfare.

Long-term agricultural policy, however, was set by the passage of the second Agricultural Adjustment Act in 1938. This AAA set price support levels between 52 percent and 75 percent of parity for the basic commodities. Like the SCDA Act, the second AAA dispensed with the processing taxes and instead funded the benefit payments through general Treasury funds. The AAA of 1938 used three methods of controlling production: soil conservation allotments to limit the production of "soil-depleting" crops, marketing quotas, and acreage allotments.

As we have seen, the passage of the AAA had been followed by three conflicts within agriculture: farmers opposed to the AAA, struggles over rural reform, and resistance by agricultural processors. Although each of these conflicts threatened the AAA to varying degrees, by 1940, supply management policy had emerged as the basic principle of long-term U.S. agricultural policy. During the Second World War, supply management policy expanded to cover more agricultural commodities and to offer greater levels of support to and regulation of farmers.[41] Still, each of these conflicts around agricultural policy during the New Deal reveals important dynamics that would influence agricultural policy for the rest of the twentieth century: the staunch support of Southern planters and some opposition from the Corn Belt and agribusiness.

The Contours of Supply Management Policy in the Twentieth Century

Over the next several decades, the retrenchment of supply management policy was pushed by many of the same groups and political coalitions that had earlier fought for its creation and expansion. This period of contraction demonstrates the same processes as the earlier period of expansion, with one additional factor: the unintended consequences of existing policies. That is, the political and economic contexts of this period were shaped in particular ways by the AAA. This policy of supply management, for instance, changed the rural class structure and commodities produced in the South. It also prompted greater exports, particularly of wheat. And, finally, supply management policy boosted overall production of all three commodities and, in some cases, fueled overproduction. None of these policy outcomes was intended during the New Deal and the creation of the AAA.

Opposition from the Corn Belt

The first legislative step in the retrenchment of supply management policy was the Agricultural Act of 1954, which reduced price supports. Importantly, this retrenchment policy was pushed by the American Farm Bureau Federation. This was the largest farm organization and, at the time, it tended to represent the interests of farmers in the Corn Belt. Between 1947 and 1954, the Farm Bureau continually called for flexible price supports that would vary in the same direction as market prices: as market prices rose, price support levels would also rise; as market prices fell, support levels would likewise decline.[42] This would fundamentally alter the purpose of price supports. Existing price supports, which were set at a fixed level, offered a safety net that ensured that farm income did not fall with market prices. The Farm Bureau's flexible price supports were not meant to support farm income directly. Instead, the Farm Bureau's proposal was aimed at correcting discrepancies between supply and demand in agriculture. Thus, the Farm Bureau sought to create a more market-oriented agricultural policy. In its official policy statement leading up to the Agricultural Act of 1954, the Farm Bureau stated, "we do not consider it the responsibility of the Government to guarantee profitable prices to any group."[43] Yet the cotton-wheat coalition remained the most important defender of supply management policy. Why did corn farmers come to oppose a policy that they had supported in previous decades and that other farmers continued to support?

Importantly, the Farm Bureau opposed high supports and production controls not only for corn but for cotton and wheat as well. This position was based on the desire 1) to keep feed grain prices low; and 2) to prevent production controls on other commodities from encouraging competing sources of soybeans and corn. We can see how these two interests led the corn segment to oppose supply management for corn in particular, as well as for other commodities.

First, corn producers' opposition to high supports for corn was tied to hog production. Between 1945 and 1975, the Corn Belt accounted for between 64 percent and 70 percent of all American hog production. Just three Corn Belt states—Iowa, Illinois, and Indiana—accounted for at least 38 percent of national hog production between 1945 and 1975. This expansive livestock sector shaped the interests of corn producers who received more revenue from hog production than from corn: "Corn producers ... do not get their farm income directly from the sale of their crop. After all, between 85 and 90 percent of corn produced is sold in the form of livestock and livestock products."[44] This reliance on hog production created an interest in maintaining low prices for corn, which was the basis of livestock feed. In fact, American meat consumption began to increase swiftly and quite steadily at this time, from 101 pounds per capita annually in 1950 to 155 pounds per capita annually in 1970.[45] Coupled with the emerging industrial livestock complex that rested on intensive and industrial production methods, this increasing consumption of animals made supply management policy less necessary for feed grains, especially corn. As Allen Matusow notes, "Since demand for meat is elastic (that is, sales rise more than proportionally as prices fall), many hog farmers saw no advantage in limiting supply to keep prices high."[46] Thus, the corn segment opposed high, rigid supports and production controls for corn.

Second, these same economic interests led the Corn Belt to oppose high supports and accompanying production controls for other basic commodities, not just for corn. Again, price supports were generally contingent on adherence to acreage allotments that limited the number of acres of any particular crop that a farm could produce. For instance, to qualify for price supports for cotton, a large landowner in the South might be limited to planting cotton on only 65 percent of the farm's total acreage. This removed sizable portions of farmland in the South from traditionally Southern crops and encouraged diversification. Corn Belt farmers feared that price supports and the accompanying production controls for cotton, in particular, might encourage increased grain production in the South. This fear was well-founded, because Southern farmers often produced soybeans, wheat, and corn on land freed from traditional Southern crops such as cotton. For this reason, then, the Farm Bureau opposed price support programs for other basic commodities as well as for corn.

While farmers in the Corn Belt favored supply management policy when they faced low market prices and low demand, their economic interests changed when the meat industry began to expand and when this policy started to spur competition from other regions. Therefore, a new political economic context for corn producers, shaped to a significant extent by New Deal agricultural policy, led the Corn Belt to oppose a policy that they had supported just years before. While the Farm Bureau and Corn Belt opposed supply management policy, cotton and wheat farmers continued to favor price supports and production controls. The political power of the cotton-wheat coalition severely limited the success of the Corn Belt's drive to weaken supply management policy.[47] The economic interests and political power of the cotton-wheat coalition, however, soon changed as this policy continued to alter the political economic context of American agriculture.

Reshaping the Global Wheat Market

While price supports were changed in 1954, production controls remained strong until the passage of the Cotton-Wheat Act of 1964, which instituted more flexible production controls for cotton and wheat. Importantly, this policy was not passed against the will of the cotton-wheat coalition but rather because this political coalition came to favor weakening supply management policy. This change in policy preferences was a clear and unintended consequence of supply management. Supply management policy altered the economic interests and policy preferences of wheat producers in two ways. First, the combination of price supports and production controls prompted an overproduction of wheat. Second, the addition of export subsidies—and food aid—in 1954 as a central supply management program reshaped the global market for wheat in a way that encouraged expanding production rather than controlling it.

The particular combination of production controls and price supports administered under supply management encouraged overproduction in wheat. Production controls were primarily based on acreage rather than the actual volume of production. Farmers faced restrictions on the acreage that they could use in production, but they faced few limitations on the actual volume of commodities that they could produce on each acre. In contrast, price supports were based on volume produced: if the price support for cotton was set at $0.35 per pound, farmers would receive that support price on all cotton that they grew within their acreage allotment. This inconsistent basis of supply management—production controls on acres, price supports on volume—produced a logic for individual farmers that undermined the primary function of the policy: managing the supply of commodities. The policy encouraged farmers to intensify their production on a smaller number of acres in order to receive the optimum benefit from price supports.

Following the Second World War, a technological revolution in chemical fertilizers, pesticides, and herbicides, as well as the spread of mechanization, allowed farmers to significantly increase their productivity (that is, production per acre). Between 1945 and 1970, wheat productivity increased significantly, from 17 to 31 bushels per acre. This, of course, led to fairly constant increases in overall production, from 30 MMT to 37 MMT.[48] This increased production was a problem, because demand for wheat did not keep up with the growing supply. Surpluses were largely averted immediately after World War II because agriculture in Europe had been decimated by the war, but European agricultural production began to recover by the early 1950s, leading U.S. wheat exports to decline. Between 1952 and 1961, wheat producers faced a chronic overproduction: the annual surplus of wheat averaged about 28 MMT between 1954 and 1959. In fact, carry-over stocks exceeded production in 1955, 1956, 1959, and 1961–1963. Thus, production controls failed to prevent chronic wheat surpluses during this period. This situation encouraged wheat producers to support supply management policy, but it also led to the creation of a policy that would alter their interests.

In response to this chronic overproduction, the United States created export subsidies through food aid, via Public Law 480 (PL 480), to replace the lost export markets in Europe. Through export subsidies in food aid, the United States found an outlet for its agricultural surpluses in the periphery of the world economy, especially newly independent nations undergoing state formation as European colonial empires collapsed. Between 1945 and 1965, more than 45 new nations formed in Asia, Africa, and the Middle East. In such nations, wheat imports "rose from a base of practically zero in the mid-1950s to almost half of world food imports in 1971."[49] This flow of agricultural commodities reshaped diets and agricultural production throughout the world. Central to this expansion in the global wheat market was PL 480. As Harriet Friedmann notes: "At its peak [*in 1965*], U.S. aid accounted for 80 percent of American wheat exports and more than 35 percent of *world* wheat trade. . . ."[50] Consequently, PL 480 became a cornerstone of supply management policy because it created new markets for American wheat exports. This, however, altered the economic interests of U.S. wheat producers because they no longer needed to control production. Expanding export markets allowed them to increase production, thereby prompting wheat producers to begin to oppose strict production controls in the 1960s.

Changing the Political Economy of the South

The South had long been an agricultural region that centered on cotton produced in a peculiar rural class structure centered on the plantation system and resting especially on planter–tenant relations and labor-intensive production. Southern cotton production remained largely un-mechanized until the 1960s. In 1957, about 35 percent of cotton in Louisiana and Texas was harvested mechanically, compared to only about 17 percent in Arkansas and Mississippi, and less than 3 percent in Alabama, Georgia, the Carolinas, and Tennessee.[51] As late as 1962, most Southern states relied heavily on laborers to pick cotton by hand. Control over a sufficiently large supply of labor was crucial largely because cotton was the most important Southern crop in terms of acreage and value. Created in part to save Southern agriculture—and planters, in particular—from the Depression and falling commodity prices, the AAA and its policy of supply management prompted changes in the rural class structure of the South. The AAA facilitated a shift away from both the plantation system and cotton production.

The rate of tenancy in the South fell sharply from 1930 to 1974. In 1930, 59 percent of Southern farms were tenant-operated, but the tenancy rate fell to less than 20 percent in 1964 and 10 percent in 1974, while the number of Southern farms using sharecroppers fell by about 90 percent by 1954.[52] Thus, by the late 1960s, the plantation system no longer characterized Southern agriculture. How did the AAA contribute to this fundamental change? Federal subsidies from price supports and production controls began to sever traditional landowner–tenant relations as planters attempted to keep most—sometimes all—of the AAA payments. T. J. Woofter and his colleagues found that planters kept almost 90 percent of AAA payments in the early New Deal.[53] Many planters avoided sharing AAA payments with tenants by simply evicting them.[54] AAA payments facilitated these trends by allowing planters to replace tenants and sharecroppers with wage-laborers, as well as through mechanization. While machines harvested only 6 percent of U.S. cotton in 1949, this figure rose to 23 percent in 1955, 51 percent in 1960, and 96 percent in 1968.[55] Such mechanization, funded in part by federal subsidies, gradually eliminated the need for tenants and sharecroppers as plantations shifted toward more capital-intensive production.

Furthermore, supply management policy prompted diversification in Southern agriculture, which also played a role in changing the class structure. Production controls required that farmers limit their production of basic commodities, including cotton and tobacco. Consequently, Southern agriculture began to diversify as farmers grew other crops on land formerly used for cotton. Southern soybean production expanded from fewer than 700,000 acres in 1945 to 18.4 million in 1975. Conversely, the number of acres devoted to cotton production fell from a high of 23 million in 1949 to 8.9 million in 1975. Soybean acres had surpassed cotton acres by 1966. Along with increased acreage, of course, came increased production: Southern soybean production increased from 35 million bushels in 1950 to 432 million bushels in 1975. Much of the expansion in Southern soybean production occurred in states that had been the highest cotton producers. Alabama, Arkansas, Georgia, Mississippi, and Texas—the top cotton states from 1938 through 1950—accounted for about 60 percent of the South's soybean production from 1950 to 1975. Increased soybean production was at the heart of the diversification of Southern agriculture following World War II, and it played an important role in the transformation of the rural class structure.

The consequences of New Deal agricultural policy—cash influx, mechanization, and crop diversification—contributed to a shift in the Southern class structure by significantly undermining tenancy. This change mirrored the national trends that emerged as a result of reshaping agriculture and farming through supply management policy.

Effects of Supply Management on Farming and the Environment

Beyond the unintended political consequences of supply management policy, there were also unforeseen effects on the structure of the farming sector and the environment. Land ownership and production became more concentrated, and each of these trends was tied to the distribution of subsidies. As farms became larger and more capital-intensive, they used more technology—such as machinery, as well as chemical fertilizers, pesticides, and herbicides—that were tied to economies of scale. These trends in agriculture often had deleterious effects on the environment.

As Figure 10.2 shows, the number of farms fell sharply between 1930 and 2000. At the start of that period, there were more than 6 million farms in the United States, but the number fell to 5 million by 1955 and to 2.8 million by 1975. In 2006, there were only 2 million farms in the United States. At the same time that the number of farms declined, the size of the average farm increased from about 151 acres in 1930, to 258 acres in 1955, and to 391 acres in 1975. Through the distribution of subsidies, supply management policy contributed to this greatly increased size of U.S farms. This policy based price supports and production control payments on

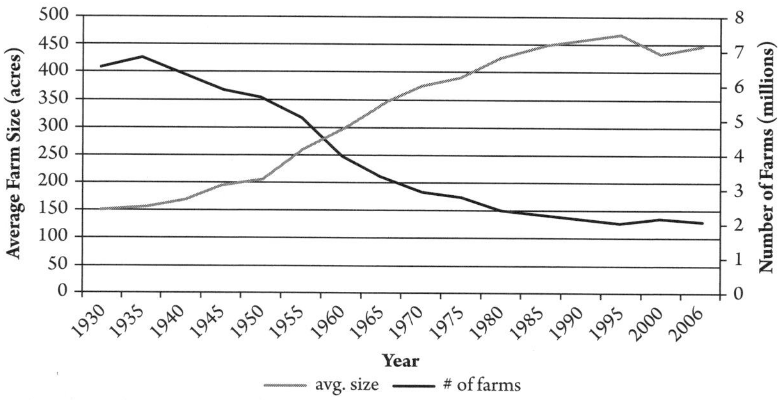

Figure 10.2 Number of Farms and Average Farm Size in the United States, 1930–2006.

historical production: that is, the more a farm had produced in the past, the more acres it could produce going forward. This "historical base," therefore, reinforced and even built on existing inequalities in American agriculture by giving the largest subsidies to the largest farms, which then had the ability to invest in more technologies and more land.

A mutually reinforcing relationship exists between farm size and the use of technologies that often rely on economies of scale and, of course, capital investment. The conventional pesticide use increased from 366 million pounds of active ingredient in 1964 to 826 million pounds in 1980.[56] These intensive agriculture techniques have also discouraged diversity in production, as the average number of commodities produced on farms has decreased from about 4.5 in 1930 to fewer than two in 2002.[57] The increased use of chemicals in farming has contributed to toxic runoff and, in turn, to a "dead zone" in the Gulf of Mexico: "One of the chief culprits behind this dead zone is American agriculture and its countless tributaries of fertilizer, pesticides and animal feces" ultimately carried by the Mississippi River.[58]

Concentration in farming has also occurred in other sectors of agriculture, most notably in meat production. The dramatic increases in the production of soybeans, corn, and other feed grains after 1945 helped fuel the expanding industrial livestock complex. As noted earlier, per capita meat consumption increased from about 50 percent from 1950 to1970.[59] As David Nibert notes, "Large confined animal feeding operations (CAFOs) allowed enormous numbers of animals to be raised in tiny areas by feeding them on surplus grain."[60] The large operations, including feedlots for beef cattle, consume large amounts of water and produce substantial amounts of pollution, and the methane produced is a significant contributor to global warming. Such dangers to the environment stemming from supply management policy and the industrial food system that it helped to create are truly ironic, given that the AAA was created in part to help stem the tide of environmental degradation found in agriculture throughout the nation.

Learning from the New Deal Experience

One important lesson of New Deal agricultural policy is the extent to which a policy may eventually come to reinforce existing social inequalities, especially in its longer-term trajectory, even if its intention is the opposite. While New Deal agricultural policy included elements that aimed to alleviate rural inequality, particularly in the South, these elements fell victim to elimination in less than two decades. The "liberal purge" in the USDA and AAA removed those interested in land reform from positions of significant policy influence, and the financial strangling of the Farm Security Administration (originally the Resettlement Administration), which had sought to purchase sub-marginal land owned by poor farmers and resettle them in group farms on land more suitable for efficient farming, ended this endeavor of rural redistribution nearly completely.[61]

By contrast, the elements of New Deal agricultural policy that persisted through the twentieth century reinforced the inequality and increasing concentration in agriculture. The combination of price supports and production controls rewarded larger farmers who had greater production and used more intensive methods, thereby encouraging concentration in farming. The number of farms declined, while the average farm size increased. These programs also encouraged and enabled more intensive farming with increased mechanization and greater use of other agricultural technologies, including chemical pesticides and herbicides, with consequent harm to the environment.

In the formation of the AAA, challenges emerged from various political quarters, including from groups promoting "liberty" and from corporations, among others. And these challenges went all the way to the Supreme Court. This process looks familiar to observers of the first Obama Administration, with the rise of the Tea Party and constitutional challenges to the Affordable Care Act. The similarities in political rhetoric, corporate support, and general political response are striking and should prompt observers to consider implications for the longevity of policies.

Over the long term, the beneficiaries of supply management policy tended to be increasingly well-off farmers, especially those in the South—despite challenges that used the rhetoric of "liberty" and "individual independence." Government policies resting on extensive regulation of the market and income support are often seen as leftwing, socialist, or un-American. Certainly, such policies are often understood to be antithetical to the market economy and to capitalism. Yet, the primary supporters of supply management policy were Southern planters, never known for supporting socialist policies. In fact, in a congressional committee hearing in 1958, Southern Democrats and Farm Bureau representatives nearly came to blows over the insinuation that the former were advocating a socialist policy.[62] In reality, however, advocates of supply management policy were truly "capitalists against markets," capitalists who sought to restrict market processes to protect their own economic and class interests.[63] This has been evident even among some of President Obama's policies that critics have accused of being "socialist," including the bank and auto industry bailouts and a healthcare reform that stands to boost the profits of the private insurance and pharmaceutical industries at the same time as it boosts the access to health care of millions of uninsured. Such support for policies restricting the market while offering social support no doubt helps explain why the long-term trajectories of policies such as supply management can increasingly favor the well-off and powerful. The crisis in the world economy in 2008 also harks back to the 1930s, in that each was preceded by a crisis in agriculture that brought unstable prices, some degree of environmental degradation, and a faltering system of international trade in agriculture. First, in the 1920s, global agricultural markets displayed instability in prices and problems with overproduction years before the world economy slid into depression. Likewise, global agricultural prices over the past twenty-five years have been quite unstable, rising dramatically in 2007 and 2008, and setting off a global food crisis. Alleviating the earlier crisis required government regulation that was successful in stabilizing prices for more than three decades. Stabilizing agricultural prices in this era may require at least a reconsideration of the successes and failures of New Deal agricultural policy.

Second, while the environmental crisis of the Dust Bowl was more immediate and clear, perhaps, than the environmental degradation related to agriculture over the past several decades, they share a link to production methods prompted by national policy. In the decades leading up to the Dust Bowl years, the federal government encouraged increased settlement and the expansion of agriculture on the Great Plains. Then, in the middle of the twentieth century, supply management policy developed in such a way as to prompt intensive and industrial agricultural production with increased reliance on chemical fertilizers, pesticides, and herbicides.[64] The use of these inputs has contributed to environmental degradation to rivers and aquifers and harm to wildlife. Coupled with a similar development in the production of animals for food, this kind of industrial agriculture has been one of the contributors to global climate change. It has also led to a sharp increase in water consumption for irrigation on some parts of the Great Plains and in feedlots and the animal slaughtering process, each of which has reduced water table levels in, for example, the Ogallala aquifer.[65] Thus, we need to pay attention to the possible unintended consequences that agricultural policy can have for the environment, as well as how federal policy can help alleviate environmental crisis, such as it did with the Soil Conservation Service.

Third, the system of world trade in agriculture has faltered over the past several decades. Once an international bastion of government regulation and support, agriculture has faced international pressures to liberalize, a trend that began in the 1980s. Yet, as the World Trade Organization (WTO) has tried to liberalize the world economy, its ministerial meetings in Cancún, Mexico, and Doha, Qatar, fell apart around the issue of agricultural liberalization, with peasant-farmer groups and environmentalists calling for more regulation. Similarly, in a world trading system based on the idea of so-called free trade, agricultural trade leading up to and during the Great Depression broke down, resulting in greater trade barriers and tariffs, greater price instability, and market collapse.[66]

Furthermore, each of these agricultural crises brought political instability. In the 1930s, farmers in some regions revolted as prices and incomes plummeted. In the United States, for example, the Farmers' Holiday movement picketed, engaged in road blockades, dumped milk, destroyed crops, disrupted and halted trains transporting livestock or crops, and challenged and disrupted government proceedings.[67] The recent food crisis also saw world hunger rise significantly and led to food riots that contributed to political instability in dozens of countries, including Argentina,

Mexico, India, Italy, Bangladesh, Egypt, Somalia, and Morocco. In 2008, for example, a week of food riots in Haiti led to the removal of its prime minister.[68] Thus, the political consequences of agricultural crises are quite significant.

Given all of this, we need to remember that the Great Depression and the current economic recession each stemmed from a world economic crisis. We should recognize that the AAA improved the economic health of agriculture and helped bolster the entire economy: "Government payments to farmers benefitted merchants and mail order houses. Even the staunchly conservative Sewell Avery, head of [*department store chain*] Montgomery Ward, conceded that the AAA had been the single greatest cause in the improvement of Ward's position."[69] The practices and rules set forth by the Soil Conservation Service played a key role in alleviating the environmental crisis of the Dust Bowl.

Nonetheless, New Deal agricultural programs were not unquestionably successful. For example, farm income in 1936 was still below what it had been in 1929; wheat and corn prices did not reach their levels of the mid-1920s until the end of World War II; and wheat and cotton production had risen only to pre–New Deal levels by 1938. Some scholars argue that this was because the U.S. government was too weak to produce an effective solution to the Depression.[70] The Great Depression, however, was a worldwide economic depression that could not be solved by policy changes within one nation. This fact made many New Deal policies relatively ineffective and played a role in the limitations of AAA and other programs. Therefore, as the Obama Administration continues to develop responses to the ongoing recession, it is useful to remember the limits of national policies in addressing turmoil in the world economy, whether in food and agriculture or in finance and industry.

Notes

1. Before the financial crisis in 2008, a global food crisis struck. Food prices rose dramatically, bringing increased world hunger and political instability around the globe. For example, see Bill Winders, "The Food Crisis and the Deregulation of Agriculture," *Brown Journal of World Affairs*, 18, no. 1 (2011): 83–95.
2. United States Department of Agriculture, *Agricultural Statistics, 1942* (Washington, DC: Government Printing Office), 662, Table 736.
3. A debate exists as to whether a depression actually hit agriculture during the 1920s. For a brief discussion of this debate, see David E. Hamilton, *From New Day to New Deal: American Farm Policy from Hoover to Roosevelt, 1928–1933* (Chapel Hill: The University of North Carolina Press, 1991), 9–10. Interestingly, gross farm income did not fall between 1925 and 1929, even though market prices fell during this period.
4. See, for example, Pete Daniel, *Breaking the Land: The Transformation of Cotton, Tobacco, and Rice Cultures since 1800* (Chicago: University of Illinois Press, 1985); and John Mark Hansen, *Gaining Access: Congress and the Farm Lobby, 1919–1981* (Chicago: The University of Chicago Press, 1991).
5. United States Department of Agriculture, *Agricultural Statistics, 1957* (Washington, DC: Government Printing Office, 1957), 579, Table 683.

6. United States Census Bureau, *Statistical Abstract of the United States, 1933* (Washington, DC: Government Printing Office), 566, Table 538.
7. John L. Shover, *Cornbelt Rebellion: The Farmers' Holiday Association* (Urbana: The University of Illinois Press, 1965), 16. Gilbert and Howe state that "In late 1932, about half of Midwestern farms were threatened by foreclosure." Jess Gilbert and Carolyn Howe, "Beyond 'State vs. Society': Theories of the State and New Deal Agricultural Policies," *American Sociological Review,* 56 (1991): 209.
8. Calculated from United States Department of Agriculture, *Agricultural Statistics, 1941* (Washington DC: Government Printing Office), 123, Table 155. Between 1929 and 1938, cotton carry-over averaged 6.5 million bales a year—nearly three times that of the period 1921–1925. Carry-over stock reached 9.7 million bales in 1931 before falling to 4.4 million in 1936.
9. Hamilton, 11.
10. After President Warren Harding died in 1923, Coolidge became president and then won re-election in 1924.
11. Thus, this "Farm Bloc" refers to a specific organization formed by representatives and senators from farm states. Over the years, the term "farm bloc" (without capital letters) has come to refer to "informal alliances of farm state lawmakers" and sometimes farm organizations. See Hansen, 31.
12. For a more complete discussion and history of these early political solutions, see Chapter 2 in Bill Winders, *The Politics of Food Supply: U.S. Agricultural Policy in the World Economy* (New Haven, CT: Yale University Press, 2009). See also Gilbert C. Fite, *George N. Peek and the Fight for Farm Parity* (Norman: University of Oklahoma Press, 1954).
13. Robert E. Snyder, *Cotton Crisis* (Chapel Hill: The University of North Carolina Press, 1984), 24.
14. Assuming that the cotton holiday had the effect of raising cotton prices, the primary beneficiaries of Long's proposal would have been cotton farmers, themselves. But such a plan would have had negative effects on sharecroppers and tenants, local merchants, and farm suppliers, as well as cotton ginners and their employees.
15. Hansen, 70.
16. Long rescinded Louisiana's holiday legislation; legislation in other states (e.g., Mississippi and South Carolina) expired due to sunset clauses that rested on other Southern states' passing reduction laws (which did not happen); and state courts declared Texas's reduction legislation unconstitutional. Snyder, 126.
17. M. C. Halleberg, *Policy for American Agriculture: Choices and Consequences* (Ames: Iowa State University Press, 1992), 345.
18. In 1933, the AAA paid farmers in the South to plow under portions of their cotton crop to reduce production because the planting season had already passed when the AAA was enacted in March of that year.
19. Hansen, 78; and Paul L. Murphy, "The New Deal Agricultural Program and the Constitution," *Agricultural History,* 29 (1955): 165.
20. David Eugene Conrad, *The Forgotten Farmers: The Story of Sharecroppers During the New Deal* (Urbana: University of Illinois Press, 1965), 23.
21. For a fuller discussion, see Winders, *Politics of Food Supply,* 56–58; or Gilbert and Howe.
22. In addition, the Senate's Minority Leader was Charles McNary, a Republican from Oregon—a wheat state—who favored government support for farmers.
23. See Ira Katznelson, *When Affirmative Action Was White: An Untold History of Racial Inequality in Twentieth-Century America* (New York: W. W. Norton, 2005); and Bill Winders, "Maintaining the Coalition: Class Coalitions and Policy Trajectories," *Politics & Society,* 33 (2005): 387–423.
24. Calculated from U.S. Congress, *Congressional Record* (Washington, DC: Government Printing Office, 1933), 3121.
25. Lawrence J. Nelson, *King Cotton's Advocate: Oscar G. Johnston and the New Deal* (Knoxville: University of Tennessee Press, 1999).

26. Jack Temple Kirby, "The Transformation of Southern Plantations, c. 1920–1960," *Agricultural History* 57 (1983): 263–264.
27. United States Department of Agriculture, *Agricultural Statistics, 1957* (Washington, DC: Government Printing Office, 1957), 597, Table 683.
28. As I explain in the next section, the economic interests of farmers in the Corn Belt were shaped by ties to the livestock industry.
29. Jean Choate, *Disputed Ground: Farm Groups That Opposed the New Deal Agricultural Program* (Jefferson, NC: McFarland & Company, 2002).
30. The NFU also opposed production controls that left farm acres idle and destroyed livestock during a period of hunger and poverty. Simpson argued that agricultural production should not be reduced until all Americans had adequate diets. Choate, 134.
31. Choate, Chapter 2; and Conrad, 28. The Missouri Farmers, Association and the Farmers Holiday Association also favored cost-of-production over parity.
32. "6,000,000 Total Ends Pig Buying," *New York Times*, September 30, 1933, 25. The FPTRA struggled unsuccessfully to get the federal government to return to farmers the money they had lost due to the processing tax on hogs. See Choate.
33. The farm organizations opposed to the AAA had little influence, in part because these groups were relatively small (only hundreds of members) and the real political power was held by Southern Democrats, the Farm Bureau, and those in the USDA—all of whom favored the AAA.
34. Conrad, *Forgotten Farmers*, 52. Sharecropping meant that "the [*land*]owner supplies everything used in production (including housing) except labor and furnishes half the cost of seed and fertilizer." Merle Prunty, Jr., "The Renaissance of the Southern Plantation," *Geographical Review*, 45 (1955): 468. Tenants, in contrast, rented portions of land and supplied the "cultivating power" (usually mules) and implements and customarily paid two-thirds of the seed and fertilizer costs"; ibid., 474. Some tenants were cash-tenants, who did not share their crop with the landowner. However, these were less common than sharecroppers or share-tenants.
35. Jess Gilbert, "Eastern Urban Liberals and Midwestern Agrarian Intellectuals: Two Group Portraits of Progressives in the New Deal Department of Agriculture," *Agricultural History*, 74 (2000): 162–180.
36. Donald H. Grubbs, *Cry from the Cotton: The Southern Tenant Farmers' Union and the New Deal* (Chapel Hill: University of North Carolina Press, 1971), 34. Grubbs notes that Chester Davis "in matters affecting the cotton reduction program . . . consulted, naturally enough, with men who 'knew' the South: men like the county agents. These were officials, in other words, who represented the planters," ibid., 33.
37. Sidney Baldwin, *Poverty and Politics: The Rise and Decline of the Farm Security Administration* (Chapel Hill: The University of North Carolina Press, 1968), 81.
38. Ibid., 82.
39. William M. Butler was a cotton manufacturer and a receiver of Hoosac Mills. Murray R. Benedict, *Farm Policies of the United States, 1790–1950: A Study of Their Origins and Development* (New York: The Twentieth Century Fund, 1957), 348.
40. For a discussion of the Supreme Court's decision and reasoning, see ibid.; Conrad Black, *Franklin Delano Roosevelt: Champion of Freedom* (New York: Public Affairs, 2003), 377; R. Douglas Hurt, *Problems of Plenty: The American Farmer in the Twentieth Century* (Chicago: Ivan R. Dee, 2002), 80–81; Arthur M. Schlesinger, Jr., *The Age of Roosevelt: The Politics of Upheaval* (Boston: Houghton Mifflin, 1960), 470–474; and Winders, *Politics of Food Supply*, 65–69.
41. Winders, *Politics of Food Supply*, 69–73.
42. Alternatively, flexible price supports could fluctuate inversely with market prices. In this situation, price support levels would be reduced as market prices rose, making supports almost irrelevant in a strong market. But support levels would increase as market prices fell, thereby providing a safety net if prices collapsed. The Farm Bureau was not advocating flexible price supports of this type.

43. United States House of Representatives, "Long Range Farm Program," Hearings before the House Committee on Agriculture, 83rd Congress, 2nd Session (Washington, DC: Government Printing Office, 1954), 2747.
44. Quoted from the testimony of Allan Kline, president of the Farm Bureau. United States House of Representatives, "General Farm Program," Hearings before the Special Subcommittee of the Committee on Agriculture, 81st Congress, 1st Session (Washington, DC: Government Printing Office, 1949), 438.
45. Economic Research Service, USDA, "Food Availability (Per Capita Data System)," accessed April 4, 2010, available at http://www.ers.usda.gov/data-products. Note that this increase in per capita meat consumption occurred at the same time as the U.S. population expanded dramatically, with the consequence that total meat production skyrocketed.
46. Allen J. Matusow, *Farm Policies and Politics in the Truman Years* (New York: Atheneum, 1967), 136.
47. For a detailed discussion of the political battle between corn interests and the cotton-wheat coalition, see Winders, *Politics of Food Supply*, 85–93.
48. This period (1945–1970) understates the change because 1970 was the only year after 1967 in which wheat production did not approach or surpass 40 MMT. Between 1967 and 1973, annual wheat production averaged 41 MMT, and annual wheat production never fell below 48 MMT after 1974.
49. Philip McMichael, *Development and Social Change: A Global Perspective* (Thousand Oaks, CA: Pine Forge Press, 2000), 63.
50. Harriet Friedmann, "The Family Farm and the International Food Regime," in *Peasants and Peasant Societies: Selected Readings,* 2nd. ed., Teodor Shanin, ed. (New York: Blackwell, 1987),. 253; emphasis in original.
51. United States Department of Agriculture, *Statistics on Cotton and Related Data, 1920–1973,* Statistical Bulletin No. 535 (Washington, DC: Government Printing Office), 218.
52. Calculated from U.S. Census Bureau, *Census of Agriculture,* 1959. After 1959, the *Census of Agriculture* stops counting sharecroppers and instead collapses sharecroppers into the larger category of "share-tenants." I estimated the number of sharecroppers for 1964 by assuming that the proportion of sharecroppers to share-tenants remained the same as in 1959, which is a conservative assumption.
53. T. J. Woofter, with Gordon Blackwell, Harold Hoffsommer, James G. Maddox, Jean M. Massell, B.O. Williams, and Waller Wynne, Jr., *Landlord and Tenant on the Cotton Plantation* (Washington, DC: Works Progress Administration, Research Monograph V, 1936), 66, Table 24.
54. Gilbert and Howe, "Beyond," 212; and Grubbs, *Cry from the Cotton*, 22–26.
55. United States Department of Agriculture, *Statistics on Cotton*, 218.
56. Timothy Kiely, David Donaldson, and Arthur Grube, "Pesticides Industry Sales and Usage 2000 and 2001: Market Estimates" (Washington, DC: U.S. Environmental Protection Agency, 2004), 31, Table 5.9.
57. Carolyn Dimitri, Anne Effland, and Neilson Conklin, "The 20th Century Transformation of U.S. Agriculture and Farm Policy" Economic Information Bulletin no. 3, (Washington, DC: Economic Research Service, USDA, 2005), 5, Figure 4.
58. Christopher D. Cook, *Diet for a Dead Planet: Big Business and the Coming Food Crisis* (New York: The New Press, 2006), 171. See also Daniel Imhoff, *Food Fight: The Citizen's Guide to a Food and Farm Bill* (Healdsburg, CA: Watershed Media), 15.
59. Economic Research Service, USDA, "Food Availability (Per Capita) Data System," accessed April 4, 2010, available at http://www.ers.usda.gov/data-products/food-availability-(per-capita)-data-system.aspx.
60. David Nibert, "The Fire Next Time: The Coming Cost of Capitalism, Animal Oppression and Environmental Ruin," *Journal of Human Rights and the Environment,* 3 (2012): 147.
61. Critics, including the Farm Bureau, strongly opposed the FSA as an experiment in collectivizing agriculture.

62. See Winders, *Politics of Food Supply*, 2–6.
63. Peter Swenson offers an excellent analysis of some political-economic contexts that can lead capitalists to oppose markets. Peter Swenson, *Capitalists Against Markets: The Making of Labor Markets and Welfare States in the United States and Sweden* (New York: Oxford University Press, 2006).
64. Cook, 175–179.
65. John Opie, *Ogallala: Water for a Dry Land* (Lincoln: University of Nebraska Press, 1993); and Michael Pollan, "Power Steer," *New York Times Magazine*, March 31, 2002, accessed May 31, 2011, available at http://www.nytimes.com/2002/03/31/magazine/power-steer.html?pagewanted=all&src=pm.
66. For information on the international regimes governing food and agriculture during these two periods, see Bill Winders, "The Vanishing Free Market: The Formation and Spread of the US and British Food Regimes," *Journal of Agrarian Change*, 9, no. 3 (2009): 315–344.
67. See, for example, John L. Shover, "The Farmers' Holiday Association Strike, August 1932," *Agricultural History* 39 (1965): 196–203. Shover notes also the influence of this movement: "Elected political officials in the Middle West and nation could not ignore such dramatic evidence of rural discontent," ibid., 202.
68. Winders, "Food Crisis."
69. William E. Leuchtenburg, *Franklin D. Roosevelt and the New Deal* (New York: Harper & Row, 1963), 77.
70. See, for example, Kenneth Finegold and Theda Skocpol, *State and Party in America's New Deal* (Madison: The University of Wisconsin Press, 1995).

11

Conclusion

Learning from the Successes and Failures of the New Deal

GERTRUDE SCHAFFNER GOLDBERG

> *We have come to a clear realization of the fact that true individual freedom cannot exist without economic security and independence....*
>
> *In our day these economic truths have become accepted as self-evident. We have accepted, so to speak, a second Bill of Rights under which a new basis of security and prosperity can be established for all—regardless of station, race, or creed.*
>
> —Franklin D. Roosevelt, Message to Congress, January 11, 1944

The New Deal grappled with one of the most serious crises ever faced by this nation. Franklin Roosevelt assumed the presidency after three years of severe depression and drift, with unemployment more than twice its peak rate during the Great Recession. The resources of the country's local and state governments were spent, and deep deprivation and despair stalked the land. With economic crisis giving birth to dictatorships elsewhere in the world, American democracy was itself on trial. An apt metaphor for a depressed nation, the Dust Bowl blackened the sky and polluted the air over huge stretches of the hinterland. Overproduction was ironically a cause of agricultural depression in a land of hunger. In struggling against the Great Depression, New Dealers, moreover, lacked the governmental institutions to deal with economic insecurity that had been established earlier in some other countries.[1] It fell to them to create those institutions in an underdeveloped state.

The Roosevelt Administration met this almost overwhelming challenge by providing unprecedented amounts of relief—though never enough—to the unemployed, much of it in the form of work that also enriched the nation's physical, social, cultural, and environmental resources. The New Deal's contribution to the nation's infrastructure was enormous: "America ran on New Deal electricity, drank New Deal water, flushed wastes down New Deal sewers, administered local government in New Deal city halls, settled cases in New Deal courthouses, drove down

New Deal roads, and traveled through New Deal tunnels."[2] During the Roosevelt tenure, the country recovered lost ground in what had been a catastrophic decline in national output, and even before World War II, it had begun to exceed the 1929 mark.[3] Reform as well as recovery was on the agenda as New Dealers enacted measures to prevent future economic disaster, guarantee collective bargaining rights to labor, and reduce the economic insecurity that the Depression had both exposed and exacerbated. More sensitive to environmental problems than his contemporaries, Roosevelt initiated important programs to conserve the land and repair the damage imposed by waste and neglect of the nation's natural resources. Whereas popular movements played their part in the enactment of other New Deal policies, the environmental interventions were largely at Roosevelt's initiative and mostly unopposed, although the progressive Republican Senator from Nebraska, George Norris, had been advocating public hydroelectric power since the 1920s.[4]

Not the least of New Deal accomplishments are its less tangible ones. Perhaps the greatest of these was to convey to the dispirited people of this nation the feeling that their government cared about them and could, as the title of this book suggests, help them solve their problems. Important, too, are a nation's aspirations and ideals, for even though we may fall far short of them, they can serve to urge us forward. Take the paradox of a declaration by slaveholders that "all men are created equal."[5] Even at the dark moment when blacks had lost the gains of Reconstruction, W. E. B. DuBois urged that they "cling unwaveringly" to "those great words" of the Declaration of Independence.[6] Like Lincoln, Roosevelt reinterpreted and expanded our ideals. Just as "created equal" became more inclusive with Lincoln's "new birth of freedom," so, with Roosevelt's reframing, liberty encompassed not only political but economic rights.

Along with many successes, both tangible and intangible, the New Deal, as the chapters in this book have shown, counted incomplete achievements and notable failures. Yet what regime, particularly one coping with an enormous crisis, can ever claim total success? For the future, of course, success and failure, however terrible at the time, can be of equal heuristic value. Here, we reflect on what we have learned about New Deal successes and failures and their relevance for our own time.

Two Great Barriers

Major New Deal failures emanated from two principal sources: Southern racists in its own Democratic Party, and antipathy to deficit spending. The first of these barriers robbed African Americans of many benefits of the New Deal. The second restraint was one that Roosevelt shared, not only with his Treasury Secretaries Lewis Douglas and Henry Morgenthau, Jr., but with Progressives like Senators Robert F. Wagner (D-New York) and Robert M. La Follette, Jr. (R, Prog.-Wisconsin).[7] The fear of deficits kept the New Deal from spending enough to conquer mass unemployment, despite its stated commitment to "the forgotten man." Moreover, deficit phobia not only impeded recovery but, at one juncture, led to a serious reversal of course. As for the recovery of jobs, not once in the 1930s did an administration that considered employment the basis of economic security manage to bring unemployment below the official rate of 14.3 percent. Even if we take into account Philip Harvey's observation (Chapter 6) that official unemployment rates included those employed in government work projects, joblessness was still high for an entire decade.

Southern Exposure

By the 1936 presidential election, blacks had switched their allegiance from "the Party of Lincoln" to the Democratic Party of Franklin Roosevelt and the New Deal. The reason: a desperate population was grateful to get some relief rather than none at all, however tainted it was with racism.[8] African Americans were aided by federal relief, housing assistance and public works, but owing to Southern legislators on whom the New Deal depended for enactment of its programs, these were, with few exceptions, discriminatory. Civil rights legislation, moreover, stood still in this decade of reform. Even outlawing so egregious a crime as lynching was off limits. Roosevelt, who undoubtedly opposed it personally, refused to speak against a Senate filibuster on the anti-lynching bill introduced by senators Edward Costigan (D-Colorado) and Robert Wagner. He told Walter White, Secretary of the NAACP, that he would keep silent because "I've got to get legislation passed by Congress to save America," and if he came out for the anti-lynching bill, Southerners, he believed, would block legislation to prevent that collapse.[9]

Often, New Deal relief and reform programs discriminated against African Americans. The occupations in which most blacks and many white women were employed were not covered by the two social insurance programs initiated by the Social Security Act, and already-beleaguered farm tenants and sharecroppers, many of them black, were further oppressed by its agricultural policies.[10] Here, discrimination based on race and class were both in evidence. The Home Owners' Loan Corporation (HOLC) instituted the policy of "red-lining" or refusing loans to homeowners in black, racially or ethnically mixed areas.[11] The Federal Housing Authority (FHA) followed HOLC's discriminatory practices. Racism in relief took various forms; for example, although regulations for the Federal Emergency Relief Administration (FERA) forbade discrimination based on race, "African-Americans experienced difficulties establishing eligibility, were paid lower rates, and were invariably assigned to unskilled, manual labor."[12] In the WPA, blacks were "routinely forced off the program entirely when their labor was needed in agriculture or in domestic service, and when reductions were ordered, they were often dismissed before whites."[13]

In decrying discrimination against blacks, one should not overlook discrimination against women in New Deal programs, an ill that Eleanor Roosevelt exposed and attempted to rectify.[14] Eleanor Roosevelt and her "Women's Network" of social reformers who had kept Progressive ideals alive during their near-eclipse in the 1920s, mobilized to protest discrimination against women in a range of New Deal programs but were unable to make equal rights for women a significant issue in the 1930s.[15] Nancy Rose, in her study of New Deal work programs, cites many instances where women were slighted by the Federal Emergency Relief Administration (FERA), but nonetheless holds that African Americans had an even harder time.[16] Of course, African American women were doubly disadvantaged.

When one considers the composition of Congress during the 1930s, it is not hard to understand why an Administration led by Northern Progressives discriminated against Negroes in programs designed to aid the poor and the hungry. Based on his study of the relationship between the Roosevelt Administration and Congress, Ira Katznelson draws this conclusion: "Each of the era's milestone laws required their [*the South's elected representatives*] support; each would have been blocked without it."[17] Black women and men paid the price for these New Deal legislative victories.

In spite of discrimination in relief and reform programs, the New Deal held some promise for blacks. Individual New Dealers, notably Eleanor Roosevelt, Interior Secretary Harold Ickes, and WPA Assistant Administrator Aubrey Williams, were known for their commitment to civil rights. Harry Hopkins and Frances Perkins opposed the exclusion from the insurance programs of occupations in which large proportions of women and blacks were employed, and Eleanor Roosevelt pushed the administration to take an official stand against lynching.[18] Black leaders, protesting discrimination in federal agencies and Roosevelt's appointment of whites as advisers on race relations in federal agencies, succeeded in getting the administration to appoint talented and well-educated blacks to these posts. Among these were Mary McLeod Bethune, director of Negro Affairs of the National Youth Administration (NYA), who headed a so-called Black Cabinet, and Robert Weaver, adviser to the Department of the Interior, who later became Secretary of Housing and Urban Development in the Johnson Administration.[19] The government's support for the expression of diverse cultural experiences through the WPA arts programs gave black artists and writers a wider audience and a boost to careers that have enriched the country's cultural heritage and exposed the public to the diversity that existed in the country. Although WPA wages for most African Americans were low, many made gains through the programs, in a number of instances owing to the intercession and protest of civil rights organizations.[20]

Blacks achieved some progress on civil rights when they threatened a march on Washington to protest discrimination in defense industries. Roosevelt, unable to dissuade them and bent on national unity, established a Fair Employment Practices Commission, an action not dependent on Congress. Still, the war that was to bring freedom to the people of the world was waged by a segregated U.S. army. Since then, owing greatly to their extraordinary mobilization in the 1950s and 1960s, blacks have gained political and civil rights that should have been granted by the Fourteenth and Fifteenth Amendments. They have, moreover, become eligible for the social insurance programs once denied the great majority of them. Today, the Federal Housing Administration that originally red-lined their neighborhoods lends disproportionately to African Americans and Hispanics. A black man in the White House was of course, unthinkable in Roosevelt's day.

Nonetheless, past and continuing discrimination continues to take its economic toll. Black unemployment rates are regularly more than double those of whites. From 2000 to 2007, the average rate of black unemployment was 9.4 percent. This was higher than the unemployment rate for the total labor force—7.6 percent in February 2009—when unemployment was considered sufficiently high for Congress to enact a $787 billion stimulus. Thus, the usual rate of black unemployment is higher than the rate that was considered a crisis for the general population.[21] Even if they manage to gain a foothold in the labor market, sporadic unemployment and low earnings drag down the social insurance benefits for which they are now eligible.

Deficit Thinking

Following his landslide re-election in 1936, Roosevelt famously acknowledged that one-third of the nation was "ill-housed, ill-clad, ill-nourished."[22] Reductions in federal spending that FDR made soon after, at the behest of Treasury Secretary Morgenthau and in pursuit of the holy grail of a balanced budget, were hardly helpful to the "one-third." (Earlier New Deal spending by the federal government was unprecedented, but not even enough to offset reductions in state and local government spending.[23]) The cutbacks made in 1937, combined with the payroll taxes for Social Security that began that year, led to a severe slump—a "depression within the Depression." Unemployment rose from 14.3 percent in 1937 to 19 percent in 1938.[24] Widespread suffering, including starvation, ensued from these sudden and drastic cuts in spending. [25] The consequences were political as well as economic, for the downturn, combined with Roosevelt's ill-advised "Court-packing" plan, led to a loss of support in Congress (particularly among more conservative former allies), a decline in the popularity of the New Deal, losses in the 1938 congressional elections, and a consequent curtailment of further reform.

After a period of delay and indecision, during which time the Morgenthau faction counseled even more fiscal restraint, a group that included Harry Hopkins, Harold Ickes, and Federal Reserve Chairman Marriner Eccles convinced Roosevelt that cutbacks in spending had caused the severe recession and that a substantial increase in spending was the remedy.[26] (Eccles, a Utah banker, was willing to go against economic orthodoxies and counseled, not less, but more government spending in a time of continuing high unemployment—and independent of Keynesian influence.) Roosevelt, in turn, requested and got Congress to agree to a $5 billion increase in spending for work relief, public works, and credit expansion. This was a significant amount, considering that the country's peacetime budget had never exceeded $10 billion.[27] In Roosevelt's rationale for the increase, Alan Brinkley discerns a new approach to federal spending on his part and one that suggests that Keynesian ideas were beginning to take hold. Whereas the president had justified earlier spending as a way to deal with specific problems such as helping the unemployed, subsidizing farmers, or developing the Tennessee Valley, the rationale for this spending package was to increase buying power and bring the economy back to health.[28] The injection of federal funds did, in fact, work. The economy picked up, for example bringing unemployment down from 19 percent in 1938 to 14.6 percent in 1940—still very high.

Hyperactive Fiscal Policy

In order to wage a world war, Roosevelt was forced to overcome the aversion to deficit spending. Many more soldiers went onto the government payroll than had been employed on work projects. Spending also skyrocketed as a result of government purchases of supplies for the United States and its allies. With this came full employment and the possibility of assuring what the New Deal had never come close to delivering in peacetime. A hyperactive fiscal policy ended the Great Depression and confirmed the Keynesian prescription that higher levels of government spending would bring higher growth rates and lower unemployment.

Despite the inability of his administration to solve the lingering problem of mass unemployment in peacetime, the right to a job at decent wages was of the utmost importance to Roosevelt. At least as early as 1932, when he was first running for the presidency, he had declared himself in favor of guaranteeing a job to all: "Every man has a right to life; and this means that he has also a right to make a comfortable living. . . ." In that 1932 speech, FDR stated further that "Our government formal and informal, political and economic, owes to every one an avenue to possess himself of a portion of that plenty sufficient for his needs, through his own work."[29] The ability to assure the right to a remunerative job was something that would only come when war cast away the fear of an unbalanced budget.

Influenced by Harry Hopkins and Aubrey Williams, who held that providing relief in the form of a job gave the unemployed dignity, not only material goods, the New Deal created work for millions of jobless men and women, although never enough to guarantee the right to a job. The aspiration, however, was there and expressed in the Report of the Committee on Economic Security that was established in 1934 to plan a permanent program of social insurance. As Philip Harvey points out in Chapter 6, the report of the Committee held that "the first objective of economic security must be maximum employment." Consequently, it proposed "employment assurance" through public works and stimulation of private employment, not only in periods of deep depression but in normal times as well.[30] As discussed in Chapter 7, Hopkins urged and came close to convincing Roosevelt that government should not only provide short-term unemployment insurance, but workers who remained jobless should be provided with employment in public works programs. However, such employment assurance was not part of the Social Security bill. Instead, FDR proposed a large-scale work program separate from permanent security legislation. The Works Progress Administration, unlike the Social Security Act, had to be reapproved annually by Congress and at varying levels of appropriation.

Fiscal Policy and Economic Rights

By the mid-1940s, Roosevelt had become convinced that it would be possible to establish in peacetime "a new basis of security and prosperity for all—regardless of station, race or creed." The centerpiece of this was to be the right to a job. In his last two Annual Messages to Congress, in 1944 and 1945, and in an important campaign speech in Chicago toward the end of his fourth presidential campaign, Roosevelt proposed a second, or "Economic Bill of Rights." This "Economic Bill of Rights" included not only the right to a job at a living wage as the most fundamental guarantee, but rights to adequate medical care, housing, old age security, and quality education.[31] In his brilliant manner of connecting new ideas to cherished traditional values, Roosevelt declared that the political rights guaranteed by the U.S. Constitution had "proved inadequate to assure us equality in the pursuit of happiness. We have come to a clear realization of the fact that true individual freedom cannot exist without economic security and independence." Roosevelt had already made this connection in his famous "Four Freedoms" speech in 1940, one of which was "freedom from want."[32]

In the 1945 restatement of his Economic Bill of Rights, FDR specifically discussed the fiscal policies that had made full employment possible:

> We have had full employment during the war. We have had it because the Government has been ready to buy all the materials of war which the country could produce—and this has amounted to approximately half our present productive capacity. After the war we must maintain full employment with Government performing its peacetime functions. This means that we must achieve a level of demand and purchasing power by private consumers—farmers, businessmen, workers, professional men, housewives—which is sufficiently high to replace wartime Government demands....[33]

Roosevelt held that the nation should rely as much as possible on private enterprise to provide the needed jobs. While private capital should finance the expansion program necessary to attain full employment, "the Government should recognize its responsibility for sharing part of any special or abnormal risk of loss attached to such financing." Furthermore, "an expanded social security program and adequate health and education programs, must play essential roles in a program designed to support individual productivity and mass purchasing power."[34]

On the campaign trail in 1944, FDR called attention to the need for government to play a role in achieving the right to housing. He estimated that a million homes per year would need to be built for at least the next decade. Private industry could build and finance the majority of this housing, and government "can and will assist and encourage private industry to do this as it has for many years." For the low income groups who could not possibly afford decent homes, "the Federal Government should continue to assist local housing authorities in meeting that need." In other words, Roosevelt was anticipating an active government role in securing these economic rights, *and there was no reference to affordability or deficits.*[35]

These were more than distant goals or aspirations. When Roosevelt first proposed this extension of the Bill of Rights in 1944, he charged Congress with their implementation, and implied political consequences if progress lagged:

> I ask the Congress to explore the means for implementing this economic bill of rights—for it is definitely the responsibility of the Congress so to do. Many of these problems are already before committees of the Congress in the form of proposed legislation. I shall from time to time communicate with the Congress with respect to these and further proposals. In the event that no adequate program of progress is evolved, I am certain that the Nation will be conscious of the fact.[36]

To this he added, "Our fighting men abroad—and their families at home—expect such a program and have the right to insist upon it." Since Roosevelt died in April 1945, we do not know how vigorously he would have supported the Murray-Wagner Full Employment Act that specifically reiterated his principle of the right of all Americans to remunerative and useful work. It was passed by the Senate in the fall of 1945 but defeated in the House a year later.[37]

Keynes for a Time

The lessons of wartime spending and their confirmation of Keynesian fiscal principles lasted for a time. However, scholars point out that the American brand was a more limited or "commercial Keynesianism" that eschewed the very expansive role for the state envisioned by some New Dealers in the mid-1930s. Instead, it confined the government's role to fiscal and monetary measures for maintaining a healthy macroeconomic environment.[38] Some thirty years after D-Day, economist Robert Lekachman observed, "Our wishes sometimes are granted in unpleasant ways. It was World War II, a giant experiment in macroeconomics that finally convinced the universe of the validity of Keynes's emphasis upon the symbiosis between employment and total spending."[39] That government spending could assure employment was one lesson, and the other, related one was that, as the New Deal historian William Leuchtenburg put it, the war had "freed the government from the taboos of a balanced budget and revealed the potentialities of spending."[40] Yet full employment, if we consider it tantamount to the right to a job for everyone who wants one, has never been achieved in peacetime.[41]

Dwight D. Eisenhower, the first Republican president to follow the New Deal, did not turn back the clock.[42] He did not simply tolerate the New Deal, but "actively embraced the idea that government could play a positive role in society by transcending the narrow self-interest of economic classes and mediating conflicts between social groups."[43] The former Allied Commander affirmed the responsibility of all levels of government, including the federal, "to reduce the fear and the incidence of destitution to a minimum."[44] Disability insurance was added to the Social Security program during his administration, and coverage of the insurance programs was extended. Eisenhower's $40 billion interstate highway program was a giant public-works program, the largest ever attempted, an anti-recessionary measure that also served a national defense function.[45] On the other hand, Eisenhower twice vetoed bills providing loans and grants for retraining unemployed workers and for public facilities needed by depressed areas or communities to attract industries.[46] Throughout Eisenhower's presidency, even after the Korean War was over, marginal tax rates were similar to those during the war years.[47] Unemployment, however, averaged 5.2 percent during the seven peacetime years of the Eisenhower presidency, and African American unemployment climbed to over twice the white rate, averaging 9.5 percent—hardly full employment.[48]

Richard Nixon, oft-quoted for declaring, "I am a Keynesian in economics," often behaved like one.[49] During his tenure, social spending continued to rise; the public assistance programs for the elderly, blind, and disabled were combined as Supplemental Security Income (SSI) and provided with a basic federal guarantee.[50] Nixon also proposed nationalizing family assistance, although he later withdrew it.[51] With unemployment rising, he signed into law the Comprehensive Employment and Training Act (CETA), which resembled New Deal job creation programs. [52]

Renewed Deficit Phobia and Its Functions

The antipathy to deficits that currently besets us is part of an attack on government and a related desire to reduce taxes on the part of upper-income groups. A belief that government could not solve our problems was evident in President Jimmy Carter's "Crisis of Confidence" speech in 1979. A Democrat, Carter alluded to people's growing lack of confidence in government and declared: "All the legislation in the world can't fix what's wrong with America."[53] Carter, moreover, began the move toward deregulation. His successor, Ronald Reagan, went much further: "government is not the solution to our problem; government *is* the problem."[54] Clearly it was the New Deal legacy, so-called big government, that was the culprit, and in getting rid of it, the deficit would play a part—but a circuitous one. Arthur Schlesinger, Jr., was among the first to identify the function of Reagan's approach to a federal deficit that he himself had greatly expanded: "Reagan aimed to shrink the role of government.... His innovation was to use tax reduction and defense spending to create a vast budgetary deficit and then to use the deficit as a pretext for a permanent reduction in the functions of the national government."[55] Similarly, as Senator Ernest Hollings (D-South Carolina) stated: "He [*Reagan*] intentionally created a deficit so large that we Democrats will never have enough money to build the sort of government programs we want.... He came to (Washington) to preside... over the dismantling of the American Government," [*on the theory that*] "if we create a big enough deficit then we can halt government and break that Democratic bureaucracy."[56] Whereas Reagan and those who share his goals have used deficit phobia as a weapon against government, for Roosevelt, these beliefs were obstacles to the expansion of government on which their relief, recovery, and reform goals depended.

With Bill Clinton, deficit reduction became an overriding policy. This "New Democrat" had been a founder in 1985 of the centrist Democratic Leadership Council, whose aim was to shed the New Deal image of the Party in order to win elections.[57] "The era of big government is over," Clinton wrote, adding without explanation that "we must not go back to an era of 'every man for himself.'"[58] It was Bill Clinton who presided over the repeal of Title IV of the Social Security Act, Aid to Families with Dependent Children. In his 1992 presidential campaign, Clinton had emphasized Progressive economic policies like job creation, but even as president-elect he had been persuaded by Robert Rubin of Goldman Sachs (an important economic advisor and later Treasury Secretary) that "the rich are running the economy," and that "putting people first," his campaign promise, would have to yield to the prerogatives of the financial markets, among them deficit reduction.[59] During Clinton's tenure, deregulation got a big boost with the repeal of that beacon of New Deal banking reform, the Glass-Steagall Act, which had separated commercial from investment banking. Unlike Reagan, however, Clinton lowered the deficit from 4.7 percent of GDP in 1992 to a surplus of 2.4 percent in 2000; at the same time, government spending shrank from 22.1 percent of GDP in 1992 to 18.2 percent in 2000.[60] With the end of the Cold War, defense spending fell by 37 percent and was responsible for the biggest proportion of the decrease. Concurrently, income security fell 18 percent, and education and science, each by 24 percent.[61] Whereas government borrowing shrank, private borrowing shot up: total household debt rose from 79 percent of disposable personal income in 1993 to 97.4 percent in 2000.[62]

Concurrent with Clinton's fiscal policies was an increase in economic inequality. Between 1992 and 2000, the bottom fifth of households, with an already-small share of total income, slipped 5.3 percent, to only 3.6 percent of total household income; while the top quintile garnered almost half of all income, having increased its share by nearly 10 percent (9.6 percent). The big winners were the top 5 percent of households, with an increase of nearly 19 percent (18.8 percent) and a share six times that of the bottom 20 percent.[63] No sooner had Clinton wiped out the deficit than his successor, George W. Bush, resumed the Reagan strategy of tax deductions and increased military spending. From surpluses of 2.4 and 1.3 percent of GDP in the last two years for which Clinton was responsible, deficits, in the six years preceding the economic crisis of 2008, rose under George Bush to an average of 2.4 percent of GDP.[64]

Lessons Half-Learned

Whether policymakers had real or bogus concerns over rising deficits, they were temporarily cast aside when economic crisis struck in 2008, the first time since the Great Depression. As Volker Janssen observes in Chapter 2, "The one lesson that decision-makers around the world learned from the Great Depression was not to allow the implosion of the financial system to happen and to restore 'market confidence.'" Initially the approach was bipartisan. Among influential members of the Bush government in 2009, there were apparently none like Hoover's Treasury Secretary Andrew Mellon, who had prescribed a harsh *laissez-faire* cleansing to wipe out speculators. At the helm of the Federal Reserve Board was Bush appointee Ben Bernanke, an academic expert on the economic and political causes of the Depression. George Bush's Treasury Secretary, Henry Paulsen, took the lead in an action resulting in the authorization by a Democratic Congress of $700 billion for the Troubled Assets Relief Program (TARP), popularly known as "the bank bailout." TARP purchased assets and equity from financial institutions to strengthen the flailing financial sector.

The banks were bailed out, and the Fed has since maintained an aggressive lending and buying program, but as Timothy Canova observes in Chapter 3, there was no "public option" in banking and finance such as a Home Owners' Loan Corporation to aid the victims of the sub-prime mortgage collapse. Canova also observes that TARP could have served as a type of revolving fund that, like the Reconstruction Finance Corporation (RFC) under Roosevelt, supported public works and jobs programs by providing funds for state infrastructure banks, relief for distressed borrowers to refinance and modify their mortgages, and loans to state and local governments to help pay for teachers' salaries and other essential needs. With public investment at only half its 1960s level, and the American Society of Civil Engineers reporting that it would take over a trillion dollars to bring the nation's infrastructure up to an acceptable standard, there was clearly a great amount for a public investment bank like the RFC to do.[65]

The American Recovery and Reinvestment Act (ARRA) or "Obama Stimulus" had some elements of a bottom-up approach but could have learned more from the New Deal than it did. Expenditures were roughly divided among entitlements, principally food stamps and extension of unemployment insurance benefits, tax benefits, and contracts, grants, and loans. Nobel laureate in economics Paul Krugman argues that the stimulus was way too small and that 40 percent of it was consumed by non-productive tax cuts.[66] In Chapter 6, Philip Harvey maintains that, had the ARRA taken a cue from the New Deal, it could have used its funds for direct job creation and could have brought the country to full employment in two years at a cost of less than $787 billion.

While the Bush-Obama response to the Great Recession could have learned more than it did from the New Deal, the intervention, nonetheless, was swift, and the catastrophe averted. Without the combined effect of the bailout and the Obama stimulus, unemployment might have risen to 16 percent instead of about 10 percent, according to an estimate by former Federal Reserve Board vice-chair Alan Blinder, and Mark Zandi, chief economist at Moody's Analytics.[67] Even so, in 2010, Blinder held that there was a "jobs emergency" that required "New Deal-style hiring of workers onto public payrolls."[68] However, Obama, as Canova points out, believes that only the private sector can create jobs—a view encouraged by Austin Goolsbee, chairman of his Council of Economic Advisors.[69] Thus, Obama bypassed the New Deal model for job creation.

If policymakers did not include enough of a "public option," especially direct job creation, they nonetheless spent a lot of money quickly. However, they failed to learn fully the fatal lesson of 1937. Having stopped the free-fall in midair, Obama pulled the plug on more relief and recovery, even though unemployment was higher than when his term began (7.6 percent in January 2009 and ranging from 9.4 to 9.9 percent during the midterm election year of 2010).[70] With the Congress still in Democratic hands, he failed to propose the needed stimulus that could have enabled him to claim a likely victory over recession and high unemployment. Instead, he has placed the imprimatur of the president on the priority of reducing annual deficits and the national debt. Obama created the Commission on Fiscal Responsibility and Reform by executive order in February 2010, appointing as its chairs two known opponents of entitlements: Democrat Erskine Bowles and Republican Allan Simpson.[71] The Tea Party movement had been launched a year earlier with its major goal of reducing the size of government and particularly taxes and government spending. If Obama's Commission was a response to that movement, it certainly did not reduce Tea Partiers' animosity to him or his administration. By elevating the deficit issue, Obama contributed to a process—the "sequester"—that has already cut entitlements and is risking a 1937-style recession. Today's policymakers did not learn the lesson of the New Deal's premature and disastrous turn toward austerity.

The turn away from recovery was premature, and arguably, the turn toward health care reform was too. Compare Roosevelt's timing. It is true that FDR set the process of social welfare reform in motion before the midterm elections of 1934, but the actual introduction of economic security legislation came *after* his party's stunning electoral triumph. Moreover, as discussed in Chapter 7, he and other New Dealers took pains to educate the public about the meaning of economic security, its relationship to basic national ideals, and the role that government must play in assuring it. It is true that the Patient Protection and Affordable Care Act (ACA) has increased access to health care, but gaining its passage cost the Obama administration political capital that could have been spent on the incomplete recovery. Waiting until he could make a stronger claim that government *can* solve problems, especially reducing unemployment below its level when he became president, would have been better timing and offered a better chance for a public option. It has been argued that if Obama were going to achieve health care reform it had to be early in the first term, but it could also be argued that if he had solved the jobs crisis first, he could have achieved health care reform subsequently and quite possibly with the public option and more public enthusiasm. Moreover, the ACA, though clearly extending access to health care, has been unpopular and poorly understood.[72] One reason is that the administration did not have a strategy for explaining to the public how the ACA was going to expand their access to health care.[73] The very name is hardly compelling: compare "Medicare," "Medicaid," "Social Security." The ACA was dubbed "Obamacare," a rather derisive title.

Popular Movements

The 1930s was a time when strong popular movements advocated more progressive policies than the New Deal proposed or could support—given its dependence for legislative victories on conservative allies in Congress, its deficit fears and "a little left of center" politics. As illustrated in Chapter 4, the New Deal relationship with popular movements was multifaceted, depending on both the extent of agreement with the organization's goals and political expediency. The New Deal was not simply pushed toward active government and progressive reforms by popular movements. Frances Perkins's acceptance of the position of Secretary of Labor was contingent on a program that included unemployment and old age insurance, abolition of child labor, an extensive public works program, and federal minimum wage and maximum hours laws. The program, Perkins wrote, "received Roosevelt's hearty endorsement, and [*he*] told me he wanted me to carry it out."[74]

At the outset of the Roosevelt and Obama administrations, the situation with respect to social movements was diametrically opposite. Early in the Depression, a militant unemployed workers' movement had risen, owing to the woeful inadequacy of relief resources on one hand, and the availability on the other hand of organizational resources, supplied initially by the Communist Party and later by other leftist sources. In 2009, when Obama took the oath of office, relief was readily available and expandable as a result of the social welfare programs established by the New Deal, and there were neither Communist nor other resources to organize what was decidedly a less desperate potential constituency.[75]

Whereas the Roosevelt Administration faced pressure from the left, Obama's strongest pressure—including a challenge to congressional leadership by his party—has come from the right. The Tea Party was partly a response to the very fiscal expansion that had stopped the economic crisis in its tracks and perhaps some resentment, on the part of grassroots Partiers, of the bailout of the bankers. The movement fell on the fertile ground of pre-existing antipathy to government and taxes that had been nourished by members of both political parties for more than a quarter century. Tea Party backers in big business, like the Koch brothers and the conservative media, are anti-entitlement as well as anti-government and anti-tax ideologues.[76] However, grassroots Tea Partiers have been found to support and often depend on Social Security, Medicare, and unemployment insurance, reserving their resentment for what they perceive as government help to "the losers" who allegedly do not pay or work for their benefits.[77]

Some of these grass roots opponents of "big government" do not seem to connect the benefits they like to their provider, as in the case of the well-publicized non sequitur: "Don't let big government take away my Medicare."[78] If the Obama Administration were interested in protecting entitlements, it could have addressed this disconnection by mounting a clever campaign to attach the benefits that the public likes with the government that provides them. Ironically, President Obama's encouragement of a deficit-reduction process that could result in cutbacks of Medicare and Social Security might well offend rather than satisfy the Tea Party grass roots—if not its elite backers.

Does the Obama Administration suffer from a lack of pressure from Progressive movements like those that contributed to New Deal reform? In health care, his public option was opposed by a vocal single-payer movement that had some support in the House but that ran up against a powerful private health care industry that also lobbied against the less radical public option. As discussed in Chapter 7, Obama was bolstered by a relatively well-funded nationwide movement that initially favored a public option but settled rather easily for increased access without it.

One potential source of pressure for Progressive action, particularly on jobs and poverty, is the black community, but that, ironically, has been stilled by the presence in the White House of a black president. According to Representative Emmanuel

Cleaver II (D-Missouri), then chairman of the Congressional Black Caucus (CBC), often referred to as "the conscience of the Congress": "If we had a white president we'd be marching around the White House." Cleaver explained that "pride" over having a black president overrides CBC concerns over the plight of African Americans.[79] Writing in the *New York Times,* Fredrick C. Harris, professor of political science and director of the Institute for Research in African American Studies at Columbia University, makes a similar point:

> ...the Obama presidency has already marked the decline, rather than the pinnacle, of a political vision centered on challenging racial inequality. The tragedy is that black elites—from intellectuals and civil rights leaders to politicians and clergy members—have acquiesced to this decline, seeing it as the necessary price for the pride and satisfaction of having a black family in the White House.[80]

Criticism of the Obama record in relation to blacks, however, has come from some black élites, not only the more militant Cornel West, professor of philosophy and Christian practice at Union Theological Seminary, but from Ben Jealous, president of the moderate National Association for the Advancement of Colored People, who holds that since Obama took office, whites are doing "a bit better" but blacks are doing "far worse."[81] Some black legislators, moreover, have introduced and actively campaigned for progressive legislation. Particularly noteworthy is Representative John Conyers (D-Michigan) who has assumed leadership on behalf of single-payer health care and full employment. Nonetheless, organized black protest, so important in earlier times, has not arisen. If Obama, like the first Catholic president, is careful not to seem to favor his own group, an assault on unemployment, though it would disproportionately aid blacks, is a class strategy aimed at all who are economically disadvantaged.

Potentially a strong push from the left was the Occupy Wall Street movement that burst onto the scene in 2011, garnering the kind of media attention that had eluded Progressive movements since the 1970s. In its representation of "the 99 percent," OWS raised public consciousness and resentment of the great economic inequality, always present in the United States, but regaining, in the last thirty years, the over-the-top levels of the pre-Depression decade. OWS seemed to offer a reprieve for those who were disappointed that the inauguration of 2009 did not, like the ascension of Roosevelt in 1933, point a finger at a major cause of the crash—the "1 percent." Contrast Roosevelt's inaugural address:

> The money changers have fled from their high seats in the temple of our civilization. We may now restore that temple to the ancient truths. The measure of the restoration lies in the extent to which we apply social values more noble than mere monetary profit.[82]

The easily understood plans of Depression-era movements like those of Long and Townsend were vital to their popularity—even if their plans were unworkable. Perhaps OWS would have arrived at a plan for reform, had it not been aborted by police action. While "We are the 99 percent" thrust inequality into the public dialogue, it did not offer a plan for redistributing income or wealth.

In writing about Occupy Wall Street, political scientist Sidney Tarrow contrasted the New Deal with the Obama administration: "the difference this time is that the White House and the Democratic Party offer no leadership to the inchoate anger that Occupy Wall Street reflects."[83] Tarrow's formulation suggests, not that FDR embraced the protest movements, but that he gave voice to their discontent and, in time, presided over changes that embodied some of their concerns, albeit never to the full extent of their aspirations. Tarrow refers to a presidential press conference following the emergence of OWS: "after acknowledging that he understands the anger of the protesters, President Barack Obama was quick to assure the financial sector of his continuing support."[84]

Perhaps a greater departure from the Roosevelt tradition that was opposed to suppression of protest was the nationwide police crackdown on OWS and the emerging evidence that it may have been coordinated by the U.S. Department of Homeland Security (DHS).[85] The involvement of the DHS implies that uncovering of and protest against deep-seated and corrosive problems in our economic and political life are somehow threats to the nation's security—subversive activities.

During the 1930s—and to an even greater extent in the subsequent Cold War—popular movements were often smeared as Communist and subversive. It is true that Communists supplied vital organizational resources to the unemployed. There were some Communist organizers in the CIO, but according to Irving Bernstein, their penetration was quite limited.[86] The vast majority of the Bonus Army was not Communist, and, indeed, the few who tried to steal the spotlight were reviled. Yet General MacArthur and Secretary of War Patrick Hurley justified the brutal attack on the nation's impoverished veterans as putting down a Communist conspiracy. President Hoover, for his part, expressed relief that the "Red plot" had been checked.[87] The Southern Farmers Tenant Union was also smeared, even though its Socialist spokesman Norman Thomas was almost as American as cherry pie. These movements—and indeed all of the popular movements treated in Chapter 4—were pointing a finger at and attempting to redress inequities in American society that should have been the focus of mainstream organizations that, in effect, often left the field to the radicals. The pension movement, however, was indeed mainstream, and that was one of its strengths.

Organized Labor: Then and Now

The New Deal's relationship with labor, one of the popular movements with which it had something of an alliance for some of the time, was complex and shifting. New

Deal legislation that strengthened collective bargaining rights and woke up the labor movement earned Roosevelt labor's vigorous backing and contributed to his landslide victory in 1936. Early in 1937, during the sit-down strike against General Motors, FDR supported Michigan governor Frank Murphy, whose restraint and desistance from armed opposition helped labor gain one of its greatest victories. Soon after, however, acting upon his reading of public opinion that the sit-down strikes were unpopular, as well as the counsel of some advisors, Roosevelt took his famous hands-off stance during labor's great and decisive battle with Little Steel. Subsequently, in the late 1930s, labor suffered from congressional Red-baiting that Roosevelt seemed relatively powerless to stop, and then from the priority he gave to gaining business support for the war effort. In Chapter 5, McIntyre points out that the labor movement has not won a legislative victory in the last fifty years and that "labor's leverage was . . . reduced because it had become so firmly wedded to the Democratic Party, a party that did not return its love."

A current case in point is the Employee Free Choice Act, legislation that was intended to make it easier for employees to join unions and harder for employers to prevent it. The labor movement considered the Act critical to a reversal of the deep decline in union density since its high point in the 1950s. Just as New Deal legislation gave vital support to a labor movement that had lost much ground, passage of the Employee Free Choice Act was expected to perform a similar function for labor today. As a senator, Barack Obama sponsored this legislation and, campaigning in 2008, said he would sign it as president. Given the assumed importance to labor, fierce business lobbying greeted the bill when a Democratic White House and congressional leadership made passage likely. Although the Democrats controlled both Houses of Congress in the first two years of the Obama Administration, the Employee Free Choice Act was bypassed, owing to a combination of White House refusal to move on it before a vote on health care reform, and reservations of moderate Democrats over one of its provisions—one that labor, however, seemed willing to forgo. With loss of Democratic control of the House and of a critical Senate seat needed for passage, the bill was doomed.[88]

While Democrats may enjoy the support of unions at little cost, there are nonetheless negative consequences for the working class as a whole, for the economy and for the political party that claims to represent the interests of that class. Research conducted by the Economic Policy Institute concluded that a major factor in the stagnation of wages for all workers has been "the ongoing erosion of unionization and the declining bargaining power of unions, along with the weakened ability of unions to set norms or labor standards that raise the wages of comparable nonunion workers."[89] With stagnating wages and labor standards, workers are likely to be discontented with politicians generally, and while unions may support the Democratic Party, workers, most of whom do not belong to unions, may feel little loyalty to the Democrats when they go to the polls. With the decline in purchasing power that diminished union power portends, the economy itself is at risk.

Environmental Crises: Then and Now

Prescient as he was about threats to the natural environment, Roosevelt could not have imagined an environmental crisis that threatens the very existence of this planet. Yet New Dealers' approach to environmental problems, even if not planetary in scope, can nonetheless guide us in coping with a disaster once unimaginable but now imminent.

It is not only New Dealers' accomplishments that inspire us, and there were many in the realm of environmental restoration. It is the willingness to face and to take action to overcome the long-standing problems they encountered in the 1930s—soil depletion, pollution of waterways, threats to wildlife, and devastation of forests. It is Roosevelt's leadership in the recognition of threats to the environment that should serve as an example to current policymakers, particularly his role as teacher and educator, informing the people of the problems the nation faced and how his administration would attempt to cope with them. "Here was a president and administration," Collins emphasizes in Chapter 9, "that was willing to think big and to go beyond the strictures of the private market."

Not the least of the New Deal's two-in-one innovations was its combination of relief to unemployed people, including the nation's young workers, and environmental restoration and conservation. The Civilian Conservation Corps was rightfully one of the most popular of New Deal programs, although it was assailable for shortcomings shared with other New Deal programs: segregated CCC camps, failure to serve blacks in proportion to their destitution, and the paucity of projects for women. Eleanor Roosevelt, "the conscience of the Administration," protested this as well as other examples of gender discrimination.[90] In eschewing the direct job-creation strategy of the New Deal, the Obama Administration has passed up an opportunity to contribute to the task of making our economy sustainable. The ARRA could have provided a stimulus, not only to recovery, but to the steps we must take to become more energy efficient if we are to make the earth habitable. Millions of the unemployed could have been put to work, as jobless workers were in the 1930s, this time in such assignments as retrofitting or making buildings more energy-efficient, upgrading storm-water systems, building more efficient waste-management systems, planting trees in urban and arid areas, preserving wilderness areas, and providing education in ecology to children and communities. It was a lost opportunity both to raise public consciousness of the problem and to take a step forward in dealing with it.

New Deal policies, while worthy of respect for their sensitivity to environmental problems, sometimes had the unintended effect of exacerbating or creating new ecological troubles. This was particularly the case in agricultural policies that, as Winders shows in Chapter 10, "promoted some farming practices and technologies that contributed to environmental decline: much greater use of chemical fertilizers, pesticides and herbicides as well as intensive irrigation in some regions...which had been struck by the Dust Bowl...."

Perhaps the most serious unintended environmental consequence of New Deal policies is the particularly American compromise with Keynesianism adopted early in the 1940s by Congress and policymakers in the Roosevelt Administration: the abandonment of long-range planning and the pursuit of fiscal policies to foster unlimited economic growth and consumerism with little emphasis on a regulatory state.[91] As Collins has pointed out in her chapter on the environment, the technological change and consumption habits driven by these growth imperatives "continuously threaten to destroy the natural basis of all economic activity." In short, climate change is an unintended consequence of fiscal policies that created unlimited growth and unparalleled, if unequally distributed, prosperity.

Some unintended consequences, it should be said, are preventable. It is important to attempt to anticipate them, to monitor outcomes as early as possible, to detect emerging undesirable results, to change course accordingly, and, for planning policies and programs, to secure the best knowledge available at the time. Learning from history can make an important contribution to this process. Careful planning is a function of a regulatory state, and so the choice of "commercial Keynesianism" is both a cause of our environmental crisis and of a loss of the capacity to cope with it.

De-Commodification: An Arrested Process

In discussing what they call "the democratization of culture" or the increased accessibility to the arts that the New Deal made possible, Collins and Rosenblum in Chapter 8 refer to their being "de-commodified" or available to people outside the marketplace. In his Economic Bill of Rights, Roosevelt included not only the right to earn enough to provide such generally accepted necessities as adequate food and clothing, but, perhaps recognizing the roots of the word, *recreation* as well. In recent years, with formerly free museums charging fees, and theater, once affordable to non-élite audiences, becoming prohibitive, culture is being re-commodified. In consequence, many Americans are losing the access to culture made possible by New Deal programs.

The term *de-commodification* has also been applied to the welfare state in the sense that it permits women and men, at various times in their lives, such as the birth of a child, illness, disability, and old age, to opt out of the market with impunity. The welfare state was a move away from treating human beings as commodities or "things" to be exchanged in the market in the sense that some classical economists used the term.[92] With cutbacks in benefits and the move toward austerity has come a regrettable process of re-commodification, a throwback to early industrialization and its sacrifice of men, women, and children to the marketplace at all costs. The attack on Social Security is an example of this process. Retirement is not a biological phenomenon. In earlier times, if one lived into old age, there was no period of rest or freedom from working for any but the well off.[93] Owing to decreased ability to find work or to gain a livelihood, it often meant impoverishment and either the poorhouse or dependence on relatives, who were usually pressed themselves. As the title of Michael Katz's history of American social welfare implies, the poor lived *In the Shadow of the Poorhouse*.[94] The dread of such institutions is vividly depicted in a number of novels by Charles Dickens. Retirement, then, is a social construction, a time of life greatly aided or made possible for the majority of older people by Social Security. If benefits decline and the retirement age rises, retirement may itself disappear or greatly diminish in length. Old age will have been re-commodified.

The effects of re-commodification in the arts may, at the outset, seem less dire and, indeed, their loss is less menacing than the absence of "necessities." Nonetheless, as Collins and Rosenblum argue, re-commodification of culture is a deep loss. The great settlement leader Jane Addams considered the arts a vital element in service to poor immigrants. To Addams, the function of art was "to preserve in permanent and beautiful form those emotions and solaces which cheer life and make it kindlier, more heroic and easier to comprehend."[95] Literature, neuroscience tells us, increases empathy and nourishes critical thinking.[96] If art, as Addams puts it "softens life," then its loss contributes to the harshness of a society that is re-commodifying itself.[97] Historian Irving Bernstein, an outstanding authority on the New Deal, credited it with the creation of "a caring society."[98] Moreover, the loss not only of exposure to the arts for so many, but also of access to participation in the creative process, cripples the public's imaginative capabilities. One loss is the diminished ability to imagine anything beyond what currently exists. Yet the conditions that now confront the human race are so grave that we will need every ounce of creativity and receptivity to change if we are to fashion a better, more sustainable world. The re-commodification of culture is still another move in the direction of a harsher, less caring, less empathetic, and ultimately unsustainable society.

A Tragic Lost Opportunity

The crisis of the 1930s was both a disaster and an opportunity for change. With overwhelming evidence that the market alone could not assure security, New Dealers helped the public understand why protecting people against what Roosevelt referred to as "the hazards and vicissitudes of life" required the participation of the federal government.[99] As Roosevelt put it, he and his fellow New Dealers were going to make the nation "more social-minded." The objectives, such as the opportunity for productive work and decent homes, were traditional, but they could no longer be achieved solely through individual responsibility or self-reliance. And thus it was necessary "to employ the active interest of the Nation as a whole through government in order to encourage a greater security for each individual who composes it."[100]

In running for the presidency in 1932, Roosevelt challenged the concept of self-reliant business, pointing out that government had subsidized the railroads and granted money to assist the merchant marine industry. "The same man who tells you that he does not want to see the government interfere in business… is the first to go to Washington and ask the government for a prohibitory tariff on his product." "When things get just bad enough," Roosevelt continued, "he will go with equal speed to the United States government and ask for a loan…."[101] Similarly, Senator Wagner, in a Senate speech in 1932, attacked the country's one-sided individualism. He approved of helping the railroads and the financial institutions. "But is there any reason why we should not likewise extend a helping hand to that forlorn American, in every village and every city of the United States, who has been without wages since 1929. Must he alone carry the cross of individual responsibility?"[102]

New Dealers took advantage of the opportunity of the 1929 Stock Market Crash and its aftermath to discredit speculation and the speculators who were largely responsible for the crisis and to make the case for regulating financial institutions. As Canova points out in Chapter 3, New Dealers stopped short of basic reforms in financial regulation and public finance but nonetheless went much further than the Obama Administration in exposing banking fraud, enacting regulatory measures like Glass-Steagall and the Federal Deposit Insurance Corporation. The financial crisis of 2008 was another opportunity to begin to set the record straight, to point the finger at the perpetrators of the financial crisis, to debunk the deregulation that had once again set loose speculation that was putting the economy at risk, and perhaps to propose reforms that not only re-regulated the financial industry, but restructured it. It was an opportunity to bring home to the public the consequences of the great inequality that was undermining the economy and, with the heavy hand of money in politics, threatening democracy itself.[103] It was an opportunity to challenge nearly three decades of reactionary attack on the capacity of government to solve problems. The Obama government provided relief and stimulated recovery for a time. During the election year of 2010, it gained passage of the Dodd-Frank Wall Street Reform and Consumer Protection Act, but, as Canova explains, parts of the bill that were "completely under the radar… left the Obama administration without a single major policy tool to provide relief and strengthen recovery in the months leading up to the 2010 mid-term elections."

Ironically, government intervention had stemmed the crisis, not only bailing out the banks but providing sustaining social benefits to millions of the unemployed. Tragically, a chance was lost to make the American people more cognizant that entitlements were rescuing them and helping to keep the economy afloat. Crisis created an opportunity for something of a paradigm shift in the perception of political and social realities or in the political economy. The Obama

Administration, however, did not consider this its mission, even though public acceptance of its health care reform rested on a belief in the government's ability to solve problems.

One reason why the crisis of the 1930s became an opportunity for change is that there was in the New Dealers and in Roosevelt an openness to new ideas. FDR welcomed the suggestion of his counsel and speechwriter Samuel Rosenman to assemble what was first called a "Brains Trust," later the "Brain Trust." These were thinkers, mostly college professors, who could help him understand the economy, the role of the state, the causes of the Depression, and how to cope with it.[104] As he governed, Roosevelt continued to listen to many voices, some orthodox and some progressive—the budget balancers on one hand, and those who counseled more government spending on the other. He met with Sir William Beveridge, who has been called the "father of the British Welfare State," and with John Maynard Keynes.[105] Eleanor Roosevelt, with her closeness to Progressive thinkers, was constantly attempting to stretch New Deal thinking in that direction.[106] It was not that the administration always went with the visionary thinkers, and, in fact, one who was close to Roosevelt regretted that he had not "led us into a new world."[107] Yet the input was welcomed and sometimes acted on.

Toward Universal Human Rights

In his Four Freedoms speech, Roosevelt had named four essential human freedoms: "freedom of speech and expression," "freedom... to worship God in his [*sic*] own way" or freedom of worship, "freedom from want," and "freedom from fear." Following each of the Four Freedoms, Roosevelt repeated, "everywhere in the world." The Four Freedoms, particularly the intrinsic relationship between freedom and economic rights, and the universality of these aspirations would be carried forward in the Universal Declaration of Human Rights of the United Nations—an achievement that owed much to the leadership of Eleanor Roosevelt.[108] According to Mary Ellen Glendon's authoritative account of the politics and origins of the Universal Declaration, "Eleanor Roosevelt's presence [*on the Human Rights Commission that framed the Declaration*] assured that Roosevelt's 'four freedoms' would be a constant touchstone for the members of the Commission." Glendon also points out that in Eleanor Roosevelt's column for VE (Victory in Europe) Day, she emphasized that "Freedom without bread... has little meaning," and referred to her husband's concept of "freedom from want."[109]

A declaration of rights is only a beginning in the often unsteady and interrupted march toward their enforcement. The world, and this nation particularly, are a long way from the achievement of the rights asserted in the Universal Declaration. Significantly, the title to Glendon's book, *A World Made New,* implies that the very declaration of universal rights, in this case, adopted by the General Assembly of the

United Nations, is an important step in the direction of their achievement; it is an assertion of rights or "aspirational law."[110]

The Current Status of Economic Rights

Absent from the indexes of most earlier works on the New Deal, the Economic Bill of Rights has received more attention in recent years. A prominent example is the 2004 book by legal scholar Cass R. Sunstein, *The Second Bill of Rights: FDR's Unfinished Revolution and Why We Need It More Than Ever*.[111] Prior to the 2012 presidential election, the AFL-CIO conducted a "Stand Up for Economic Rights for All" campaign that called attention to the Economic Bill of Rights "with its simple idea that 'true individual freedom cannot exist without economic security and independence.' "[112]

As Collins has written in Chapter 9, both the 1930s and the present are times of intertwined economic *and* environmental crises and of consequent recognition that "ecological sustainability is a necessary prerequisite for both economic security and social justice." With his deep feeling and respect for the natural environment and the abundant evidence in his speeches and writing that he understood environmental sustainability as a long-term commitment, Roosevelt would certainly have been among those to have detected impending threats to the planet and to have taken the initiative in calling for swift remedial, as well as preventive, action. Rights are asserted when they are threatened or could, from time to time, be violated. Cognizance of the threatened right to ecological sustainability must therefore take its place in an Economic Bill of Rights for the Twenty-first Century.

While a planetary environmental crisis was unimaginable in the 1940s, some omissions in the Economic Bill of Rights were recognizable at the time. Roosevelt proposed economic security "for all—regardless of station, race or creed." Consistent with the New Deal's denial of equal rights for women, gender was omitted from this thrust toward universal rights. Perhaps it was assumed that collective bargaining rights had been guaranteed by New Deal legislation, but one of the attributes of the decline of the "New Deal Order" has been the increasing precariousness of the rights of labor.[113] Labor rights are indeed threatened and incompletely endowed and should be asserted in an economic bill of rights. In its strategic decision to delay action on the Employee Free Choice Act until passage of health care reform, the Obama administration gave greater priority to the right to health care than to collective bargaining rights.

The Patient Protection and Affordable Care Act, however flawed, is moving the nation closer to the assurance of one of Roosevelt's economic rights, but current prospects for securing or even taking steps toward the achievement of other economic rights are slim. Indeed, it has become necessary to defend the right to security in old age. It is important, nonetheless, to set some goals and devise policies for the achievement of essential economic rights. When the right moment arrived, as it did in the 1930s, the work of many years by a social insurance movement was at hand to aid the economic-security planners. In fact, Edwin Witte, who headed the Committee on Economic Security, was a student of John R. Commons, who had founded the American Association for Labor Legislation that had promulgated and advocated social insurance early in the twentieth century. It is also important to take action to improve imperfect social legislation. Just as the advocates of rights for the elderly did not stop with the Social Security Act, today's health care advocates continue to press for improvements that bring us closer to the right to healthcare for all.

Government Can Help

Many people feel the federal government is both intrusive and unable to solve their problems and are placing their hopes on state or local governments or on voluntary efforts that eschew government altogether.[114] Occupy Wall Street represents an example of such despair and the search for a more participatory and democratic politics as well as a more egalitarian society. Thus, it may seem paradoxical to insist that government—particularly the federal government—can help. The nation state in concert with other countries is, however, our only hope for conquering the environmental crisis, and the federal government, often responding to popular movements, has been a major source of advances in human rights. As Arthur Schlesinger wrote, in rebuttal of the charge that government is "the problem" and not "the solution," and with the federal government in mind:

> ...the record shows that the growth of national authority...has given a majority of Americans more personal dignity and liberty than they ever had before. The individual freedoms destroyed by the increase in national authority have been in the main the freedom to deny black Americans their elementary rights as citizens, the freedom to work little children in mills and immigrant in sweatshops, the freedom to pay starvation wages and enforce barbarous working hours and permit squalid working conditions, the freedom to deceive in the sale of goods and securities, the freedom to loot national resources and pollute the environment—all freedoms that, one supposes, a civilized country can readily do without.[115]

Roosevelt envisioned a role for the state in ensuring economic rights and environmental conservation, although he assigned primary responsibility to the private sector in producing, if not in distributing, material abundance. Of course, neither economic rights nor environmental sustainability has ever been secured by the private sector. Based on short-term profit, the private sector cannot be expected to take the lead in ushering in an environmentally and economically sustainable world.

Only governments have the capacity to alter the incentives that would enable the private sector to make its contribution and individuals to change their habits and expectations.

This is not the place for detailed discussion of ideas and associated policies that would advance economic rights. Suffice it to name a few: At the top of the list is an assault on the unemployment that afflicts millions of Americans in better as well as bad times. The way to begin is to learn the New Deal lesson of direct job creation and to improve on it by planning policies and programs that are permanent and that expand and contract in relation to the number of jobless workers, and that pay living wages. Such jobs, of course, must be compatible with a sustainable economy and indeed contribute to it.

At the same time, many of the needs chronically unmet by the private sector would be addressed by such a public employment program: not only improvements of the physical infrastructure, but expansion of social services such as child and elder care, as well as increased access to cultural and educational resources. An infrastructure or national development bank could fund such ventures as the building of a national renewable energy grid and an interurban transit system run on alternative energy sources.

We must continue to counter one of the most formidable obstacles to securing economic rights: what Robert Eisner, past president of the American Association of Economics, called "deficit paranoia." Eisner, like James Galbraith, has written cogently about its harm to the great majority of people and put his finger on what motivates those who make deficit reduction a primary goal of public policy:

> Most conservative economists do not really care about the deficit. They advocate balanced budgets because their real desire is to cut government spending, particularly on the "social programs" they abhor.... The casualties, along with full employment, are Medicare and Medicaid; loans to college students; child care; job training and an expanded earned-income tax credit...; our public infrastructure of roads, bridges and airports; and the land, water and air by which we live and breathe.[116]

Such powerful indictments should be promulgated, particularly via the kinds of clever slogans and advertisements that have been used so effectively by the right to disparage progressive policies—such as dubbing the inheritance tax a "death tax." A source of revenues, no more attractive to the "1 percent" than deficit spending but appealing to the "99 percent," is a tax on financial transactions. Originally proposed by Nobel laureate James Tobin, it is being popularized as the "Robin Hood Tax," an example of the kind of packaging that can sell an idea.[117] Financial transaction taxes (FTTs) have been proposed in the House and Senate since 2009 with a number of co-sponsors.[118] A form of financial transfer tax is the proposed source of funds for the Humphrey Hawkins Full Employment and Training Act of 2013, introduced by Rep. John Conyers, Jr.[119] Legislation of this sort is unlikely to pass at this time, but nonetheless can play an educational and movement-building function. Another source of revenue, particularly for reducing inequality, is a carbon tax with a public rebate. Such a tax would provide an incentive for the transition to an economy based on renewable energy while providing those who would be hurt by higher gas and oil taxes the ability to pay them. Reductions in the military budget are a means of freeing money for domestic spending.[120] Indeed, they could be a major source of funding for mitigating climate change—what the Pentagon acknowledges is likely to be the greatest threat to national and global security.[121] Money spent now or in the near future to mitigate greenhouse gases and build resilient environments and infrastructure could help prevent the coming resource wars.[122] Still another source of funding for public projects is public banks established by local and state governments and owned by the people of a state or community. A movement to establish such banks is already under way in over twenty states across the country.[123] The costs of public projects undertaken by government bodies that establish public banks can be greatly reduced because these banks do not need to charge interest.

The assurance of a stable and sustainable environment depends on the planning and regulatory function of the state, its financial resources, and, of course, the international community of states. It is thus a cruel coincidence that a crisis utterly dependent on the state for its resolution has descended upon us at the very time when antipathy to government runs high. Yet, state action, however short of the amount needed, has drawn the nation back from the brink of financial collapse and met the needs of many who would otherwise have gone hungry. Such dependence on the federal government—like the crisis of a Great Depression—could lead us toward renewed recognition of how much we need the help of the state.

Notes

1. Alan Brinkley, "The Idea of the State," in *The Rise and Fall of the New Deal Order, 1930–1980*, Steve Fraser and Gary Gerstle, eds. (Princeton: Princeton University Press, 1989), 86.
2. Richard Walker and Gray Brechin, *The Living New Deal: The Unsung Benefits of the New Deal for the United States and California*, California Studies Center, Working Paper #220-10, Institute for Research on Labor and Employment (Berkeley, CA: University of California, August 1, 2010), accessed April 10, 2013, available at http://livingnewdeal.berkeley.edu.
3. As Volker Jansson points out (Chapter 1), GDP growth rates averaged 7.7 percent annually between 1933 and 1941. The physical volume of industrial production fell nearly 50 percent (47.2 percent) between 1929 and 1932 but had exceeded the 1929 index by 1937; it dropped down in the severe recession year of 1938, but by 1940 exceeded the 1929 level by 12 percent. Broadus Mitchell, *The Depression Decade: From New Era Through New Deal 1929–1941* (Armonk, NY: M. E. Sharpe, 1946), 446. The GNP, which had dropped 30 percent between 1929 and 1933, exceeded the 1929 level in 1937, 1939, and 1940. Lester V. Chandler, *America's Greatest Depression 1929–1941* (New York: Harper & Row, 1970), 3. According to Leuchtenburg, "marked gains had been made before the war spending had any appreciable effect." William E. Leuchtenburg, *Franklin D. Roosevelt and the New Deal 1932–1940* (New York: Harper & Row, 1963), 347.

4. Norris's proposal for a government owned and operated power station on the Tennessee River at Muscle Shoals became the prototype for the TVA.
5. Philip Harvey refers to "aspirational law." Yes, the Declaration of Independence was written by slaveholders, but "The formal recognition accorded the equality principle in the U.S. Declaration of Independence provided both encouragement and support for the efforts of those who fought to end slavery—as it does the continuing efforts of those who carry on the fight for equality today." See his "Aspirational Law," *Buffalo Law Review,* 52 (November 2004): 7–18.
6. W. E. B. DuBois, *The Souls of Black Folk* (New York: Alfred A. Knopf, 1903/1993), 51.
7. Leuchtenburg, 37.
8. Nancy J. Weiss, *Farewell to the Party of Lincoln: Black Politics in the Age of FDR* (Princeton, NJ: Princeton University Press, 1988), 211; see also Ira Katznelson, *Fear Itself: The New Deal and the Origins of Our Time* (New York: Norton), 175–176.
9. Walter White, *A Man Called White: The Autobiography of Walter White* (Athens: University of Georgia Press, 1995), 168–169, cited in Katznelson, 160.
10. Citing a number of sources, Leuchtenburg (p. 137) concludes, "The New Deal was not to blame for the social system it inherited, but New Deal policies made matters worse. The AAA's [*Agricultural Adjustment Administration*] reduction of cotton acreage drove the tenant and the cropper from the land, and landlords, with the connivance of local AAA committees which they dominated, cheated tenants of their fair share of benefits."
11. Douglas S. Massey and Nancy A. Denton, *American Apartheid: Segregation and the Making of the Underclass* (Cambridge, MA: Harvard University Press, 1993), 51–52.
12. Nancy E. Rose, *Put to Work: The WPA and Public Employment in the Great Depression,* 2nd ed. (New York: Monthly Review Press, 2009) 28, and *passim.*
13. Ibid., 82.
14. See, e.g., Blanche Wiesen Cook, *Eleanor Roosevelt 1933–1938,* Vol. 2 (New York: Viking, 1992), 86–91.
15. Ibid., 60–69, for a discussion of how ER mobilized the "Women's Network." In his authoritative work on the New Deal, Irving Bernstein considers that "the fundamental problem during the thirties was that equal rights for women were simply not a significant political issue." Irving Bernstein, *The Caring Society: The New Deal, the Worker, and the Great Depression* (Boston: Houghton Mifflin, 1985), 292. Bernstein (p. 290) goes so far as to say that "perversely the most important public policy issue of the decade was the movement to deny jobs to married women."
16. Rose, 28. Rose (p. 49) points out that there were women's divisions established in the Federal Emergency Relief Administration (FERA) and the Civil Works Administration (CWA) but no similar ones for blacks.
17. Katznelson, 252–253.
18. For a discussion of ER's role in the bi-racial movement to stop lynching and of her attempts to persuade FDR to support it, see Cook, 176–181, 243–237.
19. August Meier and Elliott Rudwick, *From Plantation to Ghetto,* 3rd ed. (New York: Hill and Wang, 1976), 259–260. In their study of the efforts of the National Urban League (NUL) and the NAACP to advocate for African-Americans in New Deal Programs, Hamilton and Hamilton report that "Negro Youth fared well in this [NYA] program. . . ." Dona Cooper Hamilton and Charles V. Hamilton, *The Dual Agenda: Race and Social Welfare Policies of Civil Rights Organizations* (New York: Columbia University Press, 1997), 16.
20. See Hamilton and Hamilton, 25, for examples of gains and the advocacy of the NAACP and the National Urban League.
21. U. S. Bureau of Labor Statistics, *Labor Force Characteristics by Race and Ethnicity, 2011,* Bulletin 1036 (Washington, DC: Author, August 2012), Table 12.
22. Franklin D. Roosevelt, Second Inaugural Address, January 20, 1937, accessed April 10, 2013, available at http://www.bartleby.com/124/pres50.html.

23. For this point, both Volker Janssen and Timothy Canova, in Chapters 2 and 3, cite E. Cary Brown, "Fiscal Policy in the 'Thirties': A Reappraisal," *American Economic Review*, 46 (December 1956): 857-879.
24. Helen Ginsburg, *Full Employment and Public Policy: The United States and Sweden* (Lexington, MA: Lexington Books, 1983), Table 1-1, 9, using data from the U.S. Bureau of Labor Statistics.
25. Leuchtenburg, citing press correspondence and other documentary evidence, gives many examples of the suffering, e.g., "In seventeen southern states Hopkins reported in May [*1938*] people were starving" (p. 249).
26. Ibid., 244–256; Brinkley, 95–97. Brinkley, 95, quoting Bruce Bliven ("Confidential: to the President," *The New Republic*, [April 29, 1938]: 328), cites evidence that there was public support for their diagnosis: "No one can doubt that the sudden withdrawal of hundreds of millions of dollars of federal relief funds, the smashing of thousands of projects all over the country, did contribute materially to the creation of our present misery."
27. Brinkley, 96.
28. Ibid., 96–97.
29. Franklin D. Roosevelt, Commonwealth Club Address, San Francisco, September 23, 1932, accessed November 11, 2012, available at http://www.americanrhetoric.com/speeches/fdrcommonwealth.htm.
30. *The Report to the President of the Committee on Economic Security*, January 15, 1935, accessed May 10, 2013, available at http://www.ssa.gov/history/reports/ces.html.
31. Franklin D. Roosevelt, Annual Message to Congress, January 11, 1944, accessed March 1, 2013, available at http://docs.fdrlibrary.marist.edu/011144.html; Campaign Address at Soldiers' Field, Chicago IL, October 29, 1944, accessed March 1, 2013, available at http://www.udhr.org/history/10-28-44.htm; Annual Message to Congress, January 6, 1945, accessed February 6, 2013, available at http://www.presidency.ucsb.edu/ws/?pid=16595.
32. Franklin D. Roosevelt, State of the Union Address, January 6, 1941, accessed November 15 2012, available at http://voicesofdemocracy.umd.edu/fdr-the-four-freedoms-speech-text/.
33. Roosevelt, Annual Message to Congress, January 6, 1945.
34. Ibid.
35. Roosevelt, Campaign Address at Soldiers' Field.
36. Roosevelt, Annual Message to Congress, January 11, 1944.
37. For a history of this legislation see Stephen Kemp Bailey, *Congress Makes a Law: The Story Behind the Employment Act of 1946* (New York: Columbia University Press, 1950).
38. Gary Gerstle and Steve Fraser, "Introduction," in Gerstle and Fraser, xiv. Gerstle and Fraser point out that the term "commercial Keynesianism" is the invention of Robert Lekachman, *The Age of Keynes* (New York: Random House, 1966), 287; see also Brinkley.
39. Lekachman, 259.
40. Leuchtenburg, 147.
41. For different definitions of full employment, see, e.g., Gertrude Schaffner Goldberg, Helen Lachs Ginsburg, and Philip Harvey, "A Survey of Full Employment Advocates," *Journal of Economic Issues*, 41, no. 4 (2007): 1161–1168.
42. See, e.g., Samuel Eliot Morison, *The Oxford History of the American People* (New York: Oxford University Press, 1965), 1079–1106. Eisenhower referred to his administration as a "mandate for change," but Morison (p. 1106) asks, "What change, except the men?"
43. Kim Phillips-Fein, *Invisible Hands: The Making of the Conservative Movement: From the New Deal to Reagan* (New York: W. W. Norton, 2009), 57. See also, Jean Edward Smith, *Eisenhower in War and Peace* (New York: Random House, 2012), 654 and *passim.*
44. Dwight D. Eisenhower, Message on Social Security, January 14, 1954, cited by Phyllis Osborn, "Aid to Dependent Children: Realities and Possibilities," *Social Service Review*, 28 (June 1954): 172.
45. Smith, 650–654. According to Hugh Wilson, Eisenhower thought of the highway program as a form of active labor market policy or job creation. Wilson, "President Eisenhower and

the Development of Active Labor Market Policy in the United States: A Revisionist View," *Presidential Studies Quarterly*, 39 (September 2009): 519–554.

46. James L. Sundquist, *Politics and Poverty: The Eisenhower, Kennedy, and Johnson Years* (Washington, D.C.: The Brookings Institution, 1968), 60–73.
47. In the Eisenhower years, the rate for the top bracket was 91 percent tax on incomes of $400,000 and above, compared to a range of 81.1 to 84 percent tax on incomes of $200,000 and above in the war years. During the Democratic regimes of John F. Kennedy and Lyndon B. Johnson, rates ranged from 70–77 percent on incomes of $200,000 and above, and for Republicans Richard Nixon and Gerald Ford, it was 70 percent on incomes of $200,000 and above. In 1989, the last year for which the Reagan Administration was responsible, it was 28 percent on incomes of $32,450 and above, and in 2011, it was 35 percent on incomes of $379,150 and above. National Taxpayers Union, History of Federal Individual Income Bottom and Top Bracket Rates, accessed April 19, 2013, available at http://www.ntu.org/tax-basics/history-of-federal-individual-1.html.
48. Ginsburg, Table 2.5, 40, using Bureau of Labor Statistics data.
49. Leonard S. Silk, "Nixon's Program—'I Am Now a Keynesian,'" *New York Times*, January 10, 1971, 1.
50. Spending on public assistance increased 85 percent between the last budget of President Johnson (1969) and the last of Richard Nixon (1974). *Social Security Bulletin Annual Statistical Supplement 1969*, Table 1, 23; *Social Security Bulletin Annual Statistical Supplement 1974*, Table 1, 39.
51. According to Nixon's Chief of Staff, H. R. Haldeman, Nixon "wants to be sure it's killed by Democrats and that we made big play for it, but don't let it pass, can't afford it." Haldeman, *The Haldeman Diaries: Inside the Nixon White House* (New York: G. P. Putnam's Sons, 1994), 181.
52. For a discussion of Nixon's social welfare policies, including the Family Assistance Plan, see Gertrude Schaffner Goldberg and Sheila D. Collins, *Washington's New Poor Law: Welfare "Reform" and the Roads Not Taken, 1935 to the Present* (New York: Apex Press 2001), 103–164.
53. Jimmy Carter, "Crisis of Confidence Speech," July 15, 1979, accessed April 10, 2013, available at http://millercenter.org/scripps/archive/speeches/detail/3402.
54. Ronald Reagan, Inaugural Address, January 20 1981, accessed March 31, 2013, available at http://www.presidency.ucsb.edu/ws/?pid=43130.
55. Arthur M. Schlesinger, Jr., *The Cycles of American History* (Boston: Houghton Mifflin 1986), 241.
56. Cited by Tom Wicker, "The Other Fritz," *New York Times*, February 3, 1984, A29.
57. James MacGregor Burns and Georgia J. Sorenson, *Dead Center: Clinton-Gore Leadership and the Perils of Moderation* (New York: Scribner, 1999), 153–163 and *passim*.
58. Bill Clinton, *Between Hope and History: Meeting America's Challenges for the 21st Century* (New York: Random House, 1996), 90.
59. Bob Woodward, *The Agenda* (New York: Simon & Schuster,1994), 165, 191, cited by Robert Pollin, *Contours of Descent: U.S. Economic Fractures and the Landscape of Global Austerity* (London: Verso, 2003), 21–22.
60. U.S. Congressional Budget Office, *Historical Budget Data—February 2013,* Table 1, accessed May 19, 2013, available at http://www.cbo.gov/publication/43904.
61. Pollin, 29.
62. Ibid., 40.
63. U.S. Census Bureau, Historical Income Tables, Table H-2, Share of Aggregate Income Received by Each Fifth and Top 5 Percent of Households, All Races: 1967 to 2011, accessed April 19, 2013, available at http://www.census.gov/hhes/www/income/data/historical/inequality/index.html.
64. U.S. Congressional Budget Office, Table 1.
65. American Society of Civil Engineers, Statement on the Federal Role in Meeting Infrastructure Needs, Testimony Before the Subcommittee on Transportation and Infrastructure, Committee

on the Environment and Public Works, U.S. Senate, July 23, 2001, accessed April 19, 2013, available at http://www.epw.senate.gov/107th/asce0723.htm.

66. Paul Krugman, "Hey, Small Spender," *New York Times,* October 10, 2010, A23.
67. Alan S. Blinder and Mark Zandi "How the Great Recession Was Brought to an End," July 27, 2010, accessed April 15, 2013, available at http://www.economy.com/mark-zandi/documents/End-of-Great-Recession.pdf.
68. John Harwood, "Mystery for White House: Where Did the Jobs Go?" *The Politics and Government Blog of the Times,* July 19, 2010, accessed April 1, 2013, available at http://thecaucus.blogs.nytimes.com/2010/07/19/mystery-for-white-house-where-did-the-jobs-go/.
69. See Canova's references in Chapter 3 for Goolsbee's views on government job creation.
70. U.S. Bureau of Labor Statistics, Labor Force Statistics from the Current Population Survey, Series Id.: LNS14000000, Unemployment Rates, January 2003–April 2013, accessed May 16, 2013, available at http://data.bls.gov/timeseries/LNS14000000.
71. In a speech to bankers in North Carolina on March 10, 2010, Bowles stated: "Anyone who has looked at the financial condition of this country knows insolvency cannot be remedied without severe cutbacks in entitlements such as Social Security, Medicare and Medicaid," accessed May 13, 2013, available at http://www.economicnoise.com/2010/03/10/a-shot-across-the-entitlement-bow/. Simpson compared Social Security to "a milk cow with 310 million tits." See Ryan Grim, "Alan Simpson, 'Social Security is a Milk Cow with 310 Million Tits,'" *Huffington Post,* August 24, 2010, accessed April 14, 2012, available at http://www.huffingtonpost.com/2010/08/24/alan_simpson_social_security_n_693277.html.
72. An analysis of public opinion survey researchers, including those at Stanford University, University of Michigan, and Princeton University, reported that "Between 2010 and 2012, public understanding of the elements of the bill [*Affordable Care Act*] we examined did not change notably." Furthermore, "If the public had perfect understanding of the elements of the bill that we examined, the proportion of Americans who favor the bill might increase from the current level of 32 percent to 70 percent." Wendy Gross et al., "Americans' Attitudes Toward the Affordable Care Act: Would Better Public Understanding Increase or Decrease Favorability?" accessed May 19, 2013, available at http://www.stanford.edu/dept/communication/faculty/krosnick/docs/2012/Health%20Care%202012%20-%20Knowledge%20and%20Favorability.pdf.
73. According to Dr. Ezekiel J. Emanuel, a physician and University of Pennsylvania vice-provost who was a top White House advisor in the development of the ACA, "We never had a spokesperson, and the public never really understood what we were doing," cited in Peter Baker, "For Obama a Signature Issue That the Public Never Embraced Looms Large," *New York Times,* June 30, 2012, A12.
74. Frances Perkins, *The Roosevelt I Knew* (New York: Harper & Row, 1946/1964), 152.
75. See Goldberg, Chapter 4, on the movement of unemployed workers.
76. Rather than being a spontaneous grassroots movement, the Tea Party has its roots in anti-tobacco control groups linked to the tobacco industry and Citizens for a Sound Economy (later merged with other organizations to form Freedom Works) founded by Koch Industries. See Amanda Fallin, Rachel Grana, and Stanton A. Glantz, "'To Quarterback Behind the Scenes, Third-Party Efforts': The Tobacco Industry and the Tea Party," *Tobacco Control,* February 8, 2013, accessed April 20, 2013, available at http://tobaccocontrol.bmj.com/content/early/2013/02/07/tobaccocontrol-2012-050815.abstract. Stuart Glantz is director of the Center for Tobacco Control Research and Education, University of California, San Francisco.
77. Vanessa Williamson, Theda Skocpol, and John Coggin, "The Tea Party and the Remaking of Republican Conservatives," *Perspectives on Politics,* 9, no. 1 (March 2011), 25–43.
78. Cited by George Lodge, "Do Americans Secretly Hate Their Government?" *Salon,* September 2, 2012, accessed April 15, 2013, available at http://www.salon.com/2012/09/27/do_americans_secretly_hate_their_government/.

79. Crystal Wright, "Congressional Black Caucus's Double Standard: Cleaver Says Obama's Blackness Trumps His Record," *Washington Post, Post Local,* September 21, 2012, accessed June 5, 2013, available at http://www.washingtonpost.com/blogs/therootdc/post/congressional-black-caucuss-double-standard-cleaver-says-obamas-blackness-trumps-his-record/2012/09/21/b3a73de8-040a-11e2-9b24-ff730c7f6312_blog.html. Cleaver told this to *The Root,* an online source of news and commentary from an African American perspective.
80. Fredrick C. Harris, "The Price of a Black President," *New York Times,* October 28, 2012, SR1.
81. On a lecture tour in the United Kingdom, West, pointing to "massive unemployment and the decrepit unemployment system, indecent housing," held that "white supremacy is still operating in the U.S., even with a brilliant black face in a high place called the White House.... He's just too tied to Wall Street." Rick Cohen, "Cornel West on Obama: 'Tied to Wall Street' and 'A War Criminal,'" *The Guardian,* May 12, 2013, accessed June 5, 2013, available at http://www.nonprofitquarterly.org/policysocial-context/22305-cornel-west-on-obama-tied-to-wall-street-and-a-war-criminal.html. Ben Jealous made this statement in an interview with David Gregory on *Meet the Press,* reported in "NAACP President Ben Jealous: Black People 'Are Doing Far Worse' Under Obama," *NEWSONE For Black America,* January 29, 2013, accessed June 5, 2013, available at http://newsone.com/2172703/ben-jealous-barack-obama/ (What Jealous said about whites' being somewhat better off is open to question.)
82. Franklin D. Roosevelt, First Inaugural Address, March 4, 1933, accessed April 20, 2013, available at http://www.bartleby.com/124/pres49.html. In accepting the Democratic nomination for a second-term as president, Roosevelt laid the responsibility for the economic collapse of 1929 on the "economic royalists" who had "created a new despotism"-- although he failed to follow his stunning rhetoric with commensurate reform. See Franklin D. Roosevelt, Acceptance Speech for Renomination for the Presidency, June 27, 1936, accessed August 12, 2013, available at http://www.presidency.ucsb.edu/ws/?pid=15314
83. Sidney Tarrow, "Why Occupy Wall Street Is Not the Tea Party of the Left," *Foreign Affairs Snapshot,* October 10, 2011, 2, accessed April 10 2013, available at http://www.relooney.info/0_New_11479.pdf.
84. Ibid., 3.
85. Government documents obtained by the Partnership for Civil Justice Fund (PCJF) through its Freedom of Information Act records request found that "As the federal and local governments and law enforcement agencies engaged in a concerted, coordinated crackdown to evict Occupy protests from public spaces in the last months of 2011, DHS [*Department of Homeland Security*] officials shared and coordinated strategies. For instance, the DHS District Commander in Detroit directly communicated with a law enforcement official who was "tasked with coming up with an exit strategy for us." After writing that he had heard in the news that encampments were "broken up in California and Georgia," the DHS District Commander continued, "What is the plan for the Occupy Detroit group in Grand Circus Park? I have been reporting daily and sending it up" (p. 115 of the documents). Partnership for Civil Justice, "New Documents Reveal: DHS Spying on Peaceful Demonstrations and Activists," April, 12, 2013, accessed April 22, 2013, available at http://www.justiceonline.org/commentary/new-documents-reveal-dhs.html. See also "Oakland Mayor Jean Quan Admits Cities Coordinated Crackdown on Occupy Movement," November 15, 2111, accessed May 13, 2013, available at http://capitoilette.com/2011/11/15/oakland-mayor-jean-quan-admits-cities-coordinated-crackdown-on-occupy-movement/; Allison Kilkenny, "Did Mayors, DHS Coordinate Occupy Wall Street Crackdown?" *In These Times,* November 16, 2011, accessed May 13, 2013, available at http://inthesetimes.com/uprising/entry/12303/mayors_dhs_coordinated_occupy_attacks; Naomi Wolf, "Revealed: How the FBI Coordinated the Crackdown on Occupy," *The Guardian,* December 30, 2012, accessed April 15, 2013, available at http://inthesetimes.com/uprising/entry/12303/mayors_dhs_coordinated_occupy_attacks/.
86. Irving Bernstein, *The Turbulent Years: A History of the American Worker, 1933–1941* (Boston: Houghton Mifflin, 1969), 780–783 and *passim.*

87. Donald J. Lisio, *The President and Protest: Hoover, Conspiracy, and the Bonus Riot* (Columbia: University of Missouri Press, 1974), 219 and *passim*.
88. See, for example, Steven Greenhouse, "Democrats Drop Key Part of Bill to Assist Unions," *New York Times*, July 17, 2009, A1, A11; Jane Hamsher, "What Happened to the Employee Free Choice Act?" *Firedoglake*, April 23, 2010, accessed April 12, 2013, available at http://workinprogress.firedoglake.com/2010/04/13/what-happened-to-the-employee-free-choice-act/.
89. Lawrence Mishel, "Unions, Inequality, and Faltering Middle-Class Wages," Washington, DC, Economic Policy Institute, accessed April 15, 2013, available at http://www.epi.org/publication/ib342-unions-inequality-faltering-middle-class/.
90. "In less than four years, Eleanor Roosevelt had established herself as the conscience of the administration"; Leuchtenburg, 192. It would seem even sooner than that, for she began by protesting the discrimination against married women workers in the federal government in one of the New Deal's earliest acts, the Economy Act of 1933.
91. Brinkley, esp. 105–111, illuminates the process that resulted in the adoption of "commercial Keynesianism."
92. De-commodification is the extent to which benefits are provided irrespective of the market status of recipients. Gøsta Esping-Andersen has developed a typology of welfare regimes based on de-commodification. Esping-Andersen, *The Three Worlds of Welfare Capitalism* (Princeton, N.J.: Princeton University Press, 1990). According to classical economist David Ricardo, "Labour, like all other things which are purchased and sold, and which may be increased or diminished in quality, has its natural and its market price." Piéro Sraffa, ed., *The Works and Correspondence of David Ricardo* (Cambridge: Cambridge University Press, 1821/1951), 93. Adam Smith wrote, "the demand for men, like that for any other commodity, necessarily regulates the production of men. . . ." Smith, *The Wealth of Nations* (New York: Random House, 1776/1991), 84.
93. Henry J. Aaron and Robert D. Reischauer, *Countdown to Reform: The Great Social Security Debate* (New York: Century Foundation Press, 1998).
94. Michael B. Katz, *In the Shadow of the Poorhouse: A Social History of Welfare in America* (New York: Basic Books, 1996).
95. Jane Addams, *The Spirit of Youth and the City Streets* (New York: Macmillan, 1901), 101, cited in Jean Bethke Elshtain, *Jane Addams and the Dream of American Democracy* (New York: Basic Books), 139.
96. See, for example, Raymond A. Mar, Keith Oatley, and Jordan B. Peterson, "Exploring the Link Between Reading Fiction and Empathy: Ruling Out Individual Differences and Examining Outcomes," *Communications*, 34 (2009): 407–428.
97. Addams, "The Call of the Social Field" (1911). Reprinted in Jane Addams, *A Centennial Reader* (New York: Macmillan, 1960), 89.
98. Note the title of one of Bernstein's books on the New Deal: *A Caring Society.*
99. Roosevelt used this phrase in signing the Social Security Act, August 4, 1935 and earlier in his Message to Congress, June 8, 1934.
100. Roosevelt, June 1934 Message to Congress.
101. Roosevelt, Commonwealth Club Address.
102. Senator Robert F. Wagner in the Senate, *Congressional Record,* 72 Cong., I Sess. (January 15, 1932; cited in Arthur M, Schlesinger, Jr., *The Crisis of the Old Order*, 1919–1933 (Boston: Houghton Mifflin, 1957), 240.
103. For the relationship between economic inequality and economic dysfunction, see Arthur MacEwan and John A. Miller, *Economic Collapse, Economic Change: Getting to the Roots of the Crisis* (Armonk, NY: M. E. Sharpe, 2011); and Gertrude Schaffner Goldberg, "Economic Inequality and Economic Crisis: A Challenge for Social Workers," *Social Work*, 57, no. 3 (July 2012): 211–224.
104. Schlesinger, *Crisis of the Old Order*, 398–405; R. G. Tugwell, *The Brains Trust* (New York: Viking, 1968).
105. Perkins, 283–284, 225–226.

106. Eleanor Roosevelt, for example, introduced him to women trade union leaders who taught FDR about the theory and history of the labor movement, about sweatshops and the improvements in health and working conditions and reduction of child labor in unionized industries. Interview of trade union leader Rose Schneiderman, cited in Brigid O'Farrell, *She Was One of Us: Eleanor Roosevelt and the American Worker* (Ithaca, NY: ILR Press, 2010), 23.
107. Tugwell, xxi.
108. Mary Ann Glendon, *A World Made New: Eleanor Roosevelt and the Universal Declaration of Human Rights* (New York: Random House, 2001). For the Declaration, see United Nations, *Universal Declaration of Human Rights,* accessed May 17, 2013, available at https://www.un.org/en/documents/udhr/.
109. Eleanor Roosevelt, *My Day: The Post-War Years, 1945–1952,* ed., David Emblidge (New York: Pharos, 1990), 17. Glendon, 43.
110. See Harvey, note 5 *supra.*
111. Cass R. Sunstein, *The Second Bill of Rights: FDR's Unfinished Revolution and Why We Need It More than Ever* (New York: Basic Books, 2004).
112. AFL-CIO, "Stand Up for Economic Rights for All," undated petition, accessed March 16, 2013, available at http://act.aflcio.org/c/18/p/dia/action3/common/public/?action_KEY=4790.
113. See, e.g., Nelson Lichtenstein, "From Corporatism to Collective Bargaining: Organized Labor and the Eclipse of Social Democracy in the Postwar Era," in Fraser and Gerstle, 122–152.
114. See esp., Gar Alperovitz, *What Then Must We Do? Straight Talk about the Next American Revolution* (White River Junction, VT: Chelsea Green Publishing, 2013).
115. Schlesinger, *The Cycles of American History,* 248.
116. Robert Eisner, "Why the Debt Isn't All Bad: Balancing Our Deficit Thinking," *The Nation,* December 11, 1995, 744–745.
117. See John Nichols, "A Robin Hood Response to the Austerity Lie: Tax Wall Street," *The Nation,* April 17, 2013, accessed May 15, 2013, available at http://www.thenation.com/blog/173879/robin-hood-response-austerity-lie-tax-wall-street.
118. For an example of legislation proposing an FTT, see H.R. 1579, Inclusive Prosperity Act of 2013, introduced by Representative Keith Ellison (D, Farm Labor-Minnesota), accessed May 10, 2013, available athttp://thomas.loc.gov/cgi-bin/query/z?c113:H.R.1579.
119. See H.R. 1000, The Humphrey Hawkins 21st Century Full Employment and Training Act of 2013, accessed September 2, 2013, available at http://www.govtrack.us/congress/bills/113/hr1000.
120. Despite cuts in military spending after the Cold War, the annual military budget remained at $300 billion. According to Pollin (p. 29), in 2000 it was triple the proportion of GDP than in the 1930s, the last decade prior to World War II and the Cold War. For discussion of prospects for reducing military spending in the future, see, for example, a policy brief by Carol Conetta and Christopher Hellman, "Talking about Military Spending and the Pentagon Budget—Fiscal Year 2013 (And Beyond)," Center for International Policy, February 8, 2012, accessed April 20, 2013, available at http://www.ciponline.org/research/entry/talking-about-military-spending-and-the-pentagon-budget-fiscal-year-2013-an.
121. Peter Schwartz and Doug Randall, *An Abrupt Climate Change Scenario and Its Implications for United States National Security,* October 2003, accessed May 16, 2013, available at http://www.climate.org/topics/PDF/clim_change_scenario.pdf; Carolyn Pumphrey, ed., *Global Climate Change: National Security Implications* (Washington, D.C.: Strategic Studies Institute, May 2008), accessed May 16, 2013, available at http://www.strategicstudiesinstitute.army.mil/pdffiles/pub862.pdf.
122. For documentation on the coming resource wars, see Michael T. Klare, *Resource Wars: The New Landscape of Global Conflict* (New York: Metropolitan Books, 2001).
123. For more information about public banks and their potential role in infrastructure improvement and economic sustainability, see the website of the Public Banking Institute, http://publicbankinginstitute.org/.

INDEX

AAA. *See* Agricultural Adjustment Act
ABS (asset-backed securities), 39
ACA (Affordable Care Act, 2010), 198, 199, 304, 314
Addams, Jane, 4, 20n7, 227, 311
adjustable rate mortgages (ARMs), 40
AFDC (Aid to Families with Dependent Children), 182, 192
Affordable Care Act (ACA, 2010), 198, 199, 304, 314
AFL (American Federation of Labor), 30, 97, 98–99, 129, 137
African Americans
  arts programs and, 295
  Brotherhood of Sleeping Car Porters, 100
  discrimination in policies of New Deal, 293, 294–295. *See also* discrimination
  housing programs and, 195, 196, 294, 296
  in labor movement, 99–100, 110, 135–136
  in social welfare programs, 99, 192
  March on Washington, 99–100
  protest against discrimination, 100
  under Obama administration, 305–306
  unemployment rates of, 296
  segregation and, 100, 216, 249
  theater companies of, 216
  work programs and, 153, 154, 249, 294
aging populations, assistance for, 103–106, 109, 189–191, 198
Agricultural Act (1954), 278
Agricultural Adjustment Act (AAA, 1933)
  efficacy of, 274
  inflationary amendment in, 57
  opposition to, 56–57, 79n36, 274–277
  price supports in, 271–273, 277, 278–280
  processing tax in, 272–273, 274, 277
  production controls in, 272–273, 279–280
  Southern planters support of, 126–127, 273, 276
  supply management policies of, xviii, 266, 271–278
Agricultural Marketing Act (1929), 270
agricultural policies of New Deal, 266–291
  Corn Belt opposition to, 278–280
  efficacy of, 274, 287
  environmental consequences of, xviii, 267, 283–284, 285, 286, 309–310
  export subsidies in food aid, 281
  farm sector, effects on, 283, 284, *284*
  lessons learned from, 284–287
  opposition to, 274–275
  origins of agricultural depression, 234, 267–269
  political responses prior to, 269–271
  Southern agriculture and class structure altered by, 281–283
  supply management policies, xviii, 266, 271–278. *See also* Agricultural Adjustment Act (AAA)
  for tenant farmers, 101–102, 110, 133, 276
  wheat market reshaped by, 280–281
Agriculture Department, U.S., 243, 245, 272
Aid to Families with Dependent Children (AFDC), 182, 192
ALI (American Law Institute), 167, 178n88
Alsberg, Henry, 212, 213
Alter, Jonathan, 9, 56
Altmeyer, Arthur, 105, 199
AMA (American Medical Association), 197
Ambrose, Stephen, 236
Amenta, Edwin, 199
American Farm Bureau Federation, 278–279
American Federation of Labor (AFL), 30, 97, 98–99, 129, 137
American Law Institute (ALI), 167, 178n88
American Medical Association (AMA), 197

American Recovery and Reinvestment Act (ARRA, 2009), 75, 85n148, 170, 181, 303. *See also* stimulus program
American scene painters, 219–220
Angelides Commission, 60
Appleby, Paul H., 12
ARMs (adjustable rate mortgages), 40
Army Corps of Engineers, 236, 248
ARRA. *See* American Recovery and Reinvestment Act
Artists' Congress, 220
Artists' Union, 220
arts programs of New Deal, 207–232
  African Americans and, 295
  Art Project, 211–212
  censorship in, 210, 213, 220, 223
  democratization and de-commodification of the arts resulting from, xvii, 218–221, 225, 310
  effects of, 208, 222–223
  lessons learned from, 223–228
  Music Project, 217–218
  neglect of artifacts from, 221
  origins of, 208
  photography program, 218
  promotion of government programs through, 8, 224–225
  Public Works of Art Project (PWAP), 209–210
  re-commodification of the arts, 222–223, 311
  Theatre Project, 215–217, 223–224
  Treasury Relief Art Project (TRAP), 210–211
  Treasury Section of Painting and Sculpture, 210
  WPA administered, 211–218
  Writers' Project, 212–214, 221, 223, 226
Ash Can painters, 219
asset-backed securities (ABS), 39
Austrian school of economics, 25–26, 46
Avery, Sewell, 287

bailouts. *See* Troubled Asset Relief Program (TARP)
Bankhead, John, 102, 273
Bankhead-Jones Farm Tenancy Act (1937), 102
bank holiday proclamation, 53, 78n10
Banking Act (1933), 34, 39, 60, 74–75, 301
Banking Act (1935), 64–65, 66
banking system
  failure of, 37, 40–41
  stabilization of, 53–56. *See also* Troubled Asset Relief Program (TARP)
Baucus, Max, 182
Benjamin, Herbert, 91, 92
Bennett, Hugh Hammond, 245, 246
Bennett, Michael, 71
Berle, Adolph, Jr., 14, 21n8
Bernanke, Ben
  background, 76–77
  on bank failures, 41, 67
  as student of Great Depression, 45, 58, 72, 302
Bernstein, Irving
  on benefits of New Deal, 311
  on Bonus Army protests, 94, 95
  on Fair Employment Practices Commission, 100
  on labor movement, 96–97
  on unemployment movement, 87, 89, 307
Beveridge, William, 313
bias. *See* discrimination
Biddle, George, 209, 225
Bilbo, Theodore, 270
bimetallism, 57
biocapacity, 251, 263n67
Blinder, Alan, 9, 303
blister rust, 236, 244
bond market, 38–39
Bonus Army protests, 2, 6, 42–43, 93–95, 114n72
bottom up approach to recovery, xv–xvi, 51–52, 58–59
Boulware, Lemuel, 131, 141
Bowles, Erskine, 68, 303
Bowyer, Jerry, 38
Brain Trust, 14, 44, 313
Brinkley, Alan, 66, 73, 107, 297
Brown, E. Cary, 45, 67
Brown, Jerry, 60, 80n59
Brown, Josephine, 188
Brown, Milton W., 219
Bruce, Edward "Ned," 209, 210
budget deficiency principle, 154, 158
bully pulpit, 8, 9
Bush, George W., 302
business class, power and cohesion of, 16–17
business loans, 61
Butler; United States v. (1935), 277
buying on margin, 35
Byrd, Harry, 193

Cahill, Holger, 211
California Infrastructure and Economic Development Bank (I-Bank), 60, 80n59
Canada, unionization rates in, 120
Canova, Timothy A., 51, 302, 303, 312
Cantwell, Robert, 213
Carson, Rachel, 19, 238
Carter, Jimmy, 252, 301
Casement, Dan, 275
categorical aid, 191–193. *See also* social welfare programs of New Deal
CCC. *See* Civilian Conservation Corps
CDOs (collateralized debt obligations), 39
censorship in arts programs, 210, 213, 220, 223

CES (Committee on Economic Security), 159–160, 161–163, 168–169, 189, 191
Chandler, Lester, 54
Children's Bureau, U.S., 192
CIO (Congress of Industrial Organizations), 97, 98–99, 127–128, 135, 137
Citizens United v. Federal Election Commission (2010), 17
Civilian Conservation Corps (CCC)
  accomplishments of, 58, 255–257
  African Americans in, 249, 309
  criticisms of, 249, 250, 309
  establishment of, 150
  gender discrimination in, 249, 309
  objectives of, xviii, 241–245
  wages provided under, 176n41
Civil Works Administration (CWA), 58, 90, 150, 151–157, 162
Civil Works Service (CWS), 152–153, 156–157
Clark, Bennett, 198
Clay East, Henry, 276
Cleaver, Emmanuel, II, 305–306
climate change, 19, 254–255, 258, 259, 286
Clinton, Bill, 34, 39, 60, 74, 301–302
Clinton, Hillary Rodham, 195–196
Cloward, Richard A., 87, 91, 92, 124
Coast and Geodetic Survey, U.S., 157
Cohen, Lizabeth, 88, 89
Cohen, Wilbur, 193
COLAs (cost-of-living adjustments), 137
Cole, John, 226
collateralized debt obligations (CDOs), 39
collective bargaining rights, 96–97, 99, 124, 308, 314. *See also* labor movement
Collins, Sheila D.
  on commodification of the arts, 207, 310, 311
  on environmental crises, 233, 309, 310, 314
  on public attitudes toward government, 1
Commerce Department, 157
commercial business loans, 61
Commission on Fiscal Responsibility and Reform, 68, 303
Committee on Economic Security (CES), 159–160, 161–163, 168–169, 189, 191
commodification of the arts, xvii, 218–221, 225, 310
Commons, John R., 315
communications. *See* media and communications
Communist Party, 4, 87–88, 93, 125–129, 305, 307
community art centers, 212, 219. *See also* arts programs of New Deal
Conference of Mayors, U.S., 89, 93
Congress of Industrial Organizations (CIO), 97, 98–99, 127–128, 135, 137
conservation practices. *See also* environmental programs of New Deal
  FDR on, 239–241
  forest-management strategies, 235–236, 238, 243–244
  soil conservation, xviii, 235, 245–246, 255
  wildlife restoration, 244
consumerism, transformation into, 27–29
Conyers, John, Jr., 306, 317
Coolidge, Calvin, 34, 43, 269–270
Coon Valley Project (Wisconsin), 246
Corcoran Gallery (Washington, D.C.), 209–210
Corn Belt, 274, 275, 278–280
corn production, 267–268, *268*, 274, 278–280. *See also* agricultural policies of New Deal
Cornwell, Elmer, Jr., 185
cost-of-living adjustments (COLAs), 137
cotton production, 267–271, 267–268, 274, 279–280, 281–282. *See also* agricultural policies of New Deal
Cotton-Wheat Act (1964), 280
Coughlin, Charles E., 5, 21n14, 106, 107, 108
court-packing plan of FDR, 65
Crash of 1929, 35–37, 41. *See also* Great Depression
cultural programs. *See* arts programs of New Deal
Cummings, Homer, 159
currency, methods for creation of, 57
Cutting, Bronson, 55
CWA (Civil Works Administration), 58, 90, 150, 151–157, 162
CWS (Civil Works Service), 152–153, 156–157

dams, electricity generated by, 248, 250
Davis, Kenneth S., 15
Dawes Plan, 31
"decade of dissent," xvi
de-commodification
  of arts, xvii, 218–221, 225, 310
  of welfare state, 310–311, 323n92
deficit phobia and paranoia, 293–294, 300–302, 316
deficit spending, 296–300
deforestation, 235–236
Democracy and Distrust (Ely), 66
democratization of the arts, xvii, 218–221, 225, 310
Department of. *See specific name of department*
Depression Economics, 46
deregulation of financial system, 74–75, 301
De Voto, Bernard, 213–214
Dies Committee, 93, 99, 217. *see also* House Committee for Investigation of Un-American Activities
Dill-Connery bill (1933), 103–104
direct job-creation initiatives, 149–166. *See also* Civilian Conservation Corps (CCC); Works Progress Administration (WPA)
  African Americans and, 153, 154, 249

direct job-creation initiatives (*Cont.*)
Civil Works Administration (CWA), 58, 90, 150, 151–157, 162
Civil Works Service (CWS), 152–153, 156–157
employment assurance proposals, 159–160, 161–163, 168–169, 194–195, 297–298
Keynesian economics and, 165, 166, 169, 171–173
National Youth Administration (NYA), 63, 150
public works initiatives vs., 149–150
social and economic benefits of, xvii, 164–166, *165*, 171–173
"twofer" effect of, 171, 172
women and, 152–153, 249
discrimination
in hiring practices, 100, 110, 136, 153
in housing programs, 195, 196, 294
in policies of New Deal, 293, 294–295
in social welfare programs, 189, 192
in work programs, 249, 294
Dodd-Frank Wall Street Reform and Consumer Protection Act (2010), 59–60, 75, 76, 77, 312
Domhoff, William, 124
dot-com bubble, 38
Douglas, Lewis, 57, 90
Douglas, Paul, 91–92, 103
Dows, Olin, 210
Drucker, Peter, 71
Dubinsky, David, 96
Dubofsky, Melvyn, 98, 129
DuBois, W. E. B., 293
Dust Bowl, 236–238, 260n11, 269, 292, 316

Eccles, Marriner
as Federal Reserve Board chairman, 64–65, 67
Keynesian economics of, 14, 64, 67, 69, 296
on public works projects, 72–73
ecological ethics, 240
Economic or Second Bill of Rights
arts and culture in, 310
collective bargaining, absence from, 97
current status of, 314–315
entitlements under, 168
as evidence of FDR's vision for U.S., 15
fiscal policy and, 298–299
Roosevelt conception of, 292, 298, 299, 314
economic recessions. *See* recessions
Economic Security Bill. *See* Social Security Act (SSA)
Edwards, George, III, 185
Eisenhower, Dwight D., 300
Eisner, Robert, 316
elderly populations, assistance for, 103–106, 109, 189–191, 198
Eliot, Thomas, 103
Ellison, Ralph, 214
Ely, John Hart, 66
Emergency Banking Act (1933), 44, 53–54, 80n68
Emergency Conservation Work program. *See* Civilian Conservation Corps (CCC)
Emergency Economic Stabilization Act (2008), 2
Emergency Relief Appropriations Act (1935), 63, 188
Emergency Unemployment Compensation Program (EUC), 181
employment. *See also* job-creation strategies of New Deal; unemployment movement
globalization and, 29, 30–31
hiring practices, discrimination in, 100, 110, 136, 153
proposals for employment assurance, 159–160, 161–163, 168–169, 194–195, 297–298
Enron Corporation, 38, 48n39
environmental challenges. *See also* conservation practices; environmental programs of New Deal
agricultural policies leading to, xviii, 267, 283–284, 285, 286
climate change, 19, 254–255, 258, 259, 286
deforestation, 235–236
Dust Bowl, 236–238, 260n11, 269
erosion, 245, 246
financial and environmental crises, relationship between, 233, 314
flood control, 236, 246, 248
of Great Depression, 18–19, 234–238
of Great Recession, 19, 258
greenhouse gas emissions, 33, 254, 255, 258
pollution, 248
environmental programs of New Deal, 233–265. *See also* Civilian Conservation Corps (CCC); conservation practices; environmental challenges
FDR's environmental protection approach, 238–241
lessons learned from, 251–259, 309
limitations of, 248–251
Soil Conservation Service, xviii, 245–246, 255
Tennessee Valley Authority (TVA), xviii, 58, 246–248, 249, 250–251
erosion, 245, 246
Essays on the Great Depression (Bernanke), 58, 72
EUC (Emergency Unemployment Compensation Program), 181
export subsidies in food aid, 281

Fair Employment Practices Commission (FEPC), 100, 295
Fair Labor Standards Act (1938), 99, 123, 187
Fannie Mae (Federal National Mortgage Association), 40

FAP (Federal Art Project), 211–212. *See also* arts programs of New Deal
Farm Bloc, 270, 273, 288n11
Farm Bureau, 278–279
Farmers Independence Council (FIC), 275
Farm Journal (FDR), 239
farm sector, 283, 284, *284*. *See also* agricultural policies of New Deal
Farm Security Administration (FSA), 102, 218
fascism, 5
FDIC (Federal Deposit Insurance Corporation), 54, 60–61
FDR. *See* Roosevelt, Franklin D.
Fechner, Robert, 243
Federal Art Project (FAP), 211–212. *See also* arts programs of New Deal
Federal Deposit Insurance Corporation (FDIC), 54, 60–61
Federal Emergency Relief Administration (FERA)
  discrimination prohibited in, 294
  efficacy of, 58, 183–184
  establishment of, 151
  predecessor of, 89
  resettlement communities and, 196
  work relief projects under, 154, 157–158, 176n41, 176n56
Federal Farm Board, 42, 43
Federal Home Loan Mortgage Corporation (Freddie Mac), 39, 40
Federal Housing Authority (FHA), 196, 294, 296
federally aided public assistance programs, 191–194. *See also* social welfare programs of New Deal
Federal Music Project, 217–218. *See also* arts programs of New Deal
Federal National Mortgage Association (Fannie Mae), 40
Federal One programs, 211. *See also* arts programs of New Deal
Federal Reserve
  authority of, 53–54, 57
  on bank failures, 37, 40–41
  banking system, stabilization of, 52, 54, 60
  efforts to curb speculation, 36–37, 73
  industrial and commercial business loans, 61
  lending authority of, 71, 80n68
  pegged period and, 72
  private sector involvement in, 66–67, 74
  structural reform of, 64–65
Federal Reserve–Treasury Accord (1951), 74
Federal Surplus Relief Corporation (FSRC), 158
Federal Theatre Project, 215–217, 223–224. *See also* arts programs of New Deal
Federal Works Agency, 149
Federal Writers' Project, 212–214, 221, 223, 226. *See also* arts programs of New Deal
Fed's Open Market Committee (FOMC), 64, 66
FEPC (Fair Employment Practices Commission), 100, 295
FERA. *See* Federal Emergency Relief Administration
FHA (Federal Housing Authority), 196, 294, 296
FIC (Farmers Independence Council), 275
filibusters, 11
Financial Crisis Inquiry Commission, 60
financial system
  deregulation of, 74–75, 301
  environmental and financial crises, relationship between, 233, 314
financial transaction taxes (FTTs), 316
Fireside Chats, 6–8, 54
First New Deal (1933–1934), 44, 56–62, 123. *See also* New Deal
fiscal and monetary policies of New Deal, 51–85
  anti-monopoly and anti-trust influence on, 64
  banking system, stabilization of, 53–56
  bottom up approach to recovery, xv–xvi, 51–52, 58–59
  comparison with policies following Great Recession, 52–53, 59–60, 63, 68–69, 75–77
  to curb speculation, 73
  deficit spending and, 296–300
  on deflation of wages and prices, 56–57
  Federal Reserve, structural reform of, 64–65
  housing programs and, 299
  industrial and commercial business loans, 61
  inflationary devices in, 57–58
  job-creation and, 298–299
  Lend-Lease program, 69
  nation-building period and, 70–71
  public option approach and, xv–xvi, 51–52, 58–59
  shortcomings and missteps in, 65–68, 69, 73–74
  for transparency in security markets, 60–61
  war effort influencing, 69–71
fiscal austerity, 67–69, 303–304
Fisher, Irving, 37
Flanagan, Hallie, 215–216, 217, 223–224
flood control, 236, 246, 248
Flood Control Act (1936), 248
FOMC (Fed's Open Market Committee), 64, 66
Fones-Wolf, Elizabeth, 130–131
food aid, export subsidies in, 281
food riots, 286–287
food stamps, 171, 181, 182, 201n3, 201n8
For All the Rights (Klein), 132
foreclosures
  in Great Depression, 31, 195, 235, 268
  in Great Recession, 195–196
foreign aid programs, 71, 281
forest-management practices, 235–236, 238, 243–244

The Forgotten Man (Shlaes), 26
Four Freedoms speech (FDR), 167, 168, 298, 313
FPTRA (National Farmers Process Tax Recovery Association), 275
Frank, Jerome, 276
Freddie Mac (Federal Home Loan Mortgage Corporation), 39, 40
Friedman, Gerald, 140
Friedman, Milton, 41, 60, 72
Friedmann, Harriet, 281
FSA (Farm Security Administration), 102, 218
FSRC (Federal Surplus Relief Corporation), 158
FTTs (financial transaction taxes), 316
full employment, 147, 166, 168, 170, 173, 174n1, 297–298, 300, 306, 316. *see also* employment assurance

Garman, Phillips L., 93
Garrison, Lloyd, 126
Geithner, Timothy, 23n43, 45, 76
Gellhorn, Martha, 13
gender differences. *See* women
General Electric, 28–29
General Motors, 28–29, 74, 97, 134–135, 137
gerrymandering, 11
G.I. Bill of Rights (1944), 70–71, 95
Glass-Steagall Act (1933), 34, 39, 60, 74–75, 301
Glendon, Mary Ellen, 313
global financial crisis. *See* Great Recession (2007–2008)
globalization
  criticisms of, 32–33
  employment and, 29, 30–31
  labor movements and, 139
global warming, 19, 254–255, 258, 259, 286
Goldberg, Gertrude Schaffner, 86, 180, 292
gold standard system, 32, 33, 43
Goolsbee, Austan, 63, 303
government
  attitudes toward. *See* public attitudes toward government
  Great Depression, response to, 2, 37, 41–45, 51. *See also* New Deal
  Great Recession, response to, 2, 45–46, 52, 302–303
  revenue sources, 316–317
graphic arts programs. *See* arts programs of New Deal
Great Depression
  agricultural markets during and prior to, 268, 285–286
  arts affected by, 207
  comparison with Great Recession, xiii, xviii, 38
  consequences of, 2, 41, 53
  cultural ideologies during, 3–5
  economic environment prior to, 28–34
  environmental concerns during, 18–19, 234–238
  FDR's response to, 2, 43–45, 51. *See also* New Deal
  foreclosures during, 31, 195, 235, 268
  Hoover's response to, 37, 41–43, 51
  income share of top percentile during, 16–17
  international political context during, 18
  international response to, 37
  lessons learned from, 46, 302
  media and communications effectiveness during, 6–8
  as opportunity for change, 311–312, 313
  popular movements during. *See* popular movements
  public response to, 2, 52
  as readjustment of values, 26–27
  stock market crash (1929) and, 35–37, 41
Great Mississippi Flood (1927), 236, 246
Great Plains, 236–238, 244, 250, 269, 286
Great Recession (2007–2008)
  agricultural markets during and prior to, 286, 287, 287n1
  arts affected by, 226–227
  comparison with Great Depression, xiii, xviii, 38
  cultural ideologies during, 5–6
  economic environment prior to, 28–34
  environmental concerns during, 19, 258
  fiscal and monetary policies following, 52–53, 59–60, 63, 68–69, 75–77
  foreclosures during, 195–196
  government response to, 2, 45–46, 52, 302–303. *See also* Obama, Barack
  income share of top percentile during, 16, 17
  international political context during, 18
  international response to, 45–46
  job-creation strategy for, 63, 170–172
  media and communications effectiveness during, 8–9
  mortgage industry collapse and, 38–41
  as opportunity for change, 312–313
  popular movements following, 305–307
  public response to, 3, 52–53
  social welfare programs, availability of, xvii, 180–183
Green, James, 99
Green, William, 96
greenbacks, 57
greenbelt towns, 196
greenhouse gas emissions, 33, 254, 255, 258
Greenspan, Alan, 40, 41
Gulick, Luther, 191

Hacker, Jacob, 11
Hamilton, Charles V., 91, 99
Hamilton, Dona, 91, 99
Hansen, Alvin, 45
Harris, Fredrick C., 306
Harvey, Philip, 146, 294, 297, 303
Haugen, Gilbert, 270
Hayek, Friedrich, 25, 131, 141
HCAN (Health Care for America Now), 199
health care, 197, 198, 199, 234, 304
Health Care for America Now (HCAN), 199
Henry Street Settlement (New York), 4, 20n7
Hickock, Lorena, 13, 234–235
Highlander Center, 135, 144n54
Hillman, Sidney, 96, 97
hiring practices, discrimination in, 100, 110, 136, 153
Hispanics, housing programs and, 196, 296
HOLC (Home Owners' Loan Corporation), 195, 294
Hollings, Ernest, 301
Holtzman, Abraham, 105
Homeland Security Department, 307
home mortgage industry collapse, 38–41
Home Owners' Loan Corporation (HOLC), 195, 294
Homestead Acts, 236–237, 260n13
Hoover, Herbert
  on agricultural depression, 269–270
  on Bonus Army protests, 42–43, 95
  Great Depression, response to, 37, 41–43, 51
  on lending authority of Federal Reserve, 80n68
  role as Secretary of Commerce, 33
  trickle-down approach to recovery, xv, 51, 76
Hopkins, Harry
  on arts programs, 215
  background of, 14, 20–21n8
  on censorship, 223
  on civil rights, 295
  Civil Works Administration and, 151–152, 154
  Committee on Economic Security and, 159
  on deficit spending, 296
  on employment assurance, 159–160, 194, 298
  Federal Emergency Relief Administration and, 151, 157–158, 183–184
  on health care, 197
  relationship with FDR, 184
  on Republican victories in midterm elections (1938), 105
  on social insurance and relief, 189
  Temporary Emergency Relief Administration and, 89
  on timing of reform, 187
  on unemployed populations, 168–169, 180, 184, 297
  Works Progress Administration and, 160
House Committee for Investigation of Un-American Activities, 93, 99, 217. *see also* Dies Committee
Housing and Urban Development (HUD), 183
housing programs, 182–183, 195–197, 294, 296, 299
Howe, Louis, 95
HUD (Housing and Urban Development), 183
Hull House (Chicago), 4, 20n7
human rights, 313–314
Humphrey Hawkins Full Employment and Training Act (2013), 316–317
Hundred Days, 44, 56–62. *See also* New Deal
Hurley, Patrick, 43, 95, 307
hydroelectric power, 248, 250, 293

I-Bank (California Infrastructure and Economic Development Bank), 60, 80n59
Ickes, Harold
  commitment to civil rights, 14, 21n8, 183, 295
  on fiscal policy, 296
  on Great Plains, 250
IMF (International Monetary Fund), 33
immigrant labor movements, 139–140
income share of top percentile, 16–17
industrial business loans, 61
Industrial Revolution, 3
inflationary devices, 57–58
infrastructure banks, 59, 60
insurance
  health care, 197, 198, 199
  social insurance, 189–191. *See also* Social Security Act (SSA)
  unemployment, 88, 91–92, 109, 181–182, 188–190
intellectual workers. *See* arts programs of New Deal
Interior Department, 211, 243, 264n87
International Monetary Fund (IMF), 33
In the Shadow of the Poorhouse (Katz), 311
isolationism, 18, 31, 32, 33

J. P. Morgan & Company, 37, 60
Jackson, Lisa, 254
Jacoby, Sanford, 131
Janssen, Volker, 25, 302
Jealous, Ben, 306
Jevons Law, 250, 262n63
job-creation strategies of New Deal, 146–179. *See also* employment
  arts programs. *See* arts programs of New Deal
  comparison with strategies following Great Recession, 63, 170–172
  criticisms of, 164–165, 166

job-creation strategies (*Cont.*)
direct job-creation, 149–166. *See also* direct job-creation initiatives
employment assurance proposals, 159–160, 161–163, 168–169, 194–195, 297–298
fiscal policy and, 298–299
lessons learned from, 164–169
origins of, 147–148
production-for-use initiatives, 158
Public Works Administration (PWA), 58, 148–149, 174n7, 196
right to work and, 162–163, 166–169
shovel-ready jobs, 76
Johnston, Oscar, 273
Jones, Cecil, 210
Jones, Jesse, 59
Jones, Marvin, 102, 273
Judiciary Reorganization Bill (1937), 65

Kahane, Gabriel, 226
Karsh, Bernard, 93
Katz, Michael, 311
Kazin, Alfred, 214
Keating, Dennis, 196
Kennedy, David, 54–55, 187
Kennedy, Roger G., 226
Keynes, John Maynard, 58, 164, 313
Keynesian economics
commercial Keynesianism, 138, 299–300, 310
demand-side strategies, 65
direct job-creation initiatives and, 165, 166, 169, 171–173
end of Great Depression as confirmation of, 70
environmental consequences of, 310
principles of, xvii, 44, 58
King, Martin Luther, 6, 136
Kirsch, Richard, 199, 200
Klein, Jennifer, 132
Korstad, Robert, 136
Krugman, Paul, 33, 68, 303

Labor Department, 243
labor movement, 120–145. *See also* employment; job-creation strategies of New Deal; unionization
African Americans and, 99–100, 110, 135–136
capitalist offensive against, 96–97, 109, 121, 122–123, 130–132
decline of, 120–121, 132–139, 308
globalization and, 139
hands-off approach by FDR, 98, 109, 308
immigrants and, 139–140
lessons learned from, 139–141
New Deal policies and, xvi, 123–124, 307–308
periods of, 122–124
radical action, impact on legislation and class struggle, 124–129
social change created through, xvi, 140
strikes, 92, 97–98, 99, 109, 134–135
tripartism and, 132–133, 134
Laffer, Arthur, 34
laissez-faire economics, 6, 76
land management. *See* conservation practices; environmental programs of New Deal
Landon, Alf, 43
Larkin, David, 226
Lasser, David, 92, 93
law of unintended consequences, xiv
Leighninger, Robert, 101, 164, 249
Lekachman, Robert, 300
Lemke, William, 108, 119n202
Lend-Lease program, 69
Leopold, Aldo, 238
Leuchtenburg, William E.
on broad vision for country held by FDR, 15
on FDR's support for National Labor Relations Act, 97
on government spending, 300
on housing programs, 197
on isolationism of U.S., 17–18
on "new style liberalism," 4
on popularity of New Deal reforms, 10
levelers, 106–108
Lewis, John L., 96, 97, 98
libertarians, 26, 33
Liberty League, 125
Lichtenstein, Nelson, 136
Lippmann, Walter, 43–44
Little Steel, 98, 109
loans
home mortgages, 38–41
for industrial and commercial businesses, 61
Long, Huey, 5, 21n14, 106–108, 110, 270
Lowi, Theodore, 66
Lubove, Roy, 197
Lundeen, Ernest, 91
Lundeen bill, 91–92, 99

MacArthur, Douglas, 43, 95, 307
Madoff, Bernard, 38
malaria control, 248, 253
Mangione, Jerre, 213, 221
March on Washington, 100
Marcuse, Peter, 196
margin buying, 35
Marshall Plan, 71
Marxism, 128, 143n29
Matusow, Allen, 279
McElvaine, Robert, 110

McIntyre, Richard, 120, 308
McNary, Charles, 270
McNary-Haugen bills, 270, 271, 273
media and communications
consumerism, promotion of, 28–29
Fireside Chats, 6–8, 54
in Great Depression, 6–8
in Great Recession, 8–9
New Deal, promotion of, 8, 224–225
Mellon, Andrew, 25, 26, 33, 302
Miller, Nathan, 62
Miller, Peter, 234
Mises, Ludwig von, 25
Mississippi River flood (1927), 236, 246
Mitchell, Charles A., 36, 37
Mitchell, H. L., 102, 276
Moley, Raymond, 44, 55, 56
Mont Pelerin Society, 131
moral suasion, 36
Morgenthau, Henry, Jr.
commitment to civil rights, 14, 21n8, 159
on restrictions to unemployment insurance, 109, 189
on spending cuts, 67, 296
mortgage industry collapse, 38–41
Muir, John, 238
mural projects, 210, 212. *See also* arts programs of New Deal
Murphy, Frank, 97, 109, 308
Murray, Philip, 97
music projects, 217–218. *See also* arts programs of New Deal
Muste, A. J., 87

NAACP (National Association for the Advancement of Colored People), 99, 306
National Credit Corporation (NCC), 42
National Endowment for the Arts (NEA), 222, 230–231n52
National Farmers Process Tax Recovery Association (FPTRA), 275
National Farmers' Union (NFU), 275, 289n30
National Forest Service, 238
National Industrial Recovery Act (NIRA, 1933), 56, 65, 123
National Labor Relations Act (NLRA, 1935)
antidiscrimination measures, lack of, 99
collective bargaining rights guaranteed under, xvi, 96–97, 109, 121
radical action influencing passage of, 109, 124–126, 127
Southern planters support of, 126–127
National Labor Relations Board (NLRB), 98–99
National Park System, 238, 255
National Public Housing Act (1937), 196
National Recovery Act (1933), 96, 109
National Resources Planning Board (NRPB), 160, 167, 251, 256, 264n87. *See also* conservation practices; environmental programs of New Deal
National Union for Social Justice, 107
National Urban League (NUL), 99
National Youth Administration (NYA), 63, 150
nation-building, 33, 70–71
NCC (National Credit Corporation), 42
NEA (National Endowment for the Arts), 222, 230–231n52
Neutrality Acts, 18, 69
New Century Financial, 40
New Deal. *See also* Roosevelt, Franklin D. (FDR)
agricultural policies. *See* agricultural policies of New Deal
arts programs. *See* arts programs of New Deal
deficit spending in, 296–300
discrimination in policies of, 293, 294–295
economic theory underlying, 44–45
environmental programs. *See* environmental programs of New Deal
failures of, 293–297
First New Deal (1933–1934), 44, 56–62, 123
fiscal and monetary policies. *See* fiscal and monetary policies of New Deal
labor relations and employment. *See* employment; job-creation strategies of New Deal; labor movement
lessons learned from, 302–304
objectives of, 311–312
popular movements, responses to, 109–111, 304. *See also* popular movements
progressivist influences on, 3–4
promotion of, 8, 224–225
Second New Deal (1935–1937), 62–65, 123
social welfare programs. *See* social welfare programs of New Deal
successes of, 292–293
Third New Deal (1937–1945), xvi, 123–124, 139
unintended consequences of, 309–310
NFU (National Farmers' Union), 275, 289n30
Nibert, David, 284
NIRA (National Industrial Recovery Act, 1933), 56, 65, 123
Nixon, Richard, 300
NLRA. *See* National Labor Relations Act
NLRB (National Labor Relations Board), 98–99
non-delegation doctrine, 65, 66
non-transported goods industries, 31
Norris, George, 293
Norris-La Guardia Act (1932), 42, 96
NRPB. *See* National Resources Planning Board
NUL (National Urban League), 99

NYA (National Youth Administration), 63, 150

OAA (Old Age Assistance) program, 104–105, 109
OAI (Old Age Insurance) program, 104–105, 106, 109, 189–191, 198
Obama, Barack
economic condition of country at start of presidency, 1, 2
on environmental challenges, 252, 254, 258
fiscal and monetary policies following Great Recession, 52–53, 59–60, 63, 68–69, 75–77
media and communications, use of, 8–9
political skills and experience of, 11–13, 14, 15
president's party in Congress, strength and composition of, 10–11, 62
sequencing of reforms by, 63
spending cuts by, 68–69, 303–304
stimulus program, 9, 45, 52, 76, 255. *See also* American Recovery and Reinvestment Act (ARRA)
trickle-down approach to recovery, xv, 63, 76
Occupy Wall Street (OWS) movement, 3, 16, 182, 306–307, 315
offshore hiring, xv, 34
Ohio River flood (1937), 252, 259
Old Age Assistance (OAA) program, 104–105, 109
Old Age Insurance (OAI) program, 104–105, 106, 109, 189–191, 198
O'Neal, Edward, 235
Operation Dixie campaign, 131, 135
organized labor movement. *See* labor movement
"Our Freedoms and Our Rights" (NRPB), 167
OWS (Occupy Wall Street) movement, 3, 16, 182, 306–307, 315

painting projects, 210, 212. *See also* arts programs of New Deal
panic selling, 37
path dependency theory, xiv
Patient Protection and Affordable Care Act (2010), 198, 199, 304, 314
Patman, Wright, 94
pattern bargaining, 138
Paulson, Henry, 2, 45, 302
Pecora, Ferdinand, 60
Pecora Investigation, 60
pegged period, 72
pension movement, 103–105, 109, 189–190, 198, 199
Perkins, Frances
background of, 20n8, 183
on civil rights, 295
as Committee on Economic Security chair, 159, 191
contingency to become Secretary of Labor, 304
on FDR's demeanor, 13–14
on health care, 197
on labor movement, 96, 97
on popular movement pressures, 104
on relationship between Hopkins and FDR, 184
on social welfare programs, 103, 185, 186, 187, 189
on unemployment, 90, 109, 194
Philips, Peter, 124–125, 126
photography programs, 218. *See also* arts programs of New Deal
Photo League, 220
Picketty, Thomas, 16, 17
Pierson, Paul, 11
Pinchot, Gifford, 238
pink collar jobs, 30
Piven, Frances Fox, 87, 91, 92, 124
planters. *See* Southern planters
plays, 215–217. *See also* arts programs of New Deal
pollution, 248
Ponzi schemes, 36
Poor Laws, 147–148, 192, 193
Poor People's Campaign, 6
popular movements, 86–119. *See also* Tea Party movement
African American, 99–100, 110, 135–136, 305–306
elderly, assistance for, 103–106, 109
following Great Recession, 305–307
levelers, 106–108
New Deal responses to, 109–111, 304
Occupy Wall Street (OWS), 3, 16, 182, 306–307, 315
organized labor movement. *See* labor movement
public attitudes toward government and, 2, 3, 4–5
Southern Tenant Farmers Union (STFU), 101–102, 110, 133, 276
Townsend (pension) movement, 103–105, 109, 189–190, 198, 199
unemployed workers movement, 87–93, 305
veterans and Bonus Army protests, 2, 6, 42–43, 93–95, 114n72
poverty in rural areas, 234–235
Powell, John Wesley, 236
Prago, Albert, 90
precautionary principle, 253
preservation of natural resources. *See* conservation practices; environmental programs of New Deal

President's Organization of Unemployment Relief, 42
price specie-flow mechanism, 32
price supports for agricultural commodities, 271–273, 277, 278–280. *See also* agricultural policies of New Deal
private non-delegation doctrine, 65, 66
private sector
  Federal Reserve, involvement in, 66–67, 74
  health insurance and, 197, 198, 199
  job-creation in, 63, 171–172, 303
  unionization in, 120, 137, 139–140
processing tax for agricultural commodities, 272–273, 274, 277. *See also* agricultural policies of New Deal
production controls for agricultural commodities, 272–273, 279–280. *See also* agricultural policies of New Deal
production-for-use initiatives, 158
progressivism, 3–4
public art projects. *See* arts programs of New Deal
public assistance programs, 191–194. *See also* social welfare programs of New Deal
public attitudes toward government, 1–24
  business class, power and cohesion of, 16–17
  communications environment and, 6–9
  cultural factors influencing, 3–6
  environmental context and, 18–19
  international political context and, 17–18
  political skills of president and, 11–15
  popular movements and, 2, 3, 4–5
  president's party in Congress, strength and composition of, 9–11
  timing of events and, 1–3
public housing programs, 182–183, 195–197, 294, 296, 299
Public Law 480 (PL 480), 281
public option approach to recovery, xv–xvi, 51–52, 58–59
Public Utilities Holding Company Act (1935), 64
Public Works Administration (PWA), 58, 148–149, 174n7, 196
Public Works of Art Project (PWAP), 209–210
PWA (Public Works Administration), 58, 148–149, 174n7, 196
PWAP (Public Works of Art Project), 209–210

racial considerations. *See* African Americans; discrimination; segregation
radio communication, 6–8, 54
Randolph, A. Philip, 100
Raskob, John Jacob, 36
Rauschenbush, Walter, 3–4
Reagan, Ronald, 34, 252, 301
recessions. *See also* Great Recession (2007–2008)
  Austrian school view of, 26
  defined, 53
  Roosevelt recession (1937–1938), 67, 98, 296
re-commodification
  of arts, 222–223, 310–311
  of welfare state, 310–311
Reconstruction Finance Corporation (RFC)
  commercial lending and, 61
  establishment of, 42
  expansion of, 58–59
  public investments and, xv–xvi, 51, 54, 71, 75
Red-baiting, xvi, 43, 98–99, 121, 308
redistribution of wealth, 108, 110
redlining policy in homeowners' loans, 195, 294
Reed, David A., 43
Rees, William E., 234
reforestation, 235–236, 238, 243–244
Regionalist painters, 220
relief programs. *See also* job-creation strategies of New Deal; social welfare programs of New Deal
  spending cuts on, 67
  for veterans, 70–71
Republic Steel massacre (1937), 98
resettlement communities, 196
retirement, social construction of, 310–311
Revenue Act (1932), 42
RFC. *See* Reconstruction Finance Corporation
right to work, 162–163, 166–169
"The Road to Serfdom" (Hayek), 131
Robinson, Joseph, 101, 273, 276
Romney, Mitt, 25
Roosevelt, Eleanor
  as humanitarian, 183, 313
  mentors of, 4
  on civil rights, 295
  on gender discrimination, 295, 309
  on Universal Declaration of Human Rights, 313
  on Workers Alliance of America, 93, 114n63
  progressivism of, 313
  public sentiment, gathering data on, 13
  veterans, work with, 95
Roosevelt, Franklin D. (FDR)
  on art, 225
  bank holiday proclamation of, 53, 78n10
  on Bonus Army protests, 95
  bottom up approach to recovery, xv–xvi, 51, 58
  Brain Trust of, 14, 44, 313
  court-packing plan of, 65
  economic condition of country at start of presidency, 1–2
  Economic or Second Bill of Rights, 292, 298, 299, 314
  environmental protection approach of, 238–241

Roosevelt (*Cont.*)
fiscal austerity of, 67–68, 69
Four Freedoms speech, 167, 168, 298, 313
Great Depression, response to, 2, 43–45, 51. *See also* New Deal
labor relations, hands-off approach to, 98, 109, 308
media and communications, use of, 6–8
missteps by, 65–68, 69
political skills and experience of, 12, 13–14, 15, 62
president's party in Congress, strength and composition of, 9–10
on right to work, 162–163, 166–168
sequencing of reforms by, 63
on social welfare programs, 185, 186
Roosevelt, Theodore, 238
Roosevelt recession (1937–1938), 67, 98, 296
Rose, Nancy, 295
Rosenblum, Naomi, 207, 310, 311
Rosenman, Samuel, 313
Rosenzweig, Roy, 88, 92
Rosswurm, Steve, 128
Rubin, Robert, 23n43
rural areas, poverty in, 234–235

Saez, Emmanuel, 16, 17
Sand County Almanac (Leopold), 238
Sarbanes-Oxley Act (2002), 39
Sass, Steven, 199
SCDA (Soil Conservation and Domestic Allotment) Act (1936), 277
Schlesinger, Arthur, Jr., 180, 239, 301, 315
Schumpeter, Joseph, 31
Schwartz, Anna, 72
sculpture projects, 210. *See also* arts programs of New Deal
SEC (Securities and Exchange Commission), 38, 39, 60, 73–74
Second Bill of Rights. *See* Economic Bill of Rights
The Second Bill of Rights: FDR's Unfinished Revolution and Why We Need It More Than Ever (Sunstein), 314
Second New Deal (1935–1937), 62–65, 123. *See also* New Deal
Securities Act (1933), 60
Securities and Exchange Commission (SEC), 38, 39, 60, 73–74
Securities Exchange Act (1934), 60
securitization of mortgages, 39
security markets, transparency in, 60–61
segregation. *See also* African Americans; discrimination
in arts funding, 216
in military, 100
in work programs, 249
Selling Free Enterprise (Fones-Wolf), 130–131
Sen, Amartya, 194–195
Servicemen's Readjustment Act (1944), 70–71, 95
settlement houses, 4, 20n7
Seymour, Helen, 91
sharecroppers, 101–102, 110, 133, 276, 281–282
Share Our Wealth, 5, 106–107
Shlaes, Amity, 26
shovel-ready jobs, 76
Silent Spring (Carson), 19, 238
silver certificates, 57
Silvers, Damon, 40
Simpson, Alan, 68, 303
Simpson, John, 275, 289n30
Sinclair, Upton, 5
sit-down strikes, 97–98, 99, 109. *See also* labor movement
Skocpol, Theda, 124
Slavkin, Heather, 40
smart growth movement, 196
Smith, Gerald L. K., 107
Smith, Howard W., 193–194
SNAP (Supplemental Nutrition Assistance Program), 171, 181, 182, 201n3, 201n8
social creed movement, 4
social gospel movement, 3–4, 20n5
social insurance, 189–191. *See also* Social Security Act (SSA)
Socialist Party, 4–5, 87, 88
social movements. *See* popular movements
Social Realist painters, 220
Social Security Act (SSA, 1935). *See also* social welfare programs of New Deal
framing and timing of, 185–187, 199–200
in Great Recession, 182
health protections in, 197
old age security programs and, 103–106, 109, 189–191, 198
Southern planters support of, 127
unemployment insurance and, 92, 99, 109, 188–189, 190
social welfare programs of New Deal, 180–206
adequacy of, 190–191, 193–194, 198
African Americans in, 192
availability during Great Recession, xvii, 180–183
categorical aid and, 191–193
de-commodification of the welfare state, 310–311, 323n92
discrimination in, 192
emergency relief efforts, 183–184. *See also* Federal Emergency Relief Administration (FERA)
employment assurance proposals, 159–160, 161–163, 168–169, 194–195, 297–298

federally aided public assistance programs, 191–194
framing and timing of, 185–187, 199–200, 304
health care and, 197
housing programs, 182–183, 195–197
lessons learned from, 197–200
origins of, 180
public employment programs, 187–188. *See also* job-creation strategies of New Deal; unemployment insurance
re-commodification of the welfare state, 311
social insurance, 189–191. *See also* Social Security Act (SSA)
taxation of, 191
soil conservation, xviii, 235, 245–246, 255
Soil Conservation Act (1935), 245
Soil Conservation and Domestic Allotment (SCDA) Act (1936), 277
Soil Conservation Service, xviii, 245–246, 255
Sokoloff, Nickolai, 217
Solis, Hilda, 183
Southern planters, 101–102, 126–127, 273, 276–277, 281–282
Southern Tenant Farmers Union (STFU), 101–102, 110, 133, 276, 307
soybean production, 282–283
speculators, 36
SSA. *See* Social Security Act
"Statement of Essential Human Rights" (ALI), 167, 178n88
Steelworkers union, 98, 128
Stepan-Norris, Judith, 128–129, 137
STFU (Southern Tenant Farmers Union), 101–102, 110, 133, 276, 307
Stiglitz, Joseph, 41, 68, 234
stimulus program, 9, 45, 52, 76, 255. *See also* American Recovery and Reinvestment Act (ARRA)
stock market crash (1929), 35–37, 41. *See also* Great Depression
strikes, 92, 97–98, 99, 109, 134–135. *See also* labor movement
Strong, Benjamin, 32
Stryker, Roy, 218
sub-prime mortgage market collapse, 38–41
suitable homes policy, 192
Summers, Larry, 23n43
Sunstein, Cass R., 314
Supplemental Nutrition Assistance Program (SNAP), 171, 181, 182, 201n3, 201n8
supply management policies for agricultural commodities, xviii, 266, 271–278. *See also* Agricultural Adjustment Act (AAA); agricultural policies of New Deal
Supreme Court, FDR's plan to pack, 65
sustainability of natural resources. *See* conservation practices; environmental programs of New Deal

Taft-Hartley Act (1947), 99, 121, 124, 133, 135
TANF (Temporary Assistance for Needy Families), 182
Tarlock, A. Dan, 253
TARP (Troubled Asset Relief Program), 52, 59–60, 75–76, 196, 302
Tarrow, Sidney, 307
taxation
financial transaction taxes (FTTs), 316
processing tax for agricultural commodities, 272–273, 274, 277
revenue from, 33–34
of social welfare programs, 191
Tax Reform Act (1986), 38
Taylor, David A., 212
Tea Party movement
compared to Austrian school economics, 26
on bailouts, 85n146
on fiscal responsibility, 46
on isolationism, 33
objectives of, 303, 305
organization of, 3
teaser rates, 38
technological change
arts affected by, 207–208
unintended consequences of, xiv
Temin, Peter, 34
Temporary Assistance for Needy Families (TANF), 182
Temporary Emergency Relief Administration (TERA), 89
tenant farmers, 101–102, 110, 133, 276, 281–282
Tennessee Valley Authority (TVA), xviii, 58, 246–248, 249, 250–251
TERA (Temporary Emergency Relief Administration), 89
Terket, Studs, 214
theatrical projects, 215–217, 223–224. *See also* arts programs of New Deal
Third New Deal (1937–1945), xvi, 123–124, 139
Thomas, Elbert D., 57
Thomas, Norman, 90, 101, 307
Thomas amendment, 57–58
Tobin, James, 316
"too big to fail" principle, 41
Townsend, Francis E., 103, 104, 105
Townsend Clubs, 5, 103
Townsend movement, 103–105, 109, 189–190, 198, 199
Trading with the Enemy Act (1917), 53
transparency in security markets, 60–61

TRAP (Treasury Relief Art Project), 210–211
Trattner, Walter, 183
Treasury Department, 52, 57, 209–211
Treasury Relief Art Project (TRAP), 210–211
Treasury Section of Painting and Sculpture, 210
trickle-down economics, xv, 33–34, 51, 63, 76
tripartism, 132–133, 134
Troubled Asset Relief Program (TARP), 52, 59–60, 75–76, 196, 302
Truman, Harry, 197
Truth in Securities Act (1933), 60
Tugwell, Rexford, 14, 21n8, 276
TVA (Tennessee Valley Authority), xviii, 58, 246–248, 249, 250–251
"twofer" effect of direct job-creation programs, 171, 172

UAW (United Auto Workers), 97, 134–135, 137
UMW (United Mine Workers), 96
Unemployed Workers Movement, 87–93. *see also* employment; job-creation strategies of New Deal
- crime and violence related to, 87–88, 90
- employed workers, support for strikes of, 92
- insurance demands of, 88, 91–92. *see also* Lundeen bill
- New Deal and, 90–93
- political affiliations of, 87, 88, 93, 305
- strategies of, 88–89, 91, 93
- Unemployed Councils, 2, 87, 89, 90, 99

unemployment insurance, 88, 91–92, 109, 181–182, 188–190
unemployment rates
- in Great Recession, 179
- from 1933–1947, 165
- of African Americans, 296

unionization
- in Canada, 120
- capitalist offensive against, 130–132
- decline in, 30
- government policies affecting, 96–99, 109
- in private sector, 120, 137, 139–140
- radical action and, 127–129
- women and, 140

United Auto Workers (UAW), 97, 134–135, 137
United Mine Workers (UMW), 96
United Nations Universal Declaration of Human Rights, 313–314
United Office and Professional Workers (UOPWA), 135
Universal Declaration of Human Rights (United Nations), 313–314
UOPWA (United Office and Professional Workers), 135
U.S. Children's Bureau, 192
U.S. Coast and Geodetic Survey, 157
U.S. Conference of Mayors, 89, 93
U.S. Department of Agriculture (USDA), 243, 245, 272
U.S. Employment Service (USES), 153
U.S. Housing Act (1937), 195, 196–197
U.S. Steel Corporation, 98

Valocchi, Steve, 87
Vanek, Jaroslav, 30–31
Van Tine, Warren, 98
veterans
- Bonus Army protests, 2, 6, 42–43, 93–95, 114n72
- reliefs programs for, 70–71

visual arts programs. *See* arts programs of New Deal

WAA (Workers Alliance of America), 92–93, 110
Wagner, Robert, 96, 102, 109, 187, 312
Wagner Act. *See* National Labor Relations Act (NLRA)
Wagner-Steagall Act (1937), 195, 196–197
Wald, Lillian, 4, 20n7
Walker, Margaret, 214
Wallace, Henry A.
- on agricultural policies, 273, 276
- commitment to civil rights, 14, 21n8, 159
- presidential campaign of, 136

War Department, 43, 243
Washington Consensus economic policy, 34
Water Pollution Control Act (1948), 248
Waters, Walter, 94
Wattenberg, Martin P., 8
Wealth Tax Act (1935), 108, 110
welfare capitalism, 131–132
welfare programs. *See* social welfare programs of New Deal
West, Cornel, 306
Wheat Belt, 275
wheat production, 267–268, *268*, *269*, 274, 280–281. *See also* agricultural policies of New Deal
When Art Worked (Kennedy & Larkin), 226
Whitcomb, Robert, 207
wildlife restoration, 244
Williams, Aubrey, 151, 159, 175n17, 295, 297
Winders, Bill, 127, 266, 309
Witte, Edwin, 104, 189, 194, 197, 315
women
- discrimination in policies of New Deal, 295
- pink collar jobs, 30
- unionization and, 140
- work programs and, 152–153, 249

Woodward, Ellen, 152–153

Woofter, T. J., 282
Woolhandler, Steffie, 198, 199
Woolner, David B., 253
Workers Alliance of America (WAA), 92–93, 110. *See also* Unemployed Workers Movement
Workers' Committees, 87, 88
Workers' Unemployment Insurance Bill (1934), 91, 99
working-class. *See* labor movement
work programs. *See* employment; job-creation strategies of New Deal
Works Progress Administration (WPA)
accomplishments of, 63, 163
arts programs under, 211–218. *See also* arts programs of New Deal
discrimination in, 294
establishment of, 123, 150, 160, 188
funding cuts to, 67, 93, 110
structure of, 160–161
wages provided under, 160, 175–176n41
WorldCom, 38, 48n39
A World Made New (Glendon), 313
World Trade Organization (WTO), 33, 59, 286
World War II (1939–1945), 52, 67, 70, 164
WPA. *See* Works Progress Administration
Wright, Richard, 214
writing projects, 212–214, 221, 223, 226. *See also* arts programs of New Deal
WTO (World Trade Organization), 33, 59, 286

yellow-dog contracts, 96

Zandi, Mark, 303
Zeitlin, Maurice, 128–129, 137